P9-CFB-431

THE

BLAIR

HANDBOOK

SECOND EDITION

TOBY FULWILER
UNIVERSITY OF VERMONT

ALAN R. HAYAKAWA

A Blair Press Book
PRENTICE HALL, UPPER SADDLE RIVER, NJ 07458

Library of Congress Cataloging-in-Publication Data

Fulwiler, Toby, 1942–
    The Blair handbook / Toby Fulwiler, Alan R. Hayakawa.—2nd ed.
       p.   cm.
    "A Blair Press Book."
    Includes indexes.
    ISBN 0-13-572181-4 (case). — ISBN 0-13-572173-3 (pbk.)
    1. English language—Rhetoric—Handbooks, manuals, etc.
    2. English language—Grammar—Handbooks, manuals, etc.
    I. Hayakawa, Alan R. II. Title.
PE1408.F78 1997
808'.042—DC20
                           96-30383
                           CIP

President, Humanities and Social Sciences: J. Philip Miller
Publisher: Nancy Perry
Acquisitions Editor: Mary Jo Southern
Development Editor: Clare Payton
Director of Production and Manufacturing: Barbara Kittle
Manufacturing Manager: Nick Sklitsis
Prepress and Manufacturing Buyer: Bob Anderson

Managing Editor: Bonnie Biller
Production Supervisor: Andrew Roney
Creative Design Director: Leslie Osher
Art Director: Anne Bonanno Nieglos
Cover Design: Thomas Nery
Interior Design: Betty Binns Design; Susan Walrath
Electronic Page Layout: Susan Walrath

This book was set in 9/11 ITC Bookman Light by Susan Walrath, and was printed and bound by Rand McNally. The cover was printed by Lehigh.

Acknowledgments

'We Real Cool' from "Blacks" by Gwendolyn Brooks, © 1991. Published by Third World Press, Chicago, 1991.

Sample PsycLit abstract. This screen is reprinted with permission of SilverPlatter Information, Inc. Copyright © 1986–1996 by the American Psychological Association, publisher of *Psychological Abstracts* and the PsycINFO Database (Copyright 1967–1996), and copyright © 1986-1996 SilverPlatter International, N.V.

Web page from U.S. government site. U.S. Geological Survey, MS804 National Center, Reston, VA 22092

"Communicate." By permission. From Merriam-Webster's Collegiate® Dictionary, Tenth Edition, © 1995 by Merriam-Webster Inc.

A Blair Press Book

© 1997 by Prentice-Hall, Inc.
Simon & Schuster/A Viacom Company
Upper Saddle River, NJ 07458

All right reserved. No part of this book may be reproduced, in any form or by any means, without permission in writing from the publisher.
Printed in the United States of America

10 9 8 7 6 5 4 3 2 1

ISBN 0-13-572173-3 (paperback Student Edition)
           0-13-572181-4 (hardcover Student Edition)
           0-13-572199-7 (Annotated Instructor's Edition)

Prentice-Hall International (UK) Limited, *London*
Prentice-Hall of Australia Pty. Limited, *Sydney*
Prentice-Hall Canada Inc., *Toronto*
Prentice-Hall Hispanoamericana, S.A., *Mexico*
Prentice-Hall of India Private Limited, *New Delhi*
Prentice-Hall of Japan, Inc., *Tokyo*
Simon & Schuster Asia Pte. Ltd., *Singapore*
Editora Prentice-Hall do Brasil, Ltda., *Rio de Janeiro*

Preface

In revising *The Blair Handbook*, we focused sharply on the needs of college writers approaching the end of the twentieth century. They continue to need what the first edition offered: clear explanations of language conventions, practices, and rules that govern good writing; strategies for negotiating all phases of the writing process; and samples of authentic student writing. In preparing the second edition, we reexamined every chapter to sharpen our treatment of these essential handbook elements, clarifying explanations, simplifying strategies, and updating writing samples.

However, even in the course of a few years, technology has greatly changed the way we read and write texts. A world of electronic textual resources now awaits us. The Internet, e-mail, software programs, and even electronic scanners all provide a dazzling array of possibilities for reading, writing, and learning. We revised *The Blair Handbook* to reflect these developments and to provide students with guidance for negotiating the electronic world.

We also renewed our commitment to making *The Blair Handbook* the most process-oriented and user-friendly handbook on the market. In preparing the second edition, we both amplified and simplified the treatment of the writing process, and we expanded and tightened the presentation of the editing process. The result is a handbook that offers the most practical and jargon-free guidance available on the crafting of writing.

PRINCIPLES UNDERLYING *THE BLAIR HANDBOOK*

Writing as a process

The organization of *The Blair Handbook* corresponds to the stages of the writing process, so that every piece of information is contextualized within the process. In particular, traditional handbook material—information on style, grammar, punctuation, and mechanics—is presented as "editing," the final stage in the writing process.

■ **Part I, Writing in College,** introduces students to the five interrelated but discrete stages of the writing process: planning, drafting, researching, revising, and editing.

■ **Part II, Planning,** discusses planning as an activity that involves purpose, audience, voice, invention and discovery writing, and journals.

■ **Part III, Drafting,** introduces students to basic drafting strategies such as finding a subject, stating a thesis, and developing a draft for five specific writing purposes: recounting, explaining, arguing, interpreting, and reflecting.

■ **Part IV, Researching,** introduces students to research methods used in writing a research essay and guides them through the challenges of using sources and documenting them according to MLA style.

■ **Part V, Revising,** focuses on revision, perhaps the most demanding and creative stage in the writing process, helping students grapple with the content and organization of their papers.

■ **Part VI, Editing,** deals with the stage in the process when writers work on not what they've said but how they've said it. "Editing" is divided into subsections on effectiveness, grammar, punctuation, and mechanics.

Students as writers
We stress that writing is a dynamic activity in which the writer continually chooses from a variety of possible options, evaluates the results, and rewrites as necessary. Thus, we outline information and possible strategies and ask students to decide what is most effective for their readers and most satisfying to themselves.

■ **Plentiful samples of student writing.** *The Blair Handbook* includes an abundance of authentic student writing samples to build confidence. There are more freewrites, journal entries, early drafts, and complete essays (nine final drafts in all) than in any other handbook.

■ **Six types of essays.** In Parts III and IV, we outline the writing purposes for the six types of essays students are most often assigned. Each of these purposes is illustrated by a complete student paper. For the research essay, we provide sample papers for three possible research assignments: an informal "I-search" essay, a literary analysis with secondary sources, and a formal research report.

■ **Hand-edited examples.** Examples in the editing part of *The Blair Handbook* use handwritten corrections to show students, problems and their solutions at a single glance.

Innovative approach to research

We introduce students to the activity of researching by pointing out that research is something they do in their everyday lives, such as when they shop for a new CD player or look for a job.

■ **Research integrated into the writing process.** Our research section appears as Part IV, exemplifying our belief that research is an essential part of the writing process, not a separate activity. For this reason, we integrate our ample section on research into the main sequence of the book rather than tuck it away at the end.

■ **Both library research and field research.** In Part IV, we stress that profitable research occurs not only in the library but also in the field. We explain two possible field techniques—interviews and site observation—and urge students to look for information wherever their search takes them.

Meaningful writing and learning activities

Rather than including exercises that drill students on isolated skills, *The Blair Handbook* features meaningful activities that help students work through their own versions of the writing process. Students explore their experiences as writers or examine the work of others in "Explorations." Students practice editing techniques on sample student texts in "Practices." They apply the principles discussed to papers they are working on in "Applications." "Suggestions for Writing and Research," appearing in Parts I through V, offer both individual and collaborative writing assignments. Many activities were deftly revised for the second edition by Sean McDowell and Dave Carlson of Indiana University.

Emphasis on the conventions of effective writing

Good writing must be more than conceptually sound and grammatically correct. If a piece of writing is to succeed in its communicative purpose, it must also be clear, vital, and stimulating to read—what we call "effective." In *The Blair Handbook*, we explain features of standard, written English as conventions that facilitate effective communication, not arbitrary rules to be memorized and followed by rote.

■ **Less jargon.** We spend less time instructing students in grammar jargon and more time showing students how to identify, analyze, and solve problems that can cause reader confusion.

■ **Support for decision making.** In *The Blair Handbook*, we show students how to engage and maintain readers' interest by expressing ideas precisely and powerfully, illustrating that "effectiveness" springs from more than just attending to "style." Students learn to decide for themselves which choice is most effective with their readers.

Comprehensive help for those who speak English as a second language (ESL)

Over fifty easily identified boxes placed throughout the book contain information not only on correct grammar and word choice but also on aspects of planning, drafting, researching, and revising that sometimes prove troublesome for ESL writers. All were written, and many were revised or added in the second edition, by ESL expert Jan Frodesen of the University of California, Santa Barbara. In addition, a strand of special writing suggestions in the first three parts asks students to draw on their experiences as nonnative speakers and writers as a means of improving their writing.

Emphasis on contemporary pedagogy

Writing classrooms today look different from those of a decade ago: Students are reading drafts to each other in groups, writing in ungraded journals, quietly conversing around computers, editing each other's work, or brainstorming on collaborative research projects. *The Blair Handbook* includes special emphasis on the soundest of the current trends in writing instruction.

■ **Critical reading.** Reading and writing are necessarily complementary processes; if students cannot read critically, they cannot possibly write well. Believing that critical reading is a keystone to the development of a student as a writer, we discuss how to read critically in Chapter 2 and ask, in subsequent sections, that students use these skills repeatedly when drafting, researching, and revising.

■ **Journals.** Because writing-to-learn is recognized as an important part of learning to write, we have included a complete chapter (Chapter 4) featuring ideas for journal writing.

We present additional suggestions for journal writing in individual chapters as activities labeled "Exploration."

■ **Voice.** "Voice" puts students themselves on display in the texts they write. Chapter 8 discusses and analyzes voice, and the drafting, revising, and editing sections of the book repeatedly ask students to consider the voices they hear in their own writing.

■ **Revising.** In Part V, we present revising as a creative activity essential to the development of good writing. We describe revision as a complex and variable process and give students concrete suggestions for a variety of methods—some conventional and some more innovative—that they can usefully apply to their writing.

■ **Writing across the curriculum.** In Part VIII, we provide detailed information on the five distinct disciplinary branches that form the context for most college writing outside the composition classroom.

NEW TO THE SECOND EDITION

We've improved—and added—coverage of a number of writing topics in the second edition of *The Blair Handbook*.

New coverage of presenting your work

"Presenting Your Work," Part VII, bridges the gap between the editing concerns of Part VI and presenting texts in final form. Three new chapters discuss designing documents, creating writing portfolios, and making oral presentations.

■ **Designing documents.** Chapter 56 covers everything students need to know for designing academic papers, beginning with the mechanics of finishing and polishing texts—formatting, printing, and proofreading—and including the consideration of such things as visuals.

■ **Creating writing portfolios.** Chapter 57 outlines the basic principles and goals behind keeping writing portfolios and shows students ways to select, assemble, and present their writing as a collective whole.

■ **Making oral presentations.** Chapter 58 focuses on the important differences between oral and written discourse as well as on how to write an oral text. The chapter also offers tips for developing the whole presentation package, including collaborating with other students, using the space, involving the audience, and implementing visual aids and other learning tools.

Enhanced coverage of researching and documentation methods

While retaining our approach to research as an activity that students already do in their everyday lives, we wanted to enhance our coverage of the more formal strategies necessary to writing an academic research paper. Thus, more is provided at every stage: from managing the project to finding sources, conducting field research, and using and documenting sources. And now, as technology becomes increasingly important, we discuss some newly established methods of using electronic sources: where to find them, how to use them, how to document them. Of course, also included are the latest documentation guidelines for using the MLA, APA, CMS (Chicago), and Science styles—clearly and expertly defined by John Clark of Bowling Green State University.

More advice about editing

A newly expanded chapter, "The Editing Process," Chapter 23, applies a hands-on and practical approach to this stage of the writing process. This chapter introduces students to thirteen major editing "moves" which they can live by—at least for their first year of college writing. All are explained with clear examples, both student and professional, and all are cross-referenced to fuller explanations in the following editing chapters on effectiveness, grammar, punctuation, and mechanics.

New tips for writing with computers

Computers have fundamentally changed the way most of us write, especially the way we revise and edit. In *The Blair Handbook*, we discuss the benefits of word processing and urge students to experiment and explore its possibilities. The second edition integrates into the book up-to-date information on the role of computers in writing, insofar as any information on computers can be up-to-date. Word-processing tips (WP TIPs), generously provided by Deborah H. Holdstein of Governors State University, offer students techniques for composing, revising, and editing on computer as well as ideas for conducting research on-line.

SUPPLEMENTS

Print supplements for instructors

■ *Annotated Instructor's Edition for The Blair Handbook, Second Edition*, by Sue Dinitz and Jean Kiedaisch, a helpful resource with answers for activities, additional activities, teaching tips,

strategies for word-processing activities, ESL advice, background information on writing, and interesting quotations
- *Blair Resources for Teaching Writing*, individual booklets presenting information on some of the most effective approaches and important concerns of composition instructors today, each written by an expert on the particular topic

Distance Education, by W. Dees Stallings (*New!*)

Computers and Composition, by Deborah H. Holdstein (*Revised edition*)

Classroom Strategies, by Wendy Bishop

Portfolios, by Pat Belanoff

Journals, by Christopher C. Burnham

Collaborative Learning, by Harvey Kail and John Trimbur

English as a Second Language, by Ruth Spack

Writing across the Curriculum, by Art Young

Print supplements for students
- *Editing Activities from The Blair Handbook, Second Edition, with Additional Items*, including both the editing activities in the handbook and additional activities, with ample space to edit on the page (Answer Key available)
- *The Blair Guide to Documentation*, assembling all the documentation information presented in *The Blair Handbook, Second Edition*, in one convenient guide
- *Prentice Hall/The New York Times Supplement* is a sixteen-page collection of timely articles from *The New York Times*, providing students with examples of rhetorical strategies and springboards for writing
- *Preparing for TASP with The Blair Handbook, Second Edition*
- *Preparing for the CLAST with The Blair Handbook, Second Edition*

Software and Audio/Visual Supplements
- *The Online Handbook*, a pop-up and abbreviated version of the handbook
- *Blue Pencil*, an interactive program that allows students to practice their editing skills on-screen
- *Bibliotech*, a bibliography generator with MLA, APA, and CBE documentation styles
- *ABC News/Prentice Hall Video Library for Composition, Volume 2*, a collection of topically arranged clips from news

programs that allows students to experience firsthand the vital relationship between traditional written discourse and video compositions

ACKNOWLEDGMENTS

To our colleagues nationwide who agreed to share their collective wisdom on the teaching of writing in the Blair resource pamphlets: Pat Belanoff, State University of New York at Stony Brook; Wendy Bishop, Florida State University; Chris Burnham, University of New Mexico at Los Cruces; Deborah H. Holdstein, Governors State University; Harvey Kail, University of Maine; Ruth Spack, Tufts University; Dees Stallings, University of Maryland; John Trimbur, Worchester Polytechnic Institute; and Art Young, Clemson University.

To Sue Dinitz and Jean Kiedaisch, colleagues at the University of Vermont, who carefully revised the second edition of the annotated instructor's edition to reflect the latest methods in teaching composition; Heidi Schultz of the University of North Carolina at Chapel Hill, who judiciously prepared new bibliographic references in "Useful Readings"; Jan Frodesen of the University of California, Santa Barbara, who again prepared "ESL Advice," incorporating the newest understandings of how students learn English as a second language; Deborah H. Holdstein of Governors State University, who implemented new strategies for teaching writing in the composition classroom, with integrated and focused "WP Strategies."

To the many students at the University of Vermont who asked and answered questions about learning to write and especially to those who allowed us to reprint samples of their essays, freewrites, and journal entries: Julie Conner, Beth Devino, Mari Engel, Rebecca Grosser, Rebecca Hart, John Jacobi, Jeff Kasden, Amanda Robertson, Zoe Reynders, Karen Santosuosso, Issa Sawabini, Lorraine White, Judith Woods, and Scott Yarochuk.

To Nancy Perry, whose vision of contemporary writing instruction guided *The Blair Handbook* from inception to completion and from edition to edition. Our warmest thanks to Clare Payton, our skillful, careful, relentless, yet diplomatic development editor; and to Jan Kasl, our helpful editorial assistant. We'd like to acknowledge the editorial guidance of Mark Gallaher and Susan Moss, who polished many chapters into completion with careful eyes and adept pens. Our handbook was taken from manuscript to bound book with the aid of an expert team: Robert

Anderson, Manufacturing Buyer; Bonnie Biller, Managing Editor; Lori Kane, Supervisor of Production Services; Anne Bonanno Nieglos, Art Director; Leslie Osher, Design Director; Andrew Roney, Production Editor; Ilene McGrath, Copyeditor; Susan Walrath, Interior Designer; and Thomas Nery, Cover Designer. We'd also like to thank Gina Sluss, Director of Marketing, and Phil Miller, President of Humanities and Social Sciences, for their enduring support of this project.

To our many, thoughtful, critical, and experienced reviewers and users of the first edition whose comments guided the major manuscript revisions: Kimberly Abels, University of North Carolina, Chapel Hill; Melanie Almeder, University of Florida; Steve Anderson, University of Arkansas at Little Rock; Richard Bullock, Wright State University; Veronica Cruz, University of Florida; Carol David, Iowa State University; Bernard J. Gallagher, Louisiana State University at Alexandra; Virginia Gibbons, Oakton Community College; Maureen Hoag, Wichita State University; Francis A. Hubbard, Marquette University; Leila Kapai, University of the District of Columbia, Washington; David Lashmet, University of Florida; Michelle LeBeau, University of New Mexico, Valencia; Erin Lebofsky, Temple University; Thomas Marshall, Robert Morris College; Lynn Langer Meeks, Utah State University; Michael Moran, University of Georgia; Katy Norton, Indiana University; J. S. Renau, University of Florida; Bryan Sandoval, Utah State University; Lucille M. Schultz, University of Cincinnati; Linda Sneed, Indiana University; Josephine Koster Tarvers, Winthrop University; Richard Veit, University of North Carolina, Wilmington; Lisa Walmsley, University of Florida; and Sam Watson, University of North Carolina, Charlotte.

To John Harvey, news editor of *The Oregonian*, who instilled respect for the language and for a writer's style; to John A. Kirkpatrick of *The Patriot-News* of Harrisburg, for his support for better news writing. To Ichiro Hayakawa and Frederick Romer Peters, who never met but shared a love of the English language that they passed on to their children.

And thanks finally and always to Laura for her continued patience with this important, yet never-ending project.

Toby Fulwiler
Alan R. Hayakawa

Contents

*The **ESL** symbol indicates sections that have ESL boxes.

II Planning   41

III Drafting   89

VI Editing   343

37 Using Adjectives and Adverbs   **565**

38 Positioning Modifiers Correctly   **576**

39 Clarifying Pronoun Reference   **585**

Editing Punctuation   627

Editing Mechanics   703

VII Presenting Your Work 753

b Classifying sentences by grammatical structure   866
c Understanding sentence patterns   867

THE

BLAIR
HANDBOOK

Writing
in College

You can count on one thing—attending college will mean writing papers. Whether you are enrolled in a writing course or any other course, you'll be asked to write critical essays, research reports, position papers, book reviews, essay exams, and laboratory reports, and sometimes to keep a journal. You may have tackled similar writing assignments in high school, so you've had some practice. Now, because college is designed to challenge you, that practice will be put to a test.

Recently we asked a class of first-year college students to talk about themselves as writers. Several began by describing where they wrote. Amy, for example, said she did most of her writing "listening to classical music and, if it is a nice day, under trees," while Jennifer felt "most comfortable writing on [her] bed and being alone." Others described their attitudes. John, for example, said he wrote best "under pressure." Becky, however, preferred writing when she "felt strongly or was angry about something," while Kevin "hated deadlines." In fact, there proved to be as many different perspectives on being a writer as there were students in the class. To continue our conversation, we asked more specific questions.

I a What is difficult about writing?

Everything about writing can seem difficult, from getting started to organizing, revising, and editing. Our own experience tells us this is so—and every published writer we know says the same thing. How, we wondered, would first-year college writers characterize their difficulties? Here is what they told us:

Jennifer: "I don't like being told what to write about."

Amy: "I never could fulfill the page requirements. My essays were always several pages shorter than they were supposed to be."

Jill: "I always have trouble starting off a paper . . . and I hate it when I think I've written a great paper and I get a bad grade. It's so discouraging and I don't understand what I wrote wrong."

Omar: "Teachers are always nitpicking about little things, but I think writing is for communication, not nitpicking. I mean, if you can read it and it makes sense, what else do you want?"

Ken: "Putting thoughts down on paper as they are in your mind is the hardest thing to do. It's like music—anyone can play a song in his head, but translating it to an instrument is the hard part."

We weren't surprised by these answers, since we too remember wondering: What did teachers want? How long was enough? How do you get thoughts into words? Why all the nitpicking?

■ WRITING 1: EXPLORATION

What do you find difficult about writing? Do you have a problem finding subjects to write about? Or do you have trouble getting motivated? Or does something about the act of writing itself cause problems for you? Explain in your own words by writing quickly for five minutes without stopping. **ESL:** Are any of your writing difficulties related to writing in a second language? For example, do you need to translate some ideas from your native language to English? Do problems with grammar or vocabulary make it difficult for you to communicate?

1 b   What do you enjoy about writing?

Though any writer will tell you writing isn't easy, most will also describe it as interesting and exciting. So we asked our first-year students what it was about writing that gave them pleasure.

Jolene: "If I have a strong opinion on a topic, it makes it so much easier to write a paper."

Rebecca: "On occasion I'm inspired by a wonderful idea. Once I get going, I actually enjoy writing a lot."

Casey: "I enjoy most to write about my experiences, both good and bad. I like to write about things when I'm upset—it makes me feel better."

Darren: "I guess my favorite kind of writing is letters. I get to be myself and just talk in them."

Like our students we prefer to write about topics that inspire or interest us, and we find personal writing such as letters especially easy, interesting, and enjoyable.

▮ WRITING 2: EXPLORATION

What kind of writing do you most enjoy doing? What do you like about it: Communicating? Exploring a subject? Playing with words? Something else?

I c What surprises are in store?

After talking with first-year students, we asked some advanced students about their writing experiences: "What has surprised you the most about writing in college?"

Carmen: "Papers aren't as hellish as I was told they'd be. In fact, I've actually enjoyed writing a lot of them—especially after they were done."

Aaron: "My style has changed a lot. Rather than becoming more complex, it's become simpler."

Kerry: "The most surprising and frustrating thing has been the different reactions I've received from different professors."

Rob: "I'm always being told that my writing is superficial. That I come up with good ideas but don't develop them."

John: "The tutor at our writing lab took out a pair of scissors and said I would have to work on organization. Then she cut up my paper and taped it back together a different way. This really made a difference, and I've been using this method ever since."

Chrissie: "Sharing papers with other students is very awkward for me. But it's extremely beneficial when I trust and like my group, when we all relax enough to talk honestly about one another's papers."

As you can see, most advanced students found ways to cope with and enjoy college writing. Several reported satisfying experiences sharing writing with each other. We are sorry that some students, even in their last year, could not figure out what their instructors wanted; we think there are ways to do that.

▇ WRITING 3: EXPLORATION

Think about your experience with writing in the last school you attended. What surprised you—pleasantly or not—about the experience? What did you learn or not learn?

▇ **I d Why is writing important?**

We also asked these advanced students why, in their last year they had enrolled in an elective writing class. "What made the subject so important to you?"

Kim: "I have an easier time expressing myself through writing. When I'm speaking, my words get jumbled—writing gives me more time, and my voice doesn't quiver and I don't blush."

Rick: "Writing allows me to hold up a mirror to my life and see what clear or distorted images stare back at me."

Glenn: "The more I write, the better I become. In terms of finding a job after I graduate, strong writing skills will give me an edge over those who are just mediocre writers."

Amy: "I'm still searching for meaning. When I write I feel I can do anything, go anywhere, search and explore."

Angel: "I feel I have something to say."

We agree with virtually all of these reasons. At times writing is therapeutic, at other times it helps us clarify our ideas, and at still other times it helps us get and keep jobs.

▇ WRITING 4: EXPLORATION

Look over the various answers given by the college seniors and select one. Do you agree or disagree with the student? Explain.

> **I** **e**   **What can you learn from the experience of others?**

Since our advanced students had a lot to say about writing, we asked them to be consultants: "What is your advice to first-year college writers?" Here are their suggestions:

Aaron: "Get something down!! The hardest part of writing is starting. Forget the introduction, skip the outline, don't worry about a thesis—just blast your ideas down, see what you've got, then go back and work on them."

Christa: "Plan ahead. It sounds dry, but planning makes writing easier than doing laundry."

Victor: "Follow the requirements of the assignment to the T. Hand in a draft for the professor to mark up, then rewrite it."

Allyson: "Don't think every piece you write has to be a masterpiece. And sometimes the worst assignment turns into the best writing. Don't worry about what the professor wants—write what you believe."

Carmen: "Imagine and create, never be content with just retelling a story."

Rick: "When someone trashes your writing, thank them and listen to their criticism. It stings, but it helps you become a better writer."

Jason: "Say what you are going to say as clearly and as straightforwardly as possible. Don't try to pad it with big words and fancy phrasing."

Angel: "Read for pleasure from time to time. The more you read, the better you write—it just happens."

Kim: "When choosing topics, choose something that has a place in your heart."

These are good suggestions to any writers: start fast, think ahead, plan to revise and edit, listen to critical advice, consider your audience, be clear, read a lot. We hope, however, that instructors respond to your writing in critically helpful ways and don't "trash" it or put it down. Whether or not you take some of the advice will depend upon what you want from your writing: good grades? self-knowledge? personal satisfaction? clear communication? a response by your audience? When we shared these suggestions with first-year students, they nodded their heads, took some notes, and laughed—often with relief.

WP TIP   Initiate an online conversation for the semester. Begin with the comments made by the students in this book and move on to sharing what each of you is learning about writing as the semester progresses.

▇ WRITING 5: EXPLORATION

What else would you like to ask advanced college students about writing? Find one and ask; report back.

I **f** **What else do you want to know about writing?**

Realizing that our first-year college writers had already received twelve years' worth of "good advice" about learning to write, we asked them one more question: "What do you want to learn about writing that you don't already know?" In parentheses, we have provided references to chapters of this handbook that answer these questions.

Emma: "Should I write to please the professor or to please myself?" (See Chapter 7, "Addressing Audiences.")

Jose: "I'm always being told to state my thesis clearly. What exactly is a thesis and why is it so important?" (See Chapter 5, " Writing for a Reason "; also Chapters 10, "Explaining Things"; 11, "Arguing Positions"; and 12, "Interpreting Texts.")

Jolene: "How do I develop a faster way of writing?" (See Chapter 6, " Inventing and Discovering.")

Amy: "Is there a trick to making a paper longer without adding useless information?" (See especially Chapter 21, "Focused Revising.")

Sam: "How do I learn to express my ideas so they make sense to common intelligent readers and not just to myself?" (See suggestions in Part VI, "Editing.")

Scott: "How can I make my writing flow better and make smooth transitions from one idea to the next?" (See Chapters 24, "Shaping Strong Paragraphs," and 26, "Strengthening Sentence Structure.")

Terry: "I want to learn to like to write. Then I won't put off assignments until the last minute." (See Chapter 3, "The Writing Process," and Part II.)

Jennifer: "I have problems making sentences sound good. How can I learn to do that?" (See Chapters 24–32.)

John P.: "I would like to develop some sort of personal style so when I write people know it's me." (See Chapter 8, "Finding a Voice.")

John K.: "I want to become more confident about what I write down on paper. I don't want to have to worry about whether my documentation is correct or my words spelled right." (See Chapters 17, "Using Sources," 18, "Documenting Sources," and 50, "Spelling.")

Woody: "Now that I'm in college, I would like to be challenged when I read and write, to think, and ask good questions, and find good answers." (See Chapter 2, "Reading Critically to Write Well.")

Pat: "I don't want to learn nose-to-the-grindstone, straight-from-the-textbook rules. I want to learn to get my mind into motion and pencil in gear." (See Chapters 3, "The Writing Process," and 6, " Inventing and Discovering.")

Heidi: "I would love to increase my vocabulary. If I had a wider range of vocabulary, I would be able to express my thoughts more clearly." (See Chapter 31, "Choosing the Right Word.")

Jess: "I'm always afraid that people will laugh at my writing. Can I ever learn to get over that and get more confident about my writing?" (See Chapters 3, "The Writing Process," and 22, "Responding to Writing.")

We can't, of course, guarantee that if you read and use *The Blair Handbook* your writing will get easier, faster, longer, clearer, or more correct. Or, for that matter, that your style will become more personal and varied, or that you will become a more confident and comfortable writer—no handbook can do that for you. Becoming a better writer depends on your own interest and hard work. It will also depend upon your college experience, the classes you take, and the teachers with whom you study. However, whether in class or on your own, if you read *The Blair Handbook* carefully and practice its suggestions, you should find possible answers to all these questions and many more.

We admit that there was at least one concern for which we really had no good response. Jessica wrote, "My biggest fear is that I'll end up one semester with four or five courses that all involve writing and I'll die." Or maybe we do have a response: If you become comfortable and competent as a writer, you'll be able to handle all the writing assignments thrown your way. Even if you can't, Jessica, you won't die. It's just college.

WP TIP Keep an electronic journal for the semester, one in which you discuss your goals in learning to write well. If you write in a notebook at times when you are away from your computer, enter your responses later. As you do, become conscious of any changes you are compelled to make to the notebook version and why. Keep dates on your entries to mark your progress.

■ WRITING 6: EXPLORATION

What else do you want to learn about writing? Refer to the table of contents and identify where in *The Blair Handbook* you think you might find the answer.

SUGGESTIONS FOR WRITING AND RESEARCH

INDIVIDUAL

1. Interview a classmate about his or her writing experiences, habits, beliefs, and practices. Include questions such as those asked in this chapter as well as others you think may be important. Write a brief essay profiling your classmate as a writer. Share your profile with a classmate.

2.   Over a two-week period, keep a record of every use you make of written language. Record your entries daily in a journal or class notebook. At the end of two weeks, enumerate all the specific uses as well as how often you did each. What activities dominate your list? Write an essay based on this personal research in which you argue for or against the centrality of writing in everyday life.

COLLABORATIVE

As a class or in small groups, design a questionnaire to elicit information about people's writing habits and attitudes. Distribute the questionnaire to both students and faculty in introductory and advanced writing classes. Compile the results. Compare and contrast the ideas of students at different levels and disciplines and write a report to share with the class. Consider writing a feature article for your student newspaper or faculty newsletter reporting what you found.   **WP TIP:** Design your questionnaire at the computer with your group. Print hard copy; then together, revise as necessary before you have it duplicated for the rest of the assignment.

Reading critically means being able to analyze the distinctions, interpretations, and conclusions of others and make sense of them. Writing critically means making distinctions, developing interpretations, and rendering conclusions in your own writing that stand up to the thoughtful scrutiny of others. Becoming a critical thinker means exercising reason and judgment in both reading and writing. While most of *The Blair Handbook* is about writing, this chapter is about critical reading and its relationship, to, and influence on, critical writing.

2 a Reading to understand

Before you can read any text critically, you need to understand what you're reading. In order to understand any text, you need some context for the new ideas you encounter, some knowledge of the text's terms and ideas, and some awareness of the rules that govern the kind of writing you are reading.

Imagine, for example, reading Mark Twain's *The Adventures of Huckleberry Finn* with no knowledge of American geography, the Mississippi River, or the institution of slavery. Imagine reading about the national debt without understanding basic mathematics, principles of taxation, or the meaning of deficit spending. The more you know about any subject, the more you are capable of learning. The more you learn, the more you know—and the more careful and critical will be your reading, writing, and thinking about that subject.

Many college instructors will ask you to read about subjects that are new to you, so you won't be spending much time reading about what you already know. As you read one unfamiliar text after another, how can you manage to read successfully? How can you create a context, learn the background, and find the rules to help you read unfamiliar texts in unfamiliar subject areas? Let's look at how this might be done.

ESL   READING STRATEGIES ACROSS LANGUAGES

If you learned to read in your native language before learning English, you can use some of the same strategies to read English that you developed in your native language. For example, some features of stories, explanations, or arguments may be the same in English as in your native language. Even if they are different, the strategies you developed in your native language for identifying and understanding the distinctive features of different kinds of texts can probably be used when you read in English as well. Whenever you feel that you do not have a good grasp of the purpose or important features of something you are reading in English, take a moment to reflect on how you would have approached a similar text in your native language, and see if you can use some of those same strategies.

You can also take advantage of information you gained through reading in your native language when you read in English. All readers relate new information in a text to what they already know; this helps them understand the text better and allows them to make predictions about what it will contain. As you read, try to be aware of any relevant information you know about the subject, whether you gained this information in English or in your native language.

As an experiment, read the following short opening paragraph from an eight-paragraph *New York Times* story entitled "Nagasaki, August 9, 1945." When you have finished, pause for a few moments and think about what you learned, how you learned it, and what you think the rest of the story will be about.

In August 1945, I was a freshman at Nagasaki Medical College. The ninth of August was a clear, hot, beautiful, summer day. I left my lodging house, which was one and one half miles from the hypocenter, at eight in the morning, as usual, to catch a tram car. When I got to the tram stop, I found that it had been derailed in an accident. I decided to return home. I was lucky. I never made it to school that day.

MICHAITO ICHIMARU

How did you do? Below, we've slowed down our own reading process to show what it was like:

1   We read the first sentence carefully, noticing the year 1945 and the name of the medical college, "Nagasaki." Through our prior historical knowledge, we *identified* Nagasaki, Japan, as the city on which the United States dropped an atomic bomb at the end of World War II—though we did not remember the precise date.

2   We noticed the city and the date (August 9) and wondered if that was when the bomb was dropped. We *asked* (silently), "Is this a story about the bomb?"

3   Still looking at the first sentence, a reference to the writer's younger self ("I was a freshman"), we guessed that the author was present at the dropping of this bomb. We *predicted* that this would be a survivor's account of the bombing of Nagasaki.

4   The word "hypocenter" in the third sentence made us pause again. We *questioned* what the word meant. The language seemed oddly out of place next to the "beautiful, summer day" described in the second sentence. It sounded technical enough to refer to the place where the bomb went off. Evidence was mounting that the narrator may have lived one and a half miles from the exact place where the atomic bomb detonated.

5   In the next to last sentence of the paragraph, the author says that he was "lucky" to miss school. Why, unless something unfortunate happened at school, would he consider missing it "lucky"? We *predicted* that had the author gone to school "as usual," he would have been closer to the hypocenter, which we now surmised was at Nagasaki Medical College.

6   We then *tested* our several predictions by reading the rest of the essay—something that you, of course, can't do here. They proved correct: Michaito Ichimaru's story is a firsthand account of witnessing and surviving the dropping of the bomb, which in fact killed all who attended the medical college, a quarter of a mile from the hypocenter.

7   Finally, out of curiosity, we *consulted* an encyclopedia for "Nagasaki" and *confirmed* that 75,000 people were killed by this second dropping of an atomic bomb on August 9, 1945.

It is possible that your reasoning went something like ours, which we have reconstructed here as best we could. Of course, these thoughts didn't occur in a seven-step sequence at all, but rather in split-second flashes, simultaneously. Even as we read a sentence for the first time, we found ourselves reading backward as much as forward to check our understanding.

You'll notice that in our example, some parts of the pattern of identifying/questioning/predicting/testing/confirming occur more than once, perhaps simultaneously, and not in any predictable order. No two readers would—or could—read this passage in exactly the same way. However, our reading process may be similar enough to yours to show that reading is a messy, trial-and-error process for everyone and that it depends as much on prior knowledge as on new information.

Whenever you read a new text or watch an unfamiliar event, you give it meaning by following a procedure similar to the one we did in the above example, trying to identify what you see, question what you don't understand, make and test predictions about meaning, and consult authorities for confirmation or information. Once you know how to read successfully for basic comprehension, you are ready to read critically.

ESL   UNDERSTANDING LANGUAGE WHEN READING

When you are reading in a language that is not your native language, vocabulary and idioms often pose a real challenge to your understanding of what you read. In addition, you may sometimes have difficulty interpreting sentences that have complex structures unlike those we typically hear in spoken English. This is especially true of difficult academic texts.

Since it is very important that you thoroughly understand any readings on which your writing assignments will be based, you may find it helpful to talk with a tutor or classmate about what you have read to check your understanding. You could ask them about idioms or vocabulary that are still unclear even after you have consulted a dictionary. You could also highlight orally difficult parts of a reading and then try paraphrasing them to check your comprehension and to identify any possible misinterpretations. In short, making sure that you understand well what you have read before you begin your first draft may save you a lot of time, effort, and possible confusion.

READING TO UNDERSTAND

1. Identify. Read first for what you recognize, know, and understand. Identify what you are reading about. Read carefully—slowly at first—and let meaning take hold where it can.

2. Question. Pause, and look hard at words and phrases you don't know or understand. See if they make sense when you reread them, compare them to what you do know, or place them in a context you understand.

3. Predict. Make predictions about what you will learn next: How will the essay, story, or report advance? What will happen? What theme or thesis will emerge? What might be the point of it all?

4. Test. Follow up on your predictions by reading further to see if they are correct or nearly correct. If they are, read on with more confidence; if they are not, read further, make more predictions, and test them. Trial and error are good teachers.

5. Confirm. Check your reading of the text with others who have also read it and see if your interpretations are similar or different. If you have questions, ask them. Share answers.

■ WRITING 1: APPLICATION

Select a book you have been assigned to read for one of your courses and find a chapter that has not yet been covered in class. Read the first page of the chapter and then stop. Write out any predictions you have about where the rest of the chapter is going. (Ask yourself, for example, What is its main theme or argument? How will it conclude?) Finish reading the chapter and check its conclusion against your predictions. If your predictions were close, you are reading well for understanding. **WP TIP:** Do this assignment on your word processor. Type out your predictions. After you finish reading, go back and write out a response to each of your predictions, creating as much space as you need between your earlier entries.

2 b   Reading critically

People read in different ways at different times. When they read a novel for pleasure or a newspaper to learn about current events, they read to find out "what happens." Doing this is reading for understanding. However, when they read a novel to write a paper on it or a newspaper to find evidence for an argument, they must read beyond this literal level of basic facts. They must analyze what they've read and assess the validity of the author's assumptions, ideas, and conclusions. Doing this is reading critically.

The rest of this chapter describes three strategies that lead readers from simply understanding texts to evaluating and interpreting them: previewing, responding, and reviewing. Although we will discuss this process of critical reading as three separate activities, it will become clear that they seldom occur in a simple one-two-three order.

One of our students, Richard, kept a detailed journal when he read a book entitled *Iron John*. Richard shared with us both his thoughts and journal entries, some of which are reproduced here as an example of critical reading.

■ WRITING 2: EXPLORATION

Describe how you read a text when you need to understand it especially well, say, before an examination on it or when you plan to use its ideas in a paper.

❶ Previewing

To preview a text, either look it over briefly before reading it or read it rapidly through once in order to get a general sense of what it says.

First questions

You should begin asking questions of a text from the moment you pick it up. Your first questions should be aimed at finding general, quickly gleaned information, such as that provided by the title, subtitle, and table of contents.

■   What does the title suggest?

■   What is the subject?

■   What does the table of contents promise?

■   What can I learn from the chapter titles or subheads?

■ Who is the author? (Have I heard of him or her?)

■ How current is the information?

You may not ask these questions methodically, in this order, and you don't have to write down your answers, but you should ask them before you read the whole text. If your answers to these questions suggest that a text is worthy of further study, continue with the previewing process.

Here are the notes Richard took in response to his first questions.

The title itself, *Iron John*, is intriguing, suggests something strong and unbreakable. I already know and admire the author, Robert Bly, for his insightful poetry, but have never read his prose.

The table of contents looks like fun:

1. The Pillow and the Key
2. When One Hair Turns Gold
3. The Road of Ashes, Descent, and Grief
4. The Hunger for the King in Time with No Father
5. The Meeting with the God-Woman in the Garden

Second questions

Once you've determined that a book or article warrants further critical attention, it's very helpful to read selected parts of it rapidly to see what they promise. Skim reading leads to second questions, the answers to which you should capture on note cards or in a journal.

■ Read the prefatory material: What can I learn from the book jacket, foreword, preface?

■ Read the introduction, abstract, or first page: What theme or thesis is promised?

■ Read a sample chapter or subsection: Is the material about what I expected?

■ Scan the index or notes: What sources have informed this text? What names do I recognize?

■ Note words or ideas that you do not understand: Do I have the background to understand this text?

■   Consider: Will I have to consult other sources to obtain a critical understanding of this one?

In skim-reading a text, you make predictions about coverage, scope, and treatment and about whether the information seems pertinent or useful for your purpose.

Here are the notes Richard took in response to his second group of questions.

> The jacket says, "*Iron John* is Robert Bly's long-awaited book on male initiation and the role of the mentor, the result of ten years' work with men to discover truths about masculinity that get beyond the stereotypes of our popular culture."

> There is no introduction or index, but the chapter notes in the back of the book (260–67) contain the names of people Bly used as sources. I recognize novelist D. H. Lawrence, anthropologist Mircea Eliade, poet William Blake, historian Joseph Campbell, and a whole bunch of psychologists—but many others I've never heard of.

These preview notes confirmed that *Iron John* is a book about men and male myths in modern American culture by a well-known poet writing a scholarly prose book in an informal style. Richard learned that Bly will not only examine current male mythology, but also make some recommendations about which myths are destructive and which constructive.

Previewing is only a first step in a process that now slows down and becomes more time-consuming and critical. As readers begin to preview a text seriously, they often make notes in the text's margin or in a journal or notebook to mark places for later review. In other words, before the preview stage of critical reading has ended, the responding stage has probably begun.

■   **WRITING 3: APPLICATION**

Select any unfamiliar book about which you are curious and preview it, using the two kinds of questions outlined here. Stop after ten minutes and write what you know about the text.

2   **Responding**

Once you understand what a text promises, you need to examine it more slowly. You need to begin the work of evaluating its ideas, assumptions, arguments, evidence, logic, and coherence. You need to start developing your own interpretation of what the text is all about. The best way to do this is to respond, or "talk back," to the text in writing.

Respond to passages that cause you to pause for a moment to reflect, to question, to read again, or to say "Aha!" If the text is informational, try to capture the statements that summarize ideas or are repeated. If the text is argumentative (and many of the texts you'll be reading in college will be), you need to examine the claims the text makes about the topic and to consider each piece of supporting evidence. (See Chapter 11 for more on arguments.) If the text is literary (a novel, play, poem, or essay), pay extra attention to language features such as images, metaphors, and dialogue. In any text, notice boldface or italicized words—they have been marked for special attention.

Ask about the effect of the text on you: How am I reacting? What am I thinking and feeling? What do I like? What do I distrust? Do I know why? But don't worry too much about answering all your questions at this point. (That's where reviewing comes in.)

Responding can take many forms, from margin notes to extensive journal entries, but it should involve writing. The more you write about something, the more you will understand it. If you own the article or book, write any questions or comments in the margins. If you don't—or even as an additional strategy if you do—try writing in a journal. A reading journal gives you a place to record responses to what you read. (Write each response on a fresh page, with the date, the title, and the author noted. In these entries, write any and all reactions you have to the text, including summaries, notes on key passages, speculations, questions, answers, ideas for further research, and connections to other books or events in your life. Note especially the ideas with which you agree or disagree. Explore ideas that are personally appealing. Record memorable quotations (with page numbers) and indicate why they strike you as memorable.

To read any text critically, begin with pen or pencil in hand. Mark places to be examined further, but be aware that mere underlining, checking, or highlighting does not yet involve you in a conversation with the text. To converse with the text, you need to engage actively in one or more of three activities: probing, freewriting, or annotating and cross-referencing.

In discussing these three activities, we will use the following brief passage from *Iron John* a text that Richard responded to in a variety of ways.

> The dark side of men is clear. Their mad exploitation of earth's resources, devaluation and humiliation of women, and obsession with tribal warfare are undeniable. Genetic inheritance contributes to their obsessions, but also culture and environment. We have defective mythologies that ignore masculine depth of feeling, assign men a place in the sky instead of earth, teach obedience to the wrong powers, work to keep men boys, and entangle both men and women in systems of industrial domination that exclude both matriarchy and patriarchy. . . .
>
> I speak of the Wild Man in this book, and the distinction between the savage man and the Wild Man is crucial throughout. The savage soul does great damage to soul, earth, and humankind; we can say that though the savage man is wounded he prefers not to examine it. The Wild Man, who has examined his wound, resembles a Zen priest, a shaman, or a woodsman more than a savage.

Although Richard's responses to *Iron John* illustrate all three activities, most students would use only one or two of these techniques to critically examine a single text.

Probing

In **probing**, ask deeper questions than you asked before. Here, for example, are the questions Richard raised about the passage from *Iron John*.

> Bly refers to the dark side of men; does he ever talk about the dark side of women? How would women's darkness differ from men's? What evidence for either does he provide?

> Bly suggests that part of men's dark behavior is genetic, part cultural; where does he get this information? Does he think it's a 50/50 split?

> What "defective mythologies" is Bly talking about? Does he mean things like religion and politics, or is he referring to nursery rhymes and folktales?

> I like the distinction Bly makes between "Wild" and "savage" men. Did he coin the terms or are they used pervasively in mythology in the same way? I wonder how sharp the line really is between the two.

Those are good questions to ask about the passage; however, any other reader could easily think of many more. These questions are "critical" in the sense that they not only request further information from the book but also challenge the author's terms, statements, and sources to see if they will stand up under scrutiny.

The questions are also written in Richard's own language. Using your own words helps in at least three ways:

1   It forces you to articulate precisely.

2   It makes the question your question.

3   It helps you remember the question for future use.

Freewriting

Write fast about an idea and see where your thoughts go. This **freewriting** often helps you clarify your own thoughts about the ideas in the text. When you freewrite, write to yourself in your own natural style, not worrying about sentence structure, spelling, or punctuation. Nobody else need ever read this; its purpose is to help you tie together ideas from your reading with the thoughts and experiences in your own mind. (For more details on freewriting, see 6b.)

In thinking about the passage from *Iron John*, Richard made the following entry in his journal.

> 9/30   Bly praises the "Wild Man" in us, clearly separating "wildness" from barbarism and savagery—hurting others. Also suggests that modern men are wounded in some way—literally?—but only those who examine their wounds gain higher knowledge. In an interview I once heard him talk about warriors—men who seek action (mountain climbing? skiing? Habitat for Humanity?) to feel whole and fulfilled. So men (why not women too?) test themselves—not necessarily against other men—against nature or even themselves. Harvey says sailing is his warrior activity. Is backpacking mine?

Richard's freewriting shows the writer reacting to one idea in the text (wildness), moving to another (being wounded), digressing by remembering a TV interview, raising a question (why not women too?), and concluding by raising a question about himself (Is backpacking mine?). Freewriting generates questions at random, catches them, and leaves the answering for later.

Annotating and cross-referencing

Annotating, or talking back to a text by writing in the margins, is an excellent way to make that text your own. Annotating is easier if you have your own copy of the text; otherwise you can make your annotations on Post-It notes or in a notebook with page numbers marked. As a critical reader, what would you write in these annotations?

■   Points of agreement or disagreement

■   Supporting examples

■   Extensions and further possibilities

■   Implications and consequences

■   Personal associations and remembrances

■   Connections to other texts, ideas, and courses

■   Recurring images and symbols

To move beyond annotating (commenting on single passages) to **cross-referencing** (finding relationships among passages), use a coding system to show that one annotation or passage is related to another. Some students write comments on different features of the text in different colors, such as reserving green for nature images, blue for key terms, red for interesting episodes, and so on. Other students write their notes first and then go back and number them, 1 for plot, 2 for key terms, and so on.

■   **WRITING 4: APPLICATION**

Keep a reading journal for an assigned reading from one of your courses. Write something in the journal after every reading session, including *probing questions* and *freewriting*. Annotate the text and create a cross-referencing system as you go along to see what patterns you can discover. Write about the results of these response methods in your journal: Did they help? Which ones worked best?

3   Reviewing

To review, you need both to reread and to *re-see* a text, reconsidering its meaning and the ideas you have about it. You need to be sure that you grasp the important points within the

The Fifties male had a clear vision of what a man was, and what male responsibilities were, but the isolation and one-sidedness of his vision were dangerous.

Examples in films? books?

During the *sixties,* another sort of man appeared. The waste and violence of the Vietnam war made men question whether they knew what an adult male really was. If manhood meant Vietnam, did they want any part of it? Meanwhile, the feminist movement encouraged men to actually look at women, forcing them to become conscious of concerns and sufferings that the Fifties male labored to avoid. As men began to examine women's history and women's sensibility, some men began to notice

How did they see it?

what was called their *feminine* side and pay attention to it. This process continues to this day, and I would say that most contemporary men are involved in it in some way.

Examples?
Easy Rider?
Platoon?

There's something wonderful about this devel opment--I mean the practice of men welcoming their own "feminine" consciousness and nurturing it--this is important--and yet I have the sense that there is something

female-associated word - loaded

Why is pleasing people wrong? contradiction?

wrong. The male in the past twenty years has become more thoughtful, more gentle. But by this process he has not become more free. He's a nice boy who pleases not only his mother but also the young woman he is living with.

How would Bly define free?

In the seventies I began to see all over the country a phenomenon that we might call the "soft male." Sometimes even today when I look out at an audience, perhaps half the young males are what I'd call soft. They're lovely, valuable people--I like them--they're not interested in harming the earth or starting wars.

Should they be?

An annotated text page

text, but you also need to move beyond that level to a critical understanding of the text as a whole. In responding, you started a conversation with the text so you could put yourself into the book's framework and context; in reviewing, you should consider how the book can fit into your own framework and context. As you review, keep responding, talking back to the text but this time do so with more purpose and focus.

Reviewing will take different forms depending on how you intend to use the text—whether or not you are using it to write a paper, for example. In general, there are two ways to review a text you have read critically: you can interpret what it means or you can evaluate its soundness or significance.

When you review to interpret or evaluate a text, you slow your reading down and ask critical questions. You move beyond an appreciation of what the text says and build your own theory of what the text means and how good or useful it is. (For more information on writing to interpret, see Chapter 12; for more on evaluating texts, see Chapter 15.)

If you plan to write a critical paper about a text, it's a good idea to confirm your interpretation by consulting what others have said about that text. The interpretations of other critics will help put your own view in perspective as well as raise questions that may not have occurred to you. Try to read more than one perspective on a text. However, it is better to consult such sources after you have established some views of your own so that you do not simply adopt the view of the first expert you read.

When you review a text, you examine its meaning and weigh its merits: What does it say? Is it credible? Why or why not? What's debatable? Texts with different purposes need to be examined accordingly. For example an argumentative text tries to do one thing, an informational text something else, and a literary text something else again.

Argumentative texts. Argumentative texts make certain claims in advance and then support those claims with evidence. When you first respond to such a text, you may simply identify and comment on the text's argument. When you review it, you examine and evaluate each part of the argument to see whether it is sound. If the text argues that *Huckleberry Finn* is a racist book, look closely at the evidence, the claims, and the whole argument.

Review the **evidence**:

- Is it a **fact**—something that can be verified and that most readers will accept without further argument?

- Is it an **inference**—a conclusion drawn from an accumulation of facts?

■ Is it an **opinion**—an idea that reflects an author's personal beliefs and may be based on faith, emotion, or myth?

While all three types of evidence have their place, the strongest arguments are based on accurate facts and reasonable inferences. Look out for opinions that are masquerading as facts and for inferences that are based on insufficient facts.

Review the **claims**. A claim is a statement that something is true or should be done.

■ Is the claim stated clearly? (On what page?)

■ Is every claim supported by sufficient evidence?

■ Are you aware of counterclaims or contradictory evidence?

If a claim is important or daring, one fact is not enough. Look for any claims that are unsupported or that are supported by insufficient evidence.

Review the **logic of the argument**. For an argument to be logical, it must be based on reason, not emotion.

■ Does the argument advance step by step to a reasonable conclusion?

■ Are there any unexplained gaps or mistakes in reasoning?

(See Chapter 11 for more on argumentative writing.)

Informational texts. Reviewing informational texts requires making sure the facts are true, the inferences are based on facts, and the opinions are based knowledge. Informational texts don't make arguments, but they often draw conclusions from the facts they present. For example, a geology text explaining the theory of continental glaciation should explain the evidence that supports the theory. Ask these kinds of questions of informational texts:

■ Do the facts justify the conclusions?

■ Is any information that you expect to be there missing?

■ Is the author's tone fair and reasonable?

■ What is the basis for the author's expertise?

(See Chapter 10 for more on informational writing.)
Literary texts. Essays, short stories, poems, and plays may contain arguments and information, but their primary goal is more elusive—to make you feel, imagine, empathize, or understand. One good way to interpret or evaluate literature is to write journal entries in response to different elements of the text:

- What is the **plot**?

- Are the **characters** believable?

- Is the **setting** convincing?

- From what **point of view** is the text written?

- What **images or themes** are repeated?

Interpreting and evaluating literature is often very personal, relying on individual associations and responses, but the strongest critical evaluations are based on textual evidence. (For information on analyzing and interpreting literary texts, see Chapter 12.)

WP TIP Enter the questions for literary texts above or any other guidelines from this section in one or more word processing files with titles that clearly reflect the contents. Draft responses to these questions in the same file(s). Print a hard copy of these guidelines whenever you need them, writing notes on them and keeping them beside you at the computer as you write.

ESL EVALUATING TEXTS

If you received reading instruction in your native language, the emphasis of your instruction may have been on understanding, remembering, and applying the information that you read rather than on critically evaluating it. You may have been taught to accept the texts you read as factual; consequently, it may seem strange or even inappropriate for you to evaluate or challenge what you read. If this is the case, you might want to discuss with your instructor this difference between your reading experience in your native language and your reading experience in English. Or you could write about it in your journal.

■ **WRITING 5: APPLICATION**

Critically review the same reading assignment you responded to in Writing 4. Review the text by asking the sorts of questions discussed here, and then record in your journal a summary of your evaluation or interpretation.

SUGGESTIONS FOR WRITING AND RESEARCH

INDIVIDUAL

Select a short text. First read it briefly for *understanding*, to be sure it makes sense to you. Second, read it *critically* according to the methods described in this chapter. Finally, write a short (two-page) *review* of the text in which you explain its meaning and recommend or don't recommend it to other readers.

COLLABORATIVE

As a class or small group, agree on a short text to read and write about, following the suggestions in the individual exercise above. Share your written reviews in small groups, paying particular attention to the claims and evidence each writer uses. Rewrite your review, using the response you received from your group. (For more information about responding to other writers' texts, see Chapter 22.)

While there is no one best way to write, some ways do seem to work for more people in more situations than do others. Learning what these ways are may save you some time, grief, or energy—perhaps all three. This chapter describes the messy business we call "the writing process." It takes a close look at how writers write from the time they select something to write about through their efforts at drafting, revising, and editing, until they send this writing out into the world. If you're interested in improving your writing, examine closely your own writing process: describe how you do it, identify what works and what doesn't, then study the ideas and strategies that work for others—some of these are bound to help you.

3   a   Describing writing as a process

It's time to examine your own writing habits: What do you do, for example, when you are assigned to write a paper due in one week? Do you sit down that day and start writing the introduction? Or do you sit down but do something else instead? If you don't work on the assignment right away, do you begin two days before deadline, or is your favorite time the night before the paper is due? Do you write a few pages a day, every day, and let your paper emerge gradually? Or do you prefer to draft it one day, revise the next, and proofread it just before handing it in?

What writing conditions do you seek? Do you prefer your own room? Do you like to listen to certain kinds of music? Do you deliberately go somewhere quiet, such as the library? Or do you prefer a coffee shop, a cafe, or a booth at McDonald's?

With what do you write? Your own computer or the school's? Your old Smith Corona portable typewriter, or a pencil on tablets of lined paper? Or do you first write with a favorite pen and then copy the result onto a computer?

Which of the habits or methods described here is the right one? Which technique yields the best results? These are trick questions, since different ones work best for different individuals. There is no single best way to write. People manage to write well under wildly different conditions.

The rest of this chapter identifies five discrete but overlapping and often nonsequential phases of the process of writing—planning, drafting, researching, revising, and editing—and explains how this handbook reflects this process.

WP TIP Use the above questions as grist for your online journal. Answer them as you also respond to the others that begin this chapter: How has online composing changed my writing process? How do more traditional methods mix with online methods in my writing process? What works best?

ESL **USING YOUR NATIVE LANGUAGE WHEN COMPOSING IN ENGLISH**

You may want to compose in both your native language and English when working on a writing assignment. For example, you might brainstorm, make notes, or create outlines in your native language, or you could use native-language words or phrases when you're not sure of the English equivalents. Using your native language this way may help you avoid writer's block and develop fluency in English. Periodically you should evaluate the effectiveness of your composing strategies. For instance, if you find that using a native language–English dictionary often results in unidiomatic constructions, you may want to become more familiar with a good English-English dictionary.

■ WRITING 1: EXPLORATION

Answer the questions posed on the opening pages of this chapter: Where, when, and how do you usually write? What are the usual results? With what do you need some extra help? **ESL:** If you sometimes write in your native language, compare the process you use when writing in it with the process you use when writing in English. Are any parts different? Why do you think this is so?

3 b   Planning

Planning consists of creating, discovering, locating, developing, organizing, and trying out ideas. Writers are doing deliberate planning when they make notes, turn casual lists into organized outlines, write journal entries, compose rough drafts, and consult with others. They also are doing less deliberate planning while they walk, jog, eat, read, browse in libraries, converse with friends, or wake up in the middle of the night thinking. Planning involves both expanding and limiting options, locating the best strategy for the occasion at hand, and focusing energy productively.

Planning comes first. It also comes second and third. No matter how careful your first plans, the act of writing usually necessitates that you keep planning all the way through the writing process, that you continue to think about why you are writing, what you are writing, and for whom. When writers are not sure how their ideas will be received by someone else, they often write to themselves first, testing their ideas on a friendly audience, and find good voices for communicating with others in later drafts.

During the planning process for *The Blair Handbook*, for instance, we were trying out ideas and exploring broadly and also narrowing our thinking to focus both on our purpose as writers and the purposes that handbooks serve. We had to consider our audience: who uses handbooks? We had to find our voice not only as classroom teachers but as writers—would we be friendly and casual or authoritative and serious? We spent some time inventing and discovering ideas—figuring out what kind of information you, our readers, require in a handbook, how much of this information we already knew, and where to find what we didn't know.

Part II of this handbook focuses on the concerns that most writers face at the initial stages of a writing project: using a journal to help you create and discover ideas (Chapter 4), writing for a reason (Chapter 5), inventing and discovering ideas through exploratory writing (Chapter 6), determining who your audience is and how to write to that audience (Chapter 7), and finding your voice as a writer (Chapter 8).

▪ WRITING 2: APPLICATION

Describe the strategies you commonly use when you plan papers. How much does your planning vary from time to time or assignment to assignment? Now use your favorite planning strategy for twenty minutes to plan one currently assigned paper.

3 **c** Drafting

At some point all writers need to move beyond thinking, talking, and planning and actually start writing. Many writers like to schedule a block of time—an hour or more—to draft their ideas, give them shape, see what they look like. One of the real secrets to good writing is simply learning to sit down and write.

Drafting is the intentional production of language to convey information or ideas to an audience. First drafts are concerned with ideas, with getting the direction and concept of the piece of writing clear. Subsequent drafting, which includes revising and editing, is concerned with making the initial ideas ever sharper, more precise and clearer.

While most writers hope their first draft will be their final draft, it seldom is. Still, try to make your early drafts as complete as possible at the time—that is, give each draft your best shot: compose in complete sentences, break into paragraphs where necessary, and aim at a satisfying form. At the same time, allow time for second and third drafts and maybe more.

Sometimes it's hard to separate drafting from planning, researching, revising, and editing. Many times in writing *The Blair Handbook*, we sat down to explore a possible idea in a notebook and found ourselves drafting part of a chapter instead. Other times, when we were trying to advance an idea in a clear and linear way, we kept returning instead to revise a section just completed. While it's useful to separate these phases of writing, don't worry too much if they refuse to stay separate. In most serious writing, every phase of the process can be considered recursive—that is, moving back and forth almost simultaneously and maybe even haphazardly, from planning to revising to editing to drafting, back to planning, and so on.

WP TIP   Be sure to save your work often when you are writing. It is safer to name a new file "Exploration" immediately upon opening it, before you begin; then save your work often as you write.

The five chapters in Part III describe strategies for drafting different college writing assignments: recounting experience (Chapter 9), explaining things (Chapter 10), arguing positions (Chapter 11), interpreting texts (Chapter 12), and reflecting on the world (Chapter 13). Each chapter contains samples of student writing, in both draft and finished stages. While there are more than five kinds of college papers, the approaches to drafting in Part III apply to any number of other writing assignments.

■ **WRITING 3: APPLICATION**

Describe the process you most commonly use to draft a paper. Is your way of starting consistent from paper to paper? Now write the first draft for the paper you planned in Writing 2: sit down, and for half an hour compose as much of the paper as you can, noting in brackets as you go along where you need to return with more information or ideas.

3 d   Researching

Writers need something to write about. Unless they are writing completely from memory, they need to locate ideas and information. Even personal essays and experiential papers can benefit from additional factual information that substantiates and intensifies what the writer remembers.

As a college student, you do a form of research every time you write an analysis or an interpretation of a text: reading and rereading the text is the research. You do research when you compare one text to another. You do research to track down the dates of historical events. You do research when you conduct laboratory experiments, visit museums, or interview people in the college community.

Whenever you write about unfamiliar subjects, you have two choices: to research and find things out, or to bluff with unsupported generalizations. Which kind of paper would you prefer to read? Which kind of writing will you profit by doing?

The six chapters in Part IV describe how to write papers that require research. We encourage you to consider research as a natural part of almost every writing assignment: The truth is, writers should know what they are writing about rather than limiting themselves to writing what they already know about. However, one common college assignment—the research essay—will require you to do more extensive research, use a more formal style and format, and write a longer paper than most other assignments; Chapter 14 provides guidance on writing research essays. Research for college papers is conducted either in the library (Chapter 15) or out in the field (Chapter 16), and after gathering your information, you'll need to decide how to use (Chapter 17) and document those sources according to the Modern Language Association (MLA) system (Chapter 18). Chapter 19 provides sample research essays written about different subjects, using a variety of styles, formats, sources, and voices.

Because the documentation system appropriate for a paper depends largely on the discipline in which it is written, we include specific instructions and models for documenting research papers in Part VIII, "Writing across the Curriculum" (Chapters 59–65). This section presents each documentation system within the context of the aims and styles of its discipline: the Chicago system for the humanities, the American Psychological Association (APA) system for the social sciences, and different number systems for the sciences.

▮ WRITING 4: APPLICATION

Describe the kind of research assignments you have done in the past. Now locate additional research information to add to the paper you began drafting in Writing 3, using any research process with which you are familiar.

3 **e** Revising

Somewhere in the midst of their writing, most writers revise the drafts they have planned, started, and researched. Revising involves rewriting to make the purpose clearer, the argument stronger, the details sharper, the evidence more convincing, the organization more logical, the opening more inviting, the conclusion more satisfying.

We consider revising to be separate from editing, yet the two tasks may not always be separable. Essentially, revising occurs at the level of ideas, whereas editing occurs at the level of the sentence. Revising means re-seeing the drafted paper and thinking again about its direction, focus, arguments, and evidence. In writing this second edition of *The Blair Handbook*, we revised ceaselessly to get each chapter even sharper than it was in the first edition.

While it is tempting to edit individual words and sentences as you revise, revising first saves time and energy. Revising to refocus or redirect often requires that you delete paragraphs, pages, and whole sections of your draft, actions that can be painful if you have already carefully edited them.

The three chapters in Part V recommend making revision a dynamic and aggressive activity. Each chapter covers a different aspect or approach to revising. Chapter 20 ("The Revising Process") discusses the revising process as a whole and recommends some general strategies. Chapter 21 ("Focused Revising") explores creative revision options, while Chapter 22 ("Responding to Writing") examines how writing groups help students become better writers.

■ WRITING 5: APPLICATION

Does your usual process for revising a paper include any of the ideas discussed in this section? Describe how your process is similar or different. Now revise the paper to which you added research information in Writing 4, using any revision techniques with which you are comfortable.

WP TIP   Don't hesitate to use word processing functions that make it fairly easy to execute your revising decisions: cutting and pasting, moving blocks of text, search and replace, and so on. Remember: the computer cannot make these decisions for you, but it can help you change the text as *you* have seen fit. Date and name your various computer-generated drafts.

3 **f**   Editing

Whether writers have written three or thirteen drafts, they want the last one to be perfect—or as near perfect as time and skill allow. When editing, writers pay careful attention to the language they have used, striving for the most clarity and punch possible. Many writers edit partly to please themselves, so their writing sounds right to their own ear. At the same time, they edit hoping to please, satisfy, or convince their intended readers.

You edit to communicate as clearly as possible. After you've spent time drafting and revising your ideas, it would be a shame for readers to dismiss those ideas because they were poorly expressed. Check the clarity of your ideas, the logic and flow of paragraphs, the precision and power of your words, and the correctness and accuracy of everything, from facts and references to spelling and punctuation.

In finishing *The Blair Handbook*, we went over every word and phrase to make sure each one expressed our ideas precisely. Then our editors did the same. Then they sent the manuscript to other experts on writing, and they too went over the whole manuscript. Then we revised and edited again.

Because there are so many different things to look for when you edit your writing, Part VI of *The Blair Handbook*, the editing section, occupies more than half the volume. It is organized into several subparts for easy reference. "Editing for Effectiveness" covers strategies for attracting and holding your readers' attention. "Editing Grammar" explains the grammatical conventions of standard English. "Editing Punctuation" describes the conventions of periods, commas, semicolons, and so on, and "Editing Mechanics" covers additional conventions of presenting language in written form.

■ WRITING 6: EXPLORATION/APPLICATION

Do you edit using any of the ideas mentioned in this section? Describe your usual editing techniques. Now edit the paper you revised in Writing 5, referring to Part VI of *The Blair Handbook* as needed.

3 *g* **Writing with computers**

Computers are great writing tools. Unlike typewriters, pens, and pencils, computers allow writers to change their writing infinitely and easily before the words are ever printed on paper. Writers are not committed to final copy until they print it out, and even then they can work on it again and again without retyping the whole thing over.

All word processing programs work in pretty much the same way: You type the words on the computer screen—plan, draft, revise, edit. When finished, you store the file on your hard drive (C) or on a floppy disk (in drive A), with a brief descriptive name (story). When you want to work on the document again, you call the file back to the screen and start all over.

WRITING WITH COMPUTERS

Following are several ways that computers can help you in the process of writing. Throughout *The Blair Handbook* you will find suggestions for using computers at each stage of the writing process.

1. Planning. Use the computer to invent and discover ideas by writing out lists of topics or tentative outlines. The computer's ability to add, delete, and rearrange makes these planning and organizing strategies easy. (See Part Two.)

2. Freewriting. Freewrite rapidly on your computer when you're exploring ideas or simply stuck. Don't worry about spelling, punctuation, grammar, or style. Let your words trigger new thoughts and suggest new plans and directions. (See Chapter 6.) Save these entries on disk to create a computer journal. (See Chapter 4.)

3. Drafting. Use the computer to compose initial ideas, taking advantage of the ease with which words, sentences, and paragraphs can be modified and moved around as your ideas and direction become clearer. It's also easy to lift whole passages from computer-written freewrites or journal writing and incorporate them directly into your draft. (See Chapters 9–13).

4. Researching. Computers equipped with modems or networked allow you to gain access to library information at the stroke of a key. Instead of traveling physically to locate books, periodicals, and special collections, search for material and receive printouts from your room. (See Chapters 14–18.)

5. Revising. Typing on a computer creates instant distance from your words and ideas, allowing you to view them more objectively. Whole paragraphs can be deleted, added, changed, and moved around—all useful activities when revising drafts. You can add new information or evidence in appropriate sections. Your computer will repaginate and reformat instantly. But remember that your paper won't *be* good simply because it *looks* good in an attractive font or after laser printing. (See Part Five.)

Improving your writing process

Computers make it easier for you to move back and forth freely as you compose. If you are like most writers, you proba-

6. Editing. Computers allow you to try out numerous possibilities when editing sentences and paragraphs. The search-and-replace function can make each sentence start a new line and be judged on its own merits. Periodically, print out a hard copy to review your text; changes you make on paper can then be incorporated easily on screen for a new printout.

7. Reference. With a keystroke you can consult online dictionaries, encyclopedias, thesauruses, grammar books, and style manuals to check and change your text.

8. Proofreading. A built-in spell checker becomes your first line of spelling defense, as it will rapidly identify which words you've mistyped or misspelled. You must still proofread with your own eyes, since the computer will not find mistyped words that spell others words (*of/if* or *dinner/diner*) or omitted words.

9. Formatting. Many word processing programs provide type styles (fonts), graphic images, and page layouts that can produce professional-looking and visually exciting papers with improved readability and aesthetic appeal. Keep in mind that an attractive presentation is no substitute for clear language, logic, and organization. Keep in mind, however, that the ways in which you use technology can also benefit from their combination with more "traditional" methods—for example, printing hard copy for editing and for preliminary revisions. Visiting the library and hunting for information there bolsters Web-generated research sources.

10. Saving. When you write with a computer, save all versions of your papers on the hard drive or on floppy disks so that you can always return to them. And be sure to make duplicate or "backup" copies of all work in case an accident destroys one copy. If you make radical revisions on one draft and don't like them, simply go back to the saved original and try again.

bly jump around—planning, drafting, and researching whenever you need to. Computers facilitate this process by keeping everything fluid and endlessly changeable.

Creating distance

Computers create instant distance from your thoughts, setting them in good-looking electronic type, where they seem less personal and easier to revise and edit. Most give you access to type styles (fonts), graphic images, and page layouts that can produce professional-looking and visually exciting papers with good readability and aesthetic appeal.

Gaining access to the library

Computers allow access to research resources via the Internet or local library via direct network. Instead of traveling physically to locate information, books, periodicals, and special collections, you can search for, find, and receive printouts from sources within the collections of many libraries, museums, and electronic bulletin boards.

Consulting reference sources

Computer programs allow you to check dictionaries, encyclopedias, thesauruses, grammar books, and style manuals, automatically coordinated with whatever text you are working on. In the future such tools will only become more numerous and better.

3 h Writing in English as a second language

All students in a writing class can grow as writers, those with extensive writing experience as well as those who have never written much. However, the ones faced with the greatest challenge may be students whose first language is not English. In addition to learning new strategies for composing and new forms for expressing what they know, nonnative speakers must attend to the conventions of language that native speakers take for granted.

Besides possible grammar and vocabulary difficulties, students who grew up speaking another language may have to adjust to the expectations and traditions of the American classroom. For example, American academic prose is often less formal than that in many other countries. Students who have learned to write in more formal systems may find instructors suggesting that they make their writing more lively or personal. Also, while U.S. schools increasingly treat writing as a multiple-draft process, instructors in many other countries may expect a piece of writing to be finished correctly the first time through.

If English is not your native language, you need to read, write, speak, and listen attentively to as much English as you can. Use your writing class as a place to try out new ideas about writing, revising, and editing, and don't be afraid to ask your instructor and classmates for help.

Throughout *The Blair Handbook*, green boxes provide information about the English language of particular interest to non-native speakers. The green letters "ESL" in the table of contents identify each section that includes one of these specially marked boxes. This symbol also appears before the special ESL writing suggestions found in many chapters in Parts I, II, and III. Finally, an ESL index is provided at the back of the book to help you locate topics that you may find helpful.

SUGGESTIONS FOR WRITING AND RESEARCH

INDIVIDUAL

Study your own writing process as you work on one whole paper from beginning to end, taking notes in your journal to document your habits and practices. Write an analytic sketch describing the way you write and speculating about the origins of your current habits.

COLLABORATIVE

With your classmates, form interview pairs and identify local professional writers or professors who publish. Make an appointment with one of these practicing writers, interview him or her about the writing process he or she practices, and report back to the class. Write a collaborative report about writers in your community; make it available to other writing classes or interested faculty.

WP TIP Interview some of your practicing writers through e-mail, others in person. Write your collaborative report with colleagues at a computer, referring to a hard copy of your online conversations.

PART TWO

Planning

Journals allow people to talk to themselves without feeling silly. They help college students figure out and reflect on what is happening in their personal and academic lives. Sometimes students focus their journal writing narrowly, on the subject matter of a single discipline; other times they speculate broadly, on the whole range of academic experience; and still other times they write personally, exploring their private thoughts and feelings. College instructors often recommend or require that students keep journals to monitor what and how the students are learning. Just as often, however, students require journals of themselves, realizing that journals are more useful for the writer than for the reader.

4 a Understanding journals

Journals are daily records of people's lives (*jour* is French for "day"). Of course, journals don't need to be written in every day, and sometimes they go by other names: daybooks, logs, learning logs, commonplace books, or simply writer's notebooks. No matter what you call them, their function is similar—to capture ideas and events that are on your mind. In this sense, a journal can be whatever you want it to be, recording whatever snippets of life you find interesting and potentially useful. What makes a journal a journal?

Sequence

Journals capture thoughts sequentially, from one day to the next. Dating each entry allows you to compare ideas to both later and earlier ones and provides an ongoing record of your constancy, change, or growth. You thus end up documenting your learning over the course of a semester or a project.

Audience

Journals are written for the writer, not some distant reader. A journal is a place to explore what's important to *you*, not to communicate information or ideas to someone else. While you may choose to share entries with people you trust, your main audience remains yourself. An assigned journal, however, may initiate an informal conversation between you and your instructor. In this role, it has much in common with notes, letters, and other informal means of communication.

Language

The language of journals is whatever writers want it to be. Since your audience is yourself, you should use whatever language you feel most comfortable with. (The exception would be a journal assigned by somebody else who wants also to read it.) Your focus should be on ideas rather than on style, grammar, spelling, or punctuation. In journal writing, focus on what you want to say rather than on the language of your thought.

Freedom

You are free to get things wrong in journals and not be penalized. Journals are practice and discovery books: you can put new concepts into your own words, try out new lines of reasoning, and not worry about completing every thought. If something doesn't work the first time, try it again in subsequent entries—or abandon it entirely.

Academic journals differ from diaries, daybooks, and private journals in important ways. Whereas diaries and the like record any and all events of the writer's day, academic journals focus more consistently on ideas under study in college. Academic journals might be described as a cross between private diaries written solely for the writer, and class notebooks, which record an instructor's words. Like diaries, journals are written in the first person about ideas important to the writer; like class notebooks, they focus on a subject under study in a college course.

Diary ──────▶ Academic Journal ◀────── Class notebook

Your journal includes your thoughts, reactions, reflections, and questions about your classes and ideas, written in your own language. Think of your academic journal as a personal record of your educational experience.

■ WRITING 1: APPLICATION

Describe your experiences with journals. Have you ever kept one for school before? In which class? With what result? Have you ever kept one on your own? With what result? Do you still keep one? What is it like? **ESL:** Have you ever kept a journal in your native language? What was it like? If you are unfamiliar with journals, what do you think of the idea of journal writing?

4 b Keeping college journals

Both personal and academic journals are useful to college writers because they provide places to record and play with thought and experience. In our classes, we recommend that students keep both, one about their private lives, one about academic matters; sometimes they do this with separate notebooks, other times by dividing a loose-leaf notebook into two sections.

WP TIP Begin an electronic journal. You have several options for its format. You can continue in the same file or initiate separate files for different dates, topics, or classes. You can also highlight and print out only what you want to share with classmates or instructors.

■ Journals in the writing class

Journals are often assigned to help student writers discover, explore, advance, and critique their writing projects and to help instructors monitor and informally assess students' development as writers.

Use your journal to find topics to write about, to try out introductions and arguments, to record relevant research and observations, to assess how the paper is turning out, and to make plans for what to do next. In the following journal entry, John tells himself what to do in the next draft of a paper describing his coaching of an eighth-grade girls' soccer team.

> 9/16 I'm going to try to use more dialogue in my paper. That is what I really think I was missing. The second draft is very dull. As I read it, it has no life. I should have used more detail.

I'll try more dialogue, lots more, in draft 3. I'll have it take place at one of my practices, giving a vivid description of what kids were like.

I have SO MUCH MATERIAL. But I have a hard time deciding what seems more interesting.

John uses his journal to critically evaluate his most recent paper draft and to catch ideas for revising next time.

Use your journal to record what you've learned about writing through class discussions, reading of other student papers, and review of your own writing. Near the end of the semester, John reflected in his journal about what he had learned so far.

11/29 I've learned to be very critical of my own work, to look at it again and again, looking for big and little problems. I've also learned from my writing group that other people's comments can be extremely helpful—so now I make sure I show my early drafts to Kelly or Karen before I write the final draft. I guess I've always known this, but now I actually do it.

WP TIP Remember that you can copy worthwhile parts of your journal directly into a working draft of a paper.

WRITING 2: APPLICATION

Keep a journal for the duration of a writing project, recording in it all of your starts, stops, insights, and ideas related to the project. At the end, consider whether the journal presents a fair portrait of your own writing process.

2 Journals across the curriculum

Journals are useful in any course, to clarify course purposes, pose and solve problems, keep track of readings, raise questions to ask in class, practice for exams, and find topics for paper assignments.

In science or mathematics, when you switch from numbers to words, you often see the problem differently. In addition, putting someone else's problem or question into your own language makes it yours and so leads you one step further toward a solution.

One of the best uses for journals is making connections between college knowledge and personal knowledge. For example, when you record personal reflections in an academic journal, you may identify with and perhaps make sense of the otherwise distant and confusing past. When you write out trial hypotheses based on personal observations, you may eventually discover good ideas for research topics, designs, or experiments.

WP TIP Review your journal entries periodically. Highlight in bold any points or ideas that you think you might like to develop in later papers. Try to make connections between your "personal" and "academic" entries and subjects when discussing them in class and in papers.

■ WRITING 3: APPLICATION

Think of any course you are now taking that does not require a journal. Could you find a use for a journal in that class? What topics would you explore?

3 Personal journals

While *The Blair Handbook* emphasizes academic writing, we believe that personal journal writing has many powerful benefits for college writers. In personal journals, feel free to explore your feelings about college, prospective majors, roommates, grades, parties, dates, friends. When you keep a journal in a writing class, mark off a section for personal entries. Whether you share these with your instructor should be up to you.

■ WRITING 4: APPLICATION

Keep a personal journal for two weeks, writing faithfully for at least ten minutes each day. Write about whatever is on your mind. Follow the "Guidelines for Keeping a Journal" at the end of this chapter. After two weeks, reread your entries and assess the worth of such writing to you.

4 Double-entry journals

Double-entry journals can help you separate initial observations from later, more reflective observations. To make such a

Summary	What I think
pp. 3–12. Celie's mother is dying so her father starts having sex with her. She got pregnant by him twice and he sold both of her babies. Celie's mother died and he got married again to a very young girl. Mr. is a man whose wife died and he has a lot of children. He wants to marry Celie's sister Nettie. Their father won't let him. He says Nettie has too much going for her so he let him have Celie.	Why did Celie's father sell her kids? How could Mr. take Celie if he wanted Nettie so much? I think Celie's father is lowdown and selfish. A very cruel man.
pp. 13–23. Celie got married to Mr. and his kids don't like her and he beats her. While Celie was in town she met the lady who has her kids. She was a preacher's wife. Nettie ran away and came to stay with Celie. Mr. still likes her and puts her out because she shows no interest in him. Celie tells her to go to the preacher's wife's house and stay with them because she was the only woman she saw with money.	I think it's wrong to marry someone to take care of your children and to keep your home clean. I think Celie was at least glad to know one of her children was in good hands. I am glad Nettie was able to get away from her dad and Mr., hopefully the preacher & wife will take her in.
pp. 24–32. Shug Avery, Mr.'s old girlfriend and also an entertainer, came to town. Mr. got all dressed up so he can go see her, he stayed gone all weekend. Celie was very excited about her.	How could he go and stay out with another woman all weekend? Why didn't he marry Shug? Why was Celie so fascinated with Shug?

A sample of a double-entry journal.

journal, divide each page in a notebook with a vertical line down the middle. On the left side of the page, record initial observations of data; on the right side, reflect on the meaning of what you first recorded, either at the same time or later. In other words, double-entry journals let you observe and reflect upon your prior observations and reflections.

Although such notebooks originated in the sciences, allowing lab scientists to collect data at one time and to speculate about them later, these notebooks also serve well in other courses. In an English class, for example, you can make initial observations about the plot of a story on the left, while raising questions and concerns on the right, as we see in Susan's entry about Alice Walker's novel *The Color Purple* shown on page 47. In the left column, she recorded the plot; in the right column, she noted her personal reaction to what she was reading.

ESL **JOURNALS FOR SECOND LANGUAGE WRITING**

Journals are useful when you are writing in a language other than your native language. Since you don't have to be concerned with correctness, you can work on developing fluency, experimenting with language, and trying out new vocabulary or sentence structures.

In an academic journal, your instructor will most likely expect you to do more than summarize assigned reading. Consider using a double-entry journal. Summarize what you have read in one column and then comment on or raise questions about the reading in the column next to it.

To help you develop your English vocabulary, keep an ongoing list of new words as described in 31c. Include both vocabulary you learn in your classes and words or idioms that you hear outside of class.

WP TIP Keep your ongoing list of words and idioms in a computer file, updating it as necessary from other notebooks that you keep with you. You will thus have easy access to your word list when drafting at the computer.

4 **c** Ideas for college journals

Journals are useful even when you're not in an academic environment, since good ideas, questions, and answers don't always wait for convenient times. We suggest that you write often, in your most comfortable voice, and not worry about someone evaluating you. The following selection of journal entries illustrates some of the ways journals can be used.

1 Planning

Journals can help you plan any project by providing a place to talk it over with yourself. Whether it's a research paper, a personal essay, or a take-home examination, you can make journal notes about how to approach it, where to start, or who else to consult before actually beginning a draft. Here is an entry from Peter's journal kept for his first-year writing class.

> 10/12 Well, I switched my research topic to something I'm actually interested in, a handicapped children's rehabilitation program right her on campus. My younger brother was born deaf and our whole family has pitched in to help him—but I've never really studied what a college program could do to help. The basis of my research will be interviews with people who run the program—I have my first appointment tomorrow with Professor Stanford.

Sometimes planning means venting frustration about what's going wrong; other times it means exploring a new direction or topic. Journal writing is ultimately unpredictable: it doesn't come out neat and orderly, and sometimes it doesn't solve your problem, but it does provide a place where you can keep trying to solve it.

2 Learning to write

Part of the content of a writing course is the business of learning to write. You can use a journal to document how your writing is going and what you need to do next to improve it. In the following example, Bruce reflects on his experience of writing a report.

10/3 I'm making this report a lot harder than it should be. I think my problem is I try to edit as I write. I think what I need to do is just write whatever I want. After I'm through, then edit and organize. It's hard for me though.

Bruce chastises himself for making his writing harder than it need be and reminds himself about the process he learned in class. Journals are good places to monitor your own version of the writing process and to document what helps you the most.

3 Writing to learn

The act of regular writing clarifies ideas and causes new ones to develop. In that sense, journal writing is an invention and discovery technique. (See Chapter 6.) Julie, who kept a journal about all the authors she studied in her American literature course, noticed a disturbing pattern and wrote in her journal to make some sense of it.

5/4 So far, the first two authors we have to read have led tragic, unhappy lives. I wonder if this is just a coincidence or if it has something to do with the personality of successful writers. Actually, of all people, writers need a lot of time alone, by themselves, thinking and writing, away from other people, including, probably, close family members. The more I think about it, writers would be very difficult people to live with, that's it—writers spend so much time alone and become hard to live with.

Julie used the act of regular journal writing to process and figure out ideas, make interpretations, and test hypotheses. To write to learn is to trust that as you write, ideas will come—some right, some wrong; some good, some bad.

WP TIP Use the sort function of your word processor to identify journal entries that share a common topic. (Or skim through your entries by scrolling quickly down.) Copy the entries, or paragraphs of entries, into a new file. Type a final entry at the bottom in which you evaluate what you've learned, or concluded, about the topic.

4 Gaining social and political awareness

Writing in a journal is a good way to examine the social and political climate in which you grew up and which perhaps you took for granted. In the following example, Jennifer uses her journal to reflect on sexist language.

> 3/8 Sexist language is everywhere. So much so that people don't even realize what they are saying is sexist. My teacher last year told all the "mothers-to-be" to be sure to read to their children. What about the fathers? Sexist language is dangerous because it so easily undermines women's morale and self-image. I try my hardest not to use sexist language, but even I find myself falling into old stereotypes.

Note that Jennifer recorded both her awareness of sexist language in society and her own difficulty in avoiding it.

5 Evaluating classes

Journals are good places in which to assess your classes, including both what you're learning and what you're not learning. In the following entry, Brian seemed surprised that writing can be fun.

> 9/28 English is now more fun. When I write, the words come out more easily and it's not like homework. All my drafts help me put together my thoughts and retrieve memories that were hidden somewhere in the dungeons of my mind. Usually I wouldn't like English, like in high school, but I pretty much enjoy it here. I like how you get to hear people's reactions to your papers and discuss them with each other.

Your journal is one place where you can raise critical questions about a class or, by sharing it, let your instructor know what is happening in class from your point of view.

6 Letting off steam

Journals are good places to vent frustration when things aren't going well, personally or academically. College instructors don't assign journals to improve students' mental health, but they know that journals can help. Kenyon writes about the value of keeping his journal for one semester.

> 10/14 This journal has saved my sanity. It got me started at writing. . . . I can't keep all my problems locked up inside me, but I hate telling others, burdening them with my problems— like what I'm going to do or with the rest of my life.

In many ways, writing in a journal is like talking to a sympathetic audience; the difference, as Kenyon noted, is that the journal is always there, no matter what's on your mind.

7 Reporting progress

Sometimes it's hard to see how much you've learned until you reread your journal at the end of a term and notice where you began and where you ended. Your writing may have been casual and fast, your thinking tentative, your assessments or conclusions uncertain, but the journal gives you a record of who you were, what you thought, and how you've changed. Rereading a term's worth of entries may be a pleasant surprise, as Jeff found out.

> 11/21 The journal to me has been like a one-man debate, where I could write thoughts down and then later read them. This seemed to help clarify many of my ideas. To be honest there is probably fifty percent of the journal that is nothing but B.S. and ramblings to fulfill assignments, but that still leaves fifty percent that I think is of importance. The journal is also a time capsule. I want to put it away and not look at it for ten or twenty years and let it recall for me this period of my life.

 GUIDELINES FOR KEEPING A JOURNAL

1. Choose a notebook you are comfortable with. A small loose-leaf binder allows you to add, delete, and rearrange entries or share selected samples with an instructor.

2. Consider using a computer. One advantage of computer journals is that they make it easy for you to copy interesting or useful entries directly into the paper you are working on.

3. Date each entry. Also include the day of the week and the time if you like having more complete records. A journal allows you to watch your thoughts change over time.

4. Write long entries. Plan to write for at least ten minutes, preferably longer, to allow your thoughts to develop as fully as possible. The more you write, the more you find to say.

5. Include both "academic" and "personal" entries. Put a divider in your loose-leaf notebook to separate them.

▥ WRITING 5: APPLICATION

Look over the examples in this section and see if you can think up additional uses for journals. Can you provide any concrete examples from your own journal?

SUGGESTIONS FOR WRITING AND RESEARCH

INDIVIDUAL

1. Select a major writer in your intended major who is known to have written a journal (for example, Mary Shelley, Ralph Waldo Emerson, or Virginia Woolf in literature; Leonardo da Vinci, Georgia O'Keeffe, or Edward Weston in the arts; B. F. Skinner or Margaret Mead in the social sciences; Charles Darwin or Marie Curie in the natural sciences). Study the writer's journals to identify important characteristics and the purpose they probably served. Write a report on what you find, and share it with your class.

2. Review your journal entries for the past two weeks, select one entry that seems especially interesting, and write a reflective essay of several pages on it. How are the entry and the essay different? Which is better? Is that a fair question?

COLLABORATIVE

Bring duplicated copies of one journal entry written during the term. Exchange entries and discuss interesting features of the entries.

5 | Writing for a Reason

People write to discover what's on their minds, figure things out, vent frustrations, keep records, remember things, communicate information, shape ideas, express feelings, recount experiences, raise questions, imagine the future, create new forms, and simply for pleasure. They also write when they're required to in school, to demonstrate knowledge and solve problems. But no matter what the task, writers write better when they do so purposefully—when they know what they want to accomplish.

This chapter examines three broad and overlapping reasons for writing—discovering, communicating, and creating—and discusses strategies to accomplish each one effectively.

5 a | Writing to discover

Writing helps people discover ideas, relationships, connections, and patterns in their lives and in the world. In college, students write to discover paper topics, develop those topics, expand and explain ideas, and connect seemingly unrelated material in coherent patterns. In this sense, writing is one of the most powerful learning tools available.

Writing is especially powerful because it makes language—and therefore thought—stand still, allowing it to be examined slowly and deliberately, allowing the ideas to be elaborated, critiqued, rearranged, and corrected. Playwright Christopher Fry once said, "My trouble is that I'm the sort of writer who only finds out what he is getting at by the time he's got to the end of it." In other words, his purpose and plan become clear only after he's written a whole draft; he knows that the act of writing will help him find his way. But rather than considering this inventive power of writing "trouble"—to use Fry's word—you can consider it a solution to many other problems. Once you know that writing can generate ideas, advance concepts, and forge connections, then you can use it deliberately and strategically to help you write college papers.

Discovery can happen in all writing. Anytime you write, you may find new or lost ideas, implications, and directions. However, sometimes it pays to write with the specific intention of discovering. Discovery writing is often used before actual drafting to explore the subject and purpose of a paper or to solve writing problems once drafting and revising have begun. (See Chapter 6.)

WP TIP Save your work often, and be sure to name each file to accurately reflect its purpose and/or content so that you can find it when you need it.

■ WRITING I: EXPLORATION

Describe a time when you used writing for discovery purposes. Did you set out to use writing this way or did it happen accidentally? Have you used it deliberately since then? With what results?

5 b Writing to communicate

The most common reason for writing in college is to say something to an audience. College students write essays, exams, and reports to instructors, as well as letters, applications, and resumés to potential employers. To communicate to instructors and employers alike, writing needs to be *purposeful*, so both writer and reader know where it's going; it needs to be *clear*, in order to be understood; and it needs to be *correct*, in order to be believed.

Thesis-based writing

Many academic assignments require a thesis, a statement of the writer's purpose which the paper is expected to assert, explain, support, or defend. A thesis, broadly speaking, summarizes the main idea of a paper and makes that idea explicit to readers.

A **thesis statement** is a generalization in one or more sentences, early or late in the paper, that summarizes the paper's point. For example, the thesis of this chapter, that *writers write better when they do so purposefully—when they know what they want to accomplish*, is stated at the close of the first paragraph and supported throughout the rest of the chapter.

Some papers, such as this chapter, present the **thesis first**, in the first paragraph or somewhere on the first page. A thesis-first paper summarizes for the readers in advance what the paper will be about. Other papers present the thesis later in what might be called a **delayed-thesis** arrangement. Delayed-thesis papers show readers different sides or aspects of an idea before presenting the writer's conclusion about that idea.

Whether first or delayed, a thesis answers the critical reader question: So what? Why does this paper exist? What's it about? A thesis-first sums up what will be demonstrated if the readers continue reading; a delayed thesis explains the point they should have gotten if their reading is nearly finished. Common thesis-based assignments in college include the following.

Explaining ideas. The purpose of explaining something is to make it clear to somebody who knows less about the subject than you do. You explain best by following a logical order, using simple language, and providing illustration and examples of what you mean. (For more on explaining, see Chapter 10.)

Arguing positions. The purpose of arguing is to persuade readers to agree with your position. College assignments frequently ask you to explore both sides of an issue or several competing interpretations of a text and then to take a stand on one side against the other. (For more on argument, see Chapter 11.)

Interpreting texts. The purpose of interpreting a text is to explain what the text means, to tell why you believe it means this, and to support your reading with reasons based on evidence from the text. (For more on interpreting texts, see Chapter 12.)

Recounting experience. The purpose of recounting an experience to somebody else is to share something about yourself and, in the process, teach them something they don't already know. (For more on recounting experience, see Chapter 9.)

Reflecting on the world. The purpose of reflective writing is to speculate, explore, or meditate on an issue or idea in order to show readers your unique way of thinking about it—without necessarily coming to a single conclusion or proving a point. (For more information on reflective writing, see Chapter 13.)

Some papers, such as those that recount personal experience and those that are reflective in nature, do not state theses directly. Instead, they often have an **implied thesis**; by the paper's end, the reader understands the point of the paper without the writer's stating it directly.

WP TIP Put into boldface type any strong statements you make that might be possible thesis statements, either direct or implied. This will make such key statements easy to find when you print hard copy or review your work on screen. Examine them carefully and revise your work, developing them into thesis statements whenever appropriate.

WRITING 2: EXPLORATION

When is the last time you wrote to communicate something? Describe your purpose and audience. How successful were these acts of communication? How do you know?

5 c Writing to create

When you write to create, you pay special attention to the way your language looks and sounds—its form, shape, rhythm, images, and texture. Though the term "creative writing" is most often associated with poetry, fiction, and drama, it's important to see any act of writing, from personal narratives to research essays, as creative.

When you write to create, you pay less immediate attention to your audience and subject and more to the act of expression itself. Your goal is not so much to change the world or to transmit information about it, but to transform an experience or idea into something that will make your readers pause, see the world from a different angle, and perhaps reflect upon what it means. You want your writing itself, not just the information it contains, to affect your readers emotionally or esthetically as well as intellectually.

In most college papers, your primary purpose will be to communicate, not to create. However, nearly every writing assignment has room for a creative dimension. When writing for emotional or esthetic effect in an otherwise communicative paper, be especially careful that your creativity serves a purpose and that the communicative part is strong on its own. You want your creative use of language to enhance, not camouflage, your ideas.

1 Intensifying experience

When Amanda recounted her experience picking potatoes on board a mechanical potato harvester on her father's farm, she made her readers feel the experience as she did by crafting her language to duplicate the sense of hard, monotonous work.

> Potatoes, mud, potatoes, mud, potatoes, that was all I saw in front of me. They moved from my right side to my left, at hip level. A conveyor belt never stopping. On and on and on.
> The potatoes passed fast, a constant stream. My hands worked deftly, pulling out clods of dirt, rotten potatoes, old shaws, and anything else I found that wasn't a potato. It was October, the ground was nearly frozen, the mud was hard and solid. Cold. Dirt had gotten into my yellow and yet brown rubber gloves, had wedged under my nails increasing my discomfort.

This is a creative approach to essay writing because the writer uses a graphic, present-tense style to put readers at the scene of her experience rather than summarizing it or explaining explicitly what it meant to her.

2 Experimenting with form

Keith created a special language effect in an otherwise traditional and straightforward academic assignment by writing a poetic prologue for a research essay about homeless people in New York City. The full essay contains factual information derived from social workers, agency documents, and library research.

> The cold cement
>   no pillow
> The steel grate
>   no mattress
> But the hot air
>   of the midnight subway
> Lets me sleep.

Using the poetic form creates a brief emotional involvement with the research subject, allowing readers to fill in missing information with their imaginations. Note, however, that the details of the poem (cold cement, steel grate, subway) spring not from the writer's imagination, but from his research notes and observations. For more information on experimenting with form, style, or language, see Chapter 21, "Focused Revising."

■ **WRITING 3: EXPLORATION**

Describe a time when your primary purpose in writing was to create rather than to discover or communicate. Were you pleased with the result? Why or why not?

5 **d** **Approaching assignments**

When you write in response to an instructor's assignment, your purpose may be to report, explain, argue, or interpret, depending upon your instructor's request. But before tackling any of these tasks, you need to take over the assignment and make the writing serve your purpose as well as your instructor's; otherwise your best energy won't be in your writing, and that attitude always shows.

How do you make your writing serve both your instructor's purpose and your own? Let's look at two typical writing assignments taken from a first-year writing class.

Assignment 1

Write a personal essay exploring a recent personal experience of some significance to you. Explain this event's importance and what you learned from it. After reading your paper, the audience should know more about both you and the experience you describe.

Assignment 2

Write a paper that takes a stand on an issue recently reported in the news media that has some local impact. In completing this paper, include both library and field research. After reading this paper, the audience should know the background for this issue and the opposing arguments as well as the argument your paper supports.

To undertake these or similar assignments, follow this procedure: First, identify the instructor's purpose in making the assignment; second, locate a specific topic that interests you; and, third, discover an approach to the topic to make it your own.

1 Identify the purpose

Identify the *direction* words: verbs that tell what action to perform and nouns that imply a specific activity. Next identify the *subject* words: nouns and their adjectives that specify the subject of the assignment. These key words will tell you what your instructor expects you to write about, what the final paper is supposed to accomplish, and what steps you are expected to take in order to write the paper.

In **Assignment 1**, for example, the direction word is *explore*, which suggests an open approach allowing the writer to investigate the subject and examine different dimensions of it. The subject words are the combination of *personal experience* and *significance*, words that define what is to be explored. The experience also needs to be recent. How recent? A good question to ask the instructor.

In **Assignment 2**, the direction words are *take a stand* and *argument*. Additional words of nearly equal importance tell you to use both *library* and *field research*, suggesting the nature of the knowledge expected. The subject words are *local* and *issue*; make sure you understand your instructor's definition of *issue* before proceeding further.

■ **WRITING 4: APPLICATION**

Identify the key words in a current writing assignment and write an analysis of how the direction words and subject words determine your purpose.

2 Locate a topic

The subject words in an assignment are usually quite broad; they define a set of possible subjects but don't tell you which one to write about. You must select a subject and then narrow it down to a workable *topic*. Subjects are large and inclusive: sports or soccer. Topics are narrow and focused: the advantage of playing competitive sports in high school or the lessons of comradeship learned playing soccer. Finding a good topic serves both your instructor's purpose (because it will result in a better paper) and your own (because it allows you to influence the direction your paper will take).

First, select a subject that attracts and holds your interest. A subject you find interesting will cause you to ask more and better questions and result in more, not less, involvement in later drafts. Second, make sure the topic is also manageable. Narrowing the focus allows for more detailed research and a written product of greater depth.

In **Assignment 1**, limit the experience to something particular that's both recent and important. If a subject that interests you is sports, limit the topic to a sport you played recently (senior high school basketball) and focus on an important event (learning to support the team while sitting on the bench).

In **Assignment 2**, you might limit the topic to pollution (water), identify an issue (the closing of a public beach because of pollution), and make a case for what to do to address this issue (install a new sewage treatment plant). This act of narrowing offers the opportunity to report more detailed and concrete information.

WRITING 5: APPLICATION

For a current writing assignment, select a subject that interests you. Make a list of ten possible topics within the subject. Then write a paragraph on each of the three that interest you most. Select the one that has the most possibilities and begin your writing or research.

3 Determine your approach

How do you approach a writing assignment? From the beginning, your approach is determined by the resources available to you as you address the assignment. But it is also determined by the limits of your imagination. In other words, while there are certain stipulations in any assignment, there are also certain freedoms to include your own unique slant that will set your writing apart from anybody else's.

To write **Assignment 1**, you would need to tap into remembered knowledge. This assignment requires organizing your memories in a meaningful way. Though your memory might contain most of what you need, you might also consider revisiting the site of the experience or talking with others involved to retrieve more useful details. At the same time, you might tell the story from a third-person point of view instead of the expected first person, or you might write in the present tense instead of the more conventional past. (For more information on experimenting with alternative approaches, see Chapter 21.)

To write **Assignment 2**, you would need to know about recent issues that will have some impact on a local institution. It may be profitable to read newspapers or listen to the news. At the same time, you might choose to report your information as a feature story in a local newspaper or as a television news documentary. (For more information on research, see Part IV.)

■ WRITING 6: APPLICATION

Identify the necessary sources of information for a current writing assignment. What do you need to know to select your topic in the first place? What else do you need to know to complete your paper?

 GUIDELINES FOR APPROACHING ASSIGNMENTS

1. Analyze the direction words and subject words that identify your instructor's purpose. If the assignment asks for analysis, be sure your writing stresses the analytical rather than the personal or persuasive.

2. Narrow the topic to one that is both interesting and manageable. Think first of as many possible topics as you can; think second about those that truly interest you; think third about the one you can best manage in the time available.

3. Write from what you know. Plan to research what you don't know. Figure out the best way to collect and organize both kinds of information.

4. Own the assignment by adopting an original approach that will separate your paper from less imaginative ones.

SUGGESTIONS FOR WRITING AND RESEARCH

INDIVIDUAL

1. Select a topic and write about it in each of the three modes described in this chapter. First, begin with discovery writing to yourself, perhaps in a journal. Second, write a letter to communicate with somebody. Third, write creatively about it in a short poem, story, or play. Conclude by describing your experience writing in these different modes.

2. Write a paper explaining your idea of a good or bad writing assignment. Support your explanation with examples from your own writing experience. Conclude by explaining whether or not this was a good writing assignment.

COLLABORATIVE

1. Select a topic that your whole writing group is interested in. Divide your labors so that some of you do discovery writing, some do communicative writing, and some write creatively. With scissors and tape, combine your efforts into a single coherent piece of collage writing, making sure that some of every member's writing is included in the finished product. Perform a reading of this collage for the other groups; listen to theirs in return.

2. As a class, research the assignments you were given in high school. Examine old notebooks and papers you have saved for evidence of teachers' instructions. Write a collaborative research essay on the topic "American School Assignments: The Good, the Bad, and the Ugly," in which you describe and analyze what is typical and explain what separates the good from the bad.

Good writing depends on good ideas. When ideas don't come easily or naturally, writers need techniques for finding or creating them. Writers need to invent new ideas or discover old ones at all phases of the writing process, from finding and developing a topic to narrowing an argument and searching for good evidence. And knowing how to invent and discover ideas when none seems apparent is also the best antidote for writer's block, helping you get going even when you think you have nothing to say.

The main premise behind the techniques discussed in this chapter is "the more you write, the more you think." Language begets more language, and more language begets ideas, and ideas beget still more ideas. Virtually all writers have had the experience of starting to write in one direction and ending up in another; as they wrote, their writing moved their thinking in new directions—a powerful, messy, but ultimately positive experience and a good demonstration that the act of writing itself generates and modifies ideas. This occurs because writing lets people see their own ideas, and doing that, in turn, allows them to change those ideas. This chapter suggests ways to harness the creative power of language and make it work for you.

WRITING I: EXPLORATION

Describe the procedures you usually use to start writing a paper. Where do you get the ideas—from speaking? listening? reading? writing? Do you do anything special to help them come? What do you do when ideas don't come?

6 a Brainstorming

Brainstorming is systematic list making. You ask yourself a question and then list as many answers as you can think of. The point is to get lots of possible ideas out to examine and review. Sometimes you can do this best by setting goals for yourself: What are five possible topics for a paper on campus issues?

1   Overcrowding in campus dormitories

2   Prohibiting cars for first-year students

3   Date rape

4   Multiculturalism and the curriculum

5   Attitudes towards alcohol on campus

Sometimes you can brainstorm best by leaving the question open-ended: What do you already know about multiculturalism and the curriculum that interests you?

Racial diversity high among campus students

Racial diversity low among faculty

Old curriculum dominated by white male agenda

New curriculum dominated by young feminist agenda

How to avoid simplistic stereotypes such as those I've just written?

In making such lists, jotting down one item often triggers the next, as is seen above. Each item becomes a possible direction for your paper. By challenging yourself to generate a long list, you force yourself to find and record even vague ideas in concrete language, where you can examine them and decide whether or not they're worth further development.

WP TIP   Brainstorming on the computer can be very liberating. Typing, deleting, changing, and moving information around quickly, you can organize your thoughts almost as fast as they come to mind.

6 b Freewriting

Freewriting is fast writing. You write rapidly, depending on one word to trigger the next, one idea to lead to another, without worrying about conventions or correctness. Freewriting helps you find a focus by writing nonstop and not censoring the words and ideas before you have a chance to look at them. Try the following suggestions for freewriting:

1 Write as fast as you can about an idea for a fixed period of time, say five or ten minutes.

2 Do not allow your pen to stop moving until the time is up.

3 Don't worry about what your writing looks like or how it's organized; the only audience for this writing is yourself.

If you digress in your freewriting, fine. If you misspell a word or write something silly, fine. If you catch a fleeting thought that's especially interesting, good. If you think of something you've never thought of before, wonderful. And if nothing interesting comes out—well, maybe next time. The following five-minute freewrite shows John's attempt to find a topic for a local research project.

> I can't think of anything special just now, nothing really comes to mind, well maybe something about the downtown mall would be good because I wouldn't mind spending time down there. Something about the mall . . . maybe the street vendors, the hot dog guy or the pretzel guy or that woman selling T and sweatshirts, they're always there, even in lousy weather—do they like it that much? Actually, all winter. Do they need the money that bad? Why do people become street vendors—like maybe they graduated from college and couldn't get jobs? Or were these the guys who never wanted anything to do with college?

John's freewrite is typical: He starts with no ideas, but his writing soon leads to some. This kind of writing needs to be free, unstructured, and digressive to allow the writer to find thoughts wherever they occur. For John, this exercise turned out to be a useful one, since he ultimately wrote a paper about "the hot dog man," a street vendor.

WP TIP   A computer can help you freewrite more freely by making your words invisible. This guarantees that you won't try to revise and edit at this early stage. Simply turn down the brightness on your monitor until it is dark, and type away, focusing only on your current thoughts. After ten minutes, turn the brightness up and see what you have written.

ESL   **FREEWRITING AS A WAY TO DEVELOP FLUENCY**

Writing in a second language can be frustrating when you are trying to pay attention to your ideas, sentence structures, word choices, and so on. Many ESL writers have discovered that freewriting helps tremendously with this problem. If you haven't tried freewriting before, you might find it hard at first not to stop and carefully check each sentence, but with continued practice this activity should help you to postpone editing and improve your fluency in English. If you have access to a computer, try invisible writing.

---

6 **c**   **Looping**

Loop writing is a sequenced set of freewrites. Each freewrite focuses on one idea from the previous freewrite and expands it. To loop, follow this procedure:

1   Freewrite for ten minutes to discover a topic or to advance the one you are working on.

2   Review your freewrite and select one sentence closest to what you want to continue developing. Copy this sentence, and take off from it, freewriting for another ten minutes. (John might have selected "Why do people become street vendors?" for further freewriting.)

3   Repeat step 2 for each successive freewrite to keep inventing and discovering.

6 **d** **Asking reporters' questions**

Writers who train themselves to ask questions are training themselves to find information. Reporters ask six basic questions about every news story they write: Who? What? Where? When? Why? and How? Following this set of questions leads reporters to new information and more complete stories.

1   *Who* or what is involved? (a person, character, or thesis)

2   *What* happened? (an event, action, or assertion)

3   *Where* did this happen? (a place, text, or context)

4   *When* did it happen? (a date or relationship)

5   *Why* did it happen? (reason, cause, or explanation)

6   *How* did it happen? (a method, procedure, or action)

While these questions seem especially appropriate for reporting an event, the questions can be modified to investigate any topic:

What is my central idea?

What happens to it?

Where do I make my main point? On what page?

Are my *reasons* ample and documented?

How does my strategy work?

6 **e** **Making outlines**

Outlines are, essentially, organized lists. In fact, outlines grow out of lists, as writers determine which ideas go first, which later; which are main, which subordinate. Formal outlines use a system of Roman numerals, capital letters, Arabic numerals, and lowercase letters to create a hierarchy of ideas. Some writers prefer informal outlines, using indentations to indicate relationships between ideas.

When Carol set out to write a research essay on the effect of acid rain on the environment in New England, she first brainstormed a random list of areas that such an essay might cover.

What is acid rain?

What are its effects on the environment?

What causes it?

How can it be stopped?

After preliminary research, Carol produced this outline:

    I. Definition of acid rain

    II. The causes of acid rain

        A. Coal-burning power plants

        B. Automobile pollution

    III. The effects of acid rain

        A. Deforestation in New England

            1. The White Mountain study

            2. Maple trees dying in Vermont

        B. Dead lakes

Note how Carol rearranged the second and third items in her original list to talk about causes before effects. The very act of making the outline encouraged her to invent a structure for her ideas. Moving entries around is especially easy if you are using a computer, because you can see many combinations before committing yourself to any one of them. The rules of formal outlining also cause you to search for ideas: If you have a Roman numeral I, you need a II; if you have an A, you need a B. Carol thought first of coal-burning power plants as a cause, then brainstormed to come up with an idea to pair with it.

Writing outlines is generative: In addition to recording your original thoughts, they actually generate new thoughts. Outlines are most useful if you modify them as you write in accordance with new thoughts or information.

6 f Clustering

A clustering diagram is a method of listing ideas visually to reveal their relationships. Clustering is useful both for inventing and discovering a topic and for exploring a topic once you have

done preliminary research. To use clustering, follow this procedure:

1   Write a word or phrase that seems to be the focus of what you
want to write about. (Carol wrote down "acid rain.")

2   Write ideas related to your focus in a circle around the central
phrase and connect them to the focus phrase. If one of the ideas
suggests others related to it, write those in a circle around *it*
(Carol did this with her idea "solutions").

3   If one idea (such as "solutions") begins to accumulate related
ideas, start a second cluster with the new term in the center of
your paper.

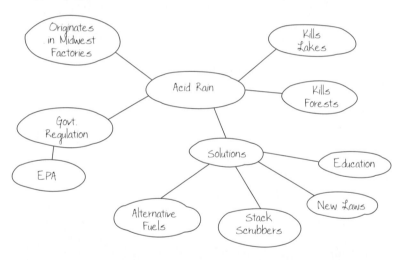

6 g   Talking with peers

One of the most powerful invention techniques is talking to
a partner with the deliberate intention of helping each other find
ideas. The directions are simple: Sit across from each other for
five or ten minutes and begin talking about possible topics or
approaches or ways of finding sources; it doesn't matter who
starts or finishes, since the principle at work here is that oral
language, like written language, begets ideas. At some point it
will be helpful to write down what you are talking about so that
you have a record to return to.

SUGGESTIONS FOR INVENTION AND DISCOVERY

1. Brainstorm a list of five possible topics to write about.

2. Freewrite for ten minutes about the most interesting topic on your list.

3. Loop back in your freewriting, selecting the most interesting or useful point, and freewrite again with that point as the focus.

4. Ask the **reporter's questions** about the topic.

5. Make an **outline** of a possible structure for your paper.

6. Cluster ideas about your topic and then on a related idea that occurs during the initial clustering.

7. Talk with a partner for seven minutes, each helping the other find or advance one idea each.

SUGGESTIONS FOR WRITING AND RESEARCH

INDIVIDUAL

Explain your own most useful invention technique for finding ideas. Explain your technique and support it with samples from your own earlier papers. Give clear directions to teach other writers how to use it.

COLLABORATIVE

Find a common writing topic by having each person in the group or class select one of the invention and discovery techniques described in this chapter and practice using it for ten minutes. Make a collective list of the topic ideas generated this way. Then ask each individual to select one topic and write for another five minutes. Again make a list of topics and the important ideas generated about them. Discuss the ideas together and try to arrive at a consensus on a common writing topic.

The better you know your audience, the better you're likely to write. Whether your writing is judged "good" or not depends largely on how well it's received by the readers for whom it's intended. Just as you change the way you speak depending upon to whom you're speaking—your boss, mother, professor, friend, younger brother—so you change the way you write depending upon to whom you're writing. You don't want to overexplain and perhaps bore the audience, nor underexplain and leave it wanting.

Speakers have an advantage over writers in that they see the effect of their words on their listeners and can adjust accordingly. A puzzled look tells the speaker to slow down, a smile and nod says keep going full speed ahead, and so on. However, writers can only imagine the reactions of the people to whom they're trying to communicate.

We believe all college papers need to be written to at least two audiences, maybe more: first, to yourself, so you understand it; second, to your instructor who has asked you to write it in the first place. In addition, you may also be writing to other students or for publication to more public audiences. This chapter examines how expectations differ from one audience to the next.

7 a Understanding college audiences

It might help to think of the different audiences you will address in college as existing along a continuum, with those closest and best known to you (yourself, friends) at one end and those farthest from and least known to you (the general public) at the other end.

Self———— Friends———— Family————Instructor————Public

While the items on your continuum will always differ in particulars from somebody else's, the principle—that you know some audiences better than others—will always be the same and will influence how you write. The audience of most concern to most college students is the instructor who will evaluate their learning on the basis of their writing.

WP TIP Create a file called "Audience." Putting the topic of your latest essay at the top of the screen page, list the characteristics of the audience you believe you are addressing. Use the criteria in the following pages—context, structure, tone, and so on—as categories to help you delineate your audience.

■ WRITING I: EXPLORATION

Think back over the past several weeks and list all the different audiences to whom you have written. To whom did you write most often? Which audiences were easy for you to address? Which were difficult? Why? **ESL:** Do you think English-speaking audiences have expectations that differ from the expectations of audiences who speak your native language?

7 b Shaping writing for different audiences

To shape your writing for a particular audience, you first need to understand the qualities of your writing that can change according to audience. The context you need to provide; the structure, tone, and style you use; and your purpose for writing can all be affected by your audience. (Structure, tone, and style are important elements of voice. See Chapter 8.)

Context

Different audiences need different contexts (different amounts or kinds of background information) in order to understand your ideas. Find out whether your audience already knows about the topic or whether it's completely new to them. Consider whether any terms or ideas need explaining. For example, other students in your writing group might know exactly who you mean if you refer to a favorite singer, but your instructor might not. Also consider what sort of explanation would work best with your audience.

Structure

Every piece of writing is put together in a certain way: some ideas are discussed early, others late; transitions between ideas are marked in a certain way; similar ideas are either grouped together or treated separately. How you structure a paper depends in large part on what you think will work best with your particular audience. For example, if you were writing an argument for someone who disagrees with your position, you might begin with the evidence with which you both agree and then later introduce more controversial evidence.

Tone

The tone of a piece of writing conveys the writer's attitude toward the subject matter and audience. How do you want to sound to your readers? Do you want them to hear you as friendly? Businesslike? Angry? Serious? Humorous? Puzzled? You may, of course, have a different attitude toward each audience you address. In addition, you may want different audiences to hear in different ways. For example, when writing to yourself, you won't mind sounding confused. When writing to instructors, though, you will want to sound confident and authoritative.

Style

Style is largely determined by the formality and complexity of your language. Writing ranges from the chatty and casual, full of contractions and sentence fragments, to the elevated and elaborate. You need to determine what style your readers expect and what style will be most effective in a given paper. Fellow students might be offended if you write in anything other than a friendly style, but some instructors might interpret the same style as disrespectful.

Purpose

The explicit purpose of your writing depends more upon you and your assignment than on your audience. (See Chapter 5.) However, certain purposes are more likely to apply to particular audiences than others. Also, there are unstated purposes embedded in any piece of writing, and these will vary depending on whom you're addressing. For example, is it important that your readers like you? Or that they respect you? Or that they give you good grades? Always ask yourself what you want a piece of writing to do for—or to—your audience and what you want your audience to do in response to your writing.

Let's follow the way writing generally needs to change as you move along the scale away from the audience you know best, yourself.

1 Writing to yourself

Every paper you write is addressed in part to yourself, and some, such as journals, primarily to yourself. However, most reports, essays, papers, and exams are also addressed to other people—instructors, peers, parents, or employers. Journal writing is your opportunity to write to yourself and yourself alone. When you write to yourself alone, you don't need to worry about context, structure, tone, or style; only purpose matters if you are the sole reader. However, if you make a journal entry that you might want to refer to later, it's a good idea to provide sufficient background and explanation to help you remember the event or the idea described if you do return to it. When you are the reader of your own writing, choose words, sentences, rhythms, images, and punctuation that come easiest and most naturally to you. (For more information, see Chapter 4).

2 Writing to peers

Your peers are your equals, your friends and classmates, people of similar age, background, or situation. Some of your assignments will ask you to consider the other students in the class to be your audience: for example, when you read papers to each other in writing groups or exchange papers to edit each other's work.

The primary difference between writing to yourself and writing to peers is the amount of context and structure you need to provide to make sure your readers understand you. If your paper is about a personal experience, you need to provide the explanations and details that will allow readers who did not have your experience to understand fully the events and ideas you describe.

If your paper is about a subject that requires research, be sure to provide background information to make the topic comprehensible and interesting in a structure (e.g., chronological,

logical, cause–effect) that makes sense. Be direct, honest, and friendly, because peers will see right through any pretentious or stuffy language.

You usually write to peers to share a response to their writing, to recount an experience, to explain an idea, or to argue a position. In a writing class, the most important implicit purpose is probably to establish a good working rapport with your classmates by being honest, straightforward, and supportive.

3 Writing to instructors

Instructors are among the most difficult audiences for whom to write. First, they usually make the assignments, so they know what they want, and it's your job to figure out what that is. Second, they often know more about your subject than you do. Third, different instructors may have quite different criteria for what constitutes good writing. And fourth, each instructor may simultaneously play several different roles: a helpful resource, a critic, an editor, a coach, and finally, a judge.

It is often difficult to know how much context to provide in a paper written for an instructor, unless the assignment specifically tells you. For example, in writing about a Shakespearean play to an English professor, should you provide a summary of the play when you know that he or she already knows it? Or should you skip the summary information and write only about ideas original with you? The safest approach is to provide full background, explain all ideas, support all assertions, and cite authorities in the field. Write as if your instructor needed all this information and it were your job to educate him or her.

When writing papers to instructors, be sure to use a structure that suits the type of paper you are writing. For example, personal experience papers are often chronological, reports may be more thematic, and so on. (The chapters in Part III describe conventional structures for each type of paper discussed there.)

One of your instructor's roles is to help you learn to write effective papers. But another role is to evaluate whether you have done so and, from a broader perspective, whether you are becoming a literate member of the college community. Therefore your implicit purpose when you write to instructors is to demonstrate your understanding of conventions, knowledge, reasoning ability, and originality.

Demonstrating understanding of conventions

The first thing your instructor may notice about your writing is what it looks like: Is it typed or handwritten? Does it have a title page? A title? A name? How long is it? How neat is it? How legible is the handwriting, or how accurate the typing? How clear and correct are the first few sentences? Did it meet the deadline? Instructors make these observations rapidly, sometimes unconsciously, before they have finished reading the paper. Such rapid observations often determine your instructor's attitude toward the whole paper. He or she is more likely to look favorably on a paper that is neat and free of spelling and grammatical errors than on one that is wrinkled and full of mechanical mistakes.

Of course, academic conventions also require correctness and accuracy in spelling, grammar, usage, and research documentation. Early in the term, your safest stance is to cover all the traditional bases of good academic writing, demonstrating that you can write about teacher-assigned subjects using a conventional structure and style, providing full explanations, supporting assertions with authority, using specialized terms carefully, and documenting all borrowed information. Later in the term, once you have established your academic legitimacy, your experiments with form, style, theme, and voice may be more readily accepted by your instructor. In truth, many instructors get tired of reading safe prose, written to satisfy requirements; they usually welcome creativity.

Demonstrating knowledge of subject

Academic papers must also have substance. Even a good-looking paper must demonstrate what you know and how well you know it. Your instructor will ask: Are the definitions, details, and explanations clear? Are they believable? Where did the information come from? How up-to-date is it? What sources were consulted? How reputable do they seem? Full knowledge needs to be there.

In writing classes, you also must demonstrate the knowledge you've gained about the writing process itself—your understanding of planning, drafting, researching, revising, and editing, as shown in your paper.

Demonstrating reasoning ability

Your papers should show your ability to reason logically, support assertions, and be persuasive whether you are writing a personal essay or an argument. In personal essays, be sure to include examples that support your generalizations; in argumentative papers, be sure to include evidence that refutes the other side and supports your side; in research essays, demonstrate that you've evaluated your sources well and are using the best and most current available ones.

Demonstrating originality

No matter what the writing assignment, you can find creative ways of doing it. When assignments are open-ended, do not choose the first topic that comes to mind or that seems easiest to do. Let your mind roam over more unusual ideas. When topics are limited, allow yourself to consider some risky or new approach. When you provide information to support your assertions, dig for something more unexpected than those most commonly known. When you open or conclude a paper, try to surprise your reader.

4 Writing to public audiences

Writing to a public audience is difficult for all writers, because the audience is usually both diverse and unknown. The public audience can include both people who know more and those who know less than the writer; it can contain experts who will correct the slightest mistake and novices who need even simple terms explained; it can contain opponents looking for reasons to argue with the writer and supporters looking for reasons to continue support. And you are unlikely to know many of these people personally.

You usually have some idea of who these anonymous readers are or you wouldn't be writing to them in the first place. Still, it is important to learn as much as you can about any of their beliefs and characteristics that may be relevant to the point you intend to make. What is their educational level? What are their political, philosophical, or religious beliefs? What are their interests?

When you don't know who your audience is, provide context for everything you say. If you are referring to even well-known groups such as NCAA or ACLU, write out the full names the first time you refer to them (National Collegiate Athletic Association or American Civil Liberties Union). If you refer to an idea as "postmodern," define or illustrate what the term means. (Good luck!) Your writing should be able to stand by itself and make complete sense to people you do not know.

Your purpose and structure should be as clear as possible, with your opening paragraph letting this audience know what's to come. Your tone will depend on your purpose, but generally it should be fair and reasonable. Your style will depend on the publication for which you are writing.

■ WRITING 2: EXPLORATION

How accurate do you find the above discussion about different college audiences? Describe circumstances that confirm or contradict the description here. If instructors are not your most difficult audience, explain who is.

SUGGESTIONS FOR WRITING AND RESEARCH

INDIVIDUAL

Select a paper written recently for an instructor. Rewrite the paper for a publication, choosing either a student newspaper or a local magazine. Before you start writing, make notes about what elements need to be changed: context, structure, tone, style, or purpose. When you finish recasting the paper to this larger, more public audience, send it to the publication.

COLLABORATIVE

In a group of five students, select a topic of common interest. Each of you select one of the following audiences to write to: yourself, a friend who is not here, your instructor, an appropriate magazine or newspaper. Each of you should share your writing with the group and together make a list of the language choices you made that characterized each audience.

8 | Finding a Voice

Each individual speaks with a distinctive voice. Some speak loudly, some softly, others with quiet authority. Some sound assertive or aggressive, while others sound cautious, tentative, or insecure. Some voices are clear and easy to follow, while others are garbled, convoluted, and meandering. Some create belief and inspire trust, while others do not.

An individual's voice can also be recognized in the writing he or she produces. A writer's voice, like a person's personality, is determined by many factors, such as ethnic identity, social class, family, or religion. In addition, some elements of voice evolve as a writer matures, such as how one thinks (logically or intuitivly) and what one thinks (a political or philosophical stance). Writers also can exert a great deal of control over their language. They create the style (simple or complex), tone (serious or sarcastic), and many other elements. Writers try to be in control of as many elements of their writing voice as they can.

WP TIP Start a written discussion of "voice" in your online journal. After exploring the writing topic, see if you can characterize your own writing voice.

8 | a | Defining voice

The word "voice" means at least two distinctly different things. First, it is the audible sound of a person speaking (*He has a high-pitched voice*). Applied to writing, this meaning is primarily metaphoric; unless writers read their work aloud, readers don't actually hear writers' voices. Speaking voices distinguish themselves by physical auditory qualities such as pitch (high, low, nasal), pace (fast, slow), tone (angry, assertive, tentative), rhythm (regular, smooth, erratic), register (soft, loud), and accent (southern, British, Boston). Writing voices do much the same when the language on the page re-creates the sound of the writer talking. Careful writers control, as much as they can, the sound of their words in their readers' heads.

Second, voice, especially when applied to writing, suggests who a person is and what he or she stands for. Written voices convey something of the writers behind the words, including their personal, political, philosophical, and social beliefs. In addition, writers' beliefs and values may be revealed in the way they reason about things—whether they do so in an orderly, scientific manner or more intuitively and emotionally.

■ WRITING I: EXPLORATION

In your own words, describe the concept of voice. Do you think writers have one voice or many? Explain what you mean.

8 b Analyzing the elements of voice

Readers experience a writer's voice as a whole expression, not a set of component parts. However, to understand and gain control of your own voice, let's examine the individual elements that combine to make the whole.

1 Tone

Tone is your attitude toward the subject and audience: angry, anxious, joyous, sarcastic, puzzled, contemptuous, respectful, friendly, and so on. Writers control their tone, just as speakers do, by adopting a particular perspective or point of view, selecting words carefully, emphasizing some words and ideas over others, choosing certain patterns of inflection, and controlling the pace with pauses and other punctuation. For example, note how your tone might change as you speak or write the following sentences:

> The English Department was unable to offer enough writing courses to satisfy the demand this semester.

> Why doesn't English offer more writing courses?

> It's outrageous that so many students were closed out of first-year writing courses!

To gain control of the tone of your writing, read drafts of your paper aloud and listen carefully to the attitudes you express. Try to hear your own words as if you were the audience: Decide whether the overall tone is the one you intended, and reread carefully to make sure every sentence contributes to this tone. (See Chapter 30 for specific examples of adjusting tone.)

2 Style

Style is the way writers express themselves according to whom they are writing and why. Style is found in the formality or informality, simplicity or complexity, clarity or muddiness of a writer's language. For example, in writing to a friend, you may adopt an informal, conversational style, characterized by contractions and simple, colloquial language:

John—Can't make it tonight. Spent the day making wood and I'm totally bushed.

In writing to professors, however, you may be more formal, careful, and precise:

Dear Professor James,

I am sorry, but my critical essay will be late. Over the weekend, I overextended myself cutting, splitting, and stacking two cords of wood for my father and ended up with a sprained back. Would you be willing to extend the paper deadline for one more day?

In other words, the style you adopt depends upon your audience, purpose, and situation. To gain control of your style, think about how you wish to present yourself and shape your words, sentences, and paragraphs to suit the occasion. (See also Chapters 5 and 7.)

3 Structure

The structure of a text is how it's put together: where it starts, where it goes next, where the thesis occurs, what evidence fits where, how it concludes. Structure is the pattern or logic that holds together thoughtful writing, revealing something of the thought process that created it. For example, a linear, logical structure may characterize the writer as a linear, logical thinker, while a circular, digressive structure may suggest more intuitive, less orderly habits of mind. Skillful writers, of course, can present themselves one way or the other depending on to whom they're writing and why.

The easiest way to gain control of an essay's structure is to make an outline that reveals visually and briefly the organization and direction you intend. Some writers outline before they start writing and stick to the outline all the way through the writing. Others outline only after writing a draft or two to help control their final draft. And still others start with a rough outline which they continue to modify as the writing modifies thought and direction. (For more on outlining, see 6e.) Also consider the structure of your paragraphs and sentences. (See Chapters 24 and 26.)

4 Values and beliefs

Your values include your political, social, religious, and philosophical beliefs. Your background, opinions, and beliefs will be part of everything you write, but you must learn when to express them directly and when not to. For example, including your values would enhance a personal essay or other autobiographical writing, but it may detract attention from the subject of a research essay.

To gain control of the values in your writing, consider whether the purpose of the assignment calls for an implicit or explicit statement of your values. Examine your drafts for words that reveal your personal biases, beliefs, and values; keep them or take them out as appropriate for the assignment.

5 Authority

Your authority comes from confidence in your knowledge and is projected through the way you handle the material about which you are writing. An authoritative voice is often clear, direct, factual, and specific, leaving the impression that the writer is confident about what he or she is saying. You can exert and project real authority only over material you know well, whether it's the facts of your personal life or carefully researched information. The more you know about your subject, the more clearly you will explain it, and the more confident you will sound.

To gain control over the authority in your writing, do your homework, conduct thorough research, and read your sources of information carefully and critically. (See Chapter 2.)

WP TIP   Explore your notion of what a writer's "voice" is in an electronic file. Examine e-mail messages sent to you from friends and instructors. What do you notice about each person's voice? How are any alike? How different? How is a writer's voice connected to his or her purpose in writing to you?

▣ WRITING 2: APPLICATION

Describe your own writing voice in terms of each of the elements outlined in this section (tone, style, structure, values, authority). Then compare your description with a recent paper you have written. In what ways does the paper substantiate your description? In what ways does it differ from your description? How do you account for any differences? **ESL:** Is your writing voice in English different from your writing voice in your native language? If you are aware of any differences, try to describe them in terms of the elements discussed in this chapter. Are there qualities of your voice in one language that you would like to transfer to your voice in the other language?

8   c   Hearing the range of one voice

All writing has a voice, even when it strives for apparent objectivity, as does the first excerpt about writing courses in the previous section. In college writing, you will need different voices to address different purposes, audiences, and situations. To illustrate this range, we have selected five samples of writing from the portfolio created by Julie during her first semester in a college writing class.

▣ Private

The first example comes from Julie's journal. In this entry, she writes to herself about her first assignment.

10/8 I'm really struggling with my personal experience paper—I can't seem to get a good balance of description, dialogue, and depth—I get carried away with one and forget the others! I'm so frustrated—I'm going to give it one more attempt—I've written more of these drafts than any other paper and I'm getting so sick of it—it seems to be getting worse instead of better. . . .

Julie's journal-writing voice was never meant for publication. The tone it projects is one of uncertainty and frustration. It is not carefully structured, worded, or punctuated. In fact, there's a raw, unfinished effect with all the dashes. Her entry reads the way personal journals read: conversationally private, unedited, off the record, but believably honest.

2 Personal

The following is the opening paragraph of a personal experience paper by Julie about her playing varsity tennis in high school.

> Bounce. Bounce. Bounce. The sound is driving me insane, but I just can't get the nerve to toss the ball and serve. Am I scared? Yes. Of what, this girl or this match? This girl, this girl scares me. She is a natural talent. How many times is that cross-court forehand shot going to rip past me? Nuts! I am going to lose plain and simple. I'll just have to deal with it.

Julie invites her readers into the inner and usually hidden reaches of her mind with her personal—but not private—voice. The tone of this informal, loosely structured voice is both flip and anxious (*Am I scared? Yes.*). The internal monologue is convincingly colloquial (*Nuts!*), inviting us to identify with her feelings of self-doubt. It is the individual voice of a good tennis player at a vulnerable moment.

3 Informative

This example is taken from the early pages of Julie's research essay focusing on a center for emotionally disturbed children.

> The Huron Center provides residential treatment for a limited number of emotionally disturbed children in the upper Midwest. The Center contains forty-five beds: thirty are reserved for long-term care, generally six months to a year; ten are assessment beds, reserved for stays of up to two months; and five are crisis beds, reserved for stays of ten days or less. The children live together, supervised by twelve staff members.

Julie's voice here is that of a reporter presenting and explaining information; she provides numerical facts in a methodical manner, carefully ordered, and makes no value judgments. By adopting this neutral, information-only tone, she puts herself in the background—a stance that suggests, nevertheless, an authoritative writer in control of her material.

4 Committed

The following is Julie's concluding paragraph from the research essay on the Huron Center.

> The Huron Center is a haven for needy people who have run out of options for helping their own children. However, the small, dedicated staff is stressed to the limit. They often work sixty-hour weeks, with children whose troubles they do not always understand. Emotionally disturbed children need more, not less, help, but federal funds have dried up. Where will future resources come from? The public must wake up and help the children!

Julie here is an advocate for the plight of the understaffed center; she now uses judgment words (*haven, needy, stressed*) and ends with an emotional plea (*wake up and help the children!*). The passionate tone here is a strong indication of her personal values. Her voice is highly structured and emotionally involved, yet precise, controlled, and focused on the facts; the voice is authoritative and committed at the same time.

5 Reflective

Julie's final paper was an examination of herself as a writer. This passage appears on the last page of her essay.

> During the semester my real growth has been in thinking rather than writing. In my first paper, I had to rewrite and rewrite until readers could actually see me playing tennis. In my research paper, I found statistics, interviewed staff members, and gathered evidence to show that the Huron Center was in trouble. In writing these papers, I've learned to slow down my thinking, to review it, to return to it and make it clearer and clearer and clearer. That's what good writing is really about, isn't it, being clear?

Here Julie leads off with what seems to be a surprising discovery—that she has grown more as a thinker than as a writer.

Her tone is thoughtful, her style informal, her structure associational, as she mulls over her experiences and then concludes whimsically with a rhetorical question aimed as much at herself as at the reader. In the end, her voice is reflective yet knowledgeable, quite different from either the neutral voice or the committed voice from her research essay.

WP TIP   Copy one passage from a paper you're working on two or three times in one file. Go back and purposely change your voice each time by considering different audiences and purposes and ranges of your voice. Write a summary at the end of the file reporting what you've discovered in doing this.

■ **WRITING 3: EXPLORATION**

How would you describe your own writing voice? How many voices do you have? Explain.

 QUESTIONS FOR EXAMINING YOUR VOICE

1. Tone. Read drafts aloud and listen to the attitude you hear. Is it what you intend? If not, how could you change it?

2. Style. What image of yourself do you create through your language? Is it formal or informal? Complex or simple?

3. Structure. What does your structure say about your manner of thinking? Is it careful and tight? Loose and flexible? Logical? Intuitive? Which do you want it to be?

4. Values. Do your beliefs show through when you speak on paper? Do you want them to?

5. Authority. Where does your writing voice sound especially knowledgeable and confident? Where does it sound tentative and unsure? What can you do to be more consistently authoritative?

SUGGESTIONS FOR WRITING AND RESEARCH

INDIVIDUAL

1.   Read a book or a substantial number of articles by one of your favorite writers of nonfiction. Make notes about the features of voice that you notice; describe them in terms of tone, style, structure, values, and authority. Write a report in which you explain and analyze the writer's voice.

2. Collect and examine as many samples of your past writing as you have saved. Also look closely at the writing you have done so far this semester. Write a paper in which you describe and explain the history and evolution of your voice and the features that most characterize your current writing voice.

COLLABORATIVE

Exchange recently written papers with a partner. Examine your partner's paper for the elements of voice. In a letter, each of you describe what you find. How does your partner's perception of your voice match or differ from your own? Now do individual assignment number 2, including your partner's assessment as part of your analysis.

PART THREE

Drafting

Good stories can be told about virtually anything. Not only can good stories be about any subject, they can be quite simple and can take place in your own backyard—and *you* can tell them. Potential stories happen all the time—daily, in fact. What makes them actually become stories is recounting them, orally or in writing. Good stories are entertaining, informative, lively, and believable; they will mean something to you who write them and to your audience, who will read them.

All stories, whether they're true (nonfiction) or imagined (fiction), are accounts of something that happened—an event or series of events, after which something or somebody is changed. Whether the story is about "The Three Little Pigs" or *Huckleberry Finn* (both fiction), or about Darwin's *Voyage of the Beagle* or your own trip last winter to Mexico (nonfiction), it includes the following elements: a character (who?) to whom something happens (what?), by some method (how?), in some place (where?), at some time (when?), for some reason (why?). In other words, any time you render a full account of a personal experience, you answer questions about who, what, how, where, when, and why. Whether your story is engaging or not depends upon the subject, your interest in telling it, and the skill with which you weave together these story elements.

WP TIP   Start a computer file in which you write down your responses to the "writings" in this chapter. Odds are you will be able to use some of this writing in a paper, so doing this gives you a head start and saves you recopying time later.

■ WRITING I: EXPLORATION

Think about the best stories you have read or listened to. What makes them memorable? What makes them believable? **ESL:** You might want to reflect on stories you have read or heard that were conveyed in your native language; do they translate into English? Why or why not?

9 **a** **Delineating character (who?)**

In personal experience writing, your main character is yourself, so try to give your readers a sense of who you are through your voice, actions, level of awareness, and description. The characters in a good story are believable and interesting; they come alive for readers.

1 Voice

Your language reveals who you are—playful, serious, rigid, loose, stuffy, honest, warm, or whatever. In the following excerpt, in which Beth relates her experience playing oboe during a two-hour Saturday morning orchestra rehearsal, we learn she's serious, fun loving, impish, and just a little lazy:

> I love that section. It sounds so cool when Sarah and I play together like that. Now I can put my reed back in the water and sit back and listen. I probably should be counting the rests. Counting would mean I'd have to pay attention and that's no fun. I'd rather look around and watch everyone else sweat.

2 Actions

Readers learn something about the kind of person you are from your actions. For example, when Karen recalls her thoughts playing in a basketball tournament, we learn something of her insecurity, fears, and skills all at once:

> This time, don't be so stupid Karen—if you don't take it up court, you'll never get the ball. Oh, God, here I go. Okay, they're in a twenty-one—just bring it up—Sarah's alone—fake up, bounce pass—yes, she hits it! I got the assist!

3 Self-awareness

One of the best ways to reveal who you are is to show yourself becoming aware of something, gaining a new insight or a new way of seeing the world. While self-awareness can occur for apparently unexplainable reasons, it most often happens when you encounter new ideas or have experiences that change you in some way. Writing his experience in the form of a journal, Jeff reveals his sense of humor and seriousness during a solo camping experience in Outward Bound, a month-long program that teaches wilderness survival skills:

Day 13. After three days of not talking to or seeing one single person, I know the three basic necessities of life. Sorry Dad, they are not Stocks, Bonds, and Spreadsheets. And no, Mom, they're not *General Hospital, Days of Our Lives,* and *All My Children.* All I have been doing is melting snow for drinking water, rationing my food so it will last, and splitting dead trees in order to get firewood.

4 Telling details

Describe yourself and other participants in your story in such a way that the details and facts help tell your story. A **telling detail** or fact is one that advances your characterization of someone without your having to render an obvious opinion. For example, when Jeff addresses his parents in his Outward Bound journal (above), he characterizes them quickly by mentioning their preoccupations with these "telling" lines: *"I know the three basic necessities of life. Sorry Dad, they are not Stocks, Bonds, and Spreadsheets. And no, Mom, they're not* General Hospital, Days of Our Lives *and* All My Children." Dan achieves a similar "telling" when he characterizes his football coach by reporting the logo on his sweatshirt: *"Winning isn't everything. It's the only thing."*

■ WRITING 2: APPLICATION

Start to characterize yourself. Write four paragraphs, and in each one, emphasize one of these individualizing elements: voice, actions, awareness, and any telling details of your life. Select any or all that seem worthy of further exploration and write a few more paragraphs.

9 b Finding a subject (what?)

People write about their personal experiences to get to know and understand themselves better, to inform and entertain others, and to leave permanent records of their lives. Sometimes people recount their experiences casually, in forms never intended for wide circulation, such as journals, diaries, and letters. Sometimes they write in forms meant to be shared with others, such as memoirs, autobiographies, or personal essays. In college, the most common narrative forms are personal experience essays.

Subjects for good stories know no limits. You already have a lifetime of experiences from which to choose, and each experience is a potential story to help explain who you are, what you believe, and how you act today. Here are some of the topics selected by a single first-year writing class.

- playing oboe in Saturday orchestra rehearsals

- counseling disturbed children at summer camp

- picking strawberries on a farm

- winning a championship tennis match

- clerking at a drugstore

- playing in a championship basketball game

- solo camping in Outward Bound

- touring Graceland in Memphis

- painting houses during the summer

When you write a paper based on personal experience, ask yourself: Which experience do I *want* to write about? Will *anybody else* want to read about it? Here are some suggestions. (See Chapter 6 for specific strategies.)

WP TIP Freewrite in a new computer file for ten minutes with the screen on your monitor turned down to black. This helps you avoid self-criticism at a stage when you need to be open to the possibilities you discover. Turn the monitor up again and read what you've written. Open a new file in a window and move phrases or sentences that seem to be leading to a topic; then explore that topic in the new file.

1 Winning and losing

Winning something—a race, a contest, a lottery—can be a good subject, since it features you in a unique position and allows you to explore or celebrate a special talent. At the same time, the exciting, exceptional, or highly dramatic subjects such as scoring the winning goal in a championship game or placing first in a creative writing contest may be difficult to write because they've been used so often that readers have very high expectations.

The truth is that in most parts of life there are more losers than winners. While one team wins a championship, dozens do not. So there's a large, empathetic audience out there who will understand and identify with a narrative about losing. Although more common than winning, losing is less often explored in writing because it is more painful to recall. Therefore there are fresher, deeper, more original stories to tell about losing.

2 Milestones

Perhaps the most interesting but also the most difficult experience to write about is one that you already recognize as a turning point in your life, whether it's winning a sports championship, being a camp counselor, or surviving a five-day solo camping trip in midwinter. People who explore such topics in writing often come to a better understanding of them. Also, their very significance challenges writers to make them equally significant for an audience that did not experience them. When you write about milestones, pay special attention to the physical details that will both advance your story and make it come alive for readers.

3 Daily life

Commonplace experiences make fertile subjects for personal narratives. You might describe practicing for, rather than winning, the big game, or cleaning up after, rather than attending, the prom. If you are accurate, honest, and observant in exploring a subject from which readers expect little, you are apt to pleasantly surprise them and draw them into your story. Work experiences are especially fruitful subjects, since you may know inside details and routines of restaurants and retail shops that the rest of us can only guess: for example, how long is it before McDonald's tosses its unsold hamburgers? how do florists know which flowers to order when?

4 A caution about love, death, and divorce

Several subjects that you may need to write about may not make good topics for formal papers that will be shared with classmates and instructors. For example, you are probably too involved in a love relationship to portray it in any but the rosiest terms; too close to the recent death of someone you care about to render the event faithfully; too angry, confused, or miserable to write well of your parents' divorce. Writing about these and other close or painful experiences in your journal or diary can be immensely cathartic, but there is no need to share them with others.

■ **WRITING 3: APPLICATION**

Make a list of a dozen experiences about which you could tell stories. Think of special insight you gained as well as commonplace events that were instructive or caused change. Share your list with classmates and find out which they would most like to hear about. **ESL:** You might want to reflect on your experiences learning English or adjusting to a new culture.

9 **C** **Establishing perspective (how?)**

The term **perspective** refers to the vantage point or position from which one is telling a story. Perspective addresses the question: How close—in time, distance, or spirit—are you to the experience? Do you write as if it happened long ago or yesterday? Do you summarize what happened or put readers at the scene? Do you explain the experience or leave it mysterious? In other words, you can control, or at least influence, how readers respond to a story by controlling the perspective from which you tell it.

Authorial perspective is established largely by **point-of-view**. Using the **first person** (*I*) puts the narrator right in the story as a participant. This point of view is usually the one used in personal experience writing, as Beth, Karen, and Jeff do in earlier examples.

The **third person** (*he* or *she*) establishes a distinction between the person narrating the events and the person experiencing them and thus tends to depersonalize the story. This perspective is more common in fiction, but it has some uses in personal essays as well. In the following example, for instance, Karen opens her personal experience essay from the imagined perspective of the play-by-play announcer who broadcasts the championship game; the point of view is first person, but from the perspective of a third person:

> 2:15 Well folks, it looks as if Belmont has given up, the coach is preparing to send in his subs. It has been a rough game for Belmont. They stayed in it during the first quarter, but Walpole has run away with it since then. Down by twenty with only six minutes left, Belmont's first sub is now approaching the table.

Verb tense establishes the time when the story happened or is happening. The tense used to relate most of the events in a story is called the **governing tense**. Personal experience stories are usually set in either the present or the past. (See 21c and 35d–f for more on tense.)

▮ Once upon a time: past tense

The most natural way to recount a personal experience is to write in the past tense; whatever you're narrating *did* happen sometime in the past. Lorraine uses the past tense to describe an automobile ride with her Native American grandfather to attend a tribal conference:

> I sat silently across from Grandfather and watched him slowly tear the thin white paper from the tip of the cigarette. He gathered the tobacco in one hand and drove the van with the other. I memorized his every move as he went through the motions of the prayer, which ended when he finally blew the tobacco out of the window and into the wind.

Even though the governing tense for your personal narrative may be the past tense, you may still want to use other tenses for special purposes.

▮ Being there: present tense

The present tense provides the illusion that the experience is happening at the moment; it leaves no time for your reflection. This strategy invites readers to become involved with your story as it is happening and invites them to interpret it for themselves.

If you want to portray yourself thinking rather than talking— in what is called **interior monologue**—you may choose to use fragment sentences and made-up words since the flow of the mind doesn't obey conventional rules of language. For example, when Beth describes her thoughts during orchestra rehearsal, she writes an interior monologue; we hear her talking to herself while trying to blow her oboe (note how she provides clues so that we understand what is going on around her):

> No you don't really mean that, do you? You do. Rats. Here we go . . . Pfff . . . Pfff . . . Why isn't this playing? Maybe if I blow harder . . . HONK!! Great. I've just made a total fool of myself in front of everyone. Wonderful.

■ **WRITING 4: APPLICATION**

Write one page of a possible story using the first person, past tense, and a second page using the first person, present tense. From which perspective do you prefer to tell the story? Why?

9 **d** **Describing the setting (where?)**

Experiences happen in some place at some time, and good stories describe these settings. To describe a believable physical setting, you need to re-create on paper the sights, sounds, smells, and physical sensations that allow readers to experience it for themselves. In addition to **telling details** that support your plot or character development, try to include **evocative details**, colorful details of setting and character that will let your readers know you were really there.

In the following example, Heather portrays details of the farm where she spent the summer picking strawberries:

> The sun is just barely rising over the treetops and there is still dew covering the ground. In the strawberry patch, the deep green leaves are filled with water droplets and the strawberries are big and red and ready to be picked. The patch is located in a field off the road near a small forest of Christmas trees. The white house, the red barn, and a checkerboard of fields can be seen in the distance. It is 5:30 A.M. and the day has begun.

The evocative details are those which appeal to your senses, such as sight, touch, and smell: *dew covering the ground, deep green leaves, strawberries . . . big . . . and red, white house, red barn,* and *checkerboard fields.*

The telling details of a setting reveal something essential about your story without your explaining them (see also 9a4). For example, in telling a story about your sister, you might describe the physical objects in her room, which in turn describe important elements of her character: *the hockey stick, soccer ball, gym bag, sweatpants, baseball jersey, and the life-size posters of Michael Jordan and Jackie Joyner-Kersee.* In other words, skillful description helps you "tell" the story without your telling it outright.

■ **WRITING 5: APPLICATION**

Describe in detail one of the settings in which your experience took place. Appeal to at least three senses, and try to include details that "tell" some of your story without needing further explanation or overt value judgments on your part.

9 **e** **Narrating a sequence of events (when?)**

In every story, events are ordered in some way. While you cannot alter the events that happened in your experience, as a writer you need to decide which events to portray and in what order to present them.

1 **Selecting events**

You have dozens of places to start and end any story, and at each point along the way, many possible details and events are worth relating. Your final selection should support the theme of your story. To decide which events to portray, figure out how much detail you intend to devote to each one. In writing about her basketball career, Karen could have told about her four years playing in high school, her senior year alone, one game, or even less. Because she wanted to focus on a climactic point in great detail, she selected "even less"—she writes her entire six-page paper about the final six minutes in her final game.

In selecting events, consider using one of two strategies that writers commonly use to maintain reader interest: showing cause and effect and building suspense. When writers recount an experience to show **cause and effect**, they pair one event (having an accident, meeting a person, taking a journey) with another event or events that was caused as a result (undergoing physical therapy, making a friend, learning a new language).

In using **suspense**, writers raise questions or pose problems but delay answering or solving them. If the writer can make the question interesting enough, the problem pressing enough, readers will keep reading to learn the answers or solutions—in other words, to find out what happens. Karen's paper asks indirectly, "What is it like to play a championship game from the perspective of a substitute player?"

2 Ordering events

The most common way to sequence events is to use **chronological order**, presenting events in the sequence in which they happened. Chronological order can be straightforward, following a day from morning to night as Heather does in her narrative about picking strawberries. Chronology also orders Jeff's twenty-two days of Outward Bound. And chronology orders Karen's six minutes at the end of one basketball game. Sometimes, however, the order is deliberately broken up, so that readers are first introduced to an event in the present and then, later in the story, are allowed to see events that happened earlier in time through **flashbacks**. For example, Jeff's Outward Bound journal could start with his first day of solo camping and then, in another entry, flash back to the early days to explain how he got there. Such a sequence has the advantage of stimulating readers' interest by opening with a point of exceptional drama or insight.

WP TIP   Type your sequence of events into a computer file. Use the outline function to view your sequence clearly. Use the cut and paste functions to rearrange the sequence of events as needed before you continue drafting.

WRITING 6: APPLICATION

Outline the sequence of events of your story in the order that makes the most sense. Is the arrangement chronological? If not, what is it? How do you decide which event to begin with? Which one to end with?

9 f Developing a theme (why?)

We can talk about the "why" of a story on two levels: First, *why* did the events occur in the story? What motivated or caused them? Well-told stories will answer this question, directly or indirectly. But we can also ask the writer. Of all the many stories you could write, *why* did you write this one? Or, more bluntly, every reader asks, at least tacitly: "So what? What's the meaning or significance of this story? What did I learn by reading it?" Well-told stories will also answer this question; readers will see and understand both why you wrote it and why they read it.

However, first drafts of personal experience narratives often do not reveal clear answers to these questions, even to the writers themselves. First drafts are for getting the events down on paper for writers to look at. In subsequent drafts, the meaning of these events—the theme—should become clearer. If it doesn't, the writer should drop the subject.

In experiential stories, the theme isn't usually explicitly stated in the first paragraph, as the thesis statement often is in expository or argumentative writing. Instead, storytellers may create a meaning that is not directly stated anywhere and that becomes clear only at the end of the narrative. Many themes fall into three broad categories: slices of life, insights, and turning points.

1 Slices of life

Some stories simply let readers see what life is like for someone else. Such stories exist primarily to record the writer's memories and to convey information in an interesting way. Their primary theme is, "This is what my life is like."

Beth's story of the Saturday orchestra rehearsal is a slice of life, as she chooses to focus on a common "practice" rather than a more dramatic "performance." After using interior monologue for nine paragraphs, in the last paragraph she speaks to the readers directly, explaining what the meaning of music is in her everyday life:

> As hard as it is to get up every Saturday morning, and as hard as it is to put up with some people here, I always feel good as I leave rehearsal. A guest conductor once said: "Music sounds how feelings feel." It's really true. Music evokes emotions that can't be described on paper. Every human feeling can be expressed through music—sadness, love, hatred. Music is an international language. Once you learn it you can't forget it.

2 Insights

In contrast to the many but routine experiences that reveal slices of life is the single important experience that leads to a writer's new insight, change, or growth. Such an experience is deeply significant to the writer, and he or she makes sure that readers see the full value of the experience, usually by explicitly commenting on its meaning. The final paragraph of Karen's championship basketball game reveals just such an insight:

> It's over now, and I've stopped crying, and I'm very happy. In the end I have to thank—not my coach, not my team—but Walpole for beating us so badly that I got to play. I can't get over

it. I played. And my dream came true, I hit a three pointer in the Boston Garden.

3 Turning points

Turning points are those moments in one's life when something happens that causes the writer to change or grow in some large or small way—more than routine, less than spectacular— perhaps somewhere in between slices of life and profound insights. In fact, many of the best personal experience stories have for themes a modest change or the beginning of growth. Although such themes may be implied throughout the story, they often become clear only in a single climactic moment or episode. Mary's camp counselor story shows her progress from insecurity to confidence in gaining the trust of a ten-year-old. The following excerpt takes place after she has rescued Josh from ridicule by other campers.

> He ran in and threw himself on my bed, crying. I held him, rubbing his head for over an hour. "I love you, Mary. You're the best big sister in the whole world and you're so pretty! I love you and don't ever want you to leave."

■ WRITING 7: APPLICATION

Freewrite for ten minutes about the meaning of your story as you have written it so far, addressing some of these questions: What have you discovered about yourself? Were there any surprises? Does your story interest you? Why or why not? What do you want readers to feel or know at the end?

9 g Shaping the whole paper

Read through the complete final draft of Karen's essay recounting her experience in the Eastern Massachusetts Basketball Championship. Note that she elects to play creatively with both time and perspective in telling her story: She opens her story by recounting the last six minutes of the game as told by the play-by-play announcer in the broadcast booth, letting us see the game from his imagined perspective. Second, she recounts the same six minutes from her own perspective on the floor. As you read this account, notice how she characterizes herself through her voice and actions, uses present tense to create suspense, and lets the theme emerge indirectly only in the last paragraph.

102 Recounting experience

The Three Pointer

Karen Santosuosso

2:15   Well folks, it looks as if Belmont has given up, the coach is preparing to send in his subs. It has been a rough game for Belmont. They stayed in it during the first quarter, but Walpole has run away with it since then. Down by twenty with only six minutes left, Belmont's first sub is now approaching the table.

Meghan Sullivan with the ball goes coast to coast and lays it in for two. She has sparked Walpole from the start.

The fans have livened up a bit, but oddly enough they aren't Walpole's fans, they're Belmont's—

"KAREN IS SMALL, SHE'S NOT TALL, WE LOVE KAREN!"

Meanwhile, Belmont's number eleven, 5' 1", Karen Santosuosso, replaces Michelle Hayes. With three minutes left, Belmont's Kristin Sullivan brings up the ball, spin dribbles—but the ball is stripped away by Meghan Sullivan, who takes it down court. She throws on fly and hits a three pointer! That girl has truly amazing talent.

Belmont with the ball. Santosuosso brings it up, passes to Jones, Jones shoots and hits it! Belmont may be out of the game, folks, but these reserves are having the time of their lives.

Walpole brings it up. Called for traveling.

Both Belmont and Walpole are now emptying their benches. As she sits down, Meghan Sullivan receives a standing ovation. An honor roll student and all-star athlete, she'll be attending Holy Cross this fall. What a night she had, eighteen points.

One and a half minutes left, D'Andrea inbounds to Santosuosso, who brings it up. Walpole sitting back in a twenty-one zone, Karen, over half court, stops, pops, swish. Santosuosso for three! The Belmont fans are going wild—

"KAREN IS SMALL, SHE'S NOT TALL, WE LOVE KAREN!"

As the clock winds down, fifteen seconds left, Walpole has started celebrating. The Belmont bench is quiet, but they have nothing to be ashamed of.

Smith misses the second freethrow, Hathaway on the rebound, gives it off to Keohane—and that will do it, folks. Walpole is the eastern Massachusetts women's basketball champion.

2:15   Where are they? Oh, there they are, Mom's waving and Dad has the camera. It's awesome, they come to every game, even to watch me bench.

"KAREN IS SMALL, SHE'S NOT TALL, WE LOVE KAREN!"

Oh, God, I'm so embarrassed, complete silence and those guys start yelling again. I can't believe them. Nothing is happening and no one else is cheering . . . Well, at least maybe coach hears them now—not that it will make any difference. With six minutes to go, we're still down by eighteen. No matter how badly the starters play, he won't let the subs play. My senior year, six minutes left in the Boston Garden—in my career as the shortest player in the history of Belmont High—and he hasn't played me yet.

At least my friends are on my side—they're all sitting in the bleachers on the Walpole side with their faces painted maroon and blue and wearing Belmont clothes. I want to wave to them again. Oh no, he caught me waving. No big deal, three months ago I would have minded, but what difference does it make now?

Meghan Sullivan with the ball goes coast to coast and lays it in for two. She has sparked Walpole from the start.

"Girls you have got to keep your heads into the game. Don't let them get you down. You have worked so hard all season, and you are as good as they are. Look at our record, 18–2–0, there's no reason you can't play with them."

"Coach, they're killing us. They are making us look like fools. We're down by eighteen with six minutes left. It's hopeless."

"I don't want to hear any of you talk like that. You have worked too hard to get to this point only to give up now. Remember every sweat-dripping, suicide-sprinting, drill-conditioning, nine o'clock Saturday morning practice!"

"All right girls, now get out there, play hard, and have fun."

"KAREN IS SMALL, SHE'S NOT TALL, WE LOVE KAREN!"

I can't believe those guys, I love them. My own personal fan club, and

they're even audible in the Boston Garden. Those guys won't stop until he plays me.

Five and a half minutes left, I wonder if he has the guts. . . .

"Karen, come here. Go in for Michelle."

Am I imagining this? There's a whole five minutes left and he's letting me play—but I'll take it!

"Hi, sub, number eleven for twenty-four. Is that your fan club in the balcony screaming for you?"

Wow, even the timekeeper noticed these guys. He pays more attention than coach. "Yeah, they're my friends. At every game, I put up three-point shot halftime shows just for them. We have a joke on the team that he only plays five and a half players, because the sixth hardly ever gets in."

"Tweet."

Too bad the timekeeper isn't our coach—anyway, I'm playing—on the parquet floor of the Boston Garden—actually playing, not just warming up or putting on a halftime show.

"Karen take the ball up."

"No way, Kristin, you take it." What am I afraid of?

Kristin's dribbling up the court and, as usual, she's showing off. Here she goes, spin dribble—no wait, Sullivan strips the ball. . . .

This time, don't be so stupid Karen—if you don't take it up court, you'll never get the ball. Oh, God, here I go. Okay, they're in a twenty-one—just bring it up—Sarah's alone—fake up, bounce pass—yes, she hits it! An assist!

There goes Sullivan again, burning up the court, right by all of us and she hits the one on the fly. <u>She</u> is truly awesome!

Kristin's got two defenders on her and . . . "Kristin, I'm open." So, she won't pass and she misses her shot clean, bricked it off the backboard, what a heave.

Walpole brings it up. Called for traveling.

"Karen, coach wants you to bring it up."

If I don't do this now, I'll hate myself tomorrow. If I miss, big deal, I tried. I have to try it. Just think of Dad . . . think of the guys.

Over half court, approaching the key, they aren't challenging me. Stop, pop, and there it goes. Oh please, please go in, please . . .

> Karen, over half court, stops, pops, swish. Santosuosso for
> three!

Yes! I did it. I can't believe . . . Oh my, oh my . . . I did it! Where's Dad?
I can't find him, where is he? I can't believe I'm crying. There he is Dad!
And Mom's jumping up and down—we must look like twins dancing
around, only she's in the stands and I'm on the court.

"KAREN IS SMALL, SHE'S NOT TALL, WE LOVE KAREN!"

Now if I could only stop crying so I could finish playing. Thirty seconds
left, I hope I make it.

> As the clock winds down, Walpole has started celebrating. The
> Belmont bench is quiet, but they have nothing to be ashamed
> of.

Walpole's jumping up and down—and so am I. . . .

> Walpole is the eastern Massachusetts women's basketball
> champion.

It's over now, and I've stopped crying, and I'm very happy. In the end I
have to thank—not my coach, not my team—but Walpole for beating us so
badly that I got to play. I can't get over it. I played. And my dream came
true, I hit a three pointer in the Boston Garden.

SUGGESTIONS FOR WRITING AND RESEARCH

INDIVIDUAL

Write a personal experience essay based on Writings 2–7 in this
chapter. Find a subject that will let you show some change or
learning on your part. Plan to write this narrative in several
drafts, each one exploring a different aspect of your experience.
See Chapter 20 for suggestions about revising this essay.

COLLABORATIVE

As a class, write the story of your writing class so far in the semester. Each class member contributes one chapter (one page) to
this tale. Each member chooses any moment (funny, momentous,
boring, routine) and describes it so that it stands on its own as a
complete episode. Choose two class members to collect all the
short narrative chapters and weave them into a larger narrative
with a beginning, middle, and end.

10 | Explaining Things

To explain something is to make it clear to somebody else who wants to understand it. Explaining is fundamental to most acts of communication and to nearly every type of writing, from personal to argumentative and research writing. Explanatory writing is also a genre unto itself; a newspaper feature on baseball card collecting, a magazine article on why dinosaurs are extinct, a textbook on the French Revolution, a recipe for chili, or a laboratory report.

10 a | Writing to explain

Explanatory writing (also called *expository* or *informational* writing), answers questions such as these:

- What is it?
- What does it mean?
- How does it work?
- How is it related to other things?
- How is it put together?
- Why did it happen?
- What will its consequences be?

To write a successful explanation, you need to find out first what your readers *want* to know, then what they *already know* and what they *don't know*. If you are able to determine—or at least make educated guesses about—these audience conditions, your writing task becomes clear. When you begin to write, keep in mind three general principles that typify much explanatory writing: (1) It focuses on the idea or object being explained rather than on the writer's beliefs and feelings; (2) it often—not always—

states its objective early in what might be called an informational thesis; and (3) it presents information systematically and logically.

In writing classes, explanation usually takes the form of research essays and reports which emphasize informing rather than arguing, interpreting, or reflecting. The assignment may be to "describe how something works" or to "explain the causes and effects" of a particular phenomenon. This chapter explains how to develop a topic, articulate your purpose, and use strategies appropriate for your audience.

■ WRITING 1: EXPLORATION

How good are you at explaining things to people? What things do you most commonly find yourself explaining? What is the last thing you explained in writing? How did your audience receive your explanation? **ESL:** How is explaining things in your native language different from or similar to explaining things in English?

10 b Focusing on a topic

Topics with a limited, or specific, scope are easier to explain carefully and in detail than topics that are vague, amorphous, or very broad. For example, it's hard to know where to start with subjects such as mountains, cities, automobiles, or stereo systems: What, exactly, are you interested in writing about? EVERYTHING? If so, the task is daunting for even the world's foremost expert. However, a specific mountain range, city, or automobile would be a better place to start. But even then you would still need to know what it is *about* this subject that sparks your curiosity. You could break the subject "stereo systems" into smaller components that may especially interest you, such as compact discs (CD's). And within the subject of CD's, there are probably several topics you might want to know about: their cost, their sound quality, their manufacturing process.

Effective explanations are detailed, developed, include examples, and focused around a central question: "Why are CD's better than tape recordings?" for example, or "Why do CD's cost more than records?" Of course, there may be other questions to be answered along the way (How do CD's work? How are CD's made?), but these are secondary.

Once you have a focused topic on a central question, you need to assemble information. If you're not an expert yourself, you'll need to consult authorities on the topic. Even if you are already an expert, finding supporting information from other experts will help make your explanation clear and authoritative. Keep your audience in mind as you begin your research. You don't want to waste time researching and writing about things your audience already knows.

■ **WRITING 2: APPLICATION**

What would you like to explain? For what purpose? To whom? If you're not sure, do some freewriting or journal writing to help you discover a question.

10 c Developing a thesis

A **thesis** is simply a writer's declaration of what the paper is about. Stating a thesis early in an explanatory work lets readers know what to expect and guides their understanding of the information to be presented. In explanatory writing, the thesis states the answer to the implied question your paper sets out to address: What is it? How does this work? Why is this so?

QUESTION Why do compact discs cost so much?

THESIS CDs cost more than records because the laser technology required to manufacture them is so expensive.

The advantage of stating a thesis in a single sentence is that it sums up the purpose of your paper in a single idea that lets readers predict what's ahead. Another way to state a single-sentence thesis is to convey an image, analogy, or metaphor that provides an ongoing reference point throughout the paper and gives unity and coherence to your explanation—a good image keeps both you and your readers focused.

QUESTION How are the offices of the city government connected?

THESIS City government offices are like an octopus, with eight fairly independent bureaus as arms and a central brain in the mayor's office.

The thesis you start with may evolve as you work on your paper—and that's okay. For example, suppose the more you learn

about city government, the less like an octopus and the more like a centipede it seems. So, your first thesis is really a **working thesis**, and it needs to be tentative, flexible, and subject to change; its primary function is to keep your paper focused to guide further research.

▪ WRITING 3: APPLICATION

Write out a working thesis for the topic you are explaining. If you are addressing a When? or How? question, find a controlling image or analogy that will hold all of the elements together. **WP TIP:** Use your computer's thesaurus to identify synonyms and antonyms that you might use to extend, compare, and/or contrast your point.

10 d Using strategies to explain

Good strategies that can be used to explain things include: defining, describing, classifying and dividing, analyzing causes and effects, and comparing and contrasting. Which strategy you select depends upon the question you are answering as well as the audience to whom you are explaining. You could offer two very different explanations to the same question depending upon who asked it: For example, if asked "Where is Westport Drive?" you would respond differently to a neighbor familiar with local reference points ("one block north of Burger King") than to a stranger who would not know where Burger King was either. With this caution in mind on considering who is the receiver of the explanation, here is a brief overview of possible strategies:

QUESTION	STRATEGY
What is it?	Define

A CD is a small plastic disc containing recorded music.

What does it mean?	Define

Today, when you talk about a "recording," you mean a cassette tape or a CD, not a grooved vinyl disc.

What are its characteristics?	Describe

A vinyl disc is round with tiny grooves covering its surface in which a needle travels to play sound.

QUESTION	STRATEGY

How does it work?   Describe process

On a CD, a laser beam reads the tiny dots on the spinning disk and sends back sound.

How is it related to other things?   Compare and contrast

A CD transmits clearer sound than a cassette tape, but it does not allow you to make inexpensive copies.

How is it put together?   Classify and divide

A basic stereo system includes an input (to generate sound), a processor (to amplify and transmit sound), and an output (to make sound audible).

To what group does it belong?   Classify and divide

CD players, along with record players and tape cassette decks, are sources of music in a stereo system.

Why did it happen?   Analyze cause and effect

The CD skips because either its surface is dirty or the player is broken.

What will its consequences be?   Analyze cause and effect

If you scratch a vinyl record with a knife, it will skip.

WP TIP   Open a new file and list the questions shown on p. 109 and above on the left as the student has done. Save it as a template that you can use over and over when beginning your explanatory essays. Next, go back and, in the right column, answer the questions for a topic you are currently trying to develop.

If your paper is on a tightly focused topic and answers a narrow, simple question, you may need to use only one strategy. More often, however, you will have one primary strategy that shapes the paper as a whole and several secondary strategies that can vary from paragraph to paragraph or even sentence to sentence. For example, to explain why the government has raised income taxes, your primary strategy would be to analyze cause and effect, but you may also need to define terms such as *income tax*, to classify the various types of taxes, and to compare and contrast raising income taxes to other budgetary options. In fact, almost every explanatory strategy makes use of other strategies: How, for example, do you describe a process without first dividing it into steps? How can you compare and contrast without describing the things compared and contrasted?

1 Defining

To define something is to identify it, to set it apart so that it can be distinguished from similar things. Writers need to define any terms central for reader understanding in order to make points clearly, forcefully, and with authority.

Formal definitions are what you find in a dictionary. They usually combine a general term with specific characteristics:

> A computer is a programmable electronic device [*general term*] that can store, retrieve, and process data [*specific characteristics*].

Usually, defining something is a brief, preliminary step accomplished before you move on to a more important part of the explanation. When you need to define something complex or difficult or when your primary explanatory strategy is definition, you will need an extended definition consisting of a paragraph or more. This was the case with Mark's paper explaining computers, in which he defined each part of a typical computer system. After defining the central processor unit (CPU), he then defined computer memory:

> Computer storage space is measured in units called "Kilobytes" (Ks). Each K equals 1024 "bytes" or approximately 1000 single typewriter characters. So one K equals about 180 English words, or a little less than half of a single-spaced typed page, or maybe three minutes of fast typing.
>
> Personal computers generally have their memories measured in "megabytes" (MBs). One MB equals 1,048,567 bytes (or 1000 Ks), which translates into approximately 400 pages of single-spaced type. A typical personal computer may have four to sixteen megabytes of this built-in storage space.

2 Describing

To describe a person, place, or thing means to create a verbal image so that readers can see what you see; hear what you hear; or taste, smell, and feel what you taste, smell, and feel. In other words, effective descriptions appeal to the senses. Furthermore, good description contains enough sensory detail for readers to understand the subject, but not so much as to distract or bore

ESL **VOCABULARY FOR EXPLAINING THINGS**

DESCRIPTION

consists of   has
displays   is characterized by

Example: The flower of the tobacco plant has a sweet fragrance.

DIVISION

consists of   can be separated into
can be divided into   is composed of

Example: The curriculum can be divided into the humanities, the
social sciences, and the natural sciences.

CLASSIFICATION

can be categorized according to   can be categorized as
can be classified according to   can be classified as
can be grouped according to

Example: History can be classified as a humanities discipline.

COMPARISON

also   resembles
both . . . and . . .   similar to
like   the same as

Example: Like English, Spanish uses articles before nouns.

CONTRAST

but   on the other hand
however   unlike
in contrast   yet

Example: Unlike English, Spanish does not always state the subject
of a sentence.

CAUSE AND EFFECT

as a result   therefore
consequently   thus
for this reason

Example: Some marathon runners do not pace themselves well,
and as a result they may be unable to finish a race.

them. Your job, then, is to include just the right amount of detail so that you put readers in your shoes.

To describe how processes work is more complicated than describing what something looks like: In addition to showing objects at rest, you need to show them in sequence and motion. You need to divide the process into discrete steps and present the steps in a logical order. This is easier to do with simple processes, such as making a peanut butter and jelly sandwich, than for complex processes, such as manufacturing an automobile.

Whenever you describe a process, show the steps in a logical sequence that will be easy for readers to follow. To help orient your readers, you may also want to number the steps, using transition words such as *first, second,* and *third*. In the following example, taken from an early draft of his paper, Keith describes the process of manufacturing compact discs.

> CD's start out as a refrigerator-sized box full of little plastic beads that you could sift your hands through. They are fed into a giant tapered corkscrew—a blown-up version of an old-fashioned meat grinder. As the beads pass down the corkscrew, they are slowly melted by the heated walls.
>
> At the bottom of their descent is a "master recording plate" onto which the molten plastic is pressed. The plastic now resembles a vinyl record, except that the disc is transparent. The master now imprints "pits," rather than grooves, around the disc, the surface resembling a ball of Play-Doh after being thrown against a stucco wall—magnified 5000 times.

3 Comparing and contrasting

To **compare** two things is to find similarities between them; to **contrast** is to find differences. Comparing and contrasting at the same time helps people understand something two ways: first, by showing how it is related to similar things, and second, by showing how it differs. College assignments frequently ask you to compare and contrast one author, book, idea, etc. with another.

People usually compare and contrast things when they want to make a choice or judgment about them: books, food, bicycles, presidential candidates, political philosophies. For this reason, the two things compared and contrasted should be similar: you'll learn more to help you vote for president by comparing two presidential candidates than one presidential candidate and a senate candidate; you'll learn more about which orange to buy by comparing it with other oranges (*navel, mandarin*) than with apples, plums, or pears. Likewise, it's easiest to see similarities and differences when you compare and contrast the same elements of each thing. If you describe one political candidate's stand on gun control, describe the other's as well; this way, voters will have a basis for choosing one over the other.

Comparison-and-contrast analysis can be organized in one of three ways: (1) A *point-to-point analysis* examines one feature at a time for both similarities and differences; (2) a *whole-to-whole analysis* first presents one object as a whole and then the other as a whole; (3) a *similarity-and-difference analysis* first presents the similarities, then the differences between the two things, or vice versa.

Use a point-to-point or similarity-and-difference analysis for long explanations of complex things, such as manufacturing an automobile, where you need to cover everything from materials and labor to assembly and inspection processes. But use a whole-to-whole analysis for simple objects that readers can more easily comprehend; for example, Keith compares and contrasts only one process—how records and CD's transmit the information that eventually becomes music:

> On a record, the stylus (needle) sits in a spiraled groove and reads the depth and width of the groove, from which it receives its audio signal. However, the depth of the groove is constantly changing by fractions of millimeters due to specks of dust and the wear caused by the needle, which reads not only the music but also the dust and wear, passing along all the sound as "music."
>
> On a CD, however, a laser sends out a beam of light, which bounces off an object, like radar, and returns with a message, which becomes the music. The CD player doesn't read an ever-changing and dirty groove. Instead, it reads either a "yes" or a "no"—a pit or no pit—from the disc. On one CD there are hundreds of thousands of tiny pits. . . The laser in your CD player reads the distance to the disc to determine if there's a pit, which will be farther away, or not.

An **analogy** is an extended comparison which shows the extent to which one thing is similar in structure and/or process to another. Analogies are effective ways of explaining something new to readers, because you can compare something they are unfamiliar with to something they already know about. For example, most of us have learned to understand how a heart functions by comparing it to a water pump. Be sure to use objects and images in analogies that will be familiar to your readers.

4 Classifying and dividing

People generally understand short more easily than long, simple more easily than complex. To help readers understand a complicated topic, it helps to classify and divide it into simpler pieces and to put the pieces in context.

To **classify** something, you put it in a category or class with other things that are like it:

> Like whales and dolphins, sea lions are aquatic mammals.

To **divide** something, you break it into smaller parts or subcategories:

> An insect's body is composed of a head, a thorax, and an abdomen.

Many complex systems need both classification and division to be clear. To explain a stereo system, for example, you might divide the whole into parts: headphones, record player, graphic equalizer, tape deck, compact disc player, preamplifier, amplifier, radio, and speakers. To better understand how these parts function, you might classify them into categories:

Inputs	Radio
	Record player
	Tape deck
	Compact disc player
Processors	Preamplifiers
	Amplifiers
	Graphic equalizers
Outputs	Speakers
	Headphones

Most readers have a difficult time remembering more than six or seven items at a time, so explaining is easier when you organize a long list into fewer logical groups, as in the preceding example. Also be sure that the categories you use are meaningful to your readers, not simply convenient for you as a writer.

5 Analyzing causes and effects

Few things happen all by themselves. Usually, one thing happens because something else happened; then it, in turn, makes

something else happen. You sleep because you're tired, and once you've slept, you wake up because you're rested, and so on. In other words, you already know about cause and effect because it's a regular part of your daily life. A **cause** is something that makes something else happen; an **effect** is the thing that happens.

Cause-and-effect analyses are most often assigned for college papers to answer *why* questions: Why are the fish dying in the river? Why do CD's cost more than records? The most direct answer is a "because" statement:

> Fish are dying *because* of low oxygen levels in the lake.

> CD's cost more than records *because* manufacturing costs are higher.

Each answer, in other words, is a **thesis**, which the rest of the paper must defend and support:

> There are three reasons for low oxygen levels. . . .

> The reason CD manufacturing costs are higher is. . . .

Cause-and-effect analyses also try to describe possible future effects:

> If nitrogen fertilizers were banned from farmland that drains into the lake, oxygen levels would rise, and fish populations would be restored.

Unless there is sound, widely accepted evidence to support the thesis, however, this sort of analysis may lead to more argumentative writing. In this example, for instance, farmers or fertilizer manufacturers might complicate the matter by pointing to other sources of lake pollution—outboard motors, paper mill effluents, urban sewage runoff—making comprehensive solutions harder to reach. Keep in mind that most complex situations have multiple causes. If you try to reduce a complex situation to an overly simple cause, you are making the logical mistake known as *oversimplification*. (See the box on pp. 136–37 in Chapter 11.)

■ **WRITING 4: APPLICATION**

Decide which of the five strategies described in this section best suits the primary purpose of the explanatory paper you are drafting. Which additional or secondary strategies will you also use?

10 e Organizing with logic

If you explain to your readers where you're taking them, they will follow more willingly; if you lead carefully, step by step, using a good road map, they will know where they are and will trust you.

Your method of organization should be simple, straightforward, and logical, and it should be appropriate for your subject and audience. For example, to explain how a stereo system works, you have a number of logical options: (1) you could start by putting a CD in a player and end with the music coming out of the speakers; (2) you could describe the system technically, starting with the power source to explain how sound is made in the speakers; (3) you could describe it historically, starting with components that were developed earliest and work toward the most recent inventions. All of these options follow a clear logic that, once explained, will make sense to readers.

WP TIP   As you draft your essays, be sure to save your work *frequently;* there's nothing worse than losing whole chunks of your drafts because of a power surge. Also, save your work in new files (or print out at the end of each session) so that you can trace your changes and improvements.

■ WRITING 5: APPLICATION

Outline three possible means of organizing the explanatory paper you are writing. List the advantages and disadvantages of each. Select the one that best suits your purpose and the needs of your audience.

10 f Maintaining a neutral perspective

First, you need to understand that absolute neutrality or objectivity is impossible when you write about anything. All writers bring with them assumptions and biases that cause them to view the world—including this explanatory project—in a particular way. Nevertheless, your explanations will usually be clearer and more accessible to others when you present them as fairly as possible, with as little bias as possible—even though doing this, too, will depend upon who your readers are and whether they agree or disagree with your biases. In general, it's more effective to emphasize the thing explained (the object) rather than your personal beliefs and feelings. This perspective allows you to get information to readers as quickly and efficiently as possible without you, the writer, getting in the way.

To adopt a neutral perspective, write from the *third-person point of view*, using the pronouns *he*, *she*, and *it*. Keep yourself in the background unless you have a good reason not to, such as explaining your personal experience with the subject. In some instances, adopting the second-person *you* adds a friendly, familiar tone that keeps readers interested.

And be fair; present *all* the relevant information about the topic, both things you like about it and things you dislike. Avoid emotional or biased language. Remember that your goal is not to win an argument, but to convey information.

10 g Shaping the whole paper

Keith's complete essay on compact discs is presented here. His topic is narrowly focused on one type of sound medium, CD's, and on one feature of that medium, the high cost. His thesis, that *CD's cost more than records because their manufacturing costs are higher*, evolves throughout the essay and is revealed only at the end, but it is clearly anticipated by the implicit question, "Why do CD's cost so much?" His organization is simple and easy to follow. First, the whole essay is framed by a description of a reader in a record store wondering why CD's cost more than records. Second, within this frame is a point-by-point comparison of the operational and manufacturing processes of records and CD's. Keith's perspective throughout is that of a knowledgeable tour guide.

Although the primary explanatory strategy in Keith's essay is an analysis of causes and effects, he uses most of the other strategies discussed in this chapter as well: definition, process description, and comparison and contrast. His essay is most remarkable for its effective use of analogy: At various points, he asks his readers to think of radar, the game of telephone, jimmies on an ice cream cone, corkscrews, meat grinders, player pianos, and Play-Doh.

CD's: What's the Big Difference?

Keith Jordan

The little package in your left hand says $14.95. The larger package in your right hand says $7.95. The question is, do you want to hear James

Taylor in true stereo quality or not? Since you don't want to settle for second best, you nestle the larger LP back between some Disney classics and head to the counter with your new JT compact disc. Wandering out of the store, you wonder what, besides seven dollars, was the difference between the CD and the LP.

Maybe you've heard the term "digital audio," the type of recording used with CD's, as opposed to "analog audio," used with LPs? If you don't know the difference, read on.

The purpose of your stereo system is to interpret recordings and reproduce them faithfully. Of course, nothing's perfect, so your music always has that quaint amount of background fuzz that never goes away. The fuzz is due to your stereo's misinterpretation of the signal it receives from the magnetic tape or vinyl record.

On a record, the stylus (needle) sits in a spiraled groove and reads the depth and width of the groove, from which it receives its audio signal. However, the depth of the groove is constantly changing by fractions of millimeters due to specks of dust and the wear caused by the needle, which reads not only the music but also the dust and wear, passing along all the sound as "music."

On a CD, however, a laser sends out a beam of light, which bounces off an object, like radar, and returns with a message which becomes the music. The CD player doesn't read an ever-changing and dirty groove. Instead, it reads either a "yes" or a "no"—a pit or no pit—from the disc. On one CD there are thousands of tiny pits that resemble those of a player piano scroll, telling the piano which keys to hit. The laser in your CD player reads the distance to the disc to determine if there's a pit, which will be farther away, or not.

What's the difference, you ask, in receiving music from grooves versus pits? Do you remember playing the "telephone game" in fifth grade? You know, the one where someone on one side of class whispers something in your ear and it gets passed along until it gets to the last person, who gets to say what he was told? This is much the way in which your stereo works: the LP or CD is like the first person and your speakers are like the last. In the case of the record, I whisper some line in your ear and you pass it on, but by the time it reaches the last person, it's been twisted about and has a few more words attached. In the case of the CD, I whisper either a "yes" or a "no" and by the time it reaches the last person it should be exactly the same—this is where the term "digital" comes from, meaning either there is a signal (yes) or there isn't one (no). After all, how much can you screw up a yes or a no?

Even when you understand the difference between a CD and a record, you still feel that seven-dollar difference in your pocket. Why does digital cost so much more?

Although a record would be nearly finished at this point, there's still important work to be done on the CD. From here the disc is metallized, a process that deposits a thin film of metal, usually aluminum, on the surface; you see it as a rainbow under a light. Since light won't bounce back from transparent plastic, the coating acts as a mirror to bounce back the laser beam.

The disc is mirrored by a spray-painting process called "sputtering" that must be extremely precise. You couldn't just dip the thing because then the pits would fill in or melt. The clear disc is inserted into a chamber and placed opposite to a piece of pure aluminum called a "target," which is bombarded with electricity, causing the aluminum atoms to jump off and embed themselves onto the surface of the disc, like jimmies to an ice cream cone.

To keep fingerprints from this critical surface, it is coated with a polymer resin—sort of like an epoxy glue. The disc is laid flat, while a mask is laid over the center hole and a thin bead of resin is laid down around the center. Then the disc is "spin-coated" with a fine film of resin, which becomes the outer coating on the CD.

Once the resin is cured by a brief exposure to ultraviolet light, your CD is pretty much idiot-proof. As long as you don't interrupt the light path to the film, your CD will perform perfectly, even with small scratches, so long as they don't diffract the laser beam—and even then you may be able to rub them out smooth with a finger. In no case should anything come in contact with the recorded surface.

The CD is finished when it is either stamped or silk-screened with the appropriate logo and allowed to dry. Though all of these steps take a mere seven seconds to produce one CD, with materials costing no more than a pack of gum, the cost of buying and operating one CD-producing machine is close to that of running a small team of Formula 1 race cars.

So next time you walk into Record Land, you know what you are paying for. A CD may be twice as expensive as a record, but the sound is twice as clear and the disc will last forever.

SUGGESTIONS FOR WRITING AND RESEARCH

INDIVIDUAL

1. Write a paper explaining any thing, process, or concept. Use as a starting point an idea you discovered in Writing 2. When you have finished one draft of this essay, look back and see if there are places where your explanation could be improved through use of one of the explanatory strategies explained in this chapter.

2. Select a writer of your choice, fiction or nonfiction, who explains things especially well. Read or reread his or her work and write an essay in which you analyze and explain the effectiveness of the explanation you find there.

COLLABORATIVE

Form writing groups based on mutual interests; agree as a group to explain the same thing, process, or concept. Write your explanations separately and then share drafts, comparing and contrasting your different ways of explaining. For a final draft, either (1) rewrite your individual drafts, borrowing good ideas from others in your group or (2) compose a collaborative single paper with contributions from each group member.

Argument is deeply rooted in the American political and social system, in which free and open debate is the essence of the democratic process. Argument is also at the heart of the academic process, in which scholars investigate scientific, social, and cultural issues, hoping through the give-and-take of debate to find reasonable answers to complex questions. Argument in the academic world, however, is less likely to be about winning or losing—as it is in political and legal systems—than about changing minds or altering perceptions about knowledge and ideas.

Argument as rational disagreement, rather than as quarrels and contests, most often occurs in areas of genuine uncertainty about what is right, best, or most reasonable. In disciplines such as English, history, and philosophy, written argument commonly takes the form of interpretation, in which the meaning of an idea or text is disputed. In disciplines such as political science, engineering, and business, arguments commonly appear as position papers in which a problem is examined and a solution proposed.

The purpose of writing argument papers is to persuade other people to agree with a particular point of view. Arguments focus on issues about which there is some debate; if there's no debate, there's no argument. College assignments commonly ask you to argue one side of an issue and defend your argument against attacks from skeptics.

11   a   Understanding the elements of argument

In a basic position paper assignment, you are asked to choose an issue, argue a position, and support it with evidence. Sometimes your investigation of the issue will lead you beyond polar positions toward compromise—a common result of real argument and debate in both the academic and political worlds. In other words, such a paper may reveal that the result of supporting one position (**thesis**) against another (**antithesis**) is to arrive at yet a third position (**synthesis**), which is possible now because both sides have been fully explored and a reasonable compromise presents itself.

This chapter explains the elements that constitute a basic position paper: an arguable issue, a claim and counterclaim, a thesis, and evidence.

1 Issues

An issue is a controversy, something that can be argued about. For instance, mountain bikes and cultural diversity are things or concepts, not in themselves issues. However, they become the foundation for issues when questions are raised about them and controversy ensues.

ISSUE   Do American colleges adequately represent the cultural diversity of the United States?

ISSUE   Should mountain bikes be allowed on wilderness hiking trails?

These questions are issues because reasonable people could answer them in different ways; they can be argued about because more than one answer is plausible, possible, or realistic.

Virtually all issues can be formulated, at least initially, as yes/no questions about which you will take one position or the other: pro (if the answer is yes) or con (if the answer is no).

ISSUE   Should mountain bikes be allowed on trails in Riverside Park?

PRO   Yes, they should be allowed to share pedestrians trails .

CON   No, they should not be allowed to share trails with pedestrians.

2 Claims and counterclaims

A **claim** is a statement or assertion that something is true or should be done. In arguing one side of an issue, you make one or more claims in the hope of convincing an audience to believe you. For example, you could make a claim that calls into question the educational experience at Northfield College:

CLAIM   Northfield College fails to provide good education because the faculty is not culturally diverse.

Counterclaims are statements that oppose or refute claims. You need to examine an opponents' counterclaim carefully in order to refute it or, if you agree with the counterclaim, to argue that your claim is more important to making a decision. For example, the following counterclaim might be offered against your claim about the quality of Northfield College education:

COUNTERCLAIM   The Northfield faculty are good scholars and teachers; therefore, their race is irrelevant.

You might agree that "Northfield faculty *are* good scholars and teachers" but still argue that the education is not as good as it would be with more diversity. In other words, the best arguments provide not only good reasons for accepting a position, but also good reasons for doubting the opposition. They are made by writers who know both sides of an issue and are prepared for the arguments of the opposition.

3 Thesis

The primary claim made in an argument is called a **thesis**, the major claim your paper makes:

THESIS   Northfield College should enact a policy to make the faculty more culturally diverse by the year 2000.

In taking a position, you may make other claims as well, but they should all work to support this major claim or thesis:

CLAIM   The faculty is not culturally diverse.

CLAIM   A culturally diverse faculty is necessary to provide a good education for today's student.

CLAIM   The goal of increased cultural diversity by the year 2000 is achievable and practical

In arguing a position, you may state your thesis up front, with the remainder of the paper supporting it (**thesis first**), or you may state it later in the paper after weighing the pros and cons with your reader (**delayed thesis**). As a writer, you can decide which approach is the stronger rhetorical strategy after you fully examine each claim and the supporting evidence. Each strategy, thesis first or delayed, has its advantages and disadvantages (see 11f).

4 Evidence

Evidence makes a claim believable. Evidence consists of facts, examples, or testimony that supports a claim. For example, to support a claim that Northfield College's faculty lacks cultural diversity, you might introduce the following evidence:

EVIDENCE   According to the names in the college catalog, 69 of 79 faculty members are male.

EVIDENCE   According to a recent faculty survey, 75 of 79 faculty members are Caucasian or white.

EVIDENCE   According to Carmen Lopez, an unsuccessful candidate for a position in the English Department, 100 percent of the faculty hired in the last ten years have been white males.

Most arguments become more effective when they include documentable source material; however, shorter and more modest argument papers can be written without research and can profitably follow a process similar to that described here.

■ WRITING 1: EXPLORATION

An issue debated by college faculty is whether or not a first-year writing course should be required of all college students. Make three claims and three counterclaims about this issue. Then select the claim you most believe in and write an argumentative thesis that could form the basis for a whole essay. **ESL:** Consider similarities and differences in how arguments are developed in English and in your native language. Do arguments in your native language use claims and counterclaims?

11 b Finding an issue

You'll write better and have a more interesting time if you select an issue that interests you and about which you still have real questions. A good issue around which to write a position paper will meet the following criteria:

1   It is a real issue, about which there is controversy and uncertainty.

2   It has at least two distinct and arguable positions.

3   Resources are available to support both sides.

4   It is manageable within the time and scope of the assignment.

In selecting an issue to research and write about, consider both national and local issues. You are likely to see national issues explained and argued in the media:

Are SATs a fair measure of academic potential?

Should handgun ownership be outlawed in the United States?

Does acid rain kill forests?

The advantages of national issues include their extensive coverage by television and radio, national newspapers such as the *New York Times* and *Washington Post*, and national news magazines. In addition, you can count on your audience's having some familiarity with the subject. The disadvantage is that it may be difficult to find local experts or a site where some dimension of the issue can be witnessed.

Local issues derive from the community in which you live. You will find these issues argued about in local newspapers and on local news broadcasts:

Should a new mall be built on the beltway?

Should mountain bikes be allowed in Riverside Park?

Should Northfield College require a one-semester course introducing students to diverse American cultures?

The advantage of local issues is that you can often visit a place where the controversy occurs, interview people who are affected by it, and find generous coverage in local news media. The disadvantage is that the subject won't be covered in the national news.

Perhaps the best issue is a national issue (hikers versus mountain bikers) with a strong local dimension (this controversy in a local park). Such an issue will enable you to find both national press coverage and local experts (see 11g).

■ WRITING 2: APPLICATION

Make a list of three national and three local issues about which you are concerned. Next, select the three issues that seem most important to you and write each as a question with a yes or no answer. Finally, note whether each issue meets the criteria for a good position paper topic.

II **c** **Analyzing an issue**

The most demanding work in writing a position paper takes place *after* you have selected an issue, but *before* you actually write the paper. To analyze an issue, you need to conduct enough research to explain it and identify the arguments of each side.

In this data collecting stage, treat each side fairly, framing the opposition as positively as you frame the position. Research as if you are in an honest debate with yourself—doing so may even cause you to switch sides—one of the best indications of open-minded research. Furthermore, empathy for the opposition leads to making qualified assertions and heads off overly simplistic right versus wrong arguments. Undecided readers who see merit in the opposing side respect writers who acknowledge an issue's complexity.

1 **Context**

Provide full context for the issue you are writing about, as if readers know virtually nothing about it. Providing context means answering these questions: What is this issue about? Where did the controversy begin? How long has it been debated? Who are the people involved? What is at stake? Use a neutral tone, as Issa does in discussing the mountain bike trail controversy:

> With all these new riders, there is a need for places to ride, and this is where the wilderness trail controversy begins. The mountain bike is designed to be ridden on dirt trails, logging roads, and fire trails in backwoods country. However, other trail users who have been around much longer than mountain bikers prefer to enjoy the woods at a slow, leisurely pace. They find the rapid and sometimes noisy two-wheel intruders unacceptable.

2 **Claims for (pro)**

List the claims supporting the pro side of the issue. Make each claim a distinctly strong and separate point, and make the best possible case for this position, identifying by name the most important people or organizations that hold this view. Issa makes the following claims for opening up wilderness trails to mountain bikes:

1 All people should have the right to explore the wilderness so long as they do not damage it.

2 Knobby mountain bike tires do no more damage to hiking trails than Vibram-soled hiking boots.

3 Most mountain bike riders are respectful of the wilderness and courteous to other trail users.

3 Claims against (con)

List the claims supporting the con side of the issue—the counterclaims. It is not important to have an equal number of reasons for and against, but you do want an approximate balance:

1 Mountain bike riders ride fast, are sometimes reckless, and pose a threat to slower moving hikers.

2 Mountain bike tires damage trails and cause erosion.

4 Annotated references

Make an alphabetical list on note cards or computer files of the references you consulted during research, briefly identifying each according to the kind of information it contains. The same article may present claims from both sides as well as provide context. Following are three of Issa's annotated references:

Buchanan, Rob. "Birth of the Gearhead Nation." *Rolling Stone* 9 July 1992: 80–85. Marin Co. CA movement advocates more trails open to mountain bike use. Includes history. (pro)

"Fearing for Desert, A City Restricts Mountain Bikes." *New York Times* 4 June 1995, A24. Controversy in Moab, Utah, over conservation damage by mountain bikes. (con)

Schwartz, David, M. "Over Hill, Over Dale on a Bicycle Built for . . . Goo." *Smithsonian* 25.3 (June 1992): 74–84. Discusses the hiker vs. biker issue, promotes peaceful co-existence, includes history. (pro/con)

Note: Annotating your list of references allows you to check and rearrange your claims at any time during the writing process. In addition, if you write and organize your references now, your reference page will be ready to go when you've finished writing your paper.

■ **WRITING 3: APPLICATION**

Select one of the issues you are interested in, establish the necessary context, and make pro and con lists similar to those described in this section, including supporters of each position. Make the best possible case for each position.

II **d** **Taking a position**

Once you have spread out the two positions fairly, weigh which side is the stronger. Select the position that you find most convincing and then write out the reasons that support this position, most compelling reasons last. This will be the position you will most likely defend; you need state it as a thesis.

Start with a thesis

Formulate your initial position as a **working thesis** early in your paper-writing process. A working thesis asserts your major claim; it is merely something to start with, not necessarily to stick with. Even though it's tentative, it serves to focus your initial efforts in one direction and it helps you articulate claims and assemble evidence to support it:

WORKING THESIS   Hikers and mountain bikers should cooperate and support each other in using, preserving, and maintaining wilderness trails.

Writers often revise their initial positions as they reshape their paper or find new evidence. Your starting thesis should meet the following criteria:

1   It can be managed within your confines of time and space.

2   It asserts something specific.

3   It proposes a plan of action.

■ **WRITING 4: APPLICATION**

Take a position on the issue you have identified. Formulate a working thesis that you would like to support. Test your thesis against the criteria listed for good theses.   **WP TIP:** List the criteria below your working thesis. Then test your thesis against each criteria and type your responses below each one (creating space as needed with the return key).

 ARG

ESL **THESIS VERSUS CONTROLLING IDEA**

You may have heard the terms *controlling idea* and *thesis* used at different times to describe the main idea of an essay. All good writing needs a controlling idea to make it coherent and to create unity. In fact, as you probably know, each paragraph in an essay needs a controlling idea as well.

A thesis is actually a type of controlling idea which, as you learned in this chapter, makes an assertion. In other words, all theses are controlling ideas, but not all controlling ideas are theses. When you define a position, you need to make sure that the thesis is not just a fact but a statement that you will need to defend. Here are some examples of the difference between controlling ideas that are facts and controlling ideas that are theses:

FACT	THESIS (ASSERTION)
Our university has many general education requirements.	Our university has too many general education requirements.
Employment opportunities for women have increased during the past two decades.	Employment opportunities for women have not increased enough, especially at higher levels of management.

---

11 **e** **Developing an argument**

Your argument is the case you will make for your position, the means by which you will try to persuade your readers that your position is correct. Good arguments need solid and credible evidence and clear and logical reasoning.

WP TIP Sometimes it is easier to see what to write on paper than on screen. So, use hard copy to help you draft, making changes on the paper, which you can later transfer to the computer.

1 **Assembling evidence**

A claim is meaningless without evidence to support it. Facts, examples, inferences, informed opinion, and personal experience all provide believable evidence.

Facts and examples

Facts are verifiable and agreed upon by everyone involved regardless of personal beliefs or values. Facts are often statistical and recorded in some place where anybody can look them up.

Water boils at 212 degrees Fahrenheit.

Northfield College employed 79 full-time faculty and enrolled 1,143 full-time students in 1996.

Five hundred Japanese-made "Stumpjumper" mountain bikes were sold in the United States in 1981.

Examples can be used to illustrate a claim or clarify an issue. If you claim that many wilderness trails have been closed to mountain biking, you can mention examples you know about:

The New Jersey trails at South Mountain, Eagle Rock, and Mills Park have all been closed to mountain bikes.

Facts and examples can, of course, be misleading and even wrong. For hundreds of years malaria was believed to be caused by "bad air" rather than, as we know today, by a parasite transmitted through mosquito bites; however, for the people who believed the bad-air theory, it was fact.

Inferences

The accumulation of a certain number of facts and examples should lead to an interpretation of what those facts mean—an inference or a generalization. For example, if you attend five different classes at Northfield College and in each class you find no minority students, you may infer that there are no minority students on campus. However, while your inference is reasonable, it is not a fact, since your experience does not allow for your meeting all the possible students at the college.

Facts are not necessarily better or more important than inferences; they serve different purposes. Facts provide information, and inferences give that information meaning.

Sometimes inference is all that's available. For example, statistics describing what "Americans" believe or do are only inferences about these groups based on information collected from a relatively small number of individuals. To be credible, however, inferences must be reasonable and based on factual evidence.

ESL **INTRODUCING EVIDENCE**

When you write an argumentative essay based on sources (written or spoken), you will need to cite them. Here are some expressions often used in academic writing to introduce information from sources.

INTRODUCING EVIDENCE: EXPRESSIONS

According to Jane Smiley

As was discussed by Jane Smiley } children should not be required to do household chores.

As Jane Smiley states

I. Follow one of these introductory expressions with a complete sentence that gives the information. Do not add a verb or use *that* after the expression.

■ According to Jane Smiley, ~~states that~~ children have better things to
   ^
   do than perform household chores.

   Jane Smiley cannot be the subject of *states*; this noun is part of the introductory phrase.

■ According to Jane Smiley, ~~that~~ making children do chores does not

   teach them to love work or to feel pride.

   That introduces a dependent clause; you need an independent clause after the introductory phrase.

2. Do not repeat the meaning of the introductory expression:

■ According to "The Case Against Chores," ~~it states that~~ with modern

   conveniences, getting housework done is no longer very time-

   consuming.

   According to means *says* or *states*; *it states that* is unnecessarily repeating the idea in the introductory phrase.

PRESENTING EVIDENCE: REPORTING VERBS

A variety of reporting verbs can be used to present evidence for arguments. Some of these verbs are objective; they do not indicate the writer's point of view about the source material. Other verbs are less objective; they reflect the writer's attitude.

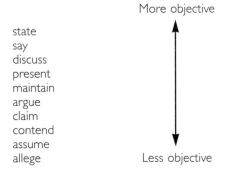

More objective

state
say
discuss
present
maintain
argue
claim
contend
assume
allege

Less objective

■ Jane Smiley says that children do not develop character by doing chores.

Says does not express the writer's attitude about this information.

■ Jane Smiley assumes that parents have the time to do all the housework themselves.

Assumes suggests that the writer may not agree with Jane Smiley's opinion.

Check your dictionary for the meaning of reporting verbs that are unfamiliar. Consider whether you want to report your information objectively or to express an evaluation of it.

When you use reporting verbs, note that some can be followed by a *that* clause and some need to be followed by a noun phrase or noun clause.

VERB + *THAT* + CLAUSE	**VERB + NOUN PHRASE/CLAUSE**
say	discuss
state	describe
explain	present
argue	summarize
maintain	tell
contend	
conclude	

■ Jane Smiley discusses ~~that~~ the reasons why she and her husband disagree about the value of assigning chores to children.

Expert opinion

Expert opinion makes powerful evidence. When a forest ranger testifies about trail damage caused by mountain bikes or lug-soled hiking boots, his training and experience make him an expert. A casual hiker making the same observation is less believable. To use expert opinion in writing arguments, be sure to cite the credentials or training that makes this person's testimony "expert."

Personal testimony

A useful kind of evidence is testimony based on personal experience. When someone has experienced something firsthand, his or her knowledge cannot easily be discounted. If you have been present at the mistreatment of a minority student, your eyewitness testimony will carry weight, even though you are not a certified expert of any kind. To use personal testimony effectively, provide details that confirm for readers that you were there and know what you are talking about.

2 Reasoning effectively

To build an effective argument, consider the audience you must persuade. In writing about the mountain bike controversy, for example, ask yourself these questions:

■ Who will read this paper?

Members of an environmentally conscious hiking club, members of a mountain bike club, or your instructor?

■ Where do I think they stand on the issue?

Hikers are often opposed to mountain bikes, mountain bikers are not, but you would need more information to predict your instructor's position.

■ How are their personal interests involved?

Hikers want the trails quiet and peaceful, bikers want to ride in the wilderness, and your instructor may or may not care.

■ What evidence would they consider convincing?

A hiker would need to see convincing examples of trails being improved by mountain bike use, bikers would accept anecdotal testimony of good intentions, and you're still not sure about your instructor.

The more you know about the audience you're trying to sway, the easier it will be to present your case. If your audience is your instructor, you'll need to make inferences about his or her beliefs based on syllabus language, class discussion, assigned readings, or personal habits. For example, if your instructor rides a mountain bike to work, you may begin to infer one thing; if he or she assigns Sierra Club readings in the course, you infer something else; and if the instructor rides a mountain bike *and* reads Sierra Club, well you've got more homework ahead. Remember that inferences based on a single piece of evidence are often wrong; find out more before you make simple assumptions about your audience. And sometimes audience analysis doesn't work very well when an instructor assumes a deliberately skeptical role in reading a set of papers. It's best to assume you will have a critical reader and to use the best logic and evidence available. Following are some ways to marshall careful and substantial evidence.

First, establish your credibility. Demonstrate to your audience that you are fair and can be trusted. Do this by writing in neutral, not obviously biased language—avoid name calling. Also do this by citing current sources by respected experts—and don't quote them out of context. Do this also by identifying elements that serve as common ground between you and the audience—be up front and admit when the opposite side makes a good point.

CREDIBLE   Northfield College offers excellent instruction in many areas; however, its offerings in multicultural education would be enhanced by a more diverse faculty.

LESS
CREDIBLE   Education at Northfield College sucks.

Second, use logic. Demonstrate that you understand the principles of reasoning that operate in the academic world: Make each claim clearly, carefully, and in neutral language. Make sure you have substantial, credible evidence to support each claim. Make inferences from your evidence with care; don't exaggerate or argue positions that are not supported by the evidence.

LOGICAL   Since 75 of 79 faculty members are white or Caucasian, and 69 of 79 are male, it would make good sense to seek to hire more black, Hispanic, and Native American women faculty when they are available.

ILLOGICAL   Since all Northfield faculty are racists, they should be sent to China.

Third, avoid false arguments. For more than two thousand years, since the time of the ancient Greeks and Romans, the principles of false logic have been recognized by careful debaters and audiences alike. Study these "logical fallacies" (see the box, "False Arguments"). Avoid using them in making your arguments, and also recognize when others try to use them on you. The illogical argument above contains three fallacies: It "begs the question" (it has not been established that the whole faculty is racist); it "does not follow" that racists should be sent to China; and it "oversimplifies" by proposing a simplistic solution to a complex problem.

Fourth, appeal to your audience's emotions. It's fair to use means of persuasion other than logic to win arguments. Write with vivid details, concrete language, and compelling examples to show your audience a situation that needs addressing. It is often helpful, as well, to adopt a personal tone and write in friendly language to reach readers' hearts as well as minds.

EMOTIONAL APPEAL   When Bridgett Jones, the only black student in
Philosophy 1, sits down, the desks on either side

 FALSE ARGUMENTS (FALLACIES)

The following false arguments are often made when a writer does not have enough evidence to support his or her claims. Learn to recognize faulty logic and avoid it.

1. Bandwagon. Encourages people to accept a position simply because others already have: *More than three-fourths of American colleges have required courses on cultural diversity; so should Northfield College.* (Is there convincing evidence that these courses are beneficial? Maybe these colleges made a mistake.)

2. Begging the question. Treats a questionable statement as if it had already been accepted: *If Northfield College is to maintain its reputation as the best liberal arts college in the state, it must hire more culturally diverse faculty members.* (Many people would question whether Northfield is the best liberal arts college in the state.)

3. Does not follow (non sequitur). Presents a conclusion that does not logically follow from its premises: *Bill Cosby is a great television comedian, so he will make an excellent college teacher.* (Simply because Cosby is good at one thing doesn't mean he will be good at another.)

4. False analogy. Uses analogy to show that two things are alike when they are—for the purpose of the argument—different: *Just as* of her remain empty. When her classmates choose partners for debate, Bridget is always the last one chosen.

■ **WRITING 5: APPLICATION**

Develop an informal profile of the audience for your position paper by answering the questions posed in this section. Make a list of the kinds of evidence most likely to persuade this audience.

II f Organizing a position paper

To organize your paper, you need to know your position on the issue: What is the main point of your argument? In other words, move from a *working thesis* to a *final thesis*: Confirm the working thesis that's been guiding your research so far, or modify it, or scrap it altogether and assert a different one. You should be able to articulate this thesis in a single sentence as the answer to the yes/no question you've been investigating. (See page 138.)

polar bears don't hang around with black panthers, so white students shouldn't be part of a community that includes black students. (Animals and humans are not necessarily alike; some communities may thrive with racial mixtures.)

5. False cause (post hoc). Assumes that if one event happened after another, the earlier event must have caused the later one: *Average SAT scores of entering students at mostly white Northfield College are twenty points lower than at integrated Southfield College, so integration is better.* (There are many possible reasons, including different programs and tuition costs, for the difference in SAT scores.)

6. False dilemma (either/or dilemma). Presents a situation as a dilemma with only two options, when there are actually more: *If we fail to hire ten minority faculty by the year 2000, Northfield College will go out of business.* (Going out of business is only one of many possible consequences of not changing the hiring practices.)

7. Oversimplification. Reduces a complex system of causes and effects to an inaccurate generalization: *The teaching of traditional American values will be eroded if the Northfield faculty becomes more culturally diverse.* (Some American values, such as equality and tolerance for difference, may be strengthened by the hiring of a more diverse faculty.)

THESIS Wilderness trails should be open to both mountain bikers and hikers.

THESIS Wilderness trails should be closed to mountain bikes.

Your next decision is where in this paper should you reveal your thesis to the reader—openly up front or strategically delayed until later?

ESL **QUALIFYING GENERALIZATIONS**

When you make general claims, you should be careful to qualify your statements so that the generalizations are accurate. Claims that are too broad may cause your readers to doubt the strength of your argument. Here are some ways to qualify your general claims:

1. Use a frequency adverb such as *often, usually* or *frequently* to qualify the verb if something is not always true.

- Due to the recent budget cuts, students $\overset{\text{often}}{\wedge}$cannot enroll in the courses they need to graduate.

2. Add a quantifier like *many, most,* or *a majority of* to qualify the subject.

- Because of the recent budget cuts, $\overset{\text{many}}{\wedge}$students cannot enroll in the courses they need to graduate.

3. Use a modal verb such as *may* or *might* if you are not certain of a claim about the future.

- Raising tuition $\overset{\text{may}}{\cancel{\text{will}}}$ deprive some students of a college education.

For more information about modals, see 66c1 (Auxiliary verbs).

4. Add a phrase that expresses probability (*it is possible/probable/ likely that . . .*) before the general claim.

It is very likely that raising tuition will prevent some students from getting a college education.

11 Thesis-first organization

When you lead with a thesis, you tell readers from the beginning where you stand on the issue. The remainder of the essay supports your claim and defends it against counterclaims. Following is one good way to organize a thesis-first argument.

1 **Introduce and explain the issue.** Make sure there are at least two debatable sides. Pose the question that you see arising from this issue; if you can frame it as a yes/no, for/against construction, both you and your reader will have the advantage throughout your answer of knowing where you stand.

> Minority students, supported by many majority students at Northfield College, have staged a week-long sit-in to urge the hiring of more minority faculty across the curriculum. Is this a reasonable position? Should Northfield hire more minority faculty members?

2 **Assert your thesis.** Your thesis states the answer to the question you have posed and establishes the position from which you will argue. Think of your thesis as the major claim the paper will make.

> Northfield College should enact a policy to make the faculty more culturally diverse as soon as is reasonably possible.

Writers commonly state their thesis early in the paper, at the conclusion of the paragraph that introduces the issue.

3 **Summarize the counterclaims.** Explain the opposition's "counterclaims" before elaborating upon your own claims, because doing that gives your own argument something to focus on—and refute—throughout the rest of the paper. Squeezing the counterclaims between the thesis (2) and the evidence (5) reserves the strongest places—the opening and closing—for your position.

COUNTERCLAIM 1   Northfield College is located in a white middle-class community, so its faculty should be white middle class also.

COUNTERCLAIM 2   The Northfield faculty are good scholars and teachers; therefore, their race is irrelevant.

4   **Refute the counterclaims.** Look for weak spots in the opposition's argument, and point them out. Use your opponent's language to show you have read closely but still find problems with the claim. To refute counterclaim 1:

> If the community in which the college is located is "white middle class," all the more reason to offer that diversity in the college.

Your reputation is often stronger when you acknowledge the truth of some of the opposition's claims (demonstrating your fairness) but point out the limitations as well. To refute counterclaim 2:

> It's true that Northfield College offers excellent instruction in many areas; however, its instruction in multicultural education would be enhanced by a more diverse faculty.

5   **Support your claims with evidence.** Spell out your own claims clearly and precisely, enumerating them or being sure to give each its own full paragraph explanation, and citing supporting evidence. This section will constitute the longest and most carefully documented part of your essay. The following evidence supports the thesis that Northfield needs more cultural diversity.

> According to the names in the college catalog, 69 of 79 faculty members are male.

> According to a recent faculty survey, 75 of 79 faculty members are Caucasian or white.

> According to Carmen Lopez, an unsuccessful job candidate for a position in the English Department, all faculty hired in the last ten years have been white males.

6   **Restate your position as a conclusion.** Near the end of your paper, synthesize your accumulated evidence into a broad general position, and restate your original thesis in slightly different language.

> While Northfield College offers a strong liberal arts education, the addition of more culturally diverse faculty members will make it even stronger.

There are several advantages to leading with a thesis. First, your audience knows where you stand from the first paragraph. Second, your thesis occupies both the first and last position in the essay. In addition, this is the most common form of academic argument.

2 Delayed-thesis organization

Using the delayed-thesis type of organization, you introduce the issue, discuss the arguments for and against, but do not obviously take a side until late in the essay. Near the end of the paper, you explain that after listening carefully to both pros and cons, you have now arrived at the most reasonable position. Concluding with your own position gives it more emphasis. The following delayed-thesis argument is derived from the sample student essay at the end of this chapter.

1 **Introduce the issue and pose a question.** Both thesis-first and delayed-thesis papers begin by establishing context and posing a question. Following is the question for the mountain bike position paper:

> Should mountain bikes be allowed on wilderness trails?

2 **Summarize the claims for one position.** Before stating which side you support, explain how the opposition views the issue:

> To traditional trail users, the new breed of bicycle [is] alien and dangerous, esthetically offensive and physically menacing.

3 **Refute these claims.** Still not stating your own position, point out your difficulties with believing this side:

> Whether a bicycle—or a car or horse for that matter—is "alien . . . and esthetically offensive" depends on your personal taste, judgment, and familiarity. And whether it is "dangerous" depends on how you use it.

In addition, you can actually strengthen your position by admitting that in some cases the counterclaims might be true.

> While it's true that some mountain bikers—like some hikers—are too loud, mountain biking at its best respects the environment and promotes peace and conservation, not noise and destruction.

4 **Summarize the counterclaims.** You are supporting these claims and so they should occupy the most emphatic position in your essay, last:

> Most mountain bikers respect the wilderness and should be allowed to use wilderness trails.

5 **Support your counterclaims.** Now give your best evidence; this should be the longest and most carefully documented part of the paper:

Studies show that bicycle tires cause no more erosion or trail damage than the boots of hikers, and far less than horses' hooves.

6   **State your thesis as your conclusion.** Your rhetorical stance or strategy is this: You have listened carefully to both the claims and counterclaims, and after giving each side a fair hearing, you have arrived at the most reasonable conclusion.

It's clear that mountain bikers don't want to destroy trails any more than hikers do. The surest way to preserve America's wilderness areas is to establish strong cooperative bonds among the hikers and bikers, as well as those who fish, hunt, camp, canoe, and bird-watch, and encourage all to maintain the trails and respect the environment.

There are many advantages also to delayed-thesis argument. First, the audience is drawn into your struggle by being asked to weigh the evidence and arrive at a thesis. Second, the audience is kept in suspense about your position; their curiosity is aroused. Finally, the audience understands your difficulty in making a decision.

WP TIP   Type thesis-first steps 1–6 into a new file. Under each step, fill in the appropriate information for your paper. Then repeat the process, this time reorganizing the material to reflect the delayed-thesis steps 1–6. View each organizational pattern and choose the one that better suits your goals for the paper.

■ WRITING 6: APPLICATION

Make two outlines for organizing your position paper, one with the thesis first, the other with a delayed thesis. Share your outlines with your classmates and discuss which seems more appropriate for the issue you have chosen.

11 g   Shaping the whole paper

In the following paper, Issa explores whether or not mountain bikers should be allowed to share wilderness trails with hikers. In the first part of the paper he establishes the context and background of the conflict; then he introduces the question his paper will address: "Is any resolution in sight?" Note his substantial use of sources, including the Internet and interviews, cited in the MLA documentation style. Issa selects a delayed-thesis strategy, which allows him to air both sides of the argument fully before revealing his solution, a compromise position: So long as mountain bikers follow environmentally sound guidelines, they should be allowed to use the trails.

On the Trail: Can the Hikers Share with the Bikers?

By Issa Sawabini

The narrow, hard-packed dirt trail winding up the mountain under the spreading oaks and maples doesn't look like the source of a major environmental conflict, but it is. On the one side are hikers, environmentalists, and horseback riders who have traditionally used these wilderness trails. On the other side, looking back, are the mountain bike riders sitting atop their modern steeds who want to use them too. But the hikers don't want the bikers, so trouble is brewing.

The debate over mountain bike use has gained momentum recently because of the increased popularity of this form of bicycling. Technology has made it easier for everyone to ride these go-anywhere bikes. These high-tech wonders incorporate exotic components including quick gear-shifting derailleurs, good brakes, and a more comfortable upright seating position—and they can cost up to $2000 each (Kelly 104). Mountain bikes have turned what were once grueling hill climbs into casual trips, and more people are taking notice.

Mountain bikes have taken over the bicycle industry, and with more bikes come more people wanting to ride in the mountains. The first mass-produced mountain bikes date to 1981, when five-hundred Japanese "Stumpjumpers" were sold; by 1983 annual sales reached 200,000; today the figure is 8.5 million. In fact, mountain biking is second only to in-line skating as the fastest growing sport in the nation: "For a sport to go from zero to warp speed so quickly is unprecedented," says Brian Stickel, director of competition for the National Off Road Bicycle Association (Schwartz 75).

With all these new riders, there is a need for places to ride, and this is where the wilderness trail controversy begins. The mountain bike is designed to be ridden on dirt trails, logging roads, and fire trails in backwoods country. However, other trail users who have been around much longer than mountain bikers prefer to enjoy the woods at a slow, leisurely pace. They find the rapid and sometimes noisy two-wheel intruders unacceptable: "To traditional trail users, the new breed of bicycle [is] alien and dangerous, esthetically offensive and physically menacing" (Schwartz 74).

"The problem arises when people want to use an area of public land for their own personal purpose," says Carl Newton, forestry professor at the University of Vermont. "Eventually, after everyone has taken their small bit of the area, the results can be devastating. People believe that because they pay taxes for the land, they can use it as they please. This makes sense to the individual, but not to the whole community." Newton is both a hiker and a mountain biker.

When mountain bikes first came on the scene, hikers and environmentalists convinced state and local officials to ban the bikes from wilderness trails (Buchanan 81; Kelly 104). The result was the closing of many trails to mountain bike use: "Many state park systems have banned bicycles from narrow trails. National Parks prohibit them, in most cases, from leaving the pavement" (Schwartz 81). These trail closings have separated the outdoor community into the hikers and the bikers. Each group is well organized, and each group believes it is right. Is any resolution in sight?

The hikers and other passive trail users have a number of organizations, from conservation groups to public park planning committees, who argue against allowing mountain bikes onto narrow trails traditionally traveled only by foot and horse in the past. They believe that the wide, deeply treaded tires of the mountain bikes cause erosion and that the high speeds of the bikers startle and upset both hikers and horses (Hanley B4; Schwartz 76).

The arrival of mountain bikes during the 1980's was resisted by established hiker groups, such as the Sierra Club, which won debate after debate in favor of closing wilderness trails to mountain bike activities. The younger and less well organized biking groups proposed compromise, offering to help repair and maintain trails in return for riding rights, but their offers were ignored. "Peace was not given a chance. Foes of the bicycle onslaught, older and better connected, won most of the battles, and signs picturing a bicycle crossed with a red slash began to appear on trail heads all over the country" (Schwartz 74).

In Milburn, New Jersey, trails at South Mountain, Eagle Rock, and Mills Park have all been closed. Anyone caught riding a bike on the trails can be arrested and fined up to $100. Local riders offered an amendment calling for trails to be open Thursday through Sunday, with the riders helping maintain the trails on the other days. The amendment was rejected. According to hiker Donald Meserlain, the bikes "ruin the tranquillity of the woodlands and drive out hikers, bird watchers, and strollers. It's like weeds taking over the grass. Pretty soon we'll have all weeds" (Hanley).

Many areas in western New York, such as Hunter's Creek, have also been closed to mountain bike use. Anti-biking signs posted on trails frequently used by bicyclists caused a loud public debate as bike riding was again blamed for trail erosion.

Until more public lands are opened to trail riding, mountain bikers must pay fees to ride on private land, a situation beneficial to ski resorts in the off season: "Ski areas are happy to open trails to cyclists for a little summer and fall income" (Sneyd). For example, in Vermont, bike trails can be found at the Catamount Family Center in Williston, Vermont, as well as at Mount Snow, Killington, Stratton, and Bolton Valley. At major resorts, such as Mount Snow and Killington, ski lifts have actually been modified to the top of the mountains and each offers a full-service bike shop at its base.

However, the real solution to the conflict between hikers and bikers is education, not separation. In response to the bad publicity and many trail closings, mountain bikers have banded together at local and national levels to educate both their own member bike riders and the non-riding public about the potential alliance between these two groups (Buchanan 81).

The largest group, the International Mountain Bike Association (IMBA), sponsors supervised rides and trail conservation classes and stresses that mountain bikers are friends, not enemies of the natural environment. "The IMBA wants to change the attitude of both the young gonzo rider bombing downhill on knobby tires, and the mature outdoors-

man bristling at the thought of tire tracks where boot soles alone did tread" (Schwartz 76). IMBA published guidelines it hopes all mountain bikers will learn to follow:

1. Ride on open trails only.
2. Leave no trace.
3. Control your bicycle.
4. Always yield trail.
5. Never spook animals.
6. Plan ahead. (JTYL)

The New England Mountain Bike Association (NEMBA), one of the largest east coast organizations, publishes a home page on the Internet outlining goals: "NEMBA is a not-for-profit organization dedicated to promoting land access, maintaining trails that are open to mountain bicyclists, and educating riders to use those trails sensitively and responsibly. We are also devoted to having fun" (Koellner).

At the local level, the Western New York Mountain Bike Association (WNYMBA) educates members on proper trail maintenance and urges its members to cooperate with local environmentalists whenever possible. For instance, when angry cyclists continued to use the closed trail at Hunter's Creek, New York, WNYMBA used the Internet to warn cyclists against continued trail use: "As WNYMBA wishes to cooperate with Erie County Parks Department to the greatest extent possible on the use of trails in open parks, WNYMBA cannot recommend ignoring posted signs. The first IMBA rule of trail is 'ride on open trails only'" (JTYL).

Educated mountain biking, like hiking and horseback riding, respects the environment and promotes peace and conservation, not noise and destruction. Making this case has begun to pay off, and the battle over who walks and who rides the trails should now shift in favor of peaceful coexistence. "Buoyed by studies showing that bicycle tires cause no more erosion or trail damage than the boots of hikers, and far less than horses' hooves, mountain bike advocates are starting to find receptive ears among environmental organizations" (Schwartz 78).

Even in the Milburn, New Jersey, area, bikers have begun to win some battles, as new trails have recently been funded specifically for mountain bike use: "After all," according to an unnamed legislator, "the bikers or their parents are taxpayers" (Hanley).

The Wilderness Club now officially supports limited use of mountain bikes, while the Sierra Club also supports careful use of trails by riders so long as no damage to the land results and riders ride responsibly on the path. "In pursuit of happy trails, bicycling organizations around the country are bending backward over their chain stays to dispel the hell-on-wheels view of them" (Schwartz 83).

Education and compromise are the sensible solutions to the hiker/biker standoff. Increased public awareness as well as increasingly responsible riding will open still more wilderness trails to bikers in the future. It's clear that mountain bikers don't want to destroy trails any more than hikers do. The surest way to preserve America's wilderness areas is to establish strong cooperative bonds among the hikers and bikers, as well as those who fish, hunt, camp, canoe, and bird-watch, and to encourage all to maintain the trails and respect the environment.

Works Cited

Buchanan, Rob. "Birth of the Gearhead Nation." Rolling Stone 9 July 1992: 80–85.

"Fearing for Desert, A City Restricts Mountain Bikes." New York Times 4 June 1995: A24.

Hanley, Robert. "Essex County Mountain Bike Troubles." New York Times 30 May 1995: B4.

JTYL (editor). Western New York Mountain Bike Association Home Page. Online. Western New York Mountain Bike Association. Available http://128.205.166.43/public/wnymba/wnymba.html.

Kelly, Charles. "Evolution of an Issue." Bicycling 31 (May 1990): 104–105.

Koellner, Ken (editor). New England Mountain Bike Association Home Page. 19 August 1995 (last update). Online. New England Mountain Bike Association. Available http://www.ultranet.com/~kvk/nemba.html.

 ARG

Newton, Carlton. Personal interview. 13 Nov. 1995.

Rau, Jordan. "Outrage at Local Officials' Desire to Restrict Mt. Biking."
Rutland Daily Herald 2 Aug. 1993: A5.

Schwartz, David, M. "Over Hill, Over Dale on a Bicycle Built for . . . Goo."
Smithsonian 25.3 (June 1992): 74–84.

Sneyd, Ross. "Mount Snow Teaching Mountain Biking." Burlington Free
Press 4 Oct. 1992: E1.

SUGGESTIONS FOR WRITING AND RESEARCH

INDIVIDUAL

1. Write a position paper on the issue you have been working with in Writings 2–6. Follow the guidelines suggested in this chapter, using as much research as you deem appropriate.

2. Write a position paper on an issue of interest to your class. Consider topics such as (1) student voice in writing topics, (2) the seating plan, (3) the value of writing groups versus instructor conferences, or (4) the number of writing assignments.

COLLABORATIVE

1. In teams of two or three, select an issue; divide up the work so that each group member contributes some work to (1) the context, (2) the pro argument, and (3) the con argument (to guarantee that you do not take sides prematurely). Share your analysis of the issue with another group and receive feedback. Finally, write your position papers individually.

2. Follow the procedure for the first collaborative assignment, but write your final position paper collaboratively.

To interpret a text is to explain what it means. To interpret a text also implies that the text can be read in more than one way—your interpretation is your reading, others may read it differently. The word *text* implies words, writing, books; however, virtually all works created by human beings can be considered as texts open to interpretation—films, music and dance performances, exhibits, paintings, photographs, sculptures, advertisements, artifacts, buildings, and even whole cultures. Perhaps the most popular forms of interpretive writing are published reviews of movies, music, books, and the like.

In college, the most common form of interpretive essay assignment is to write analytical essays about reading assignments in humanities and social science courses. Since words can mean more than one thing, texts composed of written words have multiple meanings—they can mean different things depending on who is reading them, and there is no one right answer.

To find out what a poem, essay, play, or story means, you need to hear it, look at its language, examine how it is put together, compare it with similar things, notice how it affects you, and keep asking why.

12 **a** **Writing interpretive essays**

The best texts to select for an interpretive assignment are those that are most problematic—texts whose meaning seems to you somewhat slippery and elusive—since these give you, the interpreter, the most room to argue one meaning against another. Your job is to make the best possible case that your interpretation is reasonable and deserves attention.

A typical assignment may be to interpret a poem, story, essay, or historical document—a complex task that draws upon all of your reasoning and writing skills: You may have to *describe* people and situations, *retell* events, and *define* key terms, *ana-*

lyze passages and *explain* how they work, perhaps by *comparing* or *contrasting* the text with others. Finally you will *argue* for one meaning rather than another—in other words, develop a *thesis*, and defend this thesis with sound *reasoning* and convincing *evidence.*

This chapter explores numerous ways of developing textual interpretations, using for illustrative purposes, Gwendolyn Brooks' poem "We Real Cool." Brooks' poem is especially useful because it is short, quickly read, yet full of potential meanings. Our questions about this text, as well as the strategies for finding answers, are virtually the same we would use with any text—fiction, nonfiction, or poetry.

Read, now, the following poem by Gwendolyn Brooks, and follow along as we examine different ways of determining what it means.

We Real Cool

> THE POOL PLAYERS.
> SEVEN AT THE GOLDEN SHOVEL.

> We real cool. We
> Left school. We
>
> Lurk late. We
> Strike straight. We
>
> Sing sin. We
> Thin gin. We
>
> Jazz June. We
> Die soon.

WRITING I: EXPLORATION

After reading "We Real Cool," freewrite for ten minutes to capture your initial reaction. Ask yourself questions such as: What did it remind me of? Did I like it? Do I think I understand it? What emotions did I feel?

12 b Exploring a text

A good topic for an interpretive essay addresses a question that has several possible answers. If you think the text is overly simple, you will have no real need to interpret it. In addition, choose a topic that interests or intrigues you; if it doesn't, chances are it won't interest or intrigue your readers either.

No matter what text you are interpreting, however, you need to figure out what it means to you before you can explain it well to someone else. Plan to read it more than once, first to understand what it's like, where it goes, what happens literally. As you read, mark passages that interest or puzzle you. Read the text a second time, more slowly, making marginal notes or journal entries about the interesting, questionable, or problematic passages. As you do this, look for answers and solutions to your previous concerns, rereading as many times as necessary to further your understanding.

In selecting a text to interpret, ask yourself these questions:

■ Can this text be read in more than one way?

■ What are some of the different ways of reading it?

■ With which reading do I most agree?

■ Where are the passages in the text that support this reading?

■ Who does my interpretation need to convince? (Who is my audience?)

WP TIP Open a new computer file and list the questions shown above on separate lines in boldface type with extra space between them. Save this as a template that you can use over and over when interpreting texts. Below each question, supply written responses in relation to the text you are currently analyzing.

WRITING 2: APPLICATION

Select a text that you are interested in interpreting, and write out the answers to the questions above. Do not at this time worry about developing any of these answers thoroughly.

12 c Joining an interpretive community

How you read and interpret a text depends upon who you are. Who you are depends upon the influences that have shaped you— the communities to which you belong. All of us belong to many communities: families, social and economic groups (students or teachers, middle or working class), organizations (Brownies, Boy

Scouts, Democrats, Masons), geographic locales (rural or urban, North or South), and institutions (school, church, fraternity). Your membership in one or more communities determines how you see and respond to the world.

The communities that influence you most strongly are called **interpretive communities**; they influence the meaning you make of the world. People who belong to the same community that you do are likely to have similar assumptions and therefore likely to interpret things as you would. If you live in an urban black community, jazz and rap music may be a natural and constant presence in your life; if you live in a rural white community, country and western music may be the norm; at the same time, as a member of either group you might also belong to a larger community that surrounds itself with classical music. All this means is that people who belong to different communities are likely to have different—not better or worse—perspectives from yours.

Before writing an interpretive essay, it is helpful to ask, "Who am I when writing this piece?" You ask this to examine the biases you bring to your work, for each of us sees the world—and consequently texts—from our own particular vantage point. Be aware of your age, gender, race, ethnic identity, economic class, geographic location, educational level, political or religious persuasion. Ask to what extent any of these identities emerges in your writing.

College is, of course, a large interpretive community. Various smaller communities exist within it called disciplines—English, history, business, art, and so on. Within any discipline there are established ways of interpreting texts. Often when you write an interpretive essay, you will do so from the perspective of a traditional academic interpretive community. Take care to follow the conventions of that community, whether you are asked to write a **personal interpretation** or an **analytical interpretation**.

Whether or not you deliberately identify yourself and your biases in your essay depends upon the assignment you are given. Some assignments ask you to remove your personal perspective as much as possible from your writing, others ask that you acknowledge and explain it, while others fall somewhere in between.

1 Personal interpretation

In writing from a personal or subjective perspective, the interpreter and his or her beliefs and experiences are part of the story and need to be both expressed and examined. In examining "We Real Cool," for instance, you may bring your background into your writing to help your reader understand why you view the poem as you do. You may compare or contrast your situation to that of the author or characters in the text. Or you might draw upon particular experiences that cause you to see the poem in a particular way. For example, Mitzi's response to the poem (reprinted at the end of this chapter) begins with memories inspired by the poem.

> "We Real Cool" is a sad poem. It reminds me of the gang in high school who used to skip classes and come back smelling of cigarette smoke and cheap liquor—not that I knew it was cheap back then.

It is increasingly common for good interpretive essays to include both analytical and personal discussions, allowing you to demonstrate your skill at closely reading texts while acknowledging your awareness of the subjective nature of virtually all interpretive acts. To move in a more analytic direction, Mitzi would need to quote and discuss more lines directly from the poem, as she does later in her essay.

> These "cool" dropouts paid for their rebellion in drug overdoses, jail terms, police shootouts, and short lives. They "Die soon," so we never know where else their adventurous spirits might have taken them.

2 Analytical interpretation

In analyzing a text, writers often focus on the content and deliberately leave themselves, the interpreters, in the background, minimizing personal presence and bias. If you are asked to write this way—to avoid first-person pronouns or value judgments—do your best to focus on the text and avoid language that appears biased. In reality, of course, authors reveal their presence by the choices they make: what they include, what they exclude, what they emphasize, and so on. But when you are aware of your inescapable subjectivity, aware that your own situation affects the inferences and judgments you make about others, this awareness will help you keep your focus on the subject and off yourself.

In writing about "We Real Cool," for example, your first reaction may be more personal than analytical, focusing on your own emotions by calling it a *sad poem*, as Mitzi does, or by expressing value judgments about the poem's characters:

> I think these guys are stupid, cutting their lives short drinking, stealing, and fighting.

However, a more analytical response would be to drop the first person (*I think*) and the judgment (*these guys are stupid*) and to focus more closely on the text itself, perhaps quoting parts of it to show you are paying close attention.

> The speakers in the poem, "The Pool Players," cut their lives short by hanging out at "The Golden Shovel," fighting, drinking, stealing, and perhaps worse.

12 d   Developing an interpretation

There is no formula for arriving at or presenting an interpretation in essay form, but readers, especially English instructors, will expect you to address and explain various elements of the text that usually contribute substantially to what it means.

Convincing interpretive essays commonly, but not always, include the following information:

1   an overview of the text, identifying author, title, and genre and *briefly* summarizing the whole text;

2   a description of form and structure;

3   a description of the author's point of view;

4   a summary of the social, historical, or cultural context in which the work was written;

5   an assertion or **thesis** about what the text means—your main business as an interpreter.

Your **thesis** is a clear, concise statement that identifies your interpretation, on which the readers then expect you to elaborate. While some interpretive essays include all of the above information, more commonly, essays will emphasize some aspects while downplaying others.

1 Identify and summarize the text

All interpretive essays should begin by answering basic questions: What genre is this text—poem, play, story, or essay? What is its title? Who is the author? When was it published? In addition, all such essays should provide a brief summary of the text's story, idea, or information. Summarize briefly, logically, and objectively to provide a background for what else you plan to say about the text, as in this example.

> "We Real Cool," a poem by Gwendolyn Brooks, condenses the life story of pool-playing high-school dropouts to eight short lines and foreshadows an early death on the city streets.

2 Explain the form and organization

To examine the organizational structure of a text, ask: How is it put together? Why start here and end there? What connects it from start to finish? For example, by repeating words, ideas, and images, writers call attention to them and indicate that they are important to the meaning of the text. No matter what the text, some principle or plan holds it together and gives it structure. Texts that tell stories are often organized as a sequence of events in chronological order. Other texts may alternate between explanations and examples or between first-person and third-person narrative. You will have to decide which aspects of the text's form and organization are most important for your interpretation. The following example pays close attention to Brooks' overall poetic structure.

> The poem consists of a series of eight three-word sentences, each beginning with the word "We." The opening lines "We real cool. We/left school" explain the characters' situation. The closing lines "We/Jazz June. We/Die soon" suggest their lives will be over soon.

3 Describe the author's perspective

Authorial perspective is the point of view from which the text is presented. In an article, essay, textbook, or other work of nonfiction, you can expect the author to write about truth as he or she sees it—just as we are doing in this textbook, trying to explain writing according to our own beliefs about writing. However, in a work of poetry, fiction, or drama the author's point of view may be quite different from that of the character(s) who narrate or act in the story. If you can describe or explain the author's perspective in your interpretive essay, you provide readers with clues about the author's purpose. For example, Kelly's essay (reprinted at the end of this chapter) opens by making a distinction between Brooks, the poet, and her characters, "Seven at the Golden Shovel."

Gwendolyn Brooks writes "We Real Cool" from the point of view of members of a street gang who have dropped out of school to live their lives hanging around pool halls—in this case "The Golden Shovel." These guys are semi-literate and speak in slangy street lingo that reveals their need for mutual support in their mutually rebellious attitude toward life.

What he doesn't say, but clearly implies, is that Brooks herself is a mature and highly skilled user of formal English, and that in the poem she adopts the persona or mask of semi-literate teenagers in order to tell their story more effectively.

4 Place the work in context

What circumstances (historical, social, political, biographical) produced this text? How does this text compare or contrast with another by the same author or a similar work by a different author? No text exists in isolation. Each was created by a particular author in a particular place at a particular time. Describing this context provides readers with important background information and indicates which conditions you think were most influential. "We Real Cool" could be contextualized this way:

"We Real Cool" was published in 1963, a time when the Civil Rights Movement was strong and about the time that Afro Americans coined the phrase "Black Is Beautiful." The poem may have been written to remind people that just because they were black did not mean they necessarily led beautiful lives.

5 Explain the theme of the text

In fiction, poetry, and reflective essays, the main point usually takes the form of an implicit **theme**, which in academic writing you might call a **thesis**, either stated or unstated. A main reason for writing an interpretive essay is to point out the text's theme. Examine what you think is the theme in the text. Ask yourself: so what? What is this really about? What do I think the author meant by writing this? What problems, puzzles, or ideas seem interesting? Good topics arise from material in which the meaning is not obviously stated.

When you write an interpretation from an objective or analytical perspective, you make the best case possible that, according to the evidence in the text itself, this is what the text means. In analytical writing, you generally state your thesis (about the text's theme) early in the essay, as Kelly does here about "We Real Cool" at the end of his first paragraph.

> The speakers in the poem, "We," celebrate what adults would call adolescent hedonism—but they make a conscious choice for a short intense life over a long, safe, and dull existence.

When you write from a subjective or personal perspective, you make it clear that your interpretation is based on your own emotional reactions and memories as much as on the content of the text, and that other readers will necessarily read it differently. The controlling idea or theme of Mitzi's subjective interpretation of "We Real Cool" is revealed in her first sentence, which the rest of the essay supports.

> "We Real Cool" . . . reminds me of the gang in high school who used to skip classes and come back smelling of cigarette smoke and cheap liquor—not that I knew it was cheap back then.

6 Support your interpretation

Analytical interpretations are usually built around evidence from the text itself: Summarize larger ideas in your own language to conserve space; paraphrase more specific ideas also in your own words; and quote directly to feature especially colorful or precise language. If you include outside information for supportive, comparative, or contrastive reasons, document carefully where it came from. Most of the preceding examples referred to specific lines in the poem, as does this passage from Kelly's essay.

> Instead of attending school or finding employment, these seven "Lurk late," "Strike straight," "Sing sin," "Thin gin," and "Jazz June"—actions that are illegal, frowned upon by society, or harmful to other people. This is a bunch of kids to watch out for. If you see them coming, cross the street.

Subjective interpretations also include textual evidence, but often passages from the text are cited as prompts to introduce the writer's own memories, associations, or personal ideas; the more specific and concrete your examples, the better.

> I think everybody who ever went to a public high school knows these guys—at least most of them were boys—who eventually "Left school" altogether and failed to graduate. They dressed a little differently from the rest of us—baggier pants, heavier boots,

dirtier shirts, and too long hair never washed. And if there were girls—too much makeup or none at all.

WP TIP One of the most convincing ways to show the development of a theme is to point to the repetition and progression of certain images or symbols in a text. Mark these passages in the text you are interpreting, then type the passages in order of appearance into a computer file. Next, explain and annotate each passage, pointing out the significance to the passage of the progression or pattern.

WRITING 3: APPLICATION

Look at the text you plan to interpret, and make brief notes about each of the elements described in this section.

12 e Interpreting different genres

All the examples so far have come from a single short poem. If you are interpreting a work of fiction or nonfiction, or something else altogether such as an art exhibit, a concert, or a film, the basic elements of interpretation still apply—with a few differences.

Poetry. Of all language genres and forms, poetry exhibits the most intensive, deliberate, and careful use of language. With certain exceptions, poetic texts are far shorter than even short stories or one-act plays. Consequently, when interpreting poems, pay special attention to specific words, phrases, and lines; quote exactly to support your points; and familiarize yourself with the basic poetic terms you learned in high school: line, stanza, rhyme, rhythm, meter, metaphor, and image.

Fiction. To write about a novel or short story, explain how the main elements function: the narrator (who tells the story), plot (what happens in the story), one or more characters (who are acting or being acted upon), setting (where things are happening), and theme (the meaning of the story). Be sure to keep in mind that the author who writes the story is different from the characters in the story, and that what happens in the story is different from the meaning of the story.

Drama. Plays are a special kind of fiction that are meant to be acted out upon a stage; consequently, all the elements of fiction apply, except that since the characters are acting out the story, a narrator is seldom present. In drama, the setting is limited to what is contained on the stage, what the characters are thinking is usually not available to the audience, and the actors who play the parts are crucial to the play's success. Remember, too, that plays are structured according to acts (usually from one to five), which are in turn divided into scenes.

Movies. Fictional films are discussed in terms similar to those for fiction and drama (plot, character, setting, theme). However, additional elements also come into play: camera angles, special effects, and unlimited settings. Because of the complexity of orchestrating all of these elements, the film director rather than the screenwriter is often considered the "author" of a film.

Nonfiction. The elements of a nonfiction story are similar to those of fiction, except that everything in the text is supposed to have really happened. For this reason, the author and the narrator of the story are one and the same.

Informational nonfiction—essays, reports, and textbook chapters—is also meant to be believed; however, here you might say

 GUIDELINES FOR WRITING INTERPRETIVE ESSAYS

1. Identify the text fully and correctly: author, title, date.

2. Provide a brief summary of what happens on the literal level in the text, but focus your interpretation on the larger meanings and implications.

3. In analytic interpretations, write in the third person, state the thesis early, and support it with examples from the text.

4. In personal interpretations, write in the first person, reveal the theme by essay's end, and support it with both textual and personal examples.

5. State a thesis early. Use the rest of the essay to defend it.

6. When providing evidence for assertions, **summarize to provide context**, paraphrase to point to specific passages, and use direct quotes to capture particularly strong or precise expressions.

7. Document appropriately any assertions not your own or any passages of text that you quote or paraphrase.

8. Write both analytic and personal interpretations **honestly** according to what you believe.

that "ideas" and "arguments" are the main characters to be discussed and evaluated.

Other media. In interpreting other kinds of texts—paintings, photographs, sculptures, quilts, concerts, buildings, etc.—always explain to your reader the basic identifying features, be they verbal, visual, musical, or something else: What is it? What is its name or title? Who created it? What are its main features? Where is it? When did it take place?

12 f Shaping the whole paper

This chapter concludes with two sample interpretive papers from which some of the foregoing illustrations have been taken. The first one might be called an objective or **critical essay**, while the other might be called a subjective or **personal essay**.

Analytic response to "We Real Cool"

Kelly writes a brief analytical interpretation of "We Real Cool," called "High Stakes, Short Life," keeping himself in the background, writing in the third-person point of view. He presents his thesis early and supports it afterward with frequent quotations from the text, amplifying and explaining it most fully in his last paragraph.

High Stakes, Short Life

Kelly Sachs

Gwendolyn Brooks writes "We Real Cool" (1963) from the point of view of the members of a street gang who have dropped out of school to live their lives hanging around pool halls—in this case "The Golden Shovel." These guys are semi-literate and speak in slangy street lingo that reveals their need for mutual support in their mutually rebellious attitude toward life. The speakers in the poem, "We," celebrate what adults would call adolescent hedonism—but they make a conscious choice for a short intense life over a long, safe, and dull existence.

For the "Seven at the Golden Shovel," companionship is everything. For many teenagers, fitting in or conforming to a group identity is more important than developing an individual identity. But for these kids, none of whom excelled at school or had happy home lives, their group is their life. They even speak as a group, from the plural point of view, "We," repeated at the end of each line; these seven are bonded and will stick together through boredom, excitement, and death.

From society's point of view, they are nothing but misfits—refusing to work, leading violent lives, breaking laws, and confronting polite society whenever they cross paths. Instead of attending school, planning for their future, or finding work, these seven "Lurk late," "Strike straight," "Sing sin," "Thin gin," and "Jazz June." Watch out for this bunch. If you see them coming, cross the street.

However, the most important element of their lives is being "cool." They live and love to be cool. Part of being cool is playing pool, singing, drinking, fighting, and messing around with women whenever they can. Being cool is the code of action that unites them, that they celebrate, for which they are willing to die.

The poet reveals their fate in the poem's last line. Brooks shows that the price of coolness and companionship is higher than most people are willing to pay. In this culture, the fate of rebels who violate social norms is an early death ("We/Die soon"), but to these seven, it is better to live life to the fullest than hold back and plan for a future that may never come. They choose, accept, and celebrate their lives, and "Die soon."

Personal response to "We Real Cool"

In the following essay, "Staying Put," Mitzi writes about her personal reaction to Brooks' poem, describing how it reminds her of her own high school experience. Mitzi's theme, the sad lives of ghetto gangs, opens and closes the essay and provides the necessary coherence to hold it together. While she quotes the text several times, her primary supportive examples come from her own memories.

Staying Put

Mitzi Fowler

Gwendolyn Brooks' "We Real Cool" is a sad poem. It reminds me of the gang in high school who used to skip classes and come back smelling of cigarette smoke and cheap liquor—not that I knew it was cheap back then. I think everybody who ever went to a public high school knows these guys—at least most of them were boys—who eventually "Left school" altogether and failed to graduate. They dressed a little differently from the rest of us—baggier pants, heavier boots, dirtier shirts, and too long hair never washed—and if there were girls—too much makeup or none at all.

They had their fun, however, because they stayed in their group. They came late to assemblies, slouched in their seats, made wisecracks, and often ended up like the characters in The Breakfast Club, in detention after school or Saturday morning.

And no matter how straight-laced and clean-cut the rest of us were, we always felt just a twinge of envy at these careless, jaunty rebels who refused to follow rules, who didn't care if they got detentions, who didn't do homework, and whose parents didn't care if they stayed out all night. I didn't admit it very often—at least not to my friends—but some part of me wanted to have their pool hall or whatever adventures, these adult freedoms they claimed for themselves. However, I was always afraid—chicken, they would have said—of the consequences, so I practiced piano, did my algebra, and stayed put.

Then I think of the poem's last line and know why I obeyed my parents (well, most of the time), listened to my teachers (at least some of them), and stayed put (if you don't count senior cut day). These "cool" dropouts paid for their rebellion in drug overdoses, jail terms, police shootouts, and short lives. They "Die soon," so we never know where else their adventurous spirits might have taken them. In the end, this poem just makes me sad.

SUGGESTIONS FOR WRITING AND RESEARCH

INDIVIDUAL

1. Write an interpretive essay about a short text of your choice. Write the first draft from an analytic stance, withholding all personal judgments. Then write the second draft from a personal

stance, including all relevant private judgments. Write your final draft by carefully blending elements of your first and second drafts.

2. Locate at least two reviews of a text (book, recording, exhibit) with which you are familiar, and analyze each to determine the reviewer's critical perspective. Write your own review of the text, and agree or disagree with the approach of the reviewers you analyzed. If you have a campus newspaper, consider offering your review to the editor for publication.

COLLABORATIVE

As a class or small group, attend a local concert, play, or exhibition. Have each student take good notes and, when he or she returns home, write a review of this event that includes both an interpretation and a recommendation that readers attend it (or not). Share these variations on the same theme with others in your class or group and explore the different judgments that arise as a result of different perspectives.

13   Reflecting on the World

Reflective writing is writing that raises questions about some subject, reflecting that subject back to readers, allowing a clearer view, and exposing new dimensions, as if a mirror had been held up before it. Reflective writing allows both writer and reader to consider things thoughtfully and seriously, but it demands neither resolution nor definitive answers.

Reflective essays are the modern version of writings in the essay tradition, which began some four hundred years ago when French author Michel de Montaigne first published his *Essais* in 1580. An *essai* (from the French, meaning "to try") was a short piece of writing meant to be read at a single sitting on a subject of general interest to a broad spectrum of citizens. Montaigne's essays explored education, truth, friendship, cruelty, conversation, coaches, cannibals, and many other subjects. Essays were never intended to be the last word on a subject, but rather the first thoughtful and speculative word. E. B. White, Virginia Woolf, and George Orwell are among the best-known essayists in the twentieth century; among the best-known essayists writing today are Joan Didion, Barry Lopez, and Ellen Goodman.

13   a   Writing to reflect

Writing to reflect is often done as much to figure something out for yourself as to share it with others. Such writing is commonly characterized by a slight sense of indirection—as if the writer were in the actual process of examining a subject closely for the first time. This appearance of spontaneity may be, of course, an illusion, since most good reflective writing—unlike journal writing—has been thoroughly rewritten, revised, and edited to achieve just the right reflective tone.

Perhaps the most frequently asked question in reflective essays is "Why?" Why do people live and behave the way they do? Why does society develop this way rather than that? Why does one thing happen rather than another? In posing and reflecting upon such questions, writers are trying to make sense of the world.

Reflective writing can be on any subject under the sun. However, the subject that causes the reflection in the first place is seldom the actual focus or topic of the essay. The writer focuses on something specific, then speculates upon what it means or implies: watching a dog with its owner (subject) sparks a reflection on loyalty (topic); visiting the library (subject) stimulates a reflection on knowledge and creativity (topic). The everyday object or experience comes to stand for larger issues and ideas.

Unlike the case with many college writing assignments, reflective essays ask for your opinion. Assignments that contain a direction word such as *imagine, speculate,* or *reflect* call for writing that demonstrates your ability to see a given subject from several sides and to offer tentative answers to profound questions. For these assignments, it may be important to include factual information; however, such information is background, not primary material. While reflecting, writers may explain, interpret, or argue; however, neither explanation, interpretation, nor argument is foremost on their minds.

WP TIP From the box on p. 166, copy into a new computer file the list of actions you might take when considering a topic for a reflective paper. Save as a separate file, and if you have an online journal, copy the list there as well for ready reference. When you're searching for a paper topic, try freewriting, using one of the strategies.

■ **WRITING 1: EXPLORATION**

Describe any past experiences in writing reflective essays. Did you enjoy writing them? How did readers respond to them? **ESL:** If you have written reflective essays in your native language, describe some of your experiences with that kind of writing.

13 b Finding and describing a subject

The subject of a reflective essay is often something concrete, observable, or specific that prompts a more abstract reflection. It can be any person, place, thing, or idea. If you don't have a subject, think of something that has always interested or puzzled you, review old journal entries, start freewriting, or start wander-

STRATEGIES FOR REFLECTIVE PAPERS

1. Consider the active life versus the passive life. How have you chosen to live? How have others chosen to live? Why? Populate this reflection with characters from fiction.

2. Contemplate the effect of one book, movie, song, poem, or picture on your view of the world. Cite it, quote it, sing it, recite it, draw it. Summarize your reflections on paper.

3. Deliberate upon the meaning of one institution in which you participate daily. Write down the details of your thinking. Be specific about time, place, and action.

4. Explore one square block, one square room, one square foot. List everything you see, hear, and feel. Describe the place and all that lives there.

5. Imagine a journey from your past and its influence on where you are today. What, exactly, would be different had you not made that trip? How do you know?

6. Meditate on the meaning of words that we use for abstract concepts: *life, death, love, hate, war, peace, me, you.* Choose one to discuss in depth.

7. Speculate about patterns you see in your neighborhood, education, career, spare time, or life. What do you do again and again? What do you see happening around you again and again? Why do these things recur?

8. Think about a small or common object that you see or use every day. Find out where it came from, who made it, why it's there, and what life would be like without it.

9. Fantasize about your wishes. List every birthday wish you can remember. Select one, and imagine that you had gotten this wish. In what ways would life have been different for you? In what ways would it have remained the same? Do you still wish it had happened?

10. Philosophize about the existence of things. Why one event, cause, effect, day, decision, choice rather than another? What does it mean that none of these can be reversed?

ing around deliberately looking for something about which to muse or speculate. (See Chapter 6.)

No matter what your subject, try beginning with the concrete and specific—a particular concert, a building, an encounter.

Record as much detail as you can. Make your subject visible and tangible before considering its more abstract dimensions and associations. If you ground your reflection in the everyday world, recording things that readers themselves have seen or can easily imagine, you invite their own reflecting on your subject before they share yours, which draws them more deeply into your writing.

1 People

For reflective essays, brief and casual encounters with strangers may work as well as more developed relationships. In fact, reflecting on chance encounters almost guarantees speculative and inconclusive thoughts: Why is she doing that? Where does he live? How are their lives like mine? Reflective writing about people often leads to comparisons with the writer's own circumstances, character, or behavior. What makes such writing especially interesting, of course, is that no two writers who encountered or witnessed the same person would speculate, muse, or wonder in the same way.

In the following passage, Mari writes about a chance encounter one Saturday morning.

> The sign on the front door says the store opens at eight o'-clock. It's 7:56, so I put the bag of bottles on the ground.
> An old woman with a shopping cart full of bottles stands in front of the Pearl Street Beverage Mart. Most of her long gray hair is tucked into a Red Sox baseball cap, but some of it hangs in twisted strands about her face. She wears an oversized yellow slicker, a striking contrast against the crystal blue morning sky. She looks at the bottles and her lips are moving as if she's telling them a story.
> Then the bottle lady turns and speaks to me: "These bottles in my cart here, you see which I mean? Well, I'm gonna get five hundred dollars for them and get me a fine stylin' dinner tonight. It's a good thing there's bottles, yes?"

In this early part of her essay, Mari first focuses on locating the circumstance in a particular time and place and on describing the appearance of the woman. She provides enough detail so that readers can see the woman and, perhaps, join the author in asking questions: Why is this woman wearing a raincoat when the sky is blue? Why is she speaking to the bottles?

WRITING 2: APPLICATION

Make a list of people you have observed within the past few weeks who have, for one reason or another, made a sharp impression on you. Did any of them trigger reflective thoughts? What are those thoughts? Write a paragraph that reflects on one of these people.

2 Places

Places make good reflective subjects. You can examine places right under your nose and create something interesting and reflective from them. Reflective essays that begin by describing a physical place often end up focusing on places of the heart, mind, and spirit. Places have the advantage of staying put—you can often return to a place again and again for further information and ideas. You can, of course, reflect on just about any place imaginable, including those in your memories to which you cannot return.

In the following passage, Judith turned the university library into a subject for reflection.

> Inside the smoke-colored doors, the loud and busy atmosphere vanishes, replaced by the soft, soothing hum of air-conditioning and the hushed sound of whispering voices. The repetitive sound of the copy machine has a calming effect as I look for a comfortable place in which to begin my work.
>
> I want just the right chair, with a soft cushion and a low sturdy table for a leg rest. The chairs are strategically positioned with comfortable personal space around each one, so you can stretch your arms fully without touching a neighbor. . . . People seem to respect each other's need for personal space.

In her search for the right chair, Judith's description is detailed and concrete. At the same time, she introduces the importance of quiet space to her peace of mind. She concludes with a generalization triggered by the space she describes, hinting at, but not stating, the topic of her reflection.

WRITING 3: APPLICATION

Make a list of places that would provide material for a reflective essay. Think about places you've visited recently and those to which you still have access. What associations do these places conjure up? If you can, go visit these places in person; if not, revisit in memory. Decide which place offers the best prospect for further writing.

3 Things

Any "thing" can be a subject for reflection, so long as you treat it accordingly. Perhaps the first things that come to mind are physical objects. But a very different kind of a thing is an event, whether public (a political rally, a basketball game) or private (drinking a cup of coffee, fishing for trout). A still more abstract kind of thing is a concept (multiculturalism, campus parking).

In the following example (p. 170), Scott opens with a generalized statement about water fountains.

ESL **EXPRESSING REFLECTIONS**

In written English, the following forms are often used to express reflections. They signal that the events or ideas described are possibilities, not certain or actual occurrences.

ADVERBS EXPRESSING UNCERTAINTY

maybe   possibly
perhaps

Example: Maybe next year I will visit the orchard again.

MODAL VERBS

Past	Future
may have	may
might have	might
could have	could
must have	

Example: I could have gone to the beach last week.

THE SUBJUNCTIVE MOOD

Example: If I were ten years old again, I would try to tell her how I feel.

(Note: Remember that the subjunctive is only used to express things that are untrue, not things that are uncertain. See 35g.)

INDIRECT QUESTIONS

Example: Even today I wonder whether the old dog ever made it to safety.

> There is something serene about the sound of a water foun-
> tain. The constant patter of water splashing into water. The
> sound of endless repetition, the feeling of endless cycle. . . .

Two paragraphs later, he moves to the campus water fountain.

> The fountain pipe has eighty-two nozzles. Two weeks ago,
> only fifty-five of them were spraying water vigorously, eleven
> sprayed weakly, and sixteen didn't spray at all. This week eighty-
> one are spraying; someone has fixed the fountain.

Even though Scott starts with a preliminary generalization, he
quickly gives the reader a careful, even technical description.
Readers are likely to believe Scott's reflection because he has tak-
en pains to be accurate in his observation, and so they are likely
to believe the rest of his account as well. While Scott has made it
clear that listening to fountains is peaceful for him, readers still
do not know why he chooses to write about them.

WRITING 4: APPLICATION

Make a list of things that interest you or excite your curiosity. Do so either
from memory or by walking around your room, house, or neighborhood.
Write a paragraph each on three of the things you encounter and decide
which offers the best prospect for further writing.

13 c Pausing to speculate

The three examples we have seen so far have taken everyday
people, places, and things—a woman with bottles, a library, a water fountain—as the subjects on which to reflect. The advantage of
common over spectacular subjects is that everyone has some experience with them and is automatically curious to see what you
make of them. However, your subject alone will carry interest just
so far: the rest is up to your originality, creativity, and skill as you
present the topic of your essay, the deeper and more speculative
meaning you have found.

After introducing your subject, you need to execute a pause,
saying in effect, "Wait a minute, there's something else going on
here—stop and consider." The pause is a key moment. It signals
to the reader that the essay is about to move into a new and less
predictable direction.

Often the pause is accompanied by a slight shift in voice or
tone as the writer becomes either more personal or more formal,
slightly more biased or not. The exact nature of your shift will be

determined by the point you want to make. (See Chapter 8.)

After describing the woman returning bottles, Mari steps back and shifts from the woman to the common objective that has brought them both to the store: returning bottles for a refund.

> I guess I had never thought about it before, but the world is full of bottles. They're everywhere, on shelves, in trash cans, on park benches, behind bushes, in street gutters. In the modern city, bottles are more common than grass.

By calling attention to her own new thoughts about bottles, Mari causes her readers, too, to think about a world full of bottles and about what, if anything, that may mean.

In the following passage, Scott stops observing the campus water fountain and begins wondering and remembering.

> I'm not sure where my love of fountains comes from. Perhaps it's from my father. When I was very young he bought a small cement fountain for our backyard. Its basin was an upturned shell and there was a little cherubic boy who peed into it.

This pause signals that it is not, in fact, water fountains that are on Scott's mind, but memories of his father.

▪ WRITING 5: APPLICATION

Select one of the topics you explored in Writings 2–4. Once you have described or defined it, create a reflective pause by writing one or two pages about what this person, place, or thing makes you think about.

13 d Making a point

In explanatory, argumentative, or interpretive writing, the point of the paper is commonly stated as an explicit thesis, often in the first paragraph. In successful reflective writing, however, the point may be conveyed only indirectly and nearly always emerges only at the end. Thus readers are themselves drawn into the act of reflecting and become curious to find out what the writer thinks. In other words, reflective writers muse rather than argue. In fact, reflective essays are most persuasive when they are least obviously instructive or assertive.

Mari concludes her observation of the woman returning bottles by reporting the shopkeeper's sarcastic response to the woman after he totals the deposits on her bottles.

> "Eight dollars and thirty-five cents, Alice. You must have new competition or else bottles are getting scarce. You haven't broken ten dollars in days."

As you perhaps suspected, Alice has grossly overestimated the value of the bottles in her cart. However, this transaction has a transforming effect on the observer/writer, who now adds her own bottles to the woman's pile.

> . . . I realized then that my bottles were more nuisance than necessity. They were cluttering up our back hall—the landlord had already complained once—and tonight my roommates and I were making chicken curry for our boyfriends. That wasn't the case with Alice, who seemed to have neither roommate, dinner, nor boyfriend.
>
> "Here you go, Alice. Maybe you can break ten bucks with these." I gave them to her freely, at the same time realizing their true value for the first time.

Though the essay begins with a narrative about a trip to the bottle store, it ends somewhere else. Mari is still ignorant of any real details about the woman's life, history, or prospects, although she, like us, has made educated guesses. Alice remains frozen in the essay for all time as the "bottle lady." It is what Mari makes of her that is the real topic of this essay. Mari's encounter with Alice has caused her to reassess her own relatively comfortable and privileged life as a college student with her whole future ahead of her.

Mari's essay is strong precisely because it doesn't hit us over the head with a message or champion a particular cause. Instead of writing an editorial about poverty or the homeless, Mari has raised a question about the relative value of bottles for different people in a throwaway society.

Scott's essay about water fountains has progressed from fountains in general to the campus fountain in particular, then to the memory of childhood fountains, which remind him of his father. Only in the last paragraph does he tell us more.

> My father died just after my twentieth birthday. It was very sudden and very surprising and everything felt very unfinished. They say I am a lot like him in many ways, but I'm not sure. What I know is that like him, I love the sound of water.

Even at the end, Scott's point emerges by implication rather than explication—he never tells us outright why he began this reflection or what he hopes readers will take from it.

This proved to be an especially difficult topic for Scott to write about; in fact, he might not have chosen "water fountains" had he known in advance exactly where they would lead him. Scott's early drafts focused on water and fountains and people sitting around them, but they did not mention his father. A writer may select to write about an object with only a vague idea of why it's attractive, interesting, or compelling. Often it's only through the act of reflective writing that the writer finds out the nature of the attraction, interest, or compulsion.

Remember that reflective essays raise issues but do not need to resolve them. The tradition of essay writing is the tradition of trying and attempting rather than resolving or concluding. Ending by acknowledging that you see still other questions invites your reader to join in the search for answers.

At the very end of a reflective essay, it's a good idea to return to the specific person, place, or thing that originally prompted the reflection. This brings about a sense of closure—if not for the topic itself, at least for this particular essay.

WP TIP Print out a copy of your reflective essay with the right-hand margin set at three inches. Reread your paper, and mark in this wide margin each place where a reflective pause seems appropriate. Go back and revise on screen, incorporating the new ideas.

 GUIDELINES FOR WRITING REFLECTIVE ESSAYS

1. Begin your reflection with something concrete (a person, place, or thing) that interests you.

2. Describe your subject carefully and locate it in a specific circumstance.

3. Pause and move away from your subject to the larger or different issue it brings to mind—the topic of your reflection.

4. Organize your essay to move from the concrete and specific toward the abstract and general.

5. Use a reflective voice—tentative, questioning, gentle—to advance your point.

6. Let your point emerge late in your essay.

7. Conclude by returning to where your reflective journey began.

■ **WRITING 6: APPLICATION**

Write two conclusions to the reflective essay you have been working on. In one, state your point openly; in the other, let it emerge more gradually and implicitly. Which version do you like better? Why?

13 **e** **Shaping the whole paper**

The finished draft of Judith's reflective essay, "Writing in Safety," follows the structure described in this chapter. It opens and closes with a walk to and from the library. It has a loosely narrative pattern and is written in the present tense to convey a sense of the events unfolding as we read them. Her essay does not, however, actually tell a story, since nothing happens—unless you count walking and sitting down as events. The journey emerges as a mental, almost spiritual, quest for safety—safety in which to think and create without fear. At the same time, the physical dimensions of her journey and the attention to descriptive detail make her journey believable.

Writing in Safety

Judith Woods

It is already afternoon. I fiddle with the key to lock the apartment door after me. I am not accustomed to locking doors. Except for the six months I spent in Boston, I have never lived in a place where I did not trust my neighbors. When I was little, we couldn't lock our farmhouse door; the wood had swollen and the bolt no longer lined up properly with the hole, and nobody ever bothered to fix it. I still remember the time our baby-sitter, Rosie, hammered the bolt closed and we had to take the door off the hinges to get it open.

I heft the book bag onto my shoulder and walk up College Street toward the library. As I pass and am passed by other students, I scrutinize everything around me, hoping to be struck with a creative idea for a topic for my English paper. Instead, my mind fills with a jumble of disconnected images, like a bowl of alphabet soup: the letters are there, but they don't form any words. Campus sidewalks are not the best places for creativity to strike.

Approaching the library, I see skatebcarders and bikers weaving through students who talk in clusters on the library steps. A friendly dog is tied to a bench watching for its owner to return. Subjects to write about? Nothing strikes me as especially interesting, and besides, my heart is still pounding from the walk up the hill. I wipe my damp forehead and go inside.

Inside the smoke-colored doors, the loud and busy atmosphere vanishes, replaced by the soft, soothing hum of air-conditioning and the hushed sound of whispering voices. The repetitive sound of the copy machine has a calming effect as I look for a comfortable place in which to begin my work.

I want just the right chair, with a soft cushion and a low sturdy table for a leg rest. The chairs are strategically positioned with comfortable personal space around each one, so you can stretch your arms fully without touching a neighbor. I notice that if there are three chairs in a row, the middle one is always empty. If seated at a table, people sit staggered so they are not directly across from one another. People seem to respect each other's need for personal space.

Like a dog who circles her bed three times before lying down, I circle the reading room looking for the right place to sit. I need to feel safe and comfortable so I can concentrate on mental activity. Some students, however, are too comfortable. One boy has moved two chairs together, covered himself with his coat, and is asleep in a fetal position. A girl sits at a table, head down, dozing like we used to do in first grade.

I find my place, an empty chair near a window, and slouch down into it, propping my legs on the low table in front. If my mother could see me, she'd reprimand me for not sitting up straight. I breathe deeply, close my eyes for a moment, and become centered, forgetting both last night's pizza and tomorrow's philosophy exam. I need a few minutes to acclimate to this space, relax, and feel safe before starting my work.

Two weeks ago, a female student was assaulted not far from where I live—that's why I've taken to locking my door so carefully. I am beginning to understand the importance of feeling safe in order to be creative and productive. Here, in the library, I feel secure, protected from real violence and isolated from everyday distractions. There are just enough people for security's sake but not so many that I feel crowded. And besides, I'm surrounded by all these books, all these great minds who dwell in this hallowed space! I am comfortable, safe, and beginning to get an idea.

Hours later—my paper started, my exam studied for, my eyes tired—I retrace the path to my apartment. It is dark now, and I listen closely when I hear footsteps behind, stepping to the sidewalk's edge to let a man walk briskly past. At my door, I again fumble for the now familiar key, insert it in the lock, open the door, turn on the hall light, and step inside. Here, too, I am safe, ready to eat, read a bit, and finish my reflective essay.

SUGGESTIONS FOR WRITING AND RESEARCH

INDIVIDUAL

1. Review your responses to Writings 2–6. Select the reflective possibility that interests you most, and compose a whole essay on the subject. When finished, follow the suggestions in the box on page 166 to help you write a second draft.

2. Find an object in your room, dormitory, house, or neighborhood that seems especially commonplace or routine or that you otherwise take for granted (a chair, rug, window, comb, glass, plant, fire hydrant). Describe it carefully and reflect on its possible meaning or value.

3. Look up one of the authors mentioned in this chapter—Michel de Montaigne, E. B. White, Virginia Woolf, George Orwell, Joan Didion, Barry Lopez, Ellen Goodman—or a writer of your own choice. Read several essays, then analyze the work in terms of the characteristics of reflective essays described in this chapter. Write a review of this author as an essayist.

COLLABORATIVE

As a class, select a place or event with reflective potential. Each student writes his or her own reflection on the subject, limiting each reflection to final drafts of two single-spaced pages each. Elect two class co-editors to assemble the collection of essays and publish them in bound volumes for the whole class (co-editors to add table of contents, an introduction, and afterword by the course instructor).

PART FOUR

Researching

Before agonizing too long over your next research project, stop to consider what, exactly, research entails. Keep in mind that in your nonacademic life you conduct practical research of one kind or another every time you search the want ads for a used car, browse through a library in search of a book, or read a movie review. You may not make note cards or report the results in writing, but whenever you ask questions and then systematically look for answers, you are conducting research.

In college, the research you conduct is academic rather than practical. In other words, it's designed to result in a convincing paper rather than a purchase or an action. Academic research is part of the writing process for most of your papers.

You rarely begin writing an explanation, argument, or interpretation already knowing all the facts and having all the information you'll need: to fill in the gaps in your knowledge, you conduct research. In fact, one type of assignment, the **research essay**, is specially designed to introduce you to the process of conducting research and writing a paper based on your findings. Research essays are generally longer, require more extensive research, use a more formal style and format, and take more time than other papers.

Meaningful research results from real questions that you care to answer. It's exciting work. And if you're not now excited about something, once you start engaging in research activities you may surprise yourself: Take a tour of your library and find out what's there; get on the Internet and start exploring the resources of the World Wide Web; above all, start thinking, writing, and talking to people about ideas, and exciting things will happen.

14 a Understanding research

I An example of practical research

In preparing to write this chapter, we asked ourselves about the last time we did research of a substantial nature. Toby recalled the amount of practical research he did recently when he bought a motorcycle. His current motorcycle was a small BMW that he used for riding to school and taking short trips. It was time, he thought, to buy a new motorcycle big enough for comfortable long-range touring. Finding the right machine meant shopping carefully, which meant asking good questions: What kind of motorcycle was best for touring? How large should it be? What make was most reliable? How much would it cost? Who were the best dealers?

Here's how Toby researched his questions about buying a new motorcycle:

■ Over a period of several weeks Toby talked to people who knew a lot about motorcycles—some old friends, the mechanic at the shop where his old bike was serviced, a neighbor who owned two different touring machines.

■ Toby subscribed to *Motorcyclist* and *Rider* magazines; he found the latter more interesting since it focuses primarily on touring motorcycles. The more he read, the more familiar he became with current terminology (ABS, fairings), brands (BMW, Harley-Davidson), models (sport tourers, roadsters), and performance data (roll-on speed, braking distance). On a corner of his desk, he piled the most useful magazines with many dog-eared pages.

■ Toby looked up back issues of *Rider* magazine in the local library to gain a historical perspective. He made photocopies of the most relevant articles, underlined key findings, and made notes in the margins of his photocopies.

■ Toby visited the local chapter of the BMW Motorcycle Club. Here he met more people who seemed to be expert motorcyclists (all, of course, recommending BMWs) and bought a copy of *BMW Motorcycle Owners of America News*.

■ Toby rented the video *On Any Sunday* (1972), considered by many to be the best film ever made about motorcycles, and watched it three times.

- Toby approached the owner of Frank's Motorcycle Shop and asked about the virtues of certain BMW models on display. He was most impressed by two models, the K75RT and the K100RS, both of which he sat on but did not ride. He left with literature and reread it at home. He wrote in his journal about the dreams motorcycles inspired and the difficult choices they required.

- Toby visited local dealers who sold Honda, Kawasaki, Yamaha, and Suzuki motorcycles and listened to sales pitches explaining the features of their best touring machines. He found some too racy and others too large, but he still took notes about each to facilitate his comparison.

- Toby returned to Frank's and test-drove the two BMW models that most interested him: the cheaper K75RT was smoother, but the more expensive K100RS was more powerful. Still he was undecided. He asked about the trade-in value of his old motorcycle. He took notes and made calculations and lay awake at night pondering the possibilities.

- After weighing the relative merits of smoothness versus power versus money, Toby returned to Frank's Motorcycle Shop and bought the K100RS, receiving an end-of-season discount. Then he retreated into a long Vermont winter and waited for motorcycle season to resume in the spring.

WRITING 1: EXPLORATION

What research outside of school settings have you conducted recently? Think about major changes, moves, or purchases that required you to ask serious questions. Also think about any explorations you've made in "Gopherspace," the World Wide Web, and the Internet; what electronic information has caught your attention and caused you to dig deeper and find more? (See 15c2.) Choose one of these recent research activities and list the sources you found, the questions you asked, and any steps you took to answer them. Finally, what was the result of this research?

2 Activities in the research process

While the search for motorcycle knowledge is practical rather than academic, it serves nevertheless to introduce most of the activities common to all research projects, argumentative or informational, in school or out.

I **The researcher has a genuine interest in the topic.** It's difficult to fake curiosity, but it's possible to develop it. Toby's interest in motorcycles was long-standing, but the more he investigated, the more he learned and the more he still wanted to know. Some academic assignments will allow you to pursue issues that are personally important to you; others will require that you dive into the research first and generate interest as you go.

2   **The researcher asks questions**. Toby's first questions were general rather than specific. However, as he gained more knowledge, the questions became more sharply focused. No matter what your research assignment, you need to begin by articulating questions, finding out where the answers lead, and then asking still more questions. (Read more about exploratory electronic research in 15c.)

3   **The researcher seeks answers from people**. Toby talked to both friends and strangers who knew about motorcycles. The people to whom he listened most closely were specialists with expert knowledge. All research projects profit when you ask knowledgeable people to help you answer questions or point you in directions where answers may be found. College communities abound with professors, researchers, working professionals, and nonacademic staff who can help out with research projects.

4   **The researcher visits places where information may be found**. Toby went to dealerships and a motorcycle club, not only to ask questions of experts but also to observe and experience firsthand. No matter how much other people told him, his knowledge increased when he made his own observations. In many forms of academic research, field research is as important as library research.

5   **The researcher examines texts**. Toby read motorcycle magazines and brochures and watched videotapes to become more informed about his subject. Keep in mind that texts include the vast resources of the Internet as well as any created artifact. While printed texts are helpful in practical research, they are crucial in academic research.

6   **The researcher evaluates sources**. As the research progressed, Toby double-checked information to see if it could be confirmed by more than one source. In practical research, the researcher must evaluate sources to ensure that the final decision is satisfactory. Similarly, in academic research, you must evaluate sources to ensure that your final paper is convincing.

7   **The researcher writes**. Toby made field notes, made notes about his library sources, and wrote in his journal. In practical research, writing helps the researcher find, remember, and explore information. In academic research, writing is even more important, since the results must eventually be reported in writing.

8   **The researcher tests and experiments**. In Toby's practical re-
     search, testing was simple and fairly subjective—riding different
     motorcycles to compare the qualities of each. Testing and exper-
     imentation are also regular parts of many research projects.

9   **The researcher combines and synthesizes information to ar-
     rive at new conclusions**. Toby's accumulated and sorted-out in-
     formation led to a decision to purchase one motorcycle rather
     than another. In academic research, your synthesis of informa-
     tion leads not to a purchase, but to a well-supported thesis that
     will convince a skeptical audience that your research findings are
     correct.

     What this researcher did not do, of course, is the step most
directly concerned with the subject matter of this handbook: write
down the results of his investigation in a formal report. The greatest difference between practical and academic research is that the
former leads to practical knowledge on which to act, the latter to
theoretical knowledge written for others to read. So, for academic
research, there is one more activity to consider.

10   **The researcher presents the research findings in an interest-
     ing, focused, and well-documented paper**. The remainder of
     this chapter explains how to select, investigate, and write about
     academic research topics.

■ **WRITING 2: EXPLORATION**

Explain how any of the research activities described in this section were part
of an investigation you once conducted, in school or out. How might you use
computer-based research activities to facilitate any research project you do
today—practical or academic? (If you have difficulty answering this last question, see 15c.)

14 b   Managing the research process

     A research paper is the end result of the process of finding,
evaluating, and synthesizing information that is new to you from
a wide variety of sources. Therefore, research essays occupy a
span of weeks or months and are often the most important project
you work on during a semester. It pays to study the assignment
carefully, begin working on it immediately, and allow sufficient
time for the many different activities involved.

STRATEGIES FOR MANAGING THE RESEARCH PROCESS

■ **Ask questions.** Begin by asking questions about a subject, both of yourself and of others. Preliminary questions lead to more specific inquiries.

■ **Read extensively.** Texts of all kinds—books, journal and magazine articles, and studies—are the raw material from which you will build your research paper.

■ **Question knowledgeable people.** Start with people you know. If they can't help, ask who can. Then broaden that circle to include people with specialized knowledge.

■ **Seek out firsthand information and experience.** No matter how many answers other people offer you, seek out information yourself.

■ **Evaluate your sources and double-check the information you find.** Sources vary in their accuracy and objectivity. Try to confirm the information you gather by checking more than one reliable source.

■ **Write at every stage.** The notes you take on your reading, the field notes you write, and the research log you keep all help you gain control of your subject. Everything you have written also helps you when you start drafting.

1 **Considering the assignment**

First, reflect on the course for which the paper is assigned. What is the aim of this field of study? What themes has the instructor emphasized? How would a research assignment contribute to the goals of this course? In other words, before even considering a topic, assess the instructor's probable reasons for making the assignment and try to predict what is expected from your finished paper.

Next, study the assignment directions carefully. Identify both the subject words and the direction words. **Subject words** specify the area of the investigation. **Direction words** (verbs such as *write* or *explain*) specify your purpose for writing—whether you should explain or report or argue or do something else. (See 5d.)

Finally, examine the assignment requirements: the recommended perspective, the most appropriate style, the preferred for-

 COLLABORATIVE RESEARCH PROJECTS

Of all writing assignments, those involving research profit most from collaboration. In the corporate, business, and scientific worlds, nearly all work is collaborative, including posing, processing, and solving problems; reaching decisions; evaluating production; and writing reports. For most complex problems, two heads are better than one, three better than two. If your assignment lends itself to collaboration, and if your instructor approves, find out with which classmates you could work. The following suggestions will aid collaboration.

1. Choosing a topic. Either form a group you want to work with and then choose a topic you all want to research, or choose a topic that interests you and see if you can interest others in joining you.

2. Determining size. Small groups (two to three people) work better than large groups, because they make it easier to find time to meet outside of class and to synthesize the information found.

3. Establishing organization. Divide tasks early in your project, specifying who will do what when. Divide the tasks equitably so that everyone contributes an equal amount. Divide the tasks so that members make maximum use of their different skills, abilities, and interests.

4. Doing research. Agree to take careful notes from texts or interviews and to duplicate the notes so that each group member has full sources of information. Someone should cover periodicals, someone else should check the Internet, and someone else should find local experts to interview, in person, via telephone, or through e-mail.

5. Drafting. A group writing a single paper can write together by (1) blending voices, passing the drafts back and forth, each writer overwriting the others each time; (2) sequencing voices, each writer writing a different section (as in chapters in a book); or (3) weaving voices, so that the final product has different writers' voices emerging at different times throughout the paper.

mat, the sources expected, the documentation system required, the due dates, and the paper length. Thinking about these early on may save time and help avoid false steps. (See Part VIII for information on style, format, and documentation conventions in various disciplines.)

6. Agreeing on a thesis. In the early stages of collaborative writing, each group member should write his or her own version of what the research suggests. These early drafts should be shared, with each writer reconsidering the thesis in light of points made by the other writers. If there is disagreement, continue to share the research, but write separate papers that reflect the different conclusions arrived at.

7. Revising and editing. At the end, responsibilities can be divided equitably according to abilities, with different members volunteering to type, prepare references, edit, proofread, and reproduce the final paper. This is also a good time to even out the workload, if some have done more so far than others. However, for more complete group ownership of the project, conduct a round-robin reading, whereby each member looks at the final draft.

8. Evaluating responsibility and achievement. We recommend some degree of self-assessment on all collaborative projects. The best way to achieve this is for each group member to assess both himself or herself and the group as a whole; these assessments should first be processed by the group; if disagreements arise, involve the instructor. When all group members meet their responsibilities and deadlines, all should receive the same grade. However, in cases of disagreement, give the group 100 points for their own distribution: If they do not believe everyone should receive the same points, they should work out an equitable allocation. As a last resort, the instructor or another group could referee.

> **WP TIP** If you are working on computer, date and name each file on disk and exchange disks with your co-authors. Use e-mail (and, if possible, a dedicated Listserv) to discuss the project with them. "Archive," that is, save all of the posts for ready reference.

2 Finding a topic

Your instructor may assign a specific topic, or the choice may be left up to you. If you need to find a topic, think about how your interests dovetail with the content of the course. What topics of the course do you enjoy most? What discussions, lectures, or labs have you found most engaging? What has happened recently in the news that both interests you and relates to the course material? Do some freewriting or clustering to find the topic that seems most promising to you (see again Chapter 6) or turn on your computer and surf the Internet for ideas!

At the same time, limit or narrow your topic to one you can answer with real and specific information—information that catches attention in ways that loose generalities about vast subjects cannot. Besides, if you limit your topic, your chances of managing and answering it improve dramatically.

SUBJECT   *The environment* (too broad to be called a topic).

TOPIC   *Harmful corporate practices hurt the American environment* (narrower and better but still too broad).

TOPIC   *American companies sometimes exploit people's concern for the environment by advertising "green" policies and products; the results are often false advertising, tricked consumers, and a worsened environment* (narrower, still better, more focused).

3 Developing a research question

Since research essays are among the lengthiest and most complex of all college assignments, make the project interesting and purposeful by developing a research question that will be exciting for you to answer. What makes a good research question?

1   It's a question that you really want to know the answer to.

2   It requires more than a yes or no answer.

    YES OR NO

    Do companies misrepresent the environmental advantages of their products?

    BETTER

    How do companies misrepresent the environmental advantages of their products?

3   It's sufficiently complex that you do not already know the answer.

    Some of the ways companies misrepresent green products are changing the names of chemical ingredients, hiding research that proves there are hazards, and creating advertising that suggests environmental purity.

4   It's a question that you have a reasonable chance of answering: A quick survey of library sources on false advertising reveals a wealth of books and periodicals on the subject.

How have American companies capitalized in their advertising on the American consumers' environmental consciousness?

4 Becoming an authority

Whenever you undertake research, you join an ongoing conversation among a select community of people who are knowledgeable about the subject. As you collect information, you too become something of an expert. You gain an authoritative voice, becoming a stronger, more powerful writer. Plan to become enough of an expert on your topic that you can teach your classmates and instructor something they didn't know before. The best way to exercise your new-found authority is to write in your own words all the major information and ideas connected with your research project, both periodically in your journal entries and later

---

ESL BECOMING AN AUTHORITY

If you have been educated outside the United States, your instructors may have emphasized the authority of experts rather than a student's. You may feel it is inappropriate to act as an authority, especially if the topic is one you didn't know much about before you began researching it. In U.S. colleges, however, students are expected to develop a sense of authority regarding their topics. This is to enable them to present powerful, interesting ideas of their own rather than repeating what others have said.

Becoming an authority means working hard to become an expert and thus master your writing project. The following guidelines should help.

1. Learn enough about your topic to become the class expert.

2. Think carefully about which sources to use and how to use them in your paper. (See 16a and 16b.)

3. Read your sources critically, analyzing what they say and why they might be saying it. (See Chapter 2.)

4. Make sure your paper includes ideas of your own, not just summaries of what other people have said.

when you draft. Finding your own language to express an idea makes that idea yours and increases both your understanding of and your commitment to the topic.

5 Keeping an open mind

Don't be surprised if, once you begin doing research, your questions and answers multiply and change. You ask one question, find the answer to another, pursue that, and then stumble onto the answer to your first question. Be prepared to travel in circles at times or find dead ends where you expected thoroughfares—but also thoroughfares where you expected dead ends. For example, suppose you start out researching local recycling efforts, but you stumble upon the problem of finding buyers for recycled material. One source raises the question of manufacturing with recycled materials, while another source turns the whole question back to consumer education. All of these concerns are related, but if you attempt to study them all with equal intensity, your paper will be either very long or very superficial. Follow your strongest interests, and try to answer the question you most care about.

Similarly, what began as informational research may become argumentative as the research process turns up information to tip your original neutrality one way or another. Or a research investigation that starts out to prove a thesis may result in a more neutral, informative paper if multiple causes or complexities in what had seemed a straightforward case are uncovered.

14 c Formulating a working thesis

When an answer to your research question starts to take shape, form a **working thesis**, that is, a preliminary answer from which you can investigate further. If additional research leads you in a different direction, be ready to redirect your investigation and revise your working thesis.

Whether or not you already have a working thesis will determine what type of research you undertake. **Informational research** is conducted when you don't know the answer to the question or don't have a firm opinion about the topic. You enter this kind of investigation with an open mind, focusing on the question, not on a predetermined answer. In some cases this kind of research will lead you to an argumentative position; in others you may report the results of your research in an explanatory paper. In either case, you will eventually need to develop a working thesis, and the purpose of informational research is to help you find it. Such research might be characterized as thesis-finding.

Argumentative research is conducted to prove a point. You enter the project already knowing your working thesis—the tentative answer to your question, the side of the debate you want to support: Should companies be held to stricter standards of truth in commercial advertising? You might argue yes, and then conduct research to buttress your position. A research question helps focus your energies, but argumentative research is really thesis-driven since you're hunting for support to prove your point. The process of researching may lead to a revised or entirely different thesis, so remember that any thesis is subject to revision, redirection, and clarification. Nonetheless, whatever thesis you start with will point you in one direction rather than another. (For more on informational and argumentative papers, see Chapters 10 and 11.)

As a final check, ask your instructor to respond to your intended question before you invest too much time in it. Your instructor will help direct you to projects that are consistent with the goals of the assignment or course and steer you away from questions that are too broad or too offbeat.

▉ WRITING 3: APPLICATION

Select a topic that interests you and that is compatible with the research assignment. List ten questions that you have—or that you think others might have—about this topic. Select the question that most interests you and freewrite about it for ten more minutes. Why does it interest you? Where would you start looking for answers?

14 d Keeping a research log

A research log can help you keep track of the scope, purpose, and possibilities of any research project. Such a log is essentially a journal in which you write to yourself about the process of doing research by asking questions and monitoring the results. Questions you might ask include the following:

What subject do I want to research?

What information have I found so far?

What do I still need to find?

Where am I most likely to find it?

Do I start with a working thesis or look for one?

What evidence best supports my working thesis?

What evidence challenges my working thesis?

How is my thesis changing from where it started?

Writing out answers to these questions in your log clarifies your tasks as you go along. It forces you to articulate ideas and examine supporting evidence critically. Doing this, in turn, helps you focus your research activities. Novice researchers often waste time tracking down sources that are not really useful. Answering questions in your research log as you visit the library, look for and read sources, review note cards, and write various drafts can make research more efficient. (See Chapter 4.)

When you keep notes in a research log, record them as if they were on separate note cards. Here, for example, are some entries from a first-year student's research log.

11/12 Checked the subject headings and found no books on ozone depletion. Ref. librarian suggested magazines because it takes so long for books to come out on new subjects. In the General Science Index I found about twenty articles—I've got them all on a printout. Need to come back tomorrow to actually start reading them.

11/17 Conference today with Lawrence about the ozone hole thesis—said I don't really have much of a thesis, rather a lot of information aiming in the same direction. Suggested I look at what I've found already and then back up to see what question it answers—that will probably point to my thesis.

When a project requires you to investigate only a few sources of information, you may keep all your bibliographic and research notes in your research log, in a separate part of your class notebook, or on a single computer file. (See 15e.)

WP TIP Keep your log on a computer and always date your material to keep track of your decisions. Then copy entries directly into your first draft and work with them there, or switch between two open windows.

■ WRITING 4: APPLICATION

Keep a research log for the duration of your research project. Write in it daily and record everything you think of or find in relation to the project. When your project is finished, write an account of the role the log played.

14 e Using the writing process

Research writing, like all important writing, benefits from the multistage process of planning, drafting, revising, and editing. In research writing, however, managing information and incorporating sources present special problems.

1 Planning the research process

After developing some sense of the range and amount of information available, write out a schedule of when you will do what. For example, plan a certain amount of time for trips to the library. If any of the books you need are checked out, allow time for the library to call those in. Arrange needed interviews well in advance, with time to reschedule in case a meeting has to be canceled. And allow enough time not only for writing but also for revising and editing. As you accomplish each task, you may want to check off that item in your plan or note the date. If you find yourself falling behind schedule or discover additional tasks to be accomplished, revise your plan.

WP TIP Use your online journal as a resource for recording and organizing your materials. Download any useful information from your online journal into any computer fields created for planning or drafting as well as researching.

■ WRITING 5: APPLICATION

On one page of your research log, design a research plan that includes both library and field investigations. In this plan, list sources you have already found as well as those you hope to find.

2 Researching a range of sources

To conduct any kind of research, you need to identify appropriate sources of information, consult and evaluate these sources, and take good notes recording the information you collect. You also need to understand how each source works as evidence.

Primary sources contain original material and raw information. **Secondary sources** report on, describe, interpret, or analyze someone else's work. For example, if you were exploring the development of a novelist's style, the novels themselves would be primary sources and other people's reviews and critical interpretations of the novels would be secondary sources. What constitutes a primary source will differ according to the field and your research question. For example, the novel *Moby Dick* is a primary source if you are studying it as literature and making claims about what it means. It is a secondary source if you are investigating nineteenth-century whaling and referring to chapters in it that contain descriptions of harpooning.

Most research essays use both primary and secondary sources. Primary sources ground the essay in firsthand knowledge and verifiable facts; secondary sources supply the context for your discussion and provide support for your own interpretation or argument.

Many research essays are based on library research, since libraries contain so much of the collective knowledge of the academic community. However, some of the most interesting research essays are based on **field research**. This research includes firsthand interviews with people who have expert knowledge of your subject. You can also conduct field research simply by being in the field, such as touring a local sewage treatment plant to observe the process. (See Chapter 15 for more on library research; see Chapter 16 for more on field research.)

3 Drafting a thesis statement

When you write your first draft, be sure to allow time for any needed further research. (See Chapter 17 for more information on using sources.)

You, not your audience, are the expert on your research topic, so plan to explain, define, and clarify new or unusual terms and concepts. To find out what your classmates and instructor already know, ask them to read and respond to your paper at several points during its development—for example, when you have a detailed outline or thesis and when you have completed your first draft.

In research writing, as in most writing, you need to tell your reader what you're up to. An **argumentative thesis statement** takes a position on an issue. (See Chapter 11.)

In order to reduce the annual number of violent deaths in the United States, Congress should pass a law to mandate a waiting period of ten days before all handguns can be purchased in this country.

An **informational thesis statement** presents information but does not advance one position over another. (See Chapter 10.)

Many American companies attempt to capitalize on Americans' concern for the environment by a variety of false advertising strategies.

If your research was argumentative, you probably began with a working thesis. If your research was informational, you probably began with a research question, and a working thesis evolved as you found answers.

Most research essays are long and complex enough that the thesis should be stated explicitly rather than left implicit.

TESTING YOUR THESIS STATEMENT

A good thesis statement not only helps readers understand your paper, it also helps you organize your thoughts and energies when writing. To draft a working thesis statement, ask yourself the following questions:

1. Is it interesting? An informational thesis should answer a question that is worth asking: *What tricks do advertisers use to mislead the public?* An argumentative thesis should take a position on a debatable issue and should include a proposal for change: *Mountain bikes should be allowed on wilderness trails.*

2. Is it precise and specific? Try to sharpen both your understanding of the thesis and the language you use to express it. Instead of arguing in favor of more access to the wilderness in general, argue for mountain bikes on specific wilderness trails.

3. Is it manageable? You may have collected more information than you can actually write about. If necessary, take this opportunity to narrow both the thesis and the paper you expect to write.

4. Does it adequately reflect my research and the expected shape of my paper? Your thesis should state the major point of your paper.

However, the thesis that ends up in your final paper may be different from the one you developed to help you write the paper. For example, after asking the four questions given in the box on p.193, Zoe developed this detailed statement as her thesis statement:

> To get an internship with a professional photographer in today's competitive and heavily commercialized market, you need to sell yourself effectively to busy people by developing a small and varied portfolio, making contact early and often, and demonstrating that you understand the unglamorous work involved.

In her paper, however, her explicit thesis focused on only part of this statement:

> I've learned the steps to setting up an internship: First, establish contact through writing a letter and sending a résumé, then push your portfolio.

Zoe developed her other points—about the competitive marketplace and the unglamorous work involved in being an assistant—elsewhere in her paper.

Many research essays give the thesis at the beginning, somewhere in the first or second paragraph, where it acts as a promise to the reader of what will follow (see 19c). Some research papers present the thesis at the end, where it acts as a conclusion or summary (see 11g). If you take the delayed-thesis approach, you still need to be sure that the topic and scope of your paper are clear to readers from the very beginning.

4 Revising

When drafting, you must follow your strongest research interests and try to answer the question you most care about. However, sometimes what began as informational research may become argumentative as the process of drafting the paper tips your original neutrality one way or another. Or a research investigation that starts out to prove a thesis may, as you draft, become a more neutral, informative paper of various perspectives, especially when multiple causes or complications surface in what had seemed a straightforward case.

The research process must remain flexible if it is to be vital and exciting. Keep an open mind when drafting, but when revising step back from your draft and assess just what direction your research paper is moving or has moved. Revise your paper to streamline all points and incorporate all source information to succeed in that direction.

Be ready to spend a great deal of time revising your draft, adding new research information, and incorporating sources smoothly into your prose. Such work takes a great deal of thought, and you'll want to revise your paper several times.

The revising stage of writing any paper is an important one. Consult Part V: Revising for helpful strategies on revising your draft.

5 Editing

Editing a research paper requires extra time. Not only should you check your own writing, but you should also pay special attention to where and how you use sources (see Chapter 17) and use the correct documentation style. (See Chapter 18.) The editing stage is also a good time to assess your use of quotations, paraphrase, and summary to make sure you have not misquoted or used a source without crediting it. (See 15e3.)

The editing process for any paper is covered in Part VI of this book; see Chapter 23 for details on how to strengthen your paper through editing.

For help in proofreading and formatting your final draft, see Chapter 56.

SUGGESTIONS FOR WRITING AND RESEARCH

INDIVIDUAL

I.   Select a research topic that interests you and write an exploratory draft about it. First, write out everything you already know about the topic. Second, write out everything you want to know about the topic. Third, identify experts you can talk to. Finally, make a list of questions you need answered. Plan to put this paper through a process that includes not only planning, drafting, revising, and editing but also locating, evaluating, and using sources.

2.   Keeping in mind the research topic you developed in assignment 1 above, visit the library and conduct a search of available resources. What do you find? Where do you find it? Show your questions to a reference librarian and ask what additional elec-

tronic databases he or she would suggest. Finally, don't forget the Internet, an ever-expanding source of information on virtually any topic you can think of. (Before you go much further, read Chapter 15.)

3. After completing assignments 1 and 2 above, find a person who knows something about your topic and ask him or her for leads about doing further research: Whom else would this person recommend you speak with? What books or articles would he or she recommend? What's the first thing this expert would do to find out information? Finally, look for a "virtual" person, someone available through an e-mail Listserv or on the Internet with whom you might chat to expand your knowledge. (See 15c for help here, and read Chapter 16.)

COLLABORATIVE

1. Join with a classmate or classmates to write a collaborative research essay. Develop plans for dividing tasks among members of the group.

2. After completing a collaborative research essay, write a short report in which you explain the collaborative strategies your group used and evaluate their usefulness.

Libraries are the heart—or perhaps the head—of the academic community. They provide the primary knowledge base that allows professors to teach and to conduct research in their fields. They also provide students with the sources of information that allow them to investigate any area of study.

The modern library is complex and multifaceted; you should visit your college library early and get to know it well. At first, a college library may appear intimidating, but the more you use it, the more friendly it will become.

And while you're at it, plan to learn about the electronic library of the twenty-first century, the **Internet**. Learn its entrance and exit points, its resource rooms and reference desks, and how to navigate and browse, to answer and ask. (See 15c for a detailed tour of the Internet.)

15 **a** Planning library research

To learn about the library, you need to go there, walk slowly through it, read the signs that identify special rooms and departments, poke your nose into nooks and crannies, and browse through a few books or magazines. If there is an introductory video explaining the library, pause to see it. If there is a self-paced or guided tour, take it. Read informational handouts and pamphlets. Be sure to locate the following:

The **book catalog**, computerized or on cards, that tells you which books your library owns and where they are located.

The **book stacks**, where books, periodicals, and pamphlets are stored.

The **circulation desk**, where you check out and reserve books and get information on procedures and resources.

The **periodical room**, which houses current issues of magazines, journals, and newspapers.

The **reference room**, which contains general reference works such as dictionaries and encyclopedias along with guides and indexes to more specific sources of information.

 SUGGESTIONS FOR TALKING WITH LIBRARIANS

1. Before you ask for help, try to answer your questions yourself.

2. Bring with you a copy of the research assignment.

3. Be ready to explain the assignment in your own words: purpose, format, length, number of sources, and due date.

4. Identify any special requirements about sources: Should information come from government documents? Rare books? Films?

5. Describe the particular topic you are researching and the tentative question you have framed to address the topic.

6. Describe any work you have done so far: books read, periodicals looked at, log entries written, people interviewed, and so on.

To take full advantage of library resources, keep the following suggestions in mind.

Visit the library early and often. As soon as you receive a research assignment, visit the library to find out what resources are available for your project, and plan to return often. Even if your initial research indicates a wealth of material on your topic, you may not be able to find everything the first time you look. A book you need may be checked out, or your library may not subscribe to a periodical containing important information, and you may need to order it on interlibrary loan, a process that takes some time.

Prepare to take notes. If you take careful notes from the sources you find, you will save yourself time and write a better paper. Bring index cards to the library—3″ × 5″ cards for bibliographical information and 4″ × 6″ cards for notes—from your first visit on. (See 15e for more on note taking.) Also keep a research log. Writing in it as you work on your research project will help you find ideas to research, plan your course of action, pose and solve problems related to your topic, and keep track of where you have been so far. (See 14d for more on research logs.)

Check general sources before specific ones. During your first or second visit to the library, check general sources—dictionaries, encyclopedias, atlases, and yearbooks—for information about your topic. (See 15b.) An hour or two spent with these general sources will give you a quick overview of the scope and range of your topic and will lead you to more specific information.

Ask for help. Talk to librarians. At first you might show them your assignment and describe your topic and your research plans; later you might ask them for help in finding a particular source or ask if they know of any sources that you have not checked yet. Keep in mind, however, that reference librarians are busy people; don't ask questions that you haven't tried to answer for yourself.

 PLANNING LIBRARY RESEARCH

- **Go to the library early.** Find and use resources on your subject as soon as you can because they might not be readily available.

- **Prepare to take notes**. Take careful notes the first time around so you won't have to retrieve the sources again to pick up bibliographic information.

- **Keep a research log**. Write in your research log as you work to help you keep track of what you've already done and what you still have to do.

- **Consult general sources before specific ones**. On your first visit, check general sources—dictionaries, encyclopedias, atlases, and yearbooks—for a quick overview of your topic and for guidance in locating additional sources.

- **Talk to library personnel**. Describe your assignment to your reference librarian and ask for help finding sources. Librarians often know about sources you don't—it's their job.

■ **WRITING 1: EXPLORATION**

Visit your college library and locate the areas and materials discussed in this section. Then look for a comfortable place, sit down, and write about which of these might be of most use to you as you begin a research project. Then conduct a similar tour of Gopher-space or the World Wide Web via your computer and construct a map of what such space looks like (see 15c for help).

15 b   Finding sources of information

Most of the information you need will be contained in reference books, other books, and periodicals (journals, magazines, and newspapers). Reference books are fairly easy to locate: there are relatively few of them and they are usually placed in one room or section of the library. However, even a moderately sized college library owns hundreds of thousands of books and periodicals. To simplify the researcher's task of finding the relevant ones, bibliographies and indexes have been developed. These resources either indicate which books or articles have been published on a given topic or present comprehensive lists of sources in an easy-to-use format. Once you know which book or periodical might be useful, you still need to find it. The library's catalogs tell you whether it owns the source. To find and use all these resources efficiently, follow this five-step process:

1   Consult general reference works to gain background information and basic facts. (See 15b1.)

2   Consult bibliographies and indexes to learn which books, periodicals, and articles are relevant. (See 15b2.)

3   Consult computerized databases. (See 15b3.)

4   Consult your library's catalogs to see if it owns the books and periodicals you want. (See 15b4.)

5   Consult other sources as needed. (See 15b5.)

Searching through indexes, databases, and catalogs is much easier if you have identified the key words for your research topic. A **key word** is an important word describing your topic—either a word for the topic itself, a word for the general subject, or a word describing constituent parts of the topic.

Key words are sometimes nothing more than authors' names or titles of books. For example, key words for a research paper investigating the pottery of Native Americans in the western United States could include *Indian*, *art*, and *California*. The key words you select can mean the difference between success and failure. For example, a search including the word *Sioux* might turn up nothing, but a search including the word *Dakota* (the preferred term for this group) might result in a number of sources. To find good key words for your topic, consult the *Library of Congress Subject Headings*.

1 Reference works

General reference works provide background information and basic facts about a topic. The summaries, overviews, and definitions in these sources can help you decide whether to pursue a topic further and where to turn next for information. The information in these sources is necessarily general and will not be sufficient by itself as the basis for most research projects; you will need to consult specialized sources as well. General reference works do not make strong sources to cite in research papers.

Specialized reference works contain detailed and technical information in a particular field or discipline. They often contain articles by well-known authorities and sometimes have bibliographies and cross-references that can lead to other sources. Two useful guides to finding specialized reference books are *Guide to Reference Books*, edited by Eugene P. Sheehy (10th ed., 1986) and *Walford's Guide to Reference Material* (4th ed., 1980–86).

While many reference works are published as books, increasingly they are available on CD-ROM. The following lists suggest common and useful references, although there are many more in each category.

Almanacs and yearbooks. Almanacs and yearbooks provide up-to-date information on politics, agriculture, economics, and population along with statistical facts of all kinds.

Facts on File: News Digest (1941–present). A summary and index to current events reported in newspapers worldwide. (Also CD-ROM, 1980–present.)

Statesman's Year-Book (1863–present). Annual statistics about government, agriculture, population, religion, and so on for countries throughout the world.

World Almanac and Book of Facts (1868–present). Review of important events of the past year as well as data on a wide variety of topics, including sports, government, science, business, and education.

Atlases. Atlases such as the *Hammond Atlas*, the *National Geographic Atlas of the World*, and the *New York Times Atlas of the World* can help you identify places anywhere in the world and provide information on population, climate, and industry.

Biographical dictionaries. Biographical dictionaries contain information on people who have made some mark on history in many different fields; biographical indexes tell you how to locate additional sources.

> *Contemporary Authors* (1967–present). Contains short biographies of authors who have published during the year.
>
> *Current Biography* (1940–present). Contains articles and photographs of people in the news.
>
> *Who's Who in America* (1899–present). The standard biographical reference for living Americans.

Dictionaries. Dictionaries contain definitions and histories of words along with information on their correct usage. (See 31b.)

Encyclopedias. Encyclopedias provide elementary information, explanations, and definitions of virtually every topic, concept, country, institution, historical person or movement, and cultural artifact imaginable. One-volume works such as the *Random House Encyclopedia* and *The New Columbia Encyclopedia* give brief overviews. Larger works such as *Collier's Encyclopedia* (24 volumes) and the *New Encyclopedia Britannica* (32 volumes) contain more detailed information.

Specialized reference works. Although these works provide information that is more detailed and technical than that found in general reference works, you should still use them primarily for exploratory research and background information. Each discipline has many reference works; here is a small sampling.

LANGUAGES AND LITERATURE

Cassell's Encyclopedia of World Literature
Handbook to Literature
McGraw-Hill Encyclopedia of World Drama
Oxford Companion to American Literature

HUMANITIES

Cambridge Ancient History
Dictionary of the Bible
Encyclopedia of American History
Encyclopedia of Philosophy
Encyclopedia of Religion
Encyclopedia of World History
New Grove Dictionary of Music and Musicians
Oxford Companion to Art

SOCIAL SCIENCES

Dictionary of Education
Encyclopedia of Anthropology
Encyclopedia of Crime and Justice
Encyclopedia of Psychology
Encyclopedia of Social Work
International Encyclopedia of the Social Sciences
Political Handbook and Atlas of the World

SCIENCES

Encyclopedia of Biological Sciences
Encyclopedia of Chemistry
Encyclopedia of Computer Science and Technology
Encyclopedia of Physics
Larousse Encyclopedia of Animal Life
McGraw-Hill Dictionary of Science and Technology

BUSINESS

Encyclopedia of Banking and Finance
Encyclopedia of Economics
McGraw-Hill Dictionary of Modern Economics

■ WRITING 2: APPLICATION

Look up information on your research topic, using at least three of the reference sources described in this section.

2 Bibliographies and indexes

Bibliographies and indexes are tools: they help you locate books and periodicals that contain the information you need. Periodicals consist of magazines, journals, and newspapers, which are published at set periods throughout the year. They focus on particular areas of interest, and their information is more current than that found in books. Because so many periodical issues are published each year and because every issue can contain dozens of articles on various topics, using a periodical index or database is essential to finding the article you need.

Many bibliographies and indexes are available in electronic form, either through an **online service** (which your library's computers access through a telephone line and a modem) or on a **CD-ROM disk** (a storage device much like a floppy disk, which can be read by a computer).

Bibliographies

Bibliographies list books alphabetically by title, by author, or by subject. Many books include a bibliography of the works consulted by the author in researching the book; always consult the bibliography of a book you have found helpful. Other bibliographies are published separately as reference tools. Some of the most useful are listed here.

> *Bibliographic Index: A Cumulative Bibliography of Bibliographies.* New York: Wilson, 1938–present. This index lists the page numbers of bibliographies in books over a wide variety of subjects. Such bibliographies provide you with lists of related sources already compiled by another author on a subject similar to your own.

> *Books in Print.* New York: Bowker, 1948–present. The latest edition of this yearly index lists by author, subject, and title all books currently in print. It is also available online and on CD-ROM.

> *MLA Bibliography of Books and Articles in the Modern Languages and Literature* (1921–present). This is also available online and on CD-ROM.

> *Paperbound Books in Print.* This semiannual index lists paperback books currently in print by author, subject, and title. It is also available online and on CD-ROM.

Indexes

Indexes are guides to the material published within works, sometimes within books but more often within periodicals. Each index covers a particular group of periodicals. Make sure that the index you select contains the journals, magazines, and newspapers that you want to use as sources.

Indexes list works alphabetically by author or by subject. To conduct an effective subject search, use the key words you have identified for your topic. Check under every subject heading that might be relevant. Many periodicals use the subject headings in the *Library of Congress Subject Headings*, but others use their own lists.

Most indexes are available both in printed and computerized forms. Many are also available on microfiche or microfilm—media that simulate the printed page but must be read on special machines. Indexes in book form are usually the most comprehensive; those presented on microfilm, microfiche, and computer usually cover only the past ten or twenty years.

Computerized indexes allow you to focus your search strategy most effectively. By combining key words in certain ways, you can have the computer generate a list of works that closely match your topic. For example, if your research topic is the art of the Dakota Indians, you might search for all works with the key word *Dakota* in their subject description. This search would result in hundreds of works, not only on art but on politics, economics, history, and many other topics. Something similar would happen if you searched for *art*. But if you search for *Dakota* and *art*, the computer will list only those works with both words in their subject descriptions, a much more useful list for your research topic. You can also combine key words using *or*. Searching for *Dakota* and *art or fiction* would result in a list of works that have the word *Dakota* in their subject descriptions, some of which also have *art* and some of which also have *fiction*.

General periodical indexes. These indexes list articles published in a variety of periodicals of interest to the general public. Some are listed here.

Infotrac. This monthly index, available only on CD-ROM, contains three separate indexes. The *Academic Index* covers nearly 1,000 commonly used scholarly publications. The *General Periodical Index* covers over 1,000 general-interest publications. The *Newspaper Index* covers large-circulation newspapers. Many entries include summaries.

New York Times Index (1851–present). This bimonthly index lists every article that appears in the *New York Times*. Short summaries are provided for many articles. It is also available online.

Readers' Guide to Periodical Literature (1900–present). This semimonthly index lists articles in over 200 magazines of general interest, such as *Newsweek*, *Popular Science*, and *Rolling Stone*. Online and CD-ROM versions are also available (1983–present).

Specialized periodical indexes. These indexes list articles in periodicals in specific disciplines or fields of interest. They are usually much more helpful than general indexes for college-level research. Here are some of the most common.

America: History and Life
Applied Science and Technology Index
Art Index
Biological and Agricultural Index
Business Periodicals Index
Dissertation Abstracts International

Education Index
Essay and General Literature Index
General Science Index
Humanities Index
Index to Legal Periodicals
Music Index
Psychological Index
Social Science Index

3 Computerized resources

Databases are large collections of electronically stored information that function like indexes. Often they provide summaries in addition to bibliographic information on the sources they list; occasionally they contain copies of the sources themselves. Databases can be either online or on CD-ROM. Many library catalogs today are computerized as well, in the form of **online databases**. (For more on how to use these sources, see 15c.)

DIALOG database

A major online system commonly found in college libraries is DIALOG, which keeps track of more than a million sources of information. DIALOG offers many specialized databases, 987 of which are currently listed in the manual *DIALOG Blue Sheets*. Some of the most commonly used databases within DIALOG are Arts and Humanities Search (1980–present), ERIC (Educational Resources Information Center, 1965–present), PsychINFO (1967–present), Scisearch (1974–present), and Social Scisearch (1972–present). You must decide which specialized database you need before you begin your search.

DIALOG and other search services are available online. To use an online database, you usually need the assistance of a reference librarian, who will ask you to fill out a form listing the key words you have identified for your project. The library is charged a fee for each search, calculated according to the time spent and the number of entries retrieved. Some libraries have the person requesting the search pay the fee; others limit the time allotted for each search. Be sure to ask what your library's policy is.

Some databases, including some of the specialized databases within DIALOG, are also available on CD-ROM. You can usually search through these databases without the aid of a librarian.

Internet links

Don't forget, as well, that Internet-to-library and library-to-library links (e.g., OhioLink) make exploring the vast resources of libraries such as Harvard's or Michigan's almost as quick and easy as finding a book in your campus library's electronic catalog.

WP TIP Whenever possible, print out the results of your computer searches so that you have accurate records and useful information when you start to create your working bibliography.

■ WRITING 3: APPLICATION

Use one of the bibliographies, indexes, or databases described in this section to find information on a relevant book or periodical. Locate the work, and take notes on the usefulness of the source and the process you used to obtain it.

4 The library catalog

The library catalog lists every book a library owns; many libraries also catalog their periodicals. At one time all catalogs were card catalogs, with the information printed on small cards and stored in drawers. Several decades ago, many libraries began transferring their catalogs to the more convenient microfiche and microfilm. These simulate the printed cards in a card catalog but can easily be duplicated and require much less space. More recently, libraries began computerizing their catalogs, which are now known as online catalogs (or circulation computers). Often online catalogs can be accessed through telephone lines and modems from locations outside the library.

Regardless of the format, all catalogs provide the same basic information. They list books by author, title, and subject; provide basic information about its physical format and content; and tell you where in the library to find it.

During the course of your research project, you will probably use the library catalog in two different ways. Sometimes you will already know the title of a work you want to find. The catalog can confirm that your library owns the work and can tell you where to find it. At other times you will use the catalog as you would an index or a database, searching for works that are relevant to your topic; this process is called *browsing*. Online catalogs are particu-

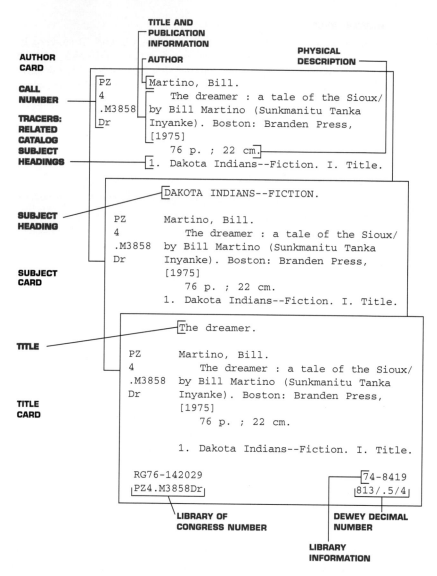

Cards from a card catalog

larly good for browsing and usually have several special features designed to facilitate it.

Even if you discover that your library doesn't own the source you want, don't despair. Many libraries can obtain a work owned by another library through an interlibrary loan, although this usually takes a few days. Ask your librarian.

Consulting online catalogs

Online catalog systems vary slightly from library to library, though all systems follow the same general principles. Locating works through author and title is much like the corresponding procedure with a card catalog, with one important exception: most online catalogs allow you to search with partial information. For example, if you know that the title of a novel begins with the words *Love Medicine* but you can't remember the rest of it, you can ask the catalog computer to search for the title *Love Medicine*. It will present you with a list of all works that begin with those words.

```
Search Request: T=LOVE MEDICINE
Search Results: 4 Entries Found                    Title Index
 -----------------------------------------------------------T257
1  LOVE MEDICINE: A NOVEL.   ERDRICH LOUISE <1984>   (BH)

   LOVE MEDICINE AND MIRACLES
2    SIEGEL BERNIE S <1986>   (BH)
3    SIEGEL BERNIE S <1988>   (DA)

   LOVE MEDICINE AND MIRACLES LESSONS LEARNED ABOUT SELFHEALING
   FROM A SURGEON'S EXPERIENCE WITH EXCEPTIONAL PATIENTS
4    SIEGEL BERNIE S <1986>   (BH)

 ---------------------------------------------------------
COMMANDS:    Type line # to see individual record
             O  Other options
             H  Help

NEXT COMMAND:
```

Results of a title search in an online catalog

Most online catalogs also allow you to perform key word searches, much like the searches conducted on computerized databases. The advantage of this kind of search is that the computer can search all three categories (author, title, and subject) at once. To perform a key word search, use the words you've identified as describing your topic, linked by *and* or *or* as appropriate. (See 15b3.) For example, if you're trying to research fictional accounts of Dakota Indians, you can search for *Dakota Indians* and *fiction*. The computer will present you with a list of works that fit that description. As with all computer searches, making your key word search request as specific as possible will result in the most useful list.

```
Search Request: T=LOVE MEDICINE
BOOK - Record 1 of 5 Entries Found                      Long View
---------------------Screen 1 of 1---------------------T259
Author:        Erdrich, Louise.
Title:         Love medicine : a novel
Edition:       1st ed.
Published:     New York : Holt, Rinehart, and Winston, c1984.
Description:   viii, 275 p. ; 22cm.
Subjects(LC):  Indians of North America--North Dakota--Fiction.

-----------------------------------------------------------
     LOCATION:          CALL NUMBER              STATUS
1    Halley Stacks      PS3555.R42 L6 1984       Not checked out


COMMANDS:       P   Previous screen
                O   Other options
                H   Help

NEXT COMMAND:
```

Full information on a book in an online catalog

Once you have found your book, you can ask the online catalog to provide complete information on it. For the most part, this is the same information you would see in the card catalog. However, many online catalogs also show circulation information, letting you know whether the book is checked out.

Using call numbers

Once you have determined through the catalog that your library owns a book you want to consult, use the book's call number to locate it in the stacks. Most academic libraries use the Library of Congress system, whose call numbers begin with letters. Some libraries still use the older Dewey Decimal system, whose call numbers consist entirely of numbers. In either case, the first letters or numbers in a call number indicate the general subject area. Because libraries shelve all books for a general subject area together, this portion of the call number tells you where in the library to find the book you want.

Be sure to copy a book's call number exactly as it appears in the catalog. Most libraries have open stacks, allowing you to retrieve the book yourself; one wrong number or letter could lead you to the wrong part of the library. If your library has closed stacks, you will need to give the call number to a librarian, who will retrieve the book for you; the wrong call number will get you the wrong book.

■ WRITING 4: APPLICATION

Use the library's catalog to see what holdings the library has on your topic. Retrieve one of these books from the stacks, and check to see if it contains a bibliography that could lead you to other books. Record these findings in your research log.

5 Other sources of information

Many libraries own materials other than books and periodicals. Often these do not circulate. If you think one of the sources listed here might contain information relevant to your research, ask a librarian about your library's holdings.

Government documents. The U.S. government publishes numerous reports, pamphlets, catalogs, and newsletters on most issues of national concern. Reference books that can lead you to these sources include the *Monthly Catalogue of United States Government Publications* (monthly) and the *United States Government Publications Index*, both available on CD-ROM and online.

Nonprint media. Records, audiocassettes, videotapes, slides, photographs, and other media are generally cataloged separately from book and periodical collections.

Pamphlets. Pamphlets and brochures published by government agencies and private organizations are generally stored in a library's vertical file. The *Vertical File Index: A Subject and Title Index to Selected Pamphlet Material* (1932/35–present) lists many of the available titles.

Special collections. Rare books, manuscripts, and items of local interest are commonly found in a special room or section of the library.

■ **WRITING 5: APPLICATION**

Identify one relevant source of information in your library's holdings other than a book or periodical. Locate it and take notes on the usefulness of the source and the process you used to obtain it.

15 c   Using electronic sources

In recent years, computers, compact disks, modems, and computer networks have put a vast array of information sources within easy reach. Once libraries began to put their card catalogs on computers, it wasn't long before those libraries and other institutions began to make their resources available for remote searching via networked or modem-linked computer.

Through this technology, you can use a personal computer—or a terminal in your school's library—to find books, articles, statistics, and government reports. You can also find people who are knowledgeable about your subject. And you can conduct your research and find these people not just in your school's library, not just on your campus, but literally all over the world.

Computer-assisted research has developed special tools and a jargon all its own—*online, browser, ftp, gopher, Archie, Web search, download*—but the basic activities are the same things you do in a physical library. You identify, retrieve, and examine documents. Using electronic mail, newsgroups, and listservs, you can also communicate with people who know about or share your interest in your subject.

You can find and retrieve documents by using an **online catalog**, searching a **CD-ROM database**, logging on to an **access port** (a computer's telephone connection) at a university library or bulletin board system, exploring an **online service** such as CompuServe or America OnLine, or "surfing" the global network of computer interconnections known as the **Internet** (**'Net**).

Whichever you use, there is nothing magic about information transferred over a computer. You will need the same critical skills you use to evaluate printed materials, although the clues may be harder to understand when you find documents online. Is the author identified? Is that person a professional in the field or an interested amateur? What are his or her biases likely to be? Does the document you have located represent an individual's opinion or peer-reviewed research?

```
SilverPlatter 3.11 Journal Articles (1/74 - 12/86)  F10=Commands
                                                     F1=Help
-------------------------------------------------------------------
                                                          1 of 3
TI: Teacher expressiveness: More important for male teachers than
female teachers?
AU: Basow.-Susan-A.; Distenfeld, -M.-Suzan
IN: Lafayette Coll
JN: Journal of-Educational-Psychology; 1985 Feb Vol 77(1) 45-52
AB: 55 male and 62 female undergraduates viewed a videotape of a
male or female actor giving a short lecture using expressive or
nonexpressive communication and rated each teacher on a 22-item
questionnaire that yielded 5 factors (Rapport, Student Orientation,
Stimulates Interest, Organization, and Knowledge of Material).
Findings show that the expressive teacher received the highest student
evaluations on the basis of a global evaluation score and on the 5
factor scores.  The nonexpressive male teacher received low ratings
on Organization and Stimulating Interest.  55 who viewed this tape
also had the poorest performance on a subsequent test.  55 who viewed
a nonexpressive female teacher had the highest performance on the
content test. It is hypothesized that differential attention as a
function of the sex-role-appropriate characteristics is a mediating
variable. It is suggested that in studies of teaching performance and
-------------------------------------------------------------------
MENU: Mark Record Select Search Term Options Find Print Download

Press ENTER to Mark records for PRINT or DOWNLOAD.
Use PgDn and PgUp to scroll.
```

Partial entry in a CD-ROM database

Many colleges and universities provide sophisticated Internet access and other computerized resources for their students and faculty. Whether or not you have your own computer, your school's computer department or library staff can help you learn computer-assisted research techniques.

1 Understanding online sources

A **host computer**—one that shares its files with other computers—keeps its information in the form of a **database**. A database is merely a structured collection of related information. You are familiar with noncomputerized databases of many kinds: the phone book, your file drawer, a library's physical card catalog. Be it a university catalog, a listing of magazine articles, or a compilation of government reports, a computer database is a familiar idea in electronic form. Whether they contain graphics files or magazine articles, computer databases are often organized like file cabinets, with a hierarchy of folders divided by subject.

Some databases are merely guides to where to find information. For example, a **bibliographic database**, like the card catalog of a library, lists articles or books by title, subject, and author, but it does not contain any text. An **abstract database** contains brief summaries of the articles it lists, which can help you tell which articles might be most valuable to you. However, when researching, you cannot rely on summaries for information, too much is lost in the process of summarizing.

A **full-text database** often contains the complete text of the articles it lists. But beware: Some texts are abbreviated when they are stored on the computer, and others omit accompanying information such as sidebars or graphics. Also, depending on how you are accessing the data, you may have to pay to retrieve the full text of an article.

2 Searching online

A detailed discussion of the technical aspects of online research is beyond the scope of this book. However, an understanding of the basic online search tools and techniques will help you get started.

The basic tools discussed here are those used on the Internet, the vast "network of networks" that connects computers all over the globe. Many online services such as CompuServe, America Online, Prodigy, and Campus Networks allow you to use these tools or variations of them, and they also have their own internal resources you can search. But the Internet tools are the most powerful and the most general, and they give access to the broadest range of resources.

WP TIP   Be sure to download any useful information you obtain from Internet or Web sources.

Electronic mail

Once you have an electronic address yourself, such as *president@whitehouse.gov* or *AHayakawa@aol.com* or *scribe@stonehouse.microserve.com*, you can send electronic messages to any of millions of people around the world, and they in turn can write to you. **E-mail** is so fast that its users have taken to referring to the U.S. Postal Service as "snail mail."

Unlike receiving junk mail, being on an Internet mailing list is voluntary. This mailing list is a system, usually automated, that distributes messages to people interested in a particular topic. If you send mail to the list, everyone on the list will get a copy. A good mailing list for people interested in computer-assisted research is *carr-l* (computer-assisted reporting and research list). To subscribe to the list in digest form (recommended), send e-mail to *listserve@ulkyvm.bitnet* containing the words *subscribe carr-l "yourname"* where "yourname" is your real name. Notice that the address to which you send subscription requests will be different from the return address that appears on the mail itself. Anything you mail to the return address will be posted (distributed) to the entire list.

Newsgroups

Whatever subject you are interested in, there probably is a **newsgroup**—a sort of public bulletin board of comments, questions, and responses—devoted to the discussion of it. Almost every online service and Internet provider offers access to newsgroups, which are also called **usenet groups**. You can learn about how they work by joining the groups called *news.announce.newusers, news.newusers.questions,* and *news.answers.* Newsgroups range from the scholarly (*sci.engr.biomed*) to the recreational (*rec.music.reggae*) to the weird and sardonic (*alt.barney.die.die.die*)

Asking a question of a mailing list or a newsgroup is a great way to get information and find people who can help you. One brief caution is in order: spend some time quietly reading the group's discussion (this is called *lurking*) before you post. Most newsgroups have files called *FAQs* (frequently asked questions, pronounced "facks"), which you should read before posting a message to the group. Make sure you are asking the right group and posing an informed question, not overlooking something answered in the first paragraph of a FAQ you haven't read. An ill-considered posting may get you *flamed*—scolded by e-mail—by 'Net veterans famed for their impatience with *newbies.* Don't worry; everyone was new once.

Internet utilities

Here are the most common Internet tools for finding and retrieving information. They are programs commonly installed on library computers and readily available for your own computer. Many are public-domain or shareware programs that you can download from sites on the 'Net. Most major online services offer version of these tools as well.

telnet. Through telnet you can *log on* or attach your computer to a remote computer (host) so that your computer acts like a terminal on the remote system, able to read directories, copy files, and in some cases even give commands to the host system. A great telnet site is *fedworld.gov*, a gateway to dozens of electronic sources within the federal government.

ftp. File transfer protocol is used to copy files—text, graphics, or software—from a remote computer to yours. A computer that accepts ftp sign-ons is called an *ftp site*. For example, at *ftp://whitehouse.gov* you can find a raft of information on pending legislation, presidential speeches, political topics, even the full text of the North American Free Trade Agreement. Many ftp sites allow you to log in with the user i.d. "anonymous" or "guest" and your own user i.d. as a password.

WP TIP   When using online sources, remember that you'll need to document these sources as well. Obtain the information you need to create a working bibliography in the documentation style you are using.

Archie. The first of several comic-book characters on the Internet, Archie searches file archives, such as ftp sites, looking for file names that match either a complete or a partial file name that you specify. If you know or have a good guess at the name of a file you want, Archie can come in handy. To use Archie, you have to telnet to an Archie site, such as *archie.internic.net* or *archie.rutgers.udu.*

Gopher. This is a search program on a remote computer, one which finds and sorts files from various Internet sites so you can easily browse through them. Once you see a file you want, the gopher handles all the details of fetching and displaying it for you to read, save, or print. Named for the lowly office minion asked to "go for" coffee and run other errands, it was developed at the University of Minnesota (the gopher state!). There are thousands of **gopher servers**; each is a little different and may retrieve a different selection of information. Two gophers you may want to try are *gopher://psulias.psu.edu* (Pennsylvania State University) and *gopher://gopher2.tc.umn.edu* (The University of Minnesota).

Veronica. Archie's friend from the comic strip can help you search gopher menus by using keywords and the Boolean logic of *and, or,* and *not.* For example, you can ask Veronica to find "*amphibians* and *endangered* not *Africa*" and the program will return references to endangered amphibians on all other continents.

Veronica appears as a menu selection on many gophers. Try, for example, *gopher://veronica.scs.unr.edu/11/veronica.*

World Wide Web. While the rest of the 'Net is primarily text-based, the Web employs text, pictures, graphics, and limited typographical design. The result is so visual that each file is called a **Web page**. The magic of the Web is that each page is linked to others by a technique called **hypertext**, so that by pointing and clicking at specially defined **links**, you can choose alternative paths through text, such as cross-references or explanatory materials. If the boldface words in this paragraph were hypertext links, for example, clicking on each of them would take you to a

---

U.S. Geological Survey

Click on an image to visit topics in geology, mapping, and water resources, or search for any topic.

....

Information about ordering USGS products!

....

Welcome to the U.S. Geological Survey, a bureau of the Department of the Interior. USGS is the Nation's largest earth science research and information agency.

- What's NEW
- USGS News Releases
- General Information
- USGS Fact Sheets
- USGS by Theme
- The Learning Web
- Publications and Data Products
- Internet Resources

U.S. Geological Survey, MS804 National Center, Reston, VA 22092, USA
URL http://www.usgs.gov/index.html
Comments and feedback: webmaster@www.usgs.gov
Last modification: 05-06-96@08:45 (mjh)

Web page from a U.S. government site

related page. To read Web pages, you need a **browser** program such as Netscape, Mosaic, or Microsoft Internet Explorer. The Web is also searchable; you can use Web Crawler, Web Worm, Yahoo, or any number of Web tools to search for keywords in Web addresses, headings, or text. One example of a Web page is *http://www.nando.net*, the Raleigh News & Observer's excellent Web newspaper. Another, *http://www.microserve.com/~scribe*, is Alan's home page. A third example, the Web Worm, is *http://www.cs.colorado.edu/home/mcbryan/WWWW.html*. One of the best-known and best-updated lists of Internet resources is *Yanoff's List*, maintained by Internet consultant Scott Yanoff. Its Web address is *http://www.uwm.edu/Mirror/inet.services.html*.

WP TIP If you use the Web in your research, create an electronic "bookmark" for every important Web page to help you retrieve it quickly for reference. Remember, in your paper you must cite Web pages according to the documentation style you are using.

15 d Reading library sources critically

You will uncover many sources through your library research, but not all of them will be equally useful. So that you don't waste time and energy taking careful notes on sources that contain unimportant or unreliable information, make sure to read each source critically by previewing, responding, and reviewing. (See 2b.)

First, *preview* the source to get a general sense of it, to determine whether the source is related closely enough to your topic to be useful, and to decide whether to read further. If you determine that the source will be useful, read it more carefully and take notes on it. Critical reading at this stage consists of *responding*—entering into a conversation with a text while you read—and *reviewing*—coming to a critical understanding of the text as a whole.

Reviewing to evaluate is particularly important when you are writing a research essay, since you are trying to determine the worth or validity of the text and the information it contains. If you determine that a source is irrelevant, unreliable, or out of date, you'll need to find a new one. Because you want to know this as soon as possible, make the effort to evaluate each source continually: when reading, when taking notes, and when considering how to incorporate the source into your final paper.

EVALUATING LIBRARY SOURCES

The more you research, the more expert you become at determining whether a source is useful. When in doubt, confer with your instructor or a librarian. Here are some questions to ask yourself.

Subject. Is the subject directly related to my research question? Does it provide information that supports my view? Does it provide helpful context or background information? Does it contain quotations or facts that I will want to quote in my paper?

Author. What do I already know about the author's reputation? Does the book or periodical provide any biographical information? Is this author cited by other sources? Am I aware of any biases that might limit the author's credibility?

Date. When was this source published? Do my field and topic require current, up-to-date sources? Or would classic, well-established sources be more credible?

Publisher. Who published this source? Is it a major publisher, a university press, or a scholarly organization that would subject material to a rigorous review procedure?

Counterauthority. Does the source address or present counterarguments on issues I intend to discuss or take? Each point of view is essential for examining an issue completely.

You can get expert help in evaluating books by consulting book reviews. To avoid a hit-and-miss search, consult one of the several indexes that identify where and when a book was reviewed.

Book Review Index. This bimonthly index lists reviews of major books published in several hundred periodicals.

Current Book Review Citations. This annual index lists reviews published in more than 1000 periodicals.

 WRITING 6: APPLICATION

For at least one source you are considering for your research paper, consult one of the book review indexes listed in this section. Look up some of these reviews and take careful notes.

15 **e** **Taking notes**

Taking good notes will make the whole research process easier, enabling you to locate and remember sources and helping you use them effectively in your writing. For short research projects requiring only a few sources, it is easy to take careful notes in a research log or class notebook and refer to them as needed when writing your paper. Or you can photocopy whole articles or chapters and take them home for further study. However, for any research project requiring more than a few sources, you should develop a card-based system for recording your sources and the information you find.

1 Developing a working bibliography

When you locate a useful source, write all the information necessary to find that source again on a 3″ × 5″ index card, using a separate card for each work. If you create bibliographic cards as you go along, then at the end you can easily arrange them in alphabetical order and prepare your reference list. (For complete information on how to record bibliographic information using the appropriate documentation style, see MLA, APA, or other documentation conventions.)

It is also easy to create bibliographic cards right on your computer, including all relevant information (see box) in briefly defined filespace (some word processing programs make card shapes on the screen to emulate the restricted space of 3″ × 5″ or 4″ × 6″ file cards). The obvious advantage of electronic card entries is that they can be sorted and alphabetized to provide a typed draft of your reference page at the end of your paper.

Annotate your bibliography cards right from the start, noting the source, its point of view, information, or possible use later on. Otherwise, it's easy to forget what each source has to offer.

2 Creating note cards

Make note cards to record the relevant information found in your sources. When writing a research essay, you will be working from these note cards, so be sure they contain all the information you need from every source you intend to use. Also try to focus them on your research question, so that their relevance is clear when you read them later.

INFORMATION TO BE RECORDED ON BIBLIOGRAPHIC CARDS

FOR BOOKS

1. Call number or other location information
2. Full name(s) of author(s)
3. Full title and subtitle
4. Edition or volume number
5. Editor or translator
6. Place of publication
7. Publisher and date of publication
8. Inclusive page numbers for relevant sections in longer works

FOR PERIODICALS

1. Full name(s) of author(s)
2. Full title and subtitle of article
3. Periodical title
4. Periodical volume and number
5. Periodical date
6. Inclusive page numbers of article
7. Library call number or other location information

To have as much room as possible on each and every note card, use 4″ × 6″ index cards. For bibliography cards, use 3″ × 5″. These different sizes will also help keep the two sets separate. (Or put notes on the smaller cards to practice condensing ideas; put bibliographic references on the larger cards, using the extra space for annotations.) A typical note card should contain only one piece of information or one idea. This system will allow you to arrange and rearrange the information in different ways as you write. At the top of each note card, identify the source through brief bibliographic identification (author and title), and note the page numbers on which the information appears. Many writers also include the category of information—a particular theme, subject, or argument for which the note provides support. Personal notes, including ideas for possible use of the information or cross-references to other information, should be clearly distinguished from material that comes from the source; they might be put at the bottom in parentheses.

```
                                                                    PE
                                                                   1405
                                                                    .U6
                                                                    M55
                                                                    1991


        Miller, Susan. Textual Carnivals.
        Carbondale: Southern Illinois UP, 1991.
```

Bibliographic card using MLA documentation style

3 Using quotation, paraphrase, and summary

When recording information on your card, you must take steps to avoid **plagiarism**. (See 17e.) Do this by making distinctions among quoting directly, paraphrasing, and summarizing. A **direct quotation** is an exact duplication of the author's words in the original source. Put quotation marks around direct quotations on your note cards so that you will know later that these words are the author's, not yours. (See 17d1.) A **paraphrase** is a restatement of the author's words in your own words. Paraphrase to simplify or clarify the original author's point. A paraphrase must restate the original facts or ideas fully and correctly. (See 17d2.) A **summary** is a brief condensation or distillation of the main point of the original source. Like a paraphrase, a summary should be in your own words, and all facts and ideas should be accurately represented. (See 17d3.)

Deciding when to quote, when to paraphrase, and when to summarize in your notes will require judgment on your part. The major advantage of quoting is that it allows you to decide later, while writing the paper, whether to include a quotation or to paraphrase or summarize. However, copying down many long quotations can be time-consuming. Also, simply copying down a quotation may prevent you from thinking about the ideas expressed in a way that will benefit your understanding of the topic. In general, copy direct quotations only when the author's words are par-

Lewis, <u>Green Delusions</u>, p. 230
Reasons for overpopulation in poor countries

Some experts believe that birth rates are linked to the "economic value"
of children to their parents. Poor countries have higher birth rates because
parents there rely on children to work for the family and to take care of
them in old age. The more children, particularly sons, the better off the
family is financially. In wealthier countries parents have fewer children because they cost more in terms of education and they contribute less.

(Based on Caldwell and Cain—check these further?)

Note card containing a paraphrase

ticularly lively or persuasive. Photocopying machines make it easy
to collect direct quotations, but highlight the pertinent material or
make notes to yourself on the copy so you can remember later
what you wanted to quote and why. For ease of organizing notes,
many researchers cut out the pertinent quotation and paste it to
a note card.

QUOTATION, PARAPHRASE, AND SUMMARY

As you take notes, use this box to help you choose which note-
taking technique is best for your purposes.

■ **Direct quotation** duplicates the exact words from a source.
Keep direct quotations brief, and put prominent quotation marks
around them on your note cards.
■ **Paraphrase** restates the author's ideas in your own words simply, clearly, and accurately. This device captures content without
exposing you to the risk of unacknowledged quotations, and thus
your text may run as long as the original.
■ **Summary** condenses the main point(s) of an original passage.
Summarize in your own words, and use quotation marks around
any of the author's language you include.

A good paraphrase can help you better understand a difficult passage by simplifying complex sentence structure and vocabulary into language with which you are more comfortable. Be careful not to distort the author's ideas. Use paraphrases when you need to record details, but not exact words.

Because a summary boils a source down to its essentials, it is particularly useful when specific details in the source are unimportant or irrelevant to your research question. You may often find that you can summarize several paragraphs or even an entire article or chapter in just a few sentences without losing any useful information. It is a good idea to note when a particular card contains a summary so you'll remember later that it leaves out detailed supporting information.

■ WRITING 7: PRACTICE

Reread this chapter as though you were researching the question: What are the most important things students need to learn about a library? First, create a bibliographic card for *The Blair Handbook*. Then write the following note cards: (1) a direct quotation; (2) a paraphrase of a two- to three-paragraph passage; (3) a summary of a longer section (for example, 15a or 15b2) in one to three sentences. On the back of each note card, explain why this material was best handled in the manner you chose.

■ WRITING 8: EXPLORATION

Describe the most important, useful, or surprising thing you have learned about the library since exploring it as part of your research project. Share your discovery with classmates, and listen to theirs. Are you comfortable in the library? Why or why not? **WP TIP:** How does technology help or hinder the research process? Explain in an online journal entry and share this with the class.

Research is an active and unpredictable process requiring serious investigators to find answers wherever those happen to be. Depending on your research question, you may need to seek answers by visiting museums, attending concerts, interviewing politicians, observing classrooms, or following leads down some other trail. Investigations that take place outside the library are commonly called **field research**.

Field researchers collect information that is not yet recorded or assessed, and so they have the chance to uncover new facts and develop original interpretations. To conduct such research, you first need to determine which people, places, things, or events can give you the information you need. Then you must go out in the field and either **observe** by watching carefully or **interview** by asking questions of a particular person. You should take careful notes to record your observations or interviews and critically evaluate the information you've collected.

A college campus is an ideal place in which to conduct field research since there are many potential sites for investigation: academic departments, administrative offices, labs, libraries, dining and sports facilities. Furthermore, accessing the Internet through your computer lab or network opens up the possibility of field research in cyberspace, from e-mail on your own campus to contact with a site halfway around the world.

16 a **Planning field research**

Unlike a library, which bundles millions of bits of every kind of information in a single location, "fields" are everywhere: your room, a dormitory, cafeteria, neighborhood, theater, mall, park, playground, and so on. Field information is not cataloged, organized, indexed, or shelved for your convenience. Obtaining it requires diligence, energy, and careful planning.

■ **Consider your research question as it now stands**. What sort of information will be most effective in your final paper?

- **Select your contacts and sites**. Find the person, place, thing, or event most helpful to you. Decide whether you will collect observations, conduct interviews, or do both.

- **Schedule field research in advance**. Interviews, trips, and events don't always work according to plan. Allow time for glitches, such as having to reschedule an interview or return for more information.

- **Do homework before you go**. Visit the library before conducting extensive field research. No matter from who, where, or what you intend to collect information, there's background information at the library that can help you make more insightful observations or formulate better interview questions. (For more information on using libraries, see Chapter 15.)

- **Take extensive notes in your research log**. Record visits, questions, phone calls, and conversations. (See 14d.) Write in your log from the very beginning about topics, questions, methods, and answers. Record even dead-end searches, to remind yourself that you tried them.

WP TIP   Consider transferring crucial recorded information from your research log to different computer files you create for subtopics. When drafting, open the file into a window next to your draft file for easy access to the results of your field research.

■ WRITING 1: APPLICATION

In your research log, write about the feasibility of using field research information to help answer your research question: What kind of field research would strengthen your paper? Where would you go to collect it?

16 b Interviewing

A good interview provides the researcher with timely, original, and useful information that often cannot be obtained by other means. Getting such information is part instinct, part skill, and part luck. If you find talking to strangers easy, then you have a head start on being a good interviewer; in many respects, a good interview is simply a good conversation. If you do not, you can still learn how to ask good interview questions that will elicit the answers you need. Your chances of obtaining good interview material increase when you've thought about it ahead of time. The following guidelines should help you conduct good interviews.

Select the right person. People differ in both the amount and kind of knowledge they have. Not everyone who knows something about your research topic will be able to give you the information you need. In other words, before you make an appointment with a local expert because the individual is accessible, consider whether this is the best person to talk to. Ask yourself (1) exactly what information you need, (2) why you need it, (3) who is likely to have it, and (4) how you might approach them to gain it.

Most research projects benefit from various perspectives, so you may want to interview several people. For example, to research Lake Erie pollution, you could interview someone who lives on the shore, a chemist who knows about pesticide decomposition, and a vice president of a paper company dumping waste into the lake. Just be sure the people you select are likely to provide you with information you really need.

Do your homework. Before you talk to an expert about your topic, make sure you know something about it yourself. Be able to define or describe your interest in it, know the general issues, and learn what your interview subject has already said about it. In this way, you will ask sharper questions, get to the point faster, and be more interesting for your subject to talk with. Plan appropriate questions.

Create a working script. A good interview doesn't follow a script, but it usually starts with one. Before you begin an interview, write out the questions you plan to ask and arrange them so that they build on each other—general questions first, specific ones later. If you or your subject digresses too much, your questions can serve as reminders about the information you need.

Ask both open and closed questions. Different kinds of questions elicit different kinds of information. Open questions place few limits on the answers given: Why did you decide to major in business? What are your plans for the future? Closed questions specify the information you want and usually elicit brief responses: When did you receive your degree? From what college? Open questions usually provide general information, while closed questions allow you to zero in on details.

Ask follow-up questions. Listen closely to the answers you receive, and when the information is incomplete or confusing, ask follow-up questions requesting clarification. Such questions can't be scripted; you just have to use your wits to direct your subject toward the information you consider most important.

Use silence. If you don't get an immediate response to a question, wait a bit before asking another one. In some cases, your question may not have been clear and you will need to rephrase it. But in many cases your interview subject is simply collecting his or her thoughts, not ignoring you. After a slight pause, you may hear thoughtful answers worth waiting for.

Read body language. Be aware of what your subject is doing while answering the questions. Does he or she look you in the eye? Fidget and squirm? Look distracted or bored? Smile? From these visual cues you may be able to infer when your subject is speaking most frankly, doesn't want to give more information, or is tired of answering questions.

Take good content notes. Most interviewers take notes on a pad that is spiral-bound on top, which allows for quick page flipping. Don't try to write down everything, just major ideas and telling statements in the subject's own words that you might want to use as quotations in your paper. Omitting small words, focusing on the most distinctive and precise language, and using common abbreviations (like *b/c* for *because* and *w/* for *with*) can make note taking more efficient.

Take good descriptive notes. Note your subject's physical appearance, facial expressions, and clothing, as well as the interview setting itself. These details will be useful later when you reconstruct the interview, helping you represent it more vividly in your paper.

Tape record with permission only. If you plan to use a tape recorder, ask for permission in advance. The advantage of tape recording is that you have a complete record of the conversation. Sometimes on hearing the person a second time, you notice important things that you missed earlier. The disadvantages are that sometimes tape recorders make subjects nervous, and transcribing a tape is time-consuming work. It's a good idea to have pen in hand to catch highlights or jot down additional questions.

Confirm important assertions. When your subject says something especially important or controversial, read back your notes aloud to check for accuracy and to allow your subject to elaborate. Some interviewers do this during the interview, others at the end.

Review your notes. Notes taken during an interview are brief reminders of what your subject said, not complete quotations. You need to write out the complete information they represent as soon after the interview as you can, certainly within 24 hours. Supplement the notes with other remembered details while they're still fresh, recording them on note cards or directly into a computer file that you can refer to as you write your paper.

Interview electronically. It is possible, and useful, to contact individuals via telephone, electronic mail, or the Internet. Phone interviews are quick and obvious ways of finding out information on short notice. If your interviewee has an e-mail address, asking questions via this medium is even less intrusive than telephones, as your subject can answer when doing so is convenient—quickly, specifically, and in writing. Usenets and listservs can also provide effective sites for initiating research conversations, and many World Wide Web sites are interactive, allowing questions and answers to flow back and forth. (For more on electronic sources, see 15c.)

ESL **CONDUCTING INTERVIEWS IN ENGLISH**

Interviewing someone in a language other than your native language can be challenging. Before you conduct an interview, consider whether you will feel comfortable taking notes and listening at the same time. If not, and if your interview subject doesn't object, you may want to use a tape recorder.

If you decide to take notes in an interview, develop a list of abbreviations beforehand to facilitate note taking. Don't hesitate to ask your interview subject to repeat information, but be polite. It is usually more polite to make a request than to use a command or statement.

LESS POLITE	**MORE POLITE**
Repeat that statistic.	Could you repeat that statistic?
I don't understand.	Would you explain that to me?

■ **WRITING 2: EXPLORATION**

Describe any experience you have had as either interviewer or interviewee. Drawing on your own experience, what additional advice would you give to researchers setting out to interview a subject?

■ **WRITING 3: APPLICATION**

Whom could you interview to find information useful and relevant to your project? Make a list of such people. Write out first drafts of possible questions to ask them.

16 c Observing

Another kind of field research calls for closely observing people, places, things, or events and then describing them accurately to show readers what you saw and experienced. While the term *observation* literally denotes visual perception, it also applies to information collected on site through other senses. The following suggestions may help you conduct field observations.

Select a good site to visit. Like interviewing, observing requires that you know where to go and what to look for. You need to have your research question in mind and then to identify those places where observation will yield useful information. For example, a research project on pollution in Lake Erie would be enhanced by on-the-scene observation of what the water smells, feels, and looks like. Sometimes the site you visit is the primary object of your research, as when the purpose of your paper is to profile the people and activities you find there. At other times the site is chosen to provide supplemental evidence.

Do your homework. To observe well, you need to know what you are looking for and what you are looking at. If you are observing a political speech, know the issues and the players; if you visit an industrial complex, know what is manufactured there. Researching background information at the library or elsewhere will allow you to use your site time more efficiently.

Plan your visit. Learn not only where the place is located on a map but also how to gain access; call ahead to ask directions. Find out where you should go when you first arrive. If relevant, ask which places are open to you, which are off limits, and which you could visit with permission. Find out about visiting hours; if you want to visit at odd hours, you may need special permission. Depending on the place, after-hours visits can provide detailed information not available to the general public.

Take good notes. At any site there's a lot going on that casual observers take for granted. As a researcher you should take nothing for granted. Keep in mind that without notes, as soon as you leave a site you forget more than half of what was there. Review and rewrite your observation notes as soon after your site visit as possible. (See 16b.)

Since you can't write everything down, be selective. Keep your research question in mind and try to focus on the impressions that are most important in answering it. Some of your observations and notes will provide the background information needed to represent the scene vividly in your paper. Some will provide the details needed to make your paper believable. Make your notes as precise as possible, indicating the color, shape, size, texture, and arrangement of everything you can.

Use a notebook that has a stiff cover so you can write standing, sitting, or squatting; a table may not be available. Double-entry notebooks are useful for site visits, because they allow you to record facts in one column and interpretations of those facts in the other. (See Chapter 4.)

If visual images would be useful, you can sketch, photograph, or videotape. If you speak your notes into a tape recorder you will also pick up the characteristic sounds of the site.

 THINKING CRITICALLY ABOUT FIELD SOURCES

When using field sources, it is important to analyze the source's underlying assumptions and reasoning, determine the reliability and credibility of the source, and develop an interpretation of your source's information that helps you answer your research question. To assess the value of field resources, ask yourself the following questions.

1. What is the most important point this source makes? How does it address my research question? How might this point fit into my paper and how should I articulate it?

2. What evidence did the source provide that supports this point? Is it strong or weak? Can I use it and build on it? Should I question or refute it?

3. Does the information support my working thesis? If so, how? How can I express the support in writing?

4. Does the information challenge my working thesis? If so, how? Can I refute the information or contradiction? Or should I revise my thesis to take the new information into account?

5. Does the information support or contradict information collected from other sources? How so? How can I resolve any contradictions? Do I need to seek other sources for confirmation?

6. Is the source reliable? Does any of the information from this source seem illogical or not credible? Has any of the information been contradicted by a more authoritative source?

7. Is the source biased? Does the interview subject have a reason to be biased in any way? Would the selection of a different site have resulted in different information?

WRITING 4: EXPLORATION

Describe a time when you used close observation in your writing. Was it deliberate or by accident? What was your readers' response?

WRITING 5: APPLICATION

List at least three physical sites to visit that would add relevant information to your study; list at least two virtual (electronic) sites as well. Then follow the suggestions in this chapter and visit at least one of each kind.

SUGGESTIONS FOR WRITING AND RESEARCH

INDIVIDUAL

1. Plan a research project that focuses on a local place (park, playground, street, building, business, or institution) and make a research plan that includes going there, describing what you find, and interviewing somebody. Make a similar plan for at least one electronic source. Conduct the research.

2. Plan a research project that begins with an issue of some concern to you. Identify a local manifestation of this issue that would profit from field research. Also consult the library or World Wide Web to place your issue in a larger context. Conduct the research, using field techniques appropriate to your topic.

COLLABORATIVE

Create a team of two to four classmates who would like to join you in researching the project you planned for suggestion 1 or 2 above. Plan the necessary activities to make this project work. Divide the labor so that each of you brings some information to the group by next week's class meeting. Make a copy of your research information for each group member, including typed transcripts of interviews, copies of e-mail interviews, and photocopies of visual information. You may each write an individual paper based on your collective research, or you may team up and write a longer paper.

17 Using Sources

Locating potential sources for a research project is one thing; deciding which ones to include, where to use them, and how to incorporate them is something else. Some writers begin making use of their sources in early exploratory drafts, perhaps by trying out a pithy quotation to see how it brings a paragraph into focus. Others prefer to sift and arrange all of their note cards in neat stacks before making any decisions about what to include in their essays. No matter how you begin writing with sources, there comes a time when you will need to incorporate them finally, smoothly, effectively, and correctly into your paper.

17 a Controlling your sources

Once you've conducted some research and are ready to begin planning and/or drafting for your essay, you need to decide which sources you will use and how you will use them. You can't make this decision on the basis of how much time you spent finding and analyzing each source; you have to decide according to how useful the source is in answering your research question. In other words, you need to control your sources rather than letting them control you.

Real research about real questions is vital and dynamic, which means it's always changing. Just as you can't expect your first working thesis to be your final thesis, you can't expect to know in advance which sources are going to prove most fruitful. And don't think that you can't collect more information once you've begun drafting. At each step in the process you see your research question and answer more clearly, so the research you conduct as you write may be the most useful of all. Similarly, and perhaps especially when you engage in field research, writers of research essays often gain an increased sense of audience as their research progresses, which pays off in increasingly reader-oriented writing.

One of the best strategies for maintaining personal control of your research essay is to make an outline first and then organize your notes accordingly. (If you compose an outline on a word processor, it will be easier to make changes later on. The same goes for your notes if you've written them on a computer.) If you do it the other way around—organizing your notes in a logical sequence and then writing an outline based on that sequence—you'll be tempted to find a place for every note and to gloss over areas where you haven't done enough research.

1 Outline your research conclusions

If you **outline** your research conclusions first, you let the logical flow of ideas create a blueprint for your paper. (Of course, your outline may change as your ideas continue to develop.) If you can't outline before you write, then be sure to begin writing—if only by drafting a "topic sentence" outline to start major sections—before you arrange your note cards.

2 Organize your supporting evidence

Once you have outlined or begun drafting and have a good sense of the shape of your paper, **organize** your notes. Arrange the note cards so that they correspond to your outline, and put bibliographic cards in alphabetical order by the author's last name. Integrate field research notes as best you can, depending on their format. Finally, go back to your outline and annotate it to indicate which source goes where. By doing this, you can see if there are any ideas that need more research.

As you prepare to draft, you need to assess all the information you have found and decide which sources are useful. Read your notes critically to evaluate each source, and **synthesize** the material into a new, coherent whole.

Synthesizing material involves looking for connections among different pieces of information and formulating ideas about what these connections mean. The connections may be similar statements made by several sources, or contradictions between two sources. Try to reach some conclusions on your own that extend beyond the information in front of you, then use those conclusions to form the goals for your paper.

Next decide how you will use your source information; base your decisions on your goals for the paper and not on the format of your research notes. Papers written in an effort "to get everything in" are source-driven and all too often read like patch jobs of quotations loosely strung together. Your goal should be to remain the director of the research production, your ideas on center stage and your sources the supporting cast. By synthesizing your information into a unique presentation, you remain at center stage.

Also, keep in mind that referring more than two or three times to a single source—unless it is itself the focus of your paper—undercuts your credibility and suggests overreliance on a single point of view. On the other hand, using synthesis to show how ideas from different sources relate to each other as well as how they relate to your own stance greatly improves the coherence of your essay. If you find yourself referring largely to one source—and therefore one point of view—make sure that you have sufficient references to add other points of view to your paper.

■ WRITING 1: EXPLORATION

Describe your experience writing a recent research paper. What kind of clues can you recall that would indicate whether you or your sources controlled that paper?

■ WRITING 2: APPLICATION

Use your research log to draft a tentative thesis and working outline for your research paper. Then arrange your note cards according to that outline. If you can, try to work out a second option for essay arrangement. This procedure is simplified if your notes are computerized. If you do rearrange your notes via computer, however, be sure to save a copy of each arrangement in case you decide to return to it.

17 d ▌ Integrating information from sources

Once you know which sources you want to use, you still have to decide how the ideas from these sources will appear in your paper. The notes you made during your research may be in many forms. For some sources, you will have copied down direct quotations; for others you will have paraphrased or summarized important information. For some field sources you may have made extensive note on background information, such as your interview subject's appearance. Simply because you've quoted or paraphrased a particular source in your notes, however, doesn't mean you have to use a quotation or paraphrase from this source in your paper. Make decisions about how to use sources based on your goals, not on the format of your research notes.

At this point, it might be helpful for you to consider our suggestion that taking notes in your own words can pay major dividends in your research-based writing. Of major importance, of course, is the fact that drafting directly from quotations leads to a source-controlled essay—and frequently to a shortage of connecting information between ideas. As was explained in 15e, taking notes in your own words also helps your comprehension of the ideas and arguments you've read. It encourages you mentally to digest material rather than simply copying, and it makes your rereading of the notes more meaningful. For these and other reasons, practices such as photocopying large chunks of material—or downloading it via computer—are no substitute for the note-*writing* portion of your research work.

Moreover, whether you quote, paraphrase, or summarize, you must acknowledge your source through documentation. Different disciplines have different conventions for documentation. The examples in this chapter use the documentation style of the Modern Language Association (MLA), the style preferred in the languages and literature field. (For more on documentation, see Chapter 18.)

1 Quoting effectively

Direct quotation provides strong evidence and can add both life and authenticity to your paper.

To quote, you must use an author's or speaker's exact words. Slight changes in wording are permitted in certain cases (see the next section), but these changes must be clearly marked. Although you can't change what a source says, you do have control over how much of it you use. Too much quotation can imply that you have little to say for yourself. Use only as long a quotation as you need to make your point. Remember that quotations should be used to support your points, not to say them for you.

Shortening quotations

Long quotations slow readers down and often have the unintended effect of inviting them to skip over the quoted material. Unless the source quoted is itself the topic of the paper (as in a

WHEN TO QUOTE

Direct quotations should be reserved for cases in which you cannot express the ideas better yourself. Use quotations when the original words are especially precise, clear, powerful, or vivid.

■ **Precise.** Use quotations when the words are important in themselves or when the author makes fine but important distinctions.

Government, even in its best state, is but a necessary evil; in its worst state, an intolerable one.

THOMAS PAINE

■ **Clear**. Use quotations when the author's ideas are complex and difficult to paraphrase.

Paragraphs tell readers how writers want to be read.

WILLIAM BLAKE

■ **Powerful**. Use quotations when the words are especially authoritative and memorable.

You shall know the truth, and the truth shall make you free.

ABRAHAM LINCOLN

■ **Vivid**. Use quotations when the language is lively and colorful, when it reveals something of the author's or speaker's character.

Writing. I'm more involved in it, but not as attached.

KAREN, A STUDENT

literary interpretation), limit brief quotations to no more than two per page and long quotations to no more than one every three pages.

Be sure that when you shorten a quotation, you have not changed its meaning. If you omit words within quotations for the sake of brevity, you must indicate that you have done so by using ellipsis points. Any changes or additions must be indicated with brackets. (See 49c-d for more on ellipses and brackets.)

ORIGINAL

The human communication environment has acquired biological complexity and planetary scale, but there are no scientists or activists monitoring it, theorizing about its health, or mounting campaigns to protect its resilience. Perhaps it's too new, too large to view as a whole, or too containing—we swim in a sea of information, in poet Gary Snyder's phrase. All the more reason to worry. New things have nastier surprises, big things are hard to change, and containing things are inescapable.

STEWART BRAND, *THE MEDIA LAB*

INACCURATE QUOTATION

In *The Media Lab*, Stewart Brand describes the control that is exerted by watchdog agencies over modern telecommunications: "The human communication environment has . . . activists monitoring it, theorizing about its health . . ." (258).

By omitting certain words, the writer has changed the meaning of the original source.

ACCURATE QUOTATION

In *The Media Lab*, Stewart Brand notes that we have done little to monitor the growth of telecommunications. Modern communication technology may seem overwhelmingly new, big, and encompassing, but these are reasons for more vigilance, not less: "New things have nastier surprises, big things are hard to change, and containing things are inescapable" (258).

Integrating quotations into your paper

Direct quotations will be most effective when you integrate them smoothly into the flow of your paper. You can do this by providing an explanatory "tag" or by giving one or more sentences of explanation. Readers should be able to follow your meaning easily and to see the relevance of the quotation immediately.

Using embedded or block format. Brief quotations should be embedded in the main body of your paper and enclosed in quotation marks. According to MLA style guidelines, a brief quotation consists of four or fewer typed lines.

> Photo editor Tom Brennan took ten minutes to sort through my images and then told me, "Most photography editors wouldn't take more than two minutes to look at a portfolio."

Longer quotations should be set off in block format. Begin a new line, indent ten spaces (for MLA), and do not use quotation marks.

Katie Kelly focuses on Americans' peculiarly negative chauvinism, in this case, the chauvinism of New York residents:

> New Yorkers are a provincial lot. They wear their city's accomplishments like blue ribbons. To anyone who will listen they boast of leading the world in everything from Mafia murders to porno movie houses. (89)

(See Chapter 48 for more on punctuating quotations.)

Introducing quotations. Introduce all quoted material so that readers know who is speaking, what the quotation refers to, and where it is from. If the author or speaker is well-known, it is especially useful to mention his or her name in an introductory signal phrase.

> Henry David Thoreau asserts in *Walden*, "The mass of men lead lives of quiet desperation" (5).

There are certain **signal phrases** to tell the reader that the words or ideas that follow come from another source. Choose a signal phrase that reflects the source's intentions, and to avoid monotony, vary the placement of the signal phrases you use.

 VERBS USED IN SIGNAL PHRASES

The verb you choose for a signal phrase should accurately reflect the intention of the source.

acknowledges	concedes	illustrates	reports
admits	concludes	implies	reveals
agrees	declares	insists	says
argues	denies	maintains	shows
asserts	emphasizes	notes	states
believes	endorses	observes	suggests
claims	finds	points out	thinks
comments	grants	refutes	writes

If your paper focuses on written works, you can introduce a quotation with the title rather than the author's name, as long as the reference is clear.

> *Walden* sets forth one individual's antidote against the "lives of quiet desperation" led by the working class in mid-nineteenth-century America (Thoreau 5).

If neither the author nor the title of a written source is well known (or the speaker in a field source), introduce the quotation with a brief explanation to give your readers some context.

> Mary Catherine Bateson, daughter of anthropologist Margaret Mead, has become, in her own right, a student of modern civilization. In *Composing a Life* she writes, "The twentieth century has been called the century of the refugee because of the vast numbers of people uprooted by war and politics from their homes" (8).

Explaining and clarifying quotations. Sometimes you will need to explain a quotation in order to clarify why it's relevant and what it means in the context of your discussion.

> In *A Sand County Almanac*, Aldo Leopold invites modern urban readers to confront what they lose by living in the city: "There are two spiritual dangers in not owning a farm. One is the danger of supposing that breakfast comes from the grocery, and the other that heat comes from the furnace" (6). Leopold sees city-dwellers as self-centered children, blissfully but dangerously unaware of how their basic needs are met.

You may also need to clarify what a word or reference means. Do this by using square brackets. (See 49d.)

Adjusting grammar when using quotations. A passage containing a quotation must follow all the rules of grammatical sentence structure: tenses should be consistent, verbs and subjects should agree, and so on. If the form of the quotation doesn't quite fit the grammar of your own sentences, you can either quote less of the original source, change your sentences, or make a slight alteration in the quotation. Use this last option sparingly, and always indicate any changes with brackets.

UNCLEAR

> In *Sand County Almanac*, Aldo Leopold follows various animals, including a skunk and a rabbit, through fresh snow. He wonders, "What got him out of bed?" (5).

CLEAR

In *Sand County Almanac*, Aldo Leopold follows various animals, including a skunk and a rabbit, through fresh snow. He wonders, "What got [the skunk] out of bed?" (5).

GRAMMATICALLY INCOMPATIBLE

If Thoreau believed, as he wrote in *Walden* in the 1850s, "The mass of men lead lives of quiet desperation" (5), then what would he say of the masses today?

The verb *lead* in Thoreau's original quotation is present tense, but the sentence might call for the past tense form *led*.

GRAMMATICALLY COMPATIBLE

If Thoreau believed, as he wrote in *Walden* in the 1850s, that the masses led "lives of quiet desperation" (5), then what would he say of the masses today?

GRAMMATICALLY COMPATIBLE

In the nineteenth century, Thoreau stated, "The mass of men lead lives of quiet desperation" (*Walden* 5). What would he say of the masses today?

GRAMMATICALLY COMPATIBLE

If Thoreau thought that in his day, the "mass of men [led] lives of quiet desperation" (*Walden* 5), what would he say of the masses today?

▮ WRITING 3: APPLICATION

Read through your research materials, highlighting any quotations you might want to incorporate into your paper. Use your research log to explore why you think these words should be quoted directly. Also note where in your essay a quotation would add clarity, color, or life; then see if you can find one to serve that purpose.

2 Paraphrasing effectively

Although it is generally wiser to write as many research notes as possible in your own words, you may have written down or photocopied many quotations instead of taking the time to put an author's or speaker's ideas into your own words.

To **paraphrase**, you restate a source's ideas in your own words. The point of paraphrasing is to make the ideas clearer (both to your readers and to yourself) and to express the ideas in the way that best suits your purpose. In paraphrasing, attempt to

preserve the intent of the original statement and to fit the paraphrased statement smoothly into the immediate context of your
essay.

 WHEN TO PARAPHRASE

Paraphrases generally re-create the original source's order,
structure, and emphasis and include most of its details.

■ **Clarity.** Use paraphrase to make complex ideas clear to your
readers.
■ **Details.** Use paraphrase only when you need to present details
that an author or speaker has described at greater length.
■ **Emphasis.** Use paraphrase when including an author's or speaker's point suits the emphasis you want to make in your paper.

The best way to make an accurate paraphrase is to stay close
to the order and structure of the original passage, to reproduce its
emphasis and details. However, don't use the same sentence patterns or vocabulary or you risk inadvertently plagiarizing the
source. (See 17e.)

If the original source has used a well-established or technical
term for a concept, you do not need to find a synonym for it. If you
believe that the original source's exact words are the best possible
expressions of some points, you may use brief direct quotations
within your paraphrase, as long as you indicate these with quotation marks.

Keep in mind why you are including this source; doing so will
help you to decide how to phrase the ideas. Be careful, though,
not to introduce your own comments or reflections in the middle
of a paraphrase, unless you make it very clear that these are your
thoughts, not the original author's or speaker's.

ORIGINAL

The affluent, educated, liberated women of the First World, who
can enjoy freedom unavailable to any woman ever before, do not
feel as free as they want to. And they can no longer restrict to the
subconscious their sense that this lack of freedom has something
to do with—with apparently frivolous issues, things that really
should not matter. Many are ashamed to admit that such trivial
concerns—to do with physical appearance, bodies, faces, hair,
clothes—matter so much.

NAOMI WOLF, *THE BEAUTY MYTH*, 9

INACCURATE PARAPHRASE

In *The Beauty Myth*, Naomi Wolf argues that First-World women, who still have less freedom than they would like to have, restrict to their subconscious those matters having to do with physical appearance—that these things are not really important to them (9).

ACCURATE PARAPHRASE

In *The Beauty Myth*, Wolf asserts that First-World women, despite their affluence, education, and liberation, still do not feel very free. Moreover, many of these women are aware that this lack of freedom is influenced by superficial things having primarily to do with their physical appearance—things which should not matter so much (9).

ESL **STRATEGIES FOR PARAPHRASING**

Writers who are inexperienced at paraphrasing in English sometimes paraphrase by substituting synonyms for some of the author's words, keeping the sentence structure and many of the words the same. This kind of paraphrasing is unacceptable in academic writing; it can be considered a form of plagiarism. (See 17e.) Here are some suggestions that may help you write effective paraphrases.

1. Before you begin writing a paraphrase of a sentence or passage, make sure that you understand the author's meaning. Look up in a dictionary any words you don't know, and ask a native speaker of English about any idioms or slang with which you are unfamiliar.

2. To write your paraphrase, look away from the original source and put the ideas into your own words.

3. If you are paraphrasing a passage, don't paraphrase the information one sentence at a time. Instead, try to express the meaning of the entire passage.

4. Consider the context of the sentence or passage you are paraphrasing. Are there any reference that are clear only from the surrounding sentences? Make sure you have given your readers enough information to understand your paraphrase.

5. Use a thesaurus to find synonyms if you need to, but remember that not every word listed together in a thesaurus is equally appropriate in every sentence. Use only words you are familiar with.

WRITING 4: APPLICATION

Read through your note cards for any passages you quoted directly from an original source. Find notes that now seem wordy, unclear, or longer than necessary. Paraphrase notes that you expect to use in your paper. Exchange your paraphrases and the originals with a classmate, and assess each other's work.

3 **Summarizing effectively**

To summarize, you distill a source's words down to the main ideas and state these in your own words. A summary includes only the essentials of the original source, not the supporting details, and is consequently shorter than the original.

✔ **WHEN TO SUMMARIZE**

As you draft, summarize often so that your paper doesn't turn into a string of undigested quotations.

■ **Main points**. Use summary when your readers need to know the main point the original source makes but not the supporting details.

■ **Overviews**. Sometimes you may want to devise a few sentences that will effectively support your discussion without going on and on. Use summary to provide an overview or an interesting aside without digressing too far from your paper's focus.

■ **Condensation**. You may have taken extensive notes on a particular article or observation only to discover in the course of drafting that you do not need all that detail. Use summary to condense lengthy or rambling notes into a few effective sentences.

Keep in mind that summaries are generalizations and that too many generalizations can make your writing vague and tedious. You should occasionally supplement summaries with brief direct quotations or evocative details collected through observation to keep readers in touch with the original source.

Summaries vary in length, and the length of the original source is not necessarily related to the length of the summary you write. Depending on the focus of your paper, you may need to summarize an entire novel in a sentence or two, or you may need to summarize a brief journal article in two or three paragraphs. Remember that the more material you attempt to summarize in a short space, the more you will necessarily generalize and abstract it. Reduce a text as far as you can while still providing all the information your readers need to know. Be careful, though, not to distort the original's meaning.

ORIGINAL

For a long time I never liked to look a chimpanzee straight in the eye—I assumed that, as is the case with most primates, this would be interpreted as a threat or at least as a breach of good manners. Not so. As long as one looks with gentleness, without arrogance, a chimpanzee will understand and may even return the look.

JANE GOODALL, *THROUGH A WINDOW 12*

INACCURATE SUMMARY

Goodall learned from her experiences with chimpanzees that they react positively to direct looks from humans (12).

ACCURATE SUMMARY

Goodall reports that when humans look directly but gently into chimpanzees' eyes, the chimps are not threatened and may even return the look (12).

■ **WRITING 5: EXPLORATION**

Review any sources on which you have taken particularly extensive notes. Would it be possible to condense these notes into a briefer summary of the entire work? Would it serve your purpose to do so? Why or why not?

■ **17** **e** **Understanding and avoiding plagiarism**

Acknowledging your sources through one of the accepted systematic styles of **documentation** is a service to your sources, your readers, and future scholars. Knowledge in the academic community is cumulative, with one writer's work building on another's. After reading your paper, readers may want to know more about a source you cited, perhaps in order to use it in papers of their own. Correct documentation helps them find the source quickly and easily.

Failure to document your sources is called **plagiarism**. Plagiarism is taking someone's ideas or information and passing them off as your own. The practice of citing sources for "borrowed" ideas or words is both customary and expected in academic writing.

Most plagiarism is not intentional; many writers are simply unaware of the conventional guidelines for indicating that they have borrowed words or ideas from someone else. Nevertheless, it is the writer's responsibility to learn these guidelines and follow them.

1 Using a documentation style

Each discipline, or area of academic study, has developed its own conventions for documentation, a standardized set of guidelines that continue to evolve as the discipline evolves. The languages and literature disciplines use the style recommended by the Modern Language Association (MLA). (See Chapter 18.) Other humanities use a system of endnotes or footnotes. Social sciences use the style recommended by the American Psychological Association (APA). Natural sciences use the style recommended by the Council of Biology Editors (CBE) or a related style. You should use the documentation of the discipline for which you are writing; if you are in doubt, ask your instructor. (See Part VIII for complete information on each of these other documentation styles.)

Basically, you must attribute any idea or wording you use in your writing to the source through which you encountered that idea or those words, *if the material is not original to yourself.* You do not need to document *common knowledge,* that is, information that an educated person can be expected to know—knowledge commonly taught in school or carried in the popular media—or knowledge that can be found in multiple sources (encyclopedias, dictionaries). Examples include the dates of historical events, the names and locations of states and cities, the general laws of science, and so on. However, when you read the work of authors who have specific opinions and interpretations of a piece of common knowledge and you use their opinions or interpretations in your paper, you must give them credit through proper documentation.

It is also important to note that even "nonpublished" ideas or words should be attributed to their sources whenever such documentation is feasible. For example, if you use opinions from a sidewalk poll, conversation, or Internet commentaries or a World Wide Web (WWW) page in your writing, you must cite that original source.

2 Avoiding plagiarism

If you are not sure what you can take from a source and what you need to cite, ask a tutor or your instructor for help before you turn in your final paper. Also find out if your school has a booklet on avoiding plagiarism.

Most campuses with Online Writing Labs (OWL's) now have information about plagiarism available through Gopher or WWW. Similarly, your campus OWL, if one exists, is also likely to provide an e-mail–based "hot line" for rapid, direct answers to important questions about plagiarism.

AVOIDING PLAGIARISM

- Place all quoted passages in quotation marks and provide source information, even if it is only one phrase.
- Identify the source from which you have paraphrased or summarized ideas, just as you do when you quote directly.
- Give credit for any creative ideas you borrow from an original source. For example, if you use an author's anecdote to illustrate a point, acknowledge it.
- Replace unimportant language with your own, and use different sentence structures when you paraphrase or summarize.
- Acknowledge the source if you borrow any organizational structure or headings from an author. Don't use the same subtopics, for example.
- Put any words or phrases you borrow in quotations marks, especially an author's unique way of saying something.

The most common incidence of inadvertent plagiarism is a writer's paraphrasing or summarizing a source but staying too close to the wording or sentence structure of the original, sometimes lifting whole phrases without enclosing them in quotation marks. Keep in mind that when you paraphrase or summarize a source, you need to identify the author of those ideas just as if you had quoted directly.

To avoid plagiarism when you paraphrase, use your own words to replace language that is not important to quote exactly;

in other words, you are attributing the ideas, but not the exact language, to the source. At the same time, make certain you cite *all* direct quotes, acknowledging that you are borrowing both the ideas *and the words.*

ORIGINAL

The World Wide Web makes world-wide publishing possible to anyone who is able to arrange disk space on a server and has some basic knowledge of how pages are created.

CAROL LEA CLARK, A STUDENT'S GUIDE TO THE INTERNET

PLAGIARIZED PARAPHRASE

World-wide publishing is possible for anyone who has access to server disk-space and who has knowledge of how Web pages are made. (Clark 77).

The above example uses too much language from the original source.

ACCEPTABLE PARAPHRASE

With the basics of Web-page construction and storage space on a network server, Clark tells us, anyone can publish, at least potentially, for audiences around the world.

This example translates source language into the writer's own language.

▇ WRITING 6: EXPLORATION

Read the following quotation from Mike Rose's *Lives on the Boundary*; then explain why each of the three sentences that follow is an example of plagiarism.

> The discourse of academics is marked by terms and expressions that represent an elaborate set of shared concepts and orientations: alienation, authoritarian personality, the social construction of self, determinism, hegemony, equilibrium, intentionality, recursion, reinforcement, and so on. This language weaves through so many lectures and textbooks, it is integral to so many learned discussions, that it is easy to forget what a foreign language it can be. (192)

1. The discourse of academics is marked by expressions that represent shared concepts.

2. Academic discourse is characterized by a particular set of coded words and ideas that are found throughout the college community.

3. Sometimes the talk of professors is as difficult for outsiders to understand as a foreign language is to a native speaker.

MLA

MLA

MLA

MLA

MLA

MLA

MLA

MLA

MLA

18   Documenting Sources: MLA Style

The Modern Language Association (MLA) system is the preferred form for documenting research sources when you write about literature or language.

- All sources are briefly documented in the text by an identifying name and page number (generally in parentheses).

- A Works Cited section at the end of the paper lists full publication data for each source cited.

- Additional explanatory information provided by the writer of the paper (but not from external sources) goes in footnotes either at the foot of the page or in a Notes section after the close of the paper.

The MLA system is explained in more detail in the *MLA Handbook for Writers of Research Papers*, 4th ed. (New York: MLA, 1995).

DIRECTORY FOR MLA DOCUMENTATION GUIDELINES

CONVENTIONS FOR IN-TEXT CITATIONS (18a)

1. Single work by one or more authors
2. Two or more works by the same author
3. Unknown author
4. Corporate or organizational author
5. Authors with the same last name
6. Works in more than one volume
7. One-page works
8. Quote from an indirect source
9. Literary works
10. More than one work in a citation
11. Long quote set off from text

DIRECTORY FOR MLA DOCUMENTATION GUIDELINES
(continued)

CONVENTIONS FOR ENDNOTES AND FOOTNOTES (18b)
CONVENTIONS FOR LIST OF WORKS CITED (18c)

MLA

MLA

MLA

MLA

MLA

MLA

MLA

MLA

MLA

MLA

The MLA system provides a simple, economical (concise), and thorough way for writers to acknowledge the sources they use in research-based papers. In the MLA system, authors use footnotes and/or endnotes to provide additional, explanatory information, but not to cite information provided by external sources (see 18b). Whenever possible, the MLA system includes explanatory information in the text itself and limits the use of footnotes or endnotes. Pay careful attention to the practical mechanics of documentation, so that readers can readily identify, understand, and locate your sources.

18 a Conventions for in-text citations

In-text citations identify ideas and information borrowed from other writers. They also refer readers to the works cited list at the end of the paper, where they can find complete publication information about each original source. The languages and literature are not primarily concerned with *when* something was written; instead, these fields of study focus on writers and the internal qualities of texts. Therefore, in-text citations following the MLA style, feature author names, text titles, and page numbers. MLA style is economical, providing only as much in-text information as readers need in order to locate more complete information in the Works Cited. Following are some examples of how in-text citation works; see section c in this chapter for the format of entries in the Works Cited, and see the next chapter for sample pages using MLA documentation.

1. Single work by one or more authors

When you quote, paraphrase, or summarize a source, include in the text of your paper the last name of the source's author, if known, and, in parentheses, the page or pages on which the original information appeared. Do not include the word *page* or the abbreviations *p.* or *pp.* You may mention the author's name in the sentence or put it in parentheses, preceding the page number(s).

Carol Lea Clark explains the basic necessities for the creation of a page on the World Wide Web (77).

Provided one has certain "basic ingredients," the Web offers potential worldwide publication to individuals (Clark 77).

Note that a parenthetical reference at the end of a sentence comes before the period. No punctuation is used between the author's last name and the page number(s).

If you cite a work with two or three authors, your in-text parenthetical citation must include all authors' names: (Rombauer and Becker 715), (Child, Bertholle, and Beck 215). For works with more than three authors, you may list all the authors or, to avoid awkwardness, use the first author's name and add "et al." without a comma: (Britton et al. 395). *Et al.* is an abbreviation for the Latin *et alii,* translated "and others."

2. Two or more works by the same author

If your paper has references to two or more works by the same author, you should clearly identify the specific work in your citation. Either mention the title of the work in the text or include a shortened version of the title (usually the first one or two important words) in the parenthetical citation.

According to Lewis Thomas in Lives of a Cell, many bacteria become dangerous only if they manufacture exotoxins (76).

According to Lewis Thomas, many bacteria become dangerous only if they manufacture exotoxins (Lives 76).

Many bacteria become dangerous only if they manufacture exotoxins (Thomas, Lives 76).

If both the author's name and a shortened version of the title are in a parenthetical citation, a comma separates them, but there is no comma before the page number.

3. Unknown author

When the author of a work you are citing is unknown, use either the complete title in the text or a shortened version of it in the parenthetical citation, along with the page number.

According to Statistical Abstracts, the literacy rate for Mexico stood at 75% in 1990, up 4% from census figures ten years earlier (374).

The literacy rate for Mexico stood at 75% in 1990, up 4% from census figures ten years earlier (Statistical 374).

4. Corporate or organizational author

When no author is listed for a work published by a corporation, organization, or association, indicate the group's full name in any parenthetical reference: (Florida League of Women Voters 3). If the name is long, cite it in the sentence and put only the page number in parentheses.

5. Authors with the same last name

When you cite works by two or more authors with the same last name, include the first initial of each author's name in the parenthetical citation: (C. Miller 63; S. Miller 101–04).

6. Works in more than one volume

When your sources are in more than one volume of a multi-volume work, indicate the pertinent volume number for each citation. Place the volume number before the page number and follow it with a colon and one space: (Hill 2: 70). If your source is in only one volume of a multivolume work, you need not specify the volume number in the in-text citation, but you should specify it in the Works Cited.

7. One-page works

When you refer to a work in your text that is only one page long, you need not include the page number in your citation. Author or title identification is sufficient for readers to find the exact page number on the Works Cited list.

8. Quote from an indirect source

When a quotation or any information in your source is originally from another source, use the abbreviation "qtd. in."

Lester Brown of Worldwatch feels that international agricultural production has reached its limit and that "we're going to be in trouble on the food front before this decade is out" (qtd. in Mann 51).

9. Literary works

In citing literary prose works available in various editions, provide additional information (such as chapter number or scene number) for readers who may be consulting a different edition. Use a semicolon to separate the page number from this additional information: (331; bk. 10, ch. 5). In citing poems, provide only line numbers for reference; include the word "line" or "lines" in the first such reference. Providing information will help your audience find the passages *in any source where those works are reprinted*, which page references alone cannot provide.

> In "The Mother," Gwendolyn Brooks remembers ". . . the children you got that
> you did not get" (line 1); children that "never giggled or planned or cried" (30).

Cite verse plays using act, scene, and line numbers, separated by periods: (*Hamlet* 4.4.31–39).

10. More than one work in a citation

To cite more than one work in a parenthetical reference, separate them with semicolons: (Aronson, *Golden Shore* 177; Didion 49–50).

11. Long quote set off from text

For quotes of four or more lines, set off the quote from the text by indentation. Indent the quote one inch or ten spaces from the left margin of the text (not from the paper's edge), double-space, and omit quotation marks. The parenthetical citation follows end punctuation (unlike shorter, integrated quotes) and is not followed by a period.

Fellow author W. Somerset Maugham had this to say about Austen's dialogue:

> No one has ever looked upon Jane Austen as a great stylist. Her spelling
> was peculiar and her grammar often shaky, but she had a good ear. Her
> dialogue is probably as natural as dialogue can ever be. To set down on
> paper speech as it is spoken would be very tedious, and some arrange-
> ment of it is necessary. (434)

18 b Conventions for endnotes and footnotes

In MLA citation style, notes are used primarily to offer comments, explanations, or additional information (especially source-related information) that cannot be smoothly or easily accommodated in the text of the paper. You might use notes also to cite several sources within a single context if a series of *in-text* references might detract from the readability of the text. In general, however, you should omit additional information, outside the "mainstream" of your text, unless it is necessary for clarification or justification.

If you conclude that a note is necessary, insert a raised (superscript) numeral at the reference point in the text; introduce the note itself with a corresponding raised numeral, and indent it. Many word processing programs provide footnote functions, which greatly simplify the entire procedure.

TEXT WITH SUPERSCRIPT

The standard ingredients for guacamole include avocados, lemon juice, onion, tomatoes, coriander, salt, and pepper.[1] Hurtado's poem, however, gives this traditional dish a whole new twist (lines 10–17).

NOTE

[1] For variations see Beard 314, Egerton 197, Eckhardt 92, and Kafka 26. Beard's version, which includes olives and green peppers, is the most unusual.

The references listed in the notes should appear in the Works Cited along with the other sources referred to in your text.

Notes may come at the bottom of the page on which the text reference appears—as footnotes—or be included as endnotes, double-spaced, on a separate page at the end of your paper. Endnote pages should be placed between the text of the paper and the Works Cited, with the title "Note" or "Notes." (For examples of format and use of endnotes, see the sample paper in Chapter 19. For more on the format for footnotes, see section 62e–f.)

18 c Conventions for list of Works Cited

All sources mentioned in an academic essay (and other types of formal or professional writing) should be identified on a concluding list of Works Cited. These entries follow specific rules for formatting and punctuation so that the reader can readily find information.

Format. After the final page of the paper, title a separate page "Works Cited," an inch from the top of the page, centered, but not underlined and not in quotation marks. Exception: If you are required to list all the works you have read in researching the topic—not just those to which you have actually referred in your text or notes—you should title this list "Works Consulted" rather than "Works Cited." Number the page, following in sequence from the last page of your paper.

Double-space between the Works Cited title and your first entry. Begin each entry at the left margin, indenting the second and all subsequent lines of each entry five spaces. Double-space both between and within entries (in other words, double-space all lines of the Works Cited list). If the list runs to more than one page, continue numbering pages in sequence but do not repeat the title.

Order of entries. Alphabetize the entries according to authors' last names. If two or more authors have the same last name, alphabetize by first name or initial. For entries by an unknown author, alphabetize according to the first word of the title, excluding an initial *A*, *An*, or *The*.

Format for entries. There are many variations on the following general formats, given the additional information needed to identify various kinds of sources. The following formats are the three most common.

GENERAL FORMAT FOR BOOKS

one space   one space   one space   one space

Author(s). Book Title. Place of publication: Publisher, year of

Indent
5 spaces ——— publication.

GENERAL FORMAT FOR JOURNAL ARTICLES

one space   one space   one space   one space

Author(s). "Article Title." Journal Title volume number (year

Indent
5 spaces ——— of publication): inclusive page numbers.

one space

GENERAL FORMAT FOR MAGAZINE AND NEWSPAPER ARTICLES

one space   one space   one space

Author(s). "Article Title." Publication Title date of

Indent 5 spaces ———publication: inclusive page numbers.

one space

Authors. Authors are listed last name first, followed by a comma and the rest of the name as it appears on the publication. A period follows the full name. If a work has more than one author, list the subsequent names first name first, and separate the names with a comma. When the Works Cited has more than one work by the same author, substitute three hyphens for the author's name after the first entry.

Titles. List the titles and subtitles fully, capitalizing them as in the original. Underline the titles of entire books and periodicals; put quotation marks around the titles of essays, poems, and other works that are part of a larger (entire) work. Put a period after a book or article title; no punctuation should follow a journal, magazine, or newspaper title.

Places of publication. For books, always give the city of publication. If several cities are listed on the title or copyright pages, give only the first. If the name of the city alone could be unfamiliar or confusing to your readers, add an abbreviation for the state or country. (See the section on abbreviations on page 259.) Use a comma to separate the city from the state or country and a colon to separate the place of publication from the publisher.

Publishers. Abbreviate publishers' names as discussed in the section on abbreviations on page 259. If the title page indicates that a book is published under an imprint—for example, Arbor House is an imprint of William Morrow—list both imprint and publisher, separated by a hyphen (Arbor-Morrow). For books, use a comma to separate the publisher from the publication date.

Dates and page numbers. For books and periodicals, give only the year of publication. Place a period after the year of publication for a book; place the year of publication for periodicals within parentheses, followed by a colon and a space. For dates of newspapers, use no commas between the elements and put the day before the month (14 June 1995). For magazines and newspapers, place a colon and a space after the date of publication. Separate inclusive page numbers with a hyphen (42–54). Up to 99, use all the digits for the second page numbers, and above 99 list the last two digits only (130–38) unless the full sequence is needed for clarity (198–210). If the page numbers are not consecutive (as in a newspaper), place a plus sign after the final consecutive page(39+, 52–55+). The plus sign represents *all* subsequent pages in the work cited, regardless of how many there are or how they are arranged.

Abbreviations. To follow MLA conventions, abbreviate state and country names—using established postal abbreviations—in the place of publication. Also abbreviate publishers' names by dropping the words *Press, Company,* and so forth (e.g., use "Blair" for "Blair Press"); by using only the first in a series of names ("Farrar" for "Farrar, Straus, & Giroux"); and by using only the last name of a person ("Abrams" for "Harry N. Abrams"). "University Press" is abbreviated UP (Southern Illinois UP; U of Chicago P). In periodical dates, abbreviate all months except May, June, and July—to the first three letters followed by a period (Jan., Apr.). If no publisher, place of publication, date of publication, or page numbers are provided for a book, use the abbreviations "n.p." (for both publisher and place, to be clarified by its relation to the separating colon), "n.d.", or "n.pag."

Following are examples of the Works Cited format for specific types of sources. For a sample Works Cited list, see Chapter 19.

1 Documenting books

I. Book by one author

Benjamin, Jessica. The Bonds of Love: Psychoanalysis, Feminism, and the Problem
of Domination. New York: Prometheus, 1988.

2. Book by two or three authors

Zweigenhaft, Richard L., and G. William Domhoff. Blacks in the White
Establishment. New Haven: Yale UP, 1991.

Author names after the first are identified first name first, and the final author's name is preceded by "and."

3. Book by more than three authors

Belenky, Mary Field, et al. Women's Ways of Knowing: The Development of Self,
Voice, and Mind. New York: Basic, 1986.

If a work has more than three authors, you may use the Latin abbreviation "et al." or list all the authors' names in full as they appear on the title page.

4. More than one book by the same author

Nelson, Mariah Burton. Are We Winning Yet?: How Women Are Changing Sports
and Sports Are Changing Women. New York: Basic, 1991.

---. The Stronger Women Get, The More Men Love Football: Sexism and the
American Culture of Sports. New York: Harcourt, 1993.

Selfe, Cynthia L. "Creating a Computer Lab that Composition Teachers Can Live
with." Collegiate Microcomputer 5 (1987): 149-58.

Selfe, Cynthia L., and Billie J. Wahlstrom. "An Emerging Rhetoric of Collaboration:
Computer Collaboration and the Composing Process." Collegiate
Microcomputer 4 (1986): 289-96.

If your Works Cited list contains more than one source by the
same author or authors, in the second and all additional entries
by that author replace the author's name with three hyphens (no
spaces) followed by a period. The hyphens represent the *exact*
name of the author in the preceding entry. If a source's author is
not identical to that in the preceding entry, list author names in
full. Two or more works with the same author are alphabetized
according to title; a work by a single author precedes works by
that author and one or more collaborators.

5. Book by a corporation, association, or organization

Society of Automotive Engineers. Effects of Aging on Driver Performance.
Warrendale, PA: Society of Automotive Engineers, 1988.

Alphabetize by the name of the organization.

6. Revised edition of a book

Peek, Stephen. The Game Inventor's Handbook. 2nd ed. Cincinnati: Betterway,
1993.

For second or any subsequent editions of a book, place the appropriate numerical designation (2nd ed., 3rd ed., etc.) after the
name of the editor, translator, or compiler, if there is one. If not,
place it after the title.

7. Edited book

Schaefer, Charles E., and Steven E. Reid, eds. Game Play: Therapeutic Use of
Childhood Games. New York: Wiley, 1986.

For books with a listed editor or editors but no author, place the
name of the editor(s) in the author position, followed by "ed." or
"eds."

8. Book with an editor and an author

Hemingway, Ernest. Conversations with Ernest Hemingway. Ed. Matthew J.
Bruccoli. Jackson: UP of Mississippi, 1986.

Books with both an editor and an author should be listed with the
editor following the title, first name first, preceded by the abbreviation "Ed." This convention holds true whether one or more editors are listed.

9. Book in more than one volume

Waldrep, Tom, ed Writers on Writing. 2 vols. New York: Random, 1985-88.

The total number of volumes is listed after the title. When separate volumes were published in different years, provide inclusive
dates.

10. One volume of a multivolume book

Waldrep, Tom, ed. Writers on Writing. Vol. 2. New York: Random, 1988.

When each volume of a multivolume set has an individual title,
list the volume's full publication information first, followed by series information (number of volumes, dates).

Churchill, Winston S. Triumph and Tragedy. Boston: Houghton, 1953. Vol. 6 of The
Second World War. 6 vols. 1948-53.

11. Translated book

Klaeber, Friedrich. Beowulf and the Finnesburg Fragment. Rev. ed. Trans. John R.
Clark Hall. London: Allen, 1950.

12. Book in a series

First NASA Workshop on Wiring for Space Applications. NASA Conference

    Publication. 10145. Washington: National Aeronautics and Space

    Administration, Office of Management, Scientific and Technical Information

    Program, 1994.

Immediately after the title, add the series information: the series
name, neither underlined nor in quotation marks, and the series
number, both followed by periods. Book titles within an underlined title are not underlined.

13. Reprinted book

Evans, Elizabeth E. G. The Abuse of Maternity. 1875. New York: Arno, 1974.

Add the original publication date after the title, then cite the current edition information.

14. Introduction, preface, foreword, or afterword in a book

Gavorse, Joseph. Introduction. The Lives of the Twelve Caesars. By Suetonius. New

    York: The Book League of America, 1937. vii-xvi.

Jacobus, Lee A. Preface. Literature: An Introduction to Critical Reading. By

    Jacobus. Upper Saddle River, NJ: Prentice, 1996. xxvii-xxxiii.

Nabokov, Vladimir. Foreword. A Hero of Our Time. By Mihail Lermontov. Garden

    City, NY: Doubleday-Anchor, 1958. v-xix.

List the author of the introduction, preface, foreword, or afterword
first, followed by the title of the book. Next insert the word "By,"
followed by the full name of the author of the whole work if different from the author of the piece, or the last name only if the same
as the author of the shorter piece.

15. Work in an anthology or chapter in an edited collection

Charen, Mona. "Much More Nasty Than They Should Be." Popular Writing in

    America: The Interaction of Style and Audience. 5th ed. Ed. Donald McQuade

    and Robert Atwan. New York: Oxford UP, 1993. 207-08.

Gay, John. The Beggar's Opera. British Dramatists from Dryden to Sheridan. Ed.
George H. Nettleton and Arthur E. Case. Carbondale: Southern Illinois UP,
1975. 530-65.

Kingston, Maxine Hong. "No Name Woman." 1976. The Blair Reader. 2nd ed. Ed.
Laurie G. Kirszner and Stephen R. Mandell. Upper Saddle River, NJ: Prentice,
1996. 46-56.

Enclose the title of the work in quotation marks unless it was
originally published as a book, in which case it should be underlined. The title of the anthology follows the book title and is underlined. At the end of the entry, provide inclusive page numbers
for the selection. For previously published nonscholarly works,
you may, as a courtesy to your reader, include the year of original
publication after the title of the anthologized work. Follow this
date with a period.

16. Two or more works from the same anthology or collection

Kingston, Maxine Hong. "No Name Woman." Kirszner and Mandell 46-56.

Kirszner, Laurie G., and Stephen R. Mandell, eds. The Blair Reader. 2nd ed. Ed.
Laurie G. Kirszner and Stephen R. Mandell. Upper Saddle River, NJ: Prentice,
1996.

Tannen, Deborah. "Marked Women." Kirszner and Mandell 362-67.

When citing two or more selections from one anthology, list the
anthology separately under the editor's name. Selection entries
will then need to include only a shortened cross-reference to the
anthology entry, as illustrated above.

17. Periodical article reprinted in a collection

Atwell, Nancie. "Everyone Sits at a Big Desk: Discovering Topics for Writing."
English Journal 74 (1985): 35-39. Rpt. in Rhetoric and Composition: A
Sourcebook for Teachers and Writers. 3rd ed. Ed. Richard Graves. Portsmouth,
NH: Boynton/Cook, 1990. 76-83.

Include the full citation for the original periodical publication, followed by "Rpt. in" (Reprinted in) and the book publication information. Provide inclusive page numbers for both sources.

18. Article in a reference book

"Behn, Aphra." The Concise Columbia Encyclopedia. 1983 ed.

"Langella, Frank." International Television and Video Almanac. 40th ed. New York:
Quigley, 1995.

Miller, Peter L. "The Power of Flight." The Encyclopedia of Insects. Ed. Christopher
O'Toole. New York: Facts on File, 1986. 18-19.

For signed articles in reference books, begin with the author's
name. For commonly known reference works (*Concise Columbia*),
you need not include full publication information or editors'
names. Page and volume numbers are also unnecessary when the
entries in the reference book are arranged alphabetically.

19. Anonymous book

The End of a Presidency. New York: Bantam, 1974.

Alphabetically arrange anonymous books (and most other sources
lacking an author name) in the Works Cited list by title, excluding
A, An, or *The.*

20. Government document

United States. Cong. House. Committee on Energy and Commerce. Ensuring
Access to Programming for the Backyard Satellite Dish Owner. Washington:
GPO, 1986.

If the author is identified, begin with that name. If not, begin with
the government (country or state), followed by the agency or organization. Most U.S. Government documents are printed/pub-
lished by the Government Printing Office in Washington, DC. You
may abbreviate this office *GPO.*

21. Dissertation
UNPUBLISHED

McGuire, Lisa C. "Adults' Recall and Retention of Medical Information." Diss.
Bowling Green State University, 1993.

Enclose the title of an unpublished dissertation in quotation
marks, followed by the abbreviation "Diss." and the name of the
university and the year.

PUBLISHED

Boothby, Daniel W. The Determinants of Earnings and Occupation for Young

    Women. Diss. U. of Cal., Berkeley, 1978. New York: Garland, 1984.

For a published dissertation, underline the title, list the university and year as for an unpublished dissertation, and then add publication information as for a book, including the order number if the publisher is University Microfilms International (UMI). The descriptive abbreviation "Diss." still follows the title.

22. A pamphlet

McKay, Hughina, and Mary Brown Patton. Food Consumption of College Men.

    Wooster: Ohio Agricultural Experiment Station, 1943.

Cite a pamphlet just as you cite a book. Remember the abbreviations *n.p.*, *n.d.*, and *n.pag.*, where publication information is missing. Also see item 23 below.

23. A book with missing publication information

Palka, Eugene, and Dawn M. Lake. A Bibliography of Military Geography. [New

    York?]: Kirby, [198-?].

The MLA practice is to provide missing publication information if possible. If the information you provide does not come from the source itself—that is, if you succeed in finding missing information through another source—you should enclose this information in brackets in the Works Cited entry [198-?]. If a date of publication can only be approximated, place a "c." before it, the abbreviation for the Latin *circa*, or "around." You may also use the abbreviations "n.p."—depending upon placement in your entry, this abbreviation stands for either "no place" or "no publisher"—"n.d." (no date), or "n. pag." (no pages).

2 Documenting periodicals

24. Article, story, or poem in a monthly or bimonthly magazine

Hawn, Matthew. "Stay on the Web: Make Your Internet Site Pay Off." Macworld

    Apr. 1996: 94-98.

Abbreviate all months except May, June, and July. Hyphenate months for bimonthlies, and do not list volume or issue numbers.

25. Article, story, or poem in a weekly magazine

Updike, John. "His Mother Inside Him." New Yorker 20 Apr. 1992: 34-36.

The publication date is inverted.

26. Article in a daily newspaper

Brody, Jane E. "Doctors Get Poor Marks for Nutrition Knowledge." New York Times
10 Feb. 1992, natl. ed.: B7.

Finn, Peter. "Death of a U-Va. Student Raises Scrutiny of Off-Campus Drinking."
Washington Post 27 Sept. 1995: D1.

If an article in a newspaper is unsigned, begin with its title. Give the name of the newspaper as it appears on the masthead, excluding *A*, *An*, or *The*. If the city is not in the newspaper's name, it should follow the name in brackets: *Blade* [Toledo, OH]. Include with the page number the letter that designates any separately numbered sections; if sections are numbered consecutively, list the section number (sec. 2) before the colon, preceded by a comma.

27. Article in a journal paginated by volume

Nelson, Jennie. "This Was an Easy Assignment: Examining How Students Interpret
Academic Writing Tasks." Research in the Teaching of English 34 (1990): 362-
96.

If page numbers are continuous from one issue to the next throughout the year, include only the volume number and year, not the issue or month. For academic or professional journals, where volume numbers separate the journal title and the year of publication, MLA practice is to enclose the year in parentheses, reducing the potential for reader confusion.

28. Article in a journal paginated by issue

Tiffin, Helen. "Post-Colonialism, Post-Modernism, and the Rehabilitation of Post
Colonial History." Journal of Commonwealth Literature 23.1 (1988): 169-81.

If each issue begins with page 1, include the volume number followed by a period and the issue number. Do not include the month of publication.

29. Anonymous article

"Fraternities Sue Hamilton College over Housing Rule." The Chronicle of Higher
Education. 41.46 (1995): A39.

As with an anonymous book, if no author is listed for an article,
begin your entry with the title and alphabetize by the first word,
excluding *A*, *An*, and *The*.

30. Microform or microfiche article

Mayer, Caroline E. "Child-resistant Caps to Be Made 'Adult-friendly.'" Washington
Post 16 June 1995: A3. CD-ROM. Newsbank (1995) CON 16: B17.

If the listing is derived from a computer-based reference source
such as *Newsbank*, which makes selected periodical articles
available on microform or microfiche, you may treat it exactly as
you would any other periodical. To help your audience locate the
source as quickly as possible, however, unless it is just as easily
located in printed form, you should include in your entry the descriptor *CD-ROM*, the name of the service (*Newsbank*), and the
available section/grid information. See also the next section,
"Documenting Electronic Sources."

31. Editorial

"Sarajevo Reborn." Editorial. New York Times 21 Feb. 1996, natl. ed.: A18.

"'Blue' Makes Man Look Amazing." Editorial. Dayton Daily News 20 Feb. 1996: 6A.

If the editorial is signed, list the author's name first.

32. Letter to the editor and reply

Kempthorne, Charles. Letter. Kansas City Star 26 July 1992: A16.

Massing, Michael. Reply to letter of Peter Dale Scott. New York Review of Books 4
Mar. 1993: 57.

33. Review

Rev. of Bone, by Faye Myenne Ng. New Yorker 8 Feb. 1992: 113.

Rosen, Steven. "Dissing 'HIStory.'" Rev. of HIStory: Past, Present, and Future—Book

    I, by Michael Jackson. Denver Post 3 July 1995: F8.

Works Cited entries for reviews should begin with the reviewer's name, if known, followed by the title of the review, if there is one. Next the abbreviation "Rev. of" precedes the title of the work reviewed, which is followed by a comma, then the word "by" and the name of the work's author. If the work of an editor, translator, etc. is being reviewed instead an author's, an abbreviation such as "ed." or "trans." replaces the word "by." The entry concludes with standard publication information. If a review is unsigned and untitled, list it as "Rev. of ____" and alphabetize it by the name of the work reviewed. If the review is unsigned but titled, begin with the title. If the review is of a performance, add pertinent descriptive information such as director, composer, or major performers.

3 Documenting electronic sources

Two major kinds of online sources are important for researchers: one is the category that includes electronic newsletters, journals, and conferences; the other is electronic texts (literary works, scientific reports, historical documents, etc.).

Following MLA guidelines, Works Cited entries for electronic newsletters, journals, and conferences should be listed as are entries for articles in printed periodicals, with some additions: cite the author's name; the article or document title in quotation marks; the newsletter, journal, or conference title; the number of volume or issue; the year or date of publication (in parentheses); the number of pages or paragraphs (or "n. pag." if no pagination is given); the medium of publication ("Online"); the computer network name; and the date of access. The electronic address may be added to the end of the entry, preceded by "Available."

Entries for electronic texts should be listed as is a printed source, followed by the medium of publication ("Online"), the electronic text name (often a library or an archive), the computer network name, and the access date.

The 1994 MLA style sheet treats electronic publications in one of two ways, depending upon whether they are portable databases (those available in published form on CD-ROM diskettes or magnetic tape) or online databases (those accessible only through services or networks).

Portable databases are much like books and periodicals. Their entries in Works Cited lists are similar to those for printed material, except you must also include the following items:

■ the medium of publication (CD-ROM, diskette, magnetic tape)

■ the name of the vendor, if known (this may be different from the name of the organization that compiled the information, which must also be included)

■ the date of electronic publication, in addition to the date the material originally may have been published (as for a reprinted book or article)

Online databases are not portable and are often updated, so their citations must also include the following items:

■ medium of publication—specifically "Online"

■ computer service or network name

■ date of access, in addition to the date that the material originally may have been published (as for a reprinted book or article)

34. CD-ROM database, periodically updated

"U. S. Population by Age: Urban and Urbanized Areas." 1990 U. S. Census of Population and Housing CD-ROM. US Bureau of the Census. 1990.

If a database comes from a printed source such as a book, periodical, or collection of bibliographies or abstracts, cite this information first, followed by the underlined title of the database, the medium of publication, the vendor name if applicable, and the date of electronic publication. If there is no printed source, include the title of the material accessed (in quotation marks), the date of the material if given, the underlined title of the database, the medium of publication, the vendor name if applicable, and the date of electronic publication. You may occasionally have difficulty determining some of the information requested in these guidelines; as for any other type of source, however, simply follow the guidelines as closely and consistently as possible.

35. CD-ROM, nonperiodical

Myst. CD-ROM. Novato, CA: Broderbund-Cyan, 1994.

"O'Keefe, Georgia." The 1995 Grolier Encyclopedia. CD-ROM. Danbury: Grolier, 1995.

List as you would a book, adding the medium of publication and information about the source, if applicable. If citing only part of a work, underline the title of this portion or place it within quotation marks, as appropriate (as you would a printed short story, poem, article, essay, or similar source).

36. Diskettes

Greco, Diane. Cyborg: Engineering the Body Electric. Diskette. Watertown: Eastgate, 1996.

Lanham, Richard D. The Electronic Word: Democracy, Technology, and the Arts. Diskette. Chicago: U of Chicago P, 1993.

List in the Works Cited as you would a book, adding the medium of publication (e.g., "Diskette") and information about the printed source, if available.

37. Electronic texts

Melville, Herman. Moby Dick. New York: Hendricks House, 1952. Online. U of Virginia Lib. Internet. 6 Jan. 1996.

"Visible Human Project Fact Sheet." Visible Human Project. Bethesda: National Library of Medicine, 1995: n. pag. Online. National Library of Medicine. Internet. 10 Feb. 1996. Available Gopher: gopher.nlm.gov:70/00/visible/visibletxt.

Entries for electronic texts should include, as possible, the author's name, the title of the work, original (printed) publication information, publication medium ("Online"), repository of the online text (name of the online library), name of the computer network, and the date you "accessed" or read the text. By providing an Internet address for the text, which is optional, you can greatly benefit readers who might wish to consult your source.

38. E-mail messages

Fallon, John. "Re: EECAP Summer Seminar." E-mail to John Clark. 6 Feb. 1996.

Krause, Steven. "Rejoining the Conversation." E-mail to the Rhetnet listserv. 25 Jan. 1996.

E-mail messages are presented in the Works Cited very much as a personal letter would be listed. Include the name of the sender

MLA **18 c**

MLA
MLA
MLA
MLA
MLA
MLA
MLA
MLA

Conventions for list of Works Cited 271

(in the author position); the title (subject line), where available, enclosed in quotation marks; a message description which includes the recipient; and the date of the message.

39. Public postings on electronic networks

Davis, Gracie. "Facts about Tori and Eric." 20 Feb. 1996: n. pag. Online posting.

Newsgroup rec.music.tori-amos. Usenet. 27 Feb. 1996.

Haneef, Omar. "Question on Nietzsche." 21 Feb. 1996: n. pag. Online posting.

Newsgroup alt.postmodern. Usenet. 27 Feb. 1996.

To list public online postings, include the author's name, the title of the posting, the date of posting, the description "Online posting," the name of the newsgroup or forum where you found the posting, the name of the network, and the date of access. Common forums for public online postings include bulletin boards, commercial online services, and Usenet groups, all of which are *asynchronous*, or non-real-time discussion formats.

40. Materials available via electronic journals, conferences, etc.

"Children of Alcoholics." Children of Alcoholics Homepage. N.d.: n. pag. Online.

American Academy of Child and Adolescent Psychiatry. Internet. 9 Jan. 1996.

Dassbach, Carl H. A. "Where Is North American Automobile Production Headed:

Low Wage Lean Production." Electronic Journal of Sociology 1 (Sept. 1994). n.

pag. Online. Internet. 3 Aug. 1995. Available WWW:http://gpu1.srv.ualberta.

ca:8010/vol1.001/dasshtm.htm.

Gray, Jerry "In Congress, G.O.P. Ponders Tactics to Regain the Edge." The New

York Times on the Web. (25 Feb. 1996): n. pag. Online. Internet. 25 Feb. 1996.

Works Cited entries for sources accessed via computer networks should be similar to entries for print-periodical articles. As possible, the entries should include the author's name; the document title, underlined or within quotation marks, as appropriate; the underlined title of the electronic journal, newsletter, or conference; volume, issue, or other identifying number; publication year or date, in parentheses; the number of pages or paragraphs, or "n. pag."; the descriptor "Online"; the name of the network; and the date you accessed the material. The electronic address may be added at the end, preceded by the word "Available."

41. Materials available via networks, with printed analogues

Clark, John M. Applications of Gopher Information Systems for Composition Classes and Programs. Urbana: ERIC Clearinghouse on Reading, English, and Communication Skills, 1994. ERIC. CD-ROM. SilverPlatter. May 1995.

"The Fortune 500." Fortune Magazine. (15 May 1995): n. pag. Online. Internet. 23 Dec. 1995. Available WWW: http://pathfinder.com.

Kraft, Kenneth. "Practicing Peace: Social Engagement in Western Buddhism." Journal of Buddhist Ethics 2 (1995): n. pag. Online. Internet. 25 Feb. 1996.

Construct Works Cited entries as for online journal articles, etc. without printed analogues (item 40). The one significant difference is that dates of publication should be much more consistently available for works with printed analogues.

42. Software programs

WordPerfect for Macintosh. Vers. 3.5 CD-ROM. Orem, UT: Novell, 1995.

List as you would a book, adding other information (e.g., version number, medium of publication, information about the printed source) as applicable.

43. Publication on magnetic tape

English Poetry Full-Text Database. Rel. 2. Magnetic tape. Cambridge, Eng.: Chadwyck, 1993.

List as you would a book; the conventions are comparable to those for software programs.

44. Publication in more than one medium

Perseus 1.0: Interactive Sources and Studies on Ancient Greece. CD-ROM videodisc. New Haven: Yale UP, 1992.

List in Works Cited as you would a nonperiodical CD-ROM publication, adding information on all media making up the work.

45. Materials available via other, Internet sources

FTP

Hart, Michael. "Short FAQ." Project Gutenberg. (1995): n. pag. Online. Internet. 24
Feb. 1996. Available FTP: mrcnext.cso.uiuc.edu/pub/etext/gutenberg/articles.

Williams, Mathew. Autoflow. (1994): n. pag. Hypercard stack. Online. Internet. 2
Feb. 1996. Available FTP: dartmouth.edu/pub/hypertexts.

GOPHER

Clinton, William. "Remarks by the President at the Tribute Dinner for Senator Byrd."
Washington: Office of the White House Press Secretary, 17 July 1994: n. pag.
Online. Internet. 27 Feb. 1996. Available Gopher: info.tamu.edu.70/00/
.data/politics/1994/byrd.0717.

Darwin, Charles. The Voyage of the Beagle. Harvard Classics Vol. 29. New York:
Collier, 1909. Rel. Sept. 1993. Online. Wiretap Electronic Library. Internet. 2
Mar. 1996. Available Gopher: wiretap.spies.com.70/00/Library/Classic/
beagle.txt.

ONLINE CHAT SESSIONS (E.G., IRC/MUD/MOO)

Callis, Rhonda. "Virtual Class Meeting." CollegeTown MOO. Online. Internet. 14
April 1994. Telnet patty.bvu.edu.

StoneHenger. Personal Interview. The Glass Dragon MOO. Online. Internet. 6 Feb.
1995. Telnet surf.tstc.edu.

TELNET

King, Jr., Martin Luther. "I Have a Dream Speech." N.p.: n.p., (28 Aug. 1963): n. pag.
Online. Internet. 3 Jan. 1996. Available Telnet: ukanaix.cc.ukans.edu.

"1993 University Guide to NASA." N.p: National Aeronautics and Space
Administration, 15 Feb. 1993: n. pag. Online. Internet. 20 Feb. 1996. Available
Telnet: spacelink.msfc.nasa.gov.

WWW

"Chicago Prep Star Fields Seriously Injured in Crash." ESPN Sportszone (27 Feb.

1996): n. pag. Online. Internet. 27 Feb. 1996. Available WWW: http://www.

sportszone.com/gen/top/0707241001.html.

Williams, Scott. "Back to School With the Quilt." AIDS Memorial Quilt Website. N.d.:

n.pag. Online. Internet. Available WWW: http://www.aidsquilt. org/newslet-

ter/stories/backto.html.

Even though the current, 4th edition of the *MLA Handbook for Writers of Research Papers* does not specifically or separately treat all of the online sources listed in item 45, these sources of information are sufficiently covered *in general* in the *MLA Handbook* to be confidently listed as explained here. For each type of resource—whether electronic or print publication—both original date of publication and date of access are required. This procedure holds true, however, only if a publication date is both provided and customary for that type of source. IRCs, MUDs, and MOOs, for example, are seldom "published" in the traditional sense; archives of these discussions are sometimes available, but publication dates are rarely cited. The Alliance for Computers and Writing, using a style sheet developed by Janice R. Walker, also extrapolates from current MLA guidelines to suggest that WWW-based sources need only an access date. Following this line of reasoning, the most logical citation date for a fast-changing Web document is the date you "visited" or read the work.

The usual online descriptors "Online" and "Internet" are used for all of the sources above, and the order of entry items is also standard. Note that optional online addresses increase in importance as the emphasis on online access of sources increases. Also note that the period that ends each online address in the examples listed is not part of the address but end punctuation for the grammatical sentence.

4 Documenting other sources

46. Cartoon

Davis, Jim. "Garfield." Cartoon. Courier [Findlay, OH] 17 Feb. 1996: E4.

Roberts, Victoria. Cartoon. New Yorker 13 July 1992: 34.

47. Film or videocassette

Casablanca. Dir. Michael Curtiz. With Humphrey Bogart and Ingrid Bergman.
Warner Bros., 1942.

Fast Food: What's in It for You. Prod. The Center for Science in the Public Interest
and Churchill Films. Videocassette. Los Angeles: Churchill, 1988.

Begin with the title, followed by the director, the studio, and the year released. Optionally, you may include the names of lead actors, producer, and the like between the title and the distribution information. If your essay is concerned with a particular person's work on a film, lead with that person's name, arranging all other information accordingly.

Lewis, Joseph H., dir. Gun Crazy. Screenplay by Dalton Trumbo. King Bros., 1950.

48. Personal interview

Holden, James. Personal interview. 12 Jan. 1993.

Morser, John. Professor of Political Science, U of Wisconsin. Telephone interview. 15
Dec. 1993.

Begin with the interviewee's name and specify the kind of interview and the date. Identify the interviewee's position if relevant to the purpose of the interview.

49. Published or broadcast interview

Sowell, Thomas. "Affirmative Action Programs." Interview. All Things Considered.
NPR. WGTE, Toledo. 5 June 1990.

Steinglass, David. Interview. Counterpoint 7 May 1970: 3-4.

For published or broadcast interviews, begin with the interviewee's name. Include appropriate publication information for a periodical or book and appropriate broadcast information for a radio or television program.

MLA

Documenting sources: MLA style

50. Print advertisement

Cadillac DeVille. Advertisement. New York Times 21 Feb. 1996, natl. ed.: A20.

Begin with the name of the product, followed by the description "Advertisement" and normal publication information for the source.

51. Unpublished lecture, public address, or speech

Graves, Donald. "When Bad Things Happen to Good Ideas." National Council of
Teachers of English Convention. St. Louis, 21 Nov. 1989.

Begin with the speaker, followed by the title (if any), the meeting (and sponsoring organization, if needed), the location, and the date. If it is untitled, use a descriptive label (such as "Speech") with no quotation marks.

52. Personal or unpublished letter

Friedman, Paul. Letter to the author. 18 Mar. 1992.

Personal letters and e-mail messages are handled nearly identically in Works Cited entries. Begin with the name of the writer, identify the type of communication (e.g., "Letter"), and specify the audience. Include the date written if known, and the date received if not. To cite an unpublished letter from an archive or private collection, include information that locates the holding (for example, "Quinn-Adams Papers. Lexington Historical Society. Lexington, KY.").

53. Published letter

King, Jr., Martin Luther. "Letter from Birmingham City Jail." 28 Aug. 1963. Civil
Disobedience in Focus. Ed. Hugo Adam Bedau. New York: Routledge, 1991.
68-84.

Cite published letters as you would a selection from an anthology. Specify the audience in the letter title (if known). Include the date of the letter immediately after its title. Place the page number(s) after the publisher information. If you cite more than one letter from a collection, cite the entire work in Works Cited, and indicate individual dates and page numbers in your text.

54. Map

Ohio River: Foster, KY to New Martinsville, WV. Map. Huntington: U. S. Corps of

   Engineers, 1985.

Cite a map as you would a book by an unknown author. Underline the title and identify it as a map or chart.

55. Performance

Bissex, Rachel. Folk Songs. Flynn Theater. Burlington, VT. 14 May 1990.

Rumors. By Neil Simon. Dir. Gene Saks. Broadhurst Theater, New York. 17 Nov.

   1988.

Identify the pertinent details such as title, place, and date of performance. If you focus on a particular person in your essay, such as the director or conductor, lead with that person's name. For a recital or individual concert, lead with the performer's name.

56. Audio recording

Young, Neil, comp. perf. Mirror Ball. CD. In part accompanied by members of Pearl

   Jam. Burbank, CA: Reprise, 1995.

Marley, Bob, and the Wailers. "Buffalo Soldier." Legend. Audiocassette. Island

   Records, 422 846 210-4, 1984.

Depending upon the focus of your essay, begin with the artist, composer, or conductor. Enclose song titles in quotation marks, followed by the recording title, underlined. Do not underline musical compositions identified only by form, number, and key. If you are not citing a compact disc, specify the recording format. End with the company label, the catalog number (if known), and the date of issue.

57. Television or radio broadcast

"Emissary." Star Trek: Deep Space Nine. Teleplay by Michael Pillar. Story by Rick

   Berman and Michael Pillar. Dir. David Carson. Fox. WFLX, West Palm Beach,

   FL. 9 Jan. 1993.

If the broadcast is not an episode of a series or the episode is untitled, begin with the program title. Include the network, the station and city, and the date of broadcast. The inclusion of other information—such as narrator, writer, director, or performers—depends on the purpose of your citation.

58. Work of art

Holbein, Hans. <u>Portrait of Erasmus</u>. The Louvre, Paris. The Louvre Museum. By

   Germain Bazin. New York: Abrams, n.d., 148.

McIntyre, Linda. <u>Colors</u>. Art Institute of Chicago.

Begin with the artist's name. Follow with the title, and conclude with the location. If your source is a book, also give pertinent publication information.

This chapter provides samples of three research papers, two following Modern Language Association (MLA) format and documentation conventions and one following American Psychological Association (APA) conventions. Each of the student papers has been edited slightly for publication but remains largely as originally written. Each contains annotations explaining the format and documentation conventions. (For a full discussion of MLA style, see Chapter 18; for a full discussion of APA style, see 63d.)

19 a   Literary research essay: MLA style

In literary research essays, students are expected to read a work of literature, interpret it, and support their interpretation through research. The research in such papers commonly uses two kinds of sources: primary sources (the literary works themselves, from which students cite pages), and secondary sources (the opinions of literary experts found in books or periodicals).

The paper that begins on page 280 was written by Andrew Turner in a first-year English class. Students were asked to focus on a topic of personal interest about the author Henry David Thoreau and to support their own reading of Thoreau's work with outside sources.

TITLE CENTERED,
ONE-THIRD
DOWN PAGE　　The Two Freedoms of Henry David Thoreau

by

NAME　　　　Andrew Turner

INSTRUCTOR　　Professor Stephany

COURSE　　　　English 2

DATE　　　　　3 October 199x

1″

TITLE IS REPEATED FROM THE TITLE PAGE.

Turner 1

WRITER'S LAST NAME AND PAGE NUMBER APPEAR ON EACH PAGE.

DOUBLE-SPACED

The Two Freedoms of Henry David Thoreau

WRITER OPENS WITH THESIS.

Henry David Thoreau led millions of people throughout the world to think about individual freedom in a new way. During his lifetime, he attempted to live free of unjust governmental constraints as well as con-

WRITER IDENTIFIES TWO WORKS TO BE EXAMINED.

tentional social expectations. In his 1849 essay "On the Duty of Civil Disobedience," he makes his strongest case against governmental interference in the lives of citizens. In his 1854 book Walden, or, Life in the Woods, he makes the case for living free from social conventions and expectations.

ABBREVI-ATED TITLE IS USED AFTER WORK HAS BEEN IDENTIFIED BY FULL TITLE.

Thoreau opens "Civil Disobedience" with his statement that "that government is best which governs not at all" (222). He argues that a government should allow its people to be as free as possible, pro-

ONLY THE PAGE NUMBER IS NEEDED WHEN SOURCE IS INTRODUCED IN THE SENTENCE.

viding for the needs of the people without infringing on their daily lives. Thoreau explains, "The government does not concern me much, and I shall bestow the fewest possible thoughts on it. It is not for many mo-ments that I live under a government" ("Civil" 238). In other words, in his daily life he attends to his business of eating, sleeping, and earning a living and not deal-ing in any noticeable way with an entity called "a gov-ernment."

SHORT TITLE IS ADDED TO PAGE NUMBER BECAUSE TWO WORKS BY SAME AUTHOR APPEAR ON WORKS CITED PAGE.

Because Thoreau did not want his freedom over-shadowed by governmental regulations, he tried to ig-nore them. However, the American government of 1845

Turner 2

would not let him. He was arrested and put in the Concord jail for failing to pay his poll tax—a tax he believed unjust because it supported the government's war with Mexico as well as the immoral institution of slavery. Instead of protesting his arrest, he celebrated it and explained its meaning by writing "Civil Disobedience," one of the most famous English-language essays ever written. In it, he argued persuasively that "Under a government which imprisons any unjustly, the true place for a just man is also a prison" (230). Thus the doctrine of passive resistance was formed, a doctrine that advocated protest against the government by nonviolent means:

PAGE NUMBER ONLY IS USED BECAUSE THE CONTEXT IDENTIFIES THE WORK.

INDENTED 10 SPACES

> How does it become a man to behave toward this American government today? I answer that he cannot without disgrace be associated with it. I cannot for an instant recognize that political organization as my government which is the slave's government also. (224)

QUOTATION OF MORE THAN 4 LINES IS PRESENTED IN BLOCK FORMAT.

SIGNAL PHRASE INTRODUCES THE NAME OF THE SECONDARY SOURCE AUTHOR.

According to Charles R. Anderson, Thoreau's other writings, such as "Slavery in Massachusetts" and "A Plea for Captain John Brown," show his disdain of the "northerners for their cowardice on conniving with such an institution" (28). He wanted all free American citizens, north and south, to revolt and liberate the slaves.

PARTIAL QUOTATION IS WORKED INTO SENTENCE IN A GRAMMATICALLY CORRECT WAY.

Turner 3

In addition to inspiring his countrymen, Thoreau's view of the sanctity of individual freedom affected the lives of later generations who shared his beliefs. "Civil Disobedience" had the greatest impact because of its "worldwide influence on Mahatma Gandhi, the British Labour Party in its early years, the underground in Nazi-occupied Europe, and Negro leaders in the modern south" (Anderson 30). For nearly one hundred and fifty years, Thoreau's formulation of passive resistance has been a part of the human struggle for freedom.

WRITER SWITCHES TO DISCUSSION OF A SECOND WORK AFTER DISCUSSION OF FIRST WORK IS COMPLETED.

Thoreau also wanted to be free from the everyday pressure to conform to society's expectations. He believed in doing and possessing only the essential things in life. To demonstrate his case, in 1845 he moved to the outskirts of Concord, Massachusetts, and lived by himself for two years on the shore of Walden Pond (Spiller et al. 396-97). Thoreau wrote Walden to explain the value of living simply, apart from the unnecessary complexity of society: "Simplicity, simplicity, simplicity! I say, let your affairs be as two or three, and not a hundred or a thousand" (66). At Walden, he lived as much as possible by this statement, building his own house and furniture, growing his own food, bartering for simple necessities, attending to his own business rather than seeking employment from others (Walden 16-17).

ABBREVIATED POPULAR TITLE IS LISTED AFTER WORK'S FIRST REFERENCE.

IDENTIFICATION FOR WORK WITH MORE THAN THREE AUTHORS

PAGE NUMBERS FOR PARAPHRASE ARE INCLUDED.

Living at Walden Pond gave Thoreau the chance

Turner 4

to formulate many of his ideas about living the simple, economical life. At Walden, he lived simply in order to "front only the essential facts of life" (66) and to center his thoughts on living instead of unnecessary details of mere livelihood. He developed survival skills that freed him from the constraints of city dwellers whose lives depended upon a web of material things and services provided by others. He preferred to "take rank hold on life and spend my day more as animals do" (117).

PAGE NUMBERS ALONE ARE SUFFICIENT WHEN CONTEXT MAKES THE SOURCE CLEAR.

While living at Walden Pond, Thoreau was free to occupy his time in any way that pleased him, which for him meant writing, tending his bean patch, and chasing loons. He wasn't troubled by a boss hounding him with deadlines nor a wife and children who needed support. In other words, he wasn't expected to be anywhere at any time for anybody except himself. His neighbors accused him of being selfish and did not understand that he sought most of all "to live deliberately" (Walden 66), as he felt all people should learn to do.

Then as now, most people had more responsibilities than Thoreau had, and could not just pack up their belongings and go live in the woods—if they could find free woods to live in. Today, people are intrigued to read about Thoreau's experiences and inspired by his thoughts, but few people can actually live or do as he suggests in Walden. In fact, most people, if faced with the prospect of spending two years removed from soci-

Turner 5

ety, would probably think of it as a punishment or ban-

ishment, rather than as Thoreau thought of it, as the

good life.

    Practical or not, Thoreau's writings about freedom

from government and society have inspired countless

people to reassess how they live their lives. Though

unable to live as he advocated, readers everywhere re-

main inspired by his ideal, that one must live as freely

as possible.

WRITER'S CONCLUSION REPEATS THESIS ASSERTION.

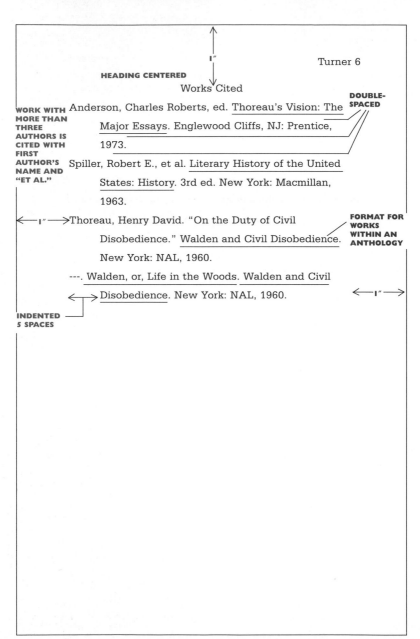

Turner 6

HEADING CENTERED

Works Cited

DOUBLE-SPACED

WORK WITH MORE THAN THREE AUTHORS IS CITED WITH FIRST AUTHOR'S NAME AND "ET AL."

Anderson, Charles Roberts, ed. Thoreau's Vision: The Major Essays. Englewood Cliffs, NJ: Prentice, 1973.

Spiller, Robert E., et al. Literary History of the United States: History. 3rd ed. New York: Macmillan, 1963.

Thoreau, Henry David. "On the Duty of Civil Disobedience." Walden and Civil Disobedience. New York: NAL, 1960.

FORMAT FOR WORKS WITHIN AN ANTHOLOGY

---. Walden, or, Life in the Woods. Walden and Civil Disobedience. New York: NAL, 1960.

INDENTED 5 SPACES

19 b Personal research essay: MLA style

The research essay, which begins on p. 288, "How to Become a Photographer's Assistant," resulted from an assignment asking students to investigate a career interest and report on it in an informal paper. Zoe Reynders writes in her own causal, personal voice yet uses careful library research (and some field research), which she documents according to the conventions of the Modern Language Association (MLA).

Reynder's paper illustrates the simple MLA style of identifying the writer of the paper and other pertinent academic information in the upper left-hand corner of the first page, followed by the title, centered. Page numbers are in the top right corner, without further punctuation or identification. Some instructors want students to put their last names at the top of each page, just before the page number, but others consider this unnecessary. (For an example of a paper with a title page as well as page numbers preceded by the writer's last name—both optional under the MLA system—see 19a.)

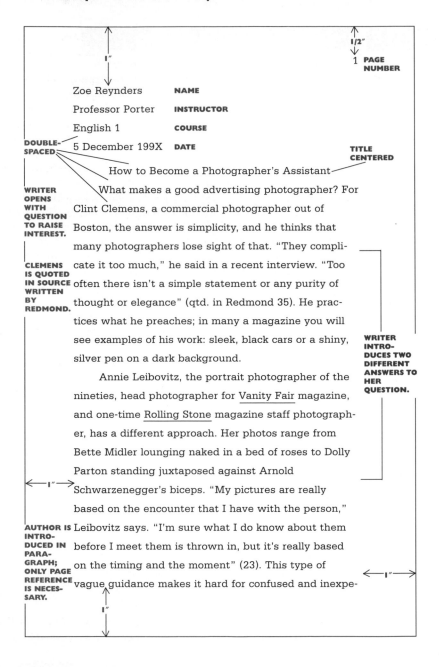

1/2″

1 PAGE
NUMBER

1″

Zoe Reynders   **NAME**

Professor Porter   **INSTRUCTOR**

English 1   **COURSE**

**DOUBLE-
SPACED** 5 December 199X   **DATE**   **TITLE
CENTERED**

How to Become a Photographer's Assistant

**WRITER
OPENS
WITH
QUESTION
TO RAISE
INTEREST.** What makes a good advertising photographer? For Clint Clemens, a commercial photographer out of Boston, the answer is simplicity, and he thinks that many photographers lose sight of that. "They compli-

**CLEMENS
IS QUOTED
IN SOURCE
WRITTEN
BY
REDMOND.** cate it too much," he said in a recent interview. "Too often there isn't a simple statement or any purity of thought or elegance" (qtd. in Redmond 35). He prac-tices what he preaches; in many a magazine you will see examples of his work: sleek, black cars or a shiny, silver pen on a dark background.

**WRITER
INTRO-
DUCES TWO
DIFFERENT
ANSWERS TO
HER
QUESTION.**

Annie Leibovitz, the portrait photographer of the nineties, head photographer for Vanity Fair magazine, and one-time Rolling Stone magazine staff photograph-er, has a different approach. Her photos range from Bette Midler lounging naked in a bed of roses to Dolly Parton standing juxtaposed against Arnold

←1″→ Schwarzenegger's biceps. "My pictures are really based on the encounter that I have with the person,"

**AUTHOR IS
INTRO-
DUCED IN
PARA-
GRAPH;
ONLY PAGE
REFERENCE
IS NECES-
SARY.** Leibovitz says. "I'm sure what I do know about them before I meet them is thrown in, but it's really based on the timing and the moment" (23). This type of vague guidance makes it hard for confused and inexpe-

←1″→

1″

2

rienced students like me to grasp any clue as to what is really wanted, what is necessary to succeed in the ever more competitive market of photography.

WRITER INTRO-DUCES HERSELF AND HER PROBLEM. Here I am, then, a lowly college student without access to a good darkroom, having no portfolio to show, attempting to get a commercial photography internship in New York City for the summer as a first step toward becoming a professional photographer. **USE OF FIRST PERSON AND CONTRACTIONS ESTABLISH INFORMAL TONE.**

WRITER STRUC-TURES PAPER ACCORD-ING TO HER QUEST FOR INFORMA-TION. With a little research, however, I've learned the steps to setting up an internship: First, establish contact through writing a letter and sending a résumé, then push your portfolio—mail it, drop it, call, recall, pester. In the process I've also learned that in commercial photography the emphasis is on commercial. Talent alone really isn't enough. If you don't represent yourself correctly, you may never get the chance to show off your photography talents.

This is understandable. An average photo shoot that will cover one full page in a relatively popular magazine can be worth anywhere from $2,000 to $200,000 and can take anywhere from one hour to three weeks to shoot. And the better known you are, the more you can charge, and the more you are used.

AUTHOR IS INTRO-DUCED IN SIGNAL PHRASE. According to Catherine Calhoun, "The current depressed market . . . is characterized by tried-and-true imagery, slick professionalism, and intense competition." But all this seemed, at first, irrelevant to me. I **NO PAGE NUMBER IS NEEDED FOR ONE-PAGE SOURCE.**

3

thought, I'm just in it for the experience, not the money, not the glamour nor the fame. Photography is fun, it is something I enjoy. Wrong. ————————— **FRAGMENT IS ACCEPTABLE IN INFORMAL PAPER.**

I've learned that not every aspect of taking photographs is that much fun. "Practically every photographer has a preconceived notion of what he will shoot **BOOK TITLE IS INTRODUCED BECAUSE IT IS POPULAR AND CATCHY.** and what he won't shoot," writes Richard Sharabura in his lively book Shoot Your Way to a $-Million. He continues, "This is probably one of the most common stumbling blocks to financial success" (56). Commercial photographers cannot pick and choose to do only the assignments they want or they would lose clients.

WRITER CONTINUES INFORMAL APPROACH BY DIRECTLY ADDRESSING THE READER. What? You're not interested in shooting a cat food ad? This can deter creative photographers because it seems more obvious today that companies approach advertising conservatively. Special-effects photography and the unconventional photo don't sell products. John Jay, creative director of Bloomingdale's, reiterates this: **POSITION OF AUTHOR IS MENTIONED TO LEND AUTHORITY.** "There's a lot more money on the line than there used to be. . . . There's not a lot of encouragement for experimentation" (qtd. in Redmond 35).

I've also learned that becoming a photographer's **STRUCTURE BASED ON QUEST FOR INFORMATION CONTINUES.** assistant is a creative void and does not entail ever taking any actual pictures. Committing myself to interning this summer won't mean blissful photo shoots with famous people. It will mean ten hours a day of getting up before the sun, packing photography equip-

4

ment, carrying supplies, loading cameras, setting up
lights, answering phones, and walking someone's dog.
Nevertheless, you have to prove that you are also competent. A highly paid photographer is not going to risk
having an idiot load preexposed film into a camera.
This is where the importance of the portfolio comes in.
You are not showing your portfolio to get a commercial
photography job for yourself . . . you have to demonstrate that you understand and respect the art of a
finely produced photo.

So, after writing my polite letters to incredibly famous New York photographers, I next took about 50 of
what I consider my best images to the leading photog-
rapher at the University of Vermont, in hopes of identi- **DATE OF PERSONAL INTERVIEW CAN BE FOUND ON WORKS CITED PAGE.**
fying 10 or 15 of my pictures that may be portfolio
quality. Photo editor Tom Brennan took ten minutes to
sort through my images and then told me, "Most photography editors wouldn't take more than two minutes
to look at a portfolio."

Again, I became nervous, not because I didn't
think I could handle the job, but because of the strict
professionalism of these people. I question if my photos
are strong enough to make an impact, if I have what it
takes to stand apart from the crowd of would-be pho-
FURTHER CITATION OF BRENNAN IS UNNECES- SARY BECAUSE SOURCE IS CLEAR. tographers. Brennan chose 12 images he thought
would be good. They do not have a consistent theme
or subject; some are in black and white, others are

5

slides or color negatives. "What I am looking for are your photos that show some kind of feeling or atmosphere," he said. Some of the photos he chose, I would have too. Others, I wouldn't have looked twice at. It's clear that I will include everything from a landscape to a portrait of my father to pictures of kids, and even an egg. The more variety, the better to demonstrate a wide range of skills.

PARA-PHRASED INFORMA-TION IS DOCU-MENTED.

Henrietta Brackman, author of The Perfect Portfolio, carefully outlines how to edit photos for a portfolio: First the work has to be good. (Who could have guessed?) But it is also important to examine every detail, to make sure that the photo is printed and developed at its best and that the picture is intelligible to the eventual viewer. I've done lots of trick photography, but I am going to stick to my traditional pho-

PARTIAL QUOTA-TION IS WORKED INTO THE SENTENCE IN A GRAMMAT-ICALLY CORRECT WAY.

tographs. Bob Lynn, the graphics director of The Ledger-Star, says he "hopes to find surprises, not clichés" (qtd. in Upton 23). I know my photos don't belong in the family album; they are not clichés.

Lost in the technicalities of this whole process, I almost forgot why I really want this internship in the first place—for the practice and hands-on experience. But I hope to learn a more important lesson—to understand how and when to take career chances. An internship, I remind myself, will also make the outside world seem a little less frightening.

6

WRITER
CONCLUDES
WITH HER
OWN
IDEAS
RATHER
THAN
BORROWED
ONES.

So I'll keep sitting around hoping for a break. I can't guarantee that this research method for landing an internship will work; it still remains to be tried and tested. To my knowledge, there is no foolproof formula for a successful start. Like everybody else before me, I'm creating my own method as I go along.

1″

7

HEADING CENTERED Works Cited

AUTHORS
ARE LISTED
ALPHABET-
ICALLY,
LAST
NAMES
FIRST.

Brackman, Henrietta. The Perfect Portfolio. New York:
     Watson, 1984.

DOUBLE-
SPACED

Brennan, Tom. Personal interview. 12 April 1992.

Calhoun, Catherine. "The Secret of Their Success."
     American Photo July 1992: 95.

Leibovitz, Annie. Annie Leibovitz Photographs. New
     York: Rolling Stone, 1983.

Redmond, Sudie. "Commercial Photography Warfare."
     American Photo July 1990: 33-37.

← 1″ →

← 1″ →

Sharabura, Richard. Shoot Your Way to a $-Million.
     Boston: Chatsworth, 1981.

INDENTED
5 SPACES

Upton, John. Photography. New York: Time-Life, 1989.

19 c **Informational research paper: APA style**

The research essay on page 296, "Green Is Only Skin Deep: False Environmental Advertising," by Elizabeth Bone, was written in response to an assignment to identify and explain one problem in contemporary American culture. Bone's essay is documented according to the conventions of the American Psychological Association (APA). This sample includes title page, abstract, and outline page; check with your instructor to find out if these are required for course papers.

ABBREVIATED TITLE (OPTIONAL)

Green
1

PAGE NUMBERING
BEGINS ON TITLE
PAGE.

Green Is Only Skin Deep: TITLE

False Environmental Marketing

TITLE PAGE IS   Elizabeth Bone   AUTHOR
CENTERED TOP TO
BOTTOM, RIGHT TO
LEFT, AND DOUBLE-   Professor John Clark   INSTRUCTOR
SPACED.
                              English 1   COURSE

                       December 6, 199X   DATE

ABSTRACT SHOULD BE PRINTED ON A SEPARATE PAGE FOLLOWING THE TITLE PAGE

Green
2

HEADING CENTERED

Abstract

NO PARAGRAPH INDENT

THE ABSTRACT SUMMARIZES THE MAIN POINT OF THE PAPER.

DOUBLE-SPACED

Most Americans consider themselves environmentalists and favor supporting environmentally friendly or "green" companies. However, companies use a number of false advertising practices to mislead the public about their green practices and products by (1) exaggerating claims, (2) masking false practices behind technical terminology, (3) mis-sponsoring green events, (4) not admitting responsibility for real problems, (5) advertising green by association, and (6) solving one problem while creating others. Consumers must be skeptical of all commercial ads and take the time to find out the truth behind advertising.

**OUTLINE SHOULD FOLLOW THE TITLE PAGE AND
CONFORM TO TRADITIONAL OUTLINE FORMAT.**

1/2″

1″

Green
3

Outline   **HEADING CENTERED**

I.   Environmental consciousness is strong in   **DOUBLE-
      Americans.**   **SPACED**

   A.   Gallop poll finds 75% are environmentalists.

   B.   False advertising betrays consumers.

II.   Definitions are exaggerated by the media and
       government.   **LETTERS
                                                     INDICATE**
ROMAN   A.   Biodegradable plastic is false advertising.   **SUBDIVISIONS**
NUMERALS   **AND**
INDICATE B.   Federal Trade Commission regulates **SUBORDINATE**
MAJOR   definitions.   **POINTS.**
DIVISIONS.

III.   Terminology is highly technical.

   A.   CFC's threaten our ozone layer.

   B.   Chrysler advertising misleads us about
       chemicals.

IV.   Some companies are green by sponsorship yet not   **OUTLINE
       green.**   **USES SEN-
                                                         TENCE
                                                         FORMAT.**

   A.   Ford supports the Smithsonian Institute Ocean
       Planet.

   B.   Ford is guilty of pollution in Michigan.

V.   It's not my problem.

   A.   CFC's are not caused by natural gas.

   B.   Natural gas causes other pollution.

VI.   Many companies are only green by association.

   A.   Advertising has nothing to do with product.

   B.   Chevrolet logo implies relationship.

Green
4

VII.   Some companies are singled-minded in their

         environmentalism.

    A.   Chevron employees do good in Mississippi.

    B.   Chevron pollutes Santa Monica Bay.

VIII. Environmental image does not match reality.

    A.   Earth First! educates consumers.

    B.   Federal Trade Commission regulates.

    C.   Consumers beware!

↑
1/2″
↓

**TITLE IS REPEATED FROM
TITLE PAGE.**

Green Is Only Skin Deep:

False Environmental Marketing

A recent Gallop poll reported that 75% of

Americans consider themselves to be environmental-

ists (Smith & Quelch, 1993). In the same study, nearly

half of the respondents said they would be more likely

**DOUBLE-
SPACED**

to purchase a product if they perceived it to be envi-

ronmentally friendly or "green." According to Smith

and Quelch (1993), since green sells, many companies

have begun to promote themselves as marketing prod-

ucts that are either environmentally friendly or manu-

factured from recycled material. Unfortunately, many of

these companies care more about appearance than re-

ality.

**AUTHOR'S
NAME, DATE,
AND PAGE
NUMBERS ARE
IN
PARENTHESES.**

**INFORMA-
TIONAL
THESIS IS AT
END OF FIRST
PARAGRAPH.**

The most common way for a company to market

itself as pro environment is to stretch the definitions of

terms such as "biodegradable" so that consumers be-

lieve one thing but the product delivers something

else. For example, so-called biodegradable plastic,

made with corn starch, was introduced to ease con-

sumers' fears that plastic lasts forever in the environ-

ment. However, the corn-starch plastic broke down on-

ly in specific controlled laboratory conditions, not

outdoors and not in compost bins. The Federal Trade

Commission has updated its regulations to prevent

such misrepresentations, so that now Glad and Hefty

**FIRST
EXAMPLE OF
FALSE
ADVERTISING
IS
INTRODUCED.**

Green
6

trash bags are no longer advertised as biodegradable

(Carlson, Grove, & Kangun, 1993).

The use of technical terms can also mislead aver- SECOND EXAMPLE IS GIVEN.

age consumers. For example, carbon fluoride com-

pounds, called CFC's, are known to be hazardous to

the protective layer of ozone that surrounds the earth,

so that their widespread use in air conditioners is con-

sidered an environmental hazard (Decker & Stammer,

1989). Chrysler Corporation advertises that it uses

CFC-free refrigerant in its automobile air conditioners

PAGE NUMBER IS NOT LISTED WHEN IT IS LISTED ON REFERENCE PAGE. to appeal to environmentally concerned consumers

("Ozone layer," 1994). However, Weisskopf (1992) AUTHOR QUOTED BY NAME IN THE TEXT IS FOLLOWED BY PUBLICATION YEAR IN PARENTHESES.

points out that the chemical compounds that replace

CFC's in their air conditioners pose other environmen-

tal hazards that are not mentioned.

TRANSI-TIONS KEEP THE READER ON TRACK. Another deceptive greening tactic is the sponsor-

ing of highly publicized environmental events such as

animal shows, concerts, cleanup programs, and educa-

tional exhibits. For example, Ocean Planet was a well-

publicized exhibit put together by the Smithsonian

Institution to educate people about ocean conservation.

Ford Motor Company helped sponsor the event, which

it then used in its car advertisements: "At Ford, we

feel strongly that understanding, preserving, and prop-

erly managing natural resources like our oceans should

be an essential commitment of individuals and corpo-

Green
7

rate citizens alike" (Smithsonian Institution's Ocean
Planet," 1995, p. 14).

While sponsoring the exhibit may be a worthwhile
public service, such sponsorship has nothing to do with
how the manufacture and operation of Ford automobiles affect the environment. In fact, Ford was ranked
as among the worst polluters in the state of Michigan
in 1995 (Parker, 1995).

Some companies court the public by mentioning
environmental problems and pointing out that they do
not contribute to those problems. For example, the natural gas industry describes natural gas as an alternative to the use of ozone-depleting CFC's ("Don't you
wish," 1994). However, according to Fogel (1985), the
manufacture of natural gas creates a host of other environmental problems from land reclamation to the car-
bon-dioxide pollution, a major cause of global warming.
By mentioning problems they don't cause, while ignoring ones they do, companies present a favorable environmental image that is at best a half truth, at worst
an outright lie.

Other companies use a more subtle approach to
misleading green advertising. Rather than make statements about environmental compatibility, these companies depict the product in unspoiled natural settings or
use green quotations that have nothing to do with the
product itself. For example, one Chevrolet advertise-

SHORTENED
TITLE IS
USED WHEN
NO AUTHOR
IS CREDITED
ON
REFERENCE
PAGE.

Green
8

QUOTE OF FEWER THAN 40 WORDS IS INTEGRATED INTO THE TEXT.

ment shows a lake shrouded in mist and quotes an environmentalist: "From this day onward, I will restore the earth where I am and listen to what it is telling me" ("From this day," 1994). Below the quote is the Chevy logo with the words "Genuine Chevrolet." Despite this touching appeal to its love of nature, Chevrolet has a history of dumping toxic waste into the Great Lakes (Allen, 1991). Has this company seriously been listening to what the earth has been telling it?

The most common manner in which companies attempt to prove they have a strong environmental commitment is to give a single example of a policy or action that is considered environmentally sound. Chevron has had an environmental advertising campaign since the mid-1970's. Most recently their ads feature Chevron employees doing environmental good deeds (Smith & Quelch, 1993). For example, a recent ad features "a saltwater wetland in Mississippi at the edge of a pine forest . . . the kind of place nature might have made," and goes on to explain that this wetland was built by Chevron employees ("The shorebirds who found," 1990). However, during the time this advertisement was running in magazines such as <u>Audubon</u>, Laganga (1993) points out that Chevron was dumping millions of gallons of nasty chemicals (carcinogens and heavy metals) into California's Santa Monica Bay, pos-

ELLIPSIS POINTS INDICATE MISSING WORDS IN QUOTATION.

Green
9

ing a health risk to swimmers. The building of the wetland in one part of the country does not absolve the
company of polluting water somewhere else.

It should be clear that the environmental image a
company projects does not necessarily match the realities of the company's practice. The products produced
by companies such as Chrysler, Ford, General Motors,
and Chevron are among the major causes of air and
water pollution: automobiles and gasoline. No amount
of advertising can conceal the ultimately negative effect these products have on the environment (Kennedy
& Grumbly, 1988). According to Shirley Lefevre, president of the New York Truth in Advertising League:

> It probably doesn't help to single out one auto-
> mobile manufacturer or oil company as signifi-
> cantly worse than the others. Despite small ef-
> forts here and there, all of these giant
> corporations, as well as other large manufactur-
> ers of metal and plastic material goods, put prof-
> it before environment and cause more harm than
> good to the environment (Personal communica-
> tion, May 1995).

Consumers who are genuinely interested in buying environmentally safe products and supporting environmentally responsible companies need to look beyond the images projected by commercial advertising
in magazines, on billboards, and on television. Organ-

DOUBLE-
SPACED

COLON IS
USED TO
INTRODUCE
A LONG
QUOTATION.

INDENTED
5 SPACES

INTERVIEW
CONDUCTED
BY
AUTHOR IS
NOT LISTED
ON THE
REFERENCE
PAGE.

izations such as Earth First! attempt to educate consumers to the realities by writing about false advertising and exposing the hypocrisy of such ads ("Do
people allow," 1994), while the Ecology Channel is

SECOND CITATION OF MORE THAN THREE AUTHORS IS SHORTENED TO FIRST AUTHOR'S NAME AND "ET AL."

committed to sharing "impartial, unbiased, multiper-
spective environmental information" with consumers
on the Internet (Ecology, 1996). Meanwhile the
Federal Trade Commission is in the process of continually upgrading truth-in-advertising regulations
(Carlson, et al., 1993). Americans who are truly environmentally conscious must remain skeptical of simplistic and misleading commercial advertisements
while continuing to educate themselves about the
genuine needs of the environment.

THESIS IS REPEATED IN MORE DETAIL AT END.

Green
11
HEADING CENTERED

References

AUTHORS ARE LISTED ALPHABETICALLY. Allen, F. E. (1991, March 10). Great Lakes cleanup enlists big volunteers. The Wall Street Journal, p. B1. **DOUBLESPACED**

INITIALS ARE USED FOR FIRST AND MIDDLE NAMES. Carlson, L., Grove, S. J., & Kangun, N. (1993). A content analysis of environmental advertising claims: a matrix methods approach. Journal of Advertising, 22 (9), 27-39. **ONLY FIRST WORD AND PROPER NAMES ARE CAPITALIZED IN ARTICLE TITLE.**

DATE FOLLOWS AUTHOR (OR TITLE IF NO AUTHOR IS IDENTIFIED). Decker. C., and Stammer, L. (1989, March 4). Bush asks ban on CFC to save ozone. Los Angeles Times, p. A1. **"P." OR "PP." IS NOT USED TO INDICATE PAGES IN A PROFESSIONAL JOURNAL.**

Do people allow themselves to be that gullible? (1994, September). Earth First! 9, 6.

Don't you wish we could just do this to CFC's natural gas advertisement. (1994, December 7). Audubon, 12, 7.

The ecology channel (1996). [Online]. Available www:http//www.ecology.com/

Fogel, B. (1985). Energy: choices for the future. New York: Franklin Watts. **BOOK AND PERIODICAL TITLES ARE UNDERLINED.**

From this day onward I will restore the earth where I am. (1994, November-December). [Chevrolet advertisement]. Audubon, 11-12, 18-19.

INDENTED 3 SPACES

Kennedy, D., & Grumbly, T.P. (1988). Automotive emissions research. In Watson, A., Bates, R.R., & Kennedy, D. (Eds.) Air pollution, the automobile, and public health (pp. 3-9). Cambridge, MA: National Academy Press. **"P." OR "PP." IS USED FOR PAGE NUMBERS IN BOOKS OR POPULAR PERIODICALS.**

Green
12

TITLES OF PERIODICAL ARE NORMALLY CAPITALIZED.

LaGanga, M. (1993, February 4). Chevron to stop
dumping waste near shoreline. Los Angeles Times,
pp. A1, A10.

The ozone layer has protected us for 1.5 billion years:
It's time we returned the favor. (1994, November-
December). [Chrysler advertisement]. Audubon, 11-
12, 40-41.

Parker, L. (1995 March 28). GM, Ford among top polluters in state. Detroit News, p. A2.

TITLE IS USED WHEN NO AUTHOR IS IDENTIFIED IN THE SOURCE.

The shorebirds who found a new wetland. (1990, July).
Audubon, 7, 38.

Smith, N.C., & Quelch, J.A. (1993). Ethics in marketing.
Boston, MA: Richard D. Irwin.

Smithsonian Institution's Ocean Planet: a special report. (1995, March). Outdoor Life, 3, 13-22.

Weisskopf, M. (1992, February 23). Study finds CFC alternatives more damaging than believed. The
Washington Post, p. A3.

PART FIVE

Revising

20 | The Revising Process

A first draft is a writer's first attempt to give shape to an idea, argument, or experience. Occasionally, this initial draft is just right and the writing is done. More often, however, the first draft shows a broad outline or general direction that needs further thinking and further revision. An unfocused first draft, in other words, is not a mistake but rather a start toward a next, more focused draft.

No matter how much prior thought writers give to complex composing tasks, once they begin writing, the draft begins to shift, change, and develop in unexpected ways. Each act of writing produces new questions and insights that must be dealt with and incorporated into the emerging piece of writing; it is during this process that active and aggressive revision strategies can help. Inexperienced writers often view revising as an alien activity that neither makes sense nor comes easy. However, most experienced writers view revising as the essence of writing, the primary way of developing thoughts to be shared with others.

20 | a | Understanding revising

The terms *revising*, *editing*, and *proofreading* are sometimes used to mean the same thing, but there is good reason to understand each as a separate process, each in its own way contributing to good finished writing. **Revising** is reseeing, rereading, rethinking, and reconstructing your thoughts on paper until they match those in your mind. It's conceptual work, generally taking place beyond the sentence, at the level of paragraph and higher.

In contrast, **editing** is changing language more than ideas. You edit to make precise what you want to say, testing each word or phrase to see that is accurate, appropriate, necessary. Editing is stylistic and mechanical work, generally taking place at the level of the sentence or word. The many dimensions of editing, including proofreading, are treated in Part VI.

Proofreading is checking a manuscript for accuracy and correctness. It is the last phase of the editing process, completed after conceptual and stylistic concerns have been addressed. When you proofread, you review spelling, punctuation, capitalization, and usage to make sure no careless mistakes have occurred that might confuse or distract readers. (See Chapter 56.)

There are two good reasons to revise before you edit. First, in revising you may cut out whole sections of a draft because they no longer suit your final purpose. If you have already edited those now-deleted sections, all that careful work goes for naught. Second, once you have invested time in carefully editing sentences, you become reluctant to cut them, even though these sections may no longer suit your purpose. Of course, writers are always circling back through the stages, editing when it makes more sense to revise, inventing when they mean to edit. Nonetheless, you will save time if you revise before editing, and edit before proofreading.

■ WRITING I: EXPLORATION

Describe any experience you've had with revising papers: Was it for a school assignment or some writing on your own? Why did you revise? How many drafts did you do? Were you pleased? Was your audience?

ESL **REVISING VERSUS EDITING**

As this chapter explains, revising the content and organization of your ideas is different from editing for word choice and grammatical correctness. When a person writes in a second language, it is often difficult to postpone concerns about word choice and grammar. Consequently, ESL writers sometimes try to edit prematurely. Although you may want to do some editing in early drafts, remember that taking time to revise content is very important and that you should work on revision before you do any extensive editing.

---

20 **b** **Planning to revise**

You cannot revise if you haven't first written, so write early and leave time to revise later. Good college papers are seldom written in one draft the night before they are due. When you plan in advance to revise, the following tools and techniques will serve you well:

Keep a revision notebook

When you begin any substantial writing project, keep a note-book or journal in which to capture all ideas related to your pa-per, including invention, drafting, research, and revision ideas. Over the span of several days or weeks, your revision may profit from your returning to earlier information, ideas, or insights. (See Chapter 4 for more about keeping a journal.)

Impose due dates

Write the due date for a final draft on your calendar, then add earlier, self-imposed due dates for first, second, or third drafts. Your self-imposed or false due dates will guarantee you the time you need to revise well.

Write and rewrite with a computer

Computers make revising easier and more effective. Any kind of word processing program allows you to change your text infi-nitely before ever calling it finished. The computer allows you to change words and sentences as well as move blocks of text from one part of your paper to another with ease—all essential acts of revising.

Read hard copy

When revising with a computer, print out hard copy of your drafts and see how they read on paper. Hard copy lets you scan several pages at a time and quickly flip pages in search of certain patterns or information.

Save draft copies

Make backup files on floppy disks of old drafts; if you become unhappy with your revisions, you can always return to the earli-er copy.

■ WRITING 2: APPLICATION

Describe your approach to writing a paper from the time it's assigned to the time you hand it in. Do you do any of the pre-revision work described above? Which of these general strategies makes sense in view of your current writing habits?

20 c Asking revision questions

To begin revising, return to the basic questions of purpose, audience, and voice: Why am I writing? To whom? In what voice?

Questions of purpose

It is often easier to see your purpose—or lack thereof—most clearly after you have written a draft or two. Ask the following questions:

1 Why am I writing this paper? (Review the assignment.)

2 Do all parts of the paper advance this purpose? (Outline by paragraph and make sure they do.)

3 What is my rhetorical strategy: to narrate, explain, interpret, argue, reflect, or something else? (Review appropriate chapters to fine-tune strategy.)

4 Have I stated the paper's theme or thesis clearly? (If not, do so, or have a good reason for not doing so.)

WP TIP Keep these basic questions of purpose in a "Purpose" file. Open the file—have it in a window if possible—and consult the questions whenever you begin a draft.

Questions of audience

Make sure your paper is aimed accurately at your readers by asking the following questions:

1 What does my audience know about this subject? (Avoid repeating elementary information.)

2 What does my audience need to know to understand the point of my paper? (Provide full context and background for information your audience is not likely to know.)

3 What questions or objections do I anticipate my audience raising? (Try to answer them before they are asked.)

WP TIP Keep these questions along with others you devise in an "Audience Profile" file. If possible, have it open in a window next to the file in which are brainstorming, drafting, or revising. Ask and answer the questions to yourself periodically.

Questions of voice

Make sure your paper satisfies you. Revise so you say what you intend in the voice you intend by asking the questions listed on page 314.

314 The revising process

1 Do I believe everything I've written in this paper? (Eliminate nonsense and filler.)

2 What doubts do I have about my paper? (Address these, don't avoid them.)

3 Which passages sound like me speaking and which don't? (Enjoy those that do, fix those that don't.)

WP TIP In a file you call "Voice," enter these and other relevant questions with the answers you provide. Bring them up easily so you can consult them as you look over your work.

■ WRITING 3: EXPLORATION

Can you think of other questions to ask about purpose, audience, and voice?

 CREATING TITLES

Titles catch the attention of readers and provide a clue to the paper's content. If a title doesn't suggest itself in the writing of your paper, try one of these strategies:

1. Use one strong short phrase from your paper.

2. Present a question that your paper answers.

3. State the answer to the question or issue your paper will explore.

4. Use a clear or catchy image from your paper.

5. Use a famous quotation.

6. Write a one-word title (or a two-word title, a three-word title, and so on).

7. Begin your title with the word "On."

8. Begin your title with a gerund (*-ing* word).

---

20 **d** **Revising strategies**

For many writers, revising seems to be an instinctive or even unconscious process—they just do it. However, even experienced writers might profit by pausing to think deliberately about what they do when they revise.

This section lists more than a dozen time-tested revision strategies that may be useful to you. While they won't all work for you all the time, some will be useful at one time or another. Notice that these suggestions start with larger concerns and progress toward smaller ones.

Some revising strategies are so important that we've treated them in a separate chapter (Chapter 21). **Limiting** is focusing on a narrow portion of a paper or concept and eliminating extraneous material; **adding** is incorporating new details and dialogue to make writing more vivid and powerful. **Switching** and **transforming** are more innovative strategies for revision: by changing the tense, point of view, form, or format of a piece of writing, writers can gain insights into their writing and present their ideas in a new light.

Establish distance

Let your draft sit for a while, overnight if possible, then reread it to see if it still makes sense. A later reading provides useful distance from your first words, allowing you to see if there are places that need clarification, explanation, or development that you did not see when drafting. You can gain distance also by reading your draft aloud—hearing instead of seeing it—and by sharing it with others and listening to their reactions. No matter how you gain it, with distance you revise better.

Reconsider everything

Reread the whole text from the beginning: Every time you change something of substance, reread again to see the effect of these changes on other parts of the text. If a classmate or instructor has made comments on some parts of the paper and not on others, do not assume that those are the only places where revision is needed.

Believe and doubt

First, reread your draft as if you wanted to believe everything you wrote (imagine a supportive friend), putting checks in the margins next to passages that create the most belief—the assertions, the dialogue, the details, the evidence. Next, reread your draft as if you were suspicious and skeptical of all assertions (imagine your most critical teacher), putting question marks next to questionable passages. Be pleased with the checkmarks, and answer the question marks.

WP TIP As you first reread your draft at the computer, just before printing a hard copy of it, underline or put into italics or "shadow" those passages that please you the most; put into bold the ones you believe merit some skepticism. When you print hard copy, you can find these various passages easily and respond accordingly. Be sure to remove these markers when you print final copy.

Test your theme or thesis

Most college papers are written to demonstrate a theme or thesis (to outlaw handguns; to legalize marijuana). However, revision generates other ideas, raises new questions, and sometimes reshapes your thesis (license handguns; legalize hemp as a cash crop). Make sure to modify all parts of your paper to keep up with your changing thesis

WP TIP Italicize and make bold your thesis statement so that you can return to it easily and recheck it.

Evaluate your evidence

To make any theme or thesis convincing, you need to support it with evidence. Do your facts, examples, and illustrations address the following questions?

1 Does the evidence support my thesis or advance my theme? (In states that license handgun ownership, crime rates have decreased.)

2 What objections can be raised about this evidence? (The decrease in crime rates has other causes.)

3 What additional evidence will answer these objections? (In states that do not license handguns, crime has not decreased.)

(For more on evaluating evidence, see Chapters 2 and 11.)

Make a paragraph outline

The most common unit of thought in a paper is the paragraph, a group of sentences set off from other groups of sentences because they focus on the same main idea. Make a paragraph outline to create a map of your whole paper and see whether the organization is effective: Number each paragraph and write a phrase describing its topic or focus. Does the subject of each paragraph lead logically to the next? If not, reorganize.

WP TIP After you have saved your paragraph, outline under one file name, copy the file and rename it. Then activate your word processing software's "Outline" function. (If you have one, it will be under "VIEW" in the menu bar for most programs.) Now view the paragraph with its key sentences set apart visually in outline form. (You can do this with an entire essay, as well.) Finally, ask yourself whether you are truly meeting your goals, and if not, create strategies for revising.

Rewrite introductions and conclusions

Once started, papers grow and evolve in unpredictable ways: An opening that seemed appropriate in an earlier draft may no longer fit. The closing that once ended the paper nicely may now fail to do so. Examine both introduction and conclusion to be sure they actually introduce and conclude. Sometimes it is more helpful to write fresh ones than to tinker with old ones. (For more on openings and conclusions, see Chapter 25.)

Listen for your voice

In informal and semiformal papers, your language should sound like a real human being speaking. Read your paper out loud when and see if the human being speaking sounds like you. If it doesn't, revise so that it does. In more formal papers, the language should sound less like you in conversation and more like you giving a presentation—fewer opinions, more objectivity, no contractions.

Let go

View change as good, not bad. Many writers become overly attached to the first words they generate, proud to have found them in the first place, now reluctant to abandon them. Learn to let your words, sentence, and even, paragraphs go. Trust that new and better ones will come.

Start over

Sometimes revising means starting over completely. Review your first draft, then turn it face down and start fresh. Starting over generates your best writing, as you automatically delete dead-end ideas, making room for new and better ones to emerge. (Many writers have discovered this fact accidentally, by deleting a file on a computer and thus being forced to reconstruct, almost always writing a better draft in the process.)

The next chapter, "Focused Revising" (Chapter 21), offers suggestions for creative revisions that may save heretofore dull papers and improve already interesting papers. The final revision chapter, "Responding to Writing" (Chapter 22), provides suggestions for obtaining thoughtful feedback from others as well as providing it to other writers yourself.

WP TIP   Print out three different drafts of the same paper and compare them. Rename the revised draft each time as a way of duplicating it.

 WRITING 4: EXPLORATION

Look over the suggestions for revision in this section. Which of them have you used in the past? Which seem most useful to you now? Which seem most far-fetched?

✔ REMINDERS FOR REVISION

1. Reread the **assignment** and state it in your own words. Does your paper address it?

2. Restate your larger **purpose**. Has your paper fulfilled it?

3. Consider your **audience**. Have you told them what they want and need to know?

4. Read the text out loud and listen to your **voice**: Does the paper sound like something you would say?

5. Restate the paper's **thesis** or **theme** in a single sentence. Is it stated in the paper? Does the paper support it?

6. List the specific **evidence** that supports this thesis or theme. Is it sufficient? Is it arranged effectively?

7. Outline the paper paragraph by paragraph. Is the development of ideas clear and logical?

8. Return to your **introduction**. Does it accurately introduce the revised paper?

9. Return to your **conclusion**. Does it reflect your most recent thoughts on the subject?

10. Return to your **title** and write five alternative titles. Which is the best one?

SUGGESTIONS FOR WRITING AND RESEARCH

INDIVIDUAL

Select any paper that you previously wrote in one draft but that you believe would profit from revision. Revise the paper by following some of the revision strategies and suggestions in this chapter.

COLLABORATIVE

Each member of the class go to the library and research the revision habits of a favorite or famous writer. If you cannot find such information, interview a professor, teacher, or person in your community who is known to write and publish. Find out about the revision process he or she most often uses. Write a report in which you explain the concept of revision as understood and used by the writer you have researched, and publish all the reports in a class anthology.   **WP TIP:**   If you can, locate a computer with access to the Internet, and with a classmate find a website about that favorite writer. Discern which information on the website is useful for your purposes (check in 18c on how to document a website as a source), and use it as part of your report.

Have you ever found yourself running out of ideas, energy, or creativity on what seemed to be a perfectly good topic for a paper? Have you ever been told to rewrite, revise, review, redo, rethink a paper, but didn't know exactly what those suggestions meant? Have you ever written a paper you thought was carefully focused and well researched but also was dull and lifeless?

Odds are you're not alone. When anyone writes a first draft—especially on an assigned topic to which he or she has given little prior thought—it's easy to summarize rather than analyze, to produce generalities and ignore specifics, to settle for clichés rather than invent fresh images, to cover too much territory in too little time. In fact, most first drafts contain more than their share of summary, generalization, superficiality, and cliché, since most first-draft writers are feeling their way and still discovering their topic. In other words, it's seldom a problem if your first draft is off the track, wanders a bit, and needs refocusing. However, it *is* a problem if, for your second draft, you don't know what to do about it.

The best way to shape a wandering piece of writing is to return to it, reread it, slow it down, take it apart, and build it back up again, this time attending more carefully to purpose, audience, and voice. Celebrate first-draft writing for what it is—a warm-up, a scouting trip—but plan next to get on with your journey in a more deliberate and organized fashion. Sometimes you already know—or your readers tell you—exactly where to go. Other times, you're not sure and need some strategies to get you moving again. This chapter offers four specific strategies for restarting, reconceiving and refocusing a stuck paper.

WP TIP As you immerse yourself in revising and "reseeing," be sure to save your work often. Create a new file for each new draft, name it, and date it for easy identification. Print hard copies, and type a heading for each, using the name of the file from which it was printed (as well as the date). Recording dates and even writing a brief note to yourself at the very beginning of a file will both help you remember what revision strategies you used and when. Later you may need to recover one or more of these drafts as you work toward a final draft.

21 **a** Limiting

Broad topics lead to superficial writing. It's difficult to recount a four-week camping trip, to explain the meaning of *Hamlet*, or to solve the problems of poverty, crime, or violence in a few double-spaced pages. You'll almost always do better to cover less ground in more pages. Instead, can you **limit** your focus to one pivotal day on the trip? Can you explain and interpret one crucial scene? Can you research and portray one real social problem in your own backyard?

Limit time, place, and action

When a first draft attempts to describe and explain actions that took place over many days, weeks, or months, try limiting the second draft to actions that took place on one day, on one afternoon, or in one hour. Limiting the amount of time you write about automatically limits the action (what happened) and place (where it happened) as well. For example, in the first draft of a paper investigating the homeless in downtown Burlington, Dan began with a broad sweep:

> In this land of opportunity, freedom takes on different meaning for different people. Some people are born to wealth, others obtain it by the sweat of their brows, while average Americans always manage to get by. But others, not so fortunate or talented, never have enough food or shelter to make even the ends of their daily lives meet.

While there is nothing inherently wrong with this start, neither is there anything new, interesting, or exciting. The generalizations about wealth and poverty tell us only what we already know; there are no new facts, information, or images to catch our attention and hold it for the pages still to come.

Before writing his second draft, Dan visited the downtown area, met some homeless people, and observed firsthand the habits of a single homeless man named Brian; then he limited his focus and described what he witnessed on one morning.

Dressed in soiled blue jeans and a ragged red flannel shirt, Brian digs curiously through an evergreen bush beside a house on Loomis Street. His yellow mesh baseball cap bears no emblem or logo to mark him a member of any team. He wears it low, concealing any expression his eyes might disclose. After a short struggle, he emerges from the bush, a Budweiser can in hand, a grin across his face. Pouring out the remaining liquid, he tosses the can into his shopping cart among other aluminum, glass, and plastic containers. He pauses, slides a Marlboro out of the crumpled pack in his breast pocket, lights it, and resumes his expedition.

While only one small act happens in this revised first paragraph—the retrieving of a single beer can—that act anticipates Dan's forthcoming story of how unemployed homeless people earn money. By starting with a single authentic scene, Dan writes more about less; in the process, he teaches his readers specific things about people he originally labeled "not so fortunate or talented." By describing instead of evaluating or interpreting this scene, he invites readers to make their own inferences about what it means. In other words, writing one specific, accurate, nonjudgmental scene asks readers to interpret and therefore engage more deeply in the text.

Limit scope

In the process of Dan's researching and writing, the scope of his paper became progressively more restricted: In draft one, he focused on the homeless in America; in draft two, he focused on the homeless in downtown Burlington; in draft three, he focused on those homeless people who collect cans for income. From his initial limitation in time came a consequent limitation in scope, and a distinct gain in specificity, detail, and reader interest.

One technique for limiting the scope of any type of paper is to identify the topic of any one page, paragraph, or sentence in which something important or interesting is introduced. Begin your next paper with that specific topic, focusing close now and limiting the whole draft to only that topic. For example, in a paper arguing against the clear-cutting of forests, focus on one page describing the cutting of Western red cedar; limit the next whole draft to that single subject. In a paper examining the exploitation of women in television advertising, focus on one paragraph describing a single beer ad; limit the next whole draft to that single subject. In a paper examining your high school soccer career, focus on one sentence describing the locker room after the loss of the championship game. By limiting your scope you expand the depth of your topic.

WP TIP If you are keeping an online journal, peruse your journal and read your draft in the same sitting. Highlight in bold, sentences that might be useful in helping you limit your topic in the draft you're working on. Start a new entry in which you copy those bold sentences and outline a plan for limiting your topic.

■ **WRITING I: APPLICATION**

Devote a portion of your journal or class notebook exclusively to exploring the revision possibilities of one paper. For your first entry, reread the paper you intend to revise, and limit either the time or scope that you intend to cover in the second draft.

21 **b** **Adding**

A sure way to increase reader interest in a paper, and your own interest as well, is to **add** new and specific material to that overly general first draft. Whether you are arguing about the effects of mountain bikes on the wilderness, explaining the situation of the homeless people downtown, or interpreting the poems of Gwendolyn Brooks, it is your job to become the most informed expert on this subject in your writing class. It's your job to read the necessary articles, visit the appropriate places, interview the relevant people who will make you the authority to write the paper. On first drafts, neither your instructor nor classmates expect you to be this authority; on subsequent drafts, their expectations increase.

Add expert voices

The surest ways to locate new information to add to next drafts is to read widely and listen carefully. Get to the library and locate sources that supplement and substantiate your own voice. Quote the experts, identifying who they are and why they should be listened to. Also get out into the field and talk to people who are the local experts on your subject. Quote these experts too, and include their voices in your next draft.

Although textual quotations are helpful and expected in academic papers, they are seldom so locally specific or lively as interview quotations from local people. In many instances where little may have been published on local issues, the only way to get up-to-date local information is from talking to people. Quoting people directly not only adds new and credible information to your paper, it invariably adds a sense of life as well. For example, as Dan continued his story of Burlington's homeless people, he interviewed a number of people, such as police officer Hardy, who had first-hand knowledge of the homeless can collectors.

> "They provide a real service to the community," he explains. "You'd see a lot more cans and bottles littering the streets if they weren't out here working hard each day. I've never had a problem with any of them. They are a real value."

While Dan himself could have made the same observation, it has greater authority and life coming from a cop on the beat.

In another instance, a team of first-year students collaborated to write a profile of the local Ronald McDonald House, a non-profit organization providing free room and board for the families of hospital patients. In their first draft, they researched the local newspaper for introductory information on the origins of this institution; it was useful information, but without much life:

> The McDonald's corporation actually provided less than 5% of the total cost of starting the Ronald McDonald House. The other 95% of the money came from local businesses and special-interest groups.

For their second draft, the group interviewed the director of the Ronald McDonald House and used her as an additional and more current source of information. In fact, they devoted the entire second draft to material collected through interviews with the director and staff at the house. In the following sample, the director substantiates the information from the initial newspaper story but adds more specific, local, and lively details.

> "Our biggest problem is that people think we're supported by the McDonald corporation. We have to get people to understand that anything we get from McDonald's is just from the particular franchise's generosity—and may be no more than is donated by other local merchants. Martins, Hood, and Ben and Jerry's provide much of the food. McDonald's is not obligated to give us anything. The only reason we use their name is because of its child appeal."

Their final profile of the Ronald McDonald House included information ranging from newspaper and newsletter stories to site descriptions and interviews with staff, volunteers, and family.

Add details

If you quickly review this chapter's samples of revision by **limiting** and **adding**, you will notice the increase in specific detail. Focusing close, interviewing people, and researching texts all produce specific information which adds both energy and evidence to whatever paper you are writing. In the can collecting paper, the visual details make Brian come alive—*the soiled blue jeans, red flannel shirt, yellow mesh cap, Budweiser can, Marlboro cigarette pack*. In the Ronald McDonald revisions, the newspaper statistics add authority (*5% McDonald Corporation contribution*) while the interview information adds specificity (*Martins, Hood, Ben and Jerry's*), both of which help explain the funding of this nonprofit organization.

WP TIP Remember that you can easily add quotations, details, and other features to your writing through word processing. Any additions can be moved or deleted later with little effort should you change your mind.

■ WRITING 2: APPLICATION

Identify texts, places, or people that contain information relevant to your paper topic and go collect it. If you are writing a paper strictly from memory, close your eyes and visit this place in your imagination: Describe the details and recreate the dialogue you find there.

21 **c** Switching

Another strategy for focusing a second or third draft is to deliberately alter your customary way of viewing and thinking about this topic. One sure way to change how you see a problem, experience, story, issue, or idea is to **switch** the perspective from which you view it (the point of view) or the language in which you portray it (the verb tense).

Switch point of view

Switching point of view from which a story, essay, or report is written means changing the perspective from which it is told. For example, in recounting personal experience, the most natural point of view is the first person (*I, we*) as we relate what happened to us. Here Karen writes in the first person in reporting her experience participating in the Massachusetts women's basketball tournament.

> *We* lost badly to Walpole in what turned out to be *our* final game. *I* sat on the bench most of the time.

However, Karen opened the final draft of her personal experience basketball narrative with a switch in point of view, writing as if she were the play-by-play announcer broadcasting the game at the moment, in this case moving to third person *and* adopting a new persona as well.

> Well folks, it looks as if Belmont has given up; the coach is preparing to send in his subs. It has been a rough game for Belmont. They stayed in it during the first quarter, but Walpole has run away with it since then. Down by twenty with only six minutes left, Belmont's first sub is now approaching the table.

In her final draft, Karen opened from the announcer's point of view for one page, then switched for the remainder of the paper to her own first-person perspective, separating the two by white space. Karen's switch to announcer is credible (she *sounds* like an announcer); if she chose to narrate the same story from the perspective of the bouncing basketball, it might seem silly. (See Chapter 9 for Karen's complete essay.)

In research writing, as opposed to personal narrative, the customary point of view for reporting research results is third person (*he, she, it*) to emphasize the information and deemphasize the writer. For example, the profile of the Ronald McDonald House begins, as you might expect, with no reference to the writers of the report.

> The Ronald McDonald House provides a home away from home for out-of-town families of hospital patients who need to visit patients for extended periods of time but cannot afford to stay in hotels or motels.

However, in one of their drafts, the writers switched to first person and wrote an impressionistic account explaining their personal feelings about reporting on this situation. While the impressionistic draft did not play a large part in the final profile, some of it remained purposefully in their final draft as they reported where they had had difficulties.

> In this documentary, we had a few problems with getting certain interviews and information. Since the house is a refuge for parents in distress, we limited the kinds of questions we asked. We didn't want to pry.

Switch tense

Switching verb tense means switching the time frame in which a story or experience occurs. While the present tense is a natural tense for explaining information (see the first Ronald McDonald example just above), the most natural tense for recounting personal experience is the past tense, as we retell occurrences that happened sometime before the present moment—the same tense Karen adopted in draft one of her basketball essay. However, her final draft is written entirely in the present tense, beginning with the announcer and continuing through to the end of her own narrative.

> It's over now, and I've stopped crying, and I'm very happy. In the end I have to thank—not my coach, not my team—but Walpole for beating us so badly that I got to play.

The advantage of switching to the present tense is that it lets you reexperience an event, and doing that in turn allows you to reexamine, reconsider, and reinterpret it—all essential activities for successful revision. At the same time, readers participate in the drama of the moment, waiting along with you to find out what will happen next. The disadvantage is that the present tense is associated with fiction—it's difficult or impossible to write while you're doing something else, like playing basketball. It's also difficult to reflect on experience if you're pretending it's occurring as you write.

WP TIP Switch tenses by highlighting the verb and immediately retyping it; for verbs that you know you have used frequently, use the search-and-replace function to change tenses. Check your changes, though; context might make a difference in the effectiveness of the change, so judge each one individually.

Switch sides

Another way to gain a new revision perspective is to switch sides in arguing a position: Write one draft supporting the "pro" side, then write a second draft supporting the "con" side. For example, Issa, a dedicated mountain bike enthusiast, planned to write in favor of opening up more wilderness trails for use by mountain bikers. However, before writing his final draft, he researched the arguments against his position and wrote an earlier draft of his paper from that point of view.

The hikers and other passive trail users argue against allowing mountain bikes onto narrow trails traditionally traveled only
by foot and horse. They point out that the wide, deeply treaded
tires of the mountain bikes cause erosion and that the high
speeds of the bikers startle and upset both hikers and horses.
According to hiker Donald Meserlain, the bikes "ruin the tran-
quillity of the woodlands and drive out hikers, bird watchers, and
strollers" (Hanley 4).

The real advantage of switching sides for a draft is that you
come to understand your opponent's point of view better and so
argue more effectively against it in your final draft. For his final
draft, Issa argues his original position in favor of mountain bikes,
but he does so with more understanding, empathy, and effectiveness because he spent a draft with the opposition. His final draft
makes it clear where he stands on the issue.

Educated mountain biking, like hiking and horseback riding,
respects the environment and promotes peace and conservation,
not noise and destruction. Making this case has begun to pay off,
and the battle over who walks and who rides the trails should
now shift in favor of peaceful coexistence. Buoyed by studies
showing that bicycle tires cause no more erosion or trail damage
than the boots of hikers, and far less than horses' hooves, mountain bike advocates are starting to find receptive ears among environmental organizations" (Schwartz 78).

The tone of the final draft of Issa's mountain bike essay is less
strident and combative than it is conciliatory and compromising;
it seems a very reasoned and reasonable approach to a difficult
problem and was, perhaps, brought about by his spending time
seriously considering the objections of the opposition. (See
Chapter 11 for the complete essay.)

WRITING 3: APPLICATION

Write in your journal about a past experience, using the present tense and/or
third-person point of view. Then reread the passage and describe its effect on
you as both writer and reader.

21 d Transforming

To **transform** a text is to change its form by casting it into a
new form or genre. In early drafts, writers often attend closely to
the content of their stories, arguments, or reports but pay little
attention to the form in which these are presented, accepting the

genre as a given. However, recasting ideas and information into different genres presents them in a different light. The possibilities for presenting information in different genres are endless, since anything can become anything else. Consequently, keep in mind that some transformations are useful primarily to help you achieve a fresh perspective during the revision process, while others are appropriate for presenting the information to readers.

In the world outside of college, it is common for research information to be reported in different genres to different audiences. For example, the same research information may be conveyed as a report to a manager, a letter to the president, a pamphlet for the stockholders, and a news release for public media—and show up later in a feature article in a trade publication or newspaper. As in the working world, so in college: Information researched and collected for any paper can be presented in a variety of forms and formats.

Transform personal experience from essay to journal

The journal form encourages informal and conversational language, creates a sense of chronological suspense, is an ideal form for personal reflection, substitutes dates for more complex transitions, and proves especially useful for conveying experience over a long period of time. For example, Jeff used the journal format to tell the story of his month-long camping trip with the organization Outward Bound; following is an excerpt, edited for brevity, in which he describes his reactions to camping alone for one week:

> *Day 14* I find myself thinking a lot about food. When I haven't eaten in the morning, I tend to lose my body heat faster than when I don't. . . . At this point, in solo, good firewood is surprisingly tough to come by. . . .

> *Day 15* Before I write about my fifth day of solo, I just want to say that it was damn cold last night. I have a –20 degree bag, and I froze. It was the coldest night so far, about –25. . . .

> *Day 17* I haven't seen a single person for an entire week. I have never done this before, and I really don't want to do it again—not having anyone to talk to. Instead of talking, I write to myself. . . . If I didn't have this journal, I think I would have gone crazy.

Transform to letters

An issue might be illuminated in a lively and interesting way by being cast as a series or exchange of letters. Each letter allows a different character or point of view to be expressed. For example, Issa's argumentative paper on mountain bike use in wilderness areas could be represented as a series of letters to the editor of a local paper arguing different sides of the controversy: from a hiker, a horseback rider, a mountain bike rider, a forest ranger, a landowner, etc.

WP TIP Consider writing your letters to the editor at the computer. The copy function will eliminate the need to retype addresses and signatures in your series of letters.

Transform to a documentary

Radio, film, and television documentaries are common vehicles for hearing news and information. Virtually any research paper could be made livelier by being cast as a documentary film or investigative feature story. Full research and documentation would be required, as for formal academic papers; however, writers would use the style of the popular press rather than the MLA or APA. In fact, the final form of the profile of the Ronald McDonald House was written as a script for *Sixty Minutes* and opened with a Mike Wallace type reporter speaking into a microphone.

> Smith: Hello, this is John Smith reporting for *Sixty Minutes*. Our topic this week is the Ronald McDonald House. Here I am, in front of the house in Burlington, Vermont, but before I go inside, let me fill you in on the history of this and many other houses like it.

The final paper included sections with the fictional Smith interviewing actual staff members as well as some sections presented neutrally from the camera's point of view.

> Toward the back of the house, three cars and one camper are parked in an oval-shaped gravel driveway. Up three steps onto a small porch are four black plastic chairs and a small coffee table containing a black ashtray filled with cigarette butts.

Transform to a book with chapters

Teams of student writers can collaborate on writing a short book with "chapters" exploring an issue of common interest. Such a form could include a table of contents, preface, foreword, afterword, introduction, and so on. For example, Dan's report on the life of a can collector could become one chapter in a collaborative "book" investigating how the homeless live:

1   Housing for the Homeless

2   Dinner at the Salvation Army

3   Shopping at Good Will

4   Brian: Case Study of a Can Collector

5   Winter Prospects

WP TIP Try keeping one "transforming" file open for easy reference as you open another next to it for another "transforming" activity.

Transform to a magazine article

If you are investigating consumer products, such as mountain bikes, CD's, stereos, and the like, consider writing the final draft as a report for *Consumer Reports*. If you are investigating an issue such as homelessness, write it as an article for *Time* or *Newsweek*. Likewise, a campus story on the Greek system could be aimed at the campus newspaper. Before writing the final draft, be sure to study the form and conventions of the periodical for which you are writing.

Transform to a talk show debate

An especially good genre for interpretative or argumentative papers would be a debate, conversation, or panel discussion. For example, students recently wrote a paper as a debate on the advantages versus disadvantages of clear-cutting timber: On one side were the environmentalists and tourist industry, on the other side the paper companies and landowners; each side had valid points in its favor. The debate format was real, as it echoed very closely a similar debate in Congress.

Transform to any medium of expression

The possibilities are endless: song, play, poem, editorial, science fiction story, laboratory report, bulletin, brochure, commercial, public address, political speech, telephone conversation, e-mail exchange, World Wide Web page, poster, "Talk of the Town" for *The New Yorker*, sound bite, environmental impact statement, conference paper, video game, philosophical debate.

■ **WRITING 4: APPLICATION**

Propose a transformation for a paper you are writing or have recently written. List the advantages and disadvantages of this transformation. Recast your paper (or a part of it) in the new genre and describe the effect.

| **21** | **e** | **Experimenting with revising versus academic convention** |

Standard **academic conventions** are accepted ways of doing certain things, such as using an objective voice in research reports and placing the thesis first in position papers. These conventions have evolved over time, for a reason. When carefully done, they transmit ideas and information in a clear, predictable, and direct manner avoiding confusion, complexity, and subjectivity. Although in many cases these conventions work well, successful writers sometimes invent unorthodox strategies and experiment with new forms to express their ideas. In order to decide whether a conventional or an unorthodox form is preferable in any part of your paper, try both to see which more appropriately presents your ideas in their best light. Sometimes an act as simple as changing time, tense, point of view, or genre, can totally change the effect of a piece of writing.

The strategies described in this chapter are useful revising tools because they force writers to resee the events in their papers in different language and from different perspectives. Writing in new forms is also intriguing, exciting, and fun—which is often what writers need after working long and hard to put together a first draft.

When and under what circumstances should you limit, add, switch, or transform? While there are no rules, you might try using these strategies whenever you feel stuck or in need of new energy or insight. But be sure to weigh gains and losses whenever you use new focusing techniques.

Disregarding academic conventions in early drafts should seldom be a problem; however, disregarding them in final drafts is riskier, so check with your instructor. Be sure that in gaining reader attention in this way, you do not lose credibility or cause confusion.

SUGGESTIONS FOR WRITING AND RESEARCH

INDIVIDUAL

1. Write the first draft of a personal experience paper as a broad overview of the whole experience. Write the second draft by limiting the story to one day or less of this experience. Write the third draft using one of the other techniques described in this chapter: adding, switching, or transforming. Write the final draft any way that pleases you.

2. Write the first draft of a research-based paper as an overview of the whole issue you intend to deal with. In the second draft, limit the scope to something you now cover in one page, paragraph, or sentence. In the third draft, adopt one of the focused revision strategies described in this chapter: adding, switching, or transforming. For your final draft, revise in any way that pleases you.

COLLABORATIVE

1. For a class research project, interview college instructors in different departments concerning their thoughts about transforming academic papers into other genres. Write up the results in any form that seems useful.

2. As a class, compile a catalog in which you list and describe as many alternative forms for college papers as you can.

22 | Responding to Writing

All writers can use a little help from their friends. Few great books or good stories were written by one author in one draft without some kind of help along the way. This is not to say that individual authors do not compose their own work, for of course they do. But even the most skillful writers benefit from suggestions by editors, reviewers, teachers, and friends. In like manner, your writing will improve if you share it with classmates, consider their reactions, and revise accordingly. This chapter explores ways to give and get writing help.

22 | a | Asking for help

Writers can profit from help at virtually every stage of the writing process—brainstorming ideas, seeking research leads, proofreading—but it's while they're revising that most writers seek the help of potential audiences to find out what in their writing is strong, what weak, because then they still have a chance to do something about it. Following are some suggestions for getting help as you seek to finish your writing.

Identify the kind of help you want

When you share a draft with a reader, specify what you want. If you want help with ideas, tell your reader not to worry about grammar, mechanics, or style. If you are firm about your ideas but want help with style or proofreading, specify that need as well. If you do want a general reaction, say so—but be prepared to hear about everything and anything.

Ask specific questions

If you wonder whether you've provided enough examples, ask about that. If you want to know whether your argument is air-tight, ask about that. If you are concerned about your tone, ask about that. Also mark specific places in your paper about which you have questions, whether a word, a sentence, or even a paragraph. (See the box on p. 321.)

Ask global questions

Ask if the larger purpose is clear. Ask if the reader can identify your theme, thesis, or main point. Ask if the paper seems right for its intended audience. Ask for general reactions about readability, evidence, and completeness. Ask what objections or problems your reader would anticipate from other readers.

Listen, don't defend

Pay close attention to what you hear. You have asked for help, so now listen to what's offered. While listening to oral comments, stay quiet and take notes, interrupting only when you don't understand something. When reading written responses, read them twice before accepting or rejecting them.

Maintain ownership

Don't act on responses with which you disagree. If you don't understand or believe what someone tells you to do, don't do it. This is your paper and you will live with the results.

■ WRITING I: EXPLORATION

Describe the best written or oral response to a piece of your writing that you remember. What were the circumstances? Who was the respondent? Explain whether the response was deserved or not.

22 b Giving constructive responses

When you find yourself in a position to help other writers, keep the following basic ideas in mind.

- ■ **Follow the Golden Rule**. Give the kind of response that you would like to receive yourself. Remember how you feel being praised, criticized, or questioned. If you remember what helps, what hurts, what makes you defensive, you'll give better help to others.

- ■ **Attend to the text, not the person**. Focus on the writer's text and not his or her person. Writers, like all people, have egos easily bruised by careless or cruel comments.

- ■ **Praise what deserves praise**. Most writers accept critical help when they also receive complimentary help, and in most papers there is something that is praiseworthy. But writers can sense hollow praise, so avoid praising what doesn't deserve it.

■ **Ask questions rather than give advice**. It's your turn, now, to respect ownership. Asking questions gives writers room to solve their own problems. Of course, when asked, give answers or suggest alternatives if you have them.

■ **Focus on major problems first**. Address conceptual problems first, mechanical ones later on. Early drafts that are marked for every possible misspelling, typo, and grammatical slip can overwhelm writers, making them reluctant to revise at all. At the same time, most writers want such proofreading help on near final drafts, so it pays to check what the writer wants when.

■ **WRITING 2: EXPLORATION**

What kind of response do you usually give to a writer when you read his or her paper? How do you know what to comment on? How have your comments been received?

22 c Responding in writing

Responding to writing in writing, as most instructors do, is both common and convenient. Writing comments directly on manuscripts takes less time and is therefore more efficient than discussing every idea orally. It is easy to make written comments specific, identifying particular words, sentences, paragraphs, or examples that need attention. Also, written comments leave a record for writers to refer to later, when they actually get around to the rewriting.

The disadvantage to writing comments directly on papers is the possibility that misunderstandings will arise because you are not present to clarify. Try to ask questions rather than give answers and, again, follow the Golden Rule. The following suggestions may help.

Comment in pencil. Ink is permanent. Red ink looks bloody. Pencil, on the other hand, is soft, gentle, and erasable. Many writers have already developed negative associations from teachers' red ink comments that correct what's wrong rather than praise what's right. Don't do that to your classmates.

Use clear symbols. Consider using professional editing symbols to comment on a classmate's paper. (They are printed on the inside back cover of this book.) Or use obvious symbols that anyone can figure out—underlining or circling phrases that puzzle you or writing question marks in the margin. Put brackets where a missing word or phrase belongs.

ESL **THE LANGUAGE OF MAKING SUGGESTIONS**

In writing, the difference between an evaluation or judgment and a suggestion often depends on phrasing and sometimes on individual words. An **evaluation or judgment** places a value or a rating on the writing and is less helpful than a **suggestion** in providing details for revising. Try to concentrate on suggesting ways to improve any weakness you encounter.

EVALUATIVE   You should give more examples.
COMMENTS   Your introduction is too short.

SUGGESTIONS   You might consider giving other examples.
                   I think your introduction could be better if you gave your reader some more background information.

Here are some tips on writing suggestions for your classmates.

1. Use words or phrases that indicate a statement is your opinion as one reader.

I think	in my opinion	from my perspective
I feel	in my viewpoint	

2. Use *could* and *might* rather than *should* or *ought*

You *could* clarify the cause-effect relationship in the last paragraph.

Not: You should clarify. . . .

3. Avoid negative phrases unless you need them to state your opinion clearly.

I didn't understand how the second example was related to the first one.

Not: Your second example wasn't related to the first.

4. Use verbs like *seems* or *appears* to qualify your opinions.

The conclusion *seems* to shift to another topic.

The ideas at the end of your essay *appear* to be repeating ones that you stated earlier. Did you intend this?

5. Use questions if you are not sure that you interpreted the writer's ideas correctly.

You seem to be disagreeing with the author in one place but agreeing with her in another. Did I misunderstand your point?

■ **WRITING 3: EXPLORATION**

Describe your most recent experience in receiving written comments from someone. Were the comments helpful? Did the respondent follow the suggestions given in this section?

22 d Responding through conferences

One-to-one conferences provide the best and most immediate help writers can get. Sitting together, you can look at a paper together, read passages aloud, and make both general and specific comments about the writing. An oral conference helps as a follow-up to written comments, as conversations between writer and reader promote community, friendship, and understanding.

Conferences also make it easy to address both global and specific writing concerns at the same time. Finally, writer and reader can clarify misunderstandings as soon as they arise. However, it is harder to make tough, critical comments face to face, so readers are often less candid than when they make written comments. Also, conferring together in any depth about a piece of writing takes time.

The suggestions for making effective written responses also apply to oral conferences; however, there are a few additional things to keep in mind.

Converse in a comfortable setting

A place that's warm and casual can make a great difference in creating a friendly, satisfying discussion. When digressions occur, as they will if you're relaxed together, use them to learn new things about the subject and about each other; many such digressions circle back and help the writer. Even in the friendliest setting, if you don't discuss the writing itself, the writer will not be helped.

Ask follow-up questions

Ask clarifying questions to help writers advance their revision. When you have already written out responses, use the oral conference time to ask deeper or follow-up questions so together you can search for appropriate solutions.

WP TIP   If you have some of these conferences online, either on a List or through e-mail, print aspects of this conversation for in-class discussion and for expansion in your online journal.

WRITING 4: APPLICATION

Confer with a writer about his or her paper. Follow the suggestions given in this section. Describe in a journal entry how they worked.

22 e **Responding in writing groups**

Many serious writer belong to writing groups in which members both give and receive help with their writing. When a particular writer's work is featured, that writer receives a response from each member of the group; in other sessions, this person gives responses.

Writing groups allow a single writer to hear multiple perspectives on a draft, which provide either more consensus or more options for revision. They also allow an interpretation to develop through the interplay of different perspectives, often creating a cumulative response that existed in no single reader's mind before the session. Finally, writing groups can give writers more confidence by providing them with a varied and supportive audience.

At the same time, groups that meet outside of a classroom setting can be difficult to coordinate, since they involve people with varied schedules. Furthermore, the multiple audiences provided by groups may be intimidating and threatening to a writer. Since writing groups involve more people, require more coordination, take more time, and are less likely to be familiar, the following suggestions may help.

Form a group along common interests

Writing groups are useful in classes because the people are usually working on similar projects. You can take advantage of having everyone together at one time and place to give each other help. Writing groups can also be created outside of class by interested people who get together regularly to share their writing.

Focus on the writing

The goal of writing groups is to improve one another's writing and to encourage one another to write more. Pass out copies of the work in advance for silent reading prior to class, or read drafts aloud during the group meetings, with other group members following along on copies. After members have read or heard the paper, share your reactions, each in turn.

Keep groups small

In-class writing groups can have as few as two or as many as five members; time constraints make groups larger than five cumbersome. Smaller groups need less time, larger groups need more. Groups that meet outside of the classroom have fewer size and time limits.

TEN QUESTIONS TO ASK WRITERS ABOUT THEIR WRITING

Although the specific questions you ask depend upon the writer's particular paper, some of the following may be helpful.

1. Where did this idea come from? (The origin of the idea may provide useful clues as an aid to further revision.)

2. What idea holds the whole piece together? (Where's the center? Can you point to a page or paragraph?)

3. When you were writing, who were your imagined readers? (Is there any place you think your readers might still be confused?)

4. Where else could you find information to support or expand this topic? (All papers profit from research knowledge.)

5. Who could you interview to provide more information or another perspective on this topic? (Interview quotes add life to most papers.)

6. Can you provide some background or context for this idea?

7. Can you provide any examples or illustrations to show what you mean?

8. Can you think of two alternate ways to begin this paper?

9. Can you think of two alternate ways to end this paper?

10. Can you think of two alternate titles?

Allocate time fairly

Sometimes a meeting is organized so that each member reads a paper or a portion of a paper. At other times a meeting may focus on the work of one member, and members thus take turns receiving responses at different meetings. If papers are to be read, it generally takes two minutes to read a typed, double-spaced page out loud. Discussion and comment time should match or exceed the oral reading time on each paper. Groups that meet on their own should experiment to determine how much they can read and discuss at each session, perhaps varying the schedule from meeting to meeting.

PARTICIPATING IN WRITING GROUPS

As a nonnative speaker of English, you may feel at a disadvantage in writing groups. Keep in mind, however, that participants usually give responses based on the content of a paper, not its grammar or word choice. Like your classmates, you can give valuable responses by pointing out what you think is successful in a paper and by providing suggestions for further developing a topic. As someone with a different cultural background, you may even be able to offer an interesting perspective on a topic that the writer hasn't considered.

SUGGESTIONS FOR WRITING AND RESEARCH

INDIVIDUAL

Investigate what has been written about peer writing groups. Check, in particular, for work by Kenneth Bruffee, Peter Elbow, Anne Ruggles Gere, Thom Hawkins, and Tori Haring-Smith. Write a report to inform your classmates about your discoveries.

COLLABORATIVE

Form interview pairs and interview local published writers about the way in which response by friends, family, editors, or critics affects their writing. Share results orally or by publishing a short pamphlet.

Editing

Good writing communicates effectively with the writers' intended audience. While you plan, draft, and revise, you focus primarily on your **purpose**—what you are trying to say to your audience. When the time comes to edit your work, your focus shifts subtly to anticipating how your **audience**—your readers—will understand what you are writing.

Anticipating how well readers will understand your words may be difficult, since you know what you wanted the words to convey, even when they do not precisely say what you intended. To edit, you must read with fresh eyes: look only at the words on the page. Anticipate any questions your reader might have and identify any lingering questions of your own. Then address them by clarifying the passage.

The main activity of editing is **testing alternatives**. When editing, you continually generate alternatives and evaluate them by anticipating their effect on your audience. Ask yourself: Given what I am trying to communicate and the audience I am writing for, which of my alternative ways is most effective?

To edit well, you need a working knowledge of the conventions of standard written English and how these conventions can be used and possibly varied according to the audience, purpose, and situation. Also, an important part of editing is polishing—refining your language to make paragraphs, sentences, and individual words communicate effectively, with clarity, style, and grace.

For your writing to be **effective**, your ideas need to come across with as much power and persuasiveness—and as few wasted words—as you can muster. Strive for **clarity**, to make your purpose readily apparent to your audience. Seek a **style** appropriate for the subject, audience, and your relation to that audience. Finally, edit for **grace**—a sense that the text is not only clear but enjoyable, moving, even memorable.

Most writers edit by attacking many issues at once, but to simplify discussion, we focus on one issue at a time. We have divided editing issues into four broad areas: effectiveness, grammar, punctuation, and mechanics.

GUIDELINES FOR EDITING

Putting yourself in the place of your reader is a primary editing skill. Here's how to develop it.

- **Budget time for editing**. Drafting is time-consuming, but so is editing. Don't assume you can rush through your paper in half an hour and make major improvements. Assume that editing will take at least as much time as drafting and/or revising did.
- **Exchange drafts with a trusted partner and/or writing group**. Jot down notes about what passages work well in your partner's writing and what elements slow your understanding. Notice how clearly such things stand out in someone else's writing. Share suggestions for improvement.
- **Work from large-scale issues to small**. Look at overall impressions, then the structure and development of ideas. Then move to paragraphs and last to sentences. The organization of this book generally follows that pattern.
- **Edit with a word processor**: Computerized text is infinitely changeable, so try different ways of expressing your ideas, then choose the best alternative. Also try changing formats and print out the paper; it's a good way to get a fresh look at your work.
- **Read with "fresh eyes" each time you sit down to edit.**

23 a Editing moves

This section outlines some major editing moves to sharpen your writing. Each move is cross-referenced to a subsequent chapter or section for more information.

1 Editing for unity

Edit paragraphs so that each advances and amplifies only one idea. One simple way to do this is to read each paragraph and make sure each sentence illustrates the main idea in some logical way. For example, Issa discovered when writing her essay "On the Trail" (see Chapter 11) that the following paragraph would be better unified if she edited out the fifth sentence, which diverges into a different topic.

■   When mountain bikes first came on the scene, hikers and environmentalists convinced state and local officials to ban the bikes from wilderness trails. The result was the closing of many trails to mountain bike use: "Many state park systems have banned bicycles from narrow trails. National Parks prohibit them, in most cases, from leaving the pavement" (Schwartz 81). These trail closings have separated the outdoor community into the hikers and the bikers. ~~Mountain bikers love their machines~~ Each group is well organized, and each group believes it is right. Is any resolution in sight?

To test this editing move, the writer read the paragraph through with and without the sentence in question and decided which was more effective. For more suggestions on editing paragraphs for a variety of purposes, see Chapter 24.

2 Editing to grab readers' attention

The most attention-catching part of your paper—the opening paragraph—needs to be interesting enough to make readers want to continue reading. There is no one way to structure a good opening. Sometimes a colorful quote or a surprising statistic works well. At other times a clear, direct thesis or a provocative question is needed. In the narrative example below, an internal monologue reveals the author's vulnerability in the middle of a championship tennis match:

> Bounce. Bounce. Bounce. The sound is driving me insane, but I just can't get the nerve to toss up the ball and serve. Am I scared? Yes. Of what, this girl or this match? This girl—this girl scares me. She's a natural talent. How many times is that cross-court forehand shot going to rip past me? Well, if I'm going to lose, let's get on with it.

For suggestions on editing openings and conclusions, see Chapter 25.

3 Editing for rhythm

Reinforce the rhythm of your sentences. Readers more easily attend to, understand, and remember sentences that sound pleasing to the ear. For example, parallel constructions create balanced, symmetrical rhythms that reinforce a comparison or contrast. You make a construction parallel by repeating an identical grammatical pattern within the same sentence, paragraph, or passage. Note the several kinds of parallel constructions used in these sentences from "On the Trail."

■ Educated mountain biking, like ~~other environmental pursuits~~ *hiking and climbing,*

respects the environment and promotes peace and

conservation, not noise and destruction. Making this case has

begun to pay off, and the battle over who walks and who rides

the trails should now shift in favor of peaceful coexistence.

Other environmental pursuits was accurate, but making the phrase parallel to the first idea made the opening more rhythmic. For more on editing for rhythm, see 26e-f.

4 Editing for emphasis

The way you structure a sentence can emphasize one point over another. For example, in an essay, a paragraph, or a sentence, the most emphatic place is usually last. To end-weight a sentence, place less-essential information early and end with the idea you want your reader to remember. However, if we rewrote the above sentence with the most important information first, it would read this way: *The most emphatic place is usually last in a whole essay, a paragraph, or a sentence, for example.* Our point has nearly vanished. To examine other ways of editing sentence structure to create emphasis, see Chapter 27.

5 Editing for variety

Varying sentence structures makes paragraphs clearer and often more enjoyable to readers. In the following example, Judith uses a variety of sentence lengths: short (4 words), medium (12 words), short (7 words), long (23 words), long (32 words); and also varies sentence types; simple (sentences 1–3), complex (sentence 4), compound complex (sentence 5):

> It is already afternoon. I fiddle with the key to lock the apartment door after me. I am not accustomed to locking doors. Except for the six months I spent in Boston, I have never lived in

a place where I did not trust my neighbors. When I was little, we couldn't lock our farmhouse door; the wood had swollen and the bolt no longer lined up properly with the hole, and nobody ever bothered to fix it.

To edit for other kinds of sentence variety, see Chapter 27.

6 Editing for specific details

Nouns label or identify persons (*woman, ballet dancer*), places (*room, dance studio*), and things (*clothes, leotards*). **Specific** nouns (*ballet dancer, dance studio, leotards*) let you see detailed images, while **general** nouns (*woman, room, clothes*) do not. Adjectives that modify nouns increase specificity by adding shape, size, color, texture, and so on. In the following paragraph, Betsy describes members of a ballet rehearsal, using a variety of specific nouns and adjectives to let us see her subjects.

> Dancers are scattered around the room, stretching, chatting, adjusting shoes and tights. Company members, the professionals who are joining us for this performance, wear tattered gray leg-warmers, sweatpants which have lost their elastic, and old faded T-shirts over mismatched tights and baggy leotards. Their hair is knotted into buns or, in the case of male dancers, held tight with sweatbands. You can tell the students by the runless pink tights, dress-code leotards, and immaculate hair.

Specific nouns and adjectives create vivid and lively images—*tattered gray leg-warmers, baggy leotards*, and *runless pink tights*—that would be lost with a more general description: *Dancers are around the room, adults and students, each group dressed differently.* For more ideas about creating vital sentences, see Chapter 28.

7 Editing for active verbs

Active verbs show the subject of a sentence doing something: *walk, stride, run, jump, fly, sing, sail, swim, stop, look, listen, hear, think, believe, doubt, sit, stumble,* or *fumble.* In contrast, **static verbs** show the subject of a sentence in a state of being, existing rather than acting: *be, appear, become, seem,* or *exist.* Changing static to action verbs makes writing more vital and holds readers' attention.

■ The water ~~is turbulent~~ swirls turbulently between the rocks.

The concluding paragraph of Judith's essay "Writing in Safety" (see Chapter 13) uses action verbs effectively.

> Hours later—my paper started, my exam studied for, my eyes tired—I retrace the path to my apartment. It is dark now, and I listen closely when I hear footsteps behind, stepping to the sidewalk's edge to let a man walk briskly past. At my door, I again fumble for the now familiar key, insert it in the lock, open the door, turn on the hall light, and step inside. Here, too, I am safe, ready to eat, read a bit, and finish my reflective essay.

Judith favors action verbs. Her two static verbs—*is* and *am*—provide a quiet contrast to the otherwise active paragraph. For a more complete discussion of editing for active verbs, see Chapter 28.

8 Editing for conciseness

Delete words that do not add meaning, rhythm, or emphasis. Look at these sentences, each of which says essentially the same thing.

> In almost every situation that I can think of, with few exceptions, it will make good sense for you to look for as many places as possible to cut out needles, redundant, and repetitive words from the papers and reports, paragraphs and sentences you write for college assignments. [48 words]
>
> In most situations it makes good sense to cut out needless words from your college papers. [16 words]
>
> Whenever possible, omit needless words from your writing. [8 words]
>
> Omit needless words. [3 words]

In the first wordy sentence, the writer struggles for clarity. In the next two, the same idea is condensed by more than half and by half again, then to a three-word command. Which version you use depends on your audience. Do you need to appear intricately involved, suggestive, direct, or authoritative? How much of readers' time can you afford to spend? For more ideas on editing for directness and conciseness, see Chapter 29.

9 Editing for tone

Your tone reveals your attitude toward your subject and audience: whether you are distant or closely involved, neutral or partisan, dispassionate or emotional. To edit for tone, think of your purpose and imagine your audience: For whom are you writing? What effect do you want to create? For example, look again at the four sentences listed in "Editing for conciseness" and notice how the tone increases in confidence and authority as you move from the tentative first version (*In almost every situation that I can think of*), through the gentle suggestion of the second (*In most situations*), to the stronger direction of the third (*Whenever possible*), to the command of the fourth (*Omit*). In each case the idea remains the same, but in each successive sentence the tone takes on more authority. For more information on editing for tone, see Chapter 30.

10 Editing to control bias

Using ethnic, racial, national, gender, or sex-preference stereotypes in your writing will make you appear biased. For example, using the word *man* or *men* to stand for *human beings* or *people* is considered sexist, because such terms ignore half of the population. Texts written since the 1970s, when this issue began to receive widespread attention, usually avoid this gender bias.

Eliminating sexism from your language can be difficult because English does not have a gender-neutral singular pronoun (*he/she, him/her, his/hers*) to match the gender-neutral plural pronouns (*they, their, them*). In the sentence *Everybody has his own opinion*, the collective singular noun *everybody* needs a singular pronoun to match. It is neutral but grammatically incorrect to write *Everybody has their own opinion*. Consider instead (1) making the sentence plural: *People have their own opinions*, (2) including both pronouns: *Everybody has his or her own opinion*, or (3) eliminating the pronoun altogether: *Everybody has an opinion*. For more information on eliminating biased language, see Chapter 32.

11 Editing for grammar

Your audience for academic writing—professors and fellow students—places a high value on grammatical correctness and the conventional use of language. Errors in sentence structure, verb agreement, or modifier placement will undermine your credibility and distract readers from your ideas. Sharpening your working knowledge of grammar will help you write better and keep you from writing nonsensical sentences such as this one.

■ ~~Studying~~ In a study of the effects of cigarette smoking, monkeys smoked the equivalent of dozens of cigarettes a day.

The monkeys were not conducting the study. This first part of the sentence is a dangling modifier.

For help in applying grammatical conventions, see **Editing Grammar**, Chapters 33–42.

12 Editing for punctuation

Correct punctuation also marks you as a skilled writer. Using commas, periods, quotation marks, colons, apostrophes, and other punctuation carefully will give you a familiarity with the rules so you will spot errors like this one:

■ The Justice Department has expanded its investigation of the tobacco industry/ and has launched several grand jury inquiries.

No comma is needed between parts of a compound predicate; the basic elements of the predicate in this sentence are expanded . . . and . . . launched.

For more detailed information, see **Editing Punctuation**, Chapters 43–49.

13 Editing for mechanics

The term **mechanics** refers to issues that arise in presenting your writing in finished form, on paper. These issues range from checking that every word is spelled correctly to capitalizing, abbreviating, and italicizing according to standard practice. The last editing act is **proofreading**—reading through your manuscript to make sure it is correct in every way. Good proofreading requires reading slowly, line by line, word by word, and letter by letter. Sharpen your proofreading skills by switching papers with a classmate. The section **Editing Mechanics** discusses all this and more in Chapters 50–55.

23 b Understanding the meaning of "error"

Getting facts wrong—identifying the North Star as Sirius rather than Polaris, for example—can destroy a reader's confidence in you. Readers also judge your reliability by your command of written language: mastery of the language implies mastery of the subject matter.

More important, writing problems can make it hard for a reader to grasp your meaning. The reader's only way of interpreting the words on a page is a knowledge of how those words have been used in the past. Every departure from **convention**—the way words are customarily used—presents a challenge to the reader. If that challenge proves too formidable, all but the most dedicated reader will turn away from reading in favor of, say, taking a nap.

Some conventions are so widely accepted that they are regarded as **rules** and departures from them are considered **errors**. These rules do not result from any one person or committee deciding what ought to be right and issuing edicts accordingly. On the contrary, the rules are based on many writers' and grammarians' descriptions of how English has been written and spoken in the past. Other conventions are more flexible. However, if you stretch the boundaries of what readers expect, you risk being misunderstood or losing the reader's attention.

■ EDITING 1: EXPLORATION

Look at the comments and corrections marked on the last draft of a paper handed back to you by your instructor. Which comments concern rules, and which concern conventions? Can you see how the change suggested by each comment would improve communication? If not, why might your instructor have made the comment? If you cannot understand the reason for the proposed change, discuss it with your instructor.

23 c Working with others

■ Editing someone else's work

When you edit someone else's writing, make constructive suggestions that the writer can act on, not critical assessments that will leave the writer feeling attacked. The most effective editing relationship relies not on one person's authority to judge a piece of writing but on cooperative efforts between writer and editor.

Focus first on understanding what the writer is trying to do—the purpose—and on the ways in which he or she has succeeded. Perhaps the writing employs good analysis, expresses a clear insight, or uses a compelling voice. Identifying such strengths helps the writer build on them. Then discuss the things you think the writer needs to clarify or correct. (For more on work with other students, see Chapter 22.)

2 Accepting editorial advice

Everyone has had the painful experience of having a paper returned with curt corrections in red ink. But being edited by others is a fact of life. In college, other students as well as teachers may comment on your writing. If you write for publication or at a job, staff editors or supervisors will edit your work. As a writer, you should accept comments with an open mind. Focus on how other people's reactions and verbal or written responses show what is working and not working in your writing. Edit your writing by adopting the suggestions you agree with and discussing further the ones you don't. No matter how tactlessly or brusquely an editor communicates with you, remember that the comments are about a particular draft—not about all the writing you've ever done and certainly not about you yourself. Respond objectively and not defensively. Adopting a professional attitude will facilitate your interactions with those editing your work.

■ EDITING 2: EXPLORATION

Think of the teacher who has helped you most with your writing. How did he or she express comments and suggestions about your work? How did you respond? Can you also recall an occasion when comments or corrections hurt your feelings? What was the impact on your writing? Were you able to distinguish between the meaning of the comments and their effect on you? How?

23 d Editing with a computer

A word processing program greatly simplifies editing by making it easy to generate alternative versions by adding, deleting, moving and changing words. To edit, place the computer's electronic marker, called the *cursor*, on the spot where you want to make a change. Then insert a new word, type over an existing one, or simply delete a word. Most word processors have a "search-and-replace" or "find" function that allows you to locate every use of a word or phrase and change it with a few keystrokes.

Even more powerful is the computer's ability to copy or move chunks of text. First "highlight" a block of text and then move, copy, or delete the block using the cursor and function keys to re-arrange phrases, sentences, and even whole paragraphs.

 EDITING STRATEGIES USING COMPUTERS

Here are some strategies on how to use the computer to help you edit.

- **Change the look of your paper**. Radical changes in appearance give you the distance you need to edit your work effectively. Change the font of your entire paper and print it out. Doing this will help you recognize weaknesses as you review.
- **Alternate between hard copy and the screen**. This strategy also allows you to see with "fresh eyes." Edit first on a printed-out draft, marking any changes in pencil. Go back to the screen and edit, transferring the changes and moving along to other issues as you spot them.
- **Print fresh drafts frequently**. Writers sometimes get blocked on a draft and don't know exactly what needs to be done. Looking at a fresh copy of the whole paper at a glance can give you a clearer picture of exactly where to focus the next round of editing. Mark in pencil in the margins where changes must occur and go back to the screen for more work.
- **Keep a file of personal trouble spots**. If you know that you overuse certain words or repeat certain grammatical errors, keep a running list of your personal trouble spots in a separate computer file. When editing, consult the list and check your latest draft. Use your computer's software tools to find and remedy some of these trouble areas.
- **Use software tools with care**. Many software packages contain a spell checker, dictionary, thesaurus, and sometimes a grammar checker and style checker. Take advantage of these features, but use them with care. Even the best spell checker cannot show you that you've written *two* when you should have written *to*, and no grammar checker can recognize every error.

A computer will store your work in a document or file each time under a name you choose. When you have finished editing a draft, either replace the unedited file with the edited one or save the edited version under a different name, thus preserving both the original and the edited text. Sometimes it's good to store each version of a paper separately so that you can see the successive stages of your creative processes. This practice also allows you to compare your most recent editing decisions with previous ones and then choose the best one.

Not least important, the ability to print any document easily eliminates the need to retype successive drafts, leaving you free to edit—and print out—your work as many times as necessary.

Word processing tips (**WP TIPS**) appear throughout *The Blair Handbook* to show you how the computer can help you at every stage of the writing process.

EDITING 3: APPLICATION

Explore the use of computers more extensively in your writing. If you have your own computer, investigate the word processing capabilities of your classmates. Do any of their programs have advantages over yours? Do any of them use particularly helpful computer editing strategies? If you don't have a computer, find out whether your college or community has computers that students can use and how to get access to them.

23 e Editing when English is your second language

Editing can be quite difficult for people who grew up speaking a language other than English, because they have had less time to develop an ear for what "sounds right"—something native speakers often rely on. Certain aspects of English are often confusing to nonnative speakers and writers, such as the sequence of verb tense used to illustrate the time at which events occurred.

> By the time the sun *sets* tomorrow, I *will have been walking* for fifteen days.

The first part of the sentence uses the present tense to describe an action in the future; the second part describes an action that began in the past and will continue into the future but will be finished by the time indicated in the first part (sunset tomorrow).

In seemingly arbitrary ways, adjectives and articles (*the, a, an*)—or their absence—convey significant information about the nouns they precede:

A book is missing from the library	ONE SPECIFIC BOOK
Books are missing.	AN INDEFINITE NUMBER
The books are missing.	ALL OF THEM
Some books are missing.	BUT NOT ALL
A biology book is missing.	ONE OF SEVERAL
The biology book is missing.	THE ONLY ONE

To edit your writing for issues of this kind, try to improve your English-language skills in general. The best way to gain a masterful command of the language is by reading widely, listening and observing how language is used, and examining your own usage of English to see how it resembles or differs from standard usage. Of course, this advice applies to all of us, native and nonnative speakers alike.

In addition, read over your papers and attend to your instructors' comments carefully so that you will learn to recognize nonstandard usage or grammatical errors. Once you identify patterns in your writing, reread your papers, looking specifically for each trouble spot. The more you review grammar points and edit for grammar and usage, the easier it will become to make the right choice the first time.

Throughout *The Blair Handbook*, special boxes will help you understand certain aspects of the English language. Read the ESL boxes for tips regarding some of the grammatical structures and established patterns of standard written English.

ESL **EDITING OTHER STUDENTS' WRITING**

As a nonnative speaker of English, you may question your ability to edit your classmates' writing. Keep in mind, however, that you probably know more than you think about what makes a piece of writing readable and effective. Also consider that you will often be a part of the audience a classmate wants to reach. As a reader you can offer helpful feedback about clarity of purpose, variety of sentence structure, words or phrases that seem unnecessary, and many other elements of an essay that are discussed in this chapter.

Many college instructors use a handbook like this one to show students how to make their writing stronger. Teachers reading dozens of student papers weekly will usually focus their written comments on large-scale issues, such as organization, logic, and the development of ideas. Rather than correct grammatical errors in detail, many instructors simply mark passages and refer students to the appropriate sections of the handbook for help.

■ What I liked most was / the opportunity to explore different
kinds of writing. No comma comes between subject and verb.
                    See commas, 44j.

This instructor suggests that the student refer to section 44j to review the use of commas, in particular the rule that a single comma should not separate a verb from its subject. If you read and understand the advice in that section, you will be less likely to repeat the error. Your instructor may also simply use a proofreading mark or correction symbol:

■ Every doctor has <u>their</u> own way of working. agr

Proofreading marks and correction symbols are widely used and largely standardized. The symbol *agr* here stands for agreement between a pronoun (*their*) and its antecedent (*doctor*). To see what a symbol means, look it up in the chart on the inside back cover of this book; the chart will refer you to a relevant section of the book. Standard proofreading marks are listed in Chapter 56c.

■ **EDITING 4: APPLICATION**

Select two or three comments that were marked on the last draft of a paper handed back to you by your instructor. Use the index or table of contents of *The Blair Handbook* to find out where the handbook addresses these issues, and then read those sections. Were the issues treated as matters of effectiveness, of grammar, of punctuation, or of mechanics? What have you learned that you didn't know before? Use the editing advice in *The Blair Handbook* to edit the relevant sentences and correct any problems.

Editing for Effectiveness

Paragraphs are the units of your writing, showing which ideas go together and how they relate to each other. Good paragraphing gives readers clues to how to read your paper. The visual pattern of paragraphs on a page helps show the paper's organization: when a new paragraph begins, readers expect a new step in the development of your ideas.

Especially in academic writing, readers expect to see how each sentence within a paragraph helps develop a single main idea—that the paragraph will be **unified**. They expect the paragraph to present its ideas in a clearly perceptible order—that it will be well **organized**. And they expect each succeeding sentence to relate to what came before, advancing and supporting the central point—that the paragraph will be **coherent**. Otherwise readers may have trouble following your ideas.

24 **a** **Ensuring that paragraphs are unified**

In most college writing, each paragraph directly states a central idea, or **topic**, which is usually contained in a **topic sentence**. Sometimes a paragraph's topic can be communicated more subtly: readers may be able to infer a topic from a series of related sentences that do not include an explicit topic sentence.

In either case, a paragraph should contain only one main idea. Elements that do not support or clarify this idea should be eliminated. You can simply delete stray words or sentences, you can move them to another paragraph, or you can create a new paragraph where they will be more effective.

In writing about minimizing the effect of divorce on children, Amy identified the first sentence as the topic sentence: *For various reasons, some unhappy couples remain married.* When she read each of the other sentences carefully to see whether they described reasons for staying married, she realized that the fourth sentence was out of place. She decided to move this sentence to the next paragraph, which dealt with a new topic.

■   For various reasons, some unhappy couples remain married. Some are forbidden to divorce by religion, others by social custom. Still others stay together "for the sake of the children." In recent years, psychologists and sociologists have studied families to determine whether more harm is done to children by divorce or by parents who stay together despite conflict. ~~But by staying together, such parents feel~~ *believing* they are sparing their children the pain of divorce.

In his study of family conflict, Robert S. Weiss found that children in such families were often happiest "when Daddy is at work.". . .

WP TIP   From one of your files, select a draft paragraph that you want to edit. Copy it one to three times in a new file. Identify your topic sentence, and edit each paragraph for unity, adding and deleting information in different ways. Choose the strongest paragraph.

■ **EDITING I: PRACTICE**

A. The following paragraph, part of an information manual for new employees at a college radio station, discusses gifts and promotions. With this audience in mind, edit the paragraph to improve unity.

College radio stations do not receive lavish gifts, but they are not neglected in the grand sweep of promotions that back college-targeted records. This station has received everything from posters to gold records to bottles of liquor. Whether the promotions actually get the records played is hard to document at college radio stations, and ours is no exception. The most common gifts are passes to performances and free copies of records.

B. This paragraph is from an editorial that explains to local citizens the workings of the city planning board. With this audience in mind, edit the paragraph to improve unity.

The idea of planning seems simple enough. Communities are asked to designate areas for specific purposes, such as commercial, residential, or industrial use. The state's new requirement that every city and township formulate a plan may create a shortage of planners. People take city planning very seriously. Sometimes such an innocuous topic as zoning leads to turmoil—for instance, when one group wants to open a restaurant in what others consider a "residential" zone. Trying to pinpoint exactly what a planner does is a little more complicated.

EDITING 2: APPLICATION

Select a paragraph from a paper that you are working on. As you reread the paragraph, ask yourself three questions: (1) Who am I writing for? (2) What is my topic sentence? and (3) How does my paragraph fit into my paper? Examine each sentence to see whether it conforms to your answers to these questions. If any sentences do not seem to contribute to the main idea of the paragraph or to the paper in general, try omitting them. Edit the paragraph by eliminating any other elements that detract from its main point. If you find that some of your ideas need elaboration, write additional sentences with the above three questions in mind.

How does your edited paragraph compare with the original? Does it target its audience more precisely? Does it advance your purpose more effectively?

24 b Organizing paragraphs

Ideas that are presented in what seems like no apparent order can confuse your readers, so clear organization within a paragraph is important. When editing, you must decide whether you have organized each paragraph in the way that most effectively accomplishes your purpose. You may decide to move your topic sentence or to reorganize the whole paragraph.

1 Placement of the topic sentence

Often the topic sentence or main idea is most effective at the beginning of a paragraph. If you find a topic sentence buried in the middle of a paragraph, consider moving it to the beginning.

^ In 1987 a man lost his job for taking a few puffs of a cigarette during his lunch break, because smoking on or off the job violated his department's policy. He took his employers to court to get his job back, but the judge ruled that smoking was not comparable to the privacy rights protected by the Constitution. Court decisions have limited smokers' rights to pursue their habit. Other cases have established nonsmokers' right to protection from second-hand smoke.

A topic sentence can also be placed at the end of a paragraph, which is a way of emphasizing it.

■ In 1987 a man lost his job for taking a few puffs of a cigarette during his lunch break, because smoking on or off the job violated his department's policy. He took his employers to court to get his job back, but the judge ruled that smoking was not comparable to the privacy rights protected by the Constitution. *like these* Court decisions, have limited smokers' rights to pursue their habit. Other cases have established nonsmokers' right to protection from second-hand smoke.

WP TIP Highlight each topic sentence in bold. Examine your placement of each paragraph and determine the appropriateness of the position. Share it with a peer for discussion.

2 Common patterns of organization

The sentences and ideas within a paragraph should follow a readily understandable order, one that is appropriate to the subject and that conveys the point of the paragraph effectively.

WP TIP Editing involves thinking up alternatives and choosing among them. Use your word processor to make copies of a passage giving you trouble. Insert returns so that each sentence begins on a new line. Then rearrange the sentences differently in the separate copies to find the best possible organization.

General to specific

One common pattern for organizing paragraphs is **general to specific**. Begin the paragraph by stating the principal idea; edit subsequent sentences to support, explain, or expand on that idea.

Many athletes have improved their performance by using steroids. One such athlete is track star Ben Johnson, who won the Olympic gold medal in 1988 in the hundred-meter dash. After a couple of days, Johnson's medal was taken away because he had tested positive for the use of steroids. His steroid use had increased his leg strength and therefore made him a faster runner. Another example is Benji

GENERAL STATEMENT

SPECIFIC EXAMPLE

Ramirez, a former student at Central State University. He played on the JV team for two years and wanted to be good enough for the varsity squad. He decided to do this by increasing his physical strength, and the method he chose was using steroids. By his senior year, he was a starter on the varsity team.

Notice that the general-to-specific pattern begins with a statement that applies to many people, then proceeds to discuss individuals who fit or contrast with the larger pattern.

Specific to general

A specific-to-general pattern of organization begins with a series of details or examples and ends with a general statement, the topic sentence. In this personal narrative, Anita saved the topic sentence for last to give it impact.

> I began by oversleeping—somehow I had forgotten to set my alarm clock. Then I had to drink my morning coffee black and eat my cereal dry because my roommate hadn't replaced the quart of milk she finished yesterday. After missing my bus and arriving late for my first class, I discovered that the history paper I thought was due next week was actually due today. And because my lab partner was still mad at me from the mess I made of things last week, we accomplished almost nothing in two hours. All in all, it was a terrible day. **SPECIFIC EXAMPLE** … **GENERAL STATEMENT**

Chronological order

A discussion of related events can be organized in chronological order, the order in which they happened. The topic sentence, a general statement summarizing the events and perhaps interpreting them, can appear at the beginning or, as in the paragraph above, at the end.

Sometimes paragraphs relating a series of events are better arranged in **reverse chronological order**, which looks back from the most recent to the most distant past, as in the example below. Here the topic sentence can appear at the end or at the beginning.

> At first a little hesitant to talk about painful memories, Leo started by describing his background. He then told me that on September first, 1939, the Germans attacked Poland. They left his town alone for three days. On the third, they collected all the **GENERAL STATEMENT** … **EVENT 1** … **EVENT 2**

males from fifteen to sixty years of age and put them
in a yard. The men were given trash and told to bury   EVENT 3
it with their hands. A friend of Leo's resisted and they
shot him. He was buried along with the refuse.   EVENT 4

*In this vignette from a personal profile, Mark shows his subject open-
ing up as he remembers the past. Mark has structured the narrative to
build up to its chilling conclusion.*

Climactic order

An appeal to logic might be arranged in **climactic order**, beginning with a general statement, presenting specific details in order of increasing importance, and ending with a dramatic statement, a climax. Here Patrick is using scientific predictions to
arouse and alarm a general, nonscientific audience.

Consider the potential effect of just a small in-   GENERAL
crease in the earth's atmospheric temperature. A rise   STATEMENT
of only a few degrees could melt the polar ice caps.   SPECIFICS IN
Rainfall patterns would change. Some deserts might   INCREASING
bloom, but lands now fertile might turn to desert, and   IMPORTANCE
many hot climates could become uninhabitable. If the
sea level rose only a few feet, dozens of coastal cities
would be destroyed, and life as we know it would be   CLIMAX
changed utterly.

Spatial order

A physical description can be organized in **spatial order**,
moving from one detail to another as the eye would move. As in
the chronological paragraph, a topic sentence summarizing and
interpreting the details can appear at the beginning or end.
Janelle intended this description to give the reader the feeling of
sitting in one place, observing carefully.

Above the mantelpiece hung an ancient wheel   SPECIFICS
lock musket that gave every indication of being in   ARRANGED
working order. A small collection of pewter, most of it   SPATIALLY
dating from the colonial period, was arrayed across
the mantel shelf. To the left of the hearth stood a collection of wrought-iron fireplace tools and a bellows of
wood and leather with brass fittings. At the right, a
brass hopper held several cut limbs of what might
have been an apple tree. On an iron hook above the
coals hung a copper kettle, blackened with age and   GENERAL
smoke. The fireplace looked as though it had changed   STATEMENT
little since the Revolution.

WP TIP   Use the "outline" function (available on most word-processing programs) as a way to view your existing text with the sentences separated. Or insert a return after every sentence. Use the "cut" and "paste" functions to rearrange sentences. Be sure to save your work every time you move a sentence or copy the work elsewhere so you can restore any original arrangements later.

■ EDITING 3: PRACTICE

The following paragraph is from a news release that was sent to local newspapers in the townships near White Glen Park. Strengthen the paragraph by improving its organization.

One Saturday each month, Mike Perkins, a local golf pro, gives a free golf clinic at White Glen Park. Enthusiasts gather round while Mike discusses the finer points of the game. He addresses one aspect of the golf swing each session. He demonstrates the relevant concept, using someone from the crowd as a model. Last month he discussed proper hip movement in the iron swing. Then, after the lesson, Mike's monthly students hit practice shots until they use up the balls. The event is quite popular. The public course donates six bushel baskets of golf balls and the use of its driving range for the event. Usually about sixty to eighty people show up. Saturday afternoons with Mike are always fun and informative.

■ EDITING 4: APPLICATION

Make a copy of a paragraph from a paper you are working on, and experiment to find the best possible organization for it. First, disassemble the paragraph so that each sentence stands alone, either by cutting with scissors or by starting each sentence on a new line on the computer screen. Next, find the topic sentence and set it aside. Then play with the order of the sentences until you find one that seems particularly effective; you may want to try some of the patterns of organization discussed in 24b. Next, decide whether the topic sentence belongs at the beginning or the end of the paragraph. Finally, rewrite the paragraph using the new organization, making any necessary changes in wording. How does this edited version compare with the original?

24 c   Making paragraphs coherent

In a **coherent** paragraph, each sentence connects with the next in a way that readers can easily recognize. Shortening long paragraphs, using transitional expressions, and sparingly repeating key words can all help achieve coherence.

▌ Shortening long paragraphs

Long paragraphs can lack coherence simply because readers may lose track of what you are saying. Breaking a long paragraph into several smaller ones can give the reader a chance to rest, and it often results in greater coherence within each of the new paragraphs.

■ During a divorce, parents have the ability to shield a child from most of the potential harm. Most couples who stay together believe that the two-parent structure is important to the child's well-being and that changing this pattern upsets a child. ¶ A child's security is based on his or her relationship with each parent individually, according to studies by Judith Wallerstein, who found that stable, caring relationships between a child and each parent are the most significant ingredient in raising a child. If these relationships are maintained, the effect of divorce on a child's emotions is much reduced. Indeed, maintaining even one stable relationship would appear to be better than a weak connection with both parents. ¶ In the early stages of a breakup, both parents are often distracted by other issues. The child may suffer as a result. A child's performance in school and interactions with others may deteriorate, so everything should be done to aid the child in transition.

Breaking up the long paragraph helped us understand important points. Amy went on to add transitions between paragraphs as outlined in 24c2.

An essay consisting of many short paragraphs, however, can seem choppy and disjointed. If several small paragraphs develop what is essentially one idea, they might be better joined into larger paragraphs.

2 Using transitional expressions

Whenever your flow of ideas shifts, let the reader know which way you are headed. Otherwise readers may be confronted with a seemingly unrelated string of facts. Words that signal a change are called **transitional expressions**. Here is a paragraph with its transitional expressions removed:

> Newspaper and magazine publishing is not usually regarded as cyclic. This recession has cut deeply into advertising revenue. The economy is gathering steam. Classified-ad buyers should return. Display advertising will lag. Publications that have sharply cut their costs should see strong upturns in their profits as advertisers return. The coming year looks rosy.

Here is the same paragraph with transitional expressions restored:

> Newspaper and magazine publishing is not usually regarded as cyclic, but this recession has cut deeply into advertising revenue. With the economy gathering steam, classified-ad buyers should return, although display advertising will lag. Meanwhile, publications that have sharply cut their costs should see strong upturns in their profits as advertisers return. For them, the coming year looks rosy.

WP TIP Add transitional words (and mark existing ones) using boldface type. Print a hard copy and discuss with a peer the choices you have made. What do you find most effective? Why?

As you edit, examine each change of subject, time, point of view, or setting to see whether you have adequately marked the transition. Changes you make while restructuring paragraphs may make new transitions necessary. Look again at the edited example from the paper about divorce, in which one long paragraph was broken into three. To clarify how the three new paragraphs and the sentences within them related to one another, Amy added two transitional sentences.

■   During a divorce, parents have the ability to shield a child

from most of the potential harm. Most couples who stay

together believe that the two-parent structure is important to the child's well-being and that changing this pattern upsets a child.

This, however, appears not to be the case.

∧ A child's security is based on his or her relationship with each parent individually, according to studies by Judith Wallerstein, who found that stable, caring relationships between a child and each parent are the most significant ingredient in raising a child. If these relationships are maintained, the effect of divorce on a child's emotions is much reduced. Indeed, maintaining even one stable relationship would appear to be better than a weak connection with both parents.

The issue during divorce, then, is how well a child can maintain at least

∧ In the early stages of a breakup, both parents are often distracted by other issues. The child may suffer as a result. A child's performance in school and interactions with others may deteriorate, so everything should be done to aid the child in transition.

one secure relationship.

The first transitional sentence emphasizes a logical contrast. The second marks a shift of subject.

3 Using deliberate repetition

Repeating key words or concepts can improve coherence by linking sentences. Selective repetition creates a path for readers. The words that you want readers to remember become stepping-stones connecting one sentence to the next. In the following example, *controversy* and *dispute* as well as *opposes, opponents,* and *proponents* are key words that help readers keep in mind the main thrust of the argument.

> The controversy over Northgate Mall has continued for at least five years. The dispute has divided the city into two camps. A small group opposes the mall, but its members are vocal and energetic. The opponents maintain that it would rob trade from existing businesses downtown and contribute to traffic congestion. Proponents say that the growth it would bring would be easily manageable.

TRANSITIONAL EXPRESSIONS

Transitional expressions connect distinct ideas, indicating how one idea expands, exemplifies, summarizes, or relates to another.

EXPANDING

also, and, besides, finally, further, in addition, moreover, then

EXEMPLIFYING

as an illustration, for example, for instance, in fact, specifically, thus

QUALIFYING

but, certainly, however, to be sure

SUMMARIZING

and so, finally, in conclusion, in short, in sum, this experiment shows, thus we see

RELATING LOGICALLY

as a result, because, by implication, for this reason, from this we can see, if, since, so, therefore

COMPARING

also, as well, likewise, similarly

CONTRASTING

but, even though, nevertheless, still, yet

RELATING IN TIME

after, before, between, earlier, later, longer than, meanwhile, since

RELATING IN SPACE

above, adjacent to, behind, below, beyond, in front of, next to, north of, over, through, within

---

ESL **SUGGESTIONS FOR USING TRANSITIONAL EXPRESSIONS**

You can learn to use transitional expressions effectively by practicing and by paying attention to how others use them in writing. Here are some guidelines for deciding whether you need a transitional expression and which one to use.

1. Shifts that readers may not expect need transitions more than those that are expected. For example, a contrast or contradiction is often unexpected and needs a transition.

The film's plot is very predictable and the characters are not especially likable. *Nevertheless,* the movie is worth seeing for the skillful cinematography and fine acting.

Other logical relationships, such as time sequence, are often obvious from the context and do not need a transitional phrase.

The main character of the film moves to Brazil. He finds a job in a large corporation and settles into a routine.

Although you could use then *in the second sentence to signal the time relationship, the reader can infer the sequence easily from the content.*

2. If you use a series of transitional expressions to signal a sequence or to list points, make sure they are parallel. For example, use *first, second,* and *last* to introduce three different points, but don't use *first, in the second place,* and *the last.* If you're not sure which expressions are used together, consult your instructor or a native speaker of English.

3. If you repeatedly use one-word transitions to begin sentences, your writing may sound choppy or monotonous. Try editing your transitions in the following ways.

■ Consider omitting some transitions. (See point number 1 above.)
■ Put some of the transitional expressions in the middle of sentences: *Keeping a journal is helpful, in addition, because. . . .* If you're not sure where in the sentence a transitional expression can or should go, ask someone for help.

4. Try to use a variety of transitional expressions. Don't use the same ones over and over. For example, instead of always using *first, second,* and *third* to list sequences, consider using *for example, also,* and *finally.*

STRATEGIES FOR EDITING PARAGRAPHS

Most writers paragraph intuitively when they draft. When you edit, make conscious decisions about paragraphs.

1. Look at length. Does each paragraph begin and end in the appropriate place? Should it be shorter? Should it include part of the following paragraph? Are there too many long paragraphs or too many short paragraphs in a row?

2. Check for unity. Does each paragraph express and develop a single idea?

3. Consider organization. Is the pattern of each paragraph apparent? Is it the most appropriate pattern of organization, given your purpose and audience?

4. Assess coherence. Do any elements distract from the main idea of each paragraph? Delete any minor points, asides, or extraneous sentences, or place them elsewhere.

EDITING 5: APPLICATION

The following paragraph is from an oral report for a debate class. Strengthen the paragraph by editing to improve coherence. Consider the use of transitional expressions, the order of sentences, and the use of repetition. More than one edited version is possible. By ready to explain your editing choices.

Accidents involving bicyclists usually increase when the college students—and their bicycles—return to classes. Many drivers in the city resent the high number of cyclists. They claim that the streets are too busy and too narrow for bike travel. Cyclists often will ignore traffic signals and stop signs and cut in and out of traffic without warning. If opposing traffic is slow in starting after a light changes, cyclists frequently will turn in front of it to move ahead. Usually few cyclists attempt to keep up with traffic, which creates a long line of cars unable to pass. These tendencies can be dangerous. At the corner of 10th Street and Indiana the other day, a cyclist was struck by a car turning right when he tried to pass on the inside. He suffered no injuries, but some victims had to be hospitalized.

■ EDITING 6: PRACTICE

The following passage is from a newspaper account summarizing the history of a zoning proposal for a new mall and its impact on a mayoral election. Revise the paragraph (1) to improve its unity, organization, and coherence, and (2) to make it more interesting. You can have fun with your revision, so long as you do not alter the facts.

The zoning board rejected the proposal. The plan was the subject of three evenings of raucous debate. Then the city council took it up on appeal. The disagreement continued there for months. Some members said their first responsibility was to promote economic development in any form. The debate on the council reflected the divisions in the community. Growth should be regulated so that it does not harm existing businesses or the city as a whole, others believed. The project was approved two weeks after the new mayor took office. Amanda Robbins campaigned for mayor by rallying downtown businesspeople, historic preservationists, and neighborhood activists against the mall. Council member Steven McMillan ran on a pro-development, pro-mall platform. Both candidates said they wanted voters to end the deadlock on the proposal. The election was won by McMillan.

■ EDITING 7: APPLICATION

From a recent paper, select a passage of three or four paragraphs that does not read quite smoothly to you. Use your word processor or a photocopier to make several copies to experiment with. Try breaking paragraphs into smaller paragraphs or even individual sentences and rearranging them for better coherence, unity, and organization.

Try at least two new versions before deciding which is best.

You never get a second chance to make a first impression. Your first words are in many ways the most important. The **opening** of an essay must engage, stimulate, and challenge readers, enticing them to read further. Your opening should give readers a reliable guide to what will follow: it should introduce your topic and your thesis or main idea and give readers some idea of what you intend to say in the rest of your paper.

An essay's **conclusion** merits equal attention because your parting words will linger in the reader's mind. A conclusion that merely repeats generalities, that focuses only on a minor point, or that wanders off the subject will undermine all your efforts. The conclusion provides your last opportunity to tie together everything you have covered in your paper and to present it in a coherent package.

There are no all-purpose formulas for openings or conclusions; each must be carefully written to suit your purpose and audience. On rare occasions, the first words of an essay may spring to mind as you begin to write, or the last words may flow effortlessly from the preceding paragraphs, and you may never need to change them. More often, however, you will find it distracting, while drafting, to worry about an opening or conclusion. Put your efforts first toward drafting the main portion of the paper, and plan to worry later about the opening and conclusion. After drafting and revising, go back to your openings and conclusions. The editing stage is the best time to sharpen your focus in each, check your directness, and polish the wording of your main ideas.

25 a Making openings engaging

In a short essay of two to three pages, you start like a sprinter and run flat-out for the full fifty meters. An opening no longer than one paragraph is standard in much college writing. In a longer paper, you can set off at a more leisurely pace, engaging readers' attention, then guiding it and focusing it by the time you state your **thesis**, or the main thrust of your argument.

In either case, readers should quickly be able to recognize both your **subject**, the general area you are writing about, and your **topic**, that particular aspect of the subject on which you are focusing. They should also understand your **main idea**, the central point you will make about that topic in your paper. In argumentative and research writing, this main point is presented in a **thesis**, an explicit statement usually placed in the opening paragraph. In personal experience and reflective writing, the thesis can take an unstated form as an implicit **theme** which is referred to throughout.

> Nikorn Phasuk, a Bangkok policeman who is also known as Plastic Man, steps onto a stage of asphalt under the glare of a blazing sun. He crouches, then retreats with mincing footwork as he coaxes vehicles toward him with fluid arm gestures, part of an artful ballet he uses to keep traffic rolling, no small feat in the city that may have the most congested streets in the world.
>
> As the last motorist accelerates by, the officer stabs a white gloved hand toward the heart of the city in a gesture that ends in a pirouette. Below dark sunglasses his teeth flash in a full grin, one that commuters irked by delays cannot help but emulate.
>
> "It relieves the tension, makes everybody less serious, and it's fun," Nikorn said. "And traffic seems to move faster."
>
> As he walked me back to my car, he held hands with a Bangkok journalist who had stopped by. Such intimacy, while common among Asian men, might be hard to imagine in New York City. But this was Thailand, where most actions seem choreographed for gentleness, and smiles are the expressions of choice.
>
> NOEL GROVE, "THE MANY FACES OF THAILAND"

Taking a few paragraphs to introduce a lengthy essay, Grove gives his readers a verbal film clip of downtown Bangkok that signals to his audience that they will be visiting an unfamiliar but delightful culture.

The type of opening you employ should be appropriate to your topic and main idea. Here are some techniques for organizing your openings to suit specific purposes.

General-to-specific pattern

Many opening paragraphs for college papers start with a general statement of the main idea in a topic sentence. Subsequent sentences contain specific examples that support, explain, and expand on that statement, and the paragraph ends with a thesis statement.

Language is the road map of a culture. It tells you where its people come from and where they are going. A study of the English language reveals a dramatic history and astonishing versatility. It is the language of survivors, of conquerors, of laughter.

RITA MAE BROWN "TO THE VICTOR BELONGS THE LANGUAGE"

Starting with a metaphor about language, Brown goes on to explain specifically what she means. In the third sentence she narrows her topic to the English language, and in the fourth sentence she states her thesis.

Striking assertion

This opening features a statement so improbable or far-reaching that the reader will demand to see proof. After grabbing his readers' attention, the writer directly states his thesis.

John Milton was a failure. In writing "Paradise Lost," his stated aim was to "justify the ways of God to men." Inevitably, he fell short of accomplishing that and only wrote a monumental poem. Beethoven, whose music was conceived to transcend Fate, was a failure, as was Socrates, whose ambition was to make people happy by making them reasonable and just. The inescapable conclusion seems to be that the surest, noblest way to fail is to set one's own standards titanically high.

LAWRENCE SHANIES,
"THE SWEET SMELL OF SUCCESS ISN'T ALL THAT SWEET"

Milton, one of the greatest poets in the English language, was a failure? How? Having whetted his readers' curiosity, Shanies quickly provides his answer.

Anecdote

Try telling an anecdote, or brief story, about people or incidents to introduce your topic and illustrate your thesis.

Once I met a woman who grew up in the small North Carolina town to which Chang and Eng, the original Siamese twins, retired after their circus careers. When I asked her how the town reacted to the twins marrying local girls and setting up adjacent households, she laughed and said: "Honey, that was nothing compared to what happened before the twins got there." Get the good gossip on any little mountain town, scratch the surface and you'll find a snake pit!

FRANCINE PROSE, "GOSSIP"

Approaching the end of this paragraph, you see Prose's thesis coming and are ready to agree with it.

Interesting detail, statistic, or quotation

An interesting detail, statistic, or quotation can grab readers' attention and situate them in an unfamiliar situation, making them eager for the context and explanation you are about to provide.

> People are often surprised, even alarmed, to learn that many of their cells crawl around inside them. Yet cell crawling is essential to our survival. Without it, our wounds would not heal; blood would not clot to seal off cuts; the immune system could not fight infections. Unfortunately, crawling contributes to some disease processes, too, such as destructive inflammation and the formation of atherosclerotic plaques in blood vessels. Cancer cells crawl to spread themselves throughout the body: were cancer just a matter of uncontrolled cell growth, all tumors would be amenable to surgical removal.
>
> THOMAS P. STOSSEL, "THE MACHINERY OF CELL CRAWLING"

Was your reaction the same as ours, "Yuck"? Then Stossel had you right where he wanted you!

Provocative question

After a few sentences of background information to establish the topic, a writer can ask a provocative question, which the essay proceeds to answer.

> Look around you in most locations in the United States and Australia, and most of the people you'll see will be of European ancestry. At the same sites 500 years ago everyone without exception would have been an American Indian or an aboriginal Australian. This is an obvious feature of our daily life, and yet it poses a difficult question, one with a far from obvious answer: Why is it that Europeans came to replace most of the native population of North America and Australia, instead of Indians or native Australians replacing the original population of Europe?
>
> JARED DIAMOND, *THE ACCIDENTAL CONQUEROR*

Before the question starts the reader wondering, Diamond points out an important but "obvious feature" that the reader may not have thought of before.

WP TIP Make the following strategies box part of a permanent file on your computer. When checking your openings, have it available for quick reference in one of your windows.

STRATEGIES FOR OPENINGS

To engage readers' interest, try using one of the following strategies.

- Move from **general to specific** in your opening paragraph.
- Make a **striking assertion** in your opening.
- Add an **anecdote** that arouses your readers' curiosity.
- Grab their attention with an **interesting detail or quotation**.
- Ask a **provocative question** that can't be easily answered.

EDITING I: PRACTICE

Edit the following opening paragraph to make it more engaging. First assume you are writing a paper on economics for an economics class. Then edit the paragraph again, assuming you are writing about economics for an audience of noneconomists. What should your opening achieve in each case? What goals are the same, and which ones differ?

Dr. Ravi Batra, an economist at Southern Methodist University, has described a long-term cycle of economic indicators. Those indicators, he believes, forecast a depression in the next few years. The World Futurist Society also predicts a global economic collapse rivaling the Great Depression of the 1930s. Both predictions cite a rash of bank failures in recent years, implying that the first indication of wider economic troubles will be the downfall of financial institutions.

25 b   Strengthening openings

Wanting to sound well informed and self-assured, writers sometimes lapse into misdirection, wordiness, overgeneralization, and cliché, which can be catastrophic in openings. Readers are more likely to keep reading when they see that each sentence, each word, is important to the purpose of the writing. To that end, edit any elements that may be distracting to your readers.

1 **Being direct**

Ernie's draft starts on one topic and moves to another. Can you tell where his paper is headed?

ESL **CROSSCULTURAL DIFFERENCES IN ESSAY OPENINGS**

In your native language you may have learned a different approach to writing openings than the one presented here. For example, you may have been taught to lead into your thesis less directly or to start with a well-known proverb or saying. Try the following methods to gain a better understanding about composing introductions in English.

1. Discuss with your instructor or your classmates what you have learned about writing openings in your native country. Try to identify the differences between the way people write in your native language and the way they write in English.

2. Ask a friend or classmate to read and respond to the openings in your drafts before you turn in your final papers.

3. Pay attention to the ways that openings are developed in published works and in your classmates' papers. You might see, for example, that using a proverb or a familiar story as an opening is appropriate and engaging in some contexts but not in others.

Isaac Asimov is among the first to have written about robotics. *I, Robot* is a collection of short stories on the subject, the earliest of which is from 1940. Even when going to the moon was science fiction, Asimov predicted that mankind would come to fear its own creation, a concept that dates back at least as far as Mary Shelly's *Frankenstein.*

A movie that demonstrates the paranoia Asimov wrote about is *Terminator,* in which a computer takes control of machines, then attempts to eradicate the human race. This is the paranoia Asimov predicted: mankind the slave master has an innate fear of rebellion among its slaves.

A robot is defined as "any mechanical device operated automatically, especially by remote control." The subject I will be addressing is the argument that robots are stealing jobs from humans, that painters, spot welders, machinists, skilled laborers of all kinds are being replaced by machines.

Ernie's problem is misdirection. Does he mean to focus on the workplace or the psyche? Keeping his literary examples as context, Ernie edited a new opening to show his true position on the subject.

The claim that robots are stealing jobs from humans is nothing new; it is an old fear in a new form. Many writers and filmmakers have explored the underlying anxiety.

Isaac Asimov was among the first to have written about robotics. . . .

Beware of *telling* the reader "My paper will be about. . . ." Edit phrases like these so that you jump right in and *show* the reader what you are going to discuss.

2 Sharpening focus

Too broad an opening can dull readers' interest. Try to limit opening generalizations so that readers understand right away what your main idea focuses on, as Julie did in this reflective essay on the relations between men and women.

Communication has become very important in our everyday lives. Without this ability to relate, friendships and marriages would fail. Furthermore, the different ways men and women communicate can result in serious problems at home and in the workplace.

Her draft sentences were too obvious, so Julie sharpened her focus. Her edited sentences outline the territory she plans to cover.

Men and women have different ways of communicating that can create problems in marriages and work relationships. Overcoming these differences is essential to friendships and marriages alike.

3 Emphasizing the main idea

An opening should move quickly to establish the topic of your paper and tell readers what your point will be. Anything that takes readers away from your main idea should be eliminated. In this draft, Dwayne intended to explore the morality of capital punishment, but he started with a dry definition, likely to bore his readers.

What exactly is capital punishment? According to the Academic Encyclopedia, capital punishment is the lawful imposition of the death penalty. In biblical times, the death penalty was prescribed for murder, kidnapping, and witchcraft. In England in the 1500s, major crimes such as treason, murder, larceny, burglary, rape, and arson carried the death penalty.

Between 1977 and 1991 in the United States alone, 2,350 persons faced the death penalty, and at least 150 were executed. Although use of the death penalty has strict legal limitations, Americans have differing views on its value in protecting society. Is capital punishment right or wrong?

By asking the definition of a commonly known term, Dwayne wasted his opening words. When editing, he sharpened the question he planned to explore, moved the background information out of the way, and tightened everywhere.

Can capital punishment be morally justified?

Americans disagree about whether the death penalty protects society. Its supporters argue that the fear of death deters some criminals and that execution stops others from striking again. Opponents believe that even noble ends cannot justify such terrible means.

Lawful execution has been around since biblical times, when it was prescribed for murder, kidnapping, and witchcraft. . . .

◼ EDITING 2: EXPLORATION

Read the following two paragraphs, which begin Ambrose Bierce's essay, "Disintroductions." Consider the strategies Bierce has used to engage the reader's interest, and evaluate the effectiveness of this opening. Be prepared to discuss your views with other members of your class.

The devil is a citizen of every country, but only in our own are we in constant peril of an introduction to him. All men are equal; the devil is a man; therefore, the devil is equal. If that is not a good and sufficient syllogism I should be pleased to know what is the matter with it.

To write in riddles when one is not prophesying is too much trouble; what I am affirming is the horror of the characteristic American custom of promiscuous, unsought and unauthorized introductions.

◼ EDITING 3: PRACTICE

Read the following opening paragraph. What do you think are the writer's audience, purpose, and thesis? Generate at least two alternative versions of the paragraph. Evaluate your alternatives according to your understanding of audience, purpose, and thesis.

My research paper is on the clunker law and why people are in favor of it or opposed to it. The controversy exists between large corporations and individuals who own old cars. The law proposes that cars dated 1981 or older that do not pass emission standards be destroyed or limited in their annual mileage. The law will affect the automobile industry and the economic welfare of the lower class. The clunker law is a short-term solution to the problem of pollution. I will state my own opinion about the clunker law. It's a fight between David and Goliath.

■ EDITING 4: EXPLORATION

Read several opening paragraphs by an author whose writing you admire, and select one that seems particularly effective to you. Jot down what you think were the writer's purpose, the intended audience, and the thesis or main idea. What techniques has the author used to engage your attention? How has the author focused your thoughts on the main idea? Which of these techniques can you use in your own writing?

■ EDITING 5: APPLICATION

Read the opening paragraph of a paper you are working on, and evaluate its effectiveness. Are you addressing your audience appropriately? Will it grab readers' attention? Have you focused attention on your central idea? Edit the paragraph with those questions in mind, and compare the edited version with the original. What are the strengths and weaknesses of each?

25 c Making conclusions satisfying

An effective conclusion leaves readers satisfied and gives them something to think about. Again, there is no magic formula for creating satisfying and memorable conclusions. Your conclusion should remind readers of your main idea, but it must go beyond a simple restatement.

Here are some common pitfalls to overcome when editing your conclusions.

■ A conclusion that simply asserts your own belief—unsupported by evidence—is unlikely to persuade anyone not already disposed to agree with you.

■ Last-minute appeals to beliefs or authority will not sway anyone who holds other beliefs or does not share your respect for your chosen authority.

■ A conclusion that goes far beyond what your evidence will support also is unlikely to be persuasive.

■ If you have not yet given readers an explicit statement of your main idea, you must do so in your conclusion.

Here are some strategies for driving your point home.

Rhetorical question

In closing an argument, one highly effective strategy is to end with a **rhetorical question**, one that is not meant to be answered but creates a situation in which the readers cannot help but agree with you.

> Drug violence will continue as long as citizens tolerate the easy availability of guns on the streets; as long as the public shells out money for violence glorified in television and film; as long as drug customers, deprived of effective treatment, pour money into disadvantaged neighborhoods. How can society sit by and do nothing?

The reader isn't really expected to answer this question but rather is expected to respond by saying, "We must do something!"

Summary

Another strategy is a concise **summary** of your main points, followed by a **reflective** point about their meaning. This works well when your exploration has raised questions rather than provided firm answers, as in Teresa's exploration of the nature of death.

> Death is a reality we are confronted with every day. Morticians tend to package death and sell it as interminable slumber. The military suggests that to be killed for a cause is an elevating experience that guarantees heroic stature. The medical profession struggles to preserve life beyond any reasonable hope for a significant future. One way or another, everyone has beliefs about an afterlife, but what happens beyond the grave, the world will never know. What happens lies beyond a door that one day each of us will unlock.

Teresa didn't want to say death was one thing and not another; she wanted her readers to ponder what death means to each of them.

Call to action

Consider concluding an argumentative paper with a **call to action**. What better purpose in marshaling all your powers of persuasion in the paper if not to mobilize your readers on behalf of change? In so doing, you have to presume that your readers believe your argument and are ready to leap up and help you change the world.

Media violence may not be the only cause of aggressive behavior, but it clearly has an adverse effect on viewers. Children are most affected because they readily learn new behavior by imitation. Their lessons are reenacted on playgrounds and on the streets. It's time the public demanded better.

Speculation

You can also conclude with **speculation** about the future, showing your readers a better world—if they act as you have urged in your argumentative paper. Anthropologist Margaret Mead ends her discussion of capital punishment by presenting a vision of a better future.

The tasks are urgent and difficult. Realistically we know we cannot abolish crime. But we can abolish crude and vengeful treatment of crime. We can abolish—as a nation, not just state by state—capital punishment. We can accept the fact that prisoners, convicted criminals, are hostages to our own human failures to develop and support a decent way of living. And we can accept the fact that we are responsible to them, as to all living beings, for the protection of society, and especially responsible for those among us who need protection for the sake of society.

MARGARET MEAD, "A LIFE FOR A LIFE"

STRATEGIES FOR CONCLUSIONS

Make your conclusions more satisfying to you and your readers by adopting one of the following strategies.

- Ask a **rhetorical question**, one that does not need answering but will ring in the readers' ears.
- **Summarize** the important points of your paper, driving home any connections you want to make or any final overarching point that needs to be made.
- Sound a **call to action** when writing papers that argue for change; it's a good way to engage your readers in further thought.
- **Speculate** about the future, leaving your readers to weigh the outcome of the issues you have presented.

EDITING 6: PRACTICE

Edit the following conclusion to make it more satisfying. More than one edited version is possible. Be ready to explain your editing choices.

Computers have already radically altered our society and will undoubtedly continue to do so. But how far will computers take us? Will we like our destination? From the banking and finance industries to recreation and art, every aspect of our lives has been affected by the ramifications of RAM and ROM. Much as the Industrial Revolution and the Agricultural Revolution did in past centuries, the Computer Revolution will fundamentally transform our culture in ways we cannot yet imagine. The three distinctive characteristics of computer transactions—speed of computation, ease of replication, and access through networking—are unremarkable in themselves, but when combined they change the very nature of information, the currency of our culture. No longer is knowledge accumulated over the centuries, unalterably fixed on pieces of paper and painstakingly consulted when needed. Today's information resembles a rushing torrent, always changing, impossible to contain or chart, and ready to sweep aside all limits or restrictions.

25 d Strengthening conclusions

An effective conclusion concisely summarizes, yet does not merely repeat, the whole message of the paper. This is your last chance to communicate with your readers. What is it that you most want readers to remember? Given everything you've demonstrated, what is the strongest statement of your position that you can make? When editing your conclusion, focus on that statement and get everything else out of the way.

1 Being direct

Wordiness undermines the vitality of any concluding statements you make, but worse, it undermines the credibility and authority you have established in the rest of your paper. Transitional phrases such as *in conclusion, all in all,* or *to sum up* shouldn't normally be used to signal that a conclusion is approaching. It is the structure and language of your concluding paragraphs that should show readers that you're winding up. Furthermore, a conclusion cluttered with unnecessary wordiness or transitional phrases makes you sound hesitant, unsure of yourself.

A **qualifying phrase** such as *I think* or *I believe* is another sort of wordiness that can weaken your conclusion. Such a construction is entirely appropriate when you need to distinguish your conclusion from someone else's: *While Robinson concludes that the data clearly link low-frequency radiation to these illnesses, I would argue that the evidence is far from conclusive.* In most cases, however, readers will understand that the ideas expressed in the conclusion are your own.

In drafting her paper on sharks, Aliah concluded with a repetition of other people's opinions or facts, ones that she had carefully documented earlier. By qualifying them in the first person, her conclusion seemed to be merely her own opinion, not a carefully formulated conclusion based on research and analysis. When editing, Aliah removed the first-person references and, rather than telling what her conclusions would be, she simply stated them.

■ ~~I can only hope that I have given some information to help~~ *Sharks* ~~you see that sharks~~ are not the fearsome creatures humans seem to think they are. *Millions of years old,* They have their place in the scheme of things like every other animal. The sooner we accept that the oceans are their domain, the sooner we can learn to share the oceans with them. ~~Sharks are millions of years old; I don't want to be part of their destruction. I hope you too will consider helping to save mankind's ancient enemy, the shark.~~

2 Broadening narrow conclusions

Take care not to limit your conclusion unnecessarily or to end by focusing on a point that is secondary to your overall intent. Mara originally drafted this conclusion arguing against religion's playing a formal role in public schools. When editing, Mara realized that she had ended on a minor point which made her conclusion seem narrower than the rest of her paper.

■ Praying, reading from the Bible, and presenting the teachings of any one religion tend to exclude people who are not believers in that religion. In the public school system, the prayers and beliefs of Christians would predominate and make non-Christians feel "different" and excluded. This is why religion should be kept out of the public schools and kept in the place of worship and the home.

~~As for the future,~~ [predict] I ~~think~~ that religion will not be integrated back into the public school system. ~~However, I do think that holiday concerts and "Season's Greetings" decorations around Christmas and Hanukkah will continue.~~

3 Focusing conclusions

You may want to conclude your essay by raising questions or making generalizations that follow from your discussion. Kyle's essay discussed his college's requirement that students acquire computers, explored the educational applications of computers, and touched on the problems students encountered using them. Yet his conclusion wandered off into speculation. When editing, Kyle decided the possible obsolescence of human thought was too fantastic even for speculation. He edited that statement out and created a smooth transition.

■   With computers becoming as prevalent in college as they are in business, people are beginning to wonder where the computer age is taking us. Will computers become an integral part of everyday life? ~~Will programmable machines make human minds obsolete?~~ [Exactly how they will change people's lives remains to be seen, but] One university official ~~seems to think~~ [predicts changes more gradual than sweeping:] ~~not~~ "When it comes to just plain living and thinking, the computer is not really much help."

WP TIP   Copy the introduction and conclusion of a paper you are working on into a new file; doing this enables you to study them closely without the distraction of the rest of the essay. Is each effective on its own? If not, what is missing? What needs clarifying? Edit them as separate units, then return them to your paper for fine-tuning.

ESL **USING TRANSITIONS IN CONCLUSIONS**

Writers sometimes use transitional phrases to introduce concluding statements in essays.

CONCLUDING/SUMMARIZING TRANSITIONS

in conclusion
to conclude
in summary
to summarize
in sum

EFFECT/RESULT TRANSITIONS

therefore
as a result
consequently

While concluding transitions may be useful to let readers know that you are summing up central points, make sure that what follows is indeed a concluding statement or a summary. Don't mechanically use a phrase such as *in conclusion* every time you end an essay.

Similarly, use a transition indicating result only when what you have written is truly a result or effect of what you have previously discussed. If it is not, omit the connector and consider another way of moving ahead with your discussion.

Take the time when reading the work of others to notice the contexts in which writers use transitions. Notice the different ways that writers create connections to what they have already written (such as repetition of key words or paraphrasing main ideas) when they begin conclusions. Try adopting some of their styles.

■ **EDITING 7: PRACTICE**

Edit the following conclusion to make it more satisfying. More than one edited version is possible. Be ready to explain your editing choices.

Everyone acknowledges that history is important, but there is a lot of debate over just what kind of history should be studied and taught. History matters. Some people mean different things when they say this, though. A form of social history which focuses on the lives and experiences of ordinary people has come into prominence in recent years. Traditionally, history was the study of "great men" and their wars. Economic conditions are also considered by some to be at the center of what we mean by "history." Issues of race and gender are now more prominent than they were before. There is no agreement. So where does that leave those of us who want to study history now? What model are we supposed to follow? There are so many facts and ideas to learn in studying history. When you don't know what facts and ideas you are supposed to be learning, it makes the whole process overwhelming. You can't learn everything, can you? If historians rethink what their discipline is all about, maybe things will work themselves out. History is too important for this issue to be ignored.

■ EDITING 8: EXPLORATION

Select an essay that looks interesting to you because of its title but that you have not read before. First read only the opening paragraph. What can you tell about the essay from this paragraph alone? What is the topic of the essay? What will the author's position on this topic be? What is the author's relation to the subject matter (expert? tourist? researcher? storyteller?)? Who is the intended audience, and how does the author relate to that audience? What is the tone or mood of the essay?

Next read the conclusion. Compare your understanding of the audience, purpose, topic, position, and tone with your impressions of the opening. How are they different? Judging only from the opening and the conclusion, try to determine what were the important points made in the essay.

Last, read the entire essay and see how accurate your predictions were. How good were your guesses?

■ EDITING 9: APPLICATION

Find two essays that you have read and enjoyed recently and compare their conclusions. Then try rewriting the conclusions of the first essay in the style of the second (and vice versa). Compare the effectiveness of the new conclusions with that of the old. Does one seem better than the other? Why? You might try this exercise using essays representing different genres (an expository essay and a proposal, a reflective essay and an essay that seeks to explain a concept, etc.). If you do so, ask yourself whether some types of conclusions seem to work well in different kinds of writing while others do not. Think about why this might be the case.

The simplest kind of **sentence** contains a single idea, but if each of your ideas stands alone in individual sentences, the reader may see them as a string of isolated facts and fail to understand the connections you wish to make. By carefully combining ideas within sentences, you can show readers how those ideas are related.

Various **sentence structures** can express closely related ideas in different ways. Each technique of structuring sentences—coordination, subordination, and creating parallel structures—has specific uses that can help clarify your meaning.

Joining ideas through **coordination**—using the coordinating conjunctions *and, but, so, or, for, nor,* and *yet*—implies that they are of equal importance. However, different kinds of coordination imply different relationships between ideas.

> Give me liberty *or* give me death. [equal alternatives]
>
> Gentlemen may cry peace, peace, *but* there is no peace. The war is actually begun! [contrast]
>
> PATRICK HENRY

Joining ideas through **subordination** implies that one element is related to, dependent upon, caused by, or less important than another. When you subordinate one element to another, you signal to the reader that one element is dependent on another for the reasons you express.

> We should all be concerned about the future *because* we will have to spend the rest of our lives there.
>
> CHARLES KETTERING, "SEED FOR THOUGHT"

Writers use **parallelism**—the repetition of a grammatical structure—to emphasize a similarity between ideas or to assert that several items should be seen in the same way. The repeated elements may be words, phrases, clauses, sentences, or even entire paragraphs. Parallelism creates symmetry, balance, and even elegance.

> No eye can see, no hand can touch, no tongue can name the devils that plague him.

STRATEGIES FOR STRENGTHENING SENTENCES

When editing, consider the following ways to clarify the relationships between your ideas.

1. Use **coordination** for alternatives, comparisons, contrasts, and extensions.
2. Use **subordination** to clarify logical relationships between ideas by subordinating one of them.
3. Combine choppy sentences using coordination or subordination.
4. Use **parallelism** to support coordination or create emphasis.

26 a Using coordination

Elements joined by **coordination** must be in the same grammatical form—two independent clauses, two dependent clauses, two phrases, or two words. As you edit, look for places where ideas of comparable importance could be linked through coordination. When considering whether to use coordination to join two sentences, ask yourself whether the meaning of the sentences is related closely enough to warrant being joined. Then consider whether they are of equal importance to your point. By using coordination skillfully, you can suggest connections, avoid repetition, and enhance readability.

Coordinating conjunctions

Coordinate two or more sentences, or **independent clauses**, by joining them into a single **compound sentence** with a **coordinating conjunction** (*and, but, or, nor, so, for, yet*) and a comma; or with just a semicolon. (For punctuation advice, see Chapter 34). Choose the method of coordination carefully to express the relationship you intend between the two ideas.

Gentlemen may cry peace, peace, *but* there is no peace. The war is actually begun!

Here revolutionary Patrick Henry states his opponents' objective, then with the contrasting conjunction but *tells them their hope for peace is in vain.*

> **COORDINATING CONJUNCTIONS, CORRELATIVE CONJUNCTIONS, CONJUNCTIVE ADVERBS**
>
> | RELATIONSHIP | COORDINATING CONJUNCTIONS |
> | --- | --- |
> | addition | *and* |
> | contrast | *but, yet* |
> | choice | *or, nor* |
> | effect | *so* |
> | causation | *for* |
>
> | RELATIONSHIP | CORRELATIVE CONJUNCTIONS |
> | --- | --- |
> | addition | *both . . . and* |
> | | *not only . . . but also* |
> | choice | *either . . . or* |
> | substitution | *not . . . but* |
> | negation | *neither . . . nor* |
>
> | RELATIONSHIP | CONJUNCTIVE ADVERBS |
> | --- | --- |
> | addition | *also, besides, furthermore, moreover* |
> | contrast | *however, instead, nevertheless, otherwise* |
> | comparison | *similarly, likewise* |
> | effect | *accordingly, consequently, therefore, thus* |
> | sequence | *first, meanwhile, next, then, finally* |
> | emphasis | *indeed, certainly* |

The joining of equivalent elements with *and* or with a semicolon implies continuation or addition.

> Nothing is illegal if one hundred businessmen decide to do it, *and* that's true anywhere in the world.
>
> ANDREW YOUNG

◼ Deforestation is a global problem/ ~~The~~ *and the* United States plays a major role in its spread.

The coordinating conjunction and *implicates the United States in the problem.*

◼ Tropical rain forests account for 60 percent of the world's deforestation/ ~~They~~ *yet they* are the most biologically diverse ecosystems in the world.

The conjunction yet *amplifies the author's objection to deforestation.*

Using coordination can shorten sentences and avoid repetition. Join nouns, verbs, modifiers, phrases, or clauses to create **compound elements** by using one of the coordinating conjunctions. (Also see 26f.) Check to make sure that the two joined elements are equal grammatically. (See 26f.)

■ The police should be interested in the results of the investigation. ~~The district attorney should also be interested.~~

[handwritten insertion: and the district attorney]

Correlative conjunctions

Another way to coordinate two independent clauses is by using a pair of correlative conjunctions such as *both . . and, either . . . or*, or *not only . . . but also*.

■ Lavar won high honors in mathematics and physics. ~~He~~ was also recognized for his achievement in biology.

[handwritten insertions: not only ... but he]

Elements joined by coordinating or correlative conjunctions must be parallel in form. See 26f.

ESL **USING CORRELATIVE CONJUNCTIONS**

If you join subjects with correlative conjunctions such as *both . . . and* or *neither . . . nor*, be sure to check for subject–verb agreement. (See 36e.)

If you join two sentences with *not only . . . but also*, you will need to change word order in the first clause.

1. If the first clause has an auxiliary verb or if the main verb is *be*, reverse the order of the subject and the auxiliary or *be*.

Not only *has the Computer Science department* added several new courses this year, but they have also updated the curriculum.

Not only *is California* a large state geographically, but it also has many cities with large populations.

2. If the first clause has no auxiliary, add an appropriate form of *do* before the subject. The verb must be in its base form.

Not only *did the voters express* a lack of confidence in their governor, but they also showed concern about the effectiveness of the Congress.

Conjunctive adverbs

A **conjunctive adverb** such as *however, moreover,* or *nevertheless* used with a semicolon can also join two independent clauses.

■ An Advanced Placement Test score will be accepted. However, the test must be taken within the last year.

however

WP TIP Highlight all examples of coordination by searching for all coordinating conjunctions. Consider the effectiveness of each use. Do the same with correlative conjunctions and conjunctive adverbs.

■ EDITING 1: PRACTICE

Edit the following passage, using coordination to relate ideas of equal importance. More than one edited version is possible. Be ready to explain your editing choices.

The workers were instructed to seal the oiled rags in cans. They forgot to do it. At night the rags caught fire. The fire spread rapidly through the storage area. A smoke detector went off. No one noticed. The alarm was relayed to the fire station. Firefighters raced to the warehouse. Flames already were darting through the windows. Smoke poured through the ceiling. Glass cracked in the heat. It shattered. The fire commander turned in a second alarm. Another company sped toward the scene.

■ EDITING 2: EXPLORATION

Read the following passage from a personal narrative by N. Scott Momaday. How has Momaday used coordination? How many examples can you find of ideas joined by coordinating conjunctions? By semicolons? Could any of these ideas have been joined in other ways? If they had been, how would the effect of the passage have been different?

Once there was a lot of sound in my grandmother's house, a lot of coming and going, feasting and talk. The summers there were full of excitement and reunion. The Kiowas are a summer people; they abide the cold and keep to themselves, but when the season turns and the land becomes warm and vital they cannot hold still; an old love of going returns upon them. The aged visitors who came to my grandmother's house when I was a child were made of lean and leather, and they bore themselves upright. They wore great black hats and bright ample shirts that shook in the wind. They rubbed fat upon their hair and wound their braids with strips of colored cloth. Some of them painted their faces and carried the scars of old and cherished enmities.

N. SCOTT MOMADAY, *THE WAY TO RAINY MOUNTAIN*

26 b Using subordination

Like coordination, **subordination** joins ideas and implies a relationship between them. In addition, it focuses attention on certain ideas by deemphasizing, or subordinating, others. When considering whether to use subordination, think about your intended meaning and what you want to emphasize. Then use the method of subordination that will most clearly express the intended relationship. By using dependent clauses or structures, you will be able to build an elaborate structure of information, buttressing main ideas with related ones.

NO SUBORDINATION	Tom Peters has become a phenomenon among business writers. He focuses on excellence and quality.
SUBORDINATION	Tom Peters, *who focuses on excellence and quality*, has become a phenomenon among business writers.

This construction emphasizes Peters's status as a phenomenon.

SUBORDINATION	Tom Peters, *who has become a phenomenon among business writers*, focuses on excellence and quality.

This construction emphasizes the focus of Peters's writing.

A subordinate element may appear as a clause, a phrase, or a single word. The less important the element is grammatically, the less attention the reader pays to it.

NO SUBORDINATION	The committee selected a plan. It seemed to leave nothing to chance.
CLAUSE	The plan *that the committee selected* seemed to leave nothing to chance.
PHRASE	The plan *selected by the committee* seemed to leave nothing to chance.
WORD	The plan *selected* seemed to leave nothing to chance.

A **dependent** or **subordinate** clause, which contains a subject and a verb but cannot stand alone as a full sentence, is usually introduced by a subordinating conjunction or a relative pronoun.

ESL   EXPRESSING LOGICAL RELATIONSHIPS USING SUBORDINATION

As you edit, notice whether you rely heavily on coordinating conjunctions and conjunctive adverbs to express logical relationships. If you do, consider using subordinating conjunctions to indicate more clearly how ideas relate.

COORDINATING CONJUNCTION	Freud believed that our dreams reflect our unconscious wishes, *but* some psychologists today believe otherwise.
CONJUNCTIVE ADVERB	Freud believed that our dreams reflect our unconscious wishes. *However,* some psychologists today believe otherwise.
SUBORDINATING CONJUNCTION	*Whereas* Freud believed that our dreams reflect our unconscious wishes, some psychologists today believe otherwise.

The first two versions direct readers to what Freud thought, which is not where you are heading. Only the third version tells readers right away that you are writing about disagreement with Freud.

The following are logical relationships expressed by the three types of connectors. Do not overuse any one type.

RELATIONSHIP	COORDINATING CONJUNCTIONS	CONJUNCTIVE ADVERBS	SUBORDINATING CONJUNCTIONS
contrast	*but*	*however*	*while, whereas*
concession	*but*	*nevertheless*	*although, though*
cause/effect	*for, so*	*therefore, consequently*	*because, since, so that*
sequence	*and*	*then, later, finally*	*after, before, until, when*

Subordinating conjunctions

Using a **subordinating conjunction**, such as *although, because, if, since, whether,* or *while*, makes the dependent clause an adverb clause, one that speaks to adverbial concerns (answering *when, where, why, how* or *under what condition*).

 The plan has a chance of success̸, ~~It~~ ^{although it} requires the efforts of several people. ^{Because one} ~~One~~ person must be available to explain each course offering to students̸, ~~Many~~ ^{many} people are needed.

✔ **SUBORDINATING CONJUNCTIONS**

RELATIONSHIP	SUBORDINATING CONJUNCTIONS
cause/effect	*as, because, since, so that, in order that*
condition	*if, even if, unless, if only*
contrast	*although, even though, though*
comparison	*than, as though, as if, whereas, while*
choice	*whether, than, rather than*
sequence	*after, as, as long as, as soon as, before, once, since, till, until, when, whenever, while*
space	*where, whenever, whence*

Relative pronouns

Using a **relative pronoun** to introduce a dependent clause usually makes the clause an adjective clause, one that modifies (or describes) a noun or pronoun elsewhere in the sentence. Common relative pronouns include *that, what, which, who,* and *whom.* (See 39f.)

The gap between rich and poor̸, ^{which has been widening for over twenty years,} has caused great concern among social thinkers. ~~The gap has been widening for over twenty years.~~

I have interviewed several economists̸, ~~They~~ ^{who} believe that the gap will continue to grow.

Noun clauses

You can also subordinate a sentence by using it as a subject or as an object. Such **noun clauses** can be introduced by *why, what, that, where, whether,* or *how.*

 ~~There are a few basic facts~~ <u>What</u> we know today about AIDS./~~They are~~ <u>is</u>

the result of years of painstaking resarch.

 The entire department became interested./ <u>in what Cate was discovering</u>. ~~Other teachers and~~

~~students wanted to learn about Cate's discoveries.~~

WP TIP To find excessive subordination, scroll through your paper placing in bold all subordinating conjunctions or relative pronouns. Check the effectiveness of each use.

✔ **PUNCTUATING SUBORDINATE STRUCTURES**

If a dependent clause is a **restrictive clause**, one that is necessary to describing the word it modifies, it is not set off by commas. If it is a **nonrestrictive clause**, one that is not needed to identify the word it modifies, it is set off by commas.

RESTRICTIVE He likes cats *that* seem self-reliant and not too familiar.

The dependent clause is restrictive because it identifies particular cats. No commas are needed.

NONRESTRICTIVE He likes his cats, *which* seem self-reliant and not too familiar.

The dependent clause is nonrestrictive because his cats has already identified the specific cats. Use commas here.

If a dependent clause precedes the independent clause, separate them with a comma.

While the trucks poured the concrete into the forms, the workers smoothed it.

See 44c for more on punctuating phrases and clauses.

26 c Creating effective coordination and subordination

Skillful coordination and subordination connect ideas appropriately and enhance readability. As you edit, restructure instances of coordination and subordination that might confuse your readers.

1 Solving problems in logic

Because coordination implies equal relationships, avoid using coordination where the meaning of the two sentences is not related closely enough to warrant joining them.

I had eggs for breakfast, and I missed the bus.

If there is a connection between these two statements, it must be explained. Showing cause and effect, for example, is better done with subordination.

Because I took time to cook eggs for breakfast, I missed the bus.

Faulty coordination can also occur when a connection made between ideas is not only confusing but inaccurate.

■ The project was a huge undertaking, ~~yet~~ so I was exhausted at the end.

The conjunction yet *implies a contrast, which is inappropriate. The conjunction* so *implies the proper cause-and-effect relationship.*

Careless subordination may suggest causal relationships that you do not intend, so be careful to check each of your subordinated structures.

■ ~~When~~ As the moon rose, the rain stopped.

The rising of the moon did not cause the rain to stop.

■ **EDITING 3: PRACTICE**

Edit the following passage from a book review to strengthen coordination and subordination. More than one edited version is possible. Be ready to explain your editing choices.

At the start of *The Bridge across Forever*, the narrator is a stunt pilot performing in small towns of the American Midwest, and the narrator and the author seem to have much in common. The author writes about flying, and the narrator takes people for rides in his plane, but he is bored with the routine, but he is convinced that he will find the perfect woman at one of these shows, so he keeps going. Disillusioned at last, he gives up flying to pursue his quest, and he encounters many women, but none of them is the soul mate he is seeking.

2 Avoiding excessive coordination or subordination

How much coordination or subordination is too much? Beware of a pattern of similar sentences, especially when you did not intend such a pattern.

■ The paper industry ~~is~~ notorious for its deep cyclical swings, *has been hit unusually hard by* ~~but~~ this recession ~~has been unusually severe~~. Prices have been cut sharply, but demand has dropped even faster.

The similarity of the original two sentences was not deliberate. Restructuring one of them solved the problem.

■ Coordination can be overdone, and when it is used too much it begins to sound repetitive. ~~and readers~~ *Readers* may begin to imagine the voice of a young child speaking in sentences that just go on and on, strung together with *and*. ~~and soon~~ *Soon* they may get tired or confused or bored. ~~and~~ *As* ~~as~~ a writer you should try to prevent that.

Here, repetitive words were eliminated and emphasis was redirected for a better effect.

A passage can rely too much on subordination, which can make it sound insipid, because every point seems to be qualified, while nothing is said directly (like this one). How much is too much depends partly on your audience, your purpose, and the level of formality you intend. To edit for proper coordination or subordination, scan your paper for common conjunctions (*and, or, but, because, if, although*) and relative pronouns (*who, which, that*) and evaluate your use of them; make such checking a part of your editing routine.

ESL **USING SUBORDINATING CONJUNCTIONS**

1. When you use *whereas, while, although, though* or *even though* in a dependent clause, do not use *but* before the independent clause.

■ *Although* a smile shows happiness in most cultures, ~~but~~ in some it

may be a sign of embarassment.

Alternatively, you could delete although *and keep* but.

2. When you use *because* or *since* in a dependent clause, do not use *so* in the independent clause.

■ *Because* Rudolf Nureyev defected from Russia, ~~so~~ for many years he

could not return to dance in his native country.

You could also delete because *and keep* so.

3. *Because* and *because of* are not interchangeable. *Because* is a conjunction, which means it introduces a clause containing both a subject and a verb.

Because snow peas die in hot weather, you should plant them early in the spring.

Because of is a two-word preposition, followed by a noun.

Because of the hot weather, the peas did not grow well.

4. *Even* cannot be a subordinating conjunction by itself; it can modify a noun (*Even adults can enjoy this cartoon*), a verb (*She can even think in Chinese now*), or an adverb (*She did it quickly, even eagerly*).

Even though is a subordinating conjunction meaning "despite the fact that."

Even though I don't play the piano well, I still enjoy taking lessons.

Even if is a subordinating conjunction meaning "whether or not."

Even if it rains tomorrow, the race will be held.

■ EDITING 4: PRACTICE

Edit the following passage to eliminate ineffective coordination. More than one edited version is possible. Be ready to explain your editing choices.

Last term I ended up with a low grade-point average, and my academic advisor thought that it was because I was taking too many difficult courses at the same time, so he recommended that I try to make a more sensible schedule this semester. I took his advice, yet I found myself with a much more manageable workload. I am taking calculus, which is difficult for me, and a photography course, which offers me different challenges, but I am finding the variety to be helpful. When I am tired of doing problem sets, I can go out and take pictures, so when the weather is bad, I can stay in and do math. I don't waste time the way I did last term. Because of this new sense of balance, right now I am doing much better in all of my classes, so I hope the pattern will continue.

■ EDITING 5: PRACTICE

Edit the following passage from an analysis of director Oliver Stone's work to eliminate ineffective subordination. More than one edited version is possible. Be ready to explain your editing choices.

The Doors completes what could be termed a sixties trilogy from Stone, since it differs greatly from *Platoon* and *Born on the Fourth of July*. Stone served in Vietnam, although that part of his work is grounded in personal experience. Because he did not experience the world of the Doors, Stone portrays it as he imagines it was, which makes his work in this film different from the others, although it is less effective and less compelling.

■ EDITING 6: EXPLORATION

The following passage from an essay argues that politics has influenced the decisions of art galleries such as the Corcoran Gallery of Art in Washington, D.C. How many examples of subordination can you find in the passage? Why has the author used subordination rather than coordination to join ideas?

Whatever grave reservations regarding Congress may have motivated the directors of the Corcoran, they weakened the entire social fabric by yielding their freedom. Their decision should have been to show the work, whose merit they must have believed in to have scheduled the exhibition. Since then individual members of Congress have revealed themselves as enemies of freedom by letting their aesthetic attitudes corrupt their political integrity as custodians of the deepest values of a democratic society.

ARTHUR C. DANTO, "ART AND TAXPAYERS"

26 d Eliminating choppy sentences

Short sentences can be very powerful, especially when used to dramatic effect. (See 27b.) However, when every idea is expressed in a separate sentence, the result is a **choppy** passage that moves in baby steps. With ideas presented in separate sentences, words must be repeated. Using coordination and subordination can smooth your reader's path and make the connections needed to express the complexity of your thoughts.

■ In 1935, researchers discovered the human sleep cycle. ~~They~~ found that sleep in humans is initiated by a hypnotic state. This hypnotic state affects those brain waves of the neocortex. ~~These~~ are measured using a device called the electroencephalograph.

How long and how complicated you should make your sentences depends in part on how well you think readers will be able to follow.

■ EDITING 7: PRACTICE

Edit the following passage, using subordination to clarify the relationships between ideas and to eliminate choppiness. More than one edited version is possible. Be prepared to explain your editing choices.

Boston Red Sox first baseman Mo Vaughn makes more money per game than many people make in a year. Vaughn's genuine humility and desire to do good in the community have endeared him to the city. He visits local hospitals to see sick children. He pays for busloads of poor kids to see theatrical shows. He pays for kids to go to cultural events. Vaughn acknowledges that he has been blessed. He shows that he appreciates the opportunities he has been given. As a result, people are less willing to resent Vaughn for his success than they are other celebrities.

26 e Creating special effects

Repeating a coordinate structure can give your writing a rhythm, create a cumulative effect, or build to a climax.

It was the best of times, it was the worst of times.

CHARLES DICKENS, *A TALE OF TWO CITIES*

Try using structures that will resonate in your reader's mind. Read your papers out loud as you edit, because the rhythm of your sentences is easily recognized when heard.

In a reflective essay on time and human mortality, E. B. White describes a circus bareback rider circling a ring on horseback again and again. The repetitive coordination emphasizes the rhythm of the scene's action.

> The rider's gaze, as she peered straight ahead, seemed to be circular, as though bent by force of circumstance; then time itself began running in circles, *and* so the beginning was where the end was, *and* the two were the same, *and* one thing ran into the next, *and* time went round and around *and* got nowhere. [Italics added.]
>
> E. B. WHITE, "THE RING OF TIME"

26 f Using parallelism

Writers use **parallelism**—the repetition of a grammatical structure—to emphasize the similarity among ideas. Parallel structures are common in everyday speech as well as in formal writing.

What goes around comes around.

I came, I saw, I conquered.

JULIUS CAESAR

To underscore the similarity of ideas, the elements of a parallel structure must balance grammatically: clauses with clauses, phrases paired with phrases, possessive nouns with possessive nouns, and so on.

CLAUSES Ask not what your country can do for you; ask what you can do for your country.

JOHN F. KENNEDY

PHRASES To die, to sleep. To sleep, perchance to dream.

WILLIAM SHAKESPEARE

WORDS Getting and spending, we lay waste our powers.

WILLIAM WORDSWORTH

1 Compound elements

Compound elements can be joined by a coordinating conjunction (*and, but, or, nor, so, for,* or *yet*) or by a pair of correlative conjunctions (*either . . . or, neither . . . nor, not only . . . but also, both . . . and, whether . . . or*). (See 26a.) When you edit, make sure that all compound elements are grammatically parallel.

- He predicted that the day of judgment would cause the earth to shake and the dead ~~would~~ *to* rise.

- Most people think of the campus as a place to get an education, not ~~where you can~~ *to* exercise and get in shape.

- He not only struggled with calculus/ but *with* chemistry ~~was hard~~ too.

2 Comparisons

When elements are compared using *than* or *as*, they should be parallel in grammatical form because they are presented as equivalent alternatives.

- He always believed that effective communication was more a matter of ~~clear~~ *clearly* thinking than ~~to try to write~~ *writing* well.

- The weather is seldom as pleasant in Boston as *in* Miami's.

3 Lists

Elements presented in a series or list should be parallel in grammatical form.

- Her favorite activities were painting, walking, and ~~she liked to visit~~ *visiting* museums.

WP TIP Use the search function to find common coordinating conjunctions (*and, but, or, nor, for, so,* and *yet*) used in your papers. They often signal compound elements, comparisons, or lists that could be made parallel.

ESL **CREATING PARALLEL STRUCTURES**

Sometimes it is difficult to see at a glance what structures need to be parallel in a sentence. You may want to try this step-by-step technique to identify and create parallel structures in your drafts:

1. Find and circle words or phrases that join structures: *and, but, or, as well as, as much as,* etc.

■ This report states that productivity in the United States has increased (but) real wages of American workers have fallen.

2. You need to make ideas on each side of the circled word(s) parallel, that is, grammatically the same. First determine what ideas are parallel by reading the entire sentence very carefully. Next find the idea to the left of the circled word(s) and put brackets around it. If the parallel ideas are at the end of the sentence, you will often find the first part right after the verb.

■ This report states [that productivity in the United States has increased] (but) real wages of American workers have fallen.

3. Find the parallel idea to the right of the circled word(s) and put brackets around it.

■ This report states [that productivity in the United States has increased] (but) [real wages of American workers have fallen.]

4. Now compare the two bracketed parts; pay attention especially to the beginning of them. Check to see if the first part begins with any of the following:

    a. Complementizer *that* (usually found after verbs)
    b. Relative pronoun: *who, which, that, whose,* etc.
    c. Subordinating conjunction: *because, since, when, after,* etc.

If not, consider whether the first part is a noun phrase, a verb phrase, or an independent clause.

5. Revise your sentence to make the second part grammatically the same as the first part:

■ This report states [that productivity in the United States has increased] (but) [that real wages of American workers have fallen.]

▪ EDITING 8: PRACTICE

Coordinating conjunctions—*and, but, so, or, for, nor, yet*—and semicolons join grammatically equal elements, creating parallel constructions. Find each instance of coordinate or parallel construction in the following sentence from Thomas Jefferson's draft of the Declaration of Independence. Identify the individual elements of each use of coordination or parallelism. What is the effect of parallelism?

We therefore, the representatives of the United States of America in General Congress assembled, in the name of and by the authority of the good people of these states reject and renounce all allegiance to the kings of Great Britain and all others who may hereafter claim by, through or under them; we utterly dissolve all political connection which may heretofore have subsisted between us and the people or parliament of Great Britain; and finally we do assert and declare these colonies to be free and independent states and that as free and independent states, they have full power to levy war, conclude peace, contract alliances, establish commerce, and do all other acts and things with independent states may of right do.

▪ EDITING 9: EXPLORATION

The following passage by the black feminist Alice Walker discusses the position of African American women. Where has she used parallelism? What ideas are emphasized through this use of parallelism? How is the passage as a whole strengthened?

When we have pleaded for understanding, our character has been distorted; when we have asked for simple caring, we have been handed empty inspirational appellations, then stuck in the farthest corner. When we have asked for love, we have been given children. In short, even our plainer gifts, our labors of fidelity and love, have been knocked down our throats. To be an artist and a black woman, even today, lowers our status in many respects, rather than raises it: and yet, artists we will be.

ALICE WALKER, "IN SEARCH OF OUR MOTHERS' GARDENS"

26 g   Creating effective parallelism

Perhaps parallel structures are so common because they are so effective. However, when the words compared are not grammatically comparable, the ideas seem less similar, and the comparison becomes ambiguous.

To bring parallels into sharp focus, supply all necessary words. Words commonly omitted from parallel structures are prepositions (*to, for, at*), subordinating conjunctions (*although, since, because*), and relative pronouns (*who, which, that*).

■ The researchers tried to ensure that interviewees were
representative of the campus population and _{that} their opinions
reflected those of the whole student body.

Without the second that, it is unclear whether the clause beginning with their opinions reflected is part of a parallel structure or the beginning of a second independent clause.

Emphasis

Few devices impart greater power, gravity, and impact than the formal, rhythmic, and forceful words of a well-constructed parallel. When you edit, consider using a parallel structure to highlight a contrast or to emphasize a major point.

■ With local leaders afraid of the "no-growth" label, the quality of
local decision making has clearly declined. The question facing
towns like Abilene is _{not} whether they will ~~do enough planning to~~ plan to have no growth but
whether they will face growth with no plan. ~~avoid uncontrolled development.~~

If you employ complex forms of parallelism, match the elements of each structure carefully, and make sure the passage as a whole warrants the emphasis. Some writers use parallel structures inside other parallel structures, like sets of concentric circles. The effect is not only clarity but also the power, grace, and rhythm of a chant, useful on the most solemn of occasions.

We can never be satisfied as long as our bodies, heavy with fatigue of travel, cannot gain lodging in the motels of the highways and the hotels of the cities. We cannot be satisfied as long as the Negro's basic mobility is from a smaller ghetto to a larger one.

MARTIN LUTHER KING, JR., "I HAVE A DREAM"

Elliptical constructions

In some cases certain words may be omitted from parallel structures, a stylistic device called an **elliptical construction**.

Words that readers can be expected to supply are deliberately omitted to improve the rhythm of the sentence. Elliptical constructions work only when the omitted words are identical to words that remain.

> All worldly pursuits have but one avoidable end, which is sorrow: acquisitions end in dispersion; buildings, in destruction; meetings, in separation; births, in death.
>
> PETER MATTHIESSEN, *THE SNOW LEOPARD*

(See 27f for a complete discussion of how to use elliptical construction.)

◼ EDITING 10: PRACTICE

Strengthen sentence structures in the following paragraph from a record review by using parallelism and elliptical structures. More than one edited version is possible. Be ready to explain your editing choices.

The first cut on *Hope Chest* by 10,000 Maniacs uses a reggae sound in the keyboard. It has an insistent bass line and a guitar that sounds like a swarm of mosquitoes. The vocals are so intricately woven that during the bridge, two sets of lyrics are being sung at once. That sound creates the effect of a breakdown. It also creates the impression of the dissolving of structure.

◼ EDITING 11: PRACTICE

Edit the following paragraph from a personal narrative to correct faulty parallelism. More than one edited version is possible. Be ready to explain your editing choices.

First it rained, then hail was falling, and finally snow came down. As the temperature dropped, we moved our bedrolls closer to the fire, hung blankets over the windows, and more logs were added to the blaze. Nothing seemed to help. The thin walls seemed to invite the cold in. The wind whistled through cracks. The windows rattled in the wind. Snow drifted under the door.

◼ EDITING 12: PRACTICE

Edit the following passage—which analyzes the "Gonzo journalism" of Hunter S. Thompson—to strengthen sentence structure, using coordination, subordination, parallel structures, and elliptical structures as you think appropriate. Many edited versions are possible. Be ready to explain your editing choices.

Whether Hunter S. Thompson's world is reality or imagined, it makes for enjoyable reading. His humor arises from situations that are so frantic or such exaggerations as to be ludicrous. The writing moves from subject to subject, and it mimics the pattern of a drunken or drugged mind. His sentences ramble. His thoughts tumble. His subjects shift like colors in a hallucination. He somehow maintains a sense of reality. Each description and each phrase somehow contain a sharp shard of observation. The reader gets the feeling that his scenes could have happened. Many of them are completely farfetched. He stretches our willingness to believe to the limit. This is the key to Thompson's style.

■ EDITING 13: APPLICATION

Select a page from a draft you are working on, and evaluate the sentence structures. First identify all examples of coordination by circling coordinating conjunctions and semicolons. Next identify all examples of subordination by drawing a line under subordinate elements. Are coordination and subordination used where they are most effective? Are there any places where two ideas would be better joined through another method? Is every conjunction or conjunctive adverb well chosen? Is either coordination or subordination overused? Then look for cases where you have used parallel structures. Are the words and ideas similar enough to be included in a parallel structure? Have you included all necessary words? Find places where you might consider using parallel structures. Edit the page by improving any weak sentence structure you find. How does the edited passage compare with the original?

Effective writing focuses the reader's attention by emphasizing, or stressing, important ideas. You can establish **emphasis** by varying sentence structures and rhythms. Sometimes, when trying to make every idea clear, writers give each idea equal attention. Some ideas, however, are more important than others, and treating those ideas differently draws attention to them.

Variety not only keeps readers focused on your important ideas, it also ensures that you don't lose their attention altogether. A strong but varied rhythm carries the reader along because the writing does not become predictable and monotonous.

When editing, decide what ideas you want to emphasize and where in your paper you might change the rhythm or sentence type to focus readers' attention.

STRATEGIES FOR ACHIEVING EMPHASIS AND VARIETY

Emphasis and variety can be established within individual sentences, within paragraphs, and even throughout an entire paper. When editing to achieve emphasis and variety, try several of the following strategies, then choose the one that best suits your goals for the paper.

1. Use the emphatic first and final positions.

2. Edit sentence length.

3. Vary sentence types.

4 Vary sentence openings.

5. Use deliberate repetition.

6. Create elliptical constructions.

27 a Using the emphatic first and final positions

If you want something to be noticed, place it at a beginning. The first words of a sentence, the first sentence of a paragraph, and the first paragraph of an essay all attract readers' attention.

> *I think that we're all mentally ill*; those of us outside the asylums only hide it a little better—and maybe not all that much better, after all. We've all known people who talk to themselves, people who sometimes squinch their faces into horrible grimaces when they believe no one is watching, people who have some hysterical fear—of snakes, the dark, the tight place, the long drop . . . and of course, those final worms and grubs that are waiting so patiently underground.
>
> STEPHEN KING, "WHY WE CRAVE HORROR MOVIES"

While first words immediately grab attention, those that come last can have an enduring impact. The last words of a sentence, a paragraph, or an entire essay resonate in the reader's mind, lingering to provoke further thought.

> Early civil rights bills nebulously state that other people shall have the same rights as "white people," indicating that there were "other people." But civil rights bills passed during and after the Civil War systematically excluded Indian people. . . . *Indians were America's captive people without any defined rights whatsoever.*
>
> VINE DELORIA, JR., "CUSTER DIED FOR YOUR SINS"

When editing, look for ways to use the emphatic first and final positions of each sentence, each paragraph, and each essay, especially in your opening and conclusion. (See Chapter 25.)

■ ~~Whatever the rewards~~ The costs of prohibition, ~~its costs~~ its rewards. will always exceed ~~them~~ Users, who will always exist, are harmed not only by drugs but also by the law. The more effective the law, the more nonusers are victimized by crimes committed for drug cash. The higher drug prices go, the more desperate and sophisticated drug gangs become. ~~With~~ with a stroke of the pen, ~~society~~ Society could eliminate drug profits and drug crime.

Editing the concluding paragraph of her argument, Darla phrased her first sentence more boldly. She then moved the phrase with the stroke of a pen *to the emphatic final position.*

OLD AND NEW INFORMATION IN SENTENCES

As you edit for emphasis and variety, consider what information you have already given your readers. Presenting information that readers already know—"old" information—before introducing "new" information helps readers see the connection to earlier ideas. This mental linking helps readers recognize what is the continuing thread of the discussion and thus keeps them interested.

■ Most artificial colorings are synthetic chemicals. These colorings are [old] suspected of increasing hyperactivity in children. [new]

If the old-to-new pattern is not observed, the ideas are hard to follow, and the reader can't identify the main point.

■ Most artificial colorings are synthetic chemicals. Hyperactivity [new?] in children may be increased by these colorings. [old?]

What is the main point that the writer will go on to explore? Colorings? Hyperactivity? As it is written, we can't know.

Watch the flow of old information to new information from this masterful writer.

Big João was born near the sea, on a sugarcane plantation in Recôncavo, the owner of which, Sir Adalberto de Gumucio, was a great lover of horses. He boasted of possessing the most spirited sorrels and the mares with the most finely turned ankles in all of Bahia and of having produced these specimens of first-rate horse-flesh without any need of English studs, thanks to astute matings which he himself supervised.

MARIO VARGAS LLOSA, *THE WAR OF THE END OF THE WORLD*

Unless you carefully manage old-to-new patterns, readers may flounder in the flood of new information and might be tempted to stop reading.

■ **EDITING 1: APPLICATION**

Select two pages from a paper you are working on. Underline the first and last sentence in each paragraph. Reading only these sentences, would a reader see the most important ideas in each paragraph? Edit each paragraph so that the most important idea is in either the first sentence or the last.

Next, on one of the edited pages underline the most important element in each sentence, whether a thing, an action, or a description. How often does the most important element fall at the very beginning or at the very end of the sentence? How often is it buried somewhere in the middle? Edit each sentence, moving important elements to the emphatic first or final position within sentences wherever possible. Compare the edited version with the original to determine which you prefer. Does strengthening emphasis help achieve the goals of this paper?

27 b Editing sentence length

Some writers write short sentences. They seldom use dependent clauses. They rarely use modifiers. They never use verbal phrases. Other writers never use simple sentences when elaborate ones, decorated with ribbons of dependent clauses, can be substituted, and thus they sometimes keep the reader waiting, hoping—perhaps even praying—eventually to find a period and, with it, a chance to pause for breath. (Whew.) Short sentences and long ones both have their uses, given a writer's purpose and intended audience. When you edit, be aware of how deliberately varying sentence length can direct and focus readers' attention; mix sentence lengths for emphasis and variety.

■ Short sentences

Short sentences sound honest and direct. They command the reader's full attention. They have the power to show an intensity in feelings, impressions, and events. In the following scene Richard Rodriguez describes distributing bread in a poor neighborhood in Tijuana. Notice how his brief sentences make his confrontation with hunger and need all the more chilling.

> Five or six children come forward. All goes well for less than a minute. The crowd has slowly turned away from the altar; the crowd advances zombie-like against the truck. I fear children will

be crushed. Silent faces regard me with incomprehension. *Cuidado* [careful], damn it!

RICHARD RODRIGUEZ, "ACROSS THE BORDERS OF HISTORY"

When you want to achieve such a dramatic effect—a critical scene in a personal narrative or in the summation of an argumentative paper—condense your ideas into as few words as possible and break up long sentences into shorter ones.

■   ~~As soon as~~ I hit the ball and took ~~my~~ a ~~first~~ step/. ~~my~~ My knee collapsed, and I was on the ground. in The pain was blinding. ~~pain~~, I heard my teammates yelling, "Get up! Run!" ~~but~~ I could no more run than ~~I could~~ fly.

2 Long sentences

Most academic writing requires that you elaborate on your ideas and show the connections between them. Long sentences give you the room you need to develop more complex thoughts and the structure to show the relationships between them. (See also Chapter 26.) If you find a patch of short sentences that say little and don't emphasize an important point, consider combining some sentences to emphasize the main ideas.

■   Recent snows have renewed a problem in the town of Palmyra/: ~~The problem is~~ sinkholes/, ~~Water~~ which are caused by water eroding underground limestone deposits. ~~causes them~~, They are like huge potholes/ that ~~They~~ appear quickly and grow rapidly. A few years ago a sinkhole opened in a car dealer's lot, swallowing a few cars. Last February a fuel truck making a delivery ended up in a sinkhole/, ~~Another~~ while another swallowed a yard and threatens a house. With heavy ~~Heavy~~ snows ~~are~~ melting rapidly/, ~~We~~ we face the problem of a sinking town.

You can create emphasis by mixing both long and short sentences. Try changing abruptly from a long sentence to a sparsely worded, simple sentence that stresses one of your key points. The break in rhythm will make readers stop in their tracks and notice your point. Try it. It works.

> Of course, the association of guitars with cowboys goes back quite a long way, almost to the beginning, you might say. The rugged and rowdy cowboy at home on the range singing songs around the campfire is a part of American mythology. Ironically, the earliest guitar-toting cowpokes urging little dogies to get along were more likely to be Mexican *vaqueros* than Yankees or northern Europeans in search of wide open spaces. *Nevertheless, the image is as American as apple pie.* [Italics added.]
>
> MICHAEL WRIGHT, "SPIRIT OF THE WEST"

You can also build up to a longer sentence for emphasis.

■   **Concern over deforestation has increased greatly in recent years. William Robinson, president of the American Plywood Association, says no environmental problem "is more life-threatening, long term, to our industry and planet." The problem today reaches beyond the simple reduction of beautiful trees. It is not just the extinction of animals and the pollution of water by clear-cutting. It is also fear of global warming due in part to the destruction of forests.**

WP TIP   Some style checkers can chart sentence length, giving you a tally of how many words each sentence contains and how many sentences of various lengths you have written. You can also determine the length of your sentences by inserting a hard return so that each sentence starts on a new line. Identify your sentence patterns, then decide which ideas could be emphasized through the use of a different sentence length.

■ **EDITING 2: PRACTICE**

Edit the following passage, which appears just before the end of a personal narrative, varying the length of the sentences to improve emphasis and variety. More than one edited version is possible. Be ready to explain your editing choices.

When I heard the mail drop through the slot in the door, my heart leapt. After I practically flew downstairs, I pounced on the mail that lay scattered on the floor. There, finally, was a letter for me from Iowa State University. "Today's the day," I said to myself, "the day that will seal my fate." At last I would have the answer to the all-important question of whether I had been accepted at the school of my choice. I wondered where I would spend the next four years. I wondered if I would be in Ames, Iowa, or home in Deerfield, Illinois. After I took a deep breath and counted to three, I ripped open the envelope.

27 c Varying sentence types

Sentences can vary by *grammatical type*, by *rhetorical type*, or by *functional type*. (Also see Chapter 68.) Because readers' attention will be drawn to an atypical sentence—a question or command, for instance—varying sentence types provides another way to create emphasis.

▮ Grammatical types

Varying grammatical sentence types usually means varying sentence lengths: short sentences are usually **simple sentences**, with a single independent clause, while long sentences are often **compound**, with more than one independent clause; **complex**, with at least one dependent clause; or **compound-complex sentences**, with a dependent clause as well as at least two independent clauses. Each type has its own typical pattern and rhythm. If you have used too many sentences of one type, you may miss a chance to create emphasis and variety.

A young-looking 43, he is a slim but strongly built man whose fast smile and self-deprecating patter convey the impression of relentless, perpetual movement. Talk slowly, or make a point twice, and an impatient glaze comes into his eyes. *He is restlessness in a designer suit.* But when I talked to him recently in his North London home, [British Labour Party leader Tony] Blair was off duty, tousled and denim'd. He has always been a cheery rock-freak, a passionate father and a weekend slob. *And he has always been surprising.* [Italics added.]

ANDREW MARR, "VANITY BLAIR"

Notice how the quick sentences keep the passage moving. The last sentence focuses attention forward, on what the writer finds "surprising."

GRAMMATICAL SENTENCE TYPES

A simple sentence consists of a single independent clause:

independent clause
■ ⌐Pollution is a growing problem.⌐

A compound sentence consists of two or more independent clauses (joined by a comma and a coordinating conjunction or by a semicolon):

independent clause   *independent clause*
■ ⌐Pollution is a growing problem⌐ and ⌐it affects every aspect of our

lives.⌐

A complex sentence consists of one independent clause and one or more dependent clauses:

dependent clause   *independent clause*
■ ⌐Because clear-cut forests hold less water,⌐⌐water quality deteriorates.⌐

A compound-complex sentence contains at least two independent clauses and one or more dependent clauses:

dependent clause   *independent clause*
■ ⌐When the rains stop,⌐⌐the ground dries out rapidly,⌐ and ⌐stream
independent clause
temperatures rise.⌐

(For more on sentence types, see Chapter 68.)

2   Rhetorical types and word order

Within a sentence, should you put the main point first and the subordinate information later? Or should you first establish the context and then deliver the main message? Such decisions refer to rhetorical sentence types. The first strategy—placing the main idea first—results in a **cumulative sentence**.

main point   *subordinate information*
■ ⌐Othello smothers the delicate Desdemona⌐⌐in a fit of anguished
main point
passion and boiling fury.⌐ ⌐He kills the person he loves most⌐
subordinate information
⌐because he has trusted the lies of the vicious Iago.⌐

The second strategy—which saves its punch for the end—results in a **periodic sentence**.

subordinate information   main point

■ ⌐In a fit of anguished passion and boiling fury,¬ ⌐Othello smothers
                                subordinate information
the delicate Desdemona.¬ ⌐Because he has trusted the lies of the
                  main point
vicious Iago,¬ ⌐he kills the person he loves most!¬

Notice how the effects differ despite the very slight variation in the actual words used.

Cumulative sentences allow a writer to make a major point, then support it. Yet writing composed solely of cumulative sentences can be monotonous, so consider using a periodic sentence to emphasize a point.

■   *A Small Place* is an unsettling book. In it Jamaica Kincaid

discloses shocking details about the tourist paradise Antigua,

where she grew up. We see the poor condition of the school,

the library, the hospital, and even the government, all problems
                                              When

she links to English and American imperialism. ~~An American~~
                                      ^

~~reader feels defensive and ashamed when~~ confronted by the
                                       an American reader feels

consumers of unthinking exploitation/ /*defensive and ashamed.*

Alternatively, you can put important information first by using **inverted word order**, in which the verb precedes the subject: *Down came the rain and washed the spider out.* Although such inversion is uncommon, it can be used to strong effect in a special situation such as an opening or an ending.

   WP TIP   Select a paragraph from a paper you are working on and copy it to a new file. Revise, implementing some of the strategies in this chapter. Compare the original and the revised paragraphs and consider which is more effective and why.

3 Functional types

Most writing relies primarily on **declarative sentences**—sentences that make statements. However, an occasional **question**,

ESL **INVERTING SUBJECTS AND VERBS**

When you place certain structures at the front of a sentence, you must reverse the order of the **subject** of the main clause and the first **auxiliary** verb (a form of *have* or *be* or a modal auxiliary such as *may, can, would, should*). If there is no auxiliary verb, then add the appropriate form of *do* and put the subject and the verb after it. The main verb changes to base form.

■ *Under no circumstances did we wish to cut funding for this program.*

introductory element | auxiliary subject | base verb

Here is a list of introductory elements that require changing subject–verb order.

NEGATIVE ADVERB OF FREQUENCY	*Seldom* has a verdict created such an outrage among citizens. (Others: *rarely, scarcely, hardly ever, only once*)
OTHER NEGATIVE ADVERBS AND ADVERB PHRASES	*In no way* should funding for this program be cut. (Others: *in no case, in no way, not until* + *[time], not since* + *[time]*)
ADVERB OF EXTENT OR DEGREE	*So* intense was the hurricane that it destroyed much of the small town.
CONDITIONAL CLAUSES	*Only if* we take measures now will we rescue our city from urban blight. *Only when* there is justice will there be peace.

Certain other elements at the beginning of a sentence require you to place the subject after both the auxiliary (if there is one) and the main verb.

ADVERB OF POSITION	*Behind the sofa* could go the larger of the two bookcases.
COMPARATIVES	*More intriguing* than the main plot of the novel are several of the subplots.
PARTICIPLES WITH MODIFIERS	*Lying on my desk* should be a large sealed envelope.

exclamation, or **command** can grab the reader's attention. (Also see 68a.)

> Yes, I love the church. *How could I not do otherwise?* I am in the rather unique position of being the son, the grandson, and the great-grandson of preachers. Yes, I see the church as the body of Christ. *But, oh! How we have blemished and scarred that body through social neglect and through fear of being nonconformists.* [Italics added.]
>
> MARTIN LUTHER KING JR., "LETTER FROM BIRMINGHAM JAIL"

Notice how the emotional color of the paragraph changes as King changes sentence types using questions and exclamations.

> The church was a hub of Black children's social existence, and caring Black adults were buffers against the segregated and hostile world that told us we weren't important. But our parents said it wasn't so, our teachers said it wasn't so, and our preachers said it wasn't so. The message of my racially segregated childhood was clear: *let no man or woman look down on you, and look down on no man or woman.* [Italics added.]
>
> MARIAN WRIGHT EDELMAN, "A FAMILY LEGACY"

Edelman stressed the message by putting it in a command—the reader can hear the message as she heard it herself.

■ EDITING 3: EXPLORATION

Extreme examples of periodic and cumulative sentences were much more common in the past than now. Here are two excerpts from an essay by the eighteenth-century writer Samuel Johnson in which he relates the demise of an "adventurer in lotteries"—a gambler. What can you infer of Johnson's audience and purpose? Which sentence is periodic, and which is cumulative? What effect does each one have on you, the reader? Try to write sentences modeled on these examples, following their general patterns and rhythms but using different topics.

> As I have passed much of life in disquiet and suspense, and lost many opportunities of advantage by a passion which I have reason to believe prevalent in different degrees over a great part of mankind, I cannot but think myself well qualified to warn those, who are yet uncaptivated of the danger which they incur by placing themselves within its influence....

My heart leaped at the thoughts of such an approach of sudden riches, which I considered myself, however contrarily to the laws of computation, as having missed by a single chance; and I could not forbear to revolve the consequences which such a bounteous allotment would have produced, if it had happened to me.

SAMUEL JOHNSON, "THE HISTORY OF AN ADVENTURER IN LOTTERIES"

27 d Varying sentence openings

As you edit, consider repositioning elements so that some sentences begin with elements other than the subject. Doing so will slightly emphasize that sentence and the element that begins it.

Modifier

■ ~~Doctors~~ *Increasingly, doctors* rely ~~increasingly~~ on advanced diagnostic equipment.

■ ~~Single~~ parents, *Overworked and often underpaid* ~~who are overworked and often underpaid,~~ are among the most marginalized members of society.

Dependent clause

■ ~~Much~~ *Until researchers learned to translate its hieroglyphs, much* of ancient Mayan culture remained a mystery. ~~until researchers learned to translate its heiroglyphs,~~

Transitional expression

■ Most teenagers are aware of the dangers of smoking. ~~They~~ *However, they* don't always realize the addictive power of cigarettes. ~~however,~~

■ EDITING 4: PRACTICE

To improve the emphasis and variety of the following passage, edit it by beginning some of the sentences with an element other than the subject. More than one edited version is possible. Be ready to explain your editing choices.

Chicken soup, a traditional remedy for colds, is a good food to eat in winter. Its temperature warms the body, like other hot liquids. Chicken soup, not difficult to prepare, is made by boiling a whole chicken in about three quarts of water until the chicken is cooked fully and begins to come away from the bone. Be sure to add plenty of salt, which brings out the flavor, before you bring the chicken to a boil. Diced carrots, onions, and celery accentuate the flavor of the broth even more. You should add these vegetables when the chicken is done, but be sure to remove the bones first. The vegetables then take another hour to cook. You know the soup is ready when they are soft enough to cut with a fork.

27 **e** **Using deliberate repetition**

Deliberately repeating words, phrases, or sentence structures links the repeated elements and emphasizes them. (See 24c for repetition and paragraph coherence.) Repetition can also create powerful rhythmic effects. A succession of similar phrases, falling on the reader's ear like the sound of waves striking the shore, can be soothing or can build to a strong climax. Getting just the right amount of repetition is difficult, however. When in doubt, err on the side of too little rather than too much. You can also use slight variations, or **synonyms**, rather than repeat the same word.

In the following passage, Annie Dillard weaves together repeated words and phrases, creating a rhythm that suggests the sense of serenity she found in the forests of Ecuador.

> The point of going somewhere like the Napo River in Ecuador is not to see the most spectacular anything. It is simply to see what is there. We are here on the planet only once, and might as well get a feel for the place. We might as well get a feel for the fringes and hollows in which life is lived, for the Amazon basin, which covers half a continent, and for the life that—there, like anywhere else—is always and necessarily lived in detail: on the tributaries, in the riverside villages, sucking this particular white-fleshed guava in this particular pattern of shade.
>
> ANNIE DILLARD, "IN THE JUNGLE"

To use repetition effectively, look for words, phrases, or structures that are important to your meaning. Make sure that the element you have repeated deserves the emphasis and that the rhythmic effect you create is appropriate for your subject and audience. In this passage, Mark was trying to recreate the magic spell his mother cast by reading to him regularly.

■ ~~When she~~ *She* read to me, I ~~could see~~ *and saw* faraway islands fringed
with coconut palms. ~~With~~ *She read to me, and with* Jim Hawkins, I shivered in the apple
barrel while the pirates plotted. *She read to me, and* I ran with Maori warriors to
raid the villages of neighboring tribes. *She read to me, and* I saw Captain Cook slain

on a beach of the Sandwich Isles. I saw the Tahitians welcome

British sailors. I watched Fletcher Christian mutiny against

Captain Bligh, and I marveled that Bligh reached England in an

open boat. I heard Ahab's peg leg thump on the deck overhead,

and I marveled at the whiteness of the whale.

■ **EDITING 5: EXPLORATION**

In the following passage, identify instances of repetition. How does repetition contribute to the effectiveness of the passage? What ideas are emphasized?

His need for food stamps, quite obviously, is minimal now. But his need is not minimal for a reminder of those days when his father worked as a shipping clerk in a refrigerator plant and his mother stayed home to raise three children before she died so prematurely that her youngest son's heart still aches to think of it.

To reach the goal he has set for himself, to reach the level Sugar Ray Leonard once occupied at the top of boxing's craggy Mount Olympus, he must not lose a fight, but just as important, he must not lose his way.

He must avoid the normal pitfalls a fighter faces like the jabs to the nose and hooks to the liver, but this fighter must avoid more than that. He must avoid the eroding powers of money and fame, two things that build a man up and bring him crashing back to earth with the same swiftness.

RON BORGES, "A GOLDEN BOY WITH A PLATINUM PLAN"

27 f Creating elliptical constructions

In an **elliptical construction**, words that your reader will be able to supply mentally are omitted for the sake of brevity or to create a special rhythm. (See also 26g.) The omitted words are almost always dropped from the second part of a parallel construction after the idea has been introduced.

- ■ Her words suggested one thing, her actions ~~suggested~~ another.

Elliptical constructions work only when the words you omit are identical to words that remain.

- ■ Of Shakespeare's female characters, Lady Macbeth is the most ruthless, Desdemona and Juliet ~are~ the most loving, and Portia ~is~ the most resourceful.

The omitted verbs must match exactly the verb that remains: is. *But the plural subject* Desdemona and Juliet *requires the verb* are, *so the omitted verbs had to be reinstated.*

Like repetition, an elliptical construction strongly affects rhythm and emphasis. It heightens rhythm by omitting words that would not have been stressed and leaving only the stressed words. But it also syncopates rhythm, so that a word occurs a beat or two sooner than the reader expected. Read out loud any elliptical constructions you create in the context of their sentences to make sure that you have achieved the right rhythm.

■ EDITING 6: EXPLORATION

The ways a writer achieves emphasis and variety are central to his or her writing style. Select a few pages of writing by your favorite author and study the sentences for the techniques mentioned in this chapter. Does the author favor one technique more than the others? Which technique(s) do you think the author uses most effectively? Why? What does the author's use of variety and emphasis say about his or her style? Answers to these questions could tell you a great deal about why you like your favorite author's work.

■ EDITING 7: PRACTICE

Edit the following passage from a personal narrative for emphasis and variety. You will, of course, have to choose what to emphasize and which elements to preserve as you create variety. Think of at least two alternatives for each choice, and note the reasons for your decisions. If you have to make assumptions about audience or purpose, note them as well.

Sunday dinner at Grandma's house was about as appealing to me as a day without recess for me, an energetic nine-year-old. It meant leaving the kids at the playing field at the bottom of the eighth inning. I had to take a bath in the middle of the day and wash behind my ears. The worst thing was that I had to put on my best clothes and try to keep them clean. For me to keep my clothes clean seemed beyond the realm of possibility in those days. My parents would look absolutely delighted as I emerged from the bath every week. I looked, frankly, nothing like myself. My father would exclaim, "She's as clean as a hound's tooth!" Yet I would arrive at Grandma's week after week looking like Raggedy Ann, despite my parents' best efforts. My shirt would inevitably be stained; my stockings would inevitably be split; my shoes would inevitably be scuffed. My mother would look at me in disbelief as I climbed out of the car. She was amazed, no doubt, that such a metamorphosis could have occurred in a twenty-minute ride. My disheveled appearance, to be honest, never seem to bother Grandma. She always exclaimed, "Don't you look nice!" I don't know to this day whether she was losing her eyesight or just being kind.

■ EDITING 8: APPLICATION

Select a passage from a paper you are working on and look for places that need emphasis or variety. Generate alternative versions using the various techniques discussed in this chapter—position, sentence length, sentence type, sentence openings, repetition, and ellipsis. Pick the version—alternative or original—that best suits your audience and purpose, and explain your choices.

What brings writing to life? Why does one writer's prose dull the senses while another's, on the same subject, rivets readers' attention? Sentence vitality —liveliness—helps create clear and compelling writing. By delighting the imagination, a vital sentence encourages readers to go on to the next sentence and the next, and to think and interact with your words. Clarity, appropriate descriptiveness, action, and specific examples all contribute to vitality in varying degrees.

In an argument paper, vitality means supporting your assertions with concrete evidence. In a reflective paper, it means providing candid insights into your perceptions and reactions. In a personal narrative, it means relating carefully observed detail in language that is fresh and accurate.

For example, most readers would find the first of these two descriptions dull and the second more vivid and powerful.

> The sky and the sunrise are reflected by the snow. There is a road in front of me that goes down the slope toward the stone formations.

> The snow-covered ground glimmers with a dull blue light, reflecting the sky and the approaching sunrise. Leading away from me the narrow dirt road, an alluring and primitive path into nowhere, meanders down the slope and toward the heart of the labyrinth of naked stone.

> EDWARD ABBEY, *DESERT SOLITAIRE*

Why is the second passage more vital than the first? The first uses general, **abstract nouns** with few modifiers: *sunrise, road, stone formations*. The second uses specific, **concrete nouns** and modifiers that create tangible images: *alluring and primitive path, labyrinth of naked stone*. The first uses weak or **static verbs**: *is, goes*. The second uses **strong verbs** that evoke actions readers can visualize: *meanders*. Finally, while the verb in the first passage is in the **passive voice** (*are reflected*), the second passage uses a verb in the **active voice** (*glimmers*).

To improve the vitality of your writing, think of each sentence as a story. Like any story, a sentence has actors—nouns and pronouns—and actions—verbs. When you make each actor and action as vivid and as tangible as possible, readers can imagine the story unfolding before their eyes. When editing, use the following techniques to give your sentences immediacy and energy.

28 a Using concrete, specific nouns and modifiers

If a sentence is to tell a story, your first task is to identify the actors in it so that readers can recognize them fully. Whether a character is a person, an object, or an idea, try to make that element come alive in readers' minds. Compare the mental pictures you get from the phrases *an old blue car* and *a rusted, baby-blue '59 Buick Electra*. The first evokes images of a number of cars, the second a specific car.

As you edit, examine your choice of language, since it plays a big part in conveying vivid and powerful images. Is your language abstract or concrete? **Abstract** words refer to ideas and concepts that cannot be perceived by the senses: *transportation, wealth, childhood, nutrition.* **Concrete** words name things that can be seen, touched, heard, tasted, or smelled: *cars, dime, child, broccoli.*

Next, is your language general or specific? **General** words refer to categories and groups: *pets, stores, doctors.* **Specific** words identify individual objects or people: *Rover; the Reading Terminal Market; pediatrician Andrea McCoy.*

The terms *abstract* and *concrete* are not absolute. Think of them as representing the ends of a continuum, with varying degrees of abstraction in between. The same is true of the terms *general* and *specific.*

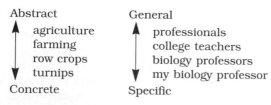

These two ways of characterizing words can overlap. *Music,* for example, is concrete in that you can hear it, but the word is also a general term embracing everything from Bartok to bagpipes to Hootie and the Blowfish.

1 Using concrete, specific nouns

Human thought depends on the ability to make connections between the general and the specific. Some kinds of thought require abstract terms: we could not think, speak, or write about *truth, insurance, constitutionality, political risk,* or *angular velocity* without using words developed for such concepts. Yet writing composed exclusively of abstractions can seem like nothing but "hot air." On the other hand, it may be hard to glean general truths from writing consisting only of details. Writers usually err on the side of too many generalizations, so look for ways to enliven abstract terms with specifics.

> We stand for a brighter future, a renewed hope, a better America.

Who doesn't want those things? How can you tell what this writer stands for?

> We stand for a brighter future, a renewed hope, a better America, in which the unemployed find work, the sick receive health care, the old and the young are nurtured, and all of us are treated with respect.

What this writer means by "a better America" is quite clear now, and the reader is free to agree or disagree with the specifics provided.

When writing about an abstract concept, provide a definition or example definition shortly after introducing it. Then make sure you ground the abstraction with clear, tangible examples so that it has meaning for your readers.

■ Concern about the national debt ̭has driven efforts to balance
 ‑money the government has borrowed in order to operate‑
the federal budget.

■ Liberal policies ̭are bringing this country to ruin.
 like those that created the welfare system

■ Conservatives ̭don't care about people, only business.
 by slashing environmental protections, show they

When writing academic papers, you may want to use broader, more general statements in openings and conclusions. Make sure that you have developed the specific and concrete details needed in the rest of the paper. (See 25d.)

ESL USING ARTICLES WITH NOUNS

The choice of an article (*a*, *an*, *the*) before a noun depends on the type of noun and the context in which it is used. All nouns are either count nouns or noncount nouns. Count nouns can be singular (*island*, *child*, *ratio*) or plural (*islands*, *children*, *ratios*). Noncount nouns generally cannot be made plural (*information*, *homework*, *justice*, *success*). (For more information on articles, see 32b.)

1. Use an article before a singular count noun unless the noun has a quantifier (*one*) or a possessive (*my*, *her*) before it.

 an island the child a ratio

Exceptions to this rule are singular proper nouns, which in most cases do not require an article.

 Italy Pearl Street Lake Erie

2. Use *a* or *an* with a singular count noun when you have not specified one particular thing or individual.

 There is *a problem* with this approach.

  Readers don't know what the problem is yet.

 We all appreciate *an understanding friend.*

  Any understanding friend, not a particular one.

3. Use *the* with a singular count noun in the following cases.

■ The noun has already been mentioned.

 There is a problem with this approach. *The problem* is a subtle one.

■ The noun is made specific by modifiers that follow it.

 The problem that I see with this approach is a subtle one.

  The modifying clause that I see with this approach makes it clear that the writer is referring to one specific problem.

■ The noun is made specific by the context.

 I entered a large lecture hall. *The teacher* was standing behind a podium. *The blackboard* seemed very far away.

  In a lecture hall, there is likely to be only one teacher and only one blackboard.

■ The noun names a unique person, place, or thing.

The moon was still hovering on *the horizon.*

> *There is only one moon and only one horizon.*

4. Use *the* with plural count nouns in the following cases.

■ The noun is made specific by modifiers that follow it.

The novels that I like best focus on characters rather than on events.

> *The modifying clause* that I like best *makes it clear that the writer is referring to a specific set of novels.*

■ The noun is made specific by the context.

We saw a play tonight. *The actors* were from London.

> *The context makes it clear that the writer is referring specifically to the actors in the play they saw tonight.*

■ The noun is a proper noun referring to a country or a set of lakes, mountain ranges, or islands.

the United States   the Rocky Mountains
the Great Lakes   the Bahamas

5. Use *some* (*any* in negative sentences) or no article with non-count nouns if the noun is not specific.

They asked for *some information* at the tourist center.

There isn't *any homework* for tomorrow.

The citizens are demanding *justice.*

6. Use *the* with noncount nouns if the noun is specific because it has been previously mentioned, it is clear from the context, or it has modifiers.

We ordered new skiing equipment. After *the equipment* arrived, we decided we didn't need it.

As class came to an end, she passed out *the homework.*

The justice of this verdict is questionable.

2 **Using concrete, specific modifiers**

Use the same considerations when selecting modifiers as you did for nouns: Choose specific and concrete modifiers over abstract and vague terms. Some descriptive modifiers, such as *pretty, dull, dumb, nice, beautiful, good, bad, young, old*, have become almost meaningless through overuse. They paint a very general picture. Rather than ask readers to accept your impression, give them the specific details so they can see things for themselves.

VAGUE   Everyone likes Alex.

SPECIFIC Everyone likes witty Alex with his dimpled chin and big laugh.

VAGUE   A row of old brick houses stands along the street.

SPECIFIC Dilapidated brick houses line the street, their shutters sagging and their windows boarded.

■ **EDITING I: PRACTICE**

Edit the following paragraph by using concrete, specific nouns and modifiers. You may invent and add whatever details you think are necessary. Create one edited version. Then repeat the exercise, providing different details.

Our college library is really good. Not only does it have lots of books on all kinds of topics, but it also has plenty of periodicals. Many resources are available to help people with any research they might need to do, and the staff is always ready to give guidance. Research librarians are there to help answer all sorts of questions about library resources. Last year the library finally finished installing the new computer system. Now we can look up an item in the library from any of the remote computer terminals located all over campus. With just a few keystrokes, we can determine whether the library owns the item and, if so, whether it is available or currently in circulation.

28 b   Choosing strong verbs

After you have clearly identified the actors in each sentence, you need to describe their actions in equally vivid language by using strong verbs.

> **ESL** **ORDER OF ADJECTIVES**
>
> Some types of adjectives typically occur before others. For example, an adjective describing size usually occurs before one describing color: *the large white house*, not *the white large house*. Shown below is the typical order of adjectives before nouns. (Keep in mind, of course, that you should generally avoid long strings of adjectives.)
>
> | 1 | 2 | 3 | 4 | 5 |
> |---|---|---|---|---|
> | *EVALUATION* | *SIZE* | *SHAPE* | *CONDITION* | *AGE* |
> | good | big | round | broken | old |
> | pretty | small | oblong | shiny | young |
> | happy | minuscule | squarish | rickety | new |
>
> | 6 | 7 | 8 |
> |---|---|---|
> | *COLOR* | *MATERIAL* | *NOUN AS ADJECTIVE* |
> | blue | wooden | sports |
> | red | cotton | flower |
> | magenta | iron | city |
>
> ■ One never forgets that first shiny new sports car.
>   (4   5   8)
>
> ■ A few large rectangular cardboard boxes were stacked on the floor.
>   (2   3   7)

■ Replacing static verbs

Verbs drive sentences the way an engine powers a car. **Action verbs**—those that express motion or create vivid images—add horsepower to your writing. **Static verbs**—verbs that simply show a state of being, such as *be, appear, become, seem, exist*—can leave your sentences underpowered. As you edit, look for static verbs and consider replacing them with action verbs.

■ Nothing ~~is more dangerous to~~ *threatens* future economic stability~~,~~ *more* than inflation.

■ Even some forest-product corporations *oppose* ~~have taken a stand against~~ deforestation, which is spreading rapidly.

Not every verb needs to be changed. In this case, the writer decided is spreading *did not need to be strengthened since it was less important to the sentence than the other verb.*

Sometimes a form of *be* precedes a phrase or clause that may suggest or even contain a stronger verb that can become the main verb of the sentence.

■ The most effective writers ~~are those who~~ write as though they were simply talking.

WP TIP Use the search-and-replace function to locate every form of the verb *be*. Consider in each case whether the sentence would benefit from a stronger verb and edit accordingly.

Expletive constructions, those that begin with somewhat empty phrases like *there is/are* and *it is*, can frequently be replaced with stronger verbs.

■ ~~There are several~~ moons ~~orbiting~~ Jupiter, Galileo found.
(Several) (orbit)

There is and *it is* usually introduce new topics, so avoid using expletive constructions in midsentence.

■ ~~There are many~~ people ~~who~~ still believe that Elvis Presley is alive, even though ~~it is~~ only tabloids ~~that~~ report such "news" seriously.
(Many)

USING EXPLETIVE CONSTRUCTIONS

Expletive constructions such as *it is* and *there are* often serve useful functions. They can create emphasis by slightly delaying the subject of the sentence and by allowing more opportunities for parallelism. (See 26f–g.)

It is a far, far better thing that I do, than I have ever done; it is a far, far better rest that I go to, than I have even known.

CHARLES DICKENS, *A TALE OF TWO CITIES*

Expletives are also necessary in certain expressions about time and the weather.

There were showers this morning, but right now it's sunny outside.

It's five o'clock, sir; it's time to go.

2 Replacing weak action verbs

Not all verbs that describe action spark clear images. Overuse has exhausted the image-making power of such verbs as *do, get, go, have, make,* and *think.* As you edit, watch for weak action verbs and substitute stronger verbs that evoke clear images.

■ He ~~has~~ several antique cars. *(owns)*

■ She ~~does her carvings~~ with great skill. *(carves)*

■ Beavers ~~make~~ dams that slow erosion. *(build)*

Often a verb that relies on a modifier or other words for its descriptive power can be replaced. Depending on the context, you may have to choose which verb best describes what you intend to convey.

■ He ~~walked rapidly~~ out of the room. *(rushed)*

■ He ~~walked rapidly~~ out of the room. *(scurried)*

■ He ~~walked rapidly~~ out of the room. *(ran)*

3 Turning nouns into verbs

The ease with which English words can be changed from one part of speech to another gives the language a marvelous flexibility. With the help of a suffix such as *-ance, -ment,* or *-ation,* verbs such as *deliver, announce,* or *tempt* can become useful nouns: *deliverance, announcement, temptation.*

Nouns thus made from verbs are called **nominalizations**. Using a nominalization can sometimes conceal the real action of a sentence by requiring the use of a static verb such as the verbs *do, have, make,* or *be.* If you have entombed the real action of your sentence in a nominalization, dig up the buried verb to give your prose new life.

■ Pickett's Charge ~~has a continuing fascination for~~ historians of the Battle of Gettysburg. *(still fascinates)*

Some nouns and verbs have the same form: *cause, dance, march, tie, love, hate.* If you use them as nouns, then you have to find new verbs, which are usually weaker. There is no reason to *perform a dance* when you can simply *dance*, no sense in *holding a march* when you can simply *march*.

■ The signs told us to ~~make a~~ detour around the construction.

■ We plan to ~~hold a~~ meet ~~meeting~~ at the courthouse tomorrow.

Also not every noun can be turned into a verb. Many grammarians object to the use of some nouns that have been transferred to verb form: *Jay Leno* hosts *the Tonight Show* instead of *Jay Leno is the* host *of the Tonight Show*. Use care when reaching for stronger verbs.

CHANGING NOUNS TO VERBS

To enliven your writing, replace these common expressions with the action verbs that are buried within them.

EXPRESSION	BURIED VERB
put forth a proposal	propose
hold a discussion	discuss
formulate a plan	plan
reach a decision	decide
arrive at a conclusion	conclude
hammer out an agreement	agree
hold a meeting	meet
call a strike	strike
make a choice	choose

 EDITING 2: EXPLORATION

Read the following paragraph, which narrates one of the murders committed by Jack the Ripper. What verbs has Colin Wilson chosen to convey the action of the scene? Are they effective? Wilson has used *be* as the main verb of a clause twice in this paragraph. Why do you think he does this?

They tiptoed down the passageway, and crept into a corner of the yard by the fence. The man moved closer; she was not even aware of the knife he held in his left hand. A moment later she was dead; the first thrust had severed her windpipe. The man allowed her to slide down the fence. He slipped out of his dark overcoat, and bent over the woman.

COLIN WILSON, "THE CRIMES OF JACK THE RIPPER"

STEPS TO SENTENCE VITALITY

Apply these two simple suggestions when editing for sentence vitality.

1. Make the person or concept that performs the action of the sentence into the grammatical subject of the sentence.

WEAK At the hearing by the selection committee, three sites were taken out of consideration, and the fourth was placed in further study.

STRONG At the hearing, *the selection committee* took three sites out of consideration and said it would study the fourth.

In the original, the real subject—the selection committee—is hidden in a prepositional phrase.

2. Express the main action of the sentence in the main verb of the sentence.

STRONG At the hearing, the selection committee *eliminated* three sites and *agreed to study* the fourth.

If you follow these two simple suggestions, your writing will spring to life.

■ **EDITING 3: PRACTICE**

Strengthen the verbs in the following sentences. Make any changes in wording that are necessary for smooth reading. More than one edited version is possible. Be ready to explain your editing choices.

1. The first witness gave an adequate report of what he saw on the night of the murder.
2. A police officer, he was the first person to arrive on the murder scene after the 911 call.
3. There was nobody standing or walking nearby, he said.
4. The witness did a good job describing specifics, such as the knife and the severity of the wounds.
5. He had a good memory and was very articulate, even when the defense attorney was asking him questions.
6. When he was finished testifying, he was told he could leave the stand.

28 c Selecting active or passive voice

When a verb is in the **active voice**, the person or thing performing the action is the subject.

Donald *spent* the money.

Donald, the actor performing the action, is the subject of the sentence. *Money*, the recipient of the action, is the direct object.

When a verb is in the **passive voice**, things get turned around. The recipient of the action—*money*—becomes the grammatical subject, and *Donald* becomes the **agent** of the action in the prepositional phrase *by Donald*.

The money *was spent* by Donald.

Donald can appear as above or disappear entirely, depending on how important it is that the reader know who the agent of the action was: *The money was spent, and the club folded.* Perhaps there is no agent at all: *The child was finally found in the bottom of a well.*

1 Using the active voice to emphasize actors and actions

By making the actor the subject of the sentence, the active voice helps readers visualize the action of a sentence. Active-voice sentences usually use fewer words and proceed more directly than passive-voice sentences. If your writing situation requires vitality, editing for the active voice is a good strategy.

■   ~~The~~ Tate and LaBianca murders Manson and his followers planned the ~~were planned by Manson~~
^
~~and his followers~~ to incite a race war. ~~Whites were expected~~ They expected whites to
^
rise up in alarm at the killings.

WP TIP   Copy a passage from a paper you are working on. Double-space it and print it out. Exchange passages with a peer, and in the space between the lines suggest ways the passage might be strengthened for vitality.

2 Using the passive voice for special purposes

The passive voice deemphasizes the actor and highlights the recipient of the action. At times, depending on your purpose, this

ESL **VERBS THAT CAN'T BE PASSIVE, VERBS THAT CAN'T BE ACTIVE**

Not all English verbs can be both active and passive. Verbs that can't be passive—because they do not have a direct object—are labeled **intransitive verbs** in a dictionary. The verbs *happen, occur, result, disappear, vanish,* and *die* are sometimes mistakenly put in the passive voice.

■ The tornado ~~was~~ happened yesterday.

■ Much improvement ~~was~~ resulted from working with a tutor.

Some verbs followed by object in active-voice sentences (**transitive verbs**), such as *have, weigh,* and *consist of,* cannot be rephrased in the passive voice either.

ACTIVE New York City has five boroughs.
INCORRECT PASSIVE Five boroughs are had by New York City.

A number of verbs in English express some type of change that a person, place, or thing undergoes. These verbs, sometimes called **change-of-state** verbs, include *increase, decrease, open, close, develop,* and *change.* When the agent is known or is not important, we use these verbs in the active voice without naming an agent.

■ Prices ~~were~~ increased last week.

■ My hometown ~~was~~ changed during the years I was away.

If, however, you think it is important to name an agent for a particular context, you may use active or passive forms.

ACTIVE Many supermarkets increased prices last week.
PASSIVE Prices were increased by many supermarkets last week.

Some verb phrases are used only in the passive voice. These include *be born, be located, be killed, be made,* and *be given.*

PASSIVE The U.S. capital was once located in Philadelphia.
INCORRECT ACTIVE The U.S. capital located in Philadelphia.

may be exactly what you want to do. Use the passive voice to accomplish the following special purposes.

To stress the results of actions

A constitutional amendment outlawing flag burning *was rejected* by the Senate.

To leave the agent unstated

According to investigators the fire *was* deliberately *set.*

By whom? No one knows at this point.

To establish objectivity in research writing

In the experiment, samples of food *were* first *contaminated* with bacteria. The samples *were* then *irradiated.* The samples *were tested* to see whether the bacteria survived.

To strengthen flow between sentences

ACTIVE   Two crises threaten the economic security of the nation. Economists, business leaders, and politicians *have documented* the first crisis, the decay of manufacturing industries. They have all but ignored the second, however.

PASSIVE   Two crises threaten the economic security of the nation. The first crisis, the decay of manufacturing industries, *has been documented* by economists, business leaders, and politicians. They have all but ignored the second, however.

Notice how the change helps the sequence of topics flow from one sentence to the next.

To take advantage of an emphatic position

Two crises threaten the economic security of the nation. The first crisis, the decay of manufacturing industries, *has been documented* by economists, business leaders, and politicians. *The second*, however, *has* all but *been ignored.*

Using the passive moves the key word ignored *to the emphatic final position.*

■ EDITING 4: EXPLORATION

The following passage by James Baldwin makes extensive use of expletive constructions and the passive voice. Read it carefully, and try to decide why the author has used these techniques. Do they influence the meaning of the passage? Its effect? Where do they focus your attention? Do they create a particular mood or atmosphere?

There is a custom in the village—I am told it is repeated in many villages—of "buying" African natives for the purpose of converting them to Christianity. There stands in the church all year round a small box with a slot for money, decorated with a black figurine, and into this box the villagers drop their francs. During the *carnival* which precedes Lent, two village children have their faces blackened   out of which bloodless darkness their blue eyes shine like ice—and fantastic horsehair wigs are placed on their blond heads; thus disguised, they solicit among the villagers for money for the missionaries in Africa. Between the box in the church and the blackened children, the village "bought" last year six or eight African natives.

JAMES BALDWIN, "STRANGER IN THE VILLAGE"

■ EDITING 5: PRACTICE

Edit the following paragraph from a paper arguing against pesticide use by substituting the active voice whenever you think it is effective. Make any changes in wording to make the passage flow better or have greater impact. More than one edited version is possible. Be ready to explain your editing choices.

We are all affected by pesticides. Hundreds of synthetic chemicals have been developed by scientists to destroy the insects and rodents that are called "pests" by farmers and Sunday gardeners. Once these deadly toxins are used, however, they are retained in the land for years sometimes. They are maintained in the environment, where our crops and water supply are contaminated and desirable species of birds and fish are killed off. Ironically, pesticides are even known not to work very well in the first place, since usually a pest population that is resistant to the chemicals is created. And within a few years, the problem is as large as ever. The effect of pesticides on the environment and on our lives should be questioned. Perhaps even the right to use them at all should be questioned.

28 d Untangling noun clusters

A remarkable quality of English is its use of nouns as modifiers. Instead of saying *a cabinet for files*, we can say *a file cabinet*. We can also string noun modifiers together. A *metal file cabinet* is far easier to say than *a cabinet of metal for files*.

Like any good thing, using nouns as modifiers can be done to excess. A long string of nouns used as modifiers is called a **noun cluster**: *do-it-yourself home improvement instruction videotape recordings*. Readers, upon finding a large noun cluster, must stop to interpret which nouns are acting as modifiers and which is the "real" noun. Vital sentences move readers along quickly and easily, so anything that causes readers to stop and struggle should be eliminated. When editing, untangle noun clusters for your readers by moving some of the modifiers elsewhere.

■ Michael Graves's architecture attempts to revitalize a ~~building~~
        of building forms
   ~~form~~ language ^that was lost during the heyday of International

   Style modernism.

Sometimes writers are tempted to introduce a person with a long string of identifying modifiers in a special kind of noun cluster called a **false title**. Pick the elements about the person that you want to emphasize and move the other descriptive modifiers elsewhere.

                    Minnie Peppers, the
■ We met ^Texas-style chili cook-off champion. ~~Minnie Peppers~~
                                Carter McIlroy, who led the   ^   in
■ The team signed 170-pound ^Big Ten Conference ^rushing and
            kick-returns.
   ~~kick-return leader Carter McIlroy~~
                           ^

■ **EDITING 6: EXPLORATION**

Read the following paragraph from Nancy Gibbs' description of modern American zoos. What choices has Gibbs made to give vitality to the passage?

At some 150 American zoos. . . , the troubles are not very different. The sharks eat the angelfish. The Australian hairy-nosed wombat stays in its cave, and the South American smoky jungle frog hunkers down beneath a leaf, all tantalizingly hidden from the prying eyes of the roughly 110 million Americans who go to zoos every year. Visitors often complain that as a result of all the elaborate landscaping, they cannot find the animals. But this, like almost everything else that goes wrong these days, is a signal that America's zoos are doing something right.

                                    NANCY GIBBS, "THE NEW ZOO: A MODERN ARK"

■ **EDITING 7: PRACTICE**

Edit the following paragraph to create vital sentences. You may invent and add any details you think are necessary. More than one edited version is possible. Be ready to explain your editing choices.

Most dog owners don't realize in advance how much time, money, and energy must be spent on a puppy. First, there is housebreaking the puppy and teaching it basic puppy obedience skills: how to accompany its owner while on a leash, how to respond to its name, how to stay near its owner. There are also other things—fetching, standing, and so on. And even when owners have the time for training, they probably don't have the necessary expertise. This means enrollment in expensive obedience school classes is required. Puppies create other expenses as well. Veterinarian visits, food and bedding, leashes and playthings, and grooming—a must for any well-bred dog—are all costly. And at least one nice rug or one pair of shoes must be replaced because a bad dog has chewed through them. Still, as any devoted dog owner will tell you, the expense is justified by the rewards: there's nothing like coming home from a hard day and being greeted by someone who loves you unconditionally and absolutely.

■ **EDITING 8: APPLICATION**

Read through a paper you are working on and pay close attention to the vitality of your sentences. Have you chosen specific, concrete nouns and modifiers wherever possible? Are your verbs precise? Do they convey action? Have you used the passive voice? If so, do you have a good reason for doing so? Can you find any noun clusters? Consider the vitality of the language and sentence structure: keep the elements that you like and improve those that you don't like.

In most writing situations, the goal is to convey information clearly and efficiently, in order to spare the reader unnecessary effort. Vagueness, wordiness, and needless complexity can tire or annoy readers. Therefore, make your writing **direct**: express your ideas plainly. Be **concise**: use as few words as possible to achieve your purpose.

It is natural—indeed a good idea—to throw lots of ideas into your first draft just to get them all down; but when editing, strive to make your writing concise and direct. Some writers call this process *boiling down*, referring to the cooking process that turns large quantities of thin broth into hearty, full-flavored soup. The drafts of this book required a lot of boiling down. The following is our original draft of a paragraph that appears later in this chapter:

> According to current wisdom, public speakers are urged, "Tell them what you're going to tell them, then say it, then tell them what you said." In other words, say the message at least three times so that the audience will understand it clearly. This advice reflects the patterns of spoken language.

The second sentence seemed to do little more than rephrase the first, so we combined it with the third sentence.

> In ~~other words, say~~ the message ~~at least three times so that~~ the audience ~~will~~ understand it clearly. ~~This advice reflects the patterns of spoken language~~
>
> (inserted: *spoken language, repeating* ... *will help*)

With further editing we eliminated other unnecessary words.

> In spoken language, ~~repeating the message will help the audience~~ understand. ~~it clearly~~
>
> (inserted: *repetition helps listeners*)

At every step, we tested our results: we compared the new edited version both with the previous one and with our understanding of what we were trying to say. We guarded against losing meaning, but we were willing to lose subtle shadings if we could state our point more clearly. If you polish relentlessly to eliminate extra words, your prose will begin to shine.

 EDITING FOR CONCISENESS AND DIRECTNESS

When editing for conciseness and directness, keep the following guidelines in mind:

- Eliminate vague generalities.
- Remove automatic or idle words.
- Simplify grammatical constructions.
- Eliminate redundant words or phrases.
- Avoid pretentious language.
- Minimize euphemism.

29 **a** **Eliminating vague generalities**

As we think and reason, we absorb specific information and experiences and then make associations to generalize about these data: *That radiator burned my hand when I touched it. Radiators can be dangerous.*

Writing that consists only of specific details may fail to convey broader ideas. On the other hand, writers can use too many generalizations and forget the details, or use such broad generalizations that details are neglected and thus meaning is lost. Overly broad generalizations are called **generalities**, and they need editing.

It is our duty today to take responsibility for our actions.

When was it not everyone's duty to be responsible?

Some generalities attempt to make a point but result in circular reasoning: *During the harsh winters of the 1870s, the weath-*

er was very cold. (A harsh winter is cold by definition.) Some don't really say anything at all: *Many factors played a part.* (What factors?)

Generalities don't advance discussion; the reader can only hope you will soon come to the point. Eliminating them will usually improve your writing.

■ Fetal alcohol syndrome affects one of every 750 newborn babies/~~It is clearly not good for them~~, causing coordination problems, malformed organs, small brains, short attention spans, and behavioral problems.

When you delete a generality, you may have to move some information from it to another sentence.

■ Is college worthwhile? ~~Whether or not to go to college is a decision that many eighteen-year-olds must face after graduating from high school~~. Each high school graduate must decide according to his or her finances, other career opportunities, and, most important, personal interests and goals.

Although unnecessary generalities can occur anywhere in a paper, look particularly in your openings and conclusions, where you may be pushing for sweeping statements or impressive summaries. (See Chapter 25.)

29 b Removing idle words

Eliminate idle words from your writing. To determine whether a word is working hard enough, test it: If removing the word does not alter meaning, leave it out.

1 Condensing automatic and wordy phrases

The speech habit of embellishing sentences with unnecessary words too easily becomes a writing habit. It is a fact that most writers do it all the time. For example, in the previous sentence, *it is a fact that* adds no meaning. Phrases such as *it appears that* or *it has come to my attention that* merely preface what the writer is about to say, a sort of authorial "throat-clearing." Most sentences are better off without them.

Think of such phrases as **automatic phrases**. They often seem to write themselves, but when examined, they prove to add little if any meaning. Automatic phrases can appear anywhere in a sentence, but they appear most often at the beginning. When you find an automatic phrase, test it for meaning: If something seems missing without it, try inserting a condensed version of the phrase.

■ ~~In order to~~ understand the effects of the law, consider the following example. *(To)*

■ ~~In this day and age~~, children ~~in many instances~~ know more about dinosaurs than they know about American history. *(Today,)* *(often)*

AUTOMATIC PHRASES

CONSIDER DELETING	OR SUBSTITUTING
it is a fact that	in fact
it is clear that	clearly
there is no question that	certainly
the reason is that	because
without a doubt	surely, certainly
it is my opinion that	I think
beyond the shadow of a doubt	certainly

Wordy phrases can usually be condensed. Look for unnecessary uses of the preposition *of* and for phrases containing *of* that can be reduced to a single word. Abstract nouns such as *area, aspect, factor, kind, manner, nature, tendency, thing,* and *type* are imprecise and can create wordiness. Often you can delete them, condense them, or find more concrete substitutes. (See 28a.)

■ The author spent little time outside ~~of~~ his small circle of friends.

■ The architect had a specific ~~type of~~ construction method in mind.

2 Deleting useless modifiers

Modifiers such as *clearly, obviously, interestingly, undoubted-ly, absolutely, fortunately, hopefully, really,* and *totally* are often used to intensify a whole sentence, making it sound more forceful or authoritative. Sometimes they add an important nuance that the writer intended, but more often they can be deleted. Always test for altered meaning.

■ The strike against General Motors ~~clearly~~ disrupted production on the Saturn assembly line. It was undoubtedly intended to do so.

Anna considered, but decided against, deleting undoubtedly, *which tells the reader that the assessment is her own conclusion.*

WORDY PHRASES

WORDY	CONCISE
most of the people	most people
all of the work	all the work
due to the fact that	since, because
despite the fact that	although
at that point in time	then
communicate to	tell
in this day and age	today
in those days	then
in any case	anyway
in the case of	regarding, concerning
in most instances	usually
in some instances	sometimes
subsequent to	after
in the event of	if
in the final analysis	finally

WP TIP   With the above list as a reference, use the search-and-replace function to help you find and eliminate useless modifiers.

29 c Simplifying grammatical constructions

To fight wordiness another way, consider simplifying grammatical constructions. Changing a **passive voice** sentence to the **active voice** usually shortens it slightly. (See 28c.) Eliminating **expletive constructions** such as *there were* and *it is* allows the use of strong verbs. (See 28b.)

Also consider shortening dependent clauses to phrases and phrases to single words. (For definitions of these terms, see 67e and 67f.) To simplify dependent clauses, look especially at **modifier clauses**—those that function as adjectives or adverbs. A modifier clause usually begins with a relative pronoun such as *which*, *that*, *who*, or *whom* or with a subordinating conjunction such as *because, before, when, where, while, if,* or *although.* To shorten a modifier clause to a phrase, try using the past participle of the clause's main verb as the basis of the phrase.

CLAUSE   The research project *that we were assigned to complete* involves a complex experiment.

PHRASE   The research project *assigned to us* involves a complex experiment.

WORD   *Our* research project involves a complex experiment.

In some situations, using the fewest words may not be the best solution. Take care that you do not create an awkward cluster by simplifying too many constructions. (See 28d.)

ORIGINAL   The committee report listed sixteen international dealers, accusing them of illegally selling military weapons.

AWKWARD   The committee report listed sixteen alleged international illegal military-weapons dealers.

BETTER   The committee report listed sixteen alleged international dealers of illegal military weapons.

29 d Eliminating redundancy

In a famous piece of advice, public speakers are urged, "Tell them what you're going to say, say it, then tell them what you said." In speaking, repetition helps listeners understand.

ESL **STRATEGIES FOR REDUCING CLAUSES**

The following are strategies for simplifying modifier clauses.

1. In addition to forming phrases with past participles from relative clauses (the project *that we were assigned*—the project *assigned to us*), you can sometimes shorten relative clauses that contain *-ing* verbs and prepositional phrases:

■ The child ~~who was~~ waiting at the bus stop seemed frightened.

■ The article ~~that was~~ about the Internet was useful.

2. Some clauses cannot be reduced, so be careful that you do not take out relative pronouns or verbs that are needed.

■ You cannot reduce clauses that have one main verb.

The course that fulfills my science requirement was cancelled.

That *cannot be taken out.*

■ You cannot reduce a clause in which a *be* verb is followed by an adjective (including *-ing* participles) or a noun phrase, unless you rewrite the sentence.

Courses that are $\begin{cases} \text{challenging} \\ \text{a challenge} \end{cases}$ tend to be more interesting.

Neither that *nor* are *can be taken out.*

You could rewrite it to read: *Challenging courses tend to be interesting.*

■ You cannot reduce a clause with *whose* + noun.

The poet whose biography I read grew up in Haiti.

Whose *cannot be taken out.*

In writing, some repetition is important, even necessary, to provide continuity. (See 24c.) Repeating a key word or phrase can also help you build a rhythmic pattern to emphasize an idea. (See

27e.) All that said, there is such a thing as too much repetition; it's called **redundancy**.

Exactly what constitutes redundancy remains for you to determine according to your purpose and your audience. Try testing each instance by omitting the repetition. Reread the passage, comparing it both to the earlier version and to what you want to say. Ask yourself whether the repetition helps link ideas, sustains an important rhythm, creates a needed emphasis, or prevents confusion. If it does none of these things, leave it out. Also consider having someone else read the passage for excessive repetition. Explain whom you are writing for and what you are trying to accomplish.

The most obvious redundancies arise from thoughtlessly using words that mean the same thing.

■ The ~~general~~ consensus ~~of opinion~~ among students was that the chancellor had exceeded her authority.

Consensus *means a general agreement of opinion.*

■ The raccoon warily circled ~~around~~ the tree.

Circled *means to go* around *something, so* around *should be omitted.* An unnecessary definition is also usually easy to spot.

■ Foresters ~~who study trees~~ report that acid rain is damaging the state's population of hemlocks.

If you find yourself repeating the same word or a similar one, look for ways to eliminate one.

■ ~~A very high percentage~~ About ninety percent of the prison's inmates take advantage of the special education program/. ~~about ninety percent~~

You can often eliminate an ineffective repetition by combining two sentences.

■ As you edit your writing, be alert to possible redundancy/. ~~One~~ any kind of ~~redundancy is an~~ unnecessary repetition.

REDUNDANT PHRASES

first and foremost	refer back
full and complete	basic fundamentals
past history	initial preparation
round in shape	terrible tragedy
red in color	final result, end result
the general consensus of opinion	free gift
a faulty miscalculation	true facts
old and outdated	completely destroyed
first ever	circle around
cross over	irregardless

■ EDITING 1: EXPLORATION

Look for examples of writing that contain generalities, idle words, and redundancies. Magazine articles and mass-market nonfiction books are often good sources. Collect two or three examples, and try editing them to make them more concise. You may want to bring your examples and edited versions to class to share with your classmates. Be ready to explain what you found wrong with the originals and how your editing improves them.

■ EDITING 2: PRACTICE

Edit the following passage to make it more concise, eliminating vague generalities, idle words, and redundancies and simplifying grammatical constructions. More than one edited version is possible. Be ready to explain your editing choices.

Many languages have influenced the development of English. The first instance of important influence came from the north in the form of Viking invaders who spoke a Scandinavian language. It appears that when these Vikings settled down and became farmers and traders who were peaceful, they wanted to be able to communicate with and speak to their Anglo-Saxon neighbors. There were several factors involved. Both groups spoke Germanic languages with similar vocabularies but with systems of grammar and inflection that were somewhat different. Clearly the easiest of the ways to smooth communication was for each group to drop the elements of their language that gave the other group difficulty. This explains why it is the case that modern English lacks the elaborate systems of verb endings and gender that characterize and distinguish other Indo-European languages.

29 e   Avoiding pretentious language

Sometimes writers believe that in order to impress their readers, they need to use technical or obscure language. They write *institutionalized populations* instead of *people in prison*. Other writers overdecorate their sentences: *In this sacrosanct institution of higher learning we continually rededicate ourselves to the elevated principle that knowledge is empowering.* In most writing situations, it would be more effective to say *In this university we believe that knowledge gives power.*

While professors do expect students to demonstrate familiarity with the technical terms of their discipline (see 31h), needlessly complex language is termed **pretentious**. A special class of pretentious language is called **bureaucratese** after the government functionaries who so often use it. Pretentious language may overwhelm readers so much that they stop reading.

Pretentious language often avoids names and personal pronouns by using the third person and the passive voice. Editing it into plain English often requires that you choose subjects for verbs and find direct ways of addressing readers.

PRETENTIOUS The range of services provided includes examinations to determine visual or auditory impairment and the specification, provision, and instruction in the use of prosthetic devices including corrective lenses and auditory amplification devices.

EDITED We can examine your eyes and ears, prescribe and sell glasses and hearing aids, and teach you to use them.

 PRETENTIOUS LANGUAGE

PRETENTIOUS	DIRECT
client populations	people served
voiced a concern	said, worried
range of selections	choice
minimizes expenditures	saves money
of crucial importance	important
institution of higher learning	college or university
have apprehension	fear

WP TIP   With the list as a reference, use the find function to locate these particular words and phrases in a paper you are currently working on. Consider what level of language your audience expects from you, and edit your word choice with this in mind.

29 f Minimizing euphemism

A **euphemism** is a word chosen for its inoffensiveness to substitute for one considered harsh or indelicate. Social conventions make it difficult for us to speak of certain subjects, especially money, death, and the human body. For example, many people would consider it more delicate to say *I lost my grandmother last week* than *My grandmother died last week.*

Euphemisms are also used by writers or speakers who fear negative reaction to plain talk about bad news. This use is called **doublespeak**, a term coined by George Orwell in his novel about totalitarianism, *1984.* Someone reading of *unemployment compensation reductions* may not understand immediately that *workers without jobs will get less money from the government.*

In academic writing, your purpose is to inform, not to obscure or mislead, so if you push too far for a delicate phrase, you will obscure meaning. When editing euphemisms from your writing, select a more direct alternative. Consider how comfortable you feel with the more direct wording and whether your audience will be offended by your directness. If in doubt, check with a peer or a professor.

■ ~~As a result of the reordering of budget priorities~~ the library ~~was forced to defer acquisitions and suspend maintenance activities~~

Short of money,

stopped buying books and maintaining its building.

ESL   IDENTIFYING EUPHEMISM

Identifying and editing euphemisms can be especially difficult when English is your second language. You may have learned euphemisms in your study of English vocabulary before you learned words that are more basic and direct. Native speakers often find it challenging to avoid euphemism too. If you're wondering whether a word or expression is a euphemism, try asking your instructor, a tutor, or other students to examine it in context.

■ EDITING 3: EXPLORATION

In the following passage, humorist Russell Baker lampoons contemporary rhetoric. How many examples of pretentious and euphemistic language can you find? Try editing the passage by replacing each example of pretentious language or euphemism with a more direct expression. Have you got "Little Red Riding Hood" back?

Once upon a point in time, a small person named Little Red Riding Hood initiated plans for the preparation, delivery and transportation of foodstuffs to her grandmother, a senior citizen residing at a place of residence in a forest of indeterminate dimension.

In the process of implementing this program, her incursion into the forest was in mid-transportation process when it attained interface with an alleged perpetrator. This individual, a wolf, made inquiry as to the whereabouts of Little Red Riding Hood's goal as well as inferring that he was desirous of ascertaining the contents of Little Red Riding Hood's foodstuffs basket, and all that.

RUSSELL BAKER, "LITTLE RED RIDING HOOD REVISITED"

■ EDITING 4: PRACTICE

Edit the following passage to make it more concise and direct by eliminating pretentious language and euphemism. More than one edited version is possible. Be ready to explain your editing choices.

We conducted employee reviews of gender or racial characteristics and maintained a high standard of objectivity. Despite high performance reviews for your department, however, we have decided to downsize the entire production staff by 40 percent. While we regret that this downsizing may inconvenience you in your relations with your subordinates, we know you, too, will understand our need to remain competitive in our market. Your continued loyalty—and that of your staff—will ensure that our company continues to set the standard of excellence for others to follow.

■ EDITING 5: PRACTICE

Edit the following passage from a paper for a history class. More than one edited version is possible. Be ready to explain your editing choices.

My great-grandfather emigrated from Poland when he was a young man. Several of his cousins already lived in small Pennsylvania mining towns. When my great-grandfather arrived in America, he joined his cousins and began working in the mines.

456 Being concise and direct

There were several things he found discouraging. The dirty work, which was also dangerous, was far different from the life of agricultural splendor he had expected to lead, but he refused to let these types of circumstances ruin his happiness. It eventually was the case that he brought two of his brothers over to this country, and together the three of them saved money that was sufficient to buy a good-sized farm. By the age of thirty-four, my great-grand-father had once again started a new life: he moved into his farmhouse, married a local woman, and began raising a family that would eventually be blessed by the arrival of fourteen bundles of joy.

■ **EDITING 6: APPLICATION**

Select a page from a paper you are working on. Examine each sentence carefully, looking for instances of wordy or indirect language. Using the checklists in this chapter, locate find euphemisms, pretentiousness, redundancy, or any other problems, and draft alternatives. Consult a friend or fellow student. Compare versions and decide which most effectively suits your purpose.

30   Adjusting Tone

A speaker's tone of voice can express warmth, anger, confidence, hesitance, friendship, hostility, enthusiasm, regret. The **tone** of a piece of writing expresses the writer's attitude toward the subject and the audience. Do you sound hesitant or authoritative about your subject? Enthusiastic? Concerned? How do you address your audience? As friends? Authority figures? Are you attempting to inform, persuade, or inspire them?

Tone isn't something you add to writing; it's already there as an important element of **voice**, which communicates a sense of the kind of person who is writing. (See Chapter 8.) The tone of your writing should represent you accurately and appropriately. Just as you wouldn't lecture to an auditorium full of people in a small, hesitant voice, you won't want to use street slang or an overly informal tone in formal academic writing.

REFINING YOUR TONE

When editing for tone, ask yourself the following questions.

1. Is the tone appropriate to the audience I am writing for and for the goal I want to accomplish? If not, you may need to adjust your point of view or level of formality.

2. Have I chosen the point of view that best illustrates my relationship to my subject? Test other points of view and then choose the one that helps you succeed in your goals for the paper.

3. Is the level of formality right for my intended audience? If not, go back and consider your presentation of ideas and choice of words throughout.

4. Have I maintained a consistent tone? If not, you need to edit your writing to eliminate elements that are incompatible with the tone you want.

30 a Making tone appropriate

The writer's tone in a piece of writing should communicate an attitude that is appropriate for the audience, the subject, and the intended purpose. In academic writing, your audience includes the instructor who assigned the paper and perhaps other students as well. Try to imagine them reading your paper, and adjust your tone if you think your readers might not get the right impression.

When you are describing personal experiences, your tone can be **informal**, as if you were capturing a conversation with a friend or addressing your audience—even the instructor—directly in a friendly manner. (See Chapter 9.) A reflective essay may strike a thoughtful, questioning, or contemplative tone as you explore the possible meanings of an experience or an event. (See Chapter 13.) You might use informal language when you want the audience to get to know something about yourself and your attitudes. Some kinds of language interfere with an informal tone, however, so edit anything, such as colloquialisms or jargon, that muddies the writing.

■ My brother and I ~~grew acquainted with~~ the other kids who
_{went to}
^met^
~~attended~~ our elementary school; Tommy even ~~went so far as to~~
^swapped^
~~exchange~~ his favorite slingshot in return for a pet frog.

To explain how something works or to interpret a work of literature, adopt a confident, authoritative tone that assures readers of your expertise. (See Chapters 10 and 12.) Avoid unnecessary qualifications that make you sound hesitant, and edit out any informalities that weaken your authority.

■ What is Title IX? ~~The original name of Beethoven's last symphony? No. Title IX~~ ^It^ is part of the Educational Amendments of 1972 that gave women the same rights as men in all aspects of education, including athletics.

Use **formal** language when you want to downplay your personal involvement and emphasize facts, reports, or descriptions that can be verified or experienced by other observers. Research papers benefit from more formal language. (See Chapter 14.)

■ ~~In a search of the library, I found~~ three 19th-century authors
(handwritten above: Three   nineteenth)
~~who~~ discuss this aspect of Mill's theory of liberty.

When writing argument essays, use a dispassionate tone to marshal evidence and appeal to readers' reason. Sometimes you can select language that appeals primarily to emotion to convince your readers, but make sure that any emotional appeals are not too strident. (See Chapter 11.)

ESL **DEVELOPING AN APPROPRIATE TONE FOR ACADEMIC WRITING**

You may have noticed that the tone of academic writing in English is sometimes different from that in academic writing in your native language. For example, you may be used to more or less emotion in argumentation than native English speakers use. If your experience learning English has been more oral than written, you may also be unsure about which words and phrases create an informal tone and which a more formal tone.

These steps can help you develop your ability to use an appropriate tone in academic English.

1. Pay attention to tone as you read many kinds of English texts; analyze how authors achieve different tones for different audiences and purposes.

2. Make a list of questions about tone to ask your instructor or a tutor. Discuss any differences you have observed between academic writing in your native language and in English.

3. Ask a friend to read your drafts and comment on the tone.

4. Read your writing aloud. Ask yourself what kind of tone you hear, and consider whether the tone sounds appropriate.

5. Start a list of terms that are considered informal (*guy*, *kid*) or slang (*awesome*, *cool*). Consult your instructor or a tutor about words you're not sure of. Use your list to edit informal words and phrases from your writing when it requires a formal tone.

EDITING 1: EXPLORATION

Read a few paragraphs aloud from your last three papers. First try to describe your tone in each paper. For whom were you writing, and what was your purpose? Does your tone vary greatly, or do you hear a similar tone throughout?

460 Adjusting tone

Next try to picture the sort of person your readers would imagine as the writer of your papers, if they could judge only from the tone of the papers. Is that image accurate? Is it the one you want them to have? Finally, decide whether you would do anything to change your tone in these papers. Are there aspects of one paper's tone that you would like to use elsewhere?

30 b Selecting a point of view

A writer's **point of view** signals to the reader the writer's relation to the subject and the audience. One principal way in which a writer articulates a point of view is by selecting a **governing pronoun**: the first person *I* or *we*, the second person *you*, or the third person *he*, *she*, *it*, or *they*.

Use the **first person** to relate personal reflection and personal experience. The first person is also appropriate in argument and research writing to describe your own observations or conclusions.

> Everyone seemed a lot more upset than necessary about my Saturdays with Miss Dawson, which then made me really want to do it. I told my mother I was going to help the poor. She was disgusted, afraid of disease, toilet seats. I even knew that the poor in Chile had no toilet seats. My friends were shocked that I was going with Miss Dawson at all. They said she was a loony, a fanatic, and a lesbian, was I crazy or what?
>
> LUCIA BERLIN, "GOOD AND BAD"

> For about a month I spent most of each day either on the Peak or overlooking Melinda Valley. . . . Piece by piece, I began to form *my* first somewhat crude picture of chimpanzee life. [Italics added.]
>
> JANE GOODALL, *IN THE SHADOW OF MAN*

Using the **second person** can thrust your readers into the center of the scene or imply a close relationship between the writer and the reader. Address them directly using *you*.

> Madrid—The window of the hotel is open and, as *you* lie in bed, *you* hear the firing in the front line seventeen blocks away. [Italics added.]
>
> ERNEST HEMINGWAY, *BY-LINE: ERNEST HEMINGWAY*

You in the sense of "people in general" is not acceptable in formal writing. Try replacing it with an impersonal construction or a more suitable noun or pronoun. (Also see 39d.)

■ ~~You can separate water~~ into its constituent elements by

Water can be separated

electrolysis by running an electric current through water and
collecting the gases at the electrodes.

A **third-person** point of view focuses the writing directly on
the subject rather than on the audience. It is the most widely
used approach in formal academic writing.

> One of the most important signs in the text is the color of
> Diane Chambers's hair. *She's* a blond, and blondness is a sign of
> considerable richness and meaning. America is a country where
> "gentlemen prefer blonds," and blond coloring is the most popu-
> lar color sold. But what does blondness signify? [Italics added.]
>
> ARTHUR ASA BERGER, "'HE'S EVERYTHING YOU'RE NOT. . . .'; A
> SEMIOLOGICAL ANALYSIS OF *CHEERS*"

Consider which point of view seems appropriate for your essay. In most cases, research papers and position or interpretive
papers do not describe your personal experience but record what
you as an investigator find and think. For these, the third-person
point of view is best; it keeps the attention on the subject and creates a sense of scholarly objectivity. (See Chapters 10–12 and 14.)
If your essay is reflective or drawn from personal experience, the
first person can convey a sense of immediacy and authenticity.
(See Chapters 9, 11, and 13.)

30 c Achieving the right level of formality

The **level of formality**, sometimes called the **register**, of writing depends on word choice, sentence structure, and rhythm. Do
you refer to your home or your pad? Are your sentences conversational in pattern, or built of elaborate sentence structures? As
you edit, check that your level of formality is appropriate.

A **familiar tone** is common in everyday speech but rare in
academic writing. Familiar language includes slang, sentence
fragments, and even vulgarity without regard to rules or conventions.

> Really got into it with Jones today. The turkey can't see the val-
> ue in anything. Thinks team sports make kids "aggressors" or
> some bull like that.

Familiar language also assumes that the audience already understands the context—who Jones is, for example.

An **informal tone** is appropriate in a letter to a friend or in a
personal experience essay. Writing informally, you give readers a
little more context than a purely familiar tone would allow.
Complete your sentences and use language that omits slang but
still allows your personal feelings to show through.

> I had a real argument with Professor Jones in my behavioral psy-
> chology class. He was trying to tell us that team sports teach peo-
> ple to be "aggressive" and "insensitive." He can't see the value in
> them at all.

Use a **formal tone** for a research paper, in which you focus
not on emotion or conflict but on evidence and argument. Choose
precise language that minimizes the personal aspects of the dispute. To establish a formal tone, write well-developed sentences,
eliminate contractions, identify sources, and use language appropriate to academic readers.

> Citing similarities between sports teams and primitive hunt-
> ing bands, some scholars, including Professor Wilkin Jones in
> his writings on Aztec ball games, have suggested that competitive
> sports breed aggression. Other researchers, however, have found
> that team sports also foster self-discipline and cooperation.

Striking a level of formality appropriate to your purpose calls
for judgment. Reflective essays, for example, are usually more formal than personal essays and less formal than research papers.
Edit your writing so that it is neither too stiff nor too casual for
the situation.

■ EDITING 2: EXPLORATION

Read the following passage taken from Oliver Goldsmith's 1765 essay "On
National Prejudice" and evaluate his tone. Then rewrite the passage, adopting
a more colloquial tone, one that you consider more appropriate for a modern audience. Think about what changes you would make and why. Then compare the two passages. Has anything been lost in the translation?

As I am one of the sauntering tribe of mortals, who spend the greatest
part of their time in taverns, coffee houses, and other places of public resort,
I have thereby an opportunity of observing an infinite variety of characters,
which, to a person of a contemplative turn, is a much higher entertainment
than a view of all the curiosities of art or nature. In one of these my late ram-

UNDERSTANDING FORMALITY

In academic writing, slang and inappropriate informality are likely to make your ideas appear less serious and committed than the work of others. An appropriate tone amounts to speaking responsibly to your fellow scholars.

■ ~~Just check out any of the cartoons today~~ Anyone who watches contemporary cartoons, such as ,Beavis & Butthead, Ren & Stimpy, Mighty Morphin Power Rangers/,~~If you watch a whole show,~~ ~~you can best believe you~~ will witness a ~~whole lot~~ great deal of violence.

bles, I accidentally fell into the company of half a dozen gentlemen, who were engaged in a warm dispute about some political affair; the decision of which, as they were equally divided in their sentiments, they thought proper to refer to me, which naturally drew me in for a share of the conversation.

Amongst a multiplicity of other topics, we took occasion to talk of the different characters of the several nations of Europe; when one of the gentlemen, cocking his hat, and assuming such an air of importance as if he had possessed all the merit of the English nation in his own person, declared that the Dutch were a parcel of avaricious wretches; the French a set of flattering sycophants; that the Germans were drunken sots, and beastly gluttons; and the Spaniards proud, haughty and surly tyrants: but that, in bravery, generosity, clemency, and in every other virtue, the English excelled all the world.

This very learned and judicious remark was received with a general smile of approbation by all the company—all, I mean, but your humble servant.

■ **EDITING 3: PRACTICE**

Edit the following two paragraphs, adjusting the tone to the appropriate level of formality. The first paragraph is from a paper relating a personal experience; the second is from a formal research paper. More than one edited version of each paragraph is possible. Be ready to explain your editing choices.

Personal Experience Essay

Who would find it credible that two adults would have trouble convincing one eight-pound feline that the time had come for his annual physical examination? Upon spotting his cage, the cat exits the room as quickly as he can.

Under the bed, over the bed, up the staircase, down the staircase, he rushes with extreme celerity from one room to the next, ever eluding our grasp. When his outrageous behavior ceases, and we have him cornered, I stealthily approach him and apprehend him. I loudly proclaim myself triumphant as I deposit him in his place of confinement and secure the top.

Formal Research Paper

At the Dryden Correctional Center, the guys who run the education department try to prepare the inmates for living on the outside. That way criminals won't (they hope!) turn back to a life of crime. OK. Sounds like a good idea. But how do they do it? Well, they make sure that as soon as the criminals get tossed in the slammer they start getting an education. This is so that they will have a better chance of getting jobs when they get out. The way they figure it is if the criminals get jobs, they won't have to turn to crime to make money. The educational programs are completely voluntary. Lots of the inmates take them, though.

30 d Maintaining consistent tone

An unnecessary shift in tone will throw your readers off balance; they won't know where your ideas are heading, and they may be reluctant to follow. Be alert to any language that suggests a shift in tone, level of formality, or point of view.

■ The assassinations of President Kennedy and Martin Luther King, Jr., the Vietnam War, the Watergate scandal—each of these events shook public confidence in the nation and made it seem that the world ~~was out of whack.~~ *had gone mad.*

Some shifts are necessitated by content. A deliberate shift in tone can be appropriately humorous, moving, or even compelling. In the following passage, Stephen Jay Gould shifts from an amusing story, told in casual language, to an argument based on logic and hard evidence, written in a more formal tone.

When Muhammad Ali flunked his army intelligence test, he quipped (with a wit that belied his performance on the exam): "I only said I was the greatest; I never said I was the smartest." In our metaphors and fairy tales, size and power are almost always balanced by a want of intelligence. Cunning is the refuge of the little guy. Think of Br'er Rabbit and Br'er Bear; David smiting

Goliath with a slingshot; Jack chopping down the beanstalk. Slow wit is the tragic flaw of a giant.

The discovery of dinosaurs in the nineteenth century provided, or so it appeared, a quintessential case for the negative correlation of size and smarts. With their pea brains and giant bodies, dinosaurs became a symbol of lumbering stupidity. Their extinction seemed only to confirm their flawed design.

STEPHEN JAY GOULD, "WERE DINOSAURS DUMB?"

Using a deliberate shift is like telling a joke in front of a group of strangers: you have to be sure it's a good joke, and you have to deliver it smoothly and with expert timing.

▮ EDITING 4: PRACTICE

Edit the following passage from a formal literary interpretation, making sure to maintain a consistent, appropriate tone. More than one edited version is possible. Be ready to explain your editing choices.

You can really see the similarities between Shakespeare's *King Lear* and Jane Smiley's novel *A Thousand Acres*. Smiley makes you think of Shakespeare's play on purpose, and she expects you to be with it enough to catch on. You can see the parallels even in the names she gives to her characters. The three sisters in *A Thousand Acres* are named Ginny, Rose, and Caroline. These names make you think of Lear's daughters, Goneril, Regan, and Cordelia. Get it? (The first letters are the same.) In both the play and the novel, one really important idea is how parents and kids get along. In Smiley's story, Caroline, the youngest daughter, doesn't like her father's plan to retire and divide his huge farm among his three daughters, so he chills her. In *King Lear*, Cordelia, also the youngest, won't compete with her sisters in telling her old dad how crazy about him she is just so she can get the largest part of his kingdom. In both works, the two older sisters tell their dad what he wants to hear, but the youngest stands up to him.

▮ EDITING 5: APPLICATION

Read through a paper you are working on, paying close attention to its tone. How would you describe the tone? How do your choices of point of view, level of formality, and wording contribute to this tone? Given your subject and your purpose, is the tone appropriate? Hove you maintained this tone throughout? If not, do your shifts in tone help the effectiveness of your paper or harm it? As you edit your paper, pay full attention to its tone, keeping the aspects that you like and improving the aspects that you don't like.

Because English has a particularly rich vocabulary, writers often must choose among many words with similar meanings. For example, the place you live could be called, in a formal manner, your *residence, domicile,* or *habitation*; less formally, it could be called your *house, quarters,* or *lodging.* Informally, it could be called your *home*; and most informally, your *shack, digs,* or *pad.* Not every word is appropriate or effective in every context. At every turn, you have to choose which word can best—given your purpose and audience—convey the shade of meaning you intend. Enlarge your vocabulary by reading widely and listening actively to the words others use. Make word lists to study; **paraphrase** new words right away and use them in sentences, and try to learn the meaning of unfamiliar words from context.

31 a Understanding the history of English

The special richness of the English vocabulary results from the merging of many languages. As waves of invasion and migration have swept over the British Isles during the past three thousand years, each group of new arrivals has brought a language that has blended with existing speech.

In the fifth century A.D., Germanic peoples from northern Europe—the Jutes, Saxons, Frisians, and Angles (for whom England is named)—invaded Great Britain, bringing with them their Germanic language, which is the basis of modern English. We refer to their early form of English as Old English. Many words in our modern vocabulary can be traced to this period: *god, gold, hand, land, under, winter, word.*

In the eighth century, new invaders, known as Danes or Vikings, brought their Scandinavian language, Old Norse.

Although they came as conquerors, many Danes settled alongside the Angles and Saxons. Words adopted from the Danes' conquest include *fellow, hit, law, rag, take, want,* and many words that begin with an *sk* sound (*scorch, scrape, scrub, skill, skirt, sky*).

In 1066 the Normans, from what is now western France, conquered England and brought with them their own language, Old French. Following the Norman Conquest, French became the language of the noble classes, the law, the monetary system, and learning. French words such as *parliament, justice, crime, marriage, money,* and *rent* seeped into common usage, as did *art, ornament, mansion, pleasure, joy,* and thousands more. English retains two sets of words for many things, an indication of the social divisions of Norman England. For example, farmers used the English words *pig, deer, sheep, cow,* and *calf,* but the ruling class, whose only contact with these animals was consumption, used French names for their meat: *pork, venison, mutton, beef,* and *veal.* Eventually English became the predominant language among all classes, but by then French words had thoroughly infiltrated its vocabulary.

In the sixteenth century, a renewed interest in classical Greek and Latin learning—history, mythology, and science—brought into English a torrent of new words. From Greek came *democracy, hexagon, monogamy, physics, rhythm,* and *theory.* From Latin came *client, conviction, index, library, medicine, orbit,* and *recipe.* In the nineteenth and twentieth centuries, Greek and Latin roots have continued to provide a wealth of scientific and technical terms, many of which are invented words made up of ancient roots, prefixes, and suffixes: *cholesterol, cyanide, radioactive, telegraph, telephone,* and *television.*

English also has absorbed words from many other languages as its speakers have spread across the globe and as many speakers of other languages have settled in English-speaking lands. Modern American English includes words from hundreds of languages, including Spanish (*canyon, mustang, poncho, rodeo*), Italian (*balcony, balloon, carnival, ghetto*), Arabic (*alcohol, algebra, candy, lemon*), Hindustani (*bungalow, cot, jungle, loot, shampoo*), Japanese (*kimono, samurai, zen, karate*), and various African languages (*banana, yam, voodoo, jazz, banjo*).

These linguistic riches place at your disposal an array of words with similar meanings. Is a particular man *male, manly, macho, virile,* or *masculine*? Does a particular woman have a *job,* a *profession*, a *vocation*, or a *calling?* The choice depends on the shade of meaning you desire and the effect you want your words to have on your readers.

■ **EDITING I: PRACTICE**

For each of the words below, think of as many synonyms and near synonyms as you can. Try to guess which words on your list came from Old English, which from French, which from Latin or Greek, and which from other languages. Use a dictionary to check your guesses. You may want to compare your word lists with those of your classmates.

home
truth
good
warmth
hope
assist

31 b   Using the dictionary and thesaurus

Writers commonly rely on reference books to guide them in their use of language. A dictionary and a thesaurus can help you through the maze of seemingly similar words. They also can help you enlarge your own word stock. If you consult them regularly, looking up and noting unfamiliar words, your word skills and your writing will improve.

1 The dictionary

An **unabridged** dictionary offers information on word origins as well as definitions and usage samples. *Webster's Third New International Dictionary* (Springfield, MA: Merriam-Webster, 1986), which contains 470,000 words, is among the most widely used. The most comprehensive is the 616,500-word *Oxford English Dictionary*, 2nd edition, 20 vols. (Oxford: Clarendon University Press, 1989), which since 1928 has attempted to chronicle the first appearance and usage history of every word in the language. A searchable edition is now available on CD-ROM.

Here is the entry from *Webster's Third* for the word *communicate*:

com•mu•ni•cate \ kə'myünə,kāt, *usu* -ād• + V\ *vb* -ED/ -ING/ -S
[L *communicatus,* past part. of *communicare* to share impart,
partake, fr. *communis* common — more at MEAN] *vt* 1 *archaic* :
partake of : use or enjoy in common : SHARE < thousands
that ~ our loss — Ben Jonson > 2 **a** : to make known : inform a person of : convey the knowledge or information of
< ~ the news > < ~ his secret to a friend> **b** : IMPART, TRANSMIT
< ~ his pleasure to us > < an odor *communicated* to one's
fingers > < *communicating* the disease to others > **c** : to make
(itself) known — used of an intangible <his tension *communicated* itself to his companion> 3 [LL *communicatus,* fr.
L] : to administer the Communion to (a person) <the priest
communicating him > 4 *archaic* : to put (oneself) into close
connection or relationship with — used with *to* 5 *archaic*
: to give or deliver over (something material or tangible) : BE-
STOW ~ *vi* 1 [L.L. *communicatus,* fr.L] : to partake of the
Lord's Supper :   receive Communion < Eastern Orthodox
Christians   ~ in both elements > 2 *obs* : to have a common
part : PARTICIPATE, SHARE 3 : to send information or messages
sometimes back and forth : speak, gesticulate, or write to
another to convey information : interchange thoughts < they
communicated with each other for years > 4 : be connected
: open into each other : afford unbroken passage : JOIN
< the two rooms ~ > < the pantry ~s with the hall > 5 *philos*
: to have something logically in common : be further specifications of a common universal : be overlapping classifications
or connotations 6 : to arouse or enlist the sympathetic
interest or understanding — used with *with* < old plays that
. . . have long since lost their ability to ~ with an audience
—Wolcott Gibbs >

An **abridged** dictionary omits some less common words and
definitions, so it may be easier to use than a huge unabridged volume. *Merriam-Webster's Collegiate Dictionary,* 10th edition
(Springfield, MA: Merriam-Webster, 1993), focuses on contemporary American usage and has 170,000 entries. The *American
Heritage Dictionary,* 2nd college edition (Boston: Houghton, 1991),
defines over 200,000 words, beginning with the most common definition and then providing comments on usage. The *Random
House Webster's College Dictionary* (New York: Random, 1991)
lists more than 180,000 entries, the most common definition first.
The entry for *communicate* from *Merriam-Webster's Collegiate
Dictionary* is explained on pages 470–71.

✔ **WHAT'S IN A DICTIONARY ENTRY?**

Most dictionaries follow the format found in the tenth edition of *Merriam-Webster's Collegiate® Dictionary*. Springfield, MA: Merriam-Webster, 1994.

③ **PART OF SPEECH LABEL**
① **ENTRY WORD** ② **PRONUNCIATION**   ④ **INFLECTED FORMS**

com•mu•ni•cate \ kə-'myü-nə-,kāt \ *vb* -cat•ed; -cat•ing [L *communicatus*, pp. of *communicare* to impart, participate, fr. *communis* common — more at MEAN] *vt* (1526) 1 *archaic* : SHARE 2 a : to convey knowledge of or information about : make known ⟨ ~ a story⟩ b : to reveal by clear signs ⟨his fear *communicated* itself to his friends⟩ 3 : to cause to pass from one to another ⟨some diseases are easily *communicated*⟩ ~ *vi* 1 : to receive Communion 2 : to transmit information, thought, or feeling so that it is satisfactorily received or understood 3 : to open into each other : CONNECT ⟨the rooms ~⟩ — com•mu•ni•ca•tee \ -,myü-ni-kə-'tē \ *n* — com•mu•ni•ca•tor \ -'myü-nə-,kā-tər \ *n*

⑤ **DERIVATION**

⑥ **DEFINITIONS**

1. The **entry word** appears in bold type. Bars, spaces, or dots between syllables show where the word may be hyphenated. If two spellings are shown, the first is more common, although both are acceptable. If two spellings are dissimilar, entries are cross-referenced: **gaol** (jal) *n. Brit. sp. of* JAIL. A superscript numeral before an entry indicates that two or more words have identical spellings.

2. Pronunciation is spelled phonetically, set in parentheses or between slashes. (The phonetic key is usually at the bottom of the page.) If two pronunciations are given, the first is more common, although both are acceptable.

3. Parts-of-speech labels are set in italic type. The abbreviations are *n* for noun, *vb* for verb, *vt* for transitive verb, and so forth.

2 **The thesaurus**

A **thesaurus** (the word comes from the Greek for "treasure") lists synonyms for each entry. Many thesauruses list antonyms as well. *Roget's Thesaurus of English Words and Phrases*, the most popular, lists words in six major classifications and many related concepts. Similarly, *Roget's 21st Century Thesaurus* lists words in alphabetical order and contains a concept index.

4. Inflected forms are shown, including plurals for nouns and pronouns, comparatives and superlatives, and principal parts for verbs. Irregular spellings also appear here.

5. The **derivation** of the word from its roots in other languages is set between brackets or slashes. *OE* and *ME* = Old English and Middle English; *L* = Latin; *Gr* = Greek; *OFr* = Old French; *Fr* – French; *G* = German; and so on.

6. Definitions appear with major meanings numbered and arranged from the oldest to the most recent or from the most common to the least common. An example of the word's use may be enclosed in brackets.

■ **Synonyms** or **antonyms** may be listed, often with comments on how the words are similar or different.

■ **Usage labels** are used for nonstandard words or meanings.

archaic: from a historic period; now used rarely if at all

colloquial [coll.]: used informally in speech or writing

dialect [dial.]: used only in some geographical areas

obsolete [obs.]: no longer used, but may appear in old writings

slang: highly informal, or an unusual usage

substandard [substand.]: widely used but not accepted in formal usage

British [Brit.], Irish, Scottish [Scot.] and so on: a word used primarily in an area other than the United States. Some dictionaries use an asterisk to mark Americanisms.

■ **Usage notes** may follow definitions. They may also comment on acceptability or unacceptability.

A thesaurus can help you find the right word for a particular context or level of formality. But be careful: a thesaurus may also suggest words entirely inappropriate to your context, and an inappropriate synonym can wreck your credibility.

WP TIP Use the dictionary and thesaurus tools on your computer as you draft, revise, and edit. Remember, however, that the final decision about your word choices is yours. Especially

when using the thesaurus, remember that the proposed words might or might not actually be appropriate in the context of the sentences you are currently working on.

3 Specialized dictionaries

Specialized dictionaries contain the vocabularies of various disciplines. For example, if you need terms for the architectural features of medieval cathedrals, consult the *Dictionary of Architecture and Construction*. There are also specialized dictionaries that cover the regional and cultural varieties of English, such as the *Dictionary of American Regional English*. The *New Dictionary of American Slang* lists words used in conversational (or colloquial) English. Some dictionaries focus on word origins, or **etymology**. Other dictionaries cover branches of the language, from Canadian to Jamaican and Bahamian English.

■ EDITING 2: PRACTICE

Use a dictionary and a thesaurus to look up any words that seem unfamiliar or that might be misused in the following passage. Edit the passage by substituting more familiar words and correcting any misuses while preserving the intended meaning. Be ready to explain your editing choices.

The role of Emma Woodhouse in Jane Austen's novel *Emma* often receives censure for her supercilious behavior. Many readers consider her attitude toward her neighbors to be unconscionable: she avoids calling on them whenever possible and suffers their visits with scarcely concealed ennui. And it's certainly true that Emma regards all social functions as opportunities to display her better charms and talents. Yet Emma may be understood as Austen's portrayal of an exceptional individual constrained by a mediocre society.

31 c Expanding your vocabulary

Words are tools of communication; improving your tool kit can help you convey your thoughts more clearly. You can enlarge your tool kit of words, your **vocabulary**, in several ways. If you pay attention to the words others use, you will learn new words and usages. When you encounter a passage containing a new word, **paraphrase** it in familiar words; doing so will help fix the new word in your mind. Here are some other ways to improve your vocabulary.

1 Learning from context

You often can infer the meaning of words from the words around them, the **context**. Suppose you read the following:

> The integration deal means that customers will be able to plug Pipes' *middleware* directly into Sybases's message server, which provides wireless communications and transaction security. Combining both vendors' message systems gives users flexible *middleware* to bridge heterogeneous systems.

Even without knowing much about computers, you can guess that *middleware* is a computer device or program (*ware*, as in *software* and *hardware*) that connects different (*heterogenous*) systems so users can send messages to each other. In the future when you see the word *middleware*, you'll go on to learn more about computers from that given context.

2 Learning from roots, prefixes, and suffixes

You can find clues to a word's meaning by looking at roots, prefixes, and suffixes.

Roots

A root is a base word, the part of a word from which other words are formed. Sometimes words are formed with two roots, as in many scientific and technical terms. For example, the word *photograph* is composed of the roots *photo*, from the Greek word meaning "light," and *graph*, meaning "writing." Other root words combined with *graph* make *telegraph*, meaning "distant writing"; *phonograph*, an instrument for recording sound; and *chronograph*, an instrument for measuring time. This process works also in words like *software*, *shareware*, and *middleware*, created by analogy with *hardware*.

One root may be spelled in several different ways, especially in words formed long ago. Thus *justice* and *jury* are both related to the Latin word *jus*, for "law." *Transcribe* and *manuscript*, as well as *inscription*, *conscript*, and *scripture*, share the Indo-European root *skeribh*, "to cut or incise," and hence, "to write."

Prefixes

A **prefix** is a group of letters attached to the beginning of a root to change its meaning. For example, the word *prefix* itself consists of a root, *fix*, meaning "attach," and a prefix, *pre-*, meaning "before." Changing a prefix can dramatically alter the meaning of a word. For example, *democracy* means "rule" (*cracy*) "by the people" (*demos*); *autocracy* means "rule by one person"; *theocracy* means "rule by God or divine authority."

Suffixes

A **suffix** is a group of letters attached to the end of a root. Adding a suffix changes the meaning of the word and often changes the part of speech. For example, the verb *educate* means "to teach"; the noun *education* means "the process of being taught"; the adjective *educational* means "having to do with education or teaching."

Knowing some prefixes, suffixes, and roots can help you guess the meanings of words. For example, the words *antebellum*, *bellicose*, and *belligerent* share the same root *bellum*, Latin for "war." If you know that *belligerent* means "warlike or at war," you can guess that *bellicose* means "prone to war or fighting" and that *antebellum* means "before the [Civil] war." Be careful to check your guesses; sometimes words closely spelled have quite different meanings. *Disinterested* means "impartial or unbiased" while *uninterested* means "not interested or not concerned." Always consult a dictionary before you write.

3 Keeping a word list

Reserve a page or two in your journal for a word list, and every time you encounter an unfamiliar word—whether heard in school or seen in a book—write it down. Write down your best guess of the word's meaning. Review the list regularly. Look up the words, and jot down the exact definitions. Immediately try out your new words in sentences in your journal and then in conversation.

WP TIP Choose which word you wish to use, then check it in the online dictionary or thesaurus. Consider whether this word is the appropriate one for your purpose. If not, choose a better word from the reference source. This method should help you build a vocabulary, starting with words you know and moving on to new words suggested by the dictionary or thesaurus.

■ EDITING 3: PRACTICE

Using context and your knowledge of prefixes, suffixes, and roots, guess the meaning of the italicized words in the sentences on page 477. Then check the accuracy of your guesses by looking up the words in a dictionary.

COMMON PREFIXES

PREFIX	MEANING	EXAMPLE
a-, an-	without	atheist, anhydrous
ante-	before	antecedent
anti-	against	antiwar
auto-	self	autopilot
co-	with	cohabit
com-, con-, cor-	with	compatriot
contra-	against	contradiction
de-	away from, off	deplane
	reverse, undo	defrost
dis-	not	dislike
en-	put into	encode
ex-	out, outside	exoskeleton
	former	ex-president
extra-	beyond, more than	extraterrestrial
hetero-	different	heterogeneous
homo-	same	homogeneous
hypo-	less than	hypobaric
il-, im-, in-, ir-	not, without	illogical, immoral, insensitive, irresponsible
in-	into	inject
inter-	between	intercollegiate
intra-	within	intravenous
macro-	very large	macroeconomics
micro-	very small	microscope
mono-	one	monomania
non-	not, without	nonsense
omni-	all, every	omnipotent
post-	after	postmodern, postmortem
pre-	before	preheat
pro-	forward	promote
sub-	under	submit
syn-	with, at the same time as	synchronize
trans-	across	transcontinental
tri-	three	triangle
un-	not	unloved
uni-	one	unicorn

 COMMON SUFFIXES

NOUN SUFFIXES

SUFFIX	MEANING	EXAMPLE
-ance, -ence	act	adherence
-ation, -ion, -sion, -tion	act, state of being	abstention, pretension
-dom	place state of being	kingdom wisdom
-er, -or	one who	pitcher
-hood	state of being	manhood
-ism	act, practice	terrorism
-ist	one who	psychologist
-ment	act	containment
-ness	state of being	wildness
-ship	state of being quality	professorship workmanship

VERB SUFFIXES

SUFFIX	MEANING	EXAMPLE
-ate	to make	activate
-en	to make	broaden
-fy	to become	liquefy
-ize	to make into	crystallize

ADJECTIVE SUFFIXES

SUFFIX	MEANING	EXAMPLE
-able, -ible	able to	acceptable
-al, -ial	pertaining to	musical
-ate	having, filled with	passionate
-ful	filled with	fanciful
-ish	resembling	devilish
-ive	having the nature of	votive, active
-less	without	shameless
-like	prone to, resembling	warlike
-ly	pertaining to	motherly
-ose, -ous	characterized by	morose

ADVERB SUFFIX

SUFFIX	MEANING	EXAMPLE
-ly	in a manner characterized by	easily

1. When the policeman pulled me over, I was *indignant.*

2. He told me that I had been *exceeding* the posted speed limit by about 30 miles per hour and that the amount of this citation would *surpass* all of the tickets he had written that day.

3. It seemed to me that he was being *spiteful,* so I grew sarcastic and thanked him for *condescending* to make me the *fortunate* recipient of such an *unprecedented* gift.

4. He looked down at me, over his sunglasses, and *dramatically* tore off my citation.

5. As I took the paper from him, he leaned forward and, in a heartfelt *monotone,* told me to have a pleasant day.

31 d Considering connotations

The direct and literal meaning of a word is its **denotation**. For example, *fragrance, odor,* and *smell* all denote something detected by the sense of smell. But their associations, differ: saying *You have a distinctive fragrance* is quite different from saying *You have a distinctive odor.* The indirect meaning, based on such associations, is a word's **connotation**. As you edit, pay attention to the connotations of your words because they will affect the meaning you convey.

Some words have such strong connotations that using them will make you sound **biased**. (See Chapter 32.) Calling someone's hobby a *fixation* or *obsession* rather than just a *pastime* implies that the person is mentally unstable, a judgment that will seem unfair unless you can support the implication with evidence. When you find words that make your writing seem biased, replace them with more balanced alternatives.

Another way in which connotations differ is in **level of formality**. (See 30c.) Some words are appropriate for informal contexts such as writing about personal experience, while others are appropriate for formal academic writing. Deciding whether you refer to an instructor as a *prof,* a *teacher,* a *professor,* an *educator,* or a *pedagogue* is partly a choice among increasing levels of formality.

EDITING 4: PRACTICE

Complete the following passage from a personal narrative, choosing one of the two words in each set of parentheses. Be sure the words you choose have the connotations you want. More than one version is possible for some sentences. Be ready to explain your choices.

As a girl, my grandmother worked in a textile mill. Recently she (revealed to/told) me what it was like for her. Every morning she had to feed her (younger/youthful) brother and sister breakfast and then take them to the house of Cousin Sophia, who looked after them. My grandmother was at the (gates/portal) of the factory by 5:25 A.M. If an employee was late, she would (forfeit/lose) half a day's pay. The work was (drab/tedious) and exhausting. My grandmother had to (patrol/watch) and tend the same machine for hours on end, with nothing to (distract/entertain) her but the whirring and clanking of the engines. Her lunch hour was just fifteen minutes long, and she often (toiled/worked) sixteen hours a day.

 Distinguishing among frequently confused words

Homonyms, words with the same sound but different spellings and meanings, frequently create confusion. Even experienced writers sometimes use *their* when they mean *there* or *they're*, or confuse *write*, *right*, and *rite*; *its* and *it's*; or *principle* and *principal*.

Sometimes the confusion arises from spelling errors. If you drop a letter from *two* or *too*, you may write *to*, and you may miss the error if you are proofreading quickly (so will your computer spell-checking program). As you edit, be aware of potentially confusing words and examine each one to be sure it is used correctly. A list of problem homonyms appears in 50a.

 Using prepositions and particles idiomatically

Idioms are expressions or speech patterns that cannot necessarily be understood or predicted by rules of logic or grammar. Why do we ride *in* a car but *on* a train? Why do we *take* a picture but *make* a recording? Why do Americans say *in school* but not *in hospital* as the British do? In each case the correct word is determined by what is conventional and customary, or idiomatic.

Idiomatic expressions can cause problems even for native speakers; prepositions, for example, are often used in unexpected ways. We know that a **preposition**—*at, by, for, out, to, with*— shows a relationship between a noun or a pronoun and other words in the sentence. The only guide to the correct use of prepositions with nouns and verbs is to learn the conventional idioms.

VERBS THAT ARE OFTEN CONFUSED

There are several pairs of verbs that are similar in form but very different in meaning. You'll want to memorize them and edit for them when checking word choice.

SIT AND SET

Sit means "to be seated."	Neighbors *sit* on their screened porches every night.
Set means "to put or place."	I *set* some milk on the stoop for our cat.

LIE AND LAY

Lie means "to recline."	She *lies* down every day and meditates.
Lay means "to put or place."	He *lays* the paper on the table every morning.

AFFECT AND EFFECT

Affect is almost always a verb; *effect* is usually a noun, although it has some uses as a verb.

Affect means "to produce an effect."	Raising prices could *affect* sales volume.
Effect, as a noun, means "the result of a change or action."	Higher prices could have a bad *effect* on sales.
Effect, as a verb, means "to make happen."	She was able to *effect* a change in policy.

COMPOSE AND COMPRISE

Compose means "to form the substance of."	The United States is *composed of* fifty states.
Comprise means "to be made up of."	Fifty states *comprise* the United States.

Other problem pairs are listed in 50a and in the Glossary of Usage.

480 **Choosing the right word**

This novel shows a great similarity *to* that one. The similarity *between* the stories is remarkable.

I will meet *with* you *in* the morning *at* the office.

Phrasal verbs are **two-word verbs**, verbs that need another word to complete their meanings. These extra words which are called **particles**, look like prepositions (*up, down, out, in, off*, and *on*) and function with the verb to convey the full meaning, which may be quite different from the meaning of the verb alone. The meanings of the phrasal verbs in the following sentences, for instance, have very little in common with the verb *to come*.

How did this *come about*? (happen)

Of course, I expected things to *come out* all right. (end)

I was unconscious for a moment, but I soon *came to*. (revived)

Check your writing for idiomatic expressions. Be aware of potential trouble spots; try to make note of how these words are

---

ESL **FREQUENTLY CONFUSED WORDS AND PHRASES**

The following are some words or phrases that can be confused.

WORD OR PHRASE	MEANING OR FUNCTION	EXAMPLE
another	an additional one	I lost my library card. May I get *another* one?
the other	the second of two items	We have two cars. One is a station wagon; *the other* is a convertible.
few	not many	Frankly, I wouldn't ask him. He usually has *few* good ideas. [He has almost no good ideas.]
a few	some	Why don't you ask him? He always has *a few* good ideas. [He does have some good ideas.]
been	past participle of *be*	She has *been* gone all day.
being	present participle of *be*	Why do you think she is *being* so difficult?

used in standard English, and whenever you are in doubt, consult a dictionary or other reference.

WP TIP If you know you frequently misuse a particular preposition or particle, use the find function to locate each preposition and edit as necessary.

IDIOMATIC EXPRESSIONS

agree	We agreed *on* a place to have lunch.
	We agreed *to* leave at 12:30.
	We agreed *that* the food was excellent.
	We seldom agree *about* anything.
amuse	My cousin was amused *by* the clown.
	I was amused *at* my cousin's delight.
	The clown amused us *with* her tricks.
arrive	They arrived *at* the airport.
	They arrived *in* Los Angeles.
	They arrived *on* the scene.
differ	Margot differs *with* Harriet on this subject.
	Each one's opinion differs *from* that of the others.
	They differ *over* whether to go skiing.
identify	You can identify her *by* her appearance.
	You must identify her *to* the authorities.
	Do you identify *with* that character?
insist	I insist *on* going along.
	She insisted *that* my help wasn't needed.
occupy	The room is occupied *by* another group.
	Mario is occupied *with* his book.
prejudice	The jury was prejudiced *against* the defendant.
	They were prejudiced *by* improper evidence.
reward	The dog was rewarded *for* its behavior.
	It was rewarded *by* praise.
	It was also rewarded *with* a steak.
trust	He trusts you.
	You may trust *in* him.
	You may trust *that* he will do the right thing.
	He trusts you *to* do the right thing.
	Do not trust him *with* your money.
vary	The colors vary *in* intensity.
	They vary *from* light to dark.
	People's tastes vary *with* time.
	Their position has varied *over* the years.

ESL **USING TWO-WORD VERBS**

Some verbs join with a preposition—a word such as *on, up, by,* or *through*—to create a new meaning. The following are some examples of two-word verbs:

VERB	PREPOSITION	MEANING
call	off	cancel
find	out	discover
get	through	finish
make	up	invent, create

Here are some guidelines for using two-word verbs.

1. When a two-word verb does not take a direct object, i.e., when it is intransitive, place the preposition directly after the verb. (For more information on intransitive and transitive verbs, see 66c.)

The photocopy machine *breaks down* often.

You can also write: *The photocopy machine often breaks down.*

Other words in this category are *come back, come out, come over, play around.*

2. Transitive two-word verbs—those with direct objects—fall into three categories:

A. Those that cannot be separated

■ **EDITING 5: PRACTICE**

Edit the following paragraph to make sure that words and expressions are used according to convention. More than one edited version is possible. Be ready to explain your editing choices.

One of the most difficult things about small classes is that you never know when the instructor might call at you. Its easier to go unnoticed in a large lecture class where your one of a hundred faces in a crowd. When I'm in a small class, I try to set in the back row and make it obvious to my teachers that I'm taking a lot of notes. My theory is that if there convinced that your trying to write down what others are saying, they are less likely to call on you. Sometimes my strategy has the opposite affect, though. Sometimes my instructors see me taking notes and assume that I'm so engaged under the material that I'll be able to answer a question. When this happens, I just have to ignore my shyness and give my best shot.

■ Please go ~~this report~~ over carefully.
  (this report) ^

Other verbs in this category are *come across, get on, get off, get over, get through* (to finish), *look into, run into, see through* (to not be deceived by).

B. Those that can be separated if the direct object is a noun

The president *called* the meeting *off*.

You can also write: *The president called off the meeting.*

If the direct object is a pronoun, you *must* separate the verb and the preposition:

■ Why did she *call ~~off~~ it*?
  (off)

Other words in this category are *cut up, fill out, fill up, find out, give up, look over, leave out, make up, put down, throw away, turn off, turn on.*

C. A few that *must* be separated by the direct object

■ I tried to get ~~through~~ the idea to him.
  (through) ^

Other words in this category are *see through* (to persevere), *do over.*

31 **g** **Using slang and regionalisms**

Everyday speech is peppered with **slang**, language that originates in and is unique to small groups such as students, musicians, athletes, or politicians. One group's slang may be unintelligible to another. Consider, for example, the slang of politics—*spin, sound bite*—or of student life—*fresh, rude.* Some slang words eventually join the mainstream and may even become part of standard English. A *jeep* was originally a general-purpose (*g.p.*) military vehicle introduced in World War II. Now it is the brand name of a four-wheel-drive vehicle.

Regionalisms are expressions used in one part of the country but not standard nationwide. The generic word for *carbonated beverages*, for example, varies by region from *pop* to *soda* to *soft drink* to *seltzer.* Some expressions from regional dialects are regarded as substandard, not acceptable in formal writing.

A **colloquialism** is an expression common to spoken language but not usually used in formal writing. For example, the noun *pot* can refer not only to a cooking vessel but also to an illegal drug, the amount of money bet on a hand of cards, and ruination (*go to pot*).

Use slang, regionalisms, and colloquialisms sparingly, if at all. Slang and some regionalisms may not be understood by everyone, and for academic writing they are usually too informal. In descriptions and dialogue, however, they can convey immediacy, authenticity, and unpretentiousness, and in some informal contexts—personal experience essays, for example—they may be effective.

▮ EDITING 6: EXPLORATION

In the following passage, where and how has the author used slang? What effect does it have on the passage? Why do you think she chose to use slang this way?

Most college students do not live in the plush, comfortable country-club-like surroundings their parents envisage, or, in some cases, remember. Open dorms, particularly when they are coeducational, are noisy, usually overcrowded, and often messy. Some students desert the institutional "zoos" (their own word for dorms) and move into run-down, overpriced apartments.

CAROLINE BIRD, "THE CASE AGAINST COLLEGE"

31 h Using jargon carefully

Each discipline develops special terms to express its ideas. Studying biology would be impossible without terms such as *chromosomes* and *osmosis*. Literary criticism employs such words as *climax* and *denouement*. Specialized language particular to a field or discipline is called **jargon**.

As you edit, you must decide whether the special terms you have used are appropriate for your audience. For example, a general audience would understand *thigh bone*, but an instructor reading a paper on a medical subject would expect you to use the technical term *femur*. To a specialized audience, correct and conventional use of technical language helps demonstrate your mastery of a subject and enhances your credibility. Less technical terms are better for a general audience.

If you adopt jargon for its own sake, however, you may sound stilted or pretentious. (See 29e.) As you edit, decide which special terms are essential to your meaning and which are merely for show.

JARGON

It is incumbent on us to challenge the prevailing proposition that critical-theoretical approaches are the most enlightened ways of introducing students to literary experience.

EDITED

We should question the widely held idea that using theories of criticism provides the best way to introduce students to literature.

Sometimes the most direct language cannot communicate a complex concept—you need a technical term. Introducing it in a certain context can help the reader grasp its meaning. An explicit definition can help too. The following passage was written for car enthusiasts but not for mechanical engineers, so the writer had to explain clearly the terms *lean* and *stoichiometric*.

Running an engine *lean* means that there is less fuel in the cylinders than is needed to completely burn all of the available air. With gasoline, 14.7 pounds of air are required to burn 1 pound of fuel. This air–fuel ratio is referred to as *stoichiometric*.

FRANK MARKUS, "LEAN-BURN ENGINES"

■ EDITING 7: PRACTICE

Edit the following paragraph from a paper describing computer enthusiasts to a general readership. Try a couple of versions, one minimizing jargon as much as possible and the other making the jargon reader friendly. What do you have to assume about your audience in either case?

Virtually all the members of the campus Internet users group regard their computers as indispensable. These people spend most of their time logged on, cruising the 'net, swapping GIFs by e-mail, chatting on-line, or waging virtual combat in a multi-user dungeon. Word processing? Spreadsheets? Old hat in this crowd! We're talking major modem traffic, personal web sites, and the latest browsers. The more adventurous of these folks speak Unix like natives and are hacking around in mainframes that are supposed to be safe behind firewalls.

31 i Using figurative language

Figurative language, which likens one thing to another in an imaginative or fanciful way, can enliven your writing. Too much literal language can shackle your prose, tethering it to the hard, dull ground. Figurative language can also unchain your thoughts, allowing an occasional leap of the imagination.

Figurative language makes connections through comparison or analogy. This process is so deeply embedded in our language that we often overlook it. For example, the verb *overlook* in the previous sentence suggests how we can fail to see a process or idea in the same way that we can fail to see a physical object. Figurative language should be fresh, not hackneyed. Take care to use it effectively, not for ornament or embellishment, but to help readers understand your meaning.

A **mixed metaphor** combines two or more unrelated images, occasionally with unintended effects. If you find a mixed metaphor, consider eliminating the weaker image and extending the stronger.

■ Jones eclipsed Smith ~~by handing him a whipping~~ in the free-throw contest, hitting a shining ten of ten while Smith hit but five.

■ EDITING 8: PRACTICE

Edit the following paragraph from a paper defending a popular TV show to improve its use of figurative language. More than one edited version is possible. Be ready to explain your editing choices.

Many people object to the television cartoon *The Simpsons* because they say it is over the top, but millions of children watch it with bated breath every week. Critics say shows like this are causing the American family to disintegrate and are teaching children that it is okay not to hit the books. They think that young people want to be like Bart Simpson, who is as proud as a peacock of being a bad student, and that the show is a stumbling block for students who want to be above par. I think it's crystal clear that children can tell the difference between television and reality. When they laugh at Bart talking back to his parents, they are just letting off steam because adults are always laying down the law.

TYPES OF FIGURATIVE LANGUAGE

■ A **simile** is a comparison that expresses a resemblance between two essentially unlike things, using *like*, *than*, or *as*.

German submarines swam the seas like sharks, suddenly seizing their prey without warning.

■ A **metaphor** equates one thing with another.

Her life became a whirlwind of design meetings, client conferences, production huddles, and last-minute decisions.

■ An **analogy** uses an extended comparison to show similarities in structure or process.

The course catalog at a large university resembles a smorgasbord. Courses range from differential calculus to American film, from Confucianism to liberation theology. Students receive little advice as to which classes are the salads, which the desserts, and which the entrees of a college education. Even amid this feast, without guidance a student may risk intellectual malnutrition.

■ **Personification** is the technique of attributing human qualities or behavior to a nonhuman event or phenomenon.

This ship sailed into the teeth of the hurricane.

■ Deliberate exaggeration is called **hyperbole**.

No book in the world is more difficult than this economics text. Reading it is absolute torture.

■ The opposite of hyperbole is deliberate **understatement**.

With temperatures remaining below zero all day, it will seem just a bit chilly outside tomorrow.

■ **Irony** is the use of words to mean the opposite of what they seem to mean on the surface.

"House guests for three weeks? Terrific."

■ A **paradox** contains a deliberately created contradiction.

For a moment after she spoke, the silence was deafening. Then the audience erupted in cheers.

31 j Eliminating clichés

An overused expression or figure of speech is called a **cliché**. The word itself, interestingly, is a metaphor. Cliché is a French word for the sound a stamping press makes in a process of making multiple identical images. In other words, something has become a cliché if it is ordinary, run-of-the-mill, like the following:

the last straw	needle in a haystack
strong as an ox	handwriting on the wall
better late than never	tried and true
lay the cards on the table	hit the nail on the head

To edit a cliché, try improving upon it. Go back to the original image and describe it in new words, add fresh detail, or introduce a play on the too-familiar words.

■ Outside, the wind ~~howled~~. keened.

If you cannot revive the cliché, replace it striving for directness.

■ It was dark ~~as night~~ inside the cave. *so* *that we waited in vain for our eyes to adjust.*

■ EDITING 9: PRACTICE

Edit the following passage for an academic audience, examining word choice. More than one edited version is possible. Be ready to explain your editing choices.

If the nineties have been a golden era for home shopping channels, it has also been one for mail-order catalogs. In the past five years the number of catalogs delivered to American homes has tripled. Vendors compose not only old favorites such as L. L. Bean and discount electronics distributors, but also newer outfits that have been created merely to take advantage of this trend. According to one survey, the average mail-order catalog junkie receives ten garb catalogs, nine catalogs for housewares and garden equipment, five catalogs for his or her favorite hobby, and six gift catalogs each month. And this doesn't even take into account the specialized catalogs that focus on children, pets, travel, and any other earmark of a consumer's life that might result in a purchase or two. Mail-order companies sell each other their lists of suckers, so once a consumer receives one catalog, chances are that he or she will be receiving catalogs to life.

■ **EDITING 10: APPLICATION**

Select one page from a paper you are working on. Remembering the purpose of the paper and its intended audience, examine your choice of words. Use the dictionary and thesaurus to check any word about which you are not sure. Does each word convey the precise meaning you intended? Do any words have connotations that are inappropriate in context? Have you misused any frequently confused words? Have you used prepositions and particles conventionally? Are your expressions idiomatically worded? Have you used any slang, regionalisms, colloquialisms, or jargon? If so, do you have a good reason and are you sure your readers will understand? Edit the page to improve word choices as necessary, and pay close attention to word choice as you edit the rest of the paper.

The structure of language enables us as thinkers, speakers, and writers to move from the general to the specific and back again. Used carefully, **generalization** offers a powerful tool for predicting future experience from past. Nevertheless, using generalization carries risks. You might generalize from faulty data or use faulty logic. If, for example, a tossed coin comes up tails ten times in a row, you might generalize that tossed coins always come up tails. But you would be wrong; the odds on the next coin toss are exactly the same as on the first—fifty-fifty.

Using generalizations about a group of people to describe, interpret, or predict the behavior or characteristics of an individual is particularly risky. Careless generalizations, especially those based on race, ethnicity, gender, cultural background, age, physical characteristics, or lifestyle, are called **stereotypes**.

Writers especially should be aware of the extent to which stereotypes can invade language, both in describing individuals (*liberal politician, chorus girl*) and in making descriptive images (*sleepy Southern town*). Referring to a doctor or lawyer as *he* reinforces the stereotype that all doctors and lawyers are men. Language that contributes to stereotypes is called **biased**, and many people—not just those being stereotyped—find biased language offensive and alienating. Using such language may offend your readers and cause them to mistrust your judgment.

32 a Eliminating stereotypes

Stereotypes are oversimplified generalizations that frequently involve gender, race, ethnicity, or sexual preference. Many stereotypes attribute undesirable behavior or characteristics to all members of a group but not all stereotypes seem negative. Expecting someone's racial or cultural background to imply skill in mathematics, for example, may seem positive at first glance, but it is still a stereotype. Such assumptions not only are as illogical as the idea that a tossed coin will always land tails up but are also demeaning in the way they substitute a simplistic formula for appreciation of an individual.

If you find you have used stereotypes, edit your writing to eliminate them. You might need to qualify a broad generalization or replace sweeping statements with relevant, specific evidence. In some cases you might need to eliminate altogether the stereotypical image or information.

■ Like most ~~teenage~~ _inexperienced_ drivers, he didn't know what to do when the car started to skid.

Inexperience is the issue, not age.

■ ~~Like so many of his race,~~ Michael Jordan is a superbly gifted athlete. His tremendous achievements have provided an inspiration to ~~black~~ _many_ children everywhere.

Jordan's race is not relevant to his skill as an athlete, and not all the children who admire him are black.

■ Frank Peters, stooped from years in the woods, ~~but still alert,~~ remembers the dry, hot summer of the Tillamook Burn.

The assumption that people of Peters' age are not alert is a stereotype.

■ **EDITING I: EXPLORATION**

Read the terms on the following list. Write down your reactions to each, and note what images and ideas spring to mind.

intellectuals	drug addicts	career politicians
lawyers	BMW drivers	actors
movie producers	chiropractors	churchgoers
generation X	baby boomers	bureaucrats
conservatives	liberals	

Now ask yourself the questions from the "Editing Stereotypes" box on page 492. Are any of your responses based on stereotypes? How many people do you know in each category? Are your reactions based on your own experience, or do they come from what you have heard or read of other people's attitudes? Do you have similar impressions of everyone you have met in the group, or have you noticed variations? If you find yourself harboring stereotypes, remember to try to counteract them when you write.

EDITING STEREOTYPES

As you edit your writing, look for stereotypes such as *Like ten-year-olds everywhere* (or *suburban families* or *Korean immigrants*). If you find one, ask yourself four questions.

1. Am I relying on stereotypes rather than on evidence to make my point? A stereotype is really shorthand: it says to your readers, "You know what I mean." But your readers may not know what you mean, or they may disagree.

2. Do my generalizations follow logically from factual evidence? Make sure your facts are accurate and adequate to support your generalization. Then make sure your conclusions are logically related to your facts. That someone is Canadian and that she likes baklava may both be facts, but it does not necessarily follow that being Canadian creates a taste for baklava.

3. Am I using generalizations responsibly? Generalizations about a group cannot predict the knowledge, abilities, attitudes, beliefs, or behavior of an individual. For example, anthropologists have suggested that Japanese culture emphasizes group values more highly than Western society, but that generalization does not support an automatic characterization of any one Japanese person.

4. Have I used euphemism to mask a stereotype? A positive stereotype often is a slur in disguise, as when someone praises a woman for being an asset to her husband, which implies that her defining role in life is as a wife, a gendered stereotype about women's roles.

32 b Using labels carefully

People often speak of themselves in terms of the racial, gender, political, professional, or ethnic groups to which they belong. Everyone who communicates, including writers, uses labels to identify such groups: *whites, females, Democrats, psychiatrists, Taiwanese.* But labels inevitably focus on a single feature and have the potential to offend those who do not want to be characterized in one particular way. Also, some labels are considered *derogatory,* that is, they go beyond simple identification and evoke stereotypes. Here are some ways to judge how to use labels in your writing.

1 Using a group's own labels

Whenever possible, refer to a group of people by the label its members themselves prefer. Sometimes doing this is easy: members of the Rotary Club call themselves *Rotarians*; members of the Ancient Free and Accepted Masons are *Masons*.

With ethnic, racial, national, cultural, sexual, or gender labels, your choices become more difficult. Sometimes even those who belong to a group do not agree on what they should be called.

Designations of race, ethnicity, and nationality

Today some Americans of Spanish heritage refer to themselves as *Hispanics*, while others prefer *Latino* and *Latina*. Some Mexican Americans prefer *Chicano* and *Chicana*. Many *Native Americans* prefer that term to *Indian*, but using the name of the tribe or nation is often a better choice: *Navaho, Lakota Sioux,* or *Seneca.* Some *Inuit* prefer that term to *Eskimo.*

The terms *black, Afro-American, African American,* and the more general *people of color* are generally accepted, while *Negro* and *colored* are no longer acceptable.

Naming the specific country of someone's origin is always correct and worth the trouble: *Japanese, Korean, Malaysian, Vietnamese, Dominican, Guatemalan, Panamanian, Chilean, Bosnian, Latvian, Ukranian, Pole, Libyan, Palestinian, Iraqi,* and so on. In some cases, you may need to identify people by ethnic origin as well as nationality: *Bosnian Serbs, German-speaking Poles.*

If the religion of a particular group has a specific relevance in your writing, use the preferred terms; for example, a *Muslim* is a believer in Islam.

 CONSIDERING OTHERS

Wherever possible, be guided by the preferences of the people you are writing about. If you cannot ask a member of the group, consult a recent dictionary. It should go without saying that derogatory labels or slang expressions denoting sexual preference, religious affiliation, or race and gender, have no place in academic writing.

ESL **USING LABELS DERIVED FROM ADJECTIVES**

Many labels that describe groups are derived from adjectives: *the rich, the poor, the homeless.* Take care to use such collective nouns correctly.

1. Always use the definite article *the* before the noun.

■ The legislature passed a law to assist ᴛʜᴇ hearing impaired.

2. Use a plural verb when the collective noun is the subject.

■ The poor ᴀʀᴇ always with us.

3. A collective noun cannot refer to an individual. If you refer to one person in a group, use an adjective-plus-noun construction.

■ We spoke to a homeless ᴡᴏᴍᴀɴ about her search for a job.

Designations of gender and sexual orientation

Most adult females prefer to be called *women* rather than *girls* or *ladies.*

When writing about sexual orientation, keep in mind that people have widely different views about the role of sexuality in our personal and public lives. Be aware that not everyone may share your perspective, and always use the preferred term for a particular group.

2 Checking labels for negative connotations

Labels that seem neutral can hide negative connotations. (See 31d.) For example, the term *AIDS victims* implies that such people are blameless, which you may intend, but also that they are helpless, which you may not.

As you edit, watch for unnecessary or unintended negative connotations, and substitute more neutral alternatives. Focus whenever possible on people's strengths, referring to people as *living with cancer* or as *cancer survivors* rather than *suffering from cancer.* Focus on individuals first and their characteristics second: *a woman with quadriplegia* rather than *a quadriplegic.*

People's preferences for certain labels change frequently, as connotations change. People with physical limitations often, but not universally, prefer *disabled* to *handicapped*, and the latter term one time seemed more neutral than *crippled*. The continuing attempt to avoid negative connotations has resulted in the use of *visually impaired* or *hearing impaired* for *blind* and *deaf* and in such constructions as *differently abled* for *disabled*. Such terms are easily lampooned as an excess of "political correctness," but you must balance the need for directness against the need for sensitivity. Sometimes the solution is not to label at all.

■ He was a fascinating ~~old~~ man with a lifelong passion for book collecting and fine cognac.

■ **EDITING 2: PRACTICE**

Identify stereotypes in the following passages and describe the ways in which they may be thoughtless or offensive. If there is any useful information in the particular passage, edit it to communicate the information in a way that is not offensive. Be ready to explain your editing choices.

I. In order to achieve more diversity on college campuses, admissions officers all over the country are eager to accept foreigners, especially from Third World countries.
2. Because of policies like this, during my freshman year I found myself living with an Oriental guy, as well as with a Jew from New York City.
3. Since I had trouble in math and science, I asked my Vietnamese roommate to help me in Calculus and Physics; I also asked him to show me some karate.
4. My other roommate, not surprisingly, was majoring in economics, but since I didn't take any economics courses we couldn't really help each other study.
5. All in all, I enjoyed the chance to live with a couple of minorities; it taught me a lot about how different people view things differently.

32 C Using nonsexist language

If you use words that embody sexual stereotypes, you run the risk of alienating half your potential audience (or more). Several kinds of gender bias arise from habits of thought and language.

1 **In pronoun choice**

English does not have a singular personal pronoun of indefinite gender. In everyday speech, people often use plural pronouns to avoid the masculine forms: *Everybody had fun on their vacations.* This is grammatically incorrect since the subject *everybody* is actually singular and requires a singular pronoun. Using a singular pronoun, however, forces a choice between the masculine *his* and the feminine *her.*

Until recently, writers and readers alike accepted the generic use of *he, him,* and *his* to refer to singular nouns or pronouns whose gender was unknown, unstated, or irrelevant: *Anyone who believes those promises should have* his *head examined.* (See 45d.) This usage has been disappearing because many people believe that the generic *he* implies the exclusion of women.

 AVOIDING THE GENERIC *HE*

Here are four strategies for avoiding using the generic *he.*

1. If you know the gender of the antecedent, you can use the pronoun of the same gender.

■ Every nun has ~~their~~ her own room.

Nuns are women, so her *is appropriate.*

2. You can make the antecedent plural and edit any other agreement problems.

■ ~~Every attorney has his~~ All attorneys have their own legal ~~specialty~~ specialties.

To avoid suggesting that all attorneys have the same specialty, specialty *must also be plural.*

3. Use *his or her.* Do this sparingly, since *his or her* becomes monotonous with repetition.

■ A lawyer is only as good as his or her preparation.

4. Eliminate the pronoun by restructuring the sentence. This approach is often the most effective because it simply eliminates the potential problem.

■ Every~~one~~ writer wrestles with this problem. ~~in his own writing.~~

2 In universal terms

The use of *man* and *mankind* to refer to the whole of humanity has fallen into disfavor because it seems to exclude or diminish the female half of the species. Substitute *humanity, the human race, humankind,* or *people.*

3 In occupational terms

In choosing terms for a person's occupation, focus on the occupation, not the person's gender. Otherwise you risk suggesting that gender is a person's most important attribute or that some jobs are "naturally" held by either men or women.

Many occupational terms have a feminine form consisting of the neutral base form and a suffix that indicates the female gender: *actor/actress, author/authoress, poet/poetess.* Some terms, like *authoress* are obsolete; others, including *poetess,* appear occasionally but are considered offensive; and still others, such as *stewardess, waitress,* and *actress,* are in the process of changing to more inclusive terms (*flight attendant, server, actor*). As you edit, avoid feminine forms and describe a person solely by occupation, not gender.

Occupational terms that end in -*man* imply that everyone who engages in that profession is a man. Sex-neutral substitutes for many occupations are readily available.

BIASED	NEUTRAL
statesman	diplomat
congressman	representative to Congress, congressional representative
mailman	letter carrier, mail carrier
policeman	police officer
fireman	firefighter
businessman	executive, businessperson
chairman	chair, head

Similarly, do not use language that implicitly assumes that an occupation determines a person's gender—that all flight attendants, nurses, secretaries, or teachers are female or that all airline pilots, business executives, or bronco busters are male.

▪ The physician was assisted by a ~~male~~ nurse, who helped prepare the patient for surgery.

4 In descriptions

Treat the sexes equally. As you edit, notice if there are comments about a woman's appearance or family life. If you would not have made the same comments about a man in a similar context, delete them.

■ Dr. Jones, mother of three, was named to the hospital's peer review board.

5 In comparisons

Whenever you use a pair of terms for male and female, make sure that the terms are directly comparable. The phrase *man and wife*, for example, identifies one partner as independent (*man*) and the other in terms of her relation to him (*wife*). Edit it as *man and woman* or *husband and wife*.

■ Her essay contrasted the British novelists Dickens and ~~Jane~~ Austen.

6 In addressing your audience

Unless you are sure that only men or only women will read your writing, do not address your audience as if it were of a single gender.

■ When you buy a house, ~~your wife~~ you will have to get used to a new kitchen.

WP TIP Use the bold function to highlight pronouns and other words or phrases that you tend to use without thinking but that might merit revision for sexist language.

■ **EDITING 3: EXPLORATION**

The following are excerpts from three political statements from earlier centuries, when ideas about the roles of the sexes and sexism in language were very different. To whom do you think Jefferson is referring? How about Lincoln? Is either statement ambiguous or open to more than one interpretation? How do you think Stanton interpreted Jefferson's text? In what ways is her use of male and female terms different from Jefferson's? In what ways is it similar to Jefferson's?

When in the course of human events it becomes necessary for one people to dissolve the political bands which have connected them with another, . . . a decent respect to the opinions of mankind requires that they should declare the causes which impel them to the separation.

We hold these truths to be self-evident, that all men are created equal, that they are endowed by their Creator with certain unalienable Rights. . . . That to secure these rights, Governments are instituted among Men deriving their just powers from the consent of the governed.

THOMAS JEFFERSON, DECLARATION OF INDEPENDENCE (1776)

Four score and seven years ago our fathers brought forth on this continent, a new nation, conceived in liberty, and dedicated to the proposition that all men are created equal.

ABRAHAM LINCOLN, GETTYSBURG ADDRESS (1863)

When in the course of human events it becomes necessary for one portion of the family of man to assume among the people of the earth a position different from that which they have hitherto occupied, . . . a decent respect to the opinions of mankind requires that they should declare the causes that impel them to such a course.

"We hold these truths to be self-evident: that all men and women are created equal; that they are endowed by their Creator with certain inalienable rights; . . . that to secure these rights governments are instituted, deriving their just powers from the consent of the governed."

ELIZABETH CADY STANTON, DECLARATION OF SENTIMENTS (1848)

■ EDITING 4: PRACTICE

Edit the following passage, eliminating any biased language that may be offensive to readers. More than one edited version is possible. Be ready to explain your editing choices.

All of the old people at White Pines Residence agree that there couldn't be a better place for them to live. The modern residence has been designed to meet their every need, and in some ways it resembles a spa more than an old-age home. For one thing, the food is terrific. Every meal offers at least one exotic dish, always cooked to perfection. This isn't surprising, considering that the chef was born in Paris. In the medical area, facilities and services are first rate. A doctor is on call around the clock to provide care to all of the residents, many of whom suffer from cancer. With the handicapped in mind, doorways have been built that are wide enough for a cripple's wheelchair to pass through, and ramps are familiar sights, both inside and outside. Staff members have been carefully chosen for both their experience with old people and their personalities. They are all extremely popular with the residents. One of the best loved is a male nurse who always makes time in his busy schedule to read to the blind residents. Another nurse is a former actress; she has arranged for a local theater group to perform regularly at the residence. In addition, volunteers from the local college visit with the residents, providing them with companionship and friendship. Like so many old people, the residents at White Pines enjoy spending time with young people and telling stories about their youth. State-of-the-art facilities are not cheap, however, and White Pines is no exception; the cost of the facility may explain the high percentage of Jewish residents. To judge from the level of satisfaction among the residents, however, it is money well spent.

■ EDITING 5: APPLICATION

Read through a paper you are working on, looking for examples of biased language. Are there any characterizations that might be considered stereotypical? If so, can you supply specific details to support your use of the stereotypes? Or should they be eliminated? Have you used any labels to describe groups of people? Would these labels be acceptable to the people themselves? Have you used male pronouns to refer to both genders? Can you find any other examples of sexist language? If you discover such stereotypes or biased language in your paper, consider carefully why you might have written that way in the first place and how you can avoid doing so in the future. Then edit the relevant passages to eliminate the biased language. How does the edited version compare with the original?

Editing Grammar

Perhaps you remember learning in grade school that a sentence "starts with a capital letter and ends with a period." Is every such group of words a sentence? As a character in *Porgy and Bess* says, "It ain't necessarily so." A group of words punctuated as a sentence that is not grammatically complete is called a **fragment**.

> There are several ways to select text with the mouse. *A few of which may be known to you.*

Fragments may lack subjects, verbs, or both. They occur often in everyday speech and in informal writing that attempts to capture the rhythms of everyday speech. While skilled writers sometimes use fragments deliberately for effect, less experienced writers tend to use them incorrectly.

In academic writing, most instructors regard sentence fragments as errors. The problem with a fragment is its incompleteness. A sentence expresses a complete idea, but a fragment neglects to tell the reader either what it is about (the subject) or what happened (the verb). Fortunately, fragments can usually be corrected by a simple change.

33 a | Editing fragments lacking subjects or verbs

You can learn to identify fragments by searching your sentences for subjects and verbs. A complete sentence—or **independent clause**—has a subject and a verb, but a fragment lacks a subject, a verb, or both. Often fragments occur when the subject or verb is only implied from the meaning of the sentence that precedes or follows. You need to edit these fragments to create complete sentences. First, decide which element is missing. Then try one of the following editing solutions.

▮ Adding missing elements

It is simple enough to fill in the missing sentence element.

■ A fleet of colorful fishing boats ^rocked^ at anchor in the bay.

The fragment is easily repaired by supplying a verb.

 RECOGNIZING FRAGMENTS

A group of words can fail to form a complete sentence (or an independent clause) because of a missing verb, subject, or both. But remember that a group of words containing a verb and a subject may also contain a subordinating word or phrase, which turns the whole into a dependent clause. If you're unsure whether a group of words is a fragment, ask yourself the following questions.

1. Does it contain a verb? If not, it is a fragment. (See 33a.)

■ A middle-aged jogger ^ran by^ in beat-up Nikes.

A gerund, an infinitive, or a participle without a helping verb cannot serve as the main verb of a sentence. (See also 65e.)

■ They had one goal ^and that was to^ ~~to~~ make others respect them.

2. Does it contain a subject? If not, it is a fragment. (See 33a.)

■ During the night the protesters talked quietly and slept ^and^ ~~And~~ prayed.

Certain sentences in the imperative mood (commands, orders, and requests) do not require explicit subjects: *Come at noon.* When the subject is understood to be *you* though it is not stated, the sentence is an **imperative sentence** and is not considered a fragment. (See 35f.)

3. If it has a subject and a verb, does it contain a subordinating word or phrase? A clause introduced by a subordinating conjunction (*until, because, after, although*) or a relative pronoun (*who, that, which*) cannot stand alone as a complete sentence. (See 33b.)

■ None of the research was completed before the deadline ^because^ ~~Because~~

of the delay in preparing the samples.

■ Out of control, the careening truck hit the guardrail. Then
It
ˆspilled chickens and feathers halfway across the Utah
landscape.

Adding a subject completes the sentence.

■ My uncle was singing to his new baby. ~~Cooing~~ back with happy

She was cooing
ˆ

sounds of her own.

Adding a subject and completing the verb repairs the sentence.

EDITING FRAGMENTS

1. Complete fragments that lack subjects or verbs or both.

■ Returning to the lab, he found that the bacterial specimens were
they were
dying. Apparently ˆkilled by some excretion from a wild mold.

2. Edit fragments that cannot stand alone.

■ This is my cousin Jacob, ~~Who~~ has never missed a day of school.
, who

3. Know when to let sentence fragments remain for special effect.

Man is the only animal that blushes. *Or needs to.*

MARK TWAIN

---

2 Joining the fragment

Another solution is to incorporate the fragment into a nearby
sentence. Sometimes phrases such as appositives are punctuated
to stand on their own, but an appositive is only a noun or noun
phrase (or pronoun) that renames or further identifies a preceding
noun or pronoun. Often you can simply change the punctuation
and join the fragment to an appropriate sentence; there may be
several ways to do that.

■ Symbolism is an important technique in Alice Walker's
a
"Everyday Use," ~~A~~ story that shows cultural differences
ˆ
between generations.

In this example, the appositive fragment is attached to the sentence containing the renamed element.

■ Few employees interviewed held the company president in high regard,̶ ~~Or~~ ⁱᵒʳ believed he could bring the business back to profitability.

Repunctuating the sentence provides a subject for believed.

■ I was in the library when I saw him,/, ~~The~~ ᵗʰᵉ new student from Hong Kong. He was looking up something in the card catalog.

The phrase the new student from Hong Kong *restates* him, *so it can be punctuated as part of the preceding sentence.*

■ I was in the library when I saw him. The new student from Hong Kong,̶ ~~He~~ was looking up something in the card catalog.

The appositive has become the subject of the following sentence.

A very brief fragment, such as the prepositional phrase in the next example, lacks so much information that it should be joined to another sentence.

■ Last month I visited Detroit's Institute of Arts,̶ ~~With~~ ʷⁱᵗʰ my mother. We saw a wonderful collection of Surrealist paintings.

Join a list or set of examples to an introductory statement using a colon or a dash.

■ Katherine Hepburn influenced a whole generation of screen actresses,̶— ~~Such as~~ Meryl Streep, Glenn Close, Sigourney Weaver, and Kathleen Turner.

■ Taking the boat out alone for the first time, I tried to think of everything my father had shown me over the summer/: ~~Centerboard,~~ ᶜᵉⁿᵗᵉʳᵇᵒᵃʳᵈ, halyards, jib sheets, main sheet, tiller, and telltales.

Note: Following a colon, the first word of a list that is not a complete sentence is not capitalized. (See 46b.)

**ESL PREPOSITION FRAGMENTS:
MULTIPLE-WORD PREPOSITIONS**

Fragments introduced by multiple-word prepositions are often more difficult to spot than those introduced by one-word prepositions. Here is a list of common multiple-word prepositions.

according to	for the sake of
along with	in contrast with
as a result of	in favor of
as compared with	in spite of
as for	instead of
aside from	on account of
as well as	regardless of
because of	relative to
contrary to	up until
due to	with respect to
except for	with the exception of

Whenever you use one of these prepositions in your writing, make sure the phrase it introduces is attached to an independent clause.

■ Our debate team was not invited to participate, ~~in~~ spite of our
   in

   winning record, which we worked hard to attain.

■ EDITING I: PRACTICE

Edit the following passage to eliminate any fragments, making small changes in wording or punctuation that are necessary for smooth reading. More than one edited version is possible. Be ready to explain your editing choices.

There he stood. In the middle of the public square. Speaking at the top of his lungs about the end of the world. After two or three hours in the hot sun, he rested. Sat down in the shade of the clock tower. He opened his satchel and took out his lunch. A banana. A small can of apple juice. Three cookies and a wedge of cheese. I walked over to talk to him. He looked me right in the eye. For a long moment. Then spoke: "Have a cookie."

33 **b** **Editing dependent clause fragments**

A **dependent clause** is a clause introduced by a **subordinating conjunction** (such as *after, although, since, because, when, where, whether*) or a **relative pronoun** (such as *who, which, that*). Even though it has a subject and a verb, a dependent clause such as *that extended from before dawn until long past dark* cannot stand alone as a sentence.

If you find a dependent clause punctuated as a sentence, try attaching it to an independent clause.

■ Contemporary accounts describe a battle, ~~That~~ that extended from before dawn until long past dark.

■ It sounds like a pretty good job, ~~Although~~ , although it can't be as good as the jobs some researchers have.

■ Tests isolated the virus, ~~Which~~ , which many researchers are calling an epidemic.

■ After the leaves had all fallen, ~~The~~ , the trees stood bare.

You might also remove the subordinating element so that the clause can stand alone. (See 26e–g.).

■ ~~After the~~ The leaves had all fallen. The trees stood bare.

On occasion, the meaning of a fragment is ambiguous, and the fragment could be attached to either the preceding or following sentence. In such a case, you will have to choose which nearby sentence should take in the independent clause. Edit the sentence to clarify your meaning.

■ It sounds like an excellent opportunity, ~~Although~~ , although the starting pay is barely minimum wage. It provides more training than many entry-level jobs.

The value of the opportunity is qualified.

■ It sounds like an excellent opportunity. Although the starting pay is barely minimum wage,~~It~~ $\overset{it}{,}$ provides more training than many entry-level jobs.

The value of the training provided is stressed.

(See 44b and 44c for punctuation of dependent clauses.)

WP TIP If your computer has a "grammar" checker in the software program, use it to locate any sentence fragments you have missed. Consider the advice the program gives you, and choose one of the suggested alternatives or devise one of your own.

■ **EDITING 2: PRACTICE**

Edit the following paragraph to eliminate dependent clause fragments. More than one edited version is possible. Be ready to explain your editing choices.

Despite the fact that doctors take an oath to protect life. Many physicians believe they should be allowed to help patients who want to commit suicide. They want to do whatever they can to ease the pain of death for those who are suffering. Because they believe people should be able to die with dignity. Although euthanasia is not legal in Europe, it is becoming more accepted in some countries, especially in the Netherlands. Which has one of the most liberal policies in the world. There, specific guidelines allow a doctor to assist in the suicide of a patient who is terminally ill. As long as the patient requests it.

33 **c** **Using sentence fragments for special effects**

Writers occasionally use fragments on purpose. Because a fragment provides a dramatic break in rhythm, it can create dramatic emphasis. For this reason, they abound in advertising copy.

The sun's harsh rays can wrinkle your skin. Even cause cancer. Introducing the ultraviolet protection of new No-ray Oil. A fluid that blends smoothly with your skin, penetrating and softening. To soothe and protect.

Here essayist Joan Didion uses fragments to underscore a major point:

I knew that I was no legitimate resident in any world of ideas. I knew I couldn't think. All I knew then was what I couldn't do. All I knew then was what I wasn't, and it took me some years to discover what I was.

Which was a writer.

By which I mean not a "good" writer or a "bad" writer, but simply a writer, a person whose most absorbed and passionate hours are spent arranging words on pieces of paper.

JOAN DIDION, "WHY I WRITE"

To capture the sound of everyday speech, intentional fragments appear in fiction, personal essays, and narratives.

"How many did you sell, Buddy?" my mother asked.

"None."

"Where did you go?"

"The corner of Belleville and Union Avenues."

"What did you do?"

"Stood on the corner waiting for somebody to buy a *Saturday Evening Post.*"

"You just stood there?"

"Didn't sell a single one."

RUSSELL BAKER, *SATURDAY EVENING POST*

Because fragments are used infrequently in academic writing, you should consider carefully before using one deliberately. How is it likely to be interpreted? Will it be seen as an effective stylistic device or as just a grammatical error? Make sure that it seems intentional, not inadvertent. Use it to create emphasis. When your point warrants disrupting readers' expectations, a fragment may be in order. If it works.

◼ EDITING 3: EXPLORATION

Look through popular magazines, essay collections, and other publications written for a general audience and note the use of intentional fragments. In each case, what effect does the fragment have on you, the reader? Defend or criticize the effectiveness of each fragment you find.

◼ EDITING 4: EXPLORATION

Read the following passage, which includes a number of intentional fragments. Identify each fragment and consider its overall effect. What do you think the writer was trying to achieve? Do you think the fragments are effective? To de-

510 Eliminating sentence fragments

termine the overall effectiveness of the passage, edit it to eliminate all fragments and then compare your edited version with the original.

There never was any question whether we would finish. Just how soon. It seemed every time we got ready to close up, another busload would come in. Tired and hungry. And the boss would say, "Can't turn away money," so we'd pour more coffee. Burn more toast. Crack more eggs. Over and over again. Because we needed the money too.

■ EDITING 5: PRACTICE

Edit the following passage to eliminate sentence fragments. Make any small changes in wording that are needed for smooth reading. More than one edited version is possible. Be ready to explain your editing choices.

Ferdinand le Menthe Morton was born in New Orleans to a Creole family. Although he took classical piano lessons, he fell in love with another kind of music. Jazz and blues. Which he heard in the part of town called Storyville. In Chicago in the 1920s, he got a recording contract with RCA. He made some records and began calling himself "Jelly Roll." He claimed to have invented jazz. By himself. George G. Wolfe wrote a musical about his life. Called *Jelly's Last Jam* and written as though looking back from the moment of his death. At the end of his life, Morton had to acknowledge the contributions of other blacks to jazz. Which he had denied all his life. He came to recognize the heritage he shared with other black musicians. To accept and understand them. Although he had always thought of himself, a Creole, as different from blacks.

■ EDITING 6: APPLICATION

Examine your recent writings for sentence fragments. Do you write one kind of fragment frequently? If so, can you explain why you might tend to make this particular mistake? Practice editing any fragments you find by correcting each one in two or three different ways. Then decide which edited version of each sentence works best in your paper.

Correcting Fused Sentences and Comma Splices

An **independent clause**, one that includes a subject and a predicate and constitutes one complete idea, can stand alone as a complete sentence.

> subject   predicate
> Professional athletes can earn huge salaries.

Any sentence that contains two or more independent clauses must be joined in one of four ways: with a comma and a coordinating conjunction; with a semicolon alone; with a semicolon and a conjunctive adverb or transitional phrase; or with a colon. These markers tell readers that a new idea is about to be presented and clarify the relationship between the ideas.

> independent clause   independent
> Professional athletes can earn huge salaries, yet some of them
>
> clause
> want still more.

In this example the comma and the conjunction *yet* mark the beginning of a new idea, a new independent clause. They help prevent misreading by limiting the number of possible ways the sentence can proceed from that point.

Two independent clauses joined without such a marker make a **fused sentence** (also called a **run-on sentence**). Readers get no warning when one independent clause ends and another begins.

> independent clause
> **FUSED SENTENCE** Professional athletes can earn huge salaries some
>
> independent clause
> are paid millions of dollars per year.

REVISED   Professional athletes can earn huge salaries; some
                    are paid millions of dollars per year.

Two independent clauses joined (or "spliced together") by only a comma make up a **comma splice**.

RECOGNIZING COMMON CAUSES OF SENTENCE ERRORS

Comma splices and fused sentences, sometimes called **sentence errors**, often occur when two clauses express ideas closely linked in the writer's mind. Understanding why sentence errors occur can help you recognize them in your own writing. Here are some common situations that can lead to sentence errors.

1. The second clause explains, elaborates, or illustrates the first.

■ Every summer the tribes gathered along the banks of the river/they ^to fished and hunted and picked berries.

2. The meaning of the second clause contrasts with the meaning of the first.

■ The Security Council supported the resolution, ^but the United States vetoed it.

3. The subject of the second clause is a pronoun that renames the subject of the first clause.

■ The professor asked us to write our thoughts down. ^He ^said just to write whatever came to mind as fast as we could.

4. A conjunctive adverb or transitional phrase is incorrectly used to join two sentences.

■ Congressional offices once were completely contained in the Capitol/^in fact/^the Supreme Court also had space there.

COMMA SPLICE Professional athletes can earn huge salaries, some are paid millions of dollars per year.

Seeing a comma without a conjunction, readers expect what follows to be part of the first clause rather than the beginning of a new clause. Since this causes the reader to stop and go back for clarity, edit out any comma splices.

34	a	Using a comma and a coordinating conjunction

The coordinating conjunctions *and, but, yet, so, for, or,* and *nor* join equal grammatical elements and specify a relationship between them, such as addition (*and*), contrast (*but, yet*), causation (*so, for*), and choice (*or, nor*). (See Chapter 26.) If the ideas in two independent clauses are equally important and their relationship can be adequately expressed by a coordinating conjunction, you can join them with a coordinating conjunction preceded by a comma. (See 44a.)

■ The cyclone was especially savage‚ₐ it struck a particularly vulnerable area.
and

■ Maya Angelou has worked as an actress and director,ₐ her greatest success came as an autobiographer and poet.
but

■ **EDITING 1: PRACTICE**

Edit each fused sentence or comma splice by using a comma and a coordinating conjunction. More than one editing option is available to you. Be ready to explain your editing choices.

David Halberstam writes about many of the events of our time, ₐhe has received numerous awards for his work.
and

1. The praise that David Halberstam has received for his nonfiction writing is due in large part to his blunt style he always says what he means.

2. He was critical of the media's involvement in the 1988 presidential election, he said so openly.

3. In his writing he not only identifies his main points he also solidifies and clarifies them.

4. He leads the reader through his thought processes, rarely is any point unsubstantiated.

5. He feels strongly about his subjects he seems to become very involved with them.

EDITING COMMA SPLICES AND FUSED SENTENCES

As you edit your work, watch for sentences that contain two independent clauses; check to see that you have joined them in an acceptable way. There are four simple ways to correct fused sentences and comma splices:

1. Use a comma and coordinating conjunction to specify the relationship between clauses.

■ Professional athletes can earn huge salaries, but million-dollar contracts are the exception, not the rule.

2. Insert a semicolon to signal the clear, close relationship of the clauses.

■ Professional athletes can earn huge salaries; some are paid millions of dollars per year.

3. Precede a conjunctive adverb or transitional phrase with a semicolon.

■ Professional athletes can earn huge salaries; in fact, some are paid millions of dollars per year.

34 b Adding a semicolon

If you choose not to join two independent clauses of equal importance with a comma and coordinating conjunction, add a **semicolon** between the clauses to signify their equality.

Semicolon alone

Joining two independent clauses with a semicolon alone is appropriate only when the clauses are closely and clearly related. (See 45a.) If they are not closely related, make them separate sentences. (See 34d.) If the relationship is unclear, use a conjunction to clarify it.

4. Use a colon when the second clause illustrates the first.

■ Professional athletes can earn huge salaries⎮⁚ Barry Bonds signed
with the San Francisco Giants for $43 million over six years.

Other methods of correcting sentence errors involve greater changes.

5. Divide the sentence into two sentences.

Professional athletes can earn huge salaries. Some are paid millions
of dollars per year.

6. Subordinate one clause to the other.

Professional athletes, some of whom earn millions of dollars per
year, can earn huge salaries.

7. Rewrite the sentence as one independent clause.

Professional athletes can earn huge salaries, up to millions of dollars in one year.

How you choose to edit a fused sentence or comma splice depends on the meaning you wish to convey, the length of the sentence, and the rhythm and wording of surrounding sentences.

■ For years the Federal Communications Commission has
advocated legislation to allow competitive auctions for
broadcast licenses⎮;so far Congress has refused.

Note: Two independent clauses joined by a semicolon constitute
only one complete, though complex, sentence; thus the second independent clause does not begin with a capital letter. (See 51a.)

Semicolons are especially useful in sentences that contain
more than two independent clauses, particularly when one or
more items in a series have internal commas.

■ The sculpture, a poor imitation of the work of Dresner, was monstrous/its surface was rough and pitted/and its colors, ranging from fuschia to lime, were garish.

When two or more independent clauses are short, closely related, and parallel in form, a semicolon is not necessary.

I washed the clothes, I dusted the furniture, I fed the children.

But it is necessary when the sentence becomes more complex, with phrases, for example.

I washed the clothes, I fed the children; after a week I was ready for a change of scenery!

Nor is a semicolon needed before a **tag question**.

A semicolon would look odd here, wouldn't it?

2 Semicolon with a conjunctive adverb or transitional expression

Conjunctive adverbs, such as *finally*, *however*, and *therefore* cannot be used with a comma to join two independent clauses. Neither can phrases such as *in fact* or *for example*, which are called **transitional expressions**. Use a semicolon instead. (See list of conjunctive adverbs on page 517; see 24c for a list of transitional expressions.)

■ The rebel forces were never completely defeated/ moreover, they still control several strategic highland passes.

You can distinguish conjunctive adverbs from coordinating conjunctions by recognizing that conjunctive adverbs, like other adverbs, can be moved around in a sentence. Coordinating conjunctions cannot.

CONJUNCTIVE ADVERB

■ The mayor presented her budget plans; (however,) the council,
however, ◄───
had its own ideas.   or?

Yes, the conjunctive adverb can be moved elsewhere to create a different, though subtle, emphasis in meaning.

COORDINATING CONJUNCTION

or?

■ The mayor presented her budget plans; ⟨but⟩ the council˄ had its own ideas.

No, the coordinating conjunction cannot be moved. If moved, it no longer serves the function of joining the two sentences.

WP TIP In a paper you are currently working on, highlight in bold the conjunctive adverbs you have used. Consider whether you have used the one that best describes your message and whether it is positioned correctly. Next, go back and look for other places to use a conjunctive adverb.

✔ CONJUNCTIVE ADVERBS

accordingly	incidentally	now
also	indeed	otherwise
anyway	instead	similarly
besides	likewise	still
certainly	meanwhile	subsequently
consequently	moreover	then
conversely	namely	therefore
finally	nevertheless	thus
furthermore	next	undoubtedly
hence	nonetheless	whereas
however		

■ **EDITING 2: PRACTICE**

Edit each fused sentence or comma splice by using either a semicolon alone or a semicolon with a conjunctive adverb or transitional expression. More than one editing option is available. Be ready to explain your editing choices.

Michael Crichton, a popular novelist, often writes about extremely technical subjects ;*however,* his novels often become bestsellers.

I. Michael Crichton's *Jurassic Park* explores the disastrous consequences of disturbing the balance of nature, it presents what could happen if scientists bring dinosaurs back from extinction.

518 Correcting fused sentences and comma splices

2. Crichton does not preach about environmental issues, he uses them to create an engaging, fast-paced story.

3. Alan Grant, the main character, is an expert in dinosaurs no one else knows as much about velociraptors as he does.

4. Grant questions the safety of the theme park, for example, having rides in the park disturbs him.

5. Crichton's characters, especially Grant, are realistic their words, thoughts, and actions are believable and true-to-life.

34 c Adding a colon

When the second clause of two independent clauses explains, elaborates, or illustrates the first, you can use a colon to join the clauses.

■ This year's team is surprisingly inexperienced‸̷seven of the players are juniors and six are sophomores.

When the second independent clause conveys the main point of the sentence, some writers capitalize the first word after the colon.

My mother gave me one important piece of advice: Never wear plaids with stripes.

Note: Capitalization is optional when you use a colon to join two independent clauses; a lowercase letter after the colon is always correct. (See Chapter 46 and 51a.)

WP TIP Use the search function to locate your use of colons to separate two independent clauses. In each case, consider whether the colon is the best choice, or edit your sentence.

■ **EDITING 3: PRACTICE**

Edit each fused sentence or comma splice by using a colon.

The ebola virus is one of the deadliest viruses on Earth‸̷it kills up to 90 percent of those who contract it.

1. The first recorded outbreak, which occurred in Zaire in 1976, took a heavy toll in human life more than 340 people died.

2. Medical researchers know very little about the disease, they have only a vague idea of where the virus originated.

3. Many people have compared ebola to AIDS because of its severity, but there is one important difference unlike AIDS ebola can kill a person in a few days.

4. Between epidemics the virus appears to go dormant many years might pass without a reported case.

5. We cannot afford to wait until the next epidemic before taking action, we must find a cure as soon as we can.

34 d Writing separate sentences

The two independent clauses in a comma splice or fused sentence may read better as two separate sentences, especially when one clause is much longer than the other or when the two clauses are dissimilar in structure or meaning.

■ The president outlined his administration's new economic

strategy on the same day that war broke out in the Middle East.
Almost
~~almost~~ no one noticed his announcement.

Making two sentences often increases emphasis on the second clause.

34 e Subordinating one clause to the other

To emphasize one of the two ideas in a fused or spliced sentence, you may choose to put the less important idea in a **subordinate clause**. Subordinating one clause to the other will make it dependent—no longer able to stand on its own.

Dependent clauses are introduced by a **subordinating conjunction** such as *after, although, as, because, if, than, whenever,* or *while* or by a **relative pronoun** such as *who, which,* or *that*. To use subordination, place the less important idea in a dependent clause and choose the subordinating conjunction or relative pronoun that best describes the relationship you want to establish between the two.

■ Because the
~~The~~ rain had frozen as it hit the ground, the streets were slick
with glare ice.

■ that
The committee studied the issue ~~it~~ decided to recommend

allowing the group to participate.

| 34 | f | Creating one independent clause |

When two independent clauses are closely related in meaning, often you can collapse them into one clause.

■ This book held my attention/~~it~~ ^{and} gave a lot of information about the colonial period.

Since book *and* it *are the same subject, it can be dropped.*

You can also turn one clause into a modifier phrase.

■ The huge chestnut oak cast a heavy blanket of shadow on the ground beneath it, ~~it dwarfed~~ ^{dwarfing} a few saplings.

■ Bobbie Ann Mason _∧, my favorite author, writes interesting stories about offbeat characters. ~~She is my favorite author~~

WP TIP   Reread a paper you are currently working on and select approximately five places where your sentences could be combined using semicolons, conjunctive adverbs, or transitional expressions. Edit each one in several ways. Then choose the best editing strategy.

■ EDITING 4: PRACTICE

Edit each fused sentence or comma splice in the following passage by creating a single sentence or separate sentences. More than one edited version is possible. Be ready to explain your editing choices.

The weather report was over, we knew the storm was rapidly approaching. We were all very nervous hurricanes had struck our town many times before they did a lot of damage. My father came back from the hardware store with several rolls of masking tape, he gave each of us a roll and told us to tape the windows to keep the glass from shattering if hit by debris. Then mom sent me to check on our next-door neighbor he is extremely scared of storms. He still remembers the violent storms of his childhood, he was born in Texas. He returned with me to our house, we all waited in the basement we played cards and we listened to the radio. Fortunately, the storm dissipated when it hit the coast south of us, all of the excitement was for nothing.

■ EDITING 5: PRACTICE

Edit the following passage to eliminate fused sentences and comma splices, using any strategy discussed in this chapter. Be ready to discuss your editing changes.

Expanding the airport will generate more flights, more flights will bring more travelers and money into the region. Each traveler spends an average of $7 in the airport on goods and services, when parking and ground transportation is added, the total approaches $25. The report said that developing the local economy would benefit the area, it said that air travel would make traffic problems worse on roads around the airport. According to the report, expanding the airport offers many advantages, including providing jobs, making travel more convenient, and boosting the economy. However, the expansion plan faces some problems, it would cost $17 million and it would have to be built on land that might be valuable as wetlands. Opponents of the airport expansion appeared before the port commission, saying that new runways would endanger the nesting grounds of several rare migratory birds. The Department of Environmental Quality studied the bird migration patterns it said that the fifteen acres of wetlands in question were home to at least nineteen different species. The Southeast Region Chamber of Commerce has supported the airport expansion, claiming that the plan could create dozens of new jobs, the chamber president called those jobs more important than a few ducks.

■ EDITING 6: APPLICATION

Examine your own recent writing for fused sentences and comma splices. If you have used any, is there a pattern to your errors? Can you see why you made these mistakes? Edit any fused sentences and comma splices you found, and think about how best to correct or avoid these errors in the future.

Effective writing uses strong verbs that show action. Verbs can convey a great deal of other information as well. They help show who performed the action by changing form according to **person**: *I talk. He talks.* They show *how many* people performed the action by changing **number**: *She sings. They sing.* They show *when* it occurred by changing **tense**: *He thinks. He thought.* They show the speaker's *attitude* toward or *relation* to the action by changing **mood**: *You are an honors student. Be an honors student.* They also show whether the subject of the sentence acts or is acted upon, by changing **voice**: *She took the picture. The picture was taken.*

Using verbs correctly in all these ways is not as difficult as it may seem. If you speak English fluently, you have been using the right person, number, tense, mood, and voice most of the time without thinking about it. In conversation, however, people often ignore the subtleties of correct usage, using gestures, intonation, or repetition to help convey meaning. Additionally, what is "correct" varies from community to community. People who grew up speaking a dialect may find their use of verbs is considered nonstandard in formal academic writing.

This chapter gives an overview of verb forms, tense, and mood. The uses of the active and passive voice are discussed in Chapter 28. For questions of agreement between verbs and subjects, see Chapter 36. **Verbals**, verb forms, which are used as nouns or adjectives, do not change form to show person or number. (See 66c.)

VERB FORMS

35 a Understanding the five verb forms

Except for the verb *be*, all English verbs have five forms.

Two forms express action occurring now: the **base form** and the **-s form**. The base form, also called the plain form or simple form, is used for present-tense action performed by *I, we, you,* or *they*; and the *-s* form is used for *he, she,* or *it* (third person singular).

 TERMS USED TO DESCRIBE VERBS

Knowing the terms used to describe verbs isn't a prerequisite for speaking good English. Nevertheless, the terms given here are useful for describing verb problems and their solutions.

■ **Person** indicates who or what performs an action. (See 35a and 35b.)

first person	the one speaking	*I read.*
second person	the one spoken to	*You read.*
third person	the one spoken about	*He reads.*

■ **Number** indicates how many people or things perform the action. (See 35a and 35b.)

singular	one	*I think.*
plural	more than one	*We think.*

■ **Tense** indicates the time of the action. (See 35d–e.)

present	at this time	*I learn.*
past	before this time	*I learned.*
future	after this time	*I will learn.*

■ **Mood** indicates the speaker's attitude toward or relation to the action. (See 35f and 35g.)

indicative	speaker states a fact or asks a question	*You are quiet.*
imperative	speaker gives a command or direction	*Be quiet!*
subjunctive	speaker expresses desire, wish, or requirement or states a condition contrary to fact	*I would be happier if you were quiet.*

■ **Voice** indicates whether the grammatical subject of the sentence performs the action or is acted upon. (See 28c.)

active	the subject acts	*She read the book.*
passive	the subject is acted upon	*The book was read by her.*

THE FIVE VERB FORMS

The five principal forms of English verbs are the base form, the -s form, the past tense, the past participle, and the present participle. Regular verbs add -d or -ed to form the past tense and past participle. Irregular verbs follow some other pattern. (The irregular verb be has more than five forms. See 35b4. For more on irregular verbs, see 35b2.)

BASE FORM	-s FORM	PAST TENSE	PAST PARTICIPLE	PRESENT PARTICIPLE
Regular				
act	acts	acted	acted	acting
seem	seems	seemed	seemed	seeming
Irregular				
know	knows	knew	known	knowing
eat	eats	ate	eaten	eating
hit	hits	hit	hit	hitting

Two verb forms express action that occurred in the past: the **past tense** and **past participle**. For **regular verbs**, the past tense and past participle are formed by adding -d or -ed to the base form. Verbs that form the past tense and past participle in other ways are called **irregular verbs**. Often the two past forms of an irregular verb differ from each other: *I knew. I have known.* The past tense and the past participle do not change to reflect who performed the action: *I tried. They tried.*

The fifth verb form, the **present participle**, is formed by adding -ing to the base form: *know, knowing.* It expresses continuing action in the present or the past. Like the past tense and past participle, it does not change according to person and number, and to serve as the main verb of a sentence it must be used with a form of *be: She is sleeping.* (See 35c.)

(For a discussion of the verb *be,* see 35b4; for more on irregular verbs, see 35b2.)

35 b Using standard verb forms

1 Using -s and -ed forms correctly

The **third-person singular form**, used when *he, she, it* or any singular noun is the subject, is formed for all present-tense verbs except *be* and *have* by adding *-s* or *-es* to the base form. *I go; she goes* (but *I am; he is* and *I have; she has*). The past tense of regular verbs is created by adding *-d* or *-ed* to the base form.

Speakers of some dialects do not use the *-s* and *-ed* endings, but such usage is considered nonstandard in formal writing. As you edit your work, watch for missing *-s* and *-ed* endings.

■ He ~~want~~ very much to go to the basketball game.
   wants

■ When I got back to class, the instructor ~~ask~~ me how I ~~like~~ the
   asked   *liked*

food at Al's Barbecue.

WP TIP If your computer has a "grammar" checker in the software program, use it to indicate incorrect verb usage. Evaluate the suggested alternatives and edit as necessary.

2 Using irregular forms correctly

Irregular verbs, unlike regular verbs, do not add *-d* or *-ed* to form the past tense or past participle. The past tense of *have*, for example, is not *haved* but *had*. The past participle of *eat* is not *eated* but *eaten*.

There are some patterns that appear among irregular verbs. For example, some verbs, such as *bet, bid, burst, cast, cut, hit,* and *quit,* do not change form for the past tense or past participle. Certain vowel changes provide another pattern: *ring, rang, rung; sing, sang, sung; drink, drank, drunk.* But these patterns are not reliable enough to predict. The past tense of *think* is not *thank,* nor is its past participle *thunk;* both the past and past participle are *thought.*

Since irregular verbs cannot easily be predicted, you need to try to memorize them. Whenever necessary, consult a dictionary that lists the forms of irregular verbs. Be sure to edit your papers carefully for the correct verb forms. (See the examples on page 528.)

ESL **GERUNDS AND INFINITIVES AS NOUNS FOLLOWING VERBS**

Gerunds and infinitives are called **verbals** because they are derived from verbs but do not function as verbs in sentences. A **gerund** is the *-ing* form of the verb functioning as a noun. An **infinitive** (*to* plus the base form of the verb) can function as a noun, adjective, or adverb.

> gerund   infinitive
>
> I stopped ⌐*eating*⌐ and started ⌐*to work.*⌐

Gerunds and infinitives often follow verbs. Some verbs can be followed only by gerunds or gerund phrases: *I enjoy eating* not *I enjoy to eat.* Other verbs can be followed only by infinitives or infinitive phrases: *I plan to swim* not *I plan swimming.* And a third category of verbs can be followed by either gerunds or infinitives (or gerund phrases or infinitive phrases): *I like reading. I like to read.*

It is sometimes difficult to remember whether to use a gerund or an infinitive with a particular verb. Here are some common verbs in each of the three categories.

1. Some verbs can be directly followed only by a gerund, not an infinitive.

■   *visiting*
    He recommended ~~to visit~~ the botanical gardens.

admit	deny	miss	resent
appreciate	dislike	postpone	risk
avoid	enjoy	practice	suggest
consider	finish	quit	tolerate
defend	imagine	recommend	understand
delay	include		

2. Some verbs can be directly followed only by an infinitive, not a gerund.

■   *to finish*
    I expect ~~finishing~~ my paper today.

agree	desire	need	refuse
appear	expect	offer	tell
ask	fail	order	tend
choose	help	plan	wait
claim	hesitate	prepare	want
decide	hope	pretend	wish
demand	intend	promise	

Some verbs followed by infinitives require a noun or pronoun between the verb and the infinitive.

- She persuaded to stay. ^my friends^ ~~my friends~~

    Verbs that require a noun or pronoun before the infinitive include

advise	command	order	remind
allow	convince	permit	tell
cause	instruct	persuade	urge
			warn

3. Some verbs can be followed by either a gerund or an infinitive.

We began *watching/to watch* the documentary.

advise	continue	permit	start
allow	forget	prefer	stop
begin	hate	regret	try
cause	like	remember	urge
cease	love		

Note that some of the verbs in this list need to be followed directly by a noun or pronoun before an infinitive.

No The instructor *allows to miss* each student one class.

Yes The instructor *allows* each student *to miss* one class.

■ She ~~seen~~ her mistake immediately.

saw

■ I've ~~knowed~~ all along that she would.

known

IRREGULAR VERBS

BASE FORM	PAST TENSE	PAST PARTICIPLE
arise	arose	arisen
awake	awoke, awaked	awaked, awoken
be	was, were	been
beat	beat	beaten, beat
become	became	become
begin	began	begun
bend	bent	bent
bet	bet	bet
bind	bound	bound
bite	bit	bitten, bit
blow	blew	blown
break	broke	broken
bring	brought	brought
broadcast	broadcast	broadcast
build	built	built
burst	burst	burst
buy	bought	bought
catch	caught	caught
choose	chose	chosen
cling	clung	clung
come	came	come
cost	cost	cost
creep	crept	crept
deal	dealt	dealt
dig	dug	dug
dive	dived, dove	dived
do	did	done
draw	drew	drawn
drink	drank	drunk
drive	drove	driven
eat	ate	eaten

IRREGULAR VERBS

BASE FORM	PAST TENSE	PAST PARTICIPLE
fall	fell	fallen
feed	fed	fed
feel	felt	felt
fight	fought	fought
find	found	found
flee	fled	fled
fly	flew	flown
forbid	forbade	forbidden
forget	forgot	forgotten, forgot
forgive	forgave	forgiven
freeze	froze	frozen
get	got	gotten, got
give	gave	given
go	went	gone
grow	grew	grown
hang (suspend)	hung	hung
hang (execute)	hanged	hanged
have	had	had
hear	heard	heard
hide	hid	hidden
hold	held	held
hurt	hurt	hurt
keep	kept	kept
know	knew	known
lay (put)	laid	laid
lead	led	led
leap	leapt, leaped	leapt, leaped
leave	left	left
lend	lent	lent
let (allow)	let	let
lie (recline)	lay	lain
light	lit, lighted	lit, lighted
lose	lost	lost
make	made	made
mean	meant	meant
meet	met	met
mistake	mistook	mistaken

(cont.)

IRREGULAR VERBS (Continued)

BASE FORM	PAST TENSE	PAST PARTICIPLE
pay	paid	paid
prove	proved	proved, proven
quit	quit	quit
read	read	read
rid	rid	rid
ride	rode	ridden
ring	rang	rung
rise	rose	risen
run	ran	run
say	said	said
see	saw	seen
seek	sought	sought
sell	sold	sold
send	sent	sent
set	set	set
shake	shook	shaken
shoot	shot	shot
show	showed	shown, showed
shrink	shrank	shrunk
sing	sang	sung
sink	sank	sunk
sit	sat	sat
sleep	slept	slept
speak	spoke	spoken
spend	spent	spent
spin	spun	spun
spit	spit, spat	spit, spat
spring	sprang	sprung
stand	stood	stood
steal	stole	stolen
stick	stuck	stuck
sting	stung	stung
stink	stank, stunk	stunk
strike	struck	struck, stricken
swear	swore	sworn
swim	swam	swum
swing	swung	swung
take	took	taken
teach	taught	taught
tear	tore	torn

IRREGULAR VERBS

BASE FORM	PAST TENSE	PAST PARTICIPLE
tell	told	told
think	thought	thought
throw	threw	thrown
wake	woke, waked	woken, waked
wear	wore	worn
win	won	won
write	wrote	written

3 Using *sit* and *set* and *lie* and *lay* correctly

The forms of *sit* and *set* and of *lie* and *lay* can cause confusion because of their similar sounds and related meanings. To distinguish them, remember that *sit* and *lie* never take direct objects (the ones with an *i* in them are **intransitive verbs**), while *set* and *lay* always take direct objects (they are **transitive verbs**). *Sit* means "to be seated"; *set* means "to put or place." *Lie* means "to recline"; *lay* means "to put or place."

INTRANSITIVE   People *sit* outside when it's warm.

I always *lie* down after lunch.

TRANSITIVE   We *set* the books on the table.

Every morning I *lay* the mail on her desk.

Part of the confusion between lay and lie comes from the similarity of their other forms. The forms of *lie* meaning "to tell a falsehood" are also similar.

WP TIP   Use the search function to locate every appearance of *sit, sat, set, lie, lying, lain, lay, laying,* and *laid* in a paper you are currently working on. Check for correct verb usage, and edit as necessary.

4 Using *be* correctly

The verb *be* is an irregular verb that has many different forms. Every other English verb uses only two forms in the present tense: the base form and the -s (or -es) form: *I work, you work, we work, they work, she works.* The verb *be*, however, has three present-tense forms, all different from the base form: *I am,*

> ### ✔ *SIT/SET* AND *LIE/LAY*
>
> | BASE FORM | PAST TENSE | PAST PARTICIPLE | PRESENT PARTICIPLE |
> |---|---|---|---|
> | sit (to be seated) | sat | sat | sitting |
> | set (to put or place) | set | set | setting |
> | lie (to recline) | lay | lain | lying |
> | lay (to put or place) | laid | laid | laying |
> | lie (to tell a falsehood) | lied | lied | lying |

you are, we are, they are, he is. Take special care to use the correct form.

■ These books ~~is~~ *are* due back at the library next week.

Some speakers use the base form of *be* instead of the correct present-tense form, and others drop the verb entirely. Such usage is regarded as nonstandard in formal writing.

■ He ~~be~~ *is* happy watching television.

■ We *are* on our way over.

Using the base form *be* as an auxiliary (see 35c2) with the past or present participle is also nonstandard.

■ I ~~be~~ *am* working harder this term than last term.

Always precede the past participle *been* by a form of the auxiliary *have.*

■ I *have* been practicing three hours every night.

WP TIP   Have your computer find all uses of the verb *be* in a paper you are currently working on by searching for *am, is, are, was, were, being,* and *been.* Doing so not only provides you with an opportunity to edit for correct verb usage, but it also gives you the chance to consider replacing some of the uses of *be,* a static verb, with an active verb to improve sentence vitality. (See 28b)

THE FORMS OF *BE*

The most irregular verb in English is *be*, which has three forms in the present tense and two forms in the past tense.

	SINGULAR	PLURAL
PRESENT	I am	we are
	you are	you are
	he, she, it is	they are
PAST	I was	we were
	you were	you were
	he, she, it was	they were

These are the principal parts of *be*:

BASE FORM	-s FORM	PAST TENSE	PAST PARTICIPLE	PRESENT PARTICIPLE
be	is	was, were	been	being

 EDITING 1: PRACTICE

Edit the following passage, using the correct -s and -ed forms and irregular forms of verbs.

The waiter sat down two hot chocolates topped with whipped cream at the table where we were setting. The bell over the door rung repeatedly as a steady stream of hungry diners enter. The winter sun shined brightly through the large glass panes next to us as we drunk our chocolate. I be resting comfortably in the corner of the booth when suddenly I seen the woman at the next table as she sprung up and walk toward the door. I gave my companion a questioning look and asked, "What do you think she meaned by that?"

 C **Using auxiliary verbs**

1 **Understanding auxiliary verbs**

In some circumstances, the main verb of a sentence requires the presence of one or more **auxiliary verbs** (also known as **help-**

ing verbs). The auxiliary and the main verb together form a **verb phrase**.

```
            verb phrase
        ┌──────────────────┐
     auxiliary      main verb
     ┌──────────┐   ┌──────┐
Tyler │has  been│   │working.│
```

The most common auxiliary verbs include forms of *be*, *have*, and *do*. They help form certain tenses (see 35d–e), add emphasis, ask questions, make negative statements, and form the passive voice.

PRESENT PROGRESSIVE   The solids *are precipitating* out of the suspension.

EMPHASIS   They *do seem* to be settling rapidly.

QUESTION   *Have* the committee members *received* the proposal?

NEGATIVE STATEMENT   They *do* not *intend* to act on it tonight.

PASSIVE VOICE   The plans *were approved* by the committee.

The auxiliary verbs *can*, *could*, *may*, *might*, *must*, *shall*, *should*, *will*, and *would* are used with a main verb to express condition, intent, permission, possibility, obligation, or desire. Known as **modal auxiliaries**, they do not change form for person, tense, number, or mood. A modal auxiliary cannot stand alone as a main verb; it must appear with the base form of a verb, unless the base form can be inferred from context.

Staying in touch with friends *can become* difficult for the elderly.

Can she *dance*? Yes, she *can*.

2 Using auxiliary verbs correctly

In standard English, neither a present participle (*running*, *believing*) nor a past participle (*gone*, *forgotten*) can function alone as the main verb of a sentence. It must be preceded by a form of *be* or *have*. (See 35d–e.)

■ Sheila ^is^ running for the city council.

■ She ^has^ spoken to our club about her campaign.

In some dialects, *don't* (for *do not*) is used with a third-person singular subject to make a negative statement: *She don't want to*

ESL **PHRASAL MODALS**

In addition to one-word modal auxiliary verbs (*can*, *should*), English has **phrasal modals**, consisting of more than one word.

PHRASAL MODAL	MEANING
be able to	possibility, ability
be allowed to	permission, possibility
be going to	future action, obligation, intent
be supposed to	obligation
had better	obligation
have got to	obligation
have to	obligation
ought to	obligation
used to	habitual past action

Unlike one-word modals, most of these phrasal modals change form to show number, person, and tense. The main verbs following them do not change form.

She *has* to take the bus today.

They *have* to take the bus today.

The phrasal modals *had better*, *ought to*, and *used to* do not change form:

We *used to* spend time in the library every day.

You *used to* spend time in the library every day.

finish the assignment. However, this usage is nonstandard. Be sure to use *doesn't* (for *does not*) with third-person singular subjects.

■ He ~~don't~~ have to work tonight.
    doesn't

■ **EDITING 2: PRACTICE**

Complete the following sentences by supplying an appropriate auxiliary verb in each blank. Some sentences may have more than one possible answer. Be ready to discuss your editing choices.

In 1993, hundreds of Midwestern residents _were_ forced to fight the rising flood waters of the Missouri and Mississippi Rivers.

1. Throughout central Missouri, no one _____ seen such severe flooding in the twentieth century.

2. The major rivers, _____ broken through their levees, threatened homes, businesses, and farms, and people _____ only watch as their lives _____ uprooted.

3. But the Great Flood of '93 created dozens of human interest stories, as scores of volunteers built new levees so that others _____ not lose their homes.

4. Even residents who _____ lost their homes already _____ stuffing sandbags alongside those of their neighbors.

5. As a result, several small towns that _____ flooded completely _____ saved.

6. As the flood waters receded, Congress approved $5.7 billion in disaster relief so that flood victims _____ begin to rebuild their homes and businesses.

VERB TENSE

35 d Understanding verb tense

The **tense** of a verb helps show when its action occurred and how the action relates in time to other actions.

The three **simple tenses** place action in the present, past, or future. Notice that the future tense is expressed with the use of a modal auxiliary, *will*.

PRESENT He *looks* happy today.

PAST He *looked* a little depressed yesterday.

FUTURE He *will look* different ten years from now.

The three **perfect tenses** indicate *action completed by a specific time.* They also are divided into present, past, and future.

■ The **present perfect tense** indicates action completed in the past or a completed action still occurring.

PRESENT PERFECT   She *has looked* for the file already.

She *has looked* for it every day this week.

■ The **past perfect tense** indicates action completed before another past action took place.

PAST PERFECT   She *had looked* for the file several times before she *found* it.

■ The **future perfect tense** indicates action that will be completed at some specific time in the future.

FUTURE PERFECT   After she checks the computer room, she *will have looked* everywhere.

The three **progressive tenses** describe *continuing action in the present, past,* or *future.*

■ The **present progressive tense** describes continuous or ongoing action in the present.

PRESENT PROGRESSIVE   She *is anticipating* the holidays.

■ The **past progressive tense** describes continuous or ongoing action in the past, although not always with a specified conclusion.

PAST PROGRESSIVE   Before her father's illness, she *was anticipating* the holidays.

■ The **future progressive tense** describes continuous or ongoing action in the future, often dependent on some other action or condition.

FUTURE PROGRESSIVE   Once her father is better, she *will be looking* forward to the holidays again.

The three **perfect progressive tenses** describe *action continuing up to a specific time of completion in the present, past, or future.*

■ The **present perfect progressive tense** describes ongoing action that began in the past and continues in the present.

PRESENT PERFECT
PROGRESSIVE   He *has been looking* for a job since August.

■ The **past perfect progressive tense** describes continuing action that was completed before some other action.

PAST PERFECT   Before he found work, he *had been looking* for a job since August.

■ The **future perfect progressive tense** describes continuous action that will be completed at some future time.

FUTURE PERFECT
PROGRESSIVE   Come August, he *will have been looking* for a job for six months.

▇ EDITING 3: PRACTICE

Edit the following passage twice, changing the verbs first to the present tense and then to the future tense.

For one week at the beginning of each semester, sororities opened their houses to prospective members. The women wore their best dresses and carefully put on their makeup. Along with frozen hair went frozen smiles. Hundreds of young women moved from house to house, where they were looked over and judged. For some women this was an exciting time; for others it was humiliating and degrading.

35 e Using verb tenses in appropriate sequence

The dominant or governing verb tense in a piece of writing affects the choice of tense for nearly every verb. "If a melody in a major key is transposed into a minor key," Theodore M. Bernstein writes in *The Careful Writer*, "it is not just the first few notes that are modified; almost every phrase that follows undergoes change." In other words, all the verbs throughout a passage must relate logically to the governing tense. This logical relation is called the **sequence of tenses**.

Within a single sentence, the tense of the main clause limits what tenses make sense in a dependent clause. For example, the present-tense sentence *I think that I am lost* becomes *I thought that I was lost* in the past tense. It would make no sense to say *I thought that I am lost*. Still, many combinations of tenses are possible. (See the examples on page 540.)

SPECIAL USES OF THE PRESENT TENSE

The present tense usually indicates action happening now, at this instant: *I feel tired*. But the present tense also has some other conventional uses.

HABITUAL OR REGULAR ACTIONS

Use the present tense to describe characteristic or regularly repeated actions.

I *run* three miles every weekday morning.

FUTURE ACTIONS

Use the present tense to indicate a future action when you use other words that locate the action in the future.

She *speaks* this afternoon; he *speaks* tomorrow night.

UNIVERSAL TRUTHS

Use the present tense to state a universal truth — that is, a scientific fact, a definition, or an accepted piece of wisdom. (See 35e1.)

Newton showed that the moon's orbit *is* an effect of gravity.

Jarosite *is* a hydrous sulfate of iron and potassium.

LITERARY PRESENT

Use the present tense to discuss literary or artistic works.

Flannery O'Connor's characters *are* often sinners, rarely saints.

If you use the literary present, use it consistently.

■ In *The Tempest,* the wizard Prospero seems to control the very
heavens. As Shakespeare ~~described~~ describes him, he ~~had~~ has extraordinary
powers.

present   present
I think that you like foreign films.

present   past
I think that you misunderstood me.

present   future
I think that you also will enjoy this movie.

Changing the tense of any verb in a sentence can change the meaning of the sentence. As you edit, check to make sure that all your choices make sense.

ESL   VERBS THAT DO NOT HAVE A PROGRESSIVE FORM

Verbs that express actions, processes, or events, can usually be used in a progressive *-ing* form to indicate that something is in progress: *She is writing lyrics for the new musical.* These verbs are called **dynamic verbs**. Most verbs fit into this category.

Other verbs express attitudes, conditions, or relationships. These verbs, called **stative verbs** cannot be used in a progressive *-ing* form.

    believe
■   I ~~am believing~~ your story.

Here are some common stative verbs that are generally not used with *-ing* forms.

admire	dislike	like	see
agree	doubt	look	seem
appear	hate	love	smell
believe	have	need	sound
belong	hear	own	taste
contain	imagine	possess	think
cost	include	prefer	understand
disagree	know	remember	want

Be aware that although these verbs are usually stative, many of them can be used as dynamic verbs to express activities or processes. In these cases, use the progressive form.

He *is thinking* about his assignment.

I *am including* two papers in this envelope.

1 Sequence with habitual actions and universal truths

When a dependent clause expresses a habitual action or a universal truth, the verb in the dependent clause remains in the present tense regardless of the tense in the main clause.

He *told* me that he *works* for Teledyne.

Copernicus *showed* that the earth *revolves* around the sun.

Notice that this use of the present tense distinguishes between statements accepted as true and assertions that may or may not be true.

He *told* me he *worked* for IBM, but I *learned* later that he *works* for Teledyne.

Only the second independent clause uses the present tense works *because only it expresses a habitual action.*

2 Sequence with direct and indirect quotation

Verbs in a direct quotation are not affected by the tense of other verbs in the sentence. The words within quotation marks should be precisely the words used by the speaker.

Nancy *said*, "My dog *is* chasing a squirrel!"

However, when you express someone else's words using indirect quotation, or indirect discourse, you should paraphrase, changing person and tense to make the quotation grammatically compatible with the rest of the sentence. (See 43a5.)

■ Nancy said that her dog ~~is~~ was chasing a squirrel.

WP TIP From a paper you are currently working on, find opportunities for quoting sources directly. Using the strategies in this chapter, write sentences using direct quotation, then rewrite them using indirect quotations. In each case, assess the effectiveness of using direct or indirect quotations depending on the meaning and emphasis you wish to convey. Edit your paper as necessary.

3 Sequence with infinitives and participles

The tense of an infinitive or a participle is affected by the tense of a main verb. The base form of a verb preceded by *to* is the

present infinitive (*to know*), sometimes called simply the infinitive. Use the present infinitive to show action occurring at the same time as or later than the action of the main verb.

PRESENT
INFINITIVE

Many children like *to play* video games.

The liking *and the* playing *take place at the same time.*

The professor wants to conduct a seminar for poets.

The seminar is in the future.

ESL **TRANSFORMING DIRECT QUOTATIONS TO INDIRECT QUOTATIONS**

You must make certain changes when you transform a direct quotation into an indirect quotation.

VERBS

You must often change the tense of quoted verbs in transforming a direct quotation to an indirect quotation.

DIRECT QUOTATION	INDIRECT QUOTATION
Present tense He said, "They *are* tired."	*Past tense* He said that they *were* tired.
Past tense She said, "They *lost* their keys."	*Past perfect tense* She said that they *had lost* their keys.
Present perfect tense He said, "She *has written* a great short story."	*Past perfect tense* He said that *she had written* a great short story.

Some modal auxiliary verbs change from present tense to future or past tense.

DIRECT QUOTATION	INDIRECT QUOTATION
can	could
may	might
must, have to	had to
will	would
He said, "They *can* watch television."	He said that they *could* watch television.

The **perfect infinitive** consists of the past participle preceded by *to have: to have known.* The perfect infinitive generally indicates action that occurred before the action of the main verb.

PERFECT INFINITIVE The mayor *appears to have decided* not to seek re-election.

The deciding has already taken place.

The **present participle**, the *-ing* form of the verb, shows action taking place at the same time as the action of the main verb.

PRONOUNS

In some cases, you may have to change pronouns when you transform a direct quotation into an indirect quotation. Pay attention to meaning when considering these changes.

DIRECT QUOTATION	INDIRECT QUOTATION
She said, "*I* was wrong."	She said that *she* was wrong.
She said to me, "*You* can sing.	She said that *I* could sing.
She said to them, "*You* can sing."	She said that *they* could sing.

FOR QUESTIONS

When a direct quotation is a question, you may need to change the word order or add a word such as *if* or *whether* when transforming it into an indirect quotation.

DIRECT QUOTATION	INDIRECT QUOTATION
She asked, "*What is the answer?*"	She asked *what the answer was.*
He asked, "*Is this correct?*"	He asked *if that was correct.*

FOR COMMANDS AND REQUESTS

When a direct quotation that is a command or a request is transformed into an indirect quotation, it should be introduced with a verb such as *tell*, *order*, or *ask* and should contain an infinitive. It may also need to specify who was given the command or request.

DIRECT QUOTATION	INDIRECT QUOTATION
I *said*, "*Don't* get up."	I *told him not to* get up.
She *said*, "*Please* leave."	She *asked him to* leave.

PERFECT INFINITIVE	*Writing* feverishly, he *worked* late into the night.
	The writing *and the* working *take place at the same time.*

The **present perfect participle**—*having* plus the past participle—shows action completed before that of the main verb.

PRESENT PERFECT PARTICIPLE	*Having worked* hard on the performance, she *was pleased* by the reviews.
	She worked hard *before* being pleased *by the reviews.*

The **past participle** can show action taking place at the same time as or completed before the action of the main verb.

PAST PARTICIPLE	*Guided* by instinct, the birds *returned* as usual on March 19.
	The guiding *and the* returning *take place at the same time.*
	John F. Kennedy, who *was born* in 1917, became the nation's youngest president in 1961.
	Kennedy was born *before he became president.*

■ **EDITING 4: PRACTICE**

Edit the following passage, using appropriate verb tenses and putting them in a logical sequence. More than one edited version is possible. Be ready to explain your editing choices.

Many people thought that it will never happen, but Los Angeles finally opened a subway system. Perhaps you imagine that the name L.A. will never be associated with public transit, because it was practically synonymous with the word "automobile." When questioned, some people say that the new system, although it is modest so far, was a turning point for the city. If you have visited New York, which has more than 450 stations and hundreds of miles of tracks, you will realize that the new system is quite small. On opening day, supporters of the new system had said that they hoped to have put the city's dollars toward building stations rather than freeways.

VERB MOOD

35 **f** **Understanding verb mood**

The **mood** of a verb expresses the speaker's attitude toward or relation to the action described.

■ The **indicative mood** is used for statements of fact and opinion and for questions—for things that have happened or will happen.

He *believes* that the theory *is* valid.

When *did* she *graduate*?

■ The **imperative mood** is used to give commands, orders, or directions. It consists of the base form of the verb and usually omits the subject, which is understood to be *you*.

Open your exam book and *read* the instructions.

Mix the eggs, milk, and vanilla and *fold* them into the dry ingredients.

■ The **subjunctive mood** expresses wishes, desires, requirements, and conditions that the speaker knows not to be factual. The **present subjunctive** is simply the base form of the verb for all persons and numbers.

I asked that she *leave* early to avoid traffic.

■ The **past subjunctive** is the same as the simple past tense for all verbs except *be*, which uses *were* for both singular and plural subjects.

Even if I *had* time, I would not take up golf.

If she *were* rich, would she be different?

■ The **perfect subjunctive** uses the past perfect tense (*had* with the past participle).

Had he *caught* the bear, he would have been very sorry.

If she *had found* one, she would have been very careful with it.

35 g Using the subjunctive mood

1 In standard idiomatic expressions

The subjunctive appears in some idiomatic expressions such as *if I were you*, *as it were*, and *far be it from me*. As with other idioms, take care to word these phrases in the customary way.

Long live the Queen!

If he were to arrive on time, then all would go smoothly.

2 After *as if*, *as though*, or *if*

In clauses beginning with *as if* and *as though*, which always specify conditions that are not factual, use the past or perfect subjunctive.

He screamed as though the house ~~was~~ were on fire.

When a dependent clause beginning with *if* describes a condition contrary to fact, use the past or perfect subjunctive.

If only it ~~was~~ were sunny, he would be happy.

Note: When the *if* clause expresses an actual condition, the subjunctive is not needed.

If it was sunny, he was happy.

To suggest that the *if* clause expresses something uncertain, rather than untrue, use the indicative rather than the subjunctive.

If she ~~were~~ was awake, she should have heard the doorbell.

3 With *might*, *could*, *should*, and *would*

When one of the modal auxiliaries that express conditionality—*might*, *could*, *should*, *would*—is used without another auxiliary in an independent clause, the verb in the dependent clause can be either a subjunctive verb—*I would go if they invited me*—or an indicative verb using another conditional modal auxiliary—*I would go if they would invite me*. However, if the dependent clause verb is a form of *be*, use the subjunctive.

■ I would go if there ~~would be~~ a good reason.
  (were)

With *might have, could have, should have,* or *would have* (the conditional perfect) in the independent clause, use the perfect subjunctive, not another conditional modal auxiliary, in the dependent clause.

■ The president could have won if he ~~would have~~ fought harder.
  (had)

4 To express a wish, a requirement, or a request

Use the past or perfect subjunctive in dependent clauses expressing wishes, which are usually contrary to fact.

■ I wished there ~~was~~ some way to help them.
  (had been)

Dependent clauses following verbs stating requirements—such as *demand, insist, require, recommend, request, suggest, specify,* and *ask*—should use the present subjunctive.

■ Courtesy requires that he ~~dresses~~ formally.
  (dress)

■ Barbara insisted that she ~~goes~~ alone.
  (go)

The subjunctive makes a request sound a little more formal, and therefore perhaps a little more polite, than the indicative or the imperative.

SUBJUNCTIVE   We ask that you *be* seated.

INDICATIVE   We ask you *to be* seated.

IMPERATIVE   *Be* seated.

■ EDITING 5: PRACTICE

Edit the following passage, using subjunctive verb forms wherever appropriate.

I was driving on the expressway when the earthquake occurred. The whole car began to shake, as if the engine was about to stall. But quickly I realized what was happening. The drivers around me panicked, their faces contorted in fear. They swerved their cars, as though switching lanes save them. If only I have stayed home! If I was home, I thought, I could find shelter in the basement. In seconds, the cars ahead of me collided, blocking all traffic. The situation demanded that I acted quickly. I slammed on the brakes. Fortunately, I came to a stop just before hitting the car in front of me.

■ EDITING 6: PRACTICE

Edit the following passage, using the correct form, tense, and mood of each verb. More than one edited version is possible. Be ready to explain your editing choices.

Until the early years of this century, the Constitution did not extend to women the right to vote. Suffragists wished that every woman citizen was able to vote and they strived to amend the Constitution so that no state can deny any citizen the right to vote on account of sex. For this to happen, the Constitution required that three-quarters of the states were in favor of the amendment. Many of the arguments against women's suffrage strike us as absurd now. Some people argued that women do not understand the business world; others said that the cost of elections will go up. If women would get the vote, some worried, next they would want to hold office. Some felt that a woman is represented by her husband and that when he voted it was as though she was voting. Some also feared that a vote for women will be a step toward feminism, which many people consider a radical and dangerous idea.

■ EDITING 7: APPLICATION

Examine your recent writing for misused verb forms, tenses, and moods. Is there one kind of verb error that you make most often? If so, think about how best to identify your verb errors when you edit your work. Practice editing sentences with incorrect verbs.

36   Making Subjects and Verbs Agree

Verbs and their subjects must agree, or correspond, in person and in number. A singular subject requires a singular verb; a plural subject requires a plural verb. The first-person pronoun *I* requires a different verbal form than a third-person subject. Such **agreement**, especially in a long sentence like this one in which many words separate the subject from the main verb, helps readers interpret relations between the parts of the sentence. After seeing a singular subject, such as *agreement* in the previous sentence, readers look for a singular verb, in this case *helps*, as the main verb of the sentence.

To solve agreement problems, first identify the subject. (See 67a.) Next, determine whether the subject is singular or plural. Then use the appropriate verb form.

Matters of agreement often come down to a single letter: *s*. Most English nouns form plurals by adding *-s* or *-es*.

SINGULAR	PLURAL
house	houses
rock	rocks
box	boxes

Most present-tense, third-person singular verbs end in *-s* or *-es*.

$$\left.\begin{matrix} I \\ you \\ we \\ they \end{matrix}\right\} \text{think} \qquad \left.\begin{matrix} he \\ she \\ it \end{matrix}\right\} \text{thinks}$$

A simple rule can guide you through many agreement problems: If the subject ends in *-s* or *-es* (is plural), the verb probably shouldn't; if the verb ends in *-s* or *-es* (is singular), the subject probably shouldn't.

The *road winds* through the mountains.

The *roads wind* through the mountains.

Irregular plurals such as *children* and *men* provide an exception to this rule. These plural nouns still require a verb without an *-s* or *-es: The children walk home.* Another exception is nouns that end in *-s* but are singular: *Politics is a dirty business.*

EDITING FOR SUBJECT–VERB AGREEMENT

To solve problems of agreement, first identify the subject. Next, determine whether it is singular or plural. Then use the corresponding verb form. Remember the following tips as you edit.

- Ignore words between the subject and the verb.
- Identify the subject even when it follows the verb.
- Identify the subject of a linking verb.
- Determine whether subjects joined by *and* are singular or plural.
- Determine whether subjects joined by *or* or *nor* are singular or plural.
- Determine whether collective nouns are singular or plural.
- Determine whether indefinite pronouns such as *everything* and *some* are singular or plural.
- Determine whether relative pronouns such as *who, which,* and *that* are singular or plural.
- Determine whether subjects that refer to amounts are singular or plural.
- Use singular verbs with noun phrases and noun clauses.
- Use singular verbs with titles and with words used as words.
- Identify singular subjects that end in *-s.*
- Use plural verbs with troublesome plurals.

36 **a** **Ignoring words between subject and verb**

When a verb follows its subject immediately, it is usually easy to tell whether the verb should be singular or plural. When a word or words come between the subject and the verb, however, confusion can arise. Restating the sentence in its simplest form—just subject and verb—can help clarify your choice.

People interested in helping reelect an incumbent representative typically [*volunteer/volunteers*] time as well as money.

Finding the subject when it follows the verb 551

> *Reduced to subject and verb, the sentence reads* People volunteer*;*
> *both subject and verb are clearly plural.*

Often, the intervening words are **prepositional phrases**, groups of words introduced by a preposition such as *of* or *with*.

> The bowl of apples [is/are] very tempting.

> *Is the subject of the verb the singular* bowl *or the plural* apples*? Here,*
> of apples *is a prepositional phrase.* Bowl *clearly is the subject, so the*
> *verb should be singular:* The *bowl* of apples *is* very tempting.

Intervening phrases that begin with such words as *including, as well as, along with, together with,* and *in addition to* are not part of a compound subject. (See 36d.) You should ignore them in making decisions about subject–verb agreement. Try to think of them as parenthetical asides.

■ The president, along with many members of his party, ~~support~~ ^supports^

stringent reforms.

36 **b** **Finding the subject when it follows the verb**

In some sentences the subject follows the verb.

> Underneath the freeway overpasses [*huddle/huddles*] a ramshackle collection of cardboard shelters.

Mentally restoring normal word order to the sentence can help you find the subject.

> A ramshackle *collection* of cardboard shelters *huddles* underneath the freeway overpasses.

> *The subject is* collection, *which is singular, so* huddles *is correct.*

In a question, part of the verb almost always precedes the subject. As you edit, look for the subject after the verb, and make sure the verb agrees with it.

> *Are* those *seats* next to you empty?

> With so many chores, is *Juan* able to finish on time?

Expletives are words such as *it*, *here*, and *there* that begin a sentence with inverted word order. *Here* and *there* are never subjects, so look for the subject elsewhere in the sentence.

There *are* a million *stories* in the Naked City.

There *is* a possibility that Agassi will beat Sampras.

However, when *it* is used in an expletive construction, it is considered the grammatical subject of the sentence. Because *it* is singular, it is always followed by a singular verb.

It is administrators who want this change, not students.

WP TIP On a passage from a paper you are currently working on, underline or italicize the subjects of your verbs. Place all verbs in boldface. Print out a hard copy. Exchange with a classmate. Together, edit for subject–verb agreement and discuss.

36 **c** **Creating agreement with linking verbs**

Linking verbs include *be*, *become*, and *seem* and the sensory verbs *appear*, *look*, *feel*, *taste*, *smell*, and *sound*. They link the subject of a sentence to an element, called a **subject complement**, that renames or identifies the subject. Think of a linking verb as an equal sign between two equivalent terms.

Angela is captain.	Angela = captain
That looks difficult.	that = difficult

The term to the left of the equal sign is the subject; the term on the right of the equal sign is the **subject complement**.

      subject   subject complement
My paper's title is "Eliot's Rite of Spring."

      subject   subject complement
"Eliot's Rite of Spring" is my paper's title.

Note that verbs describing sensations are linking verbs only when they are used to describe the subject:

Oprah *looks* happy.	Oprah = happy
The Thanksgiving turkey *smelled* delicious.	turkey = delicious

When sensory verbs describe an action, however, they are not considered linking verbs.

Oprah *looks* out the window.

Our cat *smelled* the turkey.

The verb in such a sentence should always agree with the subject, not necessarily with the complement.

■ **The thing that keeps him going ~~are~~ is his hobbies.**

Thing *is the subject;* hobbies *is the complement.*

EDITING 1: PRACTICE

Edit the following passage to make verbs agree with their subjects. Take special care in identifying the subject.

Throughout its history, the National Aeronautics and Space Administration (NASA) have been at the center of both controversy and praise. The exploration of the solar system, along with the research conducted by space shuttle crews, are hailed by pundits as significant human endeavors. The costs of these achievements, though, often becomes the subjects of newspaper headlines. Government officials and citizens at large sometimes question the value of spending billions of dollars on space exploration. Currently, there are many who think that federal government allocate too much money to NASA. Supporters, however, who credit the agency for spearheading developments in the aeronautics industry, points out that NASA's budget is the smallest of all major governmental agencies. Moreover, they say that the agency generate more revenue nationwide than it consume because of the new industries-built space exploration technology. Aeronautics, personal computers, telecommunications, and even weather forecasting depends on this technology, and these industries employ millions of Americans. Behind some of the most significant technological advances in American society are the team of researchers, engineers, and scientists working for NASA. Without them and the technology they have developed over the years, most aircraft today would not exist.

36 d Making verbs agree with subjects joined by *and*

When the conjunction *and* links two or more parts of a subject, it creates a **compound subject**. (Also see 34e.) Such a subject is almost always considered plural and thus requires a plural verb.

554 Making subjects and verbs agree

Peter and Patrick *appear* in the first act as inmates.

This rule has several exceptions. When the two elements joined by *and* are regarded as a single entity, the subject is considered singular and requires a singular verb.

■ Red beans and rice ~~are~~ *is* my favorite dish.

If all parts of a compound subject refer to the same person or thing, a singular verb is appropriate.

■ My friend, my partner, and my mentor ~~have~~ *has* brought wisdom and courage to this firm.

The writer is referring to one person who is all three things to her.

When singular elements joined by *and* are preceded by *each* or *every*, the resulting structure is singular.

■ Each river, brook, and stream in the county ~~have~~ *has* suffered pollution.

However, when *each* comes after a **compound subject** rather than before it, the subject is plural.

■ Government and industry each ~~deserves~~ *deserve* credit for the success of cleanup efforts.

36 e Making verbs agree with subjects joined by *or* and *nor*

The conjunctions *or, nor, either . . . or, not only . . . but also,* and *neither . . . nor* also create compound subjects by linking two or more elements. When one element of the subject is singular and another is plural, convention dictates that the verb agree with the part of the subject closer to it.

Neither the senator nor the witnesses *are* ready for the hearing.

Neither the witnesses nor the senator *is* ready for the hearing.

If a singular verb sounds awkward, try rearranging the subject to put the plural part closer to the verb.

■ ~~Two crabs or one~~ lobster ~~makes~~ an excellent dinner.
  One *or two crabs make*

■ **EDITING 2: PRACTICE**

Edit the following sentences to make verbs agree with their compound subjects. Circle the number of any sentence that is correct.

Neither the police officers nor the detectives ~~knows~~ how the intruder entered or left the house.
Know

1. Each window and door are locked securely.

2. In addition, the outside security system and inside motion sensors shows nothing unusual last night.

3. Nonetheless both the house and the safe was broken into, and all the money taken.

4. On the living room sofa, the banker and his wife sits weeping, lamenting their loss.

5. Not only their savings bonds but also their expensive jewelry was gone forever.

6. Police and specially trained dogs scours the grounds of the estate for clues, but not a single footprint or trace of evidence can be found.

7. Finally, the detectives and the police discover and nab the perpetrator, who were hiding in a broom closet.

36 **f** **Making verbs agree with collective nouns**

Collective nouns refer to groups of people or things: *couple, flock, crowd, herd, committee.* They can cause confusion because the words themselves have a singular form even though they refer to several individuals. Whether a collective noun takes a singular or plural verb depends on whether the members of the group are acting as individuals or as one unit. If the members of a group act individually, use a plural verb.

The jury *have* returned to their homes.

If such a construction sounds awkward to you, try replacing the subject with one that is clearly plural.

The members of the jury *have* returned to their homes.

If an action is taken by an entire group together as a unit, use a singular verb.

The crowd *roars* with delight.

The collective noun *the number* refers to a group as a single unit, so it needs a singular verb.

The number of tourists *has* declined in recent years.

However, the expression *a number* means "several" or "more than one," so it needs a plural verb.

A number of visitors *have* complimented the park management on the new trail markers.

36 **g** **Making verbs agree with indefinite pronouns**

Whether a pronoun is singular or plural usually depends on whether the word or words it refers to are singular or plural. In the sentence *My uncle enjoys fishing, and he often goes on fishing trips,* the pronoun *he* is singular (and takes a singular verb, *goes*) because it refers to a singular noun, *uncle.*

However, an **indefinite pronoun**, such as *someone, some, few, everyone, each,* or *one,* often does not refer to a specific person or thing. Most indefinite pronouns are either always singular or always plural.

SINGULAR Everybody *has* heard that old joke already.

PLURAL Luckily, few of the passengers *were* injured.

Although pronouns such as *everybody* and *someone* are singular, many people in everyday speech treat them as if they were plural in order to avoid sexist language: *Everybody has their mind*

Making verbs agree with indefinite pronouns 557

ESL **VERB AGREEMENT WITH NONCOUNT NOUNS**

Count nouns name persons, places, or things that can be counted: *one apple, two oranges.* **Noncount nouns** refer to things that can't be quantified, such as abstract concepts, emotions, and qualities.

MASS NOUNS	ABSTRACT CONCEPTS	EMOTIONS	QUALITIES
equipment	behavior	anger	confidence
furniture	education	happiness	honesty
homework	health	love	integrity
money	knowledge	surprise	sincerity

Noncount nouns are usually used only in the singular and therefore take singular verbs. In English these words usually have no plural form.

■ Good ~~equipments make~~ the job easier. *(equipment makes)*

■ ~~These informations~~ about subject–verb agreement ~~are~~ intended to *(This information ... is)*

help you with your editing.

For information on using articles (*a, an, the*) with nouns, see box in 28a.

---

made up. In formal writing, this usage is considered incorrect. (See 32c for alternatives in formal writing.)

Some, any, all, more, most, what, and *none* can be either singular or plural depending on what they mean. If the pronoun renames a person or thing mentioned elsewhere (its antecedent), the number of that noun determines the number of the pronoun.

Of the *time* that remained, more *was* spent in arguing than in making decisions.

Of the *hours* that remained, more *were* spent in arguing than in making decisions.

As you edit, try mentally recasting the sentence without the indefinite pronoun, using *it* or *they* if necessary to determine whether the pronoun is singular or plural.

Some of the children [*is/are*] eager to leave.

They are eager to leave.

All is plural when it means the total number in a group; it is singular when it means "everything" or "the only thing."

All of us *are* preparing for the examination.

All I have *is* twenty dollars.

None standing alone is always singular: *None was injured.* Followed by a prepositional phrase, *none* can be singular or plural, depending on the phrase.

None of the herd *was* missing.

None of the players *were* gone.

Be aware that some experts argue that because *none* means "not one" or "no one," only the singular is strictly correct: *None of the players was gone.*

✔ COMMON INDEFINITE PRONOUNS

ALWAYS SINGULAR

someone	anyone	no one	everyone	either
somebody	anybody	nobody	everybody	neither
something	anything	nothing	everything	each
			much	one

EITHER SINGULAR OR PLURAL

some	any	none	all	more
			most	what

ALWAYS PLURAL

few	both	several	many

ESL   **VERB AGREEMENT WITH QUANTIFIERS**

1. *Few* and *a few*

Few means "not many" or "not enough." *A few* means "some," "several," or "a small number." *Few* and *a few* take plural verbs.

> Many law students are taking the bar exam today. *A few* have taken it in other states.

> *Few* have failed it more than once.

2. *Little* and *a little*

Little means "not much" or "not enough." *A little* means "some" or "a small amount." *Little* and *a little* take singular verbs.

> Doctors have done much research on heart disease. However, *little* has been done with women as subjects.

> Be careful pouring that hot sesame oil. *A little* goes a long way.

3. *Most of the* and *most*

Most of the (or *most of*) means "the majority of": it takes a plural verb when it is followed by a plural noun or pronoun, and a singular verb when it is followed by a noncount noun or a singular pronoun. *Most* is an adjective or a pronoun; it is singular or plural depending on the noun or pronoun it modifies or refers to.

PLURAL   *Most of the dogs* in the neighborhood *bark* in the morning.

PLURAL   *Most dogs are* tied while their owners are at work. [Adjective *most* modifying plural *dogs*]

SINGULAR   *Most of the violence* on TV *is* unnecessary.

SINGULAR   *Most is* treated as harmless by TV producers. [Pronoun *most* referring to *most of the violence*]

WP TIP   When searching for subject–verb agreement, separate sentences that require editing away from the rest of your text. Next use the return key to separate parts of the sentences that affect verb choices so that you can see your task clearly. Edit for agreement, then delete all the returns and reunite the sentence back into your passage.

36	h	Making verbs agree with *who*, *which*, and *that*

To decide whether a verb following the **relative pronouns** *who*, *which*, or *that* should be singular or plural, find the word for which the pronoun stands (its antecedent).

- The dean and the department head, who ~~is~~ ^{are} working on the search committee, will meet with the candidates.

  If the dean and the department head *are both on the committee, the verb should be plural.*

- A bale of shingles that ~~slip~~ ^{slips} off the roof could hurt someone.

  That *refers to bale, so* slips *is singular.*

Relative pronouns can be troublesome when they follow the construction *one of the or the only one of the*. If the relative pronoun refers to *one*, it is singular.

The only *one* of the experiments that *works* is mine.

If the relative pronoun refers to whatever comes after *one of the* or *the only one of the*, it is plural.

One of the areas that *were* cut most heavily is social spending.

▪ EDITING 3: PRACTICE

Edit the following sentences to make verbs agree with collective noun subjects, indefinite pronoun subjects, and relative pronoun subjects. Circle the number of any sentence that is correct.

The review of the photographs, which ~~are~~ ^{is} very enthusiastic, might attract more visitors to the museum.

1. The pictures in the exhibit, which are open every night, feature children from Third World countries.

2. Many of the children photographed in Mexico was casualties of the earthquake.

3. Most people think that the look of sadness on their faces are most moving.

4. The best of the photographers, who spend three months every year in Southeast Asia, has won numerous awards.

5. The museum committee has a variety of opinions on the exhibit.

6. Adding photography exhibits to the museum was one of many good ideas of the curator, who is herself a photographer.

7. Much of her energy are spent in finding good exhibits and soliciting contributions from patrons.

36 i Making verbs agree with subjects that refer to amounts

Words that describe amounts of time, money, distance, measurement, or percentage can take singular or plural verbs. As with collective nouns, the number depends on whether the subject is considered as a group of individuals (plural) or as a single unit or sum (singular).

Four hours *have* passed since we saw each other last.

The hours pass one at a time, individually.

Fifteen minutes *is* too long to keep the boss waiting.

The minutes here are a block of time, a unit.

36 j Using noun phrases and noun clauses

Noun phrases and **noun clauses** are groups of related words that function as a subject, object, or complement in a sentence. A **noun phrase** often lacks a subject or a predicate or both; a **noun clause** has both a subject and a predicate. All noun phrases and noun clauses are singular.

NOUN PHRASE   *Planning to write* is easy; actually writing is harder.

NOUN CLAUSE   *That he would not listen to us* was surprising.

36 k Using singular verbs with titles and with words used as words

Titles of books, plays, and movies are treated as singular even if they are plural in form. The name of a company is also singular.

Happy Days was a popular TV series.

General Motors *is* an important employer in Michigan.

In discussing a word itself, use a singular verb even if the word is plural.

Hyenas was what my father lovingly called us children.

36 l Recognizing singular subjects that end in -s

Although words such as *statistics, politics, economics, athletics, acoustics,* and *aesthetics* seem to be plural because they end in -s, they take singular verbs when used in a general sense to mean a field of study, a body of ideas, or a profession. However, some of these words can be plural when referring to specific instances, activities, or characteristics.

Economics *is* sometimes called "the dismal science."

The economics of the project *make* no sense.

Words that refer to an ailment such as AIDS or measles are usually singular. So is the word *news.*

Measles *is* spreading because of a lapse in vaccinations.

No news *is* good news.

36 m Recognizing troublesome plurals

Words such as *media* and *data* look like singular words in English, but they are Latin plurals and should take plural verbs. The corresponding singular forms are *medium* and *datum.* Look out, too, for *curriculum* and *curricula, criterion* and *criteria, phenomenon* and *phenomena.* The use of *data* as singular is gaining ground, especially in reference to computers, but you should avoid it in writing.

■ The media ~~loves~~ a political scandal.
                 love

■ The experimental data ~~supports~~ the theory you advanced.
                         support

Dictionaries list the preferred plural and singular forms of these and other words of foreign origin; some, like *stadium*, have lost their original plural forms completely.

Some nouns, such as *pants, sunglasses, binoculars*, and *scissors*, refer to single objects but take plural verbs.

The scissors *are* no longer sharp.

When the construction *pair of* is used, the verb is singular.

This pair of scissors *is* sharper.

ESL **SOME NOUNS THAT TAKE PLURAL VERBS**

Some collective nouns are derived from adjectives and refer to a group of people: *the wealthy, the homeless, the elderly*. These nouns are considered plural and take plural verbs.

The young often *ignore* the advice of their elders.

The noun *people* is always plural. To indicate one, use *person*.

People *are* wondering who will be the next governor.

That person *is* wondering when to register to vote.

The noun *police* is always plural. It never refers to only one person. Likewise, *the police* is always plural. In English, the article *a* is never used before *police*. To indicate one, use *police officer*.

Police *have* been stationed in front of the house all afternoon.

A police officer *is* always on duty inside the courthouse.

EDITING 4: PRACTICE

Edit the following sentences by making verbs agree with their noun phrase or noun clause subjects, subjects that are titles or words used as words, or troublesome singular or plural subjects. Circle the number of any sentence that is correct.

Studying for classes ~~are~~ is easier when I enjoy the reading assignments.

1. Although a course in statistics often baffle college students, studying aesthetics is also challenging, particularly in courses that compare the arts.
2. Sometimes one artistic medium, like painting and sculpture, tell us something new about a novel, for instance.
3. This semester we read *Pride and Prejudice*, which were written by Jane Austen, but we also examined paintings of country houses as well.
4. Comparing the novel with the paintings provides a clearer picture of Austen's descriptions.
5. Preparing for exams for my interarts classes sometimes seem difficult because we cover a lot of material.

EDITING 5: PRACTICE

Edit the following passage to make verbs agree with their subjects. More than one edited version is possible. Be ready to explain your editing choices.

The county employees and volunteers who run the prison education program focuses on illiteracy. Statistics shows that among prison inmates nationwide, some 60 percent is illiterate, and neither substance abuse programs nor vocational training seem as effective as literacy education in limiting the return of repeat offenders. The core of the program, therefore, are reading and writing skills. Each employee and volunteer go through a three-week training program in literacy education. If they can demonstrate sufficiently high reading levels, inmates may also train to become tutors; by doing so, most earns points toward early probation. Tutoring for all participants takes place not only one-on-one but also in groups, and there is within each group inmates at various levels of reading proficiency. Even inmates who have never achieved any academic success learns without feeling intimidated. Current data shows a high rate of success.

EDITING 6: APPLICATION

Examine a paper you are working on to find any verbs that do not agree with their subjects. What kinds of mistakes did you make? Do you make one kind of mistake more than others? If so, why do you think you do?

Adjectives and adverbs *modify* other words—that is, they describe, identify, or limit the meanings of other words. **Modifiers** can enrich description, changing a simple sentence like *The explorers were lost* into an expressive one like *The polar explorers were thoroughly, hopelessly, horribly lost.* To be effective, modifiers must be used carefully. Choose carefully between adjectives and adverbs and form negatives, comparatives, and superlatives according to convention.

Although adjectives and adverbs are the most familiar types of modifiers, there are others: articles (*a, an, the*), possessives (*Michael's, my*), phrases (*used-car* buyer), and clauses (knife *that he used*). Even nouns can be used as modifiers (*music* critic, *tool* belt). This chapter focuses on choosing the correct forms for adjectives and adverbs; the placement of modifiers within a sentence is covered in Chapter 38.

37 a Choosing adjectives or adverbs

Adjectives modify nouns and pronouns.

noun   **noun**

Many *deciduous* trees in the *mid-Atlantic* states are subject to

noun

attack by *voracious* insects.

pronoun

They are especially *vulnerable* during a drought.

Adverbs modify verbs, adjectives, other adverbs, and sometimes whole clauses.

566 **Using adjectives and adverbs**

verb

Drought *rapidly* weakens the trees' natural defenses, sometimes

adjective

with *truly* devastating consequences.

clause

Obviously, fire presents another danger to a drought-weakened

forest.

Many adjectives and adverbs are formed by adding **suffixes**, or endings, to other words. (See 31c.) Adjectives are often formed by adding *-able, -ful, -ish,* and many other endings to nouns and verbs: *acceptable, beautiful, foolish.* Many adverbs are formed by adding *-ly* to an adjective: *nearly, amazingly, brilliantly.*

In speaking, some people substitute adjectives for adverbs: *It worked real well* rather than *It worked really well.* If this is a speech habit of yours, edit your writing carefully to use only adverbs to modify verbs, adjectives, or other adverbs. Use adjectives only to modify nouns and pronouns.

badly
We played ~~bad~~ in the first inning.
∧

An *-ly* suffix does not always mean that a word is an adverb: *brotherly, friendly,* and *lovely,* for example, are adjectives. Also, many adverbs do not end in *-ly: often, always, later.* Still other words can be used as either adjectives or adverbs, even though

---

✔ **CHOOSING THE RIGHT MODIFIER**

As you edit, examine your adjectives and adverbs carefully and make sure to do the following:

■ Choose an adjective or adverb according to what it modifies.
■ Use adjectives after linking verbs.
■ Choose correctly between commonly confused modifiers.
■ Avoid double negatives.
■ Use comparatives and superlatives correctly.

some of these also have *-ly* adverb forms. *Slow* can be an adjective or an adverb; *slowly* is always an adverb. If you are in doubt about the correct form, consult a dictionary. (Also see 37c.)

WP TIP Have your computer check for adverb usage by searching for all words ending in *-ly* in a paper you are currently working on. In each instance, consider whether you need an adverb or an adjective. Edit as necessary, but be careful because some words ending in *-ly* are adjectives. The computer cannot recognize the difference between adverbs and adjectives.

■ **EDITING 1: PRACTICE**

Edit the following sentences, using adjectives and adverbs in the proper places.

When I first started running ~~competitive,~~ I had all kinds of ^competitively physical ^physically problems.

1. My track coach told me that breathing too heavy was causing all my painfully cramps.

2. He suggested that I take short, evenly breaths to help me run smooth.

3. But once I perfected my breathing, my feet began to hurt real bad.

4. I found out, to my greatly surprise, that I was pigeon-toed, and that my shoes did not fit correct.

5. After a lot of looking and carefully thinking, I bought a pair of special made track shoes.

6. Now I can dedicate myself whole-hearted to the mile relay.

37 b Using adjectives after linking verbs

Confusion about whether to use an adjective or an adverb arises occasionally with **linking verbs**, such as *be, become, feel, seem, appear, look, smell, taste,* and *sound.* A modifier after a linking verb usually modifies the subject of the verb, not the verb itself, so the modifier should be an adjective, not an adverb.

■ I felt ~~badly~~ about not being able to help.
^bad

Some of these verbs can also express action, in which case they do not function as linking verbs.

LINKING VERB The ghost of Hamlet's father *appears* anxious.

Anxious *is an adjective modifying the noun* ghost.

ACTION VERB The ghost of Hamlet's father *appears* suddenly.

Suddenly *is an adverb modifying the verb* appears.

■ EDITING 2: PRACTICE

Edit the following sentences, using adjectives and adverbs correctly after link-ing verbs. Circle the number of any sentence that is correct.

I remember one time in college when my roommate, Shelly, was
very ~~siekly.~~ *sick*
    ∧

1. One day, when she first woke up, she seemed deliriously.
2. She started talking, but her voice sounded harshly and raspy.
3. I walked across the room and saw that she was pale and that her fore-head was splotchy.
4. I put my hand on it and, sure enough, her brow felt coldly and clammy.
5. Fortunately, one of our neighbors was a doctor, and she came over to see us.
6. After she gave her some antibiotics, Shelly was able to sleep and, a few days later, she felt strongly and healthy again.

37 c Choosing between commonly confused modifiers

Several pairs of modifiers frequently cause problems, either because they are commonly confused in everyday speech or be-cause their meanings are closely related.

WP TIP If you tend to misuse any of the following modifier, you can use your computer's search function to locate each one and check it.

Bad and badly

In standard English, *bad* is always an adjective; *badly* always an adverb. Although they are commonly interchanged in speech, you should be sure to use them correctly in writing, especially after linking verbs.

■ She felt ~~badly~~ about missing your party.
  ^*bad*

■ They did ~~bad~~ on the test.
  ^*badly*

Good and *well*

Good and *well* also are often confused in conversation, partly because they share the same comparative and superlative forms: *good, better, best; well, better, best.* (See 37e.) *Good* is always an adjective. *Well* can be either an adjective or an adverb. As an adjective, *well* means "healthy," the opposite of *ill.* As an adverb, *well* means, among other things, "satisfactorily" or "skillfully." Be careful not to use *good* as an adverb or *well* as an adjective meaning "satisfactory."

■ She read ~~good~~ enough to get the part.
  ^*well*

■ My hat looked ~~well~~ on my mother.
  ^*good*

Real and *really*

Real and *really* have related meanings, but *real* is properly used as an adjective meaning "genuine, true, not illusory": *They wondered whether the ghost was real. Really* is an adverb meaning "truly" or "very." Even if you sometimes use *real* as an adverb in speech, be careful as you edit to use *really* to modify adjectives and adverbs.

■ He talks ~~real~~ fast.
  ^*really*

Less and *fewer*

Use *less* to describe something considered as a whole unit: *less hope, less misery, less money.* Use *fewer* for quantities that can be counted: *fewer dreams, fewer problems, fewer dollars.*

■ The house would lose less heat if ~~less~~ windows were open.
  ^*fewer*

WP TIP Have your computer locate each appearance of the adjective/adverb combinations *bad/badly, good/well, less/fewer.* Check your usage in each instance and edit as necessary.

37 d **Avoiding double negatives**

In English, one negative modifier (*no, not, never, none*) is sufficient to change the meaning of a sentence. Although double negatives are common in some dialects, particularly when one of the negatives is a contraction, be sure in editing to make negative statements with only one negative modifier.

- He didn't want ~~no~~ ^any^ dinner.
- He ~~didn't have~~ ^had^ no money.

Using *no* or *not* with an adverb such as *hardly*, *barely*, and *scarcely* creates a double negative.

- She ~~didn't~~ hardly ~~have~~ ^had^ time to catch her breath.

Occasions do arise when you need a double negative to make a *positive* statement.

It was *not* that he had *no* money; he did not want to spend it.

He had money.

She did *not* believe that *nothing* could be done.

She believed something could be done.

EDITING 3: PRACTICE

Edit the following passage, using the correct form of any commonly confused modifiers and correcting any double negatives.

Alan whispered to me one day in class that he was real hungry. I told him that I didn't have no food with me. He started mumbling something about how he couldn't be expected to do good on a chemistry exam when his stomach felt so badly. I couldn't see hardly no reason for him to complain so much. Everybody knew that he always brought well lunches to school with him. In fact, the more I thought about it, the more I realized that nobody had less reasons to complain about being hungry than Alan. What made me even angrier, though, was that now he had made me want a snack.

Using comparatives and superlatives 571

ESL **USING NEGATIVES:** *NOT* VS. *NO*

Use *not* rather than *no* in the following situations:

■ With forms of *any* or with number modifiers

There are *not any* places to sit in the theater.

There is *not one* place to sit in the theater.

■ To negate *everybody* and *everyone*

Not everyone would have dealt with that problem as well as you did.

■ To make a verb phrase negative

I *do not agree* with the author's opinion.

To emphasize negation, you can use *no* in front of a noun instead of *not* in a verb phrase.

NEGATIVE   I do *not* see *any* reason to assume he is lying.

EMPHATIC   I see *no* reason to assume he is lying.
NEGATIVE

---

37 **e** **Using comparatives and superlatives**

The basic or **positive form** of an adjective or adverb describes a quality or property: *large, delicious, late, graciously.* The **comparative form**, which usually ends in *-er* or is preceded by *more*, compares two people or things.

She arrived *later* than I did but was greeted *more graciously.*

The **superlative form**, usually ending in *-est* or preceded by *most*, makes a comparison among three or more people or things.

Of all their guests, she always arrived *latest* and was greeted *most graciously.*

Your choice of a comparative or a superlative modifier gives readers an important clue about the nature of the comparison.

Of the brothers, Joe was the *stronger* athlete.

ESL **ARTICLES WITH COMPARATIVES AND SUPERLATIVES**

When a comparative adjective (*warmer, easier*) is used by itself, do not use an article (*a, an,* or *the*).

■ This house is ~~the~~ *larger* than the other one.

DEFINITE ARTICLE *THE*

Use *the* when a comparative or superlative adjective is followed by a specific noun or pronoun renaming a specific noun.

This house is *the larger* one.

This house is *the largest* one.

The use of *the* is optional when the comparative or superlative adjective is used without a noun but the noun is implied.

Of the two houses, which one is *the larger*? [Implied: *the larger house.*]

Of the two houses, which one is *larger*?

INDEFINITE ARTICLES *A/AN*

Use *a* or *an* with comparative adjectives modifying a noun that is not specific.

I've never seen a *larger* grapefruit.

The grapefruit mentioned is any grapefruit, not a specific grapefruit.

Use *a* or *an* with superlative adjectives only if the superlative has the meaning "very."

That was *a most refreshing* glass of grapefruit juice.

The meaning is "very refreshing."

For more information about article usage, see Using Articles with Nouns in 28a.

Of the brothers, Joe was the *strongest* athlete.

The first sentence says that there are only two brothers, while the second indicates that there are at least three brothers.

1 Forming regular comparatives and superlatives

Most one-syllable adjectives and adverbs add *-er* and *-est* to form comparatives and superlatives: *smarter, closest.* There are exceptions such as *fun, more fun,* not *funner.* Adjectives of three or more syllables, adjectives ending in *-ful,* adverbs of two or more syllables, and most adverbs ending in *-ly* generally use *more* and *most: more impressive, most hopeful, most often, most sharply.* With many two-syllable adjectives, the choice is yours (*happiest, most happy; luckiest, most lucky*), although the *-er* and *-est* endings are more common.

Negative comparisons are formed using *less* for comparatives and *least* for superlatives: *less often, least hopeful.*

2 Avoiding double comparatives and superlatives

Use either *-er* or *more,* not both. Use either *-est* or *most,* not both.

■ Eating made him feel ~~more~~ better.

3 Forming irregular comparatives and superlatives

A few adjectives and adverbs form comparatives and superlatives in irregular ways. Take care to memorize them, especially if English is not your first language.

■ Paul did ~~gooder~~ better on the test than I did.
        ∧

■ She said she felt ~~weller~~ better today.
        ∧

4 Using only the positive form of absolute modifiers

Some modifiers, called **absolutes**, do not logically form comparatives or superlatives because their meaning suggests comparison is inappropriate. Words such as *perfect, unique, equal, essential, final, total,* and *absolute* should not be intensified. As

> ✔ **IRREGULAR ADJECTIVES AND ADVERBS**
>
> | POSITIVE | COMPARATIVE | SUPERLATIVE |
> |----------|-------------|-------------|
> | good | better | best |
> | well | better | best |
> | bad | worse | worst |
> | badly | worse | worst |
> | ill | worse | worst |
> | many | more | most |
> | much | more | most |
> | some | more | most |
> | little* | less | least |
>
> *Little in the sense of "not much" is irregular. Little in the sense of "small" is regular: *She wanted a little dog, but mine is littler than hers, and my cousin's is littlest of all.*

you edit, make sure that you have not used *more* or *most* with such words.

■   The turbo engine makes this car ~~even more~~ unique.

WP TIP   If you are editing on a computer, using the search function to find every instance of the words *more, most, less,* and *least* and the letter combinations *-er* and *-est* will allow you to check your comparatives and superlatives. Note that if you search for *-er* and *-est*, you will also find words such as *swimmer* and *testing.*

■   **EDITING 4: PRACTICE**

Edit the following passage, using the correct comparative and superlative forms of adjectives and adverbs. More than one edited version is possible. Be ready to explain your editing choices.

How do American students compare with students in other countries? In general, studies show that Americans do worser on tests. Scores on SATs and other standardized tests have been dropping more steadilier over the past decade in the United States than in other countries. Perhaps we need to take a more closer look at what can be done to make our nation's young people gooder students. Perhaps it is time to admit that more traditional methods of teaching may not be most perfect. To perform more well, students need to learn more than mere memorization skills; they have to learn the bestest way to study and how best to apply what they learn. With a new approach, perhaps students will find that learning takes lesser time and can even be funner.

■ **EDITING 5: PRACTICE**

Edit the following passage, using adjectives and adverbs correctly. More than one edited version is possible. Be ready to explain your editing choices.

The snow was falling quick and the roads were becoming slickly. Since the temperature was hovering rightly around freezing, it was a wet, heavily snow. I made sure I was concentrating hardly on the road and began to drive more slow. Up ahead, I could see a car that had spun off the road with its hazard lights blinking bright. I couldn't see no icy patch where it might have slid, but I assumed there was one there. Sure enough, when I tapped my brake light I could feel the car slide a bit, so I promptly took my foot off the pedal. Since I had reacted immediate, I was able to keep the car under control. I cautious rolled past the damaged car, taking a minute to look over to see whether anyone seemed hurt. The driver looked finely, though he was clear frustrated. I turned my head back to the road and slowed down even morely. It was obvious going to be a difficult drive home.

■ **EDITING 6: APPLICATION**

Take a few moments to reflect on the difficulties you most commonly have with the correct use of adjectives and adverbs. Now examine a piece of your own writing to see whether you have incorrectly used any. Do you see any patterns in the kinds of mistakes you make most often? Did you accurately predict where your problem areas would be? Edit any sentences that contain mistakes.

In English, word order can affect meaning: *The man ate the fish* does not mean the same thing as *The fish ate the man*. Word order problems in writing often involve **modifiers**—adjectives, adverbs, and phrases or clauses used as adjectives and adverbs. If a modifier's placement within a sentence does not make clear what it modifies, readers may misinterpret the sentence. *They want only her to sing this song* means something different from *They want her to sing only this song*.

Modifiers that seem to modify the wrong thing are called **misplaced**. Those that are ambiguous about what they modify are called **squinting**. Those that have no element to modify sensibly are called **dangling**. Finally, modifiers that come between sentence elements that should not be separated are called **disruptive**.

POSITIONING MODIFIERS APPROPRIATELY

When editing to position modifiers appropriately, do the following, consulting this chapter as necessary.

- Reposition misplaced modifiers close to the word modified.
- Clarify which element is modified by a squinting modifier and move it.
- Eliminate dangling modifiers by adding the elements they should modify.
- Find a better position for any disruptive modifier that interrupts the sentence flow.

38 **a** Placing modifiers correctly

Because readers usually assume that a modifier modifies the nearest grammatically acceptable element, a **misplaced modifier** is often interpreted as modifying the wrong element, not the one the writer intended. When editing, move the modifier close to the word modified.

■ We wanted our ordeal to end desperately.

Unless the writer intended things to turn out badly, the adverb desperately *is misplaced.*

Check for misplaced modifiers by being alert to unintended meanings.

in a glass jar
■ He took a frog to biology class. in a glass jar.

It seems unlikely that the biology class was held in a glass jar.

Modifiers such as *almost, even, hardly, just, merely, nearly, only, scarcely,* and *simply* are called **limiting modifiers** because they limit the meaning of the word modified by creating an implicit contrast: to say that *Only A is true* implies that *B* and *C* are not true. Readers understand a limiting modifier to modify the sentence element that directly follows it. Consider the difference in meaning created in the following sentences by moving the limiting modifier *just.*

Just the children applauded the conductor.
Only the children, not the adults, applauded.

The children *just* applauded the conductor.
They applauded but did nothing else.

The children applauded *just* the conductor.
The children applauded the conductor and no one else.

As you edit, watch for misplaced limiting modifiers, particularly those that precede a verb when they actually modify a noun following the verb.

■ She ~~almost~~ waited until $\wedge$ the last minute.
           almost

WP TIP   If you are editing on a computer, consider searching for each instance of common limiting modifiers such as *only, almost,* and *just* in your paper so that you can evaluate the placement of each one.

▨ EDITING I: PRACTICE

Edit the following passage, moving any misplaced modifiers. More than one edited version is possible. Be ready to explain your editing choices.

Most people assume that black bears hibernate all winter incorrectly. During the winter, although sleeping deeply, a true state of hibernation is not achieved by black bears. Their body temperature only drops a little, and one can wake up a black bear with just a little effort. Preparing to sleep for several months, a very large amount of food is eaten by the bears. This way, they can store fat and feed off it all winter while they are sleeping. The female surprisingly gives birth to her young at this time.

38 b Clarifying squinting modifiers

    A **squinting modifier**, one that seems to modify two things at once, usually appears between two sentence elements that it might modify—and seems to look in both directions at once.

Students who ⌐follow directions¬ *consistently* ⌐score well¬ on standardized tests.

What occurs consistently, *the following of directions or the scoring well on tests?*

    To edit a squinting modifier, decide which sentence element you want it to modify, and then reposition it or otherwise rearrange the sentence so that no other interpretation is possible.

Eliminating dangling modifiers **579**

■ Students who *consistently* follow directions ~~consistently~~ score well on standardized tests.

■ Students who follow directions ~~consistently~~ score *consistently* well on standardized tests.

38 C Eliminating dangling modifiers

A **dangling modifier** cannot be attached logically to anything in the sentence. Either the element that the modifier is intended to modify does not appear in the sentence, or it does not appear in a grammatically appropriate form. Readers interpret a dangling modifier as modifying the nearest grammatically acceptable element, which may not be what the writer had in mind. Often a dangling modifier consists of a prepositional phrase or verbal phrase at the beginning of a sentence.

> *Running through the rain, our clothes got soaked.*

> *Clearly, it was we who were running through the rain, not our clothes. But we does not appear in the sentence, only our, which cannot be modified by the phrase* Running through the rain.

In a sense, it is the reader who is left dangling, wondering what the writer meant. When editing a dangling modifier, first introduce an element that logically can be modified, or change the form of an existing element. Then place it directly after the modifier.

■ Preparing for the experiment, *we prepped* several slides ~~were fixed~~ with dye.

> *Who was preparing? The sentence doesn't say, so insert a subject.*

■ Having done well on her research, *she earned an A on* the paper ~~earned her an A.~~

> *When her becomes she and is inserted after the modifying phrase, the sentence makes sense.*

580 Positioning modifiers correctly

When the main clause is in the passive voice, an introductory phrase often has no subject to modify. One solution is to place the sentence in the active voice. (See 28c.)

■ To study the effects of cigarette smoking, ∧researchers have forced monkeys ~~have been forced to~~ inhale the equivalent of a hundred cigarettes a day.

Clearly, the monkeys are not conducting the research.

■ **EDITING 2: PRACTICE**

Edit the following passage, clarifying squinting modifiers and eliminating dangling modifiers. More than one edited version is possible. Be ready to discuss your editing choices.

Examining the patient death rates of more than fifty doctors, the results were compared by a panel to a statistical average. Having a better than average rate, a minus score was entered for those doctors. A positive score was entered for those who had worse than average rates. Consisting of only the doctors with positive scores, the panel released a list of names to a local newspaper. After reading the article, a protest was lodged by the county medical society. Doctors who criticized the study strongly argued that the scoring was biased.

38 d Moving disruptive modifiers

A modifier that disrupts the flow of a sentence may confuse readers or distract, inadvertently, their attention from your meaning. In the previous sentence, for example, there are several better places for *inadvertently*. **Disruptive modifiers** include those that split an infinitive, those that divide a verb phrase, and those that needlessly separate major sentence elements.

WP TIP Highlight words and use the move function to rearrange the placement of any disruptive modifiers. It's the fastest way to shift words around.

Modifiers that split infinitives

An infinitive consists of the word *to* and the base form of a verb: *to fly, to grow, to achieve.* Whenever possible, avoid placing words between the word *to* and the verb. Such a construction, called a **split infinitive**, occurs often in speech but can seem awkward in writing, and some instructors and other readers consider any split infinitive a mark of careless writing.

■ She wanted to ~~as soon as possible~~ try rock climbing as soon as possible.

Sometimes it is difficult to find a natural-sounding place for the modifier. If so, edit the sentence to eliminate the infinitive altogether.

■ The director planned a vivid re-creation of ~~wanted to vividly re-create~~ a bullfight for the theater audience.

ESL **PLACING FREQUENCY ADVERBS WITHIN VERB PHRASES**

When an adverb is used between elements of a verb phrase—such as *has been happening* or *will remember*—it usually appears after the first auxiliary verb.

Our baseball stadium has *rarely* been filled to capacity this season.

In questions, the adverb appears after the first auxiliary verb and the subject and before the other parts of the verb.

In the past, have you *usually* found yourself writing a paper the day before it's due?

When *not* is used to negate another adverb, it should appear directly after the first auxiliary verb and before the other adverb.

This newspaper does *not usually* put sports news on the front page.

Not *negates usually; not usually means "seldom."*

Not should appear after the adverb when being used to negate the action expressed by the main verb.

The senators have often not paid much attention to those who elected them.

Not *negates paid.*

2 Modifiers that split verb phrases

A **verb phrase** consists of one or more auxiliary verbs, such as a form of *be* or *have*, and a participle or base form: *had been formed, does happen*. Most instructors will accept a single adverb (or *not* plus another adverb) placed between the elements of a verb phrase.

> Some early settlements in the New World have *inexplicably* vanished without a trace.

However, an intervening phrase or clause will be considered disruptive, so rewrite the sentence.

■ ~~The Roanoke colony had~~ ~~by~~ the time a supply ship arrived four
    By
    the Roanoke colony had
years later, disappeared without a trace.

3 Modifiers that separate major sentence elements

Placing modifiers often means balancing conflicting goals. On one hand, placing major sentence elements such as subjects, verbs, objects, and complements near each other helps make their relationships clear. On the other hand, any word modifying one of those elements needs to be close to that element and thus risks disrupting one of those primary relationships.

A long modifier falling between a subject and a verb, between a linking verb and a subject complement, or between a verb and its object can cause readers to forget where the sentence was originally heading.

■ *Because of her great popularity with audiences,*
Mary Pickford, ~~because of her great popularity with audiences,~~
became the first silent film actor to be publicized by name.

■ Kentucky was, *never a stronghold of slavery,* even though it had residents who fought for the
Confederacy during the Civil War, ~~never a stronghold of slavery~~

■ ~~African American spirituals influenced~~ *Through* ~~through~~ their
African American spirituals influenced
distinctive harmonic and rhythmic elements, the development
of most twentieth-century popular music.

Some modifiers may seem disruptive while others in grammatically similar situations may not. The following sentence, although similar in structure to the previous one, probably will strike you as perfectly readable.

> The partial success of Ross Perot's candidacy suggests, *at least to some analysts*, that Americans are eager for new political choices.

Because even grammatically similar examples like these must be handled differently, no sweeping rule can be made about where to put modifier phrases and clauses. When deciding where to put a modifier clause or phrase, try to minimize disruption and yet place the modifier so that what it modifies is clear.

WP TIP In a computer file, try keeping a "Modifier Log" into which you log examples of modifier problems you have had in recent papers. Copy the unedited and edited sentences into the log and write comments on your editing choices below them.

■ EDITING 3: PRACTICE

Edit the following passage, moving disruptive modifiers for easier reading. More than one edited version is possible. Be ready to discuss your editing choices.

To persuasively write, one must always keep in mind one's audience. An effective argument requires, because one cannot assume that a potential reader knows as much about the topic as the writer, a good introduction. In addition, an argumentative essay should, for the sake of clarity, define any unfamiliar terms or technical language it employs. The most important point to remember, though, is that it is necessary to clearly articulate one's thesis early in the essay. The thesis statement, because we want our readers to concentrate on the arguments we make to support our position, and to not have to needlessly struggle to figure out what that position might be, must be direct and unambiguous. If the thesis is strong, key terms are defined, and sufficient background is provided, the writer of a persuasive essay should feel confident that the reader will impartially consider the merits of the writer's argument.

■ EDITING 4: PRACTICE

Edit the following passage, eliminating dangling, disruptive, and squinting modifiers. More than one edited version is possible. Be ready to explain your editing choices.

584 Positioning modifiers correctly

Striking millions of Americans, some people only are afflicted by insomnia occasionally, while other people live with it for several years. Having experienced mild, occasional sleeplessness, your insomnia shouldn't be considered a major concern. The causes from which it stems most often are quite simple. Having something troubling or exciting on your mind, exerting too much physical or mental activity before bedtime, having a mild fever, drinking too much caffeine, or eating a heavy meal, sleeplessness might occur. Changing your schedule or surroundings, insomnia can also result. The way to best ensure a good night's sleep is to consistently follow a few simple steps. Try to go to bed at the same time every night. Sleep on a comfortable bed in a dark room. Realizing that it is still, after twenty minutes, hard to fall asleep, it is helpful for you to get up and do something, such as read, until you feel drowsy. And remember to always avoid caffeine and heavy foods as well as strenuous activity before bedtime.

■ **EDITING 5: APPLICATION**

Take a few moments to reflect on the difficulties you have with misplaced, squinting, or dangling modifiers. Make a brief list that ranks your problems in order, from greatest to least amount of difficulty. Now examine a paper you are working on and see whether you have positioned modifiers correctly. Do you notice any consistent patterns of error? How accurate was your initial prediction of where your difficulties would lie? Edit any sentences that need correction.

Pronouns serve as stand-ins for nouns, noun phrases, or other pronouns. Unless readers can understand what word a pronoun such as *she* refers to, they may find themselves asking, "She who?" Readers should know that you are talking about Maya Angelou or Joan of Arc or whomever.

The word for which a pronoun substitutes is called its **antecedent** (from Latin roots meaning "to go before"). Although antecedents normally appear before pronouns that refer to them, sometimes they follow the pronouns. In either case, there must be no conflicting choices to confuse readers. This chapter focuses on clarifying pronoun reference. (Also see Chapter 40 on ensuring that pronouns agree with their antecedents, Chapter 41 for a discussion of pronoun case, and 66b for a complete list of the various types of pronouns.)

STRATEGIES FOR CLARIFYING PRONOUN REFERENCE

To clarify pronoun reference, edit your sentences using the following strategies:

- Make sure a pronoun clearly refers to a single antecedent.
- Place a pronoun close to its antecedent.
- Provide an explicit antecedent.
- Use *it*, *they*, and *you* appropriately.
- Avoid overusing *it*.
- Choose *who*, *which*, or *that* according to the antecedent.
- Eliminate unneeded pronouns.

39 a Establishing a single antecedent

A pronoun that has more than one possible antecedent can create a confusing sentence.

Marco met Roger as *he* arrived at the gym.

Who was arriving, Marco or Roger? Because *he* could refer to either, the sentence offers the reader more than one meaning but no clue as to which is correct. Edit such a sentence so that the pronoun has only one possible antecedent. You can eliminate the pronoun, if the result does not seem too awkward.

■ Marco met Roger as ~~he~~ Roger arrived at the gym.

You can also edit the sentence to place the pronoun closer to one antecedent.

■ As Marco ~~met Roger as he~~ arrived at the gym, he met Roger.

Verbs such as *said* and *told* can create confusion about antecedents because they appear often in sentences involving more than one person. When editing such a sentence, you can often use a direct quotation.

■ Barbara told Ramona, "You ~~that she had~~ failed the test."

EDITING I: PRACTICE

Edit the following passage by making each pronoun refer clearly to a single antecedent. More than one edited version is possible. Be ready to explain your editing choices.

Diane spotted Laura as she was beginning her regimen of stretching exercises. It was twenty minutes before the race was due to begin. Diane told Laura that she thought she would win the race. She was just plain faster. Laura responded that she had a good chance, but that she was going to be tough to beat. Nodding in agreement, Diane shook hands with Laura. "Good luck," she said. "Have a good race."

39 b Placing pronouns close to antecedents

The closer a pronoun and its antecedent appear to each other, the more easily readers can spot the relationship between them. If many words intervene, the reader may lose the connection. In the following passage, by the time readers get to *he* in the fourth sentence, they may have forgotten *Galileo* is the antecedent. Find a place to introduce the pronoun earlier, or use the antecedent again.

■   In the seventeenth century, the Italian scientist Galileo Galilei upset the Catholic church by publishing a scientific paper asserting that the earth revolved around the sun. That assertion contradicted contemporary church belief, which held that the earth was the center of the universe. The paper also violated a papal order ~~of~~ [that Galileo had accepted] sixteen years earlier not to "hold, teach, or defend" such a doctrine. Under pressure from the church, ~~he~~ [Galileo] recanted his theory of the earth's motion, but even as he recanted, ~~he~~ [Galileo] is said to have whispered "Eppur si muove" ("Nonetheless it moves").

39 c Providing explicit antecedents

In general, a pronoun's antecedent should be stated explicitly. (Indefinite pronouns, such as *somebody, everybody,* and *no one,* are exceptions. See 40d.) A pronoun whose antecedent is merely implied may confuse readers.

Interviews with several computer programmers made *it* seem like a fascinating career.

What does *it* stand for? A reader might guess that *it* stands for *computer programming,* since this is a possible career, but *computer programming* does not appear in the sentence. To edit such a sentence, substitute a noun for the pronoun, use another pronoun that can refer to something already explicit in the sentence, or provide a clear antecedent for the pronoun.

■   Interviews with several computer programmers made ~~it~~ [programming] seem like a fascinating career.

■   Interviews with several computer programmers made ~~it~~ [theirs] seem like a fascinating career.

■ Interviews with several ~~computer programmers~~ made it seem
  ^people in programming
  like a fascinating career.

ESL **USING *THIS* AND *THAT***

> The demonstrative adjectives *this* and *that* mean "near" and
> "far," respectively. This concept of distance can apply to space.
>
> *This* vase right here is a better choice than *that* one in the back of
> the store.
>
> The concept can also apply to time.
>
> *That* article I showed you last week was very technical.
>
> *This* book I just found is more readable.

---

1 Providing grammatically acceptable antecedents

An antecedent must be a noun, a noun phrase, or another
pronoun. Usually, it cannot be the possessive form of a noun or
an adjective or other modifier. As you edit, make sure that any
pronoun refers to a grammatically acceptable antecedent.

■ The ~~committee's~~ bitter argument reflected badly on all of *them.*
                     ^among the committee members

A possessive form of a noun or pronoun can be an antecedent, however, if the pronoun that refers to it is also possessive.

The *committee's* argument reflected badly on all of *its* members.

2 Supplying explicit antecedents for *this, that,* and *which*

Words like *this* and *that* standing alone are **demonstrative
pronouns:** This *is real;* that *is an imitation.* Used with a noun,
they are **demonstrative adjectives**: This *book is genuine.*
Confusion can arise when a demonstrative pronoun has two possible antecedents.

No one has suggested taxing health care. *This* is unlikely.

What is unlikely, the taxing of health care or the chance that any-one would suggest it? You can usually clarify the reference by re-stating the antecedent that you intend.

■ No one has suggested taxing health care. This ͵ is unlikely.

tax (above "This")
∧

When *which* and *that* (and *who* and *whom*) introduce clauses, they are called **relative pronouns**. Usually, a relative pronoun introduces a clause that immediately follows the pronoun's antecedent.

This book, *which I heartily recommend,* is out of print.

If other elements intervene or if the relative pronoun has more than one possible antecedent, confusion can result. To clarify, you can provide an unambiguous antecedent, or you can replace *which* or *that* with another construction.

■ She took the situation seriously, which I found laughable.

a response
∧

■ She took the situation seriously, ~~which~~ I found laughable.

though (above), it (above)
∧   ∧

WP TIP   Use the search function to find *this, that,* and *which* in your papers. As you edit, make sure that these pronouns always refer to explicit antecedents.

■ **EDITING 2: PRACTICE**

Edit the following passage by making all pronouns refer to explicit antecedents. More than one edited version is possible. Be ready to explain your editing choices.

Thank you for giving me the chance to tour your videotape recycling facility. It gave me an excellent glimpse of what it is all about. I especially enjoyed the knowledge and wit of Bob Jones, our tour guide, which kept everyone in our group interested in the process. Bob showed us examples of tapes before and after they are refurbished, and that was incredible. Before processing, the tapes are scuffed and covered with labels and after the workers finish their efforts, they look brand new. I know some people are skeptical about recycled videotapes, which I find somewhat understandable. But your recycling lines help the environment, even if in a small way. Each year corporations throw thousands of videotapes away, which pollute the environment. We need to recycle not just cans, paper, and bottles, but everything we can. He made this clear to us before we left it.

---

39 **d** **Replacing a vague *it, they,* or *you***

In casual speech, people often use *it*, *they*, and *you* with no definite antecedent. In academic writing, however, indefinite uses of *it*, *they*, and *you* should be avoided in favor of more specific constructions.

■ ~~It said on the~~ news this morning that the game was canceled.
The report said

■ ~~They~~ tow away any car that is illegally parked.
The police

■ If the weather doesn't clear, ~~you~~ could see flooding.
local residents

You may be used to address the reader directly (as in *You should use specific nouns whenever possible*), but in academic writing, do not use *you* to mean "people in general." One way to avoid reliance on *you* is to use an indefinite pronoun such as *one* or *someone*, which refers to an unspecified third person.

WP TIP Use the search function of the computer to find every instance of *it*, *they*, and *you* in a paper you are currently working one. As you edit, make sure you have used these pronouns correctly.

---

39 **e** **Avoiding overuse of *it***

The pronoun *it* has three common uses. First, *it* can function as a personal pronoun: *I want to read the book, but Shana won't let me borrow it.* Second, *it* can be used to introduce a sentence in which the subject and verb are inverted: It *is necessary to apologize.* (See 36b.) Third, *it* appears in idiomatic constructions about time, weather, and distance: It *is ten past twelve.* In speech, few people notice if these senses of *it* are mixed. In writing, however, you should avoid using the same word in different senses in the same sentence.

■ ~~It is important to remember~~ that once the concert begins, it will
Remember
be two hours before ~~it breaks for~~ intermission.

Choosing *who, which,* **or** *that* 591

■ EDITING 3: PRACTICE

Edit the following passage by clarifying all uses of the pronouns *it, they,* and *you.* Make any changes in wording needed for smooth reading. More than one edited version is possible. Be ready to explain your editing choices.

They say that you shouldn't believe everything you read in the newspaper. It is foolish to assume that it is possible for it to report the news accurately all of the time. You can't expect that reporters and editors will never make mistakes. Sometimes they receive late-breaking stories and have to rush to edit them before it goes to press. Occasionally you even can see contradictions between two articles on the same topic. It will say one thing in one article and then it will say something different in the other. It is when this happens that it is hard for you to know which article you should believe.

39	f	Choosing *who, which,* **or** *that*

In general, *who* is used for people or animals with names; *which* and *that* are used for objects, ideas, unnamed animals, and anonymous people or groups of people.

Black Beauty is a fictional horse *who* lives in a world that has now disappeared.

He tried to rope the last steer, *which* twisted to avoid him.

This is the policy *that* the administration wants to enforce.

The tribes *that* built these cities have long since vanished.

(The difference between *who, whom,* and *whose* is one of case. See 41f.)

Most writers avoid using *which* to refer to people.

■ I have met hundreds of actors, of ~~which~~ Steve Martin is the funniest.
(*whom* inserted above *which*)

If using *of which* to refer to an inanimate object results in an awkward construction, you may substitute *whose.*

■ This is an idea ~~the~~ time ~~of which~~ has come.
(*whose* inserted above *the*)

■ **EDITING 4: PRACTICE**

Complete the following passage, filling in the blanks with the correct pronoun: *who, which,* or *that.*

None of the carpenters _____ I know has any use for imported nails. They swear that American-made nails are the only ones _____ are worth using. A nail _____ bends when it is driven in was probably made in Canada, they say. One box of nails, _____ they got from Japan, had heads _____ broke off if they tried to pull them out. There are problems every time the contractor brings them boxes _____ are imported. These men, every one of _____ works with nails every day, believe that they can tell where a nail comes from as soon as they hit it with a hammer. One thing is certain: a bent nail doesn't get that way because a carpenter hit it crooked.

✔ **CHOOSING BETWEEN** *WHICH* **AND** *THAT*

How can you tell whether to use *which* or *that?* It often depends on whether the modifier to be introduced is restrictive or nonrestrictive.

■ A restrictive modifier is one that is necessary to identify what it modifies. It restricts, or limits, what it modifies in such a way that it is essential to the meaning of the sentence. It can be introduced by either *which* or *that* and is never set off by commas.

All of the courses *that are offered free of charge* are held in the evenings.

The modifier that are offered free of charge *restricts (limits) the larger entity* All of the courses *to those held in the evening. The implication is that there may be other courses that are not free.*

■ By contrast, a nonrestrictive modifier merely adds more information, not affecting the meaning of the sentence. It is introduced only by *which* (but not by *that*) and is set off by commas.

All of the courses, which are offered free of charge, are listed in the catalog.

All the courses are free. The commas indicate that which are offered free of charge *doesn't limit or help identify the subject.*

39 g **Eliminating unneeded pronouns**

Speakers of some dialects use a pronoun immediately following its antecedent.

■ After the shot, the deer ~~it~~ just took off.

In formal writing or paraphrasing, delete any unneeded pronoun. Check that you have not used a personal pronoun (*he, her, it, they, them*) and a relative pronoun (*who, whom, which, that*) in the same clause to refer to the same antecedent.

■ I corrected the errors that you pointed ~~them~~ out to

me yesterday.

■ Although some people prefer *that* for all restrictive modifiers, *which* is acceptable as well.

When in the course of human events it becomes necessary for one people to dissolve the political bands *which* have connected them with another... a decent respect for the opinions of mankind requires that they should declare the reasons *which* impel them to the separation. [Italics added.]

DECLARATION OF INDEPENDENCE

■ *Who* may introduce either restrictive or nonrestrictive modifiers.

NONRESTRICTIVE Americans, *who* tend to eat a richer diet than Europeans, have rising rates of heart disease.

The nonrestrictive who *clause adds information about Americans in general.*

RESTRICTIVE Americans *who* curb their appetites for rich foods may live longer than those *who* don't.

The restrictive who *clause is necessary to identify what it modifies—in this case, just certain Americans.*

For more on restrictive and nonrestrictive clauses, see 44c.

■ EDITING 5: PRACTICE

Edit the following passage by making sure that all pronoun references are clear and that all pronouns are used appropriately. More than one edited version is possible. Be ready to explain your editing choices.

Studies have shown that alcoholism is a major problem in this city, which has a high percentage of unemployed and homeless people. This is true in other metropolitan areas as well. However, it affects not only the down-and-out but also working people, the elderly, and teenagers which have begun to experiment with drinking. We interviewed some social workers, which said that being homeless caused some people to drink.

We learned from interviewing homeless people, though, that many of those which are homeless now say they were drinking before they were on the street. Excessive drinking may force you to lose your home, if you're not careful, it seems from their experience.

■ EDITING 6: APPLICATION

Read through a paper you are working on. Are pronoun references unclear? Can you see any pattern to the problems you are having? Edit any sentences in which you found pronoun reference problems, and think about how best to identify and correct these mistakes in your future editing.

A pronoun substitutes for a noun, a phrase, or another pronoun. The word for which a pronoun substitutes is called its **antecedent** (see Chapter 39). To substitute clearly and correctly, personal pronouns should **agree** with, or correspond to, their antecedents in number, person, and gender.

■ Personal pronouns should agree with their antecedents in **number**—singular or plural. Most agreement problems involve confusion about number.

A *pronoun* is singular if *it* has a singular antecedent.

Pronouns are plural if *they* have plural antecedents.

■ Personal pronouns should agree with their antecedents in **person**—first (*I, we, my, our*), second (*you, your*), or third (*he, she, it, they, his, her, its, their*).

I write in *my* journal at least once a week.

Robert writes in *his* journal every day.

■ Singular personal pronouns should agree with their antecedents in **gender**—feminine, masculine, or neuter.

Rosanna finds that writing in *her* journal helps *her* clarify *her* thoughts.

Jimmy says it helps *him* analyze *his* research.

596 Making pronouns and antecedents agree

WP TIP When editing one of your papers, place the pronouns in boldface and their antecedents in italics. Edit for pronoun agreement. Copy the passage and prepare a second version in which you edit for pronoun agreement differently. Compare versions and choose the edited sentences that most effectively express the meanings you wish to convey.

 CHECKING FOR PRONOUN–ANTECEDENT AGREEMENT

When editing for pronoun–antecedent agreement, run through your paper, stopping to do each of the following:

■ Make pronouns agree with antecedents joined by *and.*
■ Make pronouns agree with antecedents joined by *or* or *nor.*
■ Make pronouns agree with antecedents that are collective nouns.
■ Make pronouns agree with antecedents that are indefinite pronouns.

Many questions of pronoun–antecedent agreement require the same kinds of analysis used in determining subject–verb agreement. (See Chapter 36.) Also see Chapter 39 on clarifying pronoun reference, Chapter 41 on pronoun case, and 66b for a complete list of the various types of pronouns.

40 **a** **Making pronouns agree with antecedents joined by *and***

A **compound antecedent** is one in which two or more parts are joined by a conjunction such as *and, or,* or *nor: you and I, ducks or geese, neither rain nor snow.* When *and* links elements, the resulting grouping is usually considered plural, so a pronoun that refers to a compound antecedent joined by *and* should be plural as well.

Wind energy and solar power should soon take *their* place as major energy sources.

Making pronouns agree with antecedents joined by *or* and *nor* 597

There are a few exceptions. A compound antecedent preceded by *each* or *every* takes a singular pronoun. (Also see 38d.)

Each leaf and twig was put in *its* own envelope.

When the parts of a compound antecedent refer to the same person or thing, the pronoun should be singular.

As *the systems manager and my immediate supervisor,* she oversees my work.

Also, when the elements linked by *and* constitute a single entity, use a singular pronoun.

Beans and rice is my favorite dish. *It* is always nice on cold days.

40	b	Making pronouns agree with antecedents joined by *or* and *nor*

The conjunctions *or* and *nor* can also be used to form a compound antecedent. When both elements are singular, a pronoun that refers to the compound antecedent is singular.

Either *hunger* or bad *weather* will take *its* toll on the soldiers.

When one element of a compound antecedent is singular and the other is plural, a pronoun clearly cannot agree with both of them. The convention is that the pronoun agree with the antecedent closer to it.

Either the supply problems or the bad *weather* will take *its* toll.

If following this convention seems awkward in a particular sentence, try putting the plural part of the antecedent nearer to the pronoun.

Either the bad weather or the supply *problems* will take *their* toll.

| **40** | **c** | **Making pronouns agree with collective nouns** |

Collective nouns, such as *couple, flock, crowd, herd,* and *committee,* often cause agreement problems because they are singular in form yet they refer to groups or collections that can be regarded as plural. Take your cue from the intended meaning of the sentence. Use a plural pronoun if members of the group are acting separately.

The *crew* gather *their* belongings and prepare to leave the ship.

Use a singular pronoun if the group acts as a unit.

The *flock* arose in flight and made *its* way to the shelter of the trees.

WP TIP If your paper uses a particular collective noun such as *audience* or *committee* frequently, use your word processor's search function to find every instance of this word and check each usage for correct pronoun-antecedent agreement.

■ **EDITING 1: PRACTICE**

Edit the following passage by making pronouns and antecedents agree. Be especially careful about compound and collective antecedents.

Often conflict at the workplace is inevitable, especially when an employee cannot agree with their supervisor's decisions. Sam experienced this conflict firsthand. Both he and his supervisor are unhappy with his relationship with each other. They disagree about how each regular task and special assignment should be performed, and the supervisor thinks that Sam takes too much time to complete them. The supervisor makes Sam write memos about his many overtime hours to justify it. Sam believes his boss works him too hard because she doesn't like them. Neither the personnel director nor Alicia, Sam's closest friend at work, can use their influence to help Sam transfer because the staff unanimously gives their support to the supervisor. They see nothing wrong with the supervisor's behavior.

40 d Making pronouns agree with indefinite pronouns

An **indefinite pronoun** does not require an explicit antecedent. In the sentence *Everyone likes ice cream*, for example, the pronoun *everyone* needs no other words to explain who is meant. Where there is no antecedent, it can be difficult to determine whether a pronoun that refers to an indefinite pronoun should be singular or plural.

Some indefinite pronouns are always singular: *anyone, everyone, someone, anybody, everybody, somebody, anything, everything, something, either, neither, each, nothing, much, one, no one*. Pronouns that refer to them should be singular as well.

Neither of the visitors finished *his* lunch.

Each one of the cars needs to have *its* brakes inspected.

Everybody who sees the great pyramids will be glad *she* came.

To avoid the awkward construction *he or she*, many speakers substitute *they* in such a situation, but you should avoid this solution in formal writing.

Some indefinite pronouns are always plural: *few, many, both, several.*

Few of the newly hatched turtles survive *their* first week.

Still other indefinite pronouns can be singular or plural depending on context: *some, any, all, more, most, none*.

In a survey of young *voters, some* said *they* were conservative.

Some *refers to voters, so both* some *and the pronoun* they *are plural.*

The *money* is still in the safe. *Some* is still in *its* bags.

Some *refers to money, so both* some *and the pronoun* its *are singular.*

AVOIDING THE GENERIC *HE*

A singular indefinite pronoun (such as *someone* or *anyone*) does not specify gender, yet a singular personal pronoun that refers to the indefinite pronoun must specify gender (*he* or *she*). Writers and readers once accepted the masculine pronouns *he*, *him*, or *his* in such cases, but in recent years many people have come to feel that this use of *he* in a generic sense implicitly excludes women. There are four ways to avoid the generic *he*.

1. If there is no doubt about the gender of the antecedent, use a pronoun of the appropriate gender.

■ Anyone who wants to be an operatic soprano must train ~~their~~ her voice carefully.

2. Make the antecedent plural. If you do, look out for other words in the sentence that need to be made plural as well.

■ ~~Everyone knows~~ All the singers know their ~~part.~~ parts.

3. Use *his or her*. Do so sparingly, as *his or her* becomes monotonous with repetition.

■ Everyone knows ~~their~~ his or her part.

4. Rewrite to eliminate the personal pronoun.

■ Everyone has ~~done their best~~ worked to help the recital succeed.

(For a detailed discussion of avoiding biased and sexist language, see Chapter 32.)

WP TIP If you have difficulties with pronoun–antecedent agreement when using any of these indefinite pronouns, use your computer's search function to find each instance of the troublesome pronoun. Locate its antecedent and edit for agreement as necessary.

▇ EDITING 2: PRACTICE

Edit the following passage by making pronouns and their indefinite pronoun antecedents agree. More than one edited version is possible. Be ready to explain your editing choices.

Most people make many pronoun agreement mistakes in his or her speech because spoken English is much more informal than written English. Almost everyone knows that they shouldn't say "they" when they're talking about one person but often they do so anyway when speaking. In conversation, even a professor, a freelance writer, or anyone else who works with words professionally won't always make a pronoun agree with the noun they modify. But when someone writes, they should make sure that "something" is an "it" and not a "they." Otherwise, the reader will think the writer doesn't know what they are doing.

▇ EDITING 3: PRACTICE

Edit the following passage by making pronouns agree with their antecedents. (You may have to change some verbs and nouns as well.) More than one edited version is possible. Be ready to explain your editing choices.

Changes in facial hair, a higher or a lower voice, and a decreased sex drive: this is some of the side effects of taking steroids. Yet many continue using this dangerous drug to improve their performance. Athletics is ever more competitive, and athletes are always striving to be the best he or she can be. In a race, mere seconds are a long time to an athlete when they mean the difference between a gold and a silver medal. Perhaps the athlete does not know what harm they are doing to their bodies. Someone cannot be physically addicted to steroids; any addiction to it is psychological and based on the fact that athletes like what they see. Unfortunately, the athlete cannot always see what lies ahead for them. Ben Johnson and some others should count himself lucky. All Johnson lost was a gold medal and the chance to compete again. Benjamin Ramirez was not so lucky. Nor were the many like him who lost his life.

▇ EDITING 4: APPLICATION

Read through a paper you are working on, and try to find pronouns that do not agree with their antecedents. Can you see why you made the mistakes you did? Edit any sentences with pronoun agreement problems, and think about how best to identify such problems in your future editing. In your own words, write a brief set of guidelines to help yourself in the future.

41 ⬛ Choosing Pronoun Case

In speaking, we automatically choose among the pronouns *I* or *me* or *my*, *he* or *him* or *his*. We say *I saw him* rather than *me saw he*, or *my car* rather than *I car*. These changes of form, the grammatical property of nouns and pronouns called **case**, help indicate a word's role in a sentence. The **subjective case** (*I*, *he*, *she*, or *they*, for example) serves grammatically as a subject—the person or thing that performs the action of a sentence or a clause. The **objective case** (*me*, *him*, *her*, *them*) is used for an object—the person or thing that receives the action. The **possessive case** (*my*, *mine*, *your*, *yours*, *his*, *hers*) shows possession or ownership.

Most problems with case arise from the choice between subjective and objective pronouns: *I* or *me*, *we* or *us*, *she* or *her*, *who* or *whom*. Often the difficulty arises because nonstandard usages that are acceptable in everyday speech (*It's me!*) are inappropriate in formal writing (in which you would write *It is I*). The key to choosing correct case is to analyze whether the pronoun in question is serving as a subject or as an object or is indicating possession.

 EDITING FOR CORRECT PRONOUN CASE

To edit for pronoun case, do the following:

- ▪ Check pronoun case in elements joined by *and, or,* or *nor.*
- ▪ Check the case of pronouns used as appositives.
- ▪ Determine whether you need *us* or *we* before a noun.
- ▪ Check the case of pronouns used with verbals.
- ▪ Check the case of pronouns after *than* or *as.*
- ▪ Choose between *who* or *whom*, *whoever* or *whomever.*
- ▪ Use reflexive pronouns only as objects, only when necessary.

41 **a** **Choosing case after elements joined by *and, or,* or *nor***

Joining two or more words by *and*, *or*, or *nor* and thus creating a compound element, does not affect their case. One test for correctness is to take out one pronoun and the *and* or *or* and see how the sentence reads.

■ Joe and ~~me~~ talked to him.
            I

If you mentally remove *Joe and*, you are left with *Me talked to him*. Some people, trying to avoid this mistake, assume that *and me* is always wrong and thus make errors such as *He talked to Joe and I*. But we say *He talked to me*, not *He talked to I*, so we also say *He talked to Joe and me*.

 DETERMINING PRONOUN CASE

PERSONAL PRONOUNS

	SUBJECTIVE	OBJECTIVE	POSSESSIVE
SINGULAR			
First person	I	me	my/mine
Second person	you	you	your/yours
Third person			
Masculine	he	him	his
Feminine	she	her	her/hers
Neuter	it	it	its
PLURAL			
First person	we	us	our/ours
Second person	you	you	your/yours
Third person	they	them	their/theirs

INTERROGATIVE OR RELATIVE PRONOUNS*

	SUBJECTIVE	OBJECTIVE	POSSESSIVE
	who	whom	whose
	whoever	whomever	—

*These pronouns are called **interrogative pronouns** when used to ask questions: *Whose book is that?* They are called **relative pronouns** when used to introduce dependent clauses: *The writer whose book we read visited the university.*

1 Subjective case for subjects

A subject that has two or more parts joined by *and*, *or*, or *nor* is a **compound subject**. Use the subjective case for each part of a compound subject. When one part of a compound subject is in the first person (*I*), put that part last.

■ ~~Me and~~ Sandy found five lost lottery tickets.

It sometimes helps to simplify the structure by mentally dropping everything except one pronoun: I found five lost lottery tickets.

2 Objective case for objects

With **compound objects**, as with compound subjects, case is not affected by *and*, *or*, or *nor*. Use the objective case for each part

---

✔ USING THE PRONOUN CASES

SUBJECTIVE CASE

Use the subjective case (*I, you, he, she, it, we, they, who, whoever*) for the subject of a sentence or of a dependent clause.

She researched the origins of the tune.

James knew *who* would answer.

Also use the subjective case for a subject complement, which follows a linking verb (*be, seem, become, appear*) and renames the subject.

It is *they* who will benefit most.

OBJECTIVE CASE

Use the objective case (*me, you, him, her, it, us, them, whom, whomever*) for the object of a verb or of a preposition.

The judges chose *her* first.

They awarded the prize to *us*.

of a compound object, whether it is the object of a verb or of a preposition.

■ The judges chose neither ~~he~~ ^{him} nor ~~I~~ ^{me}.

■ I spoke to Olga and ~~they~~ ^{them} about the competition.

To clarify the correct choice, mentally drop all but one pronoun from the compound object: *The judges chose him. The judges chose me. I spoke to them.*

The preposition *between* is used when clarifying the relationship between two things, *among* when clarifying the relationship between three or more. As with any preposition, the objects should be in the objective case.

■ Between Jack and ~~I~~ ^{me}, we sold more than four dozen souvenir

t-shirts. We divided the money among him, Janet, and ~~I~~ ^{me}.

USING THE OBJECTIVE CASE WITH *MAKE, LET,* AND *HAVE*

Objective case pronouns are used when infinitives follow *make, let,* and *have* even though these infinitives do not have the form *to* in front of them.

He let *us* retake the exam.

We made *him* tell us the secret recipe.

She had *me* turn the computer on.

POSSESSIVE CASE

Use the possessive case to show ownership, possession, or connection. The adjective form (*my, your, his, her, its, our, their, whose*) is used before a noun.

I wrote in *my* journal.

We heard the singer *whose* songs we liked.

The noun form (*mine, yours, his, hers, ours, theirs*) can stand alone, without a noun.

The black coat is *hers.*

His is the plaid one.

3 Subjective case following linking verbs

A **linking verb**—such as *be, become, seem, appear*—links its subject to a **complement** that follows the verb and renames the subject. In writing, both the subject and the complement should be in the subjective case.

■ The first contestants were Laura and ~~me~~.
<small>I.</small>

If you have trouble choosing case following a linking verb, try turning the sentence around and simplifying the compound structure to a single pronoun: *I was the first contestant.*

■ EDITING 1: PRACTICE

Edit the following sentences, using the appropriate pronoun case for compound subjects and objects.

Bob and ~~me~~ like to watch shows from the early days of
<small>I</small>
television whenever we get a chance.

1. To him and I they provide hours of entertainment and neither he nor me ever seems to tire of them.
2. I don't remember if it was him or me who first started watching them.
3. Others may not appreciate our passion for these shows, but they never seem boring to either he or I.
4. The best ones make me and him laugh every time we see them, and, thanks to the invention of the VCR, him and I can see them over and over.
5. Me and him have seen some shows so many times that we have practically memorized them.

41 b Choosing case for appositive pronouns

An **appositive** is a noun or pronoun that renames a preceding noun. (See 44c.) Pronouns used as appositives must be in the same case as the nouns they rename.

■ The losers—Tomoko, Rodney, and ~~me~~—all wanted a rematch.
<small>I</small>

The appositive renames the subject, losers, *so the pronoun is in the subjective case.*

■ It was her sons, Paul and ~~him~~, who missed their mother most.
     he

The appositive renames the subject complement, sons, so it is in the subjective case.

■ They asked the medalists, Katya and ~~I~~, to pose for a picture.
     me

The appositive renames medalists, the object of the verb asked, so it is in the objective case.

To decide between the subjective and objective case in such sentences, simplify the construction and substitute the appositive pronoun for the noun: *They asked me to pose for a picture.*

41 c   Choosing between *us* and *we* before a noun

Pronouns immediately followed by nouns can cause confusion, but the correct case again depends on whether the pronoun is a subject or an object. (The noun following the pronoun is an appositive renaming the pronoun. See 44c.)

■ ~~Us~~ bikers were worried about the weather.
     We

The pronoun is the subject, so the subjective case is correct.

■ They told ~~we~~ bikers not to worry about the weather.
     us

The pronoun is an object, so the objective case is correct.

Mentally dropping the noun following *us* or *we* can make the choice clearer: *We were worried about the weather. They told us not to worry about the weather.*

■ **EDITING 2: PRACTICE**

Edit the following paragraph, using the appropriate pronoun cases. Watch out for pronouns in compound subjects and objects, pronouns used as appositives, and *us* and *we* before nouns.

Fishing with our dad, Charley and me hadn't caught any fish all week. We decided it was up to the two of us, him and I, to find some way to catch something. Us two kids borrowed a rowboat and, with him and me rowing, went way out in the middle of the pond. We dropped anchor and began fishing, him out of one side of the boat and I out of the other side. Charley asked me if I was sleepy and I said, "Not me," but then a splash of water woke me, and the boat was rocking. Charley was pulling madly on his rod, and it seemed as if his catch would tip the boat over and he and I with it. It took ten minutes for us, Charley and I, to get that catfish on board. Dad said it was turning out that the real fishers in the family were Charley and me. Dad made both Charley and I feel really proud.

41 d Choosing case with verbals

Participles, gerunds, and infinitives are called **verbals** because they are derived from verbs. However, they cannot function by themselves as verbs in sentences. A **past participle** (*worked, eaten, brought*) or **present participle** (*working, eating, bringing*) without an auxiliary verb can be used as a modifier. A **gerund** is the *-ing* form of the verb used as a noun. An **infinitive** is the base form of the verb, usually preceded by *to*.

PRESENT PARTICIPLE	A person *waking* at that hour is often groggy.
PAST PARTICIPLE	He seemed *tired*.
GERUND	*Waking* at that hour can ruin my day.
INFINITIVE	I hate *to wake* so early.

1 Objective case for verbal objects

Verbals can have objects. In the sentence *I like to read books*, for example, the object of the infinitive *to read* is *books*. Choose the objective case for a pronoun that is the object of a verbal.

Watching *her* was fascinating.

He hadn't intended to lose *them*.

2 Objective or possessive case before *-ing* verbals

The choice of pronoun case before an *-ing* verbal depends on whether the verbal is used as a noun or as a modifier. Which of these sentences is correct? Either could be correct depending on the intended meaning.

He heard their shouting.

What did he hear? He heard shouting.

He heard them shouting.

What did he hear? He heard them.

In the first, *shouting* is the object of the verb, and it must be a noun, a gerund. Using the possessive *their* would then be correct because it signals that the following word is a noun. In the second, *them* is the object of the verb and *shouting* is a modifier, a present participle. The objective *them* would be correct because the pronoun is the object of the verb.

In summary, use the possessive case for pronouns preceding gerunds and the objective case for pronouns preceding present participles.

■ ~~Me~~ My leaving made them all sad.

■ He heard ~~my~~ me leaving just before midnight.

3 Objective case before infinitives

A pronoun that immediately precedes an infinitive should be in the objective case.

The study group asked *her* to stay.

41 **e** Choosing case after *than* or *as*

The subordinating conjunctions *than* and *as* often appear in **elliptical constructions**—clauses that have one or more words intentionally omitted. (See 27f.) Understanding exactly what is omitted is the key to choosing the correct case for a pronoun that follows *than* or *as*.

Alex is as strong as [I/me].

Restore the omitted word *am* at the end of the sentence, and it is easy to choose the correct pronoun: *Alex is as strong as I am.*

Sometimes the omitted words will call for the possessive case:

Jen's luggage weighs as much as *mine* [my luggage].

The subjective case could also be meaningful in this sentence:

Jen's luggage weighs as much as *I* [weigh].

The objective case, me, *would not be correct in any sense here.*

By using the correct case, you can help the reader understand sentences that offer more than one possibility for omitted words.

My sister has more respect for her friends than *I* [have].

My sister has more respect for her friends than [she has for] *me*.

WP TIP Have your computer's search function locate every use of the words *than* and *as* in your paper. Evaluate the pronoun case used in each instance.

■ EDITING 3: PRACTICE

Edit the following sentences, using the correct pronoun case after *than* and *as*. Circle the number of any sentence that is correct.

At the daily newspaper where I work, Sam receives more fan mail than ~~me~~.
 ^I.

1. We're both columnists, but I think my columns are consistently better than her.
2. Our fellow writers consider I as funny as she.
3. But apparently our readers find she funnier.
4. Maybe I just have different taste than them.
5. She writing has single-handedly increased circulation 20 percent, the circulation department says.
6. Someday I know my writing will become more popular than hers.

41 f Choosing *who* or *whom*

The distinction between *who* and *whom* and between *whoever* and *whomever* has all but disappeared from everyday speech, so your "ear" for the correct form may be of little help. Yet in formal writing, failing to use *whom* or *whomever* for the objective case is considered incorrect. When you encounter one of these pronouns, remember to use *who* and *whoever* only for subjects, *whom* and *whomever* for objects.

As a test, answer a question posed by *who* or *whom* with a sentence using *he* or *him*.

[*Who/Whom*] got here first? *He* got here first.

Who *and he are both subjective, so use* who.

[*Who/Whom*] do you trust? I trust *him*.

Whom *and* him *are both objective, so use* whom.

Use *who* when the answer uses *he*, and *whom* when it uses *him*.

1 **To introduce questions**

Who, whom, whoever, and *whomever* can introduce questions; when they do, they are **interrogative pronouns**. If the pronoun is the subject of the question, use *who* or *whoever: Who is going? Whoever could be calling at this hour?*

When the pronoun is the object of the verb, use *whom* or *whomever: Whom did you see? Whomever did he want?*

Also use *whom* or *whomever* when the pronoun is the object of a preposition: *To whom are you speaking?*

■ Who
~~Whom~~ had the authority to enter the building at night?
∧

Test: He *had the authority. Use* who.

■ Whom
~~Who~~ did you admit to the building?
∧

Test: You did admit him. *Use* whom.

■ whom
To ~~who~~ did you give authority to enter the building?
∧

Test: You did give authority to him. *Use* whom.

Be particularly careful when a preposition is left at the end of a question. Pronouns that are objects of such prepositions still need to be in the objective case:

Whom did you give it to?

Moving the preposition so that it appears just before its object can make the choice clear:

To whom did you give it?

612 Choosing pronoun case

WP TIP Use the search function to find *who*, *whom*, *whoever*, and *whomever*, and evaluate the way you have used each one. If you tell the computer to search for *[space]-w-h-o*, with no space after the *o*, it will find all four pronouns (along with some other *who*-words) with one extended search.

2 In dependent clauses

Who, *whom*, *whoever*, and *whomever* are **relative pronouns** when they introduce dependent clauses, but the same rules about case apply. Use *who* and *whoever* when the pronoun is the subject of its clause, *whom* and *whomever* when it is the object of its clause. The case of the pronoun is determined by its function in the dependent clause, not by anything in the surrounding sentence.

The man *who* lives next door is a rock climber.

Who is the subject of the clause who lives next door.

The fellow *whom* I met last week is also a rock climber.

Whom is the object of met.

As with interrogative pronouns, the question test can help you choose the right case. Turn the dependent clause into a question introduced by the pronoun, and then answer that question with *he* or *him*. If the answer uses *he* (subjective case), then *who* is correct. If the answer uses *him* (objective case), then *whom* is correct.

■ I want a list of everyone ~~whom~~ visited the plant today.
   who

Test: Who/Whom *visited the plant?* He *did, so use* who.

■ The police will interrogate ~~whoever~~ the foreman accuses.
   whomever

Test: Who/Whom *does the foreman accuse? The foreman accuses* him, *so use* whomever.

EDITING 4: PRACTICE

Edit the following passage, using *who*, *whom*, *whoever*, and *whomever* correctly.

Whomever took the last piece of German Chocolate Cake has caused an uproar in our household. Dad had vowed that he alone would be the person whom would eat it. But this afternoon, when he looked in the refrigerator, it was gone. Only an empty, crumb-filled plate remained. Mom, who saw his reaction, said that whomever ate the piece was risking Dad's wrath. Dad fumed and fussed and brooded and interrogated whoever looked guilty. None of my brothers and sisters confessed to the crime, even when he threatened whoever the guilty party was helped by. In the end, though, the culprit was Mom, whom made the cake for his birthday and said she just wanted a midafternoon snack. What could Dad say? If he complained too much, she wouldn't bake for him anymore.

41 g Using reflexive pronouns

The pronouns *myself, yourself, himself, herself, itself, ourselves, yourselves,* and *themselves* are called **reflexive pronouns**. A reflexive pronoun reflects the action of the verb back toward its subject, making it clear that the object and the subject of the verb are one and the same: *I looked at* myself *in the mirror.* A reflexive pronoun also is used to rename and emphasize an element appearing earlier in the sentence: *He did it* himself.

A reflexive pronoun is never used as a subject. This error is most common when the subject should be *I* or *me.*

■ My friend and ~~myself~~ plan to attend.
   ^I

WP TIP If you know you tend to make this mistake, you can use your computer's search function to locate every instance of the word *myself* so that you can evaluate the correctness of each one. (See also 66b on pronouns as intensifiers.)

When the subject and the object of a verb refer to the same person or persons, use a reflexive pronoun for the object:

■ John cut ~~him~~ with the scissors.
   ^himself

   Himself makes it clear that the person who has been cut is the same as the person who did the cutting.

■ John cut ~~myself~~ with the scissors when he handed them to me.
   ^me

The subject of the verb cut *is* John. *The words* myself *and* John *do not name the same person, so* myself *is incorrect.*

A reflexive pronoun should be used as the object of a preposition when it and an earlier noun or pronoun in the sentence name the same person or persons.

■ I speak only for ~~me,~~ ^myself, not for my roommate.

Myself is correct because I *precedes it in the sentence.*

■ As for Carlos and ~~myself~~ ^me, we want to work in software design.

Myself is incorrect because I *does not precede it.*

WP TIP Use the search function to locate *myself* or any other reflexive pronouns that you know you have used in a paper you are currently working on. As you edit, make sure you have used these pronouns correctly.

■ **EDITING 5: PRACTICE**

Edit the following passage, using the appropriate pronoun cases throughout.

In the memories of my siblings and myself, our house used to be surrounded by a forest on three sides. Us children—my three brothers and me—used to hunt for snakes and salamanders in the woods by overturning the rocks that they lived under. One of the best hunting grounds for ourselves was the land to the south of our yard. When I was eight years old, I saw a garter snake catch a frog and devour it whole. It eating the frog upset my brothers and I terribly. Us, with our childish minds, thought that snakes were nasty, cruel creatures and that frogs were clearly nicer than them. Now that I am grown up, I realize that the snake eating the frog was not an act of cruelty. Snakes eat frogs to survive just as frogs eat insects. Each creature on earth lives and dies according to the natural order of things.

■ **EDITING 6: APPLICATION**

Examine a paper you are working on to see if you have used inappropriate pronoun cases. Do you make one kind of error more than others? Think of ways to identify problems you have. Edit your work.

Readers, like bus riders, like to know where they are being taken. A good writer respects readers' expectations the same way that a good driver keeps passengers comfortable: by avoiding needless detours and sudden changes in destination. As you edit, check to make sure that you have not made any detours that will confuse your readers.

 COMPOSING CONSISTENT AND COMPLETE SENTENCES

As you edit, check to make sure that your sentences are consistent and complete by doing the following:

- Make sure sentences include no unnecessary or distracting shifts.
- Make subjects and predicates relate to one another grammatically and logically.
- Make sure each sentence omits no words necessary to express its ideas clearly.

---

42 a   Avoiding unnecessary shifts

Readers generally expect continuity in point of view and in references to time throughout a piece of writing. Within sentences, readers expect a logical consistency in the person and number of subjects (see Chapter 36), in the forms of verbs (see Chapter 35), and in the way quotations are reproduced. A change in any of these elements is called a **shift**. Often a writer's meaning does require a shift, such as a change of subject from third person to first person or from singular to plural.

> As *Gibson* limped around the bases, *we* in the stands erupted in frenzy.

However, a shift in verb tense in the same sentence would be unnecessary and confusing: *As Gibson limped around the bases, we in the stands erupt in frenzy.* Such unnecessary shifts disrupt effective communication.

1 Shifts in person and number

We refer to ourselves in the **first person** (*I, we*), to our audience in the **second person** (*you*), and to other subjects in the **third person** (*he, she, it, one, they*). Unnecessary shifts in **person** often arise in sentences about groups or about unidentified people. Some writers shift unnecessarily to the second person, particularly when trying to make a comprehensive statement. To avoid unnecessary shifts to the second person, use *you* in formal writing only when referring to the reader. (See 28c.)

■ The chemistry students learned that ~~you~~ *they* had to be careful with certain combinations of chemicals.

■ As one enters the building, ~~you see~~ *one sees* little evidence of fire.

Unnecessary shifts in **number**—from singular to plural and vice versa—generally occur when a writer has used a singular noun or pronoun of indeterminate gender (*student, one*) and then uses a plural pronoun to refer to it, perhaps to avoid the appearance of sexism. (See 32c and 39d.) You can avoid such shifts by making the antecedent plural or by substituting a singular pronoun.

■ ~~Every student~~ *Students* make*s* their own schedule*s*.

■ Each student is responsible for ~~their~~ *his or her* own work.

2 Shifts in tense

Tense places the action of the verb in time: *Today I go. Yesterday I went. Tomorrow I will go.* Different verbs in a sentence or paragraph may logically use different tenses to reflect actions occurring at different times. (See 35d–e.)

> We *will play* tennis before we *eat* breakfast but after we *have had* our coffee.

The tense you select to describe most of the actions in your paper is called the **governing tense**. Once you establish it, do not use another tense without a good reason.

■ When the contract was finished, it ~~sets~~ a firm deadline.
    set

The **literary present tense** is used to describe literature or art. (See 35e.) If you use it, do so consistently.

■ In *The Glass Menagerie,* Tom realizes how trapped he is after the Gentleman Caller ~~departed~~.
    departs.

ESL SHIFTING TENSE WITHIN A PARAGRAPH

Sometimes verb tense shifting within a paragraph is necessary when you support or comment on an idea. Following are some acceptable reasons for shifting tense.

SHIFTING FROM PRESENT TENSE TO PAST TENSE

■ To provide background information
■ To support a claim with an example from the past
■ To compare a present situation with a past one

Truly dedicated writers *find* time to write regardless of the circumstances. Austen *wrote* most of her novels in short bursts of activity between receiving visitors and taking care of household duties.

SHIFTING FROM PAST TENSE TO PRESENT TENSE

■ To express a comment, opinion, or evaluation

On May 6, the town council *voted* against the school bond. Their decision *is* unfortunate.

---

3 Shifts in mood

English verbs are used in one of three **moods**. The **indicative mood** is used for statements and questions: *Rain fell. Did you hear it?* The **imperative mood** expresses commands, orders, or directions: *Close the door.* Unnecessary shifts from the imperative to the indicative mood commonly occur in instructions.

■ First cover your work surface with newspapers, and then ~~you~~ make sure your materials are within easy reach.

By contrast, the **subjunctive mood** expresses wishes or statements that are known to be not factual: *He wishes chocolate were not fattening. If he were a millionaire, he'd be happy without it.* (See 35f–g.) Often, you will find that using the subjunctive mood and the indicative mood in the same sentence is appropriate. In the next two examples, the verbs in the independent clauses (*wishes* and *would be*) are in the indicative, while the verbs in the dependent clauses (*were* in both cases) are in the subjunctive.

My professor *wishes* that I *were* more diligent.

The world *would be* nicer if everyone *were* as kind as you.

Watch for and avoid shifts from the subjunctive to the indicative or to the imperative that do not make sense.

■ The contract requires that you be in Denver on July 1 and that you ~~will~~ be in Houston on August 1.

4 Shifts in voice and subject

The subject of an **active voice** verb performs the verb's action: *He hit the ball.* The subject of a **passive voice** verb is acted upon: *The ball was hit by him.* (See 28c.) If a sentence has two verbs with the same subject, a shift of voice can be acceptable.

The students *completed* the project and *were given* first prize.

*The verbs shift from active (*completed*) to passive (*were given*) but have the same subject, students. The shift is acceptable because it keeps the focus on the subject.*

A shift from the active to the passive voice (or vice versa) can be distracting and unnecessary, however, when it requires a shift in subject as well.

■ As we peered out of the tent, ∧the waning moon ~~was seen~~ we saw through the trees.

5 Shifts between direct and indirect quotation

Direct quotation, sometimes called **direct discourse**, reproduces someone's exact words, which are enclosed in quotation marks.

"I love my work," he insisted.

Indirect quotation, or **indirect discourse**, is a paraphrase of someone else's words; it is not placed in quotation marks. (See Chapter 17.)

He insisted that he loved his work.

As you edit, watch for shifts from indirect to direct quotation that are not clearly indicated. Either use indirect quotation consistently or rewrite the sentence so that the direct quotation is introduced by a new verb and is enclosed in quotation marks.

- He insisted that he loved his work and why ~~was~~ the job ~~being~~ eliminated?
  [above "and": wondered] [above "the job": had to be] [after eliminated: / .]

- He insisted that he loved his work and ~~why~~ is the job being eliminated?
  [above "why": cried, "Why] [after eliminated?: "]

Now you know that he didn't just ask such a question but that these were his exact words.

Avoid using one verb (such as *said*) to introduce both an indirect quotation and a complete sentence of direct quotation. You have three editing choices: use indirect quotation in both instances, quote less than the full sentence directly, or start a new sentence.

- Dr. Ryan claims that the play was composed before 1600 and "It ~~shows the clear hand of~~ Shakespeare."
  [above: that it was certainly written by]

- Dr. Ryan claims that the play was composed before 1600 and "It "shows the clear hand of Shakespeare."

- Dr. Ryan claims that the play was composed before 1600 ~~and~~ "It shows the clear hand of Shakespeare."
  [above: . He says,]

■ EDITING 1: EXPLORATION

Throughout the following excerpt from his essay "Computers," Lewis Thomas uses the pronouns *you* and *we* inconsistently. Consider what effect Thomas hoped to achieve with this unconventional use of pronouns. Do you think he was effective?

"It would be nice to have better ways of monitoring what we're up to so that we could recognize change while it is occurring, instead of waking up as we do now to the astonished realization that the whole century just past wasn't what we thought it was, at all. Maybe computers can be used to help in this, although I rather doubt it. You can make simulation models of cities, but what you learn is that they seem to be beyond the reach of intelligent analysis; if you try to use common sense to make predictions, things get more botched up than ever. This is interesting, since a city is the most concentrated aggregation of humans, all exerting whatever influence they can bring to bear. The city seems to have a life of its own. If we cannot understand how this works, we are not likely to get very far with human society at large."

■ EDITING 2: PRACTICE

Edit the following sentences to avoid distracting or awkward shifts. Some sentences have more than one possible answer. Be ready to explain your editing choices. Circle the number of any sentence that is correct.

> things students face. They
> Oral exams can be the hardest ~~thing a student faces, You~~ work
> they ∧
> so hard to be ready, and then ~~you~~ can just stand up there and
> freeze.

1. Last night, Karen reminded me again about the time of the exam and said, "You had better not be late this time."

2. Fortunately, this morning she also gave me a wake-up call; she says she knew that I would oversleep.

3. I arrived at the examination room about five minutes early and was given an answer booklet and a seating assignment by the proctor.

4. We were allowed one hour for the examination, and do not use any books.

5. When it was time to begin, we were told first to review, and then you can begin to answer the questions.

6. As I turn to the first section, though, I saw a truly horrible sight.

7. My test dealt with second-year organic chemistry, but I was enrolled in American history.

8. I start sweating, and then, when I looked next to me, I saw another student busily scribbling in their answer book.

9. Suddenly, it dawns on me that I don't recognize anyone in the room, and I began to panic.

10. Just then the phone rang, and I hear Karen saying "Get up!" and telling me that she knew I would oversleep.

42 b   Eliminating mixed constructions

The term **mixed construction** applies to a sentence that begins one way and then takes a sudden, unexpected turn, so that readers are unsure what it means. One kind of mixed construction uses a grammatically unacceptable element as a subject or predicate. Another kind of mixed construction links subject and verb in an illogical way.

1   Making subjects and predicates grammatically compatible

A grammatically mixed sentence can have an inappropriate element as a subject. For example, in English a prepositional phrase cannot be the subject of a sentence.

Listening
■ ~~By listening~~ closely and paying attention to nonverbal signals
       ∧
helps a doctor make a fuller diagnosis.

The prepositional phrase is converted into something that can be a subject.

A doctor can make a fuller diagnosis by
■ ~~By~~ listening closely and paying attention to nonverbal signals
     ∧   ∧
~~helps a doctor make a fuller diagnosis~~

A completely new subject is created.

A modifier clause also cannot be the subject of a sentence. A modifier clause begins with a subordinating conjunction such as *after, before, when, where, while, because, if, although,* and *unless.* To edit a sentence that has a modifier clause as a subject, provide a new subject for the sentence.

■ ~~Because the doctor is~~ an expert does not mean a patient should
  never question a diagnosis.

    The doctor's status as *(inserted above)*
    ∧

The subject is now status *rather than the modifier clause beginning
with* Because.

Another kind of grammatically mixed sentence uses an inappropriate element as a predicate. A dependent clause cannot contain the main verb of a sentence.

■ The fact that most patients are afraid to ask questions~~, which~~
  gives doctors complete control.

Removing which *turns* gives *into the main verb.*

2 Making subjects and predicates logically compatible

    Sometimes a sentence combines elements that do not quite fit logically. Although the intent is usually clear, something is wrong at the level of literal meaning. As you edit, if you sense that some elements do not work together, reduce your sentence to its most basic elements—subject and verb—to see where the problem lies.

■ ~~The opinion of most~~ people believe that dogs make better pets
  than cats.

    Most *(inserted above)*
    ∧

Reduce the sentence to subject and verb: The opinion *cannot believe;*
people *can. So* people *makes a more logical subject.*

■ ~~The increase in the~~ number of cat owners in the United States
  has doubled since 1960.

    The *(inserted above)*
    ∧

The increase *hasn't doubled;* the number of cat owners *has doubled.*

■ Repeat offenders whose licenses have already been suspended
  for drunk driving will ~~be~~ revoked.

    have their licenses *(inserted above)*
    ∧

It is not offenders *who will be revoked, but rather their* licenses.

A subject complement must rename the subject in a logical way.

■ My father's favorite kitchen appliance is ~~using~~ our microwave oven.

Using is not an appliance. When oven *functions as the subject complement renaming* appliance, *the sentence makes sense.*

3 Eliminating faulty predication

A type of mixed construction called **faulty predication** is both ungrammatical and illogical. Sentences with faulty predication use a modifier clause starting with *when, where,* or *because* to rename the subject. Some contain the phrase *The reason is because.* . . .

■ A stalemate is ~~where neither player can~~ win.
   ^ the failure of either player to

■ ~~Pop art is where~~ an artist reproduces images from commercial products and the popular media.
   ^ In pop art

Such constructions are ungrammatical because a modifier cannot rename a subject. They are illogical because a person or thing (the subject) cannot be a *when, where,* or *because.*

Reserve *when* and *where* clauses to modifiers specifying time and place. Whenever you see *the reason is because,* substitute *the reason is that* or restate the subject.

■ The reason little has been done to solve the problem is ~~because~~ the committee is deadlocked.
   ^ that

■ ~~The reason little~~ has been done to solve the problem ~~is~~ because the committee is deadlocked.
   ^ Little

WP TIP Edit a paragraph from a paper you are currently working on for shifts and mixed constructions. Save your work. Open a new file in a window next to it. Now, edit the paragraph another way. Print both versions and exchange paragraphs with a classmate. Together choose the most effective sentences.

◼ EDITING 3: PRACTICE

Edit the following passage by eliminating mixed constructions. More than one edited version is possible. Be ready to explain your editing choices.

The reason some readers feel that Ernest Hemingway's fiction is over-rated is because his style seems so simple and repetitive. By focusing on the subtleties of his language, though, can tell us a great deal about the psychology of his characters. In "The Big Two-Hearted River," for example, the intention of Hemingway tries to give the reader a sense of Nick Adams's struggle to maintain some degree of emotional stability by focusing on all of the minute details of a trout-fishing excursion. By repeatedly reminding himself that he had made a "good camp" shows that Nick feels a sense of anxiety on some other, subconscious level. In an example like this, then, we can see that Hemingway's unique style is using small details to offer deeper insights into his characters' minds.

42 c   Inserting missing words

Sentences can be incomplete because of inadvertently omitted words, faulty elliptical constructions, or ambiguous comparisons.

◼ Checking for omitted words

Little words like *the, a, an, is, was, in, at, to,* and *that* are easy to omit, either in haste or in the interest of brevity. As you edit, check that you have not omitted necessary words.

◼ Little words are easy to omit, either in haste or $\overset{in}{\wedge}$ the interest of brevity.

◼ When she told me $\overset{to}{\wedge}$ meet her at the office, I $\overset{was}{\wedge}$ sure she meant her office.

When you read silently, your eye has a tendency to "fill in" what it expects to see; therefore a good way to check for missing words is to read your writing aloud.

2 Completing elliptical constructions

In **elliptical constructions**, words are intentionally omitted that readers can be expected to understand. Elliptical structures are usually used in parallel constructions. For example, in the sentence *The sky seemed gray and the day gloomy,* the verb *seemed* has been omitted before *gloomy.* (See 26f–g, 27f.)

When you use an elliptical construction, make sure that the words omitted are identical to the words already used in the other part of the parallel. Otherwise readers may be confused about your meaning.

■ The sun shone brilliantly and the clouds ^were^ radiant.

> *The second clause requires a different verb from the verb in the first clause,* shone, *so the second verb cannot be omitted.*

For the sake of clarity, consider repeating conjunctions and prepositions, especially in long parallel structures.

■ The project was designed to measure how drinking alters metabolism and ^how^ it affects a person's body chemistry.

3 Making comparisons complete

Comparisons may be incomplete or illogical because a writer has left out words that are necessary for reader understanding. Comparisons must completely and explicitly state the persons or things compared. Beware of inadvertently equating a person with a thing.

■ Many of Melville's novels are superior to ~~Cooper,~~ ^Cooper's.^

> Novels *cannot be compared with* Cooper; *they must be compared with* Cooper's *novels.*

Do not leave readers in doubt about what you are comparing.

■ It seems that Goodall likes apes more than ^she likes^ other people.

> *Does she like apes* more than she likes *other people,* or *more than other people do? Rather than make readers choose, make the comparison clear and complete.*

(For more on comparisons, see 37e and 41e.)

■ EDITING 4: PRACTICE

Edit the following passage by adding any necessary words to elliptical structures, making all comparisons complete and adding all necessary words that may have been inadvertently omitted. More than one edited version is possible. Be ready to explain your editing choices.

It's important to keep in mind that the children at the community center are individuals. No child's problems are the same as another. Change is difficult for everyone, children more so. Some of the children here are severely emotionally disturbed. The goal of the center is assess each child's needs to discover those who need a lot of attention and those who need less attention. For youths who are severely emotionally disturbed, their disturbance is an invisible handicap and becomes more apparent at stressful times. The behavior ranges of emotionally disturbed children are wider than adults. The social workers give the children's lives a sense of structure, the schedule stability.

■ EDITING 5: PRACTICE

Edit the following passage, making all of the sentences consistent and complete. More than one edited version is possible. Be ready to explain your editing choices.

I'll bet that most people sit down to their dinner between six and seven o'clock each night. You can tell because that's when the infuriating salespeople from the local paper call. He pretends that I already have a subscription, and then he'll ask you, "Was your paper delivered on time today?" or whether it was late. It is especially annoying is where they ask the same question every time. And they think that if you say, "No, I'm not a subscriber," somehow I will agree to listen to their sales pitch. What makes it even worse is a terrible newspaper. If they were trying to sell me the *New York Times* would be a different story.

■ EDITING 6: APPLICATION

Examine a paper you are working on, and see if you have written any sentences that are inconsistent or incomplete. Is there one kind of mistake that you make frequently? Can you see why you might have made this mistake? Edit any sentences that are inconsistent or incomplete, and think about how best to avoid these problems in the future.

Editing
Punctuation

The full stop at the end of every written sentence requires one of three marks of punctuation: a **period**, a **question mark**, or an **exclamation point**. Which mark you use depends largely on the meaning you wish the sentence to express. In fact, sometimes the only clue to the meaning of a sentence is the end punctuation: *They won. They won? They won!* Periods are also used with abbreviations, and question marks are sometimes used in parentheses to indicate uncertainty.

As you edit, be aware of the conventional uses of end punctuation.

43 a Using periods

Use a period at the end of a statement, a mild command, or a polite request.

The administration has canceled classes.

Do not attempt to drive to school this morning.

Please forward an application to the address above.

Also use a period after an indirect question (one that is reported, not asked directly). (See 42a5 and 43b).

■ I wonder who made the decision̸?.

Use a period in most conventional abbreviations. Do not put a space between the parts of an abbreviation (*U.S.*), except for the initials used for a person's name (*S. E. Hinton*).

Mr., Mrs., Ms.	A.M., P.M.	U.S., U.K.
Dr., Rev., Msgr.	sec., min., hr.	B.C., B.C.E., A.D.
Atty., Gov., Sen.	wk., mo., yr.	etc., e.g., i.e., vs., ca.
B.A., M.A., Ph.d.	in., ft., yd., mi.	p., para., fig., vol.
R.N., M.D.	Mon., Tues., Wed.	St., Ave., Rd.
Jr., Sr.	Jan., Feb., Mar.	

When an abbreviation containing a period falls at the end of a sentence, use a single period to end the sentence.

■ Be ready to go fishing at 4:00 A.M./

Note that the names of government agencies, organizations, corporations, and other such entities are generally abbreviated without periods: *FBI, NCAA, CBS, SAT.* Many other familiar initial abbreviations are also written without periods: *VCR, FM, RFD.* Periods are also not used with most shortened forms of words: *lab, grad, premed, champ.* Periods are never used in **acronyms**, which are abbreviations made up of initials and pronounced as words: *NASA, NATO, HUD.* (See Chapter 55 for more on abbreviations and acronyms.)

■ **EDITING I: PRACTICE**

Edit the following sentences by using periods correctly. Example:

Sandra Booker, M̤D̤, is a role model for our community.

1. Dr Booker focuses her practice on pediatric care for homeless children, beginning her day as early as 5:00 a.m..
2. She volunteers two days a week at an A.I.D.S. clinic.
3. She has worked with the US. Department of Housing and Urban Development (H.U.D.) to develop programs for at-risk families.
4. She even conducts a learning lab. for high school students who are considering becoming doctors.
5. I wonder who else in the community does so much?

43 **b** **Using question marks**

Use a question mark at the end of every **direct question**. Direct questions are usually signaled either by an interrogative pronoun such as *what, where,* or *why,* or by inverted word order, with part of the verb before the subject.

Where is Times Square?   How can I get there?
Can I take the subway?   Do you know the fare?

A sentence that ends with a **tag question** also take a question mark. (See 44f for the use of commas with tag questions.)

■ This train goes to Times Square, doesn't it⁇

Direct questions in a series may each be followed by a question mark, even if they are not all complete sentences. (See 51a for advice on capitalizing fragmentary questions.)

Where did Mario go? Did he go to the library? the cafeteria?

When a direct question is a quotation within a declarative sentence, the question mark comes inside the quotation marks without an additional comma or period.

■ Gertrude Stein was reportedly asked on her deathbed, "What is the answer?"/ "What is the question?⁀" she replied.

When a quotation is itself a question, put the question mark inside the quotes.

■ I asked, "Should I go⁀?

When a quotation that is not a question appears in a sentence that is a question, put the question mark outside the quotes.

■ Did you say, "Should I go?⁀

When both the sentence and the quotation it contains are questions, use a question mark inside and outside the quotation marks.

■ Did you say, "May I go too?"?
⋀

The same rule applies to exclamation points; see 43c.

Writers sometimes phrase questions in normal word order, as if they were statements; a question mark indicates that they should be read as questions.

Sylvester Stallone will play Hamlet next year? Don't count on it.

On the other hand, a polite request can be phrased as a direct question and written with a period instead of a question mark, especially when compliance is expected: *Would you join us in the conference room at 10:00.*

Remember that unlike direct questions, **indirect questions**— questions which are reported rather than asked directly—are not followed by question marks. In other words, if an independent clause in a sentence is a question, then use a question mark. If the independent clause is not a question, don't use a question mark.

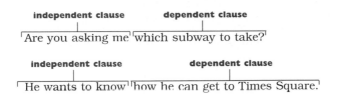

For more on indirect questions, see 42a5.

Use a question mark in parentheses to indicate uncertainty about a specific fact such as a date or the correct spelling of a word.

■ The plays of Francis Beaumont, 1584~(?)~– 1616, were as popular in their day as Shakespeare's.

Do not use question marks in parentheses to suggest sarcasm or irony.

■ Some people think it is funny ~(?)~ to humiliate others.

▨ EDITING 2: PRACTICE

Edit the following sentences by using question marks correctly. Example:

"You say that by learning another language a person can learn a lot about another culture~;~⟨?⟩" I asked.

1. I wonder how long it takes to be able to think in a different language?

2. What is the best way for me to learn to speak French. Converse with my friends. Go to the language lab. Go to France?

3. The best way to learn to speak another language is to speak it as often as possible, isn't it.

4. Some students think it's entertaining (?) when classmates make mistakes.

5. Don't you know that we learn by making mistakes.

---

43 **c** **Using exclamation points**

Use an exclamation point to convey emphasis or strong emotion in exclamations, forceful commands, interjections, and statements or questions that require special intensity.

What a mess!	Wow! It's getting late!
Stop the train!	Was that train fast!

An exclamation point in a direct quotation is enclosed within the quotation marks and is not followed by any other end punctuation.

■ "Ouch," my brother cried. "That hurts!"

Do not use an exclamation point, even in parentheses, to indicate amazement or sarcasm.

■ The judges selected Carl (!) to represent us in the regional competition.

If a sentence that requires an exclamation point ends with a quotation that does not, put the exclamation point outside the quotation marks.

■ Don't call it "Frisco!"

If both the sentence and the quotation within it require exclamation points, put one inside and one outside the quotation marks.

■ Quick, yell "Fire!"

Because exclamation points signal emphasis, they make demands on readers' attention and energy. Your writing will lose effectiveness if you use too many of them. Use only one or two in a passage; pick the most important exclamation point and replace the others with periods. You may want to use your computer's search and replace function to find and reconsider each exclamation point.

WP TIP As you edit, use your computer's search function to find and reconsider the various marks of end punctuation. For example, have the computer highlight each exclamation point you have used, and decide whether or not you've overused this particular form of emphasis.

■ **EDITING 3: EXPLORATION**

Find four or five examples of popular writing that overuse exclamation points. A good place to start your search is in advertising in newspapers or magazines. What effect do the exclamation points have?

■ EDITING 4: PRACTICE

Edit the following sentences by using exclamation points correctly. Some sentences have more than one possible answer. Be ready to discuss your editing choices. Example:

> Our mother told us to be carefu**l**/ not to slip on the ice when we were running for the bus.

1. "Be careful," she called out as we hurried down the icy driveway.
2. "Oh! No! Here comes the bus now. Hurry up."
3. "Too late. Now we'll have to walk to school."
4. "Are you crazy!? It's a four-mile walk to school."
5. "Don't tell me you can't walk four miles?" I exclaimed.

■ EDITING 5: PRACTICE

Edit the following by using all end punctuation correctly. More than one edited version is possible. Be ready to explain your editing choices.

Have you always assumed eating sugar will make you gain weight. This fact (?) is increasingly subject to debate. According to recent research, the main problem with sugar is that it usually accompanies fat in a diet Dr Adam Berg, a nutritionist, wondered what makes some people gain weight more than others? His research has led him to believe that excess fat is actually more likely than sugar to cause problems with weight and health! A study by the US Food and Drug Administration shows that the average American eats about two ounces of sugar a day. According to Berg, the level of sugar consumption found by the F.D.A. applies to both moderately overweight and obese people. Does the difference lie in amount of exercise? Genetic make-up. Calorie intake. Berg believes it is a combination of these, but he notes specifically that the eating patterns of obese people reflect a particularly high consumption of fatty foods. He suggests cutting out the doughnuts (!) and eating low-fat sweets instead. If only it could be so easy.

■ EDITING 6: APPLICATION

Take a few moments to reflect on any difficulties you have with end punctuation (periods, question marks, exclamation points). Rank the various forms of punctuation in the order of difficulty for you. Then examine a paper you are working on to see if you have misused punctuation in any way. Were you able to identify your trouble spots correctly? See if you can detect any patterns in your mistakes. Edit any sentences that have incorrect end punctuation.

The **comma** is the most frequently used mark of punctuation in English. Commas shape the phrasing of written sentences in the same way that brief pauses shape the phrasing of spoken sentences. Commas indicate how a sentence is divided into distinct but connected grammatical parts. By showing which words are related and which make up separate ideas, commas help readers understand a sentence's meaning.

Consider, for example, how difficult it is to understand the meaning of the following sentence, from which all commas have been deleted.

> A quarter of a century after the introduction of television into American society a period that has seen the medium become so deeply ingrained in American life that in at least one state the television set has attained the rank of a legal necessity safe from repossession in case of debt along with clothes cooking utensils and the like television viewing has become an inevitable and ordinary part of daily life.

With its commas restored, however, this complex sentence is actually quite clear.

> A quarter of a century after the introduction of television into American society, a period that has seen the medium become so deeply ingrained in American life that in at least one state the television set has attained the rank of a legal necessity, safe from repossession in case of debt along with clothes, cooking utensils, and the like, television viewing has become an inevitable and ordinary part of daily life.

MARIE WINN, "TELEVISION: THE PLUG-IN DRUG"

WP TIP Writers use the search function to locate commas and other forms of punctuation that they find difficult, so that they can check each use of different punctuation marks. For instance, the comma can be especially troublesome even to those who feel comfortable with its different uses. Use the search function to help you find all instances where you have used one and check.

Using commas before coordinating conjunctions joining independent clauses

An **independent clause** is a group of words that contains a subject and a predicate and that can stand alone as a complete sentence. A **compound sentence** contains two or more independent clauses. If those clauses are joined with a **coordinating conjunction** (*and*, *or*, *but*, *for*, *nor*, *yet*, *so*), use a comma before the coordinating conjunction.

The cable broke, *and* frightened passengers screamed.

She wanted to participate, *but* no one knew when the game would start.

When two independent clauses are very short, especially when they are related in meaning or parallel in structure and there is no chance of misreading, the comma between them may be omitted.

The sun rose and the fog lifted.

To prevent misreading of a compound sentence when the in dependent clauses contain internal commas, you may use a semicolon rather than a comma before the coordinating conjunction.

■ Cruise passengers may discmbark to shop, take a bus tour of the island, or snorkle/or, if they wish, they may swim, view a movie, or just relax on the ship.

Do not use a comma without a coordinating conjunction to join independent clauses. If you do, the result is an error known as a **comma splice**. (See Chapter 34.)

■ His hobby is raising geese,∧he proudly displays the blue ribbons they have won at the state fair.

Do not use a comma before a coordinating conjunction joining two dependent clauses.

■ When the board meets/and when the vote is officially recorded, the decision will be final.

Also do not use commas between other compound elements, such as compound subjects and compound verbs. (See 44j2.)

✔ **GUIDELINES FOR USING COMMAS**

As you edit, use the following guidelines for placing commas in your paper.

■ Before a coordinating conjunction that joins independent clauses

[independent clause],   [independent clause]

I had studied for hours, but I still found the exam difficult!

■ To set off an introductory element from a sentence's main clause

[introductory element],   [main clause]

Concentrating intensely, I completed the exam in twenty minutes.

■ To set off any nonrestrictive modifier or appositive at the end or in the middle of a sentence

[main clause],   [nonrestrictive modifier]

They toured the *Balclutha*, which is moored near Fisherman's Wharf.

[nonrestrictive appositive]

Dr. Parke-Cookson, our chemistry professor, gives exams weekly.

WP TIP Create a file called "Comma Guidelines," a set of worthwhile guidelines based on this book. Modify any guidelines as you, your classmates, and your instructor determine acceptable stylistic uses. Bring up this file of guidelines anytime you need help while composing a draft or revising and editing. Keep it on disk so that you can also take it to the computer lab to consult as you revise and edit.

■ **EDITING I: PRACTICE**

Edit the following sentences, using commas correctly with coordinating conjunctions joining independent clauses. Circle the number of any sentence that is correct. Example:

The highway department sets speed limits on state roads and

highways and it determines standards for intersecting roads.

■ Between items in a series and between coordinate adjectives

[item], [item],   [item]

English, history, and philosophy are my favorite subjects.

[coordinate adjective],   [coordinate adjective]   [noun]

Well-written, well-researched papers receive the best grades.

Also use commas—

■ To set off parenthetical expressions and elements of contrast
■ To set off interjections, tag sentences, and direct address
■ Between quotations and attributory phrases
■ With numbers, dates, names, and addresses
■ Whenever necessary to prevent misreading

WP TIP   If you have trouble with commas, use the search function to locate all the commas in your paper. Evaluate your use of each one and edit wherever necessary.

1.   Every new business or residence along a highway needs an access road but first the highway department must approve its design and location.

2.   The developer of a new housing development or commercial center must complete an application, and must submit it for the highway department's review.

3.   The regulations very clearly describe the standards for sight distances and markings so a developer can tell if a driveway is acceptable.

4.   The minimum sight distances vary with the speed limit and the grade of the road and the standards for driveway construction vary with the expected volume of traffic.

5.   The highway department does not have to permit a driveway that does not meet its standards or that would require modifications to the roadway.

44 b Using commas after introductory elements

An introductory element is a dependent clause, phrase, or word that precedes and introduces an independent clause. In most cases, a comma should separate the introductory element from the independent clause.

Always use a comma after an introductory **adverb clause** (a dependent clause beginning with a subordinating conjunction such as *when, because, if,* and so on).

> *When Elizabeth I assumed the throne of England in 1558,* the country was in turmoil.

In most cases, an introductory phrase should be followed by a comma.

PREPOSITIONAL PHRASE	*In every taste test,* the subjects chose the new flavor over the old.
INFINITIVE PHRASE	*To do the job properly,* they need more time.
PARTICIPIAL PHRASES	*Praised by all the critics,* the movie was still not a hit.
	Barking furiously, the little dog lunged at me.
ABSOLUTE PHRASE	*His dream of glory destroyed,* the boxer died an embittered man.

Some writers do not use a comma when the phrase is only two or three words and there is no possibility of confusion. This is particularly true with short prepositional phrases: *In 1963 an assassin's bullet shocked the world.* However, a comma is always correct in these situations and may be preferred by some instructors.

Do not use a comma after an introductory phrase when the word order of the sentence is inverted so that the verb precedes its subject.

■ In the back of the closet/was an old box.

In this sentence, box *is the subject and* was *is the verb.*

Do not use a comma after an introductory phrase that functions as the subject of the sentence rather than as a modifier.

■ Hearing that song/evokes warm memories.

In this sentence, hearing that song *is the subject.*

Introductory words should generally be separated from an independent clause by a comma.

ADJECTIVE	*Together*, we are a great team.
ADVERB	*Nervously*, I waited for my name to be called.
CONJUNCTIVE ADVERB	*However*, taxes must be raised.
TRANSITIONAL EXPRESSION	*First*, remove the plastic wrapper. *Then*, unfold the bag.
INTERJECTION	*Yes*, we need to improve our parks.

(Note that conjunctive adverbs, transitional expressions, and interjections are set off no matter where they fall in a sentence; see 44e and 44f. See 24c2 and 34b2 for more examples of transitional expressions and conjunctive adverbs.)

▪ EDITING 2: PRACTICE

Edit the following passage, using commas after introductory elements.

Despite his own admission that he had lived a life full of failings Mickey Mantle died a hero to many Americans. During the 1950s and 1960s Mantle was the most popular player on the New York Yankees. Because of that team's unsurpassed success on the baseball diamond Mantle's personal achievements took on an even greater luster than they otherwise might have. However it was not just his skills as a player that made him beloved. In fact Mantle's warmth as a human being endeared him to fans and sportswriters more than did any other trait. When Mantle died in 1995 his passing was felt deeply by many who had seen him play. Although years separated them from their childhood days at the ballpark many older Americans took time to cherish their memories of watching "the Mick" play. To many he was the symbol of a less cynical and materialistic era.

44 c Using commas to set off nonrestrictive modifiers and appositives

A modifier is **restrictive** if it provides information that readers must have in order to understand the meaning of the word or words modified. It "restricts" or limits the meaning from a general group to a more specific one.

Students *who are late* will be prohibited from taking the exam.

The modifier who are late *is restrictive because it limits the meaning of the word it modifies to a specific group of students: not all students will be prohibited from taking the exam, only those who are late.*

A modifier is **nonrestrictive** if it provides additional information but is not essential to the meaning of the word or words it modifies.

Qualified doctors, *who must be licensed*, are in short supply.

The modifier who must be licensed *is nonrestrictive because it tells the reader more about* doctors *but does not limit the meaning to a specific group of doctors.*

Note that when what is being modified is a specifically identified person or thing, its meaning cannot be limited further; therefore, the modifier is always nonrestrictive and provides only additional information: *Ernesto Seguerra, who used to run a hardware business, is now running for governor.*

Commas are used to set off nonrestrictive modifiers but not restrictive ones. Often, the only clue to whether a modifier is restrictive or nonrestrictive—and to the writer's meaning—is how the sentence is punctuated.

Company employees *who receive generous benefits* should not complain.

Company employees, *who receive generous benefits*, should not complain.

The restrictive modifier in the first sentence limits the meaning to a specific group of employees, implying that not all employees *of the company receive generous benefits. The nonrestrictive modifier in the second sentence says something different: by not specifying a specific group, it implies that* all employees *receive generous benefits.*

To determine whether a modifier is restrictive or nonrestrictive, try omitting it. Omitting a nonrestrictive modifier usually will not change the basic meaning of a sentence, but omitting a restrictive one will.

RESTRICTIVE

Athletes who take steroids want a shortcut.

Athletes want a shortcut.

These two sentences have very different meanings; the modifier is restrictive.

NONRESTRICTIVE

Olympic athletes, who all have trained intensely, are usually in top physical shape.

Olympic athletes are usually in top physical shape.

These two sentences mean about the same thing; the modifier is nonrestrictive.

Another way to see whether a modifier is restrictive or nonrestrictive is to ask a question about the identity of the subject of the clause. If the answer requires the information contained in the modifier, the modifier is restrictive.

RESTRICTIVE

A cat that neglects to groom itself will have matted fur.

What will have matted fur? A cat that neglects to groom itself.

NONRESTRICTIVE

A cat, which is a nocturnal mammal, hunts small rodents.

What hunts small rodents? A cat.

1 Adjective and adverb clauses

Adjective clauses—clauses that begin with *that, where, which, who, whom,* and *whose*—can be either restrictive or nonrestrictive. *That* is used only in restrictive clauses. *Which* is used for nonrestrictive clauses, but it can be used for restrictive as well. (For more information on *that* and *which,* see 39f.) Remember that restrictive clauses are not set off by commas because they are necessary to the meaning of the sentence; nonrestrictive clauses are set off by commas.

RESTRICTIVE

The trophy will go to the team *that scores the most points.*

Anyone *who visits the national Air and Space Museum* can touch a piece of the moon.

Note that a clause modifying an indefinite pronoun, such as anyone, is usually restrictive.

NONRESTRICTIVE

Soccer, *which dates back two centuries,* is the world's most popular sport.

The festival will honor Spike Lee, *who directed Malcolm X.*

Note that a clause modifying a proper noun, such as Spike Lee, is almost always nonrestrictive.

Adverb clauses—clauses beginning with subordinating conjunctions, such a *because, when,* and *before*—are most often restrictive. They may, however, be considered nonrestrictive when they indicate a contrast; such clauses begin with conjunctions such as *although* and *even though.* When an adverb clause introduces a sentence, it is set off with a comma (see 44b); otherwise it is not.

When I am well prepared, I always do well on tests.

Adverb clause first—use a comma.

I always do well on tests when I am well prepared.

Adverb clause last—no comma needed.

■ The jury voted to convict/ because the evidence was overwhelming.

■ The jury voted for acquittal, even though the evidence seemed overwhelming.
                            ∧

The clause may be set off with a comma because it indicates a contrast.

2 Phrases

Prepositional phrases are usually restrictive, although they occasionally serve to add nonrestrictive information. Participial phrases may be restrictive or nonrestrictive.

RESTRICTIVE

An attitude *of patience* is required *for the job.*

A house *destroyed by fire* is a terrible sight.

NONRESTRICTIVE

A "baby boom" began in 1946, *after World War II.*

The youngest "boomers," *born in 1964,* are now in their thirties.

3 Appositives

An appositive is a noun or noun phrase that immediately follows another noun and renames it. An appositive is restrictive only when it is more specific than the noun it renames.

RESTRICTIVE

Poet *Gary Soto* has written several novels for young adults.

His poem *"Oranges"* is about having a crush on someone else.

Gary Soto *is more specific than* poet. "Oranges" *specifies which of many poems.*

NONRESTRICTIVE

Gary Soto, *a popular poet,* writes novels for young adults.

"Oranges," *my favorite of his poems,* seems autobiographical.

A popular poet *is less specific than* Gary Soto. My favorite of his poems *is not more specific than* "Oranges."

WP TIP Examine an existing paragraph of your own writing, editing for punctuation. Where appropriate, highlight in **bold** those commas about which you have questions. Take hard copy to class and discuss it with a classmate.

■ EDITING 3: PRACTICE

Edit the following passage, using commas correctly with restrictive and nonrestrictive modifiers and appositives.

Anger an emotion all of us experience at one time or another generally arises, when we feel we can't control a situation or we don't get what we want. Anger may be natural, but researchers say that people, who get angry often, may be giving in to a learned response. Such uncontrolled fits of anger which can actually kill a person may be controlled if people can learn to deal with their anger, in a positive way. C. Mack Amick a counselor from North Carolina advises people to ask themselves three questions when they get angry. The first question, recommended by Amick, is "Is this really important to me?" The answer well may be "no" which means it's time to cool off. The second question that he recommends is "Is this the right time to get angry?" The final question designed specifically to help one gain control is "Do I have an effective response?" Finding a response, that is assertive but not aggressive, is the key to controlling one's anger.

| **44** | **d** | **Using commas between items in a series and between coordinate adjectives** |

A **series** consists of three or more words, phrases, or clauses that are equal in grammatical form and in importance. A coordinating conjunction—*and, or, but, nor, so, for, yet*—usually precedes the final item in the series. Use a comma after each item in the series except the last.

> He studied all of the notes, memos, letters, and reports.

> To accelerate smoothly, to stop without jerking, and to make complete turns can require many hours of driving practice.

> He reported that some economists believe the recession is over, that some believe it continues, but that most agree a slow recovery is under way.

Sometimes in a series, the comma that would normally precede the coordinating conjunction is omitted: *Participants in the peace talks included Israelis, Palestinians and Syrians.* This style is common in newspapers. In academic writing, however, using the final comma is generally preferred.

Unless a comma is required by another rule, do not use one before the first item or after the last item of a series.

■ The primary colors are/red, yellow, and blue.

■ They visited Nevada, Utah, and Arizona/on their trip West.

When individual items of a series include commas, you can help readers avoid confusion by separating the elements with semicolons instead of commas. (See 45b.)

Coordinate adjectives are two or more adjectives that modify the same noun: *warm, sunny day.* Coordinate adjectives are independent of each other in meaning and in their relationship to the noun. Use commas to separate coordinate adjectives.

To see whether adjectives are coordinate, try inserting *and* between them or reversing their order. If the resulting sentence still makes sense, the adjectives are coordinate and require commas.

ADJECTIVES COORDINATE

YES   He put on a clean, pressed shirt.

YES   He put on a clean and pressed shirt.

YES   He put on a pressed, clean shirt.

ADJECTIVES NOT COORDINATE

YES   I found five copper coins.

NO   I found five and copper coins.

NO   I found copper five coins.

Do not use a comma between coordinate adjectives and the noun they modify.

■ They walked with delicate, deliberate/steps across the ice.

■ Twelve/diseased/olive trees must be cut down.

■ **EDITING 4: PRACTICE**

Edit the following sentences, using commas correctly between items in a series and between coordinate adjectives. Circle the number of any sentence that is correct. Example:

> **Burlington International Airport, like any other airport, has a tower, a radar room,and many safety devices.**
>   ∧

1.   Inside the airport are a comfortable lounge, three departure gates, and a restaurant.

2.   The airport leases the space to a number of customers, including airlines car rental agencies food concessions and gift shops.

3.   The airport's representative explained that the airport is run like larger airports that it leases out its buildings and that it takes a percentage of the profits made by the independent businesses.

4.   The majority of air travel at the airport is between Boston Newark and Chicago, although travel is by no means limited to these three, major cities.

5.   Over the next ten years, the airport hopes to replace the few, remaining pre-1950s buildings with large modern facilities.

| 44 | e | **Using commas to set off parenthetical expressions and elements of contrast** |

Parenthetical expressions are words and phrases that interrupt the flow of a sentence to offer a comment, a supplemental explanation, or a transition. In many cases, **transitional expressions** and **conjunctive adverbs** (such as *furthermore, for* *example, as a result, therefore, however,* and *meanwhile*) serve as parenthetical expressions and are set off with commas. Other conventional parenthetical expressions include *in fact, of course, without a doubt, by the way,* and *to be honest.* Phrases that begin with *according to, such as,* and so forth are also parenthetical expressions.

Parenthetical expressions can often be moved within a sentence without affecting its meaning. No matter where they appear in a sentence, they are generally set off with commas.

ESL **PARENTHETICAL EXPRESSIONS**

Parenthetical expressions in English are often used by writers to comment on what is being said. For example, *surprisingly* and *fortunately* tell the reader that the writer thinks the facts expressed are surprising or fortunate. The expressions *to be honest* and *frankly* tell the reader that the writer is being honest or frank.

Parenthetical expressions may be placed in various parts of the sentence and should be separated from the rest of the sentence with commas. Here are some common parenthetical expressions.

clearly	I imagine	regrettably
fortunately	I suppose	sadly
frankly	I think	to be frank
honestly	it is hoped	to be honest
I believe	obviously	unfortunately

One Saturday, *for example,* we had marshmallows for breakfast.

The commissioner was not amused by the report, *however.*

Of course, these predictions may be inaccurate.

Note that if a conjunctive adverb is being used to join two independent clauses, you must use a semicolon rather than a comma before it. Otherwise, you will create a **comma splice**. (See Chapter 34 and 45a.)

Commas may also be used to set off **elements of contrast**— words, phrases, or clauses that emphasize a point by describing what it is not or by citing an opposite condition.

The experience was illuminating, but unnerving, for everyone.

The class started on Tuesday, not on Wednesday.

The article mentioned where he obtained his degree, but not when he received it.

▣ EDITING 5: PRACTICE

Edit the following sentences, using commas correctly with parenthetical expressions and elements of contrast. Circle the number of any sentence that is correct. Example:

> **Soothing music it seems is effective for reducing stress.**
>   ^   ^

1. Many physicians in fact are recommending relaxing music not tranquilizers to patients with high levels of stress.

2. One Boston doctor surprisingly enough has produced a recording of music that according to him uses the rhythms of a healthy heartbeat.

3. He believes exposure to such rhythms can promote a slower and more regular heartbeat in patients.

4. Other physicians however suggest that patients should select their own favored music not a doctor's prescription.

5. A Phoenix psychologist for example advises patients to start with music that is the same as not calmer than their energy level; they can later switch to music of a lower intensity such as new age or light jazz.

---

44 **f**   **Using commas to set off interjections, tag sentences, and direct address**

Use a comma or commas to set off mild **interjections.**

Oh, what good times we had together.

The replacement players were, *alas*, doomed from the start.

Use a comma before **tag sentences**—short statements or questions at the ends of sentences that express or elicit an opinion.

You received my application in time, *I hope.*

We are not so trusting of strangers these days, *are we*?

Use a comma or commas to set off words of **direct address**—words that name the person or group to whom a sentence is directed.

Lilith, I hope you are well.

That, *my friends*, is not the end of the story.

We appreciate your generous contribution, *Dr. Collins*.

■ EDITING 6: PRACTICE

Edit the following sentences, using commas correctly to set off interjections, tag sentences, and words of direct address. Circle the number of any sentence that is correct. Example:

We've all heard the standard politician's spiel,haven't we?

 Λ

1. Oh the promises politicians make.
2. They always begin with something like, "My fellow citizens it is my goal to follow the will of the people."
3. Then they tell us, "You realize that my first concern is my constituents I hope."
4. They can't really expect us to believe their promises can they?
5. Ah we're just disillusioned with politicians these days my friends, which is why turnout on election day gets lower every year don't you think?

44 g Using commas with quotations

Direct quotations are often accompanied by **attributory words,** which identify the source of the quotation. In general, use commas to set off attributory words, whether they appear before, after, or in the middle of the quotation. A comma before attributory words goes *inside* the quotation marks.

In 1948 Jack Kerouac first declared, "We're a *beat* generation."

"I didn't raise my boy to be a soldier," begins a 1915 poem.

"Scratch a lover," according to Dorothy Parker, "and find a foe."

Note, however, that when an attributory phrase comes between two complete quoted sentences, it is followed by a period. Note also that when a quotation ends with a question mark or exclamation point, no comma is added before an attributory phrase.

■ "Dead, did I say?" Chief Seattle ends his speech‸"There is no death, only a change of worlds."

■ "The news is terrific!‸" shouted Sharonna.

Also no comma is used when a quotation is partial and is preceded by *that*, or when there is no true attributory phrase.

■ He closed by saying that/"time will prove us right."

■ According to one critic, the program is/"a sinkhole for public dollars."

■ The slogan/ "You deserve a break today/" was particularly successful.

In general, do not use a comma before indirect quotations, which also should not be enclosed in quotation marks.

■ Jones claimed/he had not yet begun to fight.

A comma may, however, follow an introductory phrase before an indirect quotation: *According to Jones, he has not yet begun to fight.*

(See Chapter 48 for more on punctuating quotations.)

WP TIP Create a file and name it. Enter a paragraph that you have been revising, or select one from the editing activities in this chapter. As you enter the paragraph, try to punctuate as you go, putting into **bold** anything you believe might be open to dispute or discussion in class. Print hard copy and share your findings with a classmate.

■ **EDITING 7: PRACTICE**

Edit the following sentences, using commas correctly with quotations. Example:

"Love looks not with the eyes‸" according to Shakespeare "but with the mind."

I. In her novel *Jacques*, George Sand writes "No human creature can give orders to love."

2. "How do I love Thee," asked Elizabeth Barrett Browning? "Let me count the ways."

3. "Man must evolve for all human conflict a method which rejects revenge, aggression, and retaliation" said Martin Luther King, "The foundation of such a method is love."

4. Dr. King also said "I believe that unarmed truth and unconditional love will have the final word in reality."

5. "Love is heaven" wrote Walter Scott "and heaven is love."

Using commas with numbers, dates, names, places, and addresses

Various rules and conventions govern the use of commas with numbers, dates, names, places, and addresses.

1 Numbers

For numbers of five digits or more, use a comma before every three digits, counting from the right. In four-digit numbers, the comma is optional.

2700 (*or* 2,700)   79,087   1,654,220

Do not use a comma in years or page numbers of four digits or with numbers in addresses.

That example is found on page 1269.

In 1990 our address was 21001 South Street, Lodi, Ohio 43042.

2 Dates

Always use a comma between the words for the day and month and between the numbers for the date and year.

Friday, March 22   June 10, 1990

Also use a comma after the year when a date giving month, day, and year is part of a sentence.

Louis Armstrong was born on July 4, 1900, in New Orleans.

Don't use commas when only the month and year are given in a date or when the month separates the date and year.

The war broke out in August 1914 and ended on 11 November 1918.

3 Names

Use commas to set off an abbreviation or title following a name.

Joyce B. Wong, M.D., supervised the CPR training session.

Renee Dafoe, vice president, welcomed the new members.

Edwin M. Green, Jr., was the first speaker.

Do not use commas to set off roman numerals following a name: *Frank T. Winters III.*

4 Places and addresses

Use a comma before and after the state, when naming a city and state in a sentence.

She was born in Lexington, Kentucky, and raised in New York.

When a full address is given in a sentence, use a comma to separate each element except for postal zip code, which should have no comma before or after it.

My address is 169 Elm Street, Apartment 4, Boston, Massachusetts 02116 through the end of June.

However, for an address in block form, as on the front of an envelope, do not use a comma at the end of each line.

EDITING 8: PRACTICE

Edit the following sentences, using commas correctly with numbers, dates, names, places, and addresses. Example:

In the week before Christmas, the mail-order company where I worked filled 84,567 orders.

 ٨

1. I started my job in February, 1993, and the last day I worked was January 15 1994.

2. During that time, I answered 3456 calls and sold merchandise worth more than $200000.

3. The worst customers are the ones with names like Jane Jones Ph.D. or John Johnson, III, who insist on having their titles appear on all their mail.

4. You may write to my former employer at this address: National Mail-Order Products, 19123 Fifth Avenue New York New York 10001.

5. With $1500 in my savings account, I do not need to worry about getting another job until March 1994.

---

44 **i** **Using commas to prevent misreading**

Commas may occasionally be used, even when they are not required by any specific rule, when they help to prevent misreading.

We will all pitch in, in the event of a problem.

I believed, once I had seen the evidence.

Each of us who can, preserves her memory fondly.

They found that, in 1990, 256 people were infected.

■ **EDITING 9: EXPLORATION**

Try to make up two or three sentences that are awkward, confusing, or humorous without commas. Read them to your classmates to see if they are able to understand them. Examples:

In the winter time seems to stand still.

Before she had taken the wrong bus to get to the museum.

I dressed and fed my cats.

---

44 **j** **Editing misused commas**

Failing to include commas where they are conventionally expected can confuse readers and undercut your authority as a writer. It can be equally distracting, however, to use commas where they are not required by a general rule or convention.

Misuses of commas already discussed in this chapter are summarized in the box on page 653. This section covers several other common misuses.

ESL **COMMA TROUBLESHOOTING**

When editing your papers for correct use of commas, pay special attention to the commas that help readers understand your ideas. (From a reader's point of view, some commas are more important than others.)

1. As an editing strategy, put brackets around structures that need commas so that you can easily identify where phrases or clauses begin and end.

■ My English teacher [who is new this year], just graduated from Stanford.

■ [If we consider the source of humor for this joke], we see that it depends

on something that is contrary to our expectations.

2. Check for commas all adverb clauses (*because, although, when,* etc.) that begin sentences. Find the end of the clause and add a comma if necessary.

■ Since the library was closed, I studied at home.

3. When using *that* as a relative pronoun, make sure that you have not set it off by commas. (See 44j3.)

■ This writer argues very convincingly / that the freedom to think is one of

the strengths of the American educational system.

4. If you have listed three or more items in a series, make sure that you have put a comma and the word *and* before the last item. A comma alone is not sufficient. (See 44d.)

                                                      and
■ We studied similies, metaphors, analogies.

5. Delete commas that separate the subject from the verb, no matter how many words make up the subject (unless it has phrases or clauses after it that need commas). (See 44b and 44j1.)

■ *The city in the southern United States that I like the most /* is New

Orleans.

CHECKING FOR COMMAS THAT OCCUR IN PAIRS

Always make sure to use a pair of commas to set off the following when they appear in the middle of a sentence: **nonrestrictive modifiers and appositives** (44c); **parenthetical elements** and **elements of contrast** (44e); **interjections** and **words of direct address** (44f); and **years in full dates, titles and abbreviations after names**, and **state names preceded by city names** (44h).

■ This book,which he had read three times, was quite tattered.
   ∧

■ The instructors,rather than the students, are being tested.
   ∧

■ We believe, yes, the initiative should pass.
   ∧

■ It will be January 3, 1999, before I receive my degree.
   ∧

Avoid putting single commas between subjects and verbs, verbs and objects or complements, or objects and complements

Subject and verb

■ A *season* of drought/ *worried* the farmers.

Verb and object

■ The agreement *entails/ training* for part-time staff.

Verb and complement

■ The laid-off workers *seem/* surprisingly *understanding*.

Object and complement

■ The extra pay made *him/* quite *happy*.

A pair of commas, such as those used to set off parenthetical elements and nonrestrictive modifiers, may separate these elements.

David Hill, the chief researcher, developed the method.

2 **Avoid putting commas between compound elements**

Compound subject

■ The *members* of the senior class/ and their *parents* were invited.

Compound verb

■ Maria quickly *turned off* the lights/ and *locked* the door.

Compound object

■ Sean put the *books* on the shelf/ and the *pens* in the drawer.

Compound complement

■ He found the work easy to learn/ but hard to continue.

■ The weather was unbearably *hot*/ and much too *humid*.

Compound object

■ Gina tried to *save* more/ and to *spend* less.

Commas are used to separate the parts of a compound sentence. (See 44a.)

The rain stopped, and the sun came out.

3 **Avoid putting commas following a relative pronoun or subordinating conjunction**

■ The map that/ *we requested* turned out to be incorrect.

■ Our legislators have no idea how to proceed *because*/ *we have not come to a concensus.*

A pair of commas, such as those used to set off parenthetical elements, may separate these elements.

We found that, according to the latest data, the population had doubled.

See 44g for misuses of commas with quotations.

■ EDITING 10: EXPLORATION

Read the following excerpt from an essay by Isak Dinesen. What is the effect of the many commas in the opening paragraph? Are any of them unnecessary? Copy the paragraph, eliminating any unnecessary commas. Then read it aloud, comparing it to Dinesen's version. Why, do you think, did Dinesen use commas this way?

Just at the beginning of the long rains, in the last week of March, or the first week of April, I have heard the nightingale in the woods of Africa. Not the full song: a few notes only,—the opening bars of the concerto, a rehearsal, suddenly stopped and again begun. It was as if, in the solitude of the dripping woods, some one was, in a tree, tuning a small cello. It was, however, the same melody, and the same abundance and sweetness, as were soon to fill the forests of Europe, from Sicily to Elsinore.

ISAK DINESEN, "SOME AFRICAN BIRDS"

■ EDITING 11: PRACTICE

Edit the following passage by deleting any unnecessary commas.

More kids than ever before are playing video games, to fill up their leisure time. One of the most popular, games to come out in recent years is Mortal Kombat. The game is so popular, that a movie based on it became a huge, financial success. Playing the game, is thought by some to have a negative influence on behavior, though. Some, recent studies suggest that children, witnessing simulations of extreme violence, are more likely, than others, to behave violently, themselves. On the other hand, many others argue that video games are a harmless way for people, to relieve stress, and aggression. In their view, human beings are naturally prone to violence, and to claim that the elimination of a single, video game would make a difference, is sheer fantasy.

WP TIP: Enter this passage into a computer file, name it, and print it out. Then using hard copy, hand edit it for comma usage, using the proofreading marks on page 763.

EDITING UNNEEDED COMMAS

Do not use a comma for the following.

1. To join independent clauses without a coordinating conjunction (44a)

■ We won the game, *and* it was the first of many more victories.

2. After an introductory phrase when the verb precedes the subject in a sentence or when the phrase is the subject of the sentence (44b)

■ Along with every challenge, comes an opportunity for success.

■ Eating sensibly and exercising regularly, improved my health.

3. To set off restrictive clauses, phrases, or appositives (44c)

■ The materials, that you requested, have arrived.

■ A bird, with only one wing, has little chance of survival.

■ Singer and guitarist, John Hall, will appear at the benefit.

4. Before the first element or after the last element of a series, unless required by another rule (44d)

■ We contributed to, United Way, World Watch, and the Red Cross.

■ Rice, beans, and peppers, provide the basis for many local dishes.

5. Between adjectives that are not coordinate (44d)

■ There are three, different patterns of male baldness.

■ EDITING 12: PRACTICE

Edit the following passage, using commas correctly.

In two, recent scientific studies researchers have found what might be called an "excitability gene." This genetic variation as it is called is found in people who crave, excitement, thrills and new experiences. They are also themselves excitable, and prone to temper flare-ups. If the discovery holds up after further research it will represent the first link ever discovered between a gene and normal nonpathological behavior. "Success in mapping genes for a normal personality trait may signal a fruitful way to map genes for psychopathology" according to one of the researchers C. Robert Cloninger M.D. Cloninger who is on the staff of Washington University, proposed the hypothesis that, people's need for excitement is related to how dopamine a neural chemical is processed by the brain. This process is governed by a specific gene that in fact occurs in two variant ways, as a series of seven sequences or a series of four. What researchers discovered was that people, who could be called "novelty-seekers," generally had the longer seven-sequence version of the gene. This does not mean however, that the behavioral trait is governed solely by this single gene and researchers caution that other factors such as personal experience come into play.

■ EDITING 13: APPLICATION

Take a few moments to reflect on the difficulties you most commonly have in using commas. Make a brief list that ranks your problems in order, from greatest to least amount of difficulty. Now examine a paper you are working on and look for any examples of misused or omitted commas. Do you notice consistent patterns? How accurate was your initial prediction of where your difficulties would lie? Edit any sentences in which you have misused or omitted commas.

45 Semicolons

While a comma marks a pause within a sentence, a **semicolon** marks a stop within a sentence, telling readers that what precedes it is complete and that what follows is also complete and closely related. The semicolon marks a division between sentence elements of equal rank; it is not used to introduce, enclose, or end a statement.

Although using a period or a comma is often mandatory, using a semicolon is usually a choice; in certain situations it may be an alternative to either a period or a comma.

 WHEN IS A SEMICOLON NEEDED?

■ To separate two independent clauses
■ To separate items in a series containing commas

45 a Using semicolons between independent clauses

An **independent clause** is a group of words that contains a subject and a predicate and that can stand alone as a complete sentence. Two or more such clauses may be joined with a semicolon to indicate that the clauses are closely related. A semicolon is often used when the relationship between clauses is one of contrast or contradiction.

The storm raged all night; most of us slept fitfully, if at all.

Most dogs aim to please their owners; cats are more independent.

A semicolon may be used between independent clauses joined with a **conjunctive adverb** (*however, furthermore, therefore*) or a **transitional expression** (*for example, on the other hand*). (See 34b2.)

Many in the community were angry; however, they lacked an articulate leader.

The contract was approved; indeed, no one questioned the restrictions.

You may use a semicolon with a coordinating conjunction to join complex or lengthy independent clauses, particularly if they contain commas.

If the weather clears, we plan to leave at dawn; and if it doesn't, given the dangerous trail conditions, we'll pack up and go home.

Do not use a coordinating conjunction with a semicolon to join simple independent clauses.

■ **Hundreds of volunteers assisted in the cleanup effort; ~~and~~ many worked from dawn to dusk.**

(For more on joining independent clauses, see Chapter 26.)

WP TIP   Create a new file and name it. Reflect on the effect of using a semicolon to join two independent clauses. Look for or create examples to illustrate your points, perhaps showing two independent clauses joined in several ways, with a discussion evaluating the effectiveness of each. Discuss online with your peer revision group. Be sure to raise any debatable instances with your classmates and instructor.

■ **EDITING 1: EXPLORATION**

During the next two weeks, pay close attention to how the authors of essays, stories, or textbook chapters you read use semicolons. Collect ten examples that seem particularly effective to you. Why do you find them effective? What difference(s) does the semicolon make in the meaning of the sentence? Edit the examples to eliminate the semicolons. How does this change alter the effect or sense of the sentence?

■ **EDITING 2: PRACTICE**

Edit the following sentences, using semicolons as necessary to join independent clauses. Example:

The amount of crime shown on television has been criticized for inciting aggression in viewers,/in fact, it may be equally criticized for unreasonably raising viewers' fears.

1. Some experts estimate that 55 percent of prime-time characters experience a violent confrontation in the course of a week, the actual figure in life is less than 1 percent.

2. Studies have found that frequent viewers of television are likely to overestimate the statistical chance of violence in their lives, no matter what their gender, educational level, or neighborhood, and, moreover, fear, mistrust, and even paranoia can be the result.

3. For example, among city dwellers almost half of those identified as frequent viewers see crime as a very serious problem, only a quarter of infrequent viewers do.

4. Many Americans today rate crime as the country's number one problem, in fact, only a small segment of the population is actually at risk of being the victim of a violent crime.

5. Television-related misconceptions about crime may lead citizens to clamor for more protection, local governments to request additional funding, and politicians to raise taxes, and, worse, they may also contribute to increasing social mistrust.

45 b Using semicolons in a series containing commas

Items in a series are generally separated by commas. (See 44d.) In some situations, however, you can prevent confusion by separating the elements with semicolons instead.

Use a semicolon between elements in a series when at least one element of the series includes a comma.

> The candidates for the award are Maria, who won the essay competition; Elaine, the top debater; and Shelby, who directed the senior play.

Some writers use a semicolon to separate a series of long verb phrases or dependent clauses, even when they contain no internal commas.

As a nation, we need to understand why these regional conflicts occur; how they are rooted in the power vacuum that followed the fall of the Soviet Union; and what kinds of responses we can offer in settling them.

As with commas, a series should not be preceded or followed by a semicolon unless another rule requires it.

■ EDITING 3: PRACTICE

Edit the following sentences, using semicolons as necessary. Circle the number of any sentence that does not need semicolons. Example:

Our vacation to New England included trips to Mystic, Connecticut,/ ̬Ogunquit, Maine/ ̬Boston, Massachusetts,/ ̬and Keene, New Hampshire.

1. Several different craft can be seen on the Charles River, including sculls rowed by students from the universities in the area, canoes, rowboats that can be rented for a small fee, and motorboats.

2. To learn about a new place quickly, obtain a detailed map of the area you plan to visit, walk to as many places as possible, always wearing shoes with good soles, and talk to the residents, provided they look friendly.

3. If you go to Boston's Museum of Fine Arts, don't miss the Paul Revere silver, the Egyptian mummies, the Athenian vases, and the terrific collection of paintings, including works by Gauguin, Degas, Monet, van Gogh, and Whistler.

4. In addition to its art collection, New England has been home to some of the greatest writers in America: Henry David Thoreau, who wrote *Walden*, Henry Wadsworth Longfellow, whose house on Brattle Street in Cambridge is a historic landmark, and Nathaniel Hawthorne, a resident of Salem, Massachusetts, and author of *The Scarlet Letter*.

5. If you really want to fit in while you see the sights, ask someone where the locals eat, always use public transportation to find these places, and leave your maps where you're staying, relying instead on the people you meet for directions.

45 c Using semicolons sparingly

As a stylistic device, the semicolon can be overused, creating a monotonous sameness of rhythm and sentence structure. Save the semicolon for the sentences in which it is most effective.

■ Tax incentives can distort the economy; for example, real estate [*For* written above, inserting correction]
tax shelters helped create the glut of empty office buildings
that forced developers into bankruptcy and caused a banking
crisis due to defaults on loans. More tax breaks are not the
answer; they would only create more distortion. Politicians, [*They* written above]
however, compete to think up special tax cuts; it must be an
election year.

*The editing reserves the semicolon to set up the statement that requires
the most emphasis.*

WP TIP If you are using a computer to edit your paper, you
may want to use the search function to locate all instances of
semicolons. Doing this will allow you to see how often you have
used semicolons and will simplify the task of changing ineffective
semicolons to other marks of punctuation.

45 **d** **Editing misused semicolons**

The semicolon always separates sentence elements of equal
rank. If you find a semicolon not serving that purpose in your
writing, either revise the sentence or use other punctuation conventions.

I Eliminate any semicolon between an independent clause and a
dependent clause.

■ Torrential rains fell every day; when we visited Florida last
summer.

■ As soon as the rain stopped; the mosquitos came out.

■ To feel compassion is natural; but to help someone is truly
virtuous.

*In the last example, the subordinating conjunction was deleted, not the
semicolon.*

2 Eliminate any semicolon between an independent clause and a
phrase.

■ The beaches open on May 15; marking the beginning of
summer for most residents.

3 Do not use a semicolon to introduce a list.

■ It was a fine old house, but it needed work; plastering,
repainting, rewiring, and a thorough cleaning.

WP TIP Write an online journal entry or response in which
you reflect on your use of particular punctuation marks in a recent piece of writing. Have you used punctuation effectively
and/or (perhaps) less effectively than you would have liked? Is
there any pattern to your uses that you could build on or revise?

■ **EDITING 4: PRACTICE**

Edit the following sentences by replacing any incorrectly used semicolons with
the correct mark of punctuation or rewording the sentence. Some sentences
can be edited in more than one way. Circle the number of any sentence that
is correct. Be ready to explain your editing choices. Example:

> **Farley Mowat's books are not depressing; though they do make
> one think about the role of humans in the universe.**

1. His writing abounds with examples of the greedy nature of human beings; however, it does not convey a sense of helplessness.
2. Mowat clings to a spark of hope that it is not too late for humans to develop a respectful attitude toward our planet and the animals that inhabit it;
although he regards humans as covetous.
3. A self-designated advocate for nonhuman animals, Mowat reveals the
precariousness of the relationship between humans and animals; with unfor-
giving honesty for the most part.
4. He can be delightfully witty when he describes a positive, healthy relationship but also merciless when he condemns one; especially when it is destructive and exploitative.
5. After describing the harsh conditions in the village of Burgeo in the north
of Newfoundland, he reveals the paradoxical lure of the place; abundant fish,
seals, dolphins, and whales.

EDITING 5: PRACTICE

Edit the following passage, using semicolons correctly. More than one edited version is possible. Be ready to explain your editing choices.

Often students will not use the semicolon because they are unsure how to use it. They find the rules confusing; or hard to follow, or they have trouble applying the examples from textbooks to their own writing. Consequently, they avoid using semicolons whenever possible, which causes their writing to sound choppy or too simplistic at times. A person does not have to be a professional writer, however, to use semicolons correctly. He or she can develop a knack for using this elusive punctuation through practice. The following three rules might help; use semicolons between independent clauses when they are closely related, use semicolons to separate items in a complex series, and finally, do not use semicolons too often or your reader will think you don't know what you're doing—an important consideration; especially if you are writing for a professor.

EDITING 6: APPLICATION

Examine a paper you are working on to see if you have overused semicolons or overlooked opportunities to use them effectively. Is there one kind of mistake you consistently make? If so, think about how best to identify misused semicolons and about places where you might use them effectively when you edit your work. Edit any sentences in which you need to improve the use of semicolons.

Like the semicolon, the **colon** indicates a stop within a sentence. As a mark of introduction, the colon alerts the reader that the information preceding it is illustrated by what follows. The colon is also required as a mark of separation in certain other situations, such as in writing the time of day in numerals.

The colon is a strong and rather formal mark of punctuation. Be careful not to overuse it.

USES FOR COLONS

TO INTRODUCE INFORMATION	TO SEPARATE ELEMENTS
appositives	time
explanations	titles
examples	biblical citations
lists	salutations in letters and
quotations	memos

46 a Using colons to introduce lists, appositives and quotes

Use a colon to introduce an appositive, example, explanation, list, or quotation. The colon used this way must be preceded by an **independent clause**, which contains a subject and a verb and can stand alone as a complete sentence.

An appositive, example, or explanation can be a single word, a phrase, or a clause:

He has but one objective: success.

Much remains to be done: updating our computers, for example.

The budget agreement erected a wall between defense and education: No money was to be transferred between the two.

Capitalizing the first word of an independent clause following a colon is optional, but be consistent throughout a paper.

Use a colon to introduce a list that follows an independent clause. Frequently, an independent clause before a list will contain expressions such as *the following* or *as follows*.

> Almost everything you buy travels to you by truck: paper products, food, medicine, even pickup trucks.

> To complete the dish, proceed as follows: Transfer the meat to a warm platter, arrange the cooked vegetables around it, ladle on some of the sauce, and sprinkle with chopped parsley.

A colon is used to introduce a quotation when it is preceded by an independent clause.

> As he left, he quoted Puck's final lines from *A Midsummer Night's Dream*: "Give me your hands, if we be friends, / And Robin shall restore amends."

However, use a comma before a quotation if the words preceding it do not constitute an independent clause.

■ As the song from *South Pacific* puts it/, "You've got to be
⋀
carefully taught."

(See Chapter 48 for more on punctuating quotations.)

A long quotation set off from the main text in block format may also be preceded by a colon. (See 48a.)

46 b Using colons as marks of separation

Between numerals expressing hours, minutes, and seconds

Court convened promptly at 9:00 A.M.

The winning car's official elapsed time was 2:45:56.

Between a main title and a subtitle

Blue Highways: A Journey into America

"A Deep Darkness: A Review of *Out of Africa*"

Between chapter and verse numbers in biblical citations

Isaiah 14:10–11

After business letter salutations and in memo headings

Dear Mr. Nader:

To: Alex DiGiovanni

From: Paul Gallerelli

Subject: 1997 budget

Colons are also used to separate elements in bibliographies and reference lists in research papers. (See Part VIII.)

46 c Editing misused colons

In most sentences, a colon should follow only a complete independent clause or appear between items in a complex series. Otherwise, use other punctuation conventions.

1 Do not use a colon after an introductory modifying phrase or dependent clause.

▪ In order to open a shop:, you must first obtain a business license.

▪ As I learned that day:, one must always be honest with oneself.

2 Eliminate a colon that comes between a verb and its object or complement.

▪ For lunch, he usually eats: fruit, salad, or yogurt.

▪ My favorite fruits are: peaches, grapes, and bananas.

3 Delete any colon between a preposition and its object.

▪ She has traveled to: New Orleans, San Francisco, and Boston.

4 Eliminate any colon that follows an introductory expression (*including, such as, like, for example,* etc.).

▪ The show displayed several unusual pets, including: iguanas, raccoons, a civet, and a black widow spider.

5 Do not use more than one colon in a sentence.

▪ Wesley's visits always meant gifts:/ records, magazines, and books:/of pirate tales, mystery stories, and epic sagas.

WP TIP   If you find that you overuse colons in your writing, you may want to use your computer's search function to find all the colons in a paper. Doing this will allow you to see how often you have used colons and will simplify the task of changing ineffective colons to other marks of punctuation. If you find that you haven't used colons at all, use the search function to find your periods and semicolons and consider whether or not you might want to replace one of them with a colon. Discuss with a peer the ways in which these stylistic decisions will affect your writing.

◼ EDITING 1: EXPLORATION

From your local newspaper, copy five sentences that make use of colons. Now thumb through a textbook or academic journal and do the same: locate five sentences and write them down. From your research, determine which uses of the colon are the most common and which are the least. Are colons used more often in the newspaper or in the academic text? See what conclusions you can draw about colons based on your evidence.

◼ EDITING 2: EXPLORATION

In the following excerpt, Lewis Thomas uses colons in not-so-common ways. Read the passage carefully. Do you find his use of colons effective? If this were your paragraph, would you use the colons similarly or differently? Why or why not?

I am old enough by this time to be used to the notion of dying, saddened by the glimpse when it has occurred but only transiently knocked down, able to regain my feet quickly at the thought of continuity, any day. I have acquired and held in affection until very recently another sideline of an idea which serves me well at dark times: the life of the earth is the same as the life of an organism: the great round being possesses a mind: the mind contains an infinite number of thoughts and memories: when I reach my time I may find myself still hanging around in some sort of midair, one of those small thoughts, drawn back into the memory of the earth: in that peculiar sense I will be alive.

LEWIS THOMAS, "LATE NIGHT THOUGHTS ON LISTENING
TO MAHLER'S NINTH SYMPHONY"

◼ EDITING 3: PRACTICE

Edit the following sentences, using colons correctly. Example:

The first chore assigned to me as crewmate on a whale watch was not very exciting/ᴄCleaning the bathroom.

1. One thing is certain, the new person on the job always has to do the worst chores.

2. Given the terrible weather of the last few days, I was relieved by what I saw out in the distance, a nice, calm ocean.

3. I stepped on the deck and spoke these words from Melville's *Moby Dick*, "Call me Ishmael."

4. The sight of my first whale made me think of Jonah 1.17–2.10.

5. Finally, I began the job I had been hired to do, preparing snacks and beverages in the galley.

6. We spotted various kinds of whales on the excursion, right whales, humpback whales, finback whales, and minke whales.

7. There is one thing whale watch enthusiasts should always remember to do, wear rubber-soled shoes.

8. The people on the deck wore clothes to keep them dry ponchos and garbage bags.

9. When we returned to land at 6.00, I wanted nothing more than to go home and sleep.

10. One more chore awaited me, however, scrubbing the slime off the sides of the boat.

■ EDITING 4: APPLICATION

Examine your use of colons in a recent paper. Do you use colons very often? If so, is there one kind of colon mistake that you often make? If you do not use colons, can you identify a reason why you might avoid them? Try to devise a set of easy-to-remember guidelines for using colons. Then edit your paper, fixing colons that are misused and inserting others where they are appropriate.

The **apostrophe**, used primarily to form the possessive of a noun or pronoun, also indicates certain unusual plural forms and shows where a letter has been dropped in a contraction. (For this symbol's use as a single quotation mark, see Chapter 48.)

> **WHAT NEEDS AN APOSTROPHE?**
>
> - Possessive cases of nouns or indefinite pronouns: *Janey's*, *somebody's*
> - Plurals of words used as words, numbers, letters, symbols: *if's*, *10's*, *A's*, *$'s*
> - Contractions: *you're*, *we've*

Using apostrophes to form the possessive case of nouns and Indefinite pronouns

The **possessive case** of a noun or pronoun shows ownership or an association between the noun or pronoun and the word it modifies. To form the possessive case, nouns and some indefinite pronouns add an apostrophe and *-s* or add just an apostrophe. (Personal pronouns—*I, you, he, she, it, we, they*—show the possessive case by changing form in other ways. See 66b.)

Singular nouns

Use an apostrophe and *-s* to form the possessive of any singular noun that does not end in *-s*.

Denzel Washington's new movie is one of his best.

The *camera's* shutter speed is fixed.

For singular nouns ending in *-s*, it is always correct to form the possessive by adding both an apostrophe and *-s*. However, if pronouncing the additional syllable is awkward—as with last names that sound like plurals—some writers add only an apostrophe.

Don't waste the *class's* time.

John Adams' (or *Adams's*) presidency was marked by crisis and conflict.

Plural nouns

For plural nouns ending in -s, add only an apostrophe to form the possessive.

They owe her several *months'* pay.

The *Mertzes'* apartment was beneath the *Ricardos'*.

For irregular plural nouns not ending in -s, form the possessive by adding an apostrophe and -s.

We studied the *media's* coverage of *children's* issues.

WP TIP   Use the search function on your computer to help you find any words in which you've used apostrophes to form the possessive. Have your computer search for words ending in -s so that you can determine if there are any words that *need* apostrophes but don't have them.

Compound nouns

Use an apostrophe and -s on only the last word to form the possessive of a hyphenated or unhyphenated compound noun.

He borrowed his *mother-in-law's* car.

The *secretary of state's* office certified the election results.

Two or more nouns

When nouns joined by *and* are considered a unit and are jointly in possession, add an apostrophe and -s to only the last noun.

My *aunt and uncle's* anniversary party was a disaster.

When nouns joined by *and* are considered individuals in separate possession, add an apostrophe and -s to each noun.

> The documentary compared *Aretha Franklin's* and *Diana Ross's* early careers.

Indefinite pronouns

An **indefinite pronoun** is a pronoun that does not refer to any specific person or thing. Use an apostrophe and -s to form the possessive case of some indefinite pronouns, including *someone, anybody, no one, one,* and *another.*

> *Someone's* umbrella was left in the assembly hall.
>
> It is *no one's* business but mine.

Do not use an apostrophe and -s to form the possessive of the indefinite pronouns *all, any, both, each few, many, most, much, several, some,* and *such.* Indicate the possessive by using a preposition such as *of,* or use a pronoun that has a possessive form.

■ For the Dickinson and Crane seminar, we must read ~~both's~~ the^ complete works/ of both.

■ With so many applicants, we cannot respond to ~~each's~~ everyone's^ questions.

▣ EDITING I: PRACTICE

Edit the following sentences, using apostrophes correctly to form the possessive forms of nouns and indefinite pronouns. Circle the number of any sentence that is correct. Example:

> **Some people believe that student/s'^ test scores have fallen in recent years.**

I. In fact, high school juniors and seniors scores on many commercial achievement tests are higher than they have ever been.

2. It seems that the medias need to report negative news is a large factor in leading people to believe that young peoples' knowledge today is not as great as it was in the past.

3. What older people do not always realize is that no ones knowledge of the world at eighteen is as comprehensive as it will be after another ten or twenty or thirty year's worth of learning.

4. Many also do not consider that student's work today is generally more advanced than in the past, particularly in the sciences.

5. Todays' high school biology textbooks, for example, include lessons on DNA, RNA, genetic splicing, and biochemical engineering.

6. During my mother and father's high school years, such subjects were re-served for college or even graduate school.

7. Even in terms of history and geography, areas in which the current gen-erations knowledge has been shown to be weak, critic's reports of declining standards seem to be exaggerated.

8. A 1943 survey of college freshmen found that even elite students knew nothing at all about Thomas Jefferson and Abraham Lincoln's presidencies and could not identify the Mississippi Rivers' location on a map!

| **47** | **b** | **Using apostrophes to form plurals of words used as words, letters, numbers, and symbols** |

Use an apostrophe and -s to form the plural of a word used as a word.

Analysis reveals more *the*'s than *and*'s in most writing.

Also use an apostrophe and an -s to form the plural of letters, numerals, and symbols.

Tic tac toe is played on a grid with *x*'s and *o*'s.

We have no size *8*'s in that style but five size *10*'s.

Today most telephone dial pads include #'s and *'s.

A word, number, or letter used this way is usually set off by italics or underlining. (See 53c.) However, note that the apostro-phe and the -s in the plural form are not italicized or underlined.

You may use an apostrophe and -s or an -s alone to form the plural of centuries and decades, as long as you are consistent within a paper. (The Modern Language Association prefers an -s alone.) Do not use an apostrophe when the century or decade is expressed in words.

the 1800s (*or* the 1800's)

the 60s (*or* the 60's)

the sixties

Use an apostrophe and -s for plurals of abbreviations ending with periods. Use -s alone for abbreviations without periods.

My science professor has earned two Ph.D.'s.

Like all politicians, she has some IOUs.

(See Chapter 55 for more on abbreviations.)

47 c Using apostrophes to form contractions

A **contraction** joins two words into one by replacing one or more letters with an apostrophe. The following list shows the correct use of the apostrophe in some common contractions.

cannot	can't	does not	doesn't
do not	don't	would not	wouldn't
will not	won't	was not	wasn't
she would	she'd	it is	it's
who is	who's	you are	you're
I am	I'm	they are	they're
let us	let's	we have	we've
there is	there's	she has	she's

WP TIP Enter this list in a double-column file that you can call "contractions." Keep the file open for ready reference when you're writing and/or revising your next paper.

Apostrophes can also be used to indicate omitted letters in certain colloquial expressions and omitted digits in a year.

spic 'n' span   rock 'n' roll   the class of '99

Writers sometimes use apostrophes in dialogue to indicate letters omitted from certain words, suggesting the speaker's pronunciation.

"Courtin' was diff'rent in my day," the old man said.

Because they are conversational, contractions help to create a friendly, accessible tone (which is why we have used contractions in writing this book). But because of their informality, contractions tend not to be appropriate for most academic writing.

■ EDITING 2: PRACTICE

Edit the following sentences, using apostrophes correctly to form contractions. Example:

You're   you'll
If ~~your~~ a fan of the outdoors, ~~youll~~ enjoy exploring the Hudson
                                    isn't
River Valley, which ~~isnt~~ far from New York City.

I. In the summer, a boat will take passengers from the city to Bear Mountain, where hiking enthusiasts wont be disappointed.
2. The views from the mountain's 1300-foot summit cant be surpassed; youll see wilderness stretching out before your eyes in every direction.
3. A trip to the country wouldnt be complete without a stop at Buddy's Café n Deli.
4. Similarly, you shouldnt visit Hyde Park without stopping by FDR's country home, which has been preserved as it was when he died in 45.
5. Both the Hudson River Valley and New York City offer plenty to do for the outdoor buff whos interested in stunning scenery, fine hiking, and rich history.

47 d   Editing misused apostrophes

Most problems with apostrophes arise from confusing the nonpossessive forms of plural nouns or from mistaking a possessive pronoun for a contraction. Edit your paper using the following strategies.

I   Eliminate apostrophes you may have used to form nonpossessive plurals of nouns.

■ For over forty years, the Kennedy⌒s have fascinated the American public.

■ I have had two exceptional bosses' during my working life.

2 Do not use apostrophes with possessive personal pronouns.

The possessives of personal pronouns are formed without apostrophes: for example, *hers* (not *her's*), *yours* (not *your's*), *theirs* (not *their's*), *ours* (not *our's*).

■ The choice is our⌒s, not their⌒s.

3 Eliminate apostrophes you may have used by confusing possessive personal pronouns with contractions.

The possessive personal pronouns *its*, *whose*, *your*, and *their* sound like the contractions *it's*, *who's*, *you're*, and *they're*. Make sure not to substitute a contraction for a possessive personal pronoun.

■ The storm was brief, but it⌒s effects were devastating.

■ She is the candidate who's views most reflect my own.
        whose

Personal pronouns use an apostrophe only to form contractions, so, as a test, substitute the spelled-out form in each case: *The storm was brief but it's [it is] effects were devastating.* If the result makes no sense, then you have incorrectly used a contraction for a possessive form. If you confuse these, take the time to check each occurrence of these words in your writing (perhaps with the aid of your computer's search function).

WP TIP Highlight apostrophes in **bold** and check to see if any is misused. Print hard copy and examine each using the above guidelines.

■ **EDITING 3: PRACTICE**

Edit the following sentences, being careful to distinguish plurals, contractions, and possessives. Example:

Charles Dickens's brief experience of a debtor⌒s prison with it⌒s deplorable conditions had a profound effect on him.

PLURAL AND POSSESSIVE FORMS

SINGULAR	SINGULAR POSSESSIVE	PLURAL	PLURAL POSSESSIVE
school	school's	schools	schools'
box	box's	boxes	boxes'
class	class's	classes	classes'
Duvalier	Duvalier's	Duvaliers	Duvaliers'
Jones	Jones's	Joneses	Joneses'

When spoken, the plural, the singular possessive, and the plural possessive sound the same for most words. In writing, the spelling and the placement of the apostrophe help readers distinguish among the three forms.

1. Its perhaps surprising to learn that Dickens didn't start out as a novelist; instead, he trained as a lawyer's clerk.

2. The author; who's literary career began during the 1830s, started out writing for magazines' under the pseudonym "Boz."

3. Society's evil, corruption, and crime were concerns to Dickens, and their frequently found as themes throughout his novels.

4. They're style and structure were affected by the fact that Dickens wrote his novel's for publication in monthly installments.

5. Dickens's first novel, *Pickwick Papers*, was illustrated by a popular artist, who's plates contributed to the success of the work.

■ EDITING 4: EXPLORATION

During the next week, keep your eye out for what you consider mistakes in the use of apostrophes and write down any that you find. Look in newspapers, in magazines, on billboards, on the sides of commercial vehicles, on storefronts, and in television advertising. Do these mistakes make any difference in how the words are read and understood? What would be the advantages or disadvantages in leaving out apostrophes?

■ EDITING 5: PRACTICE

Edit the following passage, using apostrophes correctly.

The computer industrys' most important "enhancement" these days may be many software companies expansion of they're call-in help desks. With the enormous growth in the number of computer owners' over the past five years has come a corresponding growth in those owners need for truly helpful technical support, particularly considering that the average first-time buyer of a computer today has very little understanding of it's operation or functions. Just a few years ago, most companies technical support staff's consisted only of technicians and computer experts, who's attitude often suggested that a customers' questions were too stupid to be taken seriously, implying that "the problem is yours' not our's." Worse, their advice could be so technical that it's usefulness to customers was almost nonexistent. Today, however, companies are beginning to realize that ones success in an increasingly competitive market will depend on good customer service. Now when all those Es for "Error" appear on a users' screen, real help will be only a telephone call away.

▇ EDITING 6: APPLICATION

Examine one of your past papers for misused or omitted apostrophes. Do you consistently make one kind of mistake in using apostrophes? Which kinds of mistakes are the most difficult to spot? Why? As you review your paper, think about how best to identify misused apostrophes or places where you tend to omit apostrophes. When you're finished, write down, in your own words, a set of guidelines for using apostrophes correctly. Then, as a final test, apply these guidelines to a different paper. Do the guidelines help? Correct any mistakes that you find.

Quotation can be a powerful tool. By using quotations, you can document exactly what was said at a crucial time, portray people speaking to each other, clarify an idea you are analyzing, or enlist an expert's support for an argument you are making.

Using another person's exact words is called **direct quotation**. When you quote directly, you must tell readers you are doing so by indicating the source and by enclosing the person's exact words in quotation marks (or by setting off long quotations). Restating someone else's idea in your own words is called **paraphrasing** or **indirect quotation**. When quoting indirectly, you must still identify the source, but you do not use quotation marks.

Quotation marks are also used to distinguish certain words, such as titles, from the main body of the text. Italics are used for this purpose as well. (See Chapter 53.)

USING QUOTATION MARKS

Quotation marks are like shoes: use them in pairs. In written American English, there are two types of quotation marks: **double quotation marks** (" ") which identify quotations, titles, and so on, and **single quotation marks** (' ') which identify quotations within quotations (or titles within titles). In print and in handwriting, a distinction is made between an opening quotation mark (") and a closing quotation mark ("). Most typewriters and personal computers, however, use the same quotation mark or marks at both ends of a quotation.

The guidelines for presenting quotations vary somewhat from discipline to discipline. This chapter follows the conventions of the Modern Language Association, the authority for papers written in the languages and literature. For information on this and other disciplinary styles, see Chapters 18 and 61–65.

| 48 | a | Using quotation marks for brief direct quotations |

The conventions are different for using quotation marks when quoting short passages and long ones.

Short passages

Use quotation marks to enclose brief quotations, those from one word up to four typed lines of prose or three lines of poetry. If a parenthetical citation of the source is provided, place it after the closing quotation marks but before the period or other punctuation. (See 48e for advice about using other punctuation marks with quotation marks.)

> Boswell calls this relationship a "collateral adoption" (97), a
> term other experts do not use.

> In *Lives under Siege*, Ratzenburger argues that "most adoles-
> cents are far too worried about the next six months and far
> too unconcerned about the next sixty years" (84).

When quoting poetry, use a slash preceded and followed by a single space to indicate line breaks. (See 49e.)

> Shakespeare concludes Sonnet 18 with this couplet:
> "So long as men can breathe or eyes can see, / So
> long lives this, and this gives life to thee."

WP TIP Forgetting the quotation marks at the end of a quotation is a common typographical error, so check for these carefully as you edit. To do so, you might use your computer's search function, having the computer find each opening set of quotation marks and then making sure each quotation ends with quotation marks as well.

Long passages

Longer direct quotations are set off from the main text in **block format**. Start a new line for the quotation, indent all lines of the quotation ten spaces, and do not use quotation marks. If the words introducing a block quotation form a complete sentence, they are usually followed by a colon, although a period is also acceptable. (See 46a). If the introductory words do not constitute a complete sentence, a comma or no punctuation at all is used, depending on context. If a parenthetical citation of the source is provided, place it two spaces after the final mark of end punctuation.

> A recent editorial describes the problem:
>
>> In countries like the United States, breastfeeding, though always desirable, doesn't mean the difference between good and poor nutrition—or life and death. But it does in developing countries, where for decades infant food manufacturers have been distributing free samples of infant formulas to hospitals and birthing centers. (<u>Daily Times</u> 17)
>
> The editorial goes on to argue that the samples last only long enough for the mothers' own milk to dry up; then the mothers find they cannot afford to buy the formula.

A single paragraph or part of a paragraph in block format does not use a paragraph indent. For two or more quoted paragraphs, the first line of each new paragraph after the first is indented three additional spaces.

When quoting poetry, reproduce as precisely as possible the line breaks, indents, spacing, and capitalization of the original.

> Lawrence Ferlinghetti's poem opens with a striking image of the poet's work:
>
>> Constantly risking absurdity
>>> and death
>> whenever he performs
>>> above the heads
>>>> of his audience
>> the poet like an acrobat
>>> climbs on rime
>>>> to a high wire of his own making

If a quotation appears within a quotation, use single quotation marks for the inner quotation.

> After the election, the incumbent said, "My opponent will soon learn, as someone once said, 'You can't fool all of the people all of the time.' "

If a quotation appears within a quotation that is displayed in block format, and that therefore is not within quotation marks, use double quotation marks for the inner quotation.

■ EDITING 1: EXPLORATION

In your own writing or in professional writing, look for examples of quotations taken from other sources. Locate at least one example that uses quotation marks within text and one that uses block format set off from text. Rewrite each example using the alternative format. How do the different ways of presenting the information affect the readability of the passages?

■ EDITING 2: PRACTICE

Edit the following sentences, using quotation marks correctly with brief direct quotations. Example:

> **Remembering a trip with her parents in 1947, black American poet Audre Lorde writes in her memoir, *Zami*,"The first time I went to Washington, D.C., was on the edge of the summer when I was supposed to stop being a child."**

1. "Preparations were in the air around our house before school was even over, she recalls. We packed for a week."

2. Once in Washington, Lorde remembers, I spent the whole next day after Mass squinting up at the Lincoln Memorial where Marian Anderson had sung after the D.A.R. refused to allow her to sing in their auditorium because she was Black. Or because she was "Colored," my father said as he told me the story. Except that what he probably said was "Negro," because for his times, my father was quite progressive.

3. Lorde goes on to observe that later in the evening, "The family stopped for a dish of vanilla ice cream at a Breyer's ice cream and soda fountain.

4. When the waitress first spoke, they didn't understand her, so then, writes Lorde, "The waitress moved along the line of us closer to my father and spoke again. 'I said I kin give you to take out, but you can't eat here. Sorry."

5. The young Lorde's feelings about this casual racism in the nation's capital seems to be summarized by the first lines of a poem she wrote many years later: There are so many roots to the tree of anger / that sometimes the branches shatter / before they bear.

48 b Using quotation marks for dialogue

Use quotation marks when reproducing dialogue, whether real or fictional. Start a new paragraph to show every change of speaker. Once the pattern is established, readers can tell who is speaking even if not every quote has attributory words.

> "Early parole is not the solution to overcrowding," the prosecutor said. "We need a new jail."
>
> The chairman of the county commission asked, "How do you propose we should pay for it?"
>
> "Increase taxes if you must, but whatever you do, act quickly."

If one speaker's words continue for more than a single paragraph, use quotation marks at the beginning of each new paragraph but at the end of only the last paragraph.

(See 44g for advice about using commas to set off attributions.)

■ EDITING 3: APPLICATION

Look through some of your recent papers and locate a passage that could have been written in dialogue. Edit the passage to turn it into dialogue, following the guidelines described in this section.

WP TIP Copy one of your existing papers on computer. Renaming the file. Use the "Outline" function available in many word processing programs. Put in **bold** any dialogue you have used. Print hard copy. Edit your use of quotation marks as needed. Use the search function to check that you have a complete set of quotation marks with your dialogue.

48 c Using quotation marks for certain titles

Use quotation marks for titles of brief poems, short stories, essays, book chapters and parts, magazine and journal articles, episodes of television series, and songs. (Italics are used to indicate titles of longer works such as books, magazines, journals, television series, recordings, films, and plays. See 53a.)

"Araby" is the third story in James Joyce's book *Dubliners*.

This chart appeared with the article "Will Your Telephone Last?" in November's *Consumer Reports*.

In my favorite episode of *I Love Lucy*, "Job Switching," Lucy and Ethel work in a chocolate factory.

The Beatles' *Sgt. Pepper's Lonely Hearts Club Band* includes the song "A Day in the Life."

If the title of a part of a work or series is generic rather than specific—for example, Chapter 8—do not use either quotation marks or italics.

Use single quotation marks to indicate quoted material that is part of a title enclosed in double quotation marks.

We read " 'This Is the End of the World': The Black Death" by historian Barbara Tuchman.

Titles are indicated by quotation marks only in text, so do not put quotation marks around the title at the beginning of your own essay, poem, or story. However, use quotation marks wherever your title includes a quotation or title.

An Analysis of the "My Turn" Column in *Newsweek*

■ EDITING 4: PRACTICE

Edit the following sentences, using quotation marks correctly with titles. Circle the number of any sentence that is correct. Example:

"The Theater,"

Jeff read a review of Sunset Boulevard in The ~~Theater,~~ a column in *The New Yorker* magazine, and he wants to see the play tonight.

1. Jan prefers to stay at home and finish reading *A View from the Woods*, one of the stories in Flannery O'Connor's *Everything that Rises Must Converge*.

2. As usual, Kim will be watching *Star Trek* reruns on television. Her favorite episode is Who Mourns for Adonis?

3. Erik will spend the evening reading "Why I Write," an essay that Orwell wrote the year *after* he published his novel *Animal Farm*.

4. Alan wants to stay home and study Thomas Hardy's poem *At the Word "Farewell."*

5. Jeff decides to stay at home and listen to his jazz records. He always turns up the volume when the song *Basin Street Blues* comes on.

✔ **TITLES WITHIN TITLES**

Use the following models when presenting titles within other titles. These same guidelines apply to other words that normally are
indicated by quotation marks or italics (such as foreign words or
quotations) when they appear in titles.

1. A title enclosed in quotation marks within an italicized title

"A Curtain of Green" and Other Stories

2. An italicized title within a title enclosed in quotation marks

"Morality in Death of a Salesman"

3. A title enclosed in quotation marks within another title enclosed
in quotation marks

"The Symbolism in 'Everyday Use' "

4. An italicized title within another italicized title:

Modern Critics on Hamlet and Other Plays

For more information on using italics, see 53a.

 48 d | **Using quotation marks for translations,
specialized terms, ironic usages, and
nicknames**

Translations

When a word or phrase from another language is translated
into English, the translation may be enclosed in quotation marks.
The original word or phrase is italicized (see 53d).

I've always called Antonio *fratellino*, or "little brother," because he
is twelve years younger than I.

Specialized terms

A specialized term or new coinage is often introduced in quotation marks when it is first defined.

The ecology of this "chryocore"—a region of perpetual ice and
snow—has been studied very little.

He called the new vegetable a "broccoflower," a yellow-green cross between broccoli and cauliflower.

Irony

You may indicate that you are using a word in an ironic sense—that is, with a meaning opposed to its literal one—by putting the word in quotation marks; but use this technique sparingly in academic writing.

Jonathan Swift's essay "A Modest Proposal" offers a quick "solution" to Ireland's poverty and overpopulation: eat the children.

Nicknames

An unusual nickname may be enclosed in quotation marks at first mention, particularly when it is introduced as part of the full name.

When I joined the firm, the president was a man named Garnett E. "Ding" Cannon.

48 e Using other punctuation with quotation marks

Periods and commas

Periods and commas go inside quotation marks.

After Gina finished singing "Memories," Joe began to hum "The Way We Were."

Juliet Schor refers to "the rise of what some have called 'post-materialist values.' "

Note that the period or comma goes inside both single and double quotation marks.

Colons and semicolons

Colons and semicolons go outside quotation marks.

The sign read "Closed": there would be no sodas for us.

In 1982, Bobbie Ann Mason wrote "Shiloh"; it is considered one of her finest works.

Question marks, exclamation points, and dashes

Question marks, exclamation points, and dashes go inside the quotation marks if they are part of the quotation or title.

> Dr. King asked, "How does one determine whether a law is just or unjust?"

> "Something is wrong with my baby!" she cried.

> Robert Frost's famous poem "Out, Out—" was published in 1916.

When they are not part of the quotation or title but rather apply to the whole sentence, these marks go outside the quotation marks.

> Who invented the expression "Have a nice day"?

> To make matters worse, from the altar the bride sang "I Got You, Babe"!

> Who said, "Is there anymore?"?

If the logic of a sentence dictates that a quotation end with a question mark or an exclamation point but sentence grammar calls for a period or comma as well, use the stronger mark (the question mark or exclamation point) and delete the weaker one (the period or comma).

> ■ As soon as we heard someone shout "Fire!", we began to run for the exit.

> Emma's first word—"dada"—caused her father to beam.

■ EDITING 5: PRACTICE

Edit the following sentences, adding quotation marks as needed and making sure that they, as well as other punctuation marks, are used correctly. Example:

> "No matter how many times you say it, Christie," Malcolm said, "I still can't accept the idea that international law should have no bearing on how nations act."

1. "Wait a minute"! she retorted. That's not what I said at all.
2. Well, what did you say, then? Malcolm asked.

3. "My point, Christie said, is that a government can't allow itself to be constrained from acting to preserve its interests without some kind of guarantee that other countries won't take advantage of the opportunity".

4. But that's what international law is designed to do, isn't it? Clearly, there's an element of self-interest in any collective security arrangement, he argued, but that doesn't mean that there are no restraints on that interest.

5. "That's true", she replied, wearily. "But sometimes"—wait, let me finish"—governments use international law as a smokescreen. Besides, she continued, you have to admit that powerful countries are more likely to get what they want in the United Nations or the World Court."

6. I'm not so sure, Malcolm mused, grinning. I guess I'm just not as cynical as you are.

7. "Spare me, she replied, and will you stop jabbering and help me fix this flat"?

---

48 **f** **Editing misused quotation marks**

Quotation marks are used frequently in academic writing, and they can be tricky. Examining some of their common misuses can help you as you edit your own papers.

I Quotation marks are like shoes: use them in pairs. (The only exception is in extended dialogue; see 35b.)

■ "There are always a few students who boycott the assembly," he said, "but that's no reason for us to call it off."

2 As a rule, do not use quotation marks to indicate emphasis. Emphasis is achieved through rhythm and sentence structure. There are times, however, when you may find it necessary to use italics for emphasis.

■ He was guilty of a ⁄felony,⁄ not a misdemeanor.

■ People think if an answer ⁄looks⁄ right, it must ⁄be⁄ right.

3 Do not use quotation marks to call attention to slang or other terms. Instead, consider substituting another word or phrase.

■ Several of these companies should go into a ⁄hall of shame⁄ for their employment practices.

WP TIP   To ensure you are using quotation marks in pairs, have your computer search for opening quotation marks. Then each time, move the cursor through the quotation until you reach the closing quotation mark. If you can't find one, then insert one at the appropriate place.

■ EDITING 6: PRACTICE

Edit the following passage to make sure that quotation marks and related punctuation are used correctly.

Tennessee Williams's play "The Glass Menagerie" opens with the character Tom speaking directly to the audience: "Yes, I have tricks in my pocket, I have things up my sleeve." "But I am the opposite of a stage magician." This opening monologue serves to set the stage for the story to come. "I am the narrator of the play, continues Tom, "And also a character in it. The other characters are my mother, Amanda, my sister, Laura, and a gentleman caller who appears in the final scenes." Amanda is an aging "Southern belle" living with her two adult children in a dingy St. Louis apartment and desperate to find a match for her daughter. Crippled and painfully shy, Laura often retreats to a fantasy world of glass animal figurines and old songs like Dardanella and La Colondrina played on a scratchy victrola. When asked by Amanda how many gentlemen callers are expected one afternoon, Laura replies "I don't believe we're going to receive any, Mother. "Not one gentleman caller?, Amanda exclaims. "It can't be true! There must be a flood, there must have been a tornado"! When Amanda enlists Tom to bring home a potential "beau" for Laura, the gentleman caller turns out to be a former high school classmate, Jim, whose nickname for Laura was Blue Roses. "Whenever he saw me, Laura recalls at one point, he'd holler, "Hello, Blue Roses!" Jim is already engaged, however, a situation that leads to a climactic confrontation between Amanda and Tom.

■ EDITING 7: APPLICATION

Examine a paper you are working on to see if you have incorrectly punctuated any quotations. Is there one kind of mistake in punctuating quotations that you consistently make? If so, think about how best to identify misused quotation marks or places where you have omitted quotation marks when you edit your work. Edit any sentences in which you have incorrectly punctuated quotations.   **WP TIP:** To ensure you are using quotation marks in pairs, have your computer search for opening quotation marks. Then each time, move the cursor through the quotation until you reach the closing quotation mark. If you can't find one, then insert one at the appropriate place.

Parentheses, dashes, ellipsis points, brackets, and slashes each have specific functions in sentences, and using them appropriately can bring extra polish to your writing. Use them sparingly, however, and for specific purposes; otherwise, they will distract readers from your meaning.

49 a | Using parentheses

Parentheses enclose elements that would otherwise interrupt a sentence: explanations, examples, asides, and supplementary information. They are also used to set off cross-references, citations, and numbers in a list. Parentheses can be distracting, so use them sparingly.

1 Enclosing explanations, examples, and asides

In setting off explanations, examples, and asides, writers often have the choice of using commas, parentheses, or dashes. (For more information, see box on page 696.) Because parentheses tend to deemphasize what they enclose, use them for material that is not essential to the meaning of the sentence or to the point being made.

> Current Hollywood stars whose parents were stars include Anjelica Houston (daughter of John) and Michael Douglas (son of Kirk).

> The use of corporal punishment (paddling, for example) has been banned in most public schools.

> Speaking little English (he had immigrated to the United States only a few months earlier), my grandfather found his first job in a tuna-packing factory.

Parentheses may also be used to enclose dates, a brief translation, abbreviations, or initials.

The Oxford English Dictionary was first published under the editorship of James A. H. Murray (1888–1933).

English also borrowed the Dutch word *koekje* (cookie).

The North American Free Trade Agreement (NAFTA) continues to spark controversy.

2 Enclosing cross-references and citations

Use parentheses to enclose cross-references to other parts of your paper and to identify references and sources for quotations.

The map (p. 4) shows the areas of heaviest rainfall.

Nick Carraway felt unsettled to see Gatsby at the end of his dock beckoning in the direction of a "single green light" (21).

(See 48a and Chapters 18 and 61–65 for more information about citing sources for quotations.)

3 Enclosing numbers or letters in a list

Use parentheses to enclose numbers or letters that introduce items in a list within a sentence.

The dictionary provides (1) pronunciation, (2) etymology, (3) past meanings, and (4) usage citations for almost 300,000 words.

4 Using other punctuation with parentheses

When information placed within parentheses falls at the end of a sentence, end punctuation appears outside the final parenthesis, thereby punctuating the sentence as a whole.

The strikers protested the company's practice of buying parts from other companies (out sourcing).

When one complete sentence is enclosed in parentheses but stands alone, the end punctuation is placed inside the final parenthesis, and the first word is capitalized.

The damage caused by the storm is estimated at $1.5 million. (This does not include the costs of emergency medical aid.)

When a complete sentence enclosed by parentheses falls within another sentence, the first word is not capitalized, and no period is used. A question mark or exclamation mark may be used for effect.

> The damage caused by the storm (estimates run as high as $1.5 million) was the worst in more than three decades.

> After a visit to Buffalo (how can people there stand the cold weather?), it was a relief to return South.

A comma never comes directly before a set of parentheses. If a comma is required by the sentence structure, place it directly after the parentheses.

■ **Working for the minimum wage,/($2.30 an hour at the time),I had very little money to spare.**

ESL **PLACEMENT OF PUNCTUATION**

Only a few kinds of punctuation can begin a line of text in English: ellipsis points, an opening quotation mark, an opening parenthesis, and an open bracket. However, an opening quotation mark, an opening parenthesis, or an opening bracket may not be placed at the end of a line. All other types of punctuation should be placed within or at the end of a line.

If you are using a word processor with a "wraparound" screen or a "soft return" feature, the word processor will avoid most problems for you automatically, as long as you have not incorrectly inserted a space before or after a mark of punctuation.

■ **EDITING 1: PRACTICE**

Edit the following sentences, inserting parentheses where appropriate, deleting unnecessary parentheses, and correcting any nonstandard use of other punctuation with parentheses. (You may need to make other changes in punctuation.) Some sentences can be edited in more than one way. Be ready to explain the changes you made. Example:

> **Buddhism is a religion and philosophy that was founded in, India around 535 B.C.E. by Siddhartha Gautama, who is called Buddha,/("the Enlightened One\,").**

I. Other names for Buddha are the Tathagata, "he who has come thus," Bhagavat, "the Lord," and Sugata, "well-gone."

2. Tradition has it that Gautama, also spelled Gotama, was born a prince but renounced the world at twenty-nine years to seek to understand the inevitability of human suffering.

3. Eventual spiritual enlightenment led him to the "four noble truths" of Buddhism: 1 existence is suffering; 2 suffering is caused by attachment to the physical world; 3 the suffering humans experience can cease; 4 the path to release from suffering involves eight stages of thinking and behavior.

4. For the next forty-five years, (He was thirty-five when he reached enlightenment.) Buddha traveled and taught his doctrine to a growing number of disciples.

5. Central to the practice of Buddhism are meditation (and adherence to a set of clearly defined moral precepts).

6. These moral precepts, for example, injunctions against taking life, stealing, and dishonesty, continue to provide a primary basis of Buddhist practice.

49 b Using dashes

Dashes serve many of the same purposes as parentheses—that is, they set off explanations, examples, asides, and supplementary information that would otherwise interrupt the meaning of the sentence. However, dashes tend to emphasize the material they set off rather than subordinate it, as parentheses do. Dashes can also be used to emphasize contrast and to indicate interruptions and changes in tone. Because dashes break the flow of a sentence, use them sparingly.

On the typewriter, use two hyphens with no space on either side to create a dash.

A dash--when you use one--should look like this.

Note that unlike a single parenthesis, a dash can be used singly to set off material at the end of a sentence.

WP TIP Some word processors will end a line by breaking in the middle of a dash represented by two hyphens or a set of ellipsis points, putting part of the punctuation on one line and part on the next. You can correct these breaks by inserting "hard returns" to start the next line either with the word before the dash or with the complete set of ellipsis points. Be sure to save your changes before you close your file.

Dashes for explanations, examples, and asides

She donates a considerable sum to Georgetown University—her alma mater—every year.

At first we did not notice the rain—it began so softly—but soon we were soaked through.

Of all the oddities in Richard's apartment, the contents of the bathtub—transistors, resistors, circuit boards, and odd bits of wire—were the strangest of all.

Dashes to emphasize contrast

The restaurant is known for its excellent food—and its astronomical prices.

Dashes to indicate a pause, interruption, or change of tone

"Well, I guess I was a little late—OK, an hour late," I admitted.

"Hold on," she shouted, "while I grab this—"

The candidate claims he didn't know about his staff's illegal activities—and we're expected to believe that.

Dashes with other marks of punctuation

If the words enclosed by dashes within a sentence form a sentence, do not capitalize the first word of the inner sentence or use a period. If the enclosed sentence is a question or an exclamation, you may use a question mark or an exclamation point, but do not capitalize the first word.

Ward and June Cleaver—who can forget their orderly world?—never once question their roles in life.

Do not use a comma or a period immediately before or after a dash.

■ My cousin Eileen—she is from Ireland|—brought a strange flute with her when she came to visit.

■ With so many things happening at once—graduation, a new job—,Marcelle felt she had become a different person.

Avoid using more than two dashes in a sentence.

> ✔ **CHOOSING AMONG COMMAS, PARENTHESES, AND DASHES**
>
> Commas, parentheses, and dashes can all be used to set off nonessential material within a sentence. Use commas when the material being set off is closely related to the rest of the sentence. (See Chapter 44.)
>
> A dusty plow, the kind the early Amish settlers used, hung on the wall of the old barn.
>
> Use parentheses when the material being set off is not closely related to the main sentence and when you want to deemphasize it. (See 49a.)
>
> Two young boys found an old plow (perhaps as old as the first Amish settlement) hidden in an unused corner of the barn.
>
> Use dashes when material being set off is not closely related to the main sentence—when you want to emphasize it.
>
> The old plow—one his great-grandfather had used—was still in good working order.

▪ He never told his father about his dreams—he couldn't explain them—but silently began to make plans⁄plans that would one day lead him away from this small town. ∧

WP TIP The search function is an easy tool for checking your use of commas, parentheses, and dashes. Here's another: review a completed draft, highlighting in **bold** your various uses of these forms of punctuation. Print hard copy and edit your choices for appropriateness, as necessary.

▦ **EDITING 2: EXPLORATION**

Read the following excerpt from an essay by Joyce Carol Oates. What does the use of punctuation say about the author's attitude toward her subject? Do you find the author's use of parentheses and dashes effective? What effect is the author trying to achieve? Try to imagine the paragraph without parentheses and dashes. In what ways would the paragraph be different?

The mystique of high-performance cars has always intrigued me with its very opacity. Is it lodged sheerly in speed?—mechanical ingenuity?—the 'art' of a finely tuned beautifully styled vehicle (as the mere physical fact of a Steinway piano constitutes 'art')?—the adrenal thrill of courting death? Has it primarily to do with display (that of male game fowl, for instance)? Or with masculine prowess of a fairly obvious sort? (Power being, as the cultural critic Henry Kissinger once observed, the ultimate aphrodisiac.)

JOYCE CAROL OATES,
"'STATE OF THE ART CAR': THE FERRARI TESTAROSSA"

▉ EDITING 3: PRACTICE

Edit the following passage, deleting dashes where they are not effective. More than one edited version is possible. Be ready to explain your editing choices.

Jamaica Kincaid's most openly opinionated—and, to my mind, best—book—*A Small Place*—is a social critique of her home island—Antigua. In this book, her voice—humble yet strong, and sometimes filled with anger—speaks for her people. Her feelings—stemming from years of living in Antigua in the aftermath of British imperialism—are expressed in a simple—yet beautiful—manner.

49 c Using ellipsis points

Ellipsis points are three periods, each preceded and followed by a space. They are used to mark an **ellipsis**, any deliberate omission of words from a direct quotation. Quotations are generally shortened either to make a passage more emphatic or to reduce it to a usable length, but writers doing so must be careful not to change the original passage's meaning. (See 17d).

Consider the following paragraph from Betty Edwards's *Drawing on the Right Side of the Brain.*

> Drawing is not really very difficult. *Seeing* is the problem, or, to be more specific, *shifting to a particular way of seeing.* You may not believe me at this moment. You may feel that you are seeing things just fine and that it's the drawing that is hard. But the opposite is true, and the exercises in this book are designed to help you make the mental shift and gain a twofold advantage: first, to open access by *conscious volition* to the right side of your brain in order to experience a slightly altered mode of awareness; second, to see things in a different way. Both will enable you to draw well.

Use ellipsis points to indicate an omission within a sentence.

> Edwards tells the reader, "You may feel that . . . it's the drawing that is hard."

If an omission comes at the end of a complete sentence, include the period or other end punctuation before the ellipsis points.

> Edwards addresses the reader directly with a provocative assertion: "Drawing is not really very difficult. . . . You may not believe me at this moment."

Likewise, if you end the quotation before the end of the original sentence, include a period before the ellipsis. (Note that in such cases, there is no space between the last quoted word and the period or between the final ellipsis point and the closing quotation mark.)

> In Edwards's view, "Drawing is not really difficult. *Seeing* is the problem. . . ."

However, when parenthetical documentation is included after a quote ending with an ellipsis, the period follows the parentheses.

> Betty Edwards writes, "Drawing is not really difficult. *Seeing* is the problem . . ." (2).

Ellipsis points are not necessary when what you quote ends a sentence in the original or when what you quote is obviously not a complete sentence.

> According to Edwards, "Drawing is not really very difficult."

> Edwards offers the reader paths to "a slightly altered mode of awareness."

If you omit a whole line or more when quoting poetry, indicate the omission by using ellipsis points for the length of a line.

> She walks in beauty, like the night
> . . . .
> And all that's best of dark and bright
> Meet in her aspect and her eyes.

In dialogue, ellipsis points can indicate a hesitation or a trailing off of speech, and in informal writing they may be used to create a pause for dramatic effect.

I could only stammer, "What I mean is . . . well. . . ."

For a moment there was silence . . . followed by a rush as the cat bolted from the underbrush.

■ **EDITING 4: PRACTICE**

Using ellipsis points, edit the following paragraph to shorten it for a paper on racism. More than one edited version is possible. Be ready to explain your editing choices.

Until we label an out-group it does not clearly exist in our minds. Take the curiously vague situation that we often meet when a person wishes to locate responsibility on the shoulders of some out-group whose nature he cannot specify. In such a case he usually employs the pronoun 'they' without an antecedent. 'Why don't they make these sidewalks wider?' 'I hear they are going to build a factory in this town and hire a lot of foreigners.' 'I won't pay this tax bill; they can just whistle for their money.' If asked 'who?' the speaker is likely to grow confused and embarrassed. The common use of the orphaned pronoun *they* teaches us that people often want and need to designate out-groups (usually for the purpose of venting hostility) even when they have no clear conception of the out-group in question. And so long as the target of wrath remains vague and ill-defined specific prejudice cannot crystallize around it. To have enemies we need labels.

GORDON ALLPORT, "THE LANGUAGE OF PREJUDICE"

49 **d** **Using brackets**

Brackets are used to enclose words that are added to or changed within direct quotations. (See 17d1.) They can also enclose comments about quotations and about material that is already inside parentheses. (If your typewriter or printer does not have brackets, you can write them in by hand.)

Consider this passage from an article entitled "Interview with a Sparrow" by E. B. White.

As yet the onset of Spring is largely gossip among the sparrows. Any noon, in Madison Square, you may see one pick up a straw in his beak, put on an air of great business, twisting his head and glancing at the sky. Nothing comes of it. He hops three or four times and drops both the straw and the incident.

In quoting from this passage, it would be permissible to make small changes in order to clarify a pronoun reference, to add an explanatory phrase, or to make the quoted words read correctly within the context of the new sentence.

> E. B. White describes just such a spring day: "Any noon, in Madison Square, you may see [a sparrow] pick up a straw in his beak, put on an air of great business, twisting his head and glancing at the sky."

> E. B. White describes a sparrow on a spring day: "Any noon, in Madison Square [in New York City], you may see one pick up a straw in his beak, put on an air of great business, twisting his head and glancing at the sky."

> White concludes by noting that the bird "[hopped] three or four times and [dropped] both the straw and the incident."

Brackets are also used to change capitalization in the original quotation to make it correct in the new sentence.

> The fact that "[n]othing comes of it" is, for White, what makes the sparrow's activity worth noting.

You may add italics for emphasis in a quotation, but always indicate that you have done so by enclosing the phrase "italics added" in brackets at the end of the passage.

> According to this study, in 1992 "the *average* major league base-ball player earned more than a million dollars a year [italics added]."

Brackets can be used to indicate a spelling or punctuation error in quoted material that was present in the original. By enclosing the word *sic* (Latin for "such") in brackets directly after the error, you inform the reader that you see the error but are not responsible for it.

> In its statement, the commission said that its new health insurance program "will not effect [sic] the quality of medical care for county employees."

Within parentheses, use brackets to avoid double parentheses.

> (These findings are summarized in Table C [p. 12].)

■ **EDITING 5: PRACTICE**

Edit the following passage, using brackets correctly.

According to the findings of a new study, people who smoke may be hurting not only themselves. "It (tobacco smoke) can be just as detrimental to nonsmokers as to smokers," a spokesperson for the study told reporters. "In fact, secondhand smoke may be even more dangerous," she added, "since they (nonsmokers) are inhaling it without a filter." This latest finding adds to the growing list of the dangers of cigarette smoking. (See related article on the effects of smoking on fetal development (p. 14).)

49 **e** **Using slashes**

A **slash** (/) is a slanted line, also known as a **solidus** or **virgule**. Use a slash, preceded and followed by a space, to mark the end of a line of poetry incorporated in text.

> Shakespeare opens *The Passionate Pilgrim* with a seeming paradox: "When my love swears that she is made of truth, / I do believe her, though I know she lies."

(See 48a for more on quoting poetry.)

Use a slash with no space before or after it in some common expressions indicating alternatives.

either/or proposition   pass/fail system   true/false test

When possible, however, in most formal writing use a conjunction and hyphens between the alternatives rather than a slash.

■ A small business can be a win‸or‸lose investment.

In particular, the slashed alternatives *and/or* and *he/she* are considered inappropriate for writing in the humanities.

Also use a slash without spaces to separate numerals when they represent the parts of a date (*1/3/96*) and the numerator and denominator in a fraction (*1/2*). (Use a hyphen to separate a whole number from its fraction: *2-1/2*.)

■ EDITING 6: EXPLORATION

Locate two or three examples of professional writing that includes slashes used to present alternatives. Have the authors used the slashes correctly? Do you think that the information has been presented in the best way possible? Is there a better way to present it?

■ EDITING 7: PRACTICE

Edit the following paragraph, using parentheses, dashes, and brackets correctly. (You may have to alter some other punctuation.) More than one edited version is possible. Be ready to discuss your editing choices.

One of my biggest pleasures when I am out driving is reading other drivers' bumper stickers. These little messages, often provocative, always revealing of the people who stick them so proudly on the backs of their cars, serve a number of functions. They allow people to express their views on politicians, "Impeach Clinton or whoever happens to be in office," for example, or "Vote for Nobody," as well as their views on political issues more generally, "Imagine World Peace" and "Who Needs the Whales?" They work as advertisements, "Ask me about Avon," and as personal statements, "I live to fish." They even give parents a chance to show their pride in their children, "My child is an honor student at Pineview School," or to display their ignorance, "My child can beat up you're (sic) honor student." I don't have a bumper sticker myself, but I definitely will, once an "I Love Bumper Stickers" version appears on the market!

■ EDITING 8: APPLICATION

Examine a paper you are working on for misused or omitted parentheses, dashes, ellipsis points, brackets, and slashes. Do you make one kind of error often? Which of these marks seems the most difficult to use? In your own words, write a brief set of guidelines for using each of these marks correctly. Now reread your paper and see if you can find opportunities for using any of these marks that you have not used before. Also edit sentences in which you have misused any punctuation marks.

Editing
Mechanics

The spelling of English words seems sometimes to defy reason. Some words sound exactly the same even though they are spelled differently (*their, there, they're*), and the same sound may be represented by different letters or letter combinations—as with the long *e* sound in *meet, seat, concrete, petite, conceit,* and *piece.* Conversely, the same letter or letter combinations can represent different sounds—such as the *a*'s in *amaze;* the *g*'s in *gorgeous;* and the *ough* in *tough, though,* and *through.*

English spelling reflects the language's many etymological sources. As English has absorbed words from other languages, it has assumed or adapted their spellings; thus the spelling of a word in English often cannot be determined simply by its pronunciation. (See 31a for more on the history of the English language.)

Misspellings can seriously undermine your credibility and, in some cases, can lead readers to misunderstand. Always edit carefully for spelling, keeping in mind the guidelines that follow.

50 a Checking for commonly confused words

Distinguishing between homonyms

Homonyms are words with the same sound but different meanings: *great, grate; fair, fare.* When you are drafting and revising, it is easy to confuse homonyms, writing *their* instead of *there,* for example, or *rite* instead of *write.* As you edit, check carefully to make sure you've chosen the correct word in every case.

Memory aids can help you distinguish between some homonyms. For example, *piece,* what you slice a pie into, has a *pie* in it, whereas *peace* does not. Knowing word origins or related words can also help. *Rite* is related to *ritual,* in the sense of ceremony. *Write* is descended from an Old English word, *writan,*

SPELLING TIPS

- Always consult a dictionary when you are in doubt about how to spell a word.
- When checking the spelling of an unfamiliar word, note its *etymology*, or origin, and the history of its usage. This information will help you understand why a word is spelled in a particular way and thus fix the correct spelling in your mind.
- In your notebook or journal keep a personal spelling list of difficult words you encounter. Check to see if a word that you find troublesome shares a root, prefix, or suffix with a word you already know; the connection helps you learn the meaning, as well as the spelling, of the new word.
- Use the spell checker on your word processor to proofread your papers. It locates transposed or dropped letters as well as misspellings.
- Proofread your work carefully, even when you use a spell checker. If your spelling is right but the word is wrong, even the computer can't help. For example, if you confuse *to, too,* and *two,* or *its* and *it's,* the spell checker won't catch the error because it can't recognize the context in which a word is used.

WP TIP   Keep a list of words you frequently misspell in a special file on your computer disk. Use the search-and-replace function to locate and correct the words on your list.

meaning "to scratch, draw, or engrave." Sometimes examining roots, prefixes, and suffixes is helpful. For example, *migrate* ("to move from one place to another") serves as the root for both *emigrate* and *immigrate.* The prefix *e-* means "out of" or "away from," so to *emigrate* is to leave one's homeland (*She emigrated from Korea*). The prefix *im-,* on the other hand, means "into" or "toward," so to *immigrate* is to take up life in a new country (*She immigrated to Canada*).

WP TIP   If you frequently confuse certain homonyms, have your computer search for them and then make sure you have used the right spelling for each one. Highlight the homonyms in *italics* or **bold**; when you print hard copy, you can examine them more closely as you revise.

2 Distinguishing between expressions written as two words

Some words can be written either as one word or two: *We'll go there sometime. We spent some time there.* In almost all cases, the two spellings have two different meanings.

 HOMONYMS AND SIMILAR-SOUNDING WORDS

accept (receive)
except (leave out)

access (approach)
excess (too much)

adapt (change)
adopt (choose)

affect (influence)
effect (result)

allude (suggest)
elude (escape)

allusion (suggestion)
illusion (deception)

altar (church table)
alter (change)

ascent (climb)
assent (agree)

bare (uncovered)
bear (carry; the animal)

bazaar (market)
bizarre (weird)

birth (childbearing)
berth (place of rest)

board (plank; food)
bored (drilled; uninterested)

born (given birth to)
borne (carried)

break (smash, split)
brake (stopping device)

canvas (fabric)
canvass (examine)

capital (city; wealth)
capitol (building)

censor (prohibit)
sensor (measuring device)

cite (mention)
site (place)
sight (vision)

coarse (rough)
course (way, path)

complement (make complete)
compliment (praise)

conscience (moral sense)
conscious (aware)

cursor (computer marker)
curser (swearer)

council (committee)
counsel (advise; adviser)

dairy (milk-producing farm)
diary (daily book)

Checking for commonly confused words 707

all ready (completely prepared) already (previously)
all together (all in one place) altogether (thoroughly)
all ways (all methods) always (at all times)
a lot (a large amount) allot (distribute, assign)
every day (each day) everyday (ordinary)

dessert (sweet food) forward (to the front)
desert (abandon) foreword (preface)

dissent (disagreement) gorilla (ape)
descent (movement down- guerrilla (fighter)
ward)

hear (perceive)
dual (having two parts) here (in this place)
duel (fight between two peo-
ple) heard (perceived)
herd (group of animals)

dye (color)
die (perish) heroin (drug)
heroine (principal female character)

elicit (draw forth)
illicit (improper) hole (opening)
whole (entire)

eminent (noteworthy)
imminent (impending) holy (sacred)
wholly (entirely)

ensure (make certain)
insure (indemnify) immigrate (come in)
emigrate (leave)

exercise (activity)
exorcise (drive out) its (possessive of *it*)
it's (contraction of *it is*)

fair (just)
fare (food; fee) know (be aware)
no (negative, not yes)

faze (disturb)
phase (stage) lead (metal)
led (guided)

formerly (at an earlier time)
formally (according to a pattern) lesson (instruction)
lessen (reduce)

forth (forward)
fourth (follows third) (cont.)

HOMONYMS AND OTHER SIMILAR-SOUNDING WORDS (cont.)

lightning (electric flash)
lightening (making less heavy)

meat (food)
meet (encounter)

miner (excavator)
minor (person under a given age)

pair (two)
pear (fruit)
pare (peel; reduce)

passed (went by)
past (an earlier time)

peace (absence of war)
piece (part; portion)

peer (look; equal)
pier (pillar)

plain (simple; flat land)
plane (flat surface; smooth off; aircraft)

pray (ask, implore)
prey (hunt down; what is hunted)

principle (rule)
principal (chief person; sum of money)

quiet (silent)
quite (really, positively, very much)

rain (precipitation)
reign (rule)

right (proper, entitlement)
rite (ritual)

road (path)
rode (past of *ride*)

scene (setting, stage setting)
seen (perceived)

sense (perception)
since (from that time)

may be (could be)   maybe (perhaps)
some time (an amount of time)   sometime (at some unspecified time)

In others, the spelling depends on how the word is used in the sentence.

WP TIP   Choose a piece of writing that you are currently working on. Use the search-and-replace function to find some of the troublesome words from the list above. Put them into bold, and print out a hard copy. Go back and examine each usage more closely, then revise if neessary on screen.

shone (past of *shine*)
shown (displayed)

stationary (not moving)
stationery (writing paper)

straight (not curved)
strait (narrow place)

tack (angle of approach)
tact (sensitivity, diplomacy)

taut (tight)
taught (past of *teach*)

than (word of comparison)
then (at that time)

their (possessive of *them*)
there (in that place)
they're (contraction of *they are*)

threw (past of *throw*)
through (by way of)

to (in the direction of)
too (also)
two (the number)

waist (middle of the torso)
waste (squander)

weak (feeble)
week (seven days)

wear (carry on the body)
where (in what place)

weather (atmospheric conditions)
whether (if, in case)

which (what one)
witch (sorceress)

whose (possessive of *who*)
who's (contraction of *who is*)

write (inscribe, record)
wright (builder)
right (correct)

your (possessive of *you*)
you're (contraction of *you are*)

Patricia will try to *work out* her frustrations by exhausting herself at her afternoon *workout*.

The two words work out *are a verb; the word* workout *is a noun.*

Remember that *cannot* is always spelled as one word and that most dictionaries suggest spelling *all right* as two words.

WP TIP If you use a spell checker to help you proofread your papers, remember that it won't help you find **errors in meaning**— that is, when you want *affect* instead of *effect;* or *you're,* not *your;* or *dinner,* not *diner.* It's still up to you as a writer and careful proofreader to catch these problems.

CONFUSING CONTRACTIONS AND POSSESSIVE PRONOUNS

The words on the left are contractions; the words on the right are possessive pronouns. It's easy to make a spelling error by confusing these words, so be careful when you use them.

it's (it is)   its (of or belonging to it)
they're (they are)   their (of or belonging to them)
who's (who is)   whose (of or belonging to whom)
you're (you are)   your (of or belonging to you)

3 Distinguishing between words with similar spellings and meanings

Misspellings often occur with words that are closely related in meaning and spelled and pronounced similarly. The following pairs of words can be confusing because their meanings are related and the spelling in each case differs by only a single letter.

advice (noun)   advise (verb)
breath (noun)   breathe (verb)
chose (past tense)   choose (present tense)
cloths (fabrics)   clothes (garments)
device (noun)   devise (verb)
envelope (noun)   envelop (verb)
later (after more time)   latter (in the final position)
prophecy (noun)   prophesy (verb)

Similar problems can occur where the only spelling difference is in the prefix or suffix: *perspective, prospective; personal, personnel.* If you have trouble with words like these, remembering differences in pronunciation can help you distinguish the correct spelling of the word you intend.

WP TIP When editing for these particular similar-sounding words, you might want to add them, especially the two-word constructions, if they are not already there. The checker can correct the spelling of a particular word for you, but remember that even if you've spelled it correctly, you might have used one word when you *intended* to use the other. Using hard copy sometimes helps you see things more readily than on screen.

RECOGNIZING BRITISH SPELLINGS

For some words, British spelling—also used widely in other countries including Australia, Canada, and India—differs from the preferred American spelling: *centre* rather than *center*, *labour* rather than *labor*. In general, writers in the United States are expected to conform to American spellings, so if you've learned British spellings, you'll need to take note of such differences and edit your work accordingly.

WP TIP After typing a piece of writing on the computer, run the spell checker. Make note of the words it caught. Is the software always correct? Are there any misspellings the software missed, those based on **errors in meaning** (rather than spelling errors)?

 PRONUNCIATION AND SPELLING

Pronunciation is sometimes a poor guide to spelling. If you try to spell the following words exactly as you say them, you will probably misspell some of them. As you edit, try to pronounce such words in your mind as they are spelled, not as you normally say them.

accident*a*lly	memento	re*l*evant
ar*c*tic	mischie*vou*s	roo*mm*ate
arith*m*etic	nuc*l*ear	san*d*wich
ath*l*ete	possi*b*ly	similar
can*d*idate	preju*dic*e	sur*p*rise
envir*on*ment	(noun)	temperature
extr*a*ordinary	prejudic*ed*	tentative
Feb*r*uary	(adjective)	use*d* to
interference	prob*a*bly	usu*a*lly
laboratory	pronunciation	veteran
library	quantity	We*d*nesday
literature	re*a*ltor	win*t*ry
mathematics	recognize	

■ **EDITING I: PRACTICE**

Edit the following passage, looking for commonly confused words and for words misspelled because of how they may be pronounced.

"Were just about to have our desert. Would you care to join us?"

"Thanks allot, but no. I've all ready eaten—a four-coarse meal."

"Oh, just have one small peace of pie. You can have it plane, without any topping."

"It looks extrordinary, but to tell you the truth, I'm a little afraid of the affect it'll have on my waste. I've been trying to loose wait; my cloths are getting so tight that I can hardly breath."

"Are you getting any exorcise? Their is probly no better way to lose weight."

"Well, I never was much of an athalete, as you know. I have a stationery bike, but I just can not seem to motivate myself to workout. I always seem to find an excuse to put it off until latter."

"I no just what you mean. Its really difficult. And than when I don't exorcise, I have such a guilty conscious."

"Here's an idea: Why don't we lesson our guilt, and meat tomorrow morning at the tennis courts?"

"Alright! Your on!"

50 b Using basic spelling rules

■ **Remembering the *ie/ei* rule and its exceptions**

You may already be familiar with the rule about using "*i* before *e*": Put *i* before *e* except after *c*, or when it sounds like "ay" as in *neighbor* and *weigh*. In most cases the rule holds true.

i before **e**: belief, field, friend, mischief, niece, patience, piece, priest, review, shield, view

ei after **c**: ceiling, conceit, conceive, deceit, deceive, receipt

ei sounding like "ay": eight, feign, freight, sleigh

There are, however, several common exceptions to remember.

ie *after* **c**: ancient, conscience, financier, science, species

ei *not after* **c** or sounding like "ay": *caffeine, codeine, counterfeit, either, feisty, foreign, forfeit, height, leisure, neither, seize, weird*

2 Adding suffixes according to spelling rules

A **suffix** is a syllable or group of letters attached to the end of a word to change its meaning and, sometimes, its part of speech: *tap + ed- = tapped, reverse* (verb) *+ -ible = reversible* (adjective). (See 31c). Adding a suffix can sometimes change the spelling of the base word. In addition, remember to watch for similar-sounding suffixes that are commonly confused with one another. Adding a **prefix,** a syllable attached to the beginning of a word, almost never causes a spelling change in the base word. However, some prefixes require hyphens. (See 52b.)

 USING *-CEDE, -CEED,* AND *-SEDE*

Because they have identical sounds, the syllables *-cede, -ceed,* and *-sede* are often confused. The most common is *-cede,* as in *accede, concede, intercede, precede, recede,* and *secede. -Ceed* appears in the words *exceed, proceed,* and *succeed. -Sede* appears only in the word *supersede.*

Suffixes after words ending in *y*

If the letter before the final *y* is a consonant, the *y* changes to *i* when a suffix is added, *unless* the suffix itself begins with *i.*

CONSONANT BEFORE y
friendly + -er = friendlier
happy + -ly   = happily
apply + -ing = applying
baby + -ish   = babyish

If the letter before the *y* is a vowel, the *y* doesn't change to *i.*

VOWEL BEFORE y
convey + -ed   = conveyed
annoy + -ance = annoyance
pay + -ment   = payment

The few exceptions to these rules include (1) some short words ending in -*y* when the suffix begins with a consonant (*dryness, shyly*); (2) the adverb form of very short words ending in -*ay* (*daily, gaily*); and (3) the past tense of three irregular verbs ending in -*ay* (*laid, paid, said*).

Proper nouns ending in *y* generally do not change spellings when suffixes are added (for example, *McCarthyism, Kennedyesque*).

(See 50b3 for rules about plurals of words ending in *y*.)

Suffixes after words ending in e

If the suffix begins with a consonant, keep the final *e* of the base word.

SUFFIX STARTING WITH CONSONANT
sure + -ly = surely
polite + -ness = politeness
hate + -ful = hateful
state + -ment = statement

There are a few exceptions to this rule, which should be memorized: *acknowledgment, argument, judgment, duly, truly, wholly, awful, ninth.*

If the suffix begins with a vowel, usually drop the final *e* of the base word.

SUFFIX STARTING WITH VOWEL
admire + -able = admirable
insure + -ing = insuring
dance + -er = dancer

However, keep the *e* when it is necessary to prevent misreading: *dye* + -*ing* = *dyeing* (not *dying*); *canoe* + -*ing* = *canoeing* (not *canoing*). In addition, to conform to conventions of pronunciation, keep the *e* when it follows a soft *c* (one that sounds like *s*, not *k*) or a soft *g* (one that sounds like *j* or *jh*) and the suffix starts with *a* or *o*; dropping the *e* in such cases would give the *c* or *g* a hard pronunciation.

BASE WORD WITH SOFT c OR g
enforce + -able = enforceable
outrage + -ous = outrageous

Suffixes after words ending in a consonant

If a suffix begins with a consonant and is added to a word that ends in a consonant, simply add the suffix, even if this results in a double consonant.

SUFFIX STARTS WITH CONSONANT	cup + -ful = cupful
	defer + -ment = deferment
	open + -ness = openness
	girl + -like = girllike

If a suffix beginning with a vowel is added to a word ending in a consonant, you may be unsure whether to double the final consonant of the base word. The rules are simple. Double the final consonant only if (1) the base word is one syllable or the stress in the base word is on the last syllable _and_ (2) the final consonant is preceded by a single vowel.

slap + -ed = slapped	refer + -al = referral
hop + -ing = hopping	occur + -ence = occurrence
abet + -or = abettor	admit + -ing = admitting

If the stress in the base word is not on the last syllable, or if the final consonant is preceded by a consonant or two vowels, do not double the final consonant.

FINAL CONSONANT FOLLOWS CONSONANT	hurt + -ing = hurting
	doubt + -able = doubtable
	enact + -ed = enacted

FINAL CONSONANT FOLLOWS TWO VOWELS	fuel + -ing = fueling
	sweep + -er = sweeper
	repeat + -ed = repeated

STRESS NOT ON FINAL SYLLABLE	barter + -ing = bartering
	envelop + -ed = enveloped
	danger + -ous = dangerous

Two exceptions to this rule are _format_ (_formatted, formatting_) and program (_programmed, programming_). In addition, if the base word is stressed on the last syllable but adding the suffix changes the pronunciation so the stress of the base word is no longer on that syllable, do not double the final consonant: _refer + ence = reference._

-ly or -ally

The suffix _-ly_ or _-ally_ turns a noun into an adjective or an adjective into an adverb. Add _-ally_ to words that end in _ic_.

automatically	characteristically
basically	dynamically

An exception is *publicly*.
Add *-ly* to words that do not end in *-ic*.

absolutely	differently
actually	instantly

Most other words that end in *-ally* are formed by adding *-ly* to the adjective suffix *-al*: *nation, national, nationally*. When adding *-ly* to a word that ends in *l*, keep both *l*'s: *real + ly = really*.

3 Forming plurals according to spelling rules

Most English nouns are made plural by adding *-s*: *book, books*; *page, pages*. There are, however, many exceptions. Fortunately, most of these follow the general rules described here.

General rules for plurals

Nouns ending in *ch, s, sh, or x* usually are made plural by adding *-es*.

church, churches   glass, glasses   wish, wishes   box, boxes

Nouns ending in *y* are made plural by adding *-s* if the letter before the *y* is a vowel. Otherwise, the plural is formed by changing the *y* to *i* and adding *-es*.

day, days	dairy, dairies
alloy, alloys	melody, melodies

Nouns ending in *o* are often made plural by adding *-s*.

video, videos	trio, trios	duo, duos
burro, burros	Latino, Latinos	inferno, infernos

However, several nouns ending in *o* preceded by a consonant form their plurals by adding *-es*.

embargo, embargoes	hero, heroes
veto, vetoes	tomato, tomatoes

Other nouns ending in *o* may take either *-s* or *-es* in forming the plural.

cargo, cargos, cargoes   tornado, tornados, tornadoes
volcano, volcanos, volcanoes   zero, zeros, zeroes

Many writers make it a habit to refer to a dictionary for the accepted plural form of words ending in *o*.

Nouns ending in *f* sometimes change the *f* to *v* and add *-es* to make the plural.

leaf, leaves	calf, calves	half, halves
self, selves	loaf, loaves	thief, thieves

Other nouns ending in *f* simply add *-s*.

brief, briefs	chief, chiefs	proof, proofs
belief, beliefs	reef, reefs	oaf, oafs

Still others form the plural either way: *hoof, hooves, hoofs*.

Nouns ending in *fe* may change the *f* to *v* before adding *-s*: *wife, wives; life, lives; knife, knives*. But not all nouns ending in *fe* follow this pattern: *safe, safes; fife, fifes; strife, strifes*.

Irregular and unusual plural forms

A few nouns are made plural without adding an *-s* or *-es*.

child, children	foot, feet	goose, geese
man, men	mouse, mice	woman, women

A handful of words have the same form for singular and plural.

moose, moose	sheep, sheep	series, series

Many loan words are made plural according to the rules of their original language. Words borrowed from Latin keep the endings used in Latin when forming plurals: *alumnus, alumni; alumna, alumnae; alga, algae; datum, data; medium, media*. Words from the Greek also keep their original endings: *criterion, criteria; analysis, analyses*.

However, some loan words have Anglicized plurals that are more widely accepted than their original Latin or Greek plurals: *stadiums* rather than *stadia*. Some foreign plurals are regarded as singular in English because the singular form is so rarely used: *The agenda is brief.*

Plurals of proper nouns

In general, proper nouns form plurals by adding -s or -es. Adding -s when forming the plural does not create an extra syllable in pronunciation: *the Simpsons, the Kims, several Lisas.* When the plural is pronounced with one more syllable than the singular, add -es. This usually occurs with proper nouns that end in *ch, s, sh, x,* or *z*: *the Bushes, the Joneses, the Koches, the Ruizes.* Do not use an apostrophe to indicate the plural of a proper name.

Plurals of compound nouns

A **compound noun** consists of two or more words regularly used together. If the compound is written as one word, make the last part plural: *newspapers, henhouses, notebooks.* An exception to this rule is the word *passersby.*

If a compound noun is written as separate words or if it is hyphenated, make plural the word that expresses the central idea. This is usually the noun in the compound: *attorneys general, presidents-elect, professors emeritus.* When both parts of the compound are nouns, make plural the word that is modified by another word or by a prepositional phrase: *bath towels, sisters-in-law, soldiers of fortune.*

Plurals of letters, numbers, and words

To form the plural of a letter, number, or symbol, use an apostrophe and *s*:

There are two *m*'s in *programmer.*

No sentence should end with two *?*'s.

For the plural of numbers referring to decades or centuries expressed in numerals, an apostrophe and *s* may be used, but the letter *s* alone is also correct. Be consistent.

the 1700s   the 1700's
the nineties

Plurals of abbreviations

If an abbreviation includes periods, form its plural with an apostrophe and *s*.

Several of my classmates have become M.D.'s.

Abbreviations without periods simply add *s*.

She keeps her money in two IRAs.

◼ EDITING 2: PRACTICE

Edit the following passage, using basic spelling rules to eliminate misspelled words.

Of all the holidaies, one of my least favorite is Thanksgiving. I know that it is traditionnal to beleive in Thanksgiving as a time for shareing a hearty meal with family and freinds, but to me all that outragous food—the huge turkey with two different gravies, the spicey dressing, the rich potatos, along with the butterred vegetables, the breads and rolls, and the multiple peices of pumpkin pie—just excedes the boundarys of civilized dinning. Then after the guestes ahve all stuffed themselfs, one group—usualy the women, of course—spend the rest of the afternoon cleanning up while the others—mostly the man, naturally—head for the den, ploping down in front of the television for a truely stimulateing afternoon of armchair quarterbackking. I conceed that I am in the minority, but I just can't concieve what anyone possibally enjoies about Thanksgiving.

◼ EDITING 3: APPLICATION

Keep a word list for one week. Look up in a dictionary any unfamiliar words that you encounter in your reading or writing, noting the origin and spelling of each word. Record these words on your word list. At the end of the week, review your list. Have a friend give you a spelling test, and cross off the words you get right. Start a new list with any you miss.

51 | Capitalization

Capital letters are conventionally used to indicate the beginning of a sentence and to distinguish names, titles, and certain other words. (For information on the capitalization of abbreviations, see Chapter 55.)

 WHAT NEEDS CAPITALIZATION?

As you edit, make sure you've capitalized the following words.

- The first word of every sentence
- The first word of a quoted sentence within a sentence
- Proper nouns and their derivatives
- Important words in titles of books and other works

51 a | Capitalizing the first word of a sentence

Use a capital letter at the beginning of a sentence or a deliberate sentence fragment.

The gymnast could not have been more pleased. A perfect ten.

What was the occasion? A holiday? Someone's birthday?

In a series of fragmentary questions, it is equally acceptable to use lowercase for each fragment.

What was the occasion? a holiday? someone's birthday?

Whichever style of capitalization you choose for such questions, be sure to use it consistently throughout your paper.

Sentences following colons

When two independent clauses are joined by a colon, capitalizing the first word of the second clause is optional, but be consistent throughout a paper.

> The senators' courage failed them: The [*or* the] term-limits bill was dead for another decade.

Always capitalize a numbered list of sentences (but not phrases) following a colon.

> His philosophy can be reduced to three basic rules: (1) Think for yourself. (2) Take care of your body. (3) Never hurt anyone.

Sentences between parentheses or dashes

Capitalize the first word of a complete sentence within parentheses if it is not inside another sentence.

> Congress attacked sex discrimination in sports with a 1972 law called Title IX. (Changes added in 1974 are called the Bayh amendments.)

Do not capitalize the first word of a complete sentence set off by parentheses or dashes when it falls within another sentence.

> Title IX (the name refers to a section of U.S. civil rights law) has changed collegiate sports a great deal over twenty years. On many campuses Title IX has increased the number of competitive sports offered to women—even opponents of the law agree this is true—but its effect on men's sports is more difficult to assess.

 Capitalizing quotations and lines of poetry

1 Quotations

Capitalize the first word of a quoted sentence, wherever it falls in your own sentence.

> "We'd like to talk to you about the budget for women's sports," Jeannine told the athletic director. "The first question is from Ryan."

Ryan asked, "How many sports are offered?"

Do not capitalize the first word of the continuation of a quotation interrupted by attributory words.

"Indeed," Mr. Kott responded, "we field men's and women's teams in track, swimming, tennis, and golf."

If the first word of a quotation does not begin a sentence of yours or a sentence in the original, do not capitalize it.

Recognizing details familiar from his childhood, E. B. White feels "the same damp moss covering the worms in the fishing can."

When quoting from published prose sources, you may have to change the capitalization of the original to fit into your sentence. If you use a capital letter where the original has a lowercase letter, or vice versa, use brackets to show the change. (See 49d.)

2 Capitalizing quotations from poetry

When quoting poetry, always follow the capitalization of the original.

The poem opens with Frost's usual directness and rhythmic formality: "Whose woods these are, I think I know. / His house is in the village, though." Compare this to Lucille Clifton's offhanded "boys / i don't promise you nothing. . . ."

(See Chapters 48 and 49 for more on punctuating quotations.)

51 c Capitalizing proper nouns and their derivatives

Proper nouns name particular persons, places, or things: *Toni Cade Bambera, Gulf of Mexico, Mercedes Benz.* In general, proper nouns are capitalized. (Articles, coordinating conjunctions, and prepositions in proper nouns are not capitalized.) **Common nouns,** on the other hand, name general classes of persons, places, or things: *writer, gulf, automobile.* Common nouns are not capitalized unless they are part of a proper noun.

WP TIP Use your computer's search-and-replace function to find all such errors and replace them with correctly capitalized

Capitalizing proper nouns and their derivatives 723

names. Be careful, however, when searching for words whose capitalization depends on context, such as *ocean* in the *Atlantic Ocean* and the *vast ocean*. You may want to use the find function so that you can stop at each instance and decide whether the word should be capitalized.

 FAMILY MEMBERS

Words describing family relationships are capitalized only when they are used as names, not when they are preceded by a possessive pronoun.

The family gave a party for Dad and Uncle Fritz.

My dad and my uncle are twins.

In general, the following should be capitalized.

Names of individual people and animals

Eleanor Roosevelt	Catherine the Great
Karl Marx	Magic Johnson
Snoopy	Vincent van Gogh
Sitting Bull	Martin Van Buren

Note that capitalization of *van, de, la,* and so on varies, so consult a reliable print source for the conventional spelling of a particular name.

Religions, religious terms, deities, and sacred works

Judaism, Jews	Christianity, Christians
Roman Catholic	Protestant
God	Allah
the Koran	the Bible

Nationalities, ethnic groups, and languages

French	Chinese	Hindustani
Chicano	African Americans	Seminole

Titles

Formal and courtesy titles and their abbreviations are capitalized when they are used before a name and not set off by commas.

General Colin Powell	Senator Dianne Feinstein
Judge Marilyn Harris	Coach Bill Walsh
Dame Agatha Christie	Prof. Mitchell Cox
Ms. Sheenah Taggert	Dr. Wu

They are lowercased when used alone or separated from the name by commas.

Dianne Feinstein, senator from California

my physics professor, Mitchell Cox

Titles indicating high station or office may be capitalized when they are not followed by a name: *the President of the United States, the Queen, the Pope.* Derivatives of such titles, however, are not capitalized: *presidential, papal.*

Months, days of the week, and holidays

August 12, 1914	the Fourth of July
Tuesday, the twentieth of April	Presidents' Day

Seasons are not capitalized: *summer, fall.*

Geographic names

Little Rock, Arkansas	the Western Hemisphere
Puerto Rico	the Midwest
the Grand Canyon	the Colorado River
the Windy City	Madison Avenue

Note that common nouns like *river, avenue,* and *street* are lowercase when they are preceded by two or more proper nouns: *Bleecker and MacDougal streets.*

Although direction words are capitalized when they name a region (*the South*), they are not when they indicate compass directions: *We headed south on U.S. 61.*

Institutions, organizations, businesses, and trade names

Oberlin College	the Beatles
the United Nations	Congress
the English Department	Habitat for Humanity
Microsoft Corporation	the League of Women Voters
Big Mac	Aquafresh toothpaste

Be sure to capitalize only the proper name of an institution, not a generic term referring to it: *Oberlin is ranked among the best small colleges in the country.*

Words such as *company, incorporated,* and *limited* and their abbreviations are capitalized when they are used as part of a business's formal name: *Jones Brothers Limited.* They are not capitalized when they are not part of the formal name: *The company is on the verge of bankruptcy.*

Historical documents, legislation, events, periods, and movements

the Constitution	the Norman Conquest
the Stone Age	World War II
the Stamp Act	the Renaissance
the Romantic poets	Public Law 100-13
an Impressionist painter	the Rationalist movement

Ships, aircraft, spacecraft, and trains

the *U.S.S. Constitution*	the *Spirit of St. Louis*
the *Challenger*	the *Orient Express*

(See 53e for guidelines on italicizing names of vehicles.)

Derivatives of proper nouns

Newtonian	Texan
Marxist	Beatlemania

Prefixes before such derivatives are not capitalized: *neo-Marxist, anti-American.* (See 52b for information on hyphenating prefixes before proper adjectives.)

Words derived from proper nouns that have taken on independent meanings often are no longer capitalized: *french fries, herculean, quixotic, ohm, vulcanization.*

51 d Capitalizing titles

For the title of a book, play, essay, story, poem, movie, television series, piece of music, or work of art, capitalize the first word, the last word, and all other words except articles (*the, a, an*), coordinating conjunctions (*and, or, for, but, nor, so, yet*), and prepositions (*in, on, with,* and so on).

Sense and Sensibility	"What I Did for Love"
The Taming of the Shrew	*Beauty and the Beast*

"Home Improvement"   *Nude Descending a Staircase*
"The East Is Red"

Follow the same rule for subtitles, including capitalizing the first word: *Women Playwrights: The Best Play of 1994.*

If a title contains words joined by a hyphen, both words usually are capitalized, with the exception of articles, conjunctions, and prepositions (*The One-Minute Grammarian; The Social History of the Jack-in-the-Box*).

(See 48c and 53a on the use of quotation marks and italics for titles.)

WP TIP If you're not already doing so, consider completing one of the editing activities at the computer. Once you've identified letters that need to be changed from upper to lower case, and vice versa, it will be simple to correct them as you go through the passage. Be sure to save your changes once you've finished.

 _I_ AND _O_

Always capitalize the personal pronoun *I*, no matter where it falls in a sentence.

Whatever I play, I play to win.

Also capitalize the interjection *O*, used in prayers and to express wonder and surprise.

Descend on us, O Spirit of Peace.

Note that the interjection *oh* is not capitalized unless it begins a sentence: *We didn't succeed, but, oh, how we tried.*

 EDITING 1: PRACTICE

Edit the following passage, using capital letters according to the guidelines in this chapter.

The Library of congress, established in Washington in 1800, has been called "The United states's national library." Primarily responsible for its creation was vice president Thomas Jefferson (He was himself an avid book collector), who also supported it strongly during the course of his Presidency. When a fire destroyed much of the Collection in 1814, Jefferson donated his own personal library as a replacement. Ruined by another fire in 1851—Some 35,000 volumes were lost—the library languished until congress passed the copyright act of 1870, which required that all material copyrighted in the Country be deposited there. Today the imposing building on Independence avenue—beloved by many washingtonians—contains some 75 million items, including maps, prints, photographs, and an extensive collection of asian art and artifacts. Of course, it also houses such diverse prose works as a rare edition of *The Federalist papers* and a copy of Gary Larsen's *It Came From the Far Side*.

EDITING 2: APPLICATION

Examine a paper you are working on for mistakes in capitalization. Is there one kind of mistake in using capitalization that you consistently make? If so, think about how best to identify words that should and should not be capitalized when you edit your work. Edit any sentences in which you have made capitalization mistakes.

52 Hyphenation

The hyphen helps readers understand how words are to be read. A hyphen can link parts of a word that might otherwise be seen as separate, can separate parts of a word that might be misleading or hard to read if written together, and can be used conventionally in numbers, fractions, and units of measure.

 GUIDELINES FOR HYPHENATION

As you edit, make sure you have used hyphens appropriately for the following:

- For dividing words at the ends of lines, if necessary
- After certain prefixes
- In certain compound words
- In some fractions, numbers, and units of measure

52 a Hyphenating words at the ends of lines

If a word is too long to fit at the end of a line, you can divide it, using a hyphen to signal that the word continues on the next line. It is better not to divide words, but if you must, be sure to do so at an acceptable point. When in doubt, consult a dictionary. The divisions in the entry word indicate where it may be hyphenated. Here are a few guidelines.

- **Divide only between pronounced syllables**. Note that one-syllable words such as *eighth*, *through*, *dreamed*, and *urged* cannot be divided. Words with internal double letters can usually divide between those letters (*wil-low*, *cut-ting*), which generally indicate syllable breaks. Watch out, however, for double letters before a suffix; words with these should divide between base word and suffix (*pass-age*, not *pas-sage*).

■ **Do not leave just one letter on a line**. Words like *amount* (*a-mount*) and *ideal* (*i-deal*) cannot be divided; *abandon* can be divided only as *aban-don*, and *idolize* as *idol-ize*.

■ **Divide at prefixes or suffixes**. Try to leave both parts of the word recognizable: not *an-tibody* but *anti-body*; not *ea-gerness* but *eager-ness*.

■ **Divide between words in compounds**. The most natural place to divide a compound word is where its parts join: *mother-land*, *sword-fish*. Divide a hyphenated compound at the existing hyphen: *self-esteem*, *son-in-law*.

WP TIP **Double-check your computer's hyphenation**. Many computer word processing programs can automatically hyphenate a document. If you choose not to hyphenate any words, most programs allow you to turn off hyphenation. If you take advantage of your computer's ability to hyphenate, be sure to double-check its choices, which may be less than perfect.

■ **EDITING I: PRACTICE**

Indicate the best place, if any, for hyphenating each of the following words. If a word contains more than two syllables, indicate all possible hyphenation points. You may want to consult a dictionary.

1.	coordinated	**6.**	minibus
2.	acquitted	**7.**	ignite
3.	preparedness	**8.**	overcast
4.	width	**9.**	commitment
5.	crossbones	**10.**	antidote

52 b | **Hyphenating after some prefixes**

While prefixes are attached without hyphens, there are a few exceptions. When in doubt, consult your dictionary. The following guidelines cover most of the common uses of hyphens following prefixes.

Use a hyphen to attach a prefix to a capitalized word or to a date. (The prefix itself is usually not capitalized.)

anti-Washington sentiment   post-1994 guidelines

Use a hyphen to attach a prefix to a term of more than one word.

pro-school choice candidates   pre-space age technology

Use a hyphen after *all-*, *ex-*, *self-*, and *quasi-*.

all-inclusive   ex-convict   self-hypnosis

A hyphen may be used when a prefix ends with the same letter that begins the base word: *anti-intellectual*, *co-ownership*. However, the hyphen has been dropped from many such words (*cooperate*, *preexisting*, *unnatural*). It is usually best to check a dictionary.

A hyphen is occasionally used to distinguish between two different words spelled with the same letters, especially when there is a strong chance of a misreading.

We asked them to *refund* [give back] our money.

Congress will *re-fund* [fund again] the program for another year.

When two prefixes separated in a sentence by a conjunction apply to the same base word, add a hyphen after both prefixes, with a space after the first prefix.

We compared the *pre-* and *post-election* analyses.

52 **c** **Hyphenating compound words**

Two or more words used as a single unit form a **compound word**. Many compounds are written as one word, sometimes called a closed compound: *workhorse*, *schoolteacher*. Other compounds are written as two words, or open compounds: *hope chest*, *lunch break*, *curtain rod*. Still others are hyphenated: *great-grandson*, *mother-in-law*, and *stick-in-the-mud*.

In deciding whether to hyphenate **compound nouns**, check a dictionary. If the compound is not listed in the dictionary, write it as separate words. Note that most compound nouns consisting of three or more words are hyphenated: *attorney-at-law*, *jack-in-the-box*.

Compound adjectives consist of two or more words that function together as a single adjective before a noun: *a well-written essay*, *a late-night party*, *a touch-and-go-situation*. They are usually hyphenated to make it clear which words go together to form the adjective. It is often necessary to do this to prevent a misreading. For example, compare the meanings of the following sentences.

Mr. Donovan is an old car collector.

He is an old *person who* collects cars.

Mr. Donovan is an old-car collector.

He is a person who collects old cars.

Note, however, that where a well-established compound noun functions as an adjective, misreading is unlikely and no hyphen is needed.

post office box   high school student

Also, a hyphen is never used between an adverb ending in *-ly* and the adjective it modifies.

highly motivated employees   a strongly worded statement

When multiple-word modifiers come *after* a noun, they are generally not hyphenated.

The out-of-work actor auditioned every day.

The actor was out of work for over a year.

When two compound adjectives before a noun have the same base word and are linked by a conjunction, the base word can be dropped from the first and a space added after the hyphen.

full- and part-time employees

Coined compounds are compounds made up by writers to express an idea in a particularly concise or vivid way. Such coinages are generally hyphenated.

We worked to the whirr-whoosh-click of the packing machine.

52 d | **Hyphenating numbers, fractions, and units of measure**

Hyphenate two-word numbers from twenty-one to ninety-nine. Do not hyphenate before or after the words *hundred*, *thousand*, or *million*.

fifty-seven	twenty-two hundred
two hundred fifty-seven	six hundred twenty thousand

Remember that long numbers are often easier to read when expressed in figures. (See 54a.)

Use a hyphen between the numerator and denominator of a spelled-out fraction unless one of them is already hyphenated.

one-half	two-thirds
twenty-one fiftieths	

When a number includes a unit of measure (feet, inches, miles, pounds), hyphenate modifiers but not nouns.

An ordinary dump truck has a *nine-cubic-yard* bed.

Only a gardener would delight in *nine cubic yards* of manure.

Use a hyphen in ages when the expression functions as a noun or as an adjective preceding a noun.

I threatened to trade in my *ten-year-old* twins for a *twenty-year-old.*

Do not hyphenate when the word indicating time—in this case *years*—is plural: *The boy is ten years old.*

A hyphen can be used to suggest a range between numbers: *1987–90, 120–140 times a year.* However, readers generally find it clearer if the range is described in words: *from 1987 to 1990; between 120 and 140 times a year.* Do not combine the two methods: *they attended the college from 1987 to 1990* (not *from 1987-1990*).

▣ EDITING 2: PRACTICE

Edit the following passage, hyphenating all words where necessary and deleting unnecessary hyphens. You may have to consult a dictionary.

Widely-available desktop publishing systems have led to an explosion in the publication of *zines*, the low tech equivalent of magazines. Generally published out of the editor owner's home, the average zine has a small print run (from 250-350 copies) and very low production costs (around $500). Zines, which are similar to under-ground publications of the 1960s and 1970s, reflect the offbeat personalities of their owners. Most make very-little money but enjoy a devoted reader-ship, approximately two thirds of which is under thirty-years-old in most cases. One of the best known zines is *Ersatz*, published by Sam Pratt, twenty seven, out of his loft in Manhattan's Hells' Kitchen. Reflecting the ir- reverent sensibilities of the postReagan era, *Ersatz* has included such pieces as a quasiserious article on the deeper significance of the Trix rabbit. As zines become more-and-more popular, bigger publishers have begun to look for ways to coopt them.

■ EDITING 3: APPLICATION

Examine a paper you are working on for hyphenation mistakes. Is there one kind of mistake in using hyphens that you consistently make? If so, think about how best to remember hyphenation rules when you edit your work. Edit any sentences in which you have misused or omitted hyphens.

Most publications use a **roman** typeface—like this one—for the main body of the text. **Italic** typeface—*which looks like this*—is then used to distinguish certain words, usually to indicate that they must be interpreted somewhat differently.

The equivalent of italics in typed and handwritten work is <u>underlining</u>. Many word processing programs now allow writers to shift to italic type, but make sure this is acceptable to your instructor; he or she may still prefer underling for italics in student work.

 COMMON USES OF ITALICS

As you edit, check for your use of italics with the following:

- Titles of long published works, musical works, and works of art
- Specific words you wish to give special emphasis
- Words, numerals, and letters used as words
- Words from languages other than English
- Names of trains, ships, and other specific vehicles

---

53 | a | Italicizing titles

Italicize the titles of books, long poems considered to be independent works, plays, operas and other long musical works, movies, long-play recordings, newspapers, magazines and journals, television or radio series, and works of art. Use quotation marks rather than italics for titles that are subdivisions of a larger work. (See 48c for more on using quotation marks for titles and for marking titles within titles.)

The titles of sacred works, parts of sacred works, and ancient manuscripts are not italicized.

the Bible   the Koran   Genesis

The titles of public documents also are not in italics.

the Constitution   the Declaration of Independence

Most academic stylesheets recommend neither capitalizing nor italicizing the article (*a, an,* or *the*) in the name of a newspaper or magazine, even if the newspaper or magazine includes it in its own name, as does [*The*] *New York Times.* However, consider following its particular style when writing for a publication.

 ITALICS AND QUOTATION MARKS FOR TITLES

ITALICS	QUOTATION MARKS
Holy the Firm (book)	"Newborn and Salted" (chapter)
Here Lies (story collection)	"Big Blonde" (short story)
North of Boston (poetry collection)	"Mending Wall" (poem)
Song of Roland (long poem, independent work)	
Waiting for Godot (play)	
Porgy and Bess (opera)	
Carmina Burana (long musical work)*	
Pulp Fiction (movie)	
Voodoo Lounge (LP recording)	"Mean Disposition" (song)
Los Angeles Times (newspaper)	"Icy Words on Global Warming" (article)
New Republic (magazine)	
The Simpsons (television series)	"Homer Meets Godzilla" (episode)
All Things Considered (radio series)	
The Boating Party (painting)	
Reclining Nude (sculpture)	

*Note that a musical work identified by form and key is neither italicized nor put in quotation marks: Beethoven's Symphony No. 5 in D Minor.

53 b Italicizing for emphasis and clarity

Italics can be used to indicate that a certain word or words should receive special emphasis in a sentence.

Despite popular perception, the rate of violent crime is actually *lower* today than it was fifteen years ago.

Whether something *is* true is less important than whether people *believe* it to be true.

Such emphasis can also help writers clarify the specific point they wish to make.

Then Ms. Dillon asked *me* to sing.

Of all people, me!

Then Ms. Dillon asked me to *sing*.

Of all things, sing!

Be careful not to overuse italics for such purposes. Too much emphasis can make the sentence seem overstated or simply lose impact. Effective emphasis can often better be achieved through other means. (See Chapter 27.)

53 c Italicizing words, numerals, and letters used as words

Use italics when you refer to a word or numeral as itself rather than for its usual meaning in the context of a sentence. Also italicize letters referred to as part of the alphabet or as mathematical symbols.

How would you define the terms *liberal* and *conservative*?

Because I read the *1* as a *7*, my calculations were incorrect.

When I type quickly, I often substitute *w* for *s*.

Let *x* stand for test scores and *y* for hours of study.

53 d Italicizing words from other languages

Words and phrases from languages other than English are usually italicized unless they have become a familiar part of English usage.

Many old castles in Spain have been turned into *paradors* where visitors can spend the night.

The *tour de France* is a bicycle race of more than 2,500 miles.

The menu offered spaghetti, lasagne, and *pasticcio di faglioni.*

In deciding whether to italicize words from other languages, check a recent English dictionary. Words that do not appear should be italicized. Words that do appear should be italicized only if they are clearly not part of the English language and are seldom used by English speakers.

Always italicize a word or phrase from another language that you are defining for the first time.

The Hawaiian word for that smooth, ropelike lava is *pahoehoe.*

The Latin names used to classify plants and animals by genus and species are also italicized.

The biologists named their discovery *Symbian pandora.*

 Italicizing the names of individual trains, ships, airplanes, and spacecraft

Italicize the official names of individual trains, ships, airplanes, and spacecraft, but not the names of classifications of such vehicles.

the *Shasta Daylight* (train)	*Spirit of St. Louis* (airplane)
the U.S.S. *Arizona* (ship)	*Voyager* (spacecraft)
a Polaris rocket	a Trident submarine

 EDITING 1: PRACTICE

Edit the following passage, making sure words are italicized according to convention.

Before planting a garden, it is a good idea to consult a reputable source for tips on successful gardening. Many newspapers, such as the New York Times, have a weekly column devoted to gardening. There are also many useful books, such as "A Guide to Growing Gorgeous Greenery," with its especially helpful introductory chapter, Plan before You Plant.

First a gardener should learn about the different types of plants. Annuals is the term given to plants that complete their lifetime in one year; the term *perennials* is used for plants that grow back every year. Many annuals are popular with gardeners, especially the Begonia semperflorens and the Petunia hybrida.

Another issue for gardeners to consider is pesticides. Environmentally conscious gardeners are not opposed to pesticides *per se*, but they use only organic pesticides, which derive from *natural* rather than *synthetic* substances.

Gardening books are useful sans doute, and they may prevent the worst *faux pas* in the garden, but in the end there is no one way to make a garden— chacun à son goût!

■ EDITING 2: APPLICATION

Examine a paper you are working on for mistakes in italicizing. Is there one kind of mistake in using italics that you consistently make? If so, think about how best to remember which words to italicize when you edit your work. Edit any sentences in which you have misused or omitted italics.

54 Numbers

Many techniques of analysis and persuasion depend on numbers. When doing research, you need to present the numbers that describe your findings. As you write, you include statistics that support your position. When you edit, you must ensure that numbers are presented effectively and clearly. The more numbers used in a piece of writing, the more likely readers are to become confused or intimidated.

54 a Choosing between figures and words according to context

Conventions for choosing between figures and words for numbers vary according to discipline. For more information, consult the style guide of your discipline.

In most nontechnical academic writing (including writing in literature and the humanities), spell the numbers one to one hundred as well as all fractions. (See 52d about using hyphens in numbers.)

thirty universities   fifty-three graduates
three-fourths of the class

Also spell out round numbers over one hundred if they can be expressed in two words. Otherwise, use figures.

five hundred students   517 students
more than fifty thousand trees   52,317 trees

It is sometimes clearer to express very large round numbers using a combination of words and figures: *The Census Bureau says that the U.S. population exceeds 250 million.*

In most technical writing (including writing in the social and natural sciences), most numbers, especially measurements and statistics, are written in figures.

The pressure increased by 3 kilograms per square centimeter.

Fewer than 1/10 of the eggs failed to hatch.

In both nontechnical and technical writing, spell out any number that begins a sentence. If doing so is awkward, rewrite the sentence.

■ ~~547~~ *Five hundred forty-seven* students attended the concert.

■ *Attending the concert were* 547 students. ~~attended the concert.~~

Consistency is important. Express any numbers that readers must compare with each other in the same way. If convention requires using figures for one number, do the same for the other numbers.

■ In Midville last year, ~~eighty-seven~~ *87* cats and 114 dogs were destroyed by the humane society.

✔ **FIGURES OR SPELLED-OUT NUMBERS?**

When trying to choose between spelling out numbers or using figures, ask yourself the following:

■ Is it a round number that can be expressed in one or two words? For most writing situations, spell these out.

■ Does the number begin a sentence? Spell it out or edit the sentence so that it appears elsewhere.

■ Are you addressing a technical audience? Use the conventions for technical writing and those explained in the discipline's documentation guidelines.

---

54 b Using figures when required by convention

The following cases, by convention, require the use of figures, even in nontechnical writing.

ESL SINGULAR AND PLURAL FORMS OF NUMBERS

When the word for a number is used as a plural noun without another number before it, use the plural form of the word. You may also need to use the word *of* after it.

The news report said there were only a few protesters at the nuclear power plant, but we saw *hundreds*.

Dozens of geese headed south today.

When the word for a number is preceded by another number, use the singular form of the word, and do not use *of* with it.

There were approximately *two hundred* protesters.

At least *three dozen* geese flew over the lake today.

When a word expressing a unit of weight, money, time, or distance is used with the word for a number as a hyphenated adjective, always use the singular forms for both words.

That movie lasted *three hours*.

It was a *three-hour* movie.

In dates

11 April 1994   the year 2001
July 16, 1896

In addresses

2551 Polk Street, Apt. 3
San Francisco, CA 94109

With abbreviations and symbols

3500 rpm   37°C
65 mph $62.23
74%   53¢

In discussions that use numbers infrequently, you may use words to express percentages and amounts of money if you can do so in two or three words: *seventy-four percent* and *fifty cents*, but not *sixty-two dollars and twenty-three cents*. If you spell out numbers, also spell out *percent, dollars,* and *cents*.

For time

12:15 A.M.   2330 hours

Note that numbers used with *o'clock, past, to, till,* and *until* are generally written out as words.

at seven o'clock   twenty past one

For decimal fractions

2.7 seconds   35.4 miles

For cross-references and citations

Chapter 56   line 25
volume 3, pages 13–17   act 3, scene 2

(See Chapters 18 and 61–64 for specific documentation formats.)

WP TIP   Highlight in bold any use of numbers (even those written in words) after you've completed a draft of an essay. Print hard copy and then discuss with your peer revision group whether your use is appropriate.

ESL PUNCTUATING NUMBERS

Numbering systems throughout the world differ in their punctuation. Some numbering systems use a period to mark divisions of thousands, so that *ten thousand* is written *10.000*. In the United States, commas are used to mark divisions of thousands.

In 1989 the population of Ecuador was 10,262,271.

In the United States, the period is used as a decimal point to separate whole numbers from decimal fractions.

Seven and a half can also be written 7.5.

■ EDITING I: PRACTICE

Edit the following passage, making sure all numbers are handled appropriately for nontechnical writing.

For the last 10 years, I have been running at least five miles a day, six days a week, fifty-two weeks a year. That adds up to eighteen hundred and twenty miles yearly. I figure that by the year two thousand, I will have run well over 20,000 miles. My running schedule almost never varies. I hit the streets just after I awaken, at 6 o'clock, and run for 3/4 of an hour. Then I make a ten-minute stop at a nearby diner for a quick orange juice before circling back toward home. 1,750 footfalls later I arrive home to shower and get ready for the day.

EDITING 2: APPLICATION

Examine a paper you are working on for numbers that you have handled incorrectly. Is there one kind of mistake in using numbers that you consistently make? If so, think about how best to remember how to handle numbers when you edit your work. Edit any sentences in which you have handled numbers incorrectly.

Abbreviations are frequently used in tables, footnotes, endnotes, and bibliographies to help readers proceed through the material quickly and easily. (Documentation and its acceptable abbreviations are discussed in Chapters 18 and 61–65.) They are also used quite often in scientific and technical writing. With a few exceptions, however, you should avoid abbreviations in the body of a general, nontechnical essay, paper, or report. This chapter discusses abbreviations that are acceptable in nontechnical text.

When using an abbreviation, be sure it is appropriate for the particular writing situation, is easy for readers to understand, and is correctly punctuated and capitalized.

 WHAT CAN BE ABBREVIATED?

The following kinds of information can be abbreviated in most writing situations:

- Titles and degrees
- Numbers, symbols, and amounts
- Addresses
- Common Latin terms
- Initials and acronyms

55 a Abbreviating titles and degrees

Personal or courtesy titles such as *Mr.*, *Mrs.*, *Dr.*, and *St.* may be abbreviated when they precede a full name. For such titles, capitalize the first letter and end with a period.

Mr. Samuel Taylor Darling   Dr. Ellen Hunter
St. Francis of Assisi   Prof. Karen Greenberg
Gen. Colin Powell   Rep. Ben Nighthorse
the Rev. Martin Luther King, Jr.   Sen. Dianne Feinstein

ABB **55 b**

Abbreviating time, dates, amounts, and symbols 745

Never abbreviate *president* or *mayor.* (Note that *Miss* is not an abbreviation, so it is written without a period. The courtesy title *Ms.* ends with a period even though it is not an abbreviation.)

Except for *Mr., Mrs.,* and *Dr.,* spell out titles used before a surname alone: *Professor Greenberg, Senator Boxer.*

Titles that do not precede a name are not abbreviated or capitalized.

■ Raisha Goldblum has been named assistant ~~prof.~~ professor of chemistry.

Titles or degrees such as *Esq., M.D., LL.D., J.D.,* and *Ph.D.* that follow a name are always abbreviated, as are generational titles such as *Jr.* and *Sr.* They are set off by commas in a sentence.

A new book by Dana Clark, M.D., criticizes animal testing.

Do not use both *Dr.* and a degree.

■ ~~Dr.~~ Barry Qualls, Ph.D., will speak at commencement.

55 b Abbreviating time, dates, amounts, and symbols

The following abbreviations and symbols are used only preceding or following numbers.

Time

Use *A.M.* and *P.M.* (or *a.m.* and *p.m.*) for specific times of day. 12:15 P.M. (*or* p.m.) 9:00 A.M. (*or* a.m.)

Avoid using these abbreviations without a specific hour.

■ We studied late into the ~~P.M.~~ night.

Dates

Use *B.C.* (*before Christ*) and *A.D.* (*anno Domini,* Latin for "in the year of the Lord") when necessary to distinguish dates. To avoid a religious reference, some writers substitute the abbreviations *B.C.E.* (*before Common Era*) and *C.E.* (*Common Era*). Note that *A.D.* precedes the date, except when century is used.

425 B.C. (or 425 B.C.E.)

A.D. 376 (or 376 C.E.)

the first century A.D.

Amounts or numbers

Acceptable abbreviations with amounts or numbers in nontechnical writing include *F* for *degrees Fahrenheit* and *C* for *degrees Celsius* in temperatures; *mph* (or *m.p.h.*) for *miles per hour*; and *No.* or *no.* for *number*.

The speed limit has been raised from 55 mph to 75 mph.

The prime minister's official address is No. 10 Downing Street.

In scientific and technical writing, units of measure are abbreviated when they follow amounts, usually without periods.

To 750 ml of this solution was added 200 mg of sodium cyanate.

In other situations, abbreviations are often acceptable if they are clearly defined at the first mention.

The engine develops maximum torque at 2900 revolutions per minute (rpm). Peak power is achieved at 6500 rpm.

Symbols can also be used as abbreviations with amounts. Symbols acceptable in nontechnical writing include those for degrees (°), percentage (%), and dollars ($), when they are used with figures denoting specific quantities. Spell out the words for symbols when they are used without figures.

By definition, 100°C equals 212°F, the boiling point of water.

The bill came to $35.99.

The percent of positive responses was surprising.

55 C Abbreviating geographic names

It is acceptable to abbreviate geographic names in addresses on mail. For state names, use abbreviations recommended by the U.S. Postal Service (see the accompanying box).

Lila Martin
100 W. Glengarry Dr.
Birmingham, MI 48009

When presenting a full address in text, spell out everything but the state name. When presenting less than a full address, spell out everything.

ABB **55** c

Abbreviating geographic names 747

His address was 1109 West Green Street, Harrisburg, PA 17102.

She was born in Harrisburg, Pennsylvania.

 STATE ABBREVIATIONS

Use these U.S. Postal Service abbreviations (capitalized, with no periods) for the names of the fifty states and the District of Columbia only on mail, in full addresses in text, or in documentation.

STATE	ABBRE-VIATION	STATE	ABBRE-VIATION
Alabama	AL	Missouri	MO
Alaska	AK	Montana	MT
Arizona	AZ	Nebraska	NE
Arkansas	AR	Nevada	NV
California	CA	New Hampshire	NH
Colorado	CO	New Jersey	NJ
Connecticut	CT	New Mexico	NM
Delaware	DE	New York	NY
District of	DC	North Carolina	NC
Columbia		North Dakota	ND
Florida	FL	Ohio	OH
Georgia	GA	Oklahoma	OK
Hawaii	HI	Oregon	OR
Idaho	ID	Pennsylvania	PA
Illinois	IL	Rhode Island	RI
Indiana	IN	South Carolina	SC
Iowa	IA	South Dakota	SD
Kansas	KS	Tennessee	TN
Kentucky	KY	Texas	TX
Louisiana	LA	Utah	UT
Maine	ME	Vermont	VT
Maryland	MD	Virginia	VA
Massachusetts	MA	Washington	WA
Michigan	MI	West Virginia	WV
Minnesota	MN	Wisconsin	WI
Mississippi	MS	Wyoming	WY

It is acceptable to abbreviate *District of Columbia* in text: *Washington, D.C.* Also the United States may be abbreviated *U.S.*

when used as an adjective, but it is generally spelled out as a noun.

> The U.S. government is divided into three branches.

> Voter turnout in the United States is disturbingly low.

55 d Abbreviating common Latin terms

The following abbreviations for common Latin terms are not generally used in text but can be used in documentation or notes. (See Chapters 18 and 61–65.)

ABBREVIATION	LATIN	MEANING
c. or ca.	*circa*	about
cf.	*confer*	compare
e.g.	*exempli gratia*	for example
et al.	*et alii*	and others
etc.	*et cetera*	and so forth
ibid.	*ibidem*	in the same place
i.e.	*id est*	that is
N.B.	*nota bene*	note well
vs. or v.	*versus*	against (used in legal case names)

WP TIP As you revise at the computer, be sure to examine your use of abbreviations closely. Highlight any that you're unsure of in bold (use search-and-replace to help you find ones you remember having used) and check them against the conventions described in this section. Take a hard copy to class to discuss any unresolved ones.

55 e Using initials and acronyms

Initials or **initial abbreviations** consist of the first letter of each word in a phrase or name, such as *IMF* for International Monetary Fund, *U.K.* for the United Kingdom, or *CD* for compact disc. An **acronym** is a word consisting of initials and pronounced as a word: *NATO* for North Atlantic Treaty Organization, *UNICEF* for United Nations International Children's Emergency Fund. Both initials and acronyms consist entirely of capital letters.

Most initial abbreviations and all acronyms are written without periods. Abbreviated names of some countries do use periods:

ABB **55** e

Using initials and acronyms 749

U.S., U.K. Initials that stand for people's names also use periods, followed by a space: *B. B. King, Norman H. Schwarzkopf.* (Note, however, that conventional references to American presidents by their three initials use neither periods nor spaces: *JFK.*) If you are not sure how to punctuate an abbreviation, consult a dictionary.

Keep in mind that unfamiliar initials or acronyms can bewilder readers. Before using one, decide whether it will be recognizable and whether it is essential to your writing. It is often helpful to provide the full name at the first mention in your text followed by the abbreviation or acronym in parentheses.

> World commerce is governed in large part by a set of treaties called the General Agreement on Tariffs and Trade (GATT).

In later references you can then use just the abbreviation or acronym.

> It is GATT that keeps prices from rising too quickly.

▮ EDITING 1: EXPLORATION

Look for examples of abbreviations in your textbooks as well as in popular writing in magazines, newspapers, and fiction. Does the use of abbreviations in both types of writing follow the rules outlined in this chapter? Why do you think words have been abbreviated as they have in each kind of writing?

▮ EDITING 2: PRACTICE

Edit the following passage, using abbreviations correctly.

Although the United States Constitution is supposed to guarantee equal rights to all people regardless of color, in the first half of this century most African Americans in the southern U.S. lived in deplorable conditions. E.g., African Americans had to use separate washrooms, and they could not attend schools with whites. Not until the 1940s did the United States Supreme Court finally begin to outlaw practices that deprived African Americans of their rights. One small step toward equality was made when representatives from the National Association for the Advancement of Colored People (N.A.A.C.P.) persuaded the Court that maintaining separate schools for African Americans and whites was not equal. In 1954, under Chief Justice Earl Warren of Calif., the Court ordered the desegregation of schools in the U.S. Despite the new legislation, however, the southern states still resisted integration, and only Senator Lyndon Johnson from TX and two sen. from Tenn. (Estes

---

Before **degree abbreviations** in the singular, you need to use an article: *a*, *an*, or *the*. The choice of *a* or *an* depends on how the first letter in the abbreviation is pronounced.

■ Use *an* if the first letter of the abbreviation is a vowel or is a consonant that is pronounced with a vowel sound at the beginning.

He just finished *an* A.A. degree.

An M.S. is a Master of Science degree. [*The letter M is pronounced em.*]

■ Use *a* if the first letter of the abbreviation is a consonant that is pronounced with a consonant sound.

She has *a* Ph.D. in physics.

For **initial abbreviations** and **acronyms**, check a reference book to see if an article is needed before them.

■ Many of these words do not require an article when they are used as nouns:

I just read a new article about *NATO*.

The conference discussed *AIDS* as a global problem.

■ Some initial abbreviations require the article *the* just as the spelled-out version would.

The FBI was called in to investigate the fire.

If you spelled it out, you would write The Federal Bureau of Investigation.

■ If you use an abbreviation as an adjective, you may need to add the article *a* or *an* before it, depending on the meaning of the noun that follows. As with degrees, pronunciation of the abbreviation determines whether you should use *a* or *an*.

Both of my parents work in television: my mother at *an* NBC affiliate and my father at *a* CBS station. [*N is pronounced /en/; C is pronounced /see/.)*]

The photograph on the front page showed *a* NATO session.

The acronym NATO is pronounced as a word, not as individual letters.

ABB **55** e

Using initials and acronyms 751

Kefauver and Albert Gore, Senior) were in favor of desegregating the schools. Racial conflict raged throughout the southern states over the issue of integration; one area of conflict was Little Rock, Ark., where resistance was so great that the National Guard had to be used to enforce integration. Even this drastic step did not solve the problem, however, and the struggle for equal education and other civil rights for African Americans went on for many years.

■ EDITING 3: APPLICATION

Examine a paper you are working on for misused or omitted abbreviations. Is there one kind of mistake in using abbreviations that you consistently make? If so, think about how, in editing your work, you might best remember to abbreviate words correctly. Edit any sentences in which you have made errors in abbreviating.

PART SEVEN

Presenting
Your Work

Presenting your writing on paper in a neat, attractive, and readable way makes a positive first impression on readers. On the other hand, negative impressions created by a careless or hard-to-read presentation can be difficult to overcome, no matter how compellingly you write.

To **design** your document means deciding how to present your material visually for the strongest effect. Your design should simply, clearly, and unobtrusively display your writing in a manner appropriate to an academic audience and make its organization apparent. The paper you write on, the typeface you use, your spacing, titles, and headings—all contribute to your design.

Good design is transparent; that is, it should call attention to your work, not to itself. If the first thing someone notices about your paper is an unusual design element, the design is detracting from, not contributing to, readability.

Word processors place a vast array of design tools at your fingertips for **desktop publishing**—generating elaborately designed newsletters, brochures, advertising materials, or mass mailings. However, design for academic writing is much more conservative than that of, say, magazine articles. Even if your professor requires a simple manuscript format achievable in longhand or with a typewriter, there are things you can do to make your paper visually appealing. Also note that for college papers, you should follow any format guidelines your instructor provides and consider the style of your discipline. (See Chapters 18 and 61–64 for detailed discussions of academic styles.)

56 a | Designing your pages

Your design should be simple and clear, and it should help readers understand your paper's organization. The size of margins, the typefaces you select for text and titles, the spacing, and the placement of page numbers all contribute to the appearance of a page. Together they constitute a document's **style**, which should be consistent from page to page. A word processor can automatically carry these choices from page to page or document to document.

I Creating a design style

Typefaces

Pick a **typeface** that is easy to read and conventional. Your instructor may prefer a typeface that looks like a typewriter's, such as Courier. Otherwise use a **serif** typeface—with little strokes at the end of each letterform—such as Times Roman, New Century Schoolbook, Bookman, Marin, or Palatino. **Sans serif** typefaces—those without serifs—become hard to read in large blocks of text. Script, italic, or outline typefaces are inappropriate for the text of academic papers. If your instructor permits, you may use italics rather than underlining for quoted titles and emphasis.

Spacing and margins

White space, the area on your paper not filled by type, is an important design element. For example, the indentation at the beginning of a paragraph or an extra line of space before a heading gives readers a place to pause and helps them understand your organization.

Use a **margin** of at least one inch on the top, bottom, and sides of each page. Most word processors let you preview a page of text, reduced in size, to give you an idea of the proportion of type to white space.

Although most word processors can set type in two or more columns on a page, most academic papers use a single column. If you use a word processor, select a **type size**—10 point or 12 point—that is easy to read. Generally, the wider each line of type, the larger the point size you need for easy reading.

If you typewrite, your text will come out **ragged right**: the lines will be of unequal length. A word processor can be set to **justify** type so that all lines are of equal length, like the lines in this book. The appearance is pleasing, but make sure that the computer does not leave large spaces between words or within words, which can hinder reading. If you justify your text, also check to see that the computer has hyphenated correctly. Most word processors allow you to insert a hyphen where you want one. The manuscript for this book was printed on a desktop laser printer in 12-point Univers type, double-spaced and fully justified, as shown on p.756.

Fulwiler/Hayakawa 56-4

56a Designing your pages

Your design should be simple and clear, and it should help readers understand your paper's organization. The size of margins, the typefaces you select for text and titles, the spacing, the placement of page numbers, and justification all contribute to the appearance of a page. Together they constitute a **style,** which should be consistent from page to page. A word processor can automatically carry these choices from page to page or document to document.

White space, the area on your paper not filled by type, is an important design element. For example, the indentation at the beginning of a paragraph or an extra line of space before a heading gives readers a place to pause and helps them understand your organization.

Designing your text

Headings

Highlight the organization of your paper by using slightly different type styles for the title, headings, and subheads. You can do this quite simply on a typewriter with position, capitalization, and underlining.

Center and Capitalize Your Title
First-level heading
Second-level heading

On a word processor, you can vary the type size or use boldface.

Center and Capitalize Your Title
First-level heading
Second-level heading

Creating a Design Style

Highlight the organization of your paper by using slightly different type styles for the title, headings, and subheads. You can do this quite simply on a typewriter with position, capitalization, and underlining.

Headings

On a word processor, you can vary the type size or use boldface to create headings that clearly reflect your paper's organization.

To emphasize a point that can be broken out of your main text—a key definition, a biographical sketch, or a list—place it in a **sidebar,** a boxed or shaded area next to the main flow of text. Sidebars give readers a quick explanation of an issue important to understanding the text itself.

Charts and graphics

Charts and graphics can be very useful for showing patterns or comparing data; keep them clear and easy to read, and make sure to refer to each illustration from the text.

Organizing text visually

Charts and graphics

Charts and **graphics** can be very useful for showing patterns or comparing data; keep them clear and easy to read, and make sure to refer to each illustration from the text.

If you have an important point to emphasize that can be broken out of your main text, such as a key definition, a biographical sketch, or a list, consider putting it in a **sidebar**, a boxed or shaded area of text next to the main flow of text. Sidebars give readers a quick explanation of a side issue that will aid in their understanding.

Another way to present a list is with **bullets**, centered dots, usually boldface, at the beginning of each item. If you use bullets, keep these points in mind.

- Use a simple bullet rather than a fancy dingbat that will attract attention to itself.

- Reserve bulleted lists for points you really want to emphasize.

- Indent all lines of your bulleted list to set them off from the rest of your text.

Roberts 2

Governor Ridge proposed that, for the first time in 25 years, spending would go down. The proposal would have cut overall state spending by about $30 million. He proposed $60 million in business tax cuts, a portion of which were to be linked to the creation of new jobs.

Pennsylvania Budget 1995-96

Total: $31.198 billion

REVENUE SOURCES

3.2% 5.1%

11.6%

51.6%

28.5%

☐ State taxes	$16 billion
■ Federal funds	$8.9 billion
■ Fees and charges	$3.6 billion
■ Motor license funds	$1.6 billion
☐ Other	$998 million

WHERE IT GOES

5.7% 3.9%

10.7% 1.3%

27.9% 9.8%

41.7%

☐ Administration	$1.2 billion
■ Economic development	$1.8 billion
☐ Education	$8.7 billion
■ Health & human services	$13 billion
☐ Law enforcement	$3.1 billion
☐ Recreation	$405 million
☐ Transportation	$3.3 billion

Rather than reintroducing the school-voucher proposal that legislators had recently rejected, the governor instead proposed to spend more money to provide computers in classrooms.

"Our goal is to make computers as commonplace as the chalkboard," Ridge said.

In introducing his proposal, the governor praised what he saw as its positive aspects. If he saw at the time what controversies would arise over his budget, he gave no indication.

Integrating charts and graphics

2 Creating academic writing for the Internet

Academic writing can now be placed on the World Wide Web section of the Internet. The Web allows text, illustrations, and graphics to be presented together, along with electronic "links" to related pages or articles. When you publish on the Web, your ideas are made available to networked computers around the world. Thus you can quickly and inexpensively reach a potentially vast audience. Conventions for all kinds of communications, including academic writing, are evolving rapidly. The page shown on page 759 is one student's academic paper on the Web illustrating how technology and design can combine to create an attractive presentation.

Women in the Work Force
Are We Catching Up?

No, if. . . .

☐ Society still tells girls they have a choice as to whether or not they will work for pay. Yet, women are nine times as likely as men to be single parents. For these women work is a necessity.

☐ Females continue to be shuffled into traditionally female occupations.

☐ Present trends continue and girls are not encouraged to pursue math or science. In computer programming, they will be trained only in data and information-retrieval capacities. These are still secretarial/clerical skills, and females will remain at the low end of the service-oriented pay scale.

Yes, if. . . .

☐ Nine out of ten women work at some point during their lives.

☐ Employment growth in women-owned firms exceeds the national average by a substantial margin. 1991-1994 employment grew by 11.5% among commercially-active, women-owned firms in the U.S. compared to 5.4% among all firms.

☐ Eight out of ten women between the ages of 20 and 44 are working.

The last twenty years witnessed the women's invasion in the working market. In 1985 the female laborer represented 36.9%. According to statistics, women represent 41.4% of today's economically-active population. Most women are employed by the service sector (65.7%), followed by the industrial (19%), and the agricultural (15.3%).

🔘 To find more statistics on women in the work force click here!

🔘 To find out how it all started, click here or here!

Student home page on the World Wide Web

56 b **Creating title pages and page numbers**

For most college papers, the title and other general information appear on the first page of text rather than on a separate title page. Start at the top left margin and, without indenting, write your name, your instructor's name, the course title, and the date the paper is due, each on a separate, double-spaced line.

On the next double-spaced line, center the title of the paper, following the rules for capitalizing and punctuating titles. A type size slightly larger than your body type can make your title stand out, but don't overdo it. Do not underline your title or put it in quotation marks. Double-space again before beginning the body of the text. (See 19b for an example of an opening page using this format.)

If your instructor requires a separate title page, follow his or her guidelines or those of your discipline. (See 19a and 19c for examples of title pages using MLA and APA formats.)

Number each page of your manuscript in the upper right-hand corner, one-half inch from the top of the page. Put your last name or an abbreviated title just before the page number, separated by a single space. Do not use slashes, parentheses, periods, the abbreviation *p.* or the word *page.* (See Chapter 19 for models.) Most word processors can automatically insert the page number at the top of the page when printing.

 RULES FOR INDENTING AND SPACING

■ Indent the first word of each paragraph five spaces.

■ Space once after each word. Space twice after end punctuation.

■ Space once after a comma, semicolon, or colon.

■ Do not space between words and quotation marks, parentheses, or brackets. (See 48, 49a and 49d.)

■ Do not space between quotation marks and end punctuation or between double and single quotation marks. (See 49a.)

■ Do not space after a hyphen except in a suspended construction: *The rest of the staff are half- and quarter-time employees.* (See 52b–52d.)

■ Do not space on either side of a dash, which consists of two hyphens: *Only two players remained--Jordan and Mario.* (See 49b.)

■ Space before and after a slash only when it separates lines of poetry. (See 49e.)

■ To display quotations of more than four typed lines, use block format. (See 48a.)

■ Underlining spaces between underlined words is optional, but be consistent.

---

56 c Proofreading

When you **proofread**, you check for errors. The key to proof-reading is to see what is *actually* on the page rather than what you *intended* to put there. Somehow you must look with fresh eyes at words you have already read several times. Plan to proof-read twice: once on the final, edited draft from which you prepare your final manuscript, and once on the final manuscript itself.

Proofread to correct punctuation and typographical errors, but of course fix any others you find as well. Listing errors in your journal may may help you avoid them in the future. Here are some useful techniques to help you proofread.

1   **Proofread on hard copy**. If you have been composing on a word processor, proofread on a printout. You will be surprised how many errors or awkward passages leap out at you from the printed page. Make changes on the computer text as you go, or note all the changes on the printout before going back to enter them on the screen.

2   **Read your paper aloud**. One test of good writing is whether it sounds clear and natural when read aloud. Reading aloud is also an effective way to find dropped words, misspellings, and punctuation errors.

3   **Ask someone else to read your paper**. You can get a pair of fresh eyes by borrowing someone else's. Ask a friend to proofread your final draft for errors, omissions, or passages that seem unclear. Have your friend read your work aloud and listen for awkward wordings, usage problems, and unclear punctuation.

4   **Read your text backward**. In proofreading for spelling, the idea is to read the manuscript one word at a time. In practice, this is hard to do, since most people read at the level of phrases and sentences. To avoid being distracted by meaning, try reading backward, starting at the last word and proceeding to the first. Some writers use a ruler to help them focus on one line at a time; other writers use a pencil to point out each word.

5   **Use your computer's spell checker**. If your word processor has a spell-checking function, use it. However, be aware that it can tell you only when you have misspelled a word, not when you have used the wrong word (such as *their* for *there*), repeated one, or left one out. On the other hand, a computer will never make the mistake of seeing what it expects to see instead of what is there. (See 3g and Chapter 50 for more on spelling and using a spell checker.)

6   **Make corrections**. Use standard proofreading marks to fix errors. (See the box on p. 762.) To correct a misspelled word, draw a line through it and write out the whole word.

■   This word is ~~misspeled~~. *misspelled*
                        ∧

If you make more than two corrections per page, retype or reprint the page.

STANDARD PROOFREADING MARKS

To mark errors, use the proofreading marks listed here. Then incorporate the changes as you prepare your final manuscript. If you find errors in the final manuscript itself, you may also use these marks to make corrections; however, if you have to make more than two corrections on a page, you should probably retype or reprint the page.

⌒	close up space
#	add space between words
∧	insert *these words* at this point
— or ⌐	delete this ~~unneeded~~ material
⌐/ or ⌐⌐	delete and close up
⌐ or ⌐⌐	make a change
∼	transpose letters words or
≡	capitalize
/	lowercase
___	italicize
¶	¶ start a new paragraph

Add any symbols that are not available on computer or typewriter—such as accent marks—to your final manuscript neatly by hand, using dark blue or black ink.

◼ EDITING 1: EXPLORATION

Reflect on your usual practices when it comes to proofreading your papers. Do you proofread them at all? How do you go about proofreading? Do your methods of proofreading produce good results? Are your papers returned to you with proofreading errors marked?

◼ EDITING 2: PRACTICE

Proofread the following passage, correcting all errors in spelling, grammar, punctuation, and mechanics. Use standard proofreading marks.

Marian Anderson, who died in 1993, was the first black opera singer to preform at the Metropoliton Opera 1955 and became an inspiracion to gen-

ESL STRATEGIES FOR PROOFREADING

In addition to the suggestions given in this section for effective proofreading, you may need to read your paper very carefully to check for common grammatical errors such as missing articles *the* or *a*, wrong verb endings, and incorrect word forms. Here are some more tips for proofreading your paper:

1. Plan to read your paper several times to look for grammatical errors.

2. Make a list of any frequent errors you are aware of. For example, you may consistently leave the final *-s* off plural nouns or the *-ed* ending off past participles. Or you may use *have* instead of *has* for third person singular in the present tense. If you are not sure of your frequent errors, ask your instructor or tutor to help you create a list of them.

3. Read your paper through once for each of these error types. In other words, concentrate on only one error type at a time. At first this process will be slow, but gradually your proofreading skills will improve; you will be able to proofread faster and to check more items at one time.

4. You could also make a list of words that you frequently misspell. (For example, you might often write "develope" instead of "develop" or "writen" instead of "written.") When you proofread for spelling, refer to your list and pay special attention to such words.

---

erations of black performers thoughout the U.S. Yet she was not able to make a name for herself in her own county until late in her life because of raical crimmination. Althrough her grate talent was recognised early in her life (she won a voice contest in New York in 1925,) she could not get any rolls in opera, and her carrer was going nowhere. In the 1930s, Anderson decided to go to Europe to perform, and she quicky became an international singing star. When she returned to the U.S. and was invited to sing in Washington, DC, the D.A.R. (Daughters of the American Revolution) denied her acess to Constitution Hall, it's national headquarters. Eleanor Roosvelt (along with several other women) resined from the D.A.R. over this disgracefull incident, and she arranged for Anderson to perform outside at the Lincoln Memorial. 75,000 people came to hear Anderson sing, and her peformence in front of Lincolns statute became a powerful cymbal of the civil right's movement.

56 d Choosing a printing method and paper

1 Printing, typing, or handwriting

Computer printing generally gives excellent results. Corrections are easy, since you can reprint a single page if necessary. If your printer's output is faint and hard to read—as is that of many dot-matrix printers—put in a fresh ribbon, or take your manuscript on diskette (a copy, that is) to someone who has better equipment, perhaps even to a commercial copy shop.

Typing yields good results too, but accuracy is harder to achieve than with a computer. Make sure the ribbon is fresh and the typewriter keys are clean. You can save time and effort by making some corrections before removing each page from the typewriter. Lift-off film works better than correction fluid, which in turn works better than erasure.

No matter how neat, a **handwritten paper** will seem less formal than a typed paper; submit a typed manuscript whenever you can. Before submitting a handwritten paper, make sure it will be acceptable to your instructor. Take special care to write simply, uniformly, and legibly. If your handwriting is hard to read, write very carefully or have your paper typed.

2 Paper

For computer printing or typing, use $8\frac{1}{2}'' \times 11''$ white bond paper of medium weight and good quality. Do not use very light paper, onionskin, or so-called erasable paper, all of which are hard to handle and make writing corrections or comments difficult. Unless your instructor specifies otherwise, double-space your manuscript no matter whether you type, write by hand, or print from a computer.

If your printer uses continuous paper, remove the perforated edges, separate the pages, and put them in the proper order.

If you write longhand, use blue or black ink on white, ruled paper, using only one side. Do not use legal-sized paper or paper torn from a spiral binder.

■ EDITING 3: APPLICATION

As you prepare the final manuscript of your next paper, look at it from a design perspective. Are the page layout and typeface appropriate? Does the design reinforce your paper's organization? Is your presentation orderly and neat? Make sure that you have followed all of the conventions of format and style discussed in this chapter. Pay attention to the indentation and spacing, as well as the positioning of the various elements on the page (heading, titles, page numbers). Make sure that you have corrected all typographical errors and that your paper is neat and legible.

In simplest terms, a **writing portfolio** is a collection of your writing contained within a single folder. This writing may have been done over a number of weeks, months, or even years. A writing portfolio may contain writing that you wish to keep for yourself; in this case you decide what's in it and what it looks like. Or a portfolio may contain work you intend to share with an audience to demonstrate your writing and reasoning abilities.

One kind of writing portfolio, accumulated during a college course, presents a record of your work over a semester and will be used to assign a grade. Another type of portfolio presents a condensed, edited story of your semester's progress in a more narrative form. In addition, portfolios are often requested by prospective employers in journalism and other fields of professional writing; these samples of your best work over several years may determine whether or not you are offered a job as a writer or editor.

57 a Preparing a course portfolio

The most common type of portfolio assigned in a writing course contains the cumulative work collected over the semester plus a cover letter in which you explain the nature and value of these papers. Sometimes you will be asked to assign yourself a grade based on your own assessment.

The following suggestions may help you in preparing a course portfolio.

Make your portfolio speak for you. If your course portfolio is clean, complete, and carefully organized, that's how you will be judged. If it's unique, colorful, creative, and imaginative, that, too, is how you'll be judged. So, too, will you be judged if your folder is messy, incomplete, and haphazardly put together. Before giving your portfolio to somebody else for evaluation, consider if it reflects how you want to be presented.

Include exactly what is asked for. If an instructor wants three finished papers and a dozen sample journal entries, that's the minimum your course portfolio should contain. If an employer wants to see five samples of different kinds of writing, be sure to include five samples. Sometimes you can include more than asked for, but do not include less.

Add supplemental material judiciously. Course portfolios are among the most flexible means of presenting yourself. If you believe that supplemental writing will present you in a better light, include that too, but only after the required material. If you include extra material, attach a note to explain why it is there. Supplemental writing might include journals, letters, sketches, or diagrams that suggest other useful dimensions of your thinking.

Include perfect final drafts. At least make them as close to perfect as you can. Show that your own standard for finished work is high. Final drafts should be printed double spaced on one side only of high-quality paper, be carefully proofread, and follow the language conventions appropriate to the task—unless another format is requested.

Demonstrate growth. This is a tall order, of course, but course portfolios, unlike most other assessment instruments, can demonstrate positive change. The signal value of portfolios in writing classes is that they allow you to demonstrate how a finished paper came into being. Consequently, instructors commonly ask for early drafts to be attached to final drafts of each paper, the most recent on top, so they can see how you followed revision suggestions, how much effort you invested, how many drafts you wrote, and how often you took risks. To build such a record of your work, date every draft of each paper and keep it in a safe place.

Demonstrate work in progress. Course portfolios allow writers to present partially finished work that suggests future directions and intentions. Both instructors and potential employers may find such preliminary drafts or outlines as valuable as some of your finished work. When you include such tentative drafts, be sure to attach a note explaining why you still believe it has merit and in which direction you want to take it.

Attach a table of contents. For portfolios containing more than three papers, attach a separate table of contents. For those containing only a few papers, embed your table of contents in the cover letter.

Attend to the mechanics of the portfolio. Make sure the folder containing your writing is the kind specified and that it is clean and attractive. In the absence of such specification, use a pocket folder, which is an inexpensive means of keeping the contents organized and secure. Put your name and address on the outside cover. Organize the material inside as requested. And turn it in on time.

Include a cover letter. For many instructors, the cover letter will be the most important part of your course portfolio since it represents your own most recent assessment of the work you completed over the semester. A cover letter serves two primary purposes: (1) as an introduction describing and explaining the portfolio's contents and organization, including accounting for any missing or unusual pieces to be found therein; and (2) as a self-assessment of the work, from earliest to latest draft of each paper, and from earliest to latest work over the course of the semester. The following excerpt is from Kelly's letter describing the evolution of one paper:

> In writing the personal experience paper, I tried three different approaches, two different topics, and finally a combination of different approaches to my final topic. My first draft [about learning the value of money] was all summary and didn't show anything actually happening. My second draft wasn't focused because I was still trying to cover too much ground. At this point, I got frustrated and tried a new topic [the hospital] but that didn't work either. Finally, for my last draft, I returned to my original topic, and this time it worked. I described one scene in great detail and included dialogue, and I liked it better and so did you. I am pleased with the way this paper came out when I limited my focus and zeroed in close.

The following excerpt describes Chris's assessment of her work over the whole semester:

> As I look back through all the papers I've written this semester, I see how far my writing has come. At first I thought it was stupid to write so many different drafts of the same paper, like I would beat the topic to death. But now I realize that all these different papers on the same topic all went in different directions. This happened to some degree in the first paper, but I especially remember in my research project, when I interviewed the director of the Ronald McDonald House, I really got excited about the work they did there, and I really got involved in the other drafts of that paper.

I have learned to shorten my papers by editing and cutting out needless words. I use more descriptive adjectives now when I'm describing a setting and try to find action verbs instead of "to be" verbs in all of my papers. I am writing more consciously now—I think that's the most important thing I learned this semester.

 GUIDELINES FOR CREATING COURSE PORTFOLIOS

1. Date, collect, and save in a folder all papers written for the course.

2. Arrange papers in chronological or qualitative order, depending on the assignment, last drafts on top, earlier drafts in descending order behind.

3. In an appendix, attach supplemental writing such as journal excerpts, letters, class exercises, quizzes, or other relevant writing.

4. Review your writing and compose a cover letter explaining the worth or relevance of the writing in the portfolio: Consider the strengths and weaknesses of each individual paper as well as of the combined collection. Provide a summary statement of your current standing as a writer as your portfolio represents you.

5. Attend to the final presentation: Include all writing in a clean, attractive folder; organize contents logically; attach a table of contents; write explanatory memos to explain unusual materials; and make sure the portfolio meets the minimum specifications of the assignment.

---

57 b Preparing a story portfolio

A story portfolio is a shorter, more fully edited and finely crafted production than a cumulative course portfolio. Instead of including a cover letter and all papers and drafts written during the term as evidence for your self-assessment, a story portfolio presents the evolution of your work and thought over the course of the semester in narrative form. In a story portfolio, you include excerpts of your papers insofar as they illustrate points in your development as a writer. In addition, you include excerpts of supplemental written records accumulated at different times during the semester, including the list on the next page.

- early and dead-end drafts of papers
- journal entries
- lecture and discussion notes
- in-class writing and freewriting
- comments on papers from your instructor
- letters to or from your instructor
- comments from classmates about your papers

In other words, to write a story portfolio, you conduct something like an archeological dig through the written remains of your work in a class. By assembling this evidence in chronological order and choosing the most telling snippets from these various documents, you write the story that explains, amplifies, or interprets the documents included or quoted. The best story portfolios commonly reveal a theme or set of issues that run from week to week or paper to paper throughout the semester. As you can see, a story portfolio is actually a small research paper, presenting a claim about your evolution as a writer with the evidence coming from your own written sources.

We encourage students to write their story portfolios using an informal voice as they might in a journal or letter. However, some students choose a more formal voice. Some prefer to write in the third person, analyzing the semester's work as if they did not know the writer (themselves). We also encourage them to experiment with the form and structure of their story portfolios, so that some present their work as a series of dated journal entries or snapshots while others write a more fluid essay with written excerpts embedded as they illustrate this or that point. Following are a few pages from Karen's story portfolio that illustrate one example of such a portfolio.

When I entered English 1, I was not a confident writer and only felt comfortable writing factual reports for school assignments. Those were pretty straightforward, and personal opinion was not involved. But over the course of the semester I've learned that I enjoy including my own voice in my writing. The first day of class I wrote this in my journal:

8/31 Writing has always been hard for me. I don't have a lot of experience writing papers except for straightforward things like science reports. I never did very well in English classes, usually getting B's and C's on my papers.

But I began to feel a little more comfortable when we read and discussed the first chapter of the book—a lot of other students besides me felt the same way, pretty scared to be taking English in college.

Our first assignment was to write a paper about a personal experience that was important to us. At first, I couldn't think where to start, but when we brainstormed topics in class, I got some good ideas. Three of the topics listed on the board were ones I could write about:

—high school graduation
—excelling at a particular sport (basketball)
—one day in the life of a waitress

I decided to write about our basketball season last year, especially the last game that we lost. Here is a paragraph from my first draft:

We lost badly to Walpole in what turned out to be our final game. I sat on the bench most of the time.

As I see now, that draft was all telling and summary—I didn't show anything happening that was interesting or alive. But in a later draft I used dialogue and wrote from the announcer's point of view and the result was fun to write and my group said fun to read:

Well folks, it looks as if Belmont has given up, the coach is preparing to send in his subs. It has been a rough game for Belmont. They stayed in it during the first quarter, but Walpole has run away with it since then. Down by twenty with only six minutes left, Belmont's first sub is now approaching the table.

You were excited about this draft too, and your comment helped me know where to go next. You wrote:

> Great draft, Karen! You really sound like a play-by-play announc-
> er—you've either been one or listened closely to lots of basketball
> games. What would happen if in your next draft you alternated
> between your own voice and the announcer's voice? Want to try
> it?

This next excerpt comes from a story portfolio that included twelve pages of discussion and writing samples and concluded with this paragraph:

> I liked writing this story portfolio at the end of the term be-
> cause I can really see how my writing and my attitude have
> changed. I came into class not liking to write, but now I can say
> that I really do. The structure was free and we had plenty of time
> to experiment with different approaches to each assignment. I
> still have a long way to go, especially on my argumentative writ-
> ing, since neither you nor I liked my final draft, but now I think I
> know how to get there: rewrite, rewrite, rewrite.

 GUIDELINES FOR CREATING STORY PORTFOLIOS

1. Assemble your collected writing in chronological order, from beginning to end of each paper, from beginning to end of the semester.
2. Reread all your informal work (in journals, letters, instructor comments) and highlight passages that reflect the story of your growth
as a writer.
3. Reread all your formal work (final papers, drafts) and highlight
passages that illustrate your growth as a writer. Note especially if a
particular passage had evolved over several drafts in the same paper—these would show you learning to revise.
4. Arrange all highlighted passages in order and write a story that
shows (a) how one passage connects to another and (b) the significance of each passage.
5. Before writing your conclusion, reread your portfolio and identify common themes or ideas or concerns that have occurred over
the semester; include these in your portfolio summary.

58 Making Oral Presentations

Public speaking is another way of "publishing" ideas that originate in written form. In speaking, as in writing, it's important to present ideas with confidence, clarity, accuracy, and grace: In the professions, in business, and in government, good writers and speakers get listened to, promoted, and rewarded; poor ones do not. While the art of public speaking can be addressed more comprehensively in speech class, we believe all writers should pay some attention to the oral publication of their ideas.

If asked to present a report to your classmates and teacher, approach it as you would the writing of a paper—in stages. Allow time to analyze the assignment's purpose and scope as well as your audience; time to research, organize, and add visual aids; and time to rehearse for timing, delivery, and understanding.

58 a Interpreting the assignment

The following suggestions have proven useful to successful public speakers.

Identify your purpose. Know the objective of your oral report task: What is your report supposed to accomplish? Is the purpose to present information, raise questions, argue a position, or lead the class in an activity? If you are not sure, reread the assignment and check with your instructor (after class or via E-mail). Regardless of your instructor's reason for making this assignment, to do a good job you'll need to believe in, understand, and know your subject—just as in any writing assignment. Choose a subject and a point of departure that you care about and believe in so you have the curiosity to do effective research and the passion to speak with conviction. If you don't care about gun control legislation, don't choose that for your topic.

Know your audience. Exactly what you say and how you say it depends upon to whom you are speaking. In most class settings, your audience is comprised of both your instructor and your classmates; the best oral report will reach both effectively. Use your time in front of the class to teach them something they don't already know. Consequently, don't spend much time covering material already covered in class or in the textbook. At the other extreme, don't cover material that's totally unrelated to the course. Instead, build deliberately on issues, ideas, or information that stems from familiar class material, and present new information in that context. For example, if the class has been discussing multicultural issues, report on a small but specific and, to them, unfamiliar example.

Collaborate. If collaboration is called for or allowed—a common practice in classroom oral reporting—follow these procedures: (1) Arrive at a consensus understanding of what your task entails, and don't proceed until all of you know what is expected. (2) Divide tasks according to ability, do your own part promptly, and hold others accountable for doing theirs. (3) Meet often enough outside class so that your material is ready when the oral report is due. (4) Plan in advance who will report what and for how long.

58 b Preparing a speaking text

Texts that are spoken need to be simple, clear, and direct. The best way to prepare such a text is to follow essentially the same process as that for writing a paper: invent, draft, research, revise, and edit the material for your oral report until you know and trust it. The following ideas follow such a process.

Invent. Allow time for thinking, planning, inventing, discovering—don't try to prepare your whole oral report the night before it is due. Use your journal, notebook, or computer to brainstorm and discover the best ideas to speak about and the best strategies for preparing these ideas.

Draft. Use your computer to draft and develop ideas. Even if you don't intend to read your report out loud, it makes good sense to write it out in full to see how it looks and where it's going. Once a talk is drafted, it's easy to make an outline from it from which to speak.

Research. To teach audience members something they don't already know, research your topic so that you have fresh and detailed information to convey. Cite textual sources, quote local experts, report survey results, explain on-site visits. The more you've prepared, the more your audience will believe you.

Outline. The most effective oral reports are spoken rather than read, the speaker making eye contact with the audience as much as possible. Consequently, the "final draft" of an oral report is not a polished, proofread paper, but a "speaking outline" or notes to be glanced at as needed.

Create listening signposts. The old advice for making speeches goes like this: "Tell what you're gonna tell 'em. Tell 'em. Then tell 'em what you've told 'em." It makes sense to be repetitious in this way with oral presentations because it's hard for audiences to remember and keep track of what they hear. Signposts—words that signal what's coming—will help you do this. For example, tell your audience you are going to make three points against gun control legislation, then enumerate each as you get to it: "The first point against gun control is . . . ; the second point against gun control . . . , " and so on.

Prepare note cards. In a short report a one-page speaking outline may be the only thing you need. If your report is longer, is more complex, or includes quotations and statistics, organize note cards (3" × 5" or 4" × 6" index cards) to follow as you move from point to point in your talk.

Start strong. In speaking, as in writing, your opening sets the tone and expectations for what is to follow. In oral delivery it's especially important to get everyone listening at the same time, so speakers commonly use questions, stories, or jokes to catch quick attention. If you tell a story or joke, make sure it pertains to your subject.

Finish strong. Once they know their topic, their point, their audience, and the time available, many speakers map out their conclusion first, then work backward to make sure the text leads them there. With only five, ten, or fifteen minutes, be sure that when time is up, you've made the point you intended.

Write simply for oral delivery. Write an outline and notes with an emphasis on simplicity of language and repetition of main ideas, because listening audiences cannot pause as readers can to double-check what you mean. Simple jargon-free language is easiest to understand on a single hearing; repeating key words and phrases helps reinforce the listening memory.

Edit your reading text. If your material is complex and your time short, you may choose to read your report out loud. Reading is often less engaging than speaking, but it does guarantee that you say exactly what you wrote and meant precisely and economically. Be sure to double- or triple-space your reading copy, leave wide margins to pencil in extra notes, and start new paragraphs on new pages. For timing purposes, plan two and a half minutes for each page of double-spaced text ($8\frac{1}{2}"$ × 11").

ESL DEVELOPING ORAL PRESENTATION SKILLS

Giving presentations in a language that is not your native one can be a special challenge. Here are some suggestions for improving your skills:

1. Remember that in English the most important words (often nouns and verbs) receive the most stress in a sentence, and less important words such as articles (*a, the*), prepositions (*of, in,* etc.), and pronouns (*she, they, it,* etc.) should not be stressed unless you need to give them special emphasis. Putting equal stress on all words can make your speech difficult to understand.

2. If time permits, rehearse your presentation with a native speaker of English (a friend or tutor) as a "coach." As you give your speech, ask your coach to write down any key words that are mispronounced, with special attention to syllable stress, and any places where you need to work on your intonation (for example, rising intonation at the end of questions). Then have your coach give the corrections orally. Tape-record both your presentation and your coach's corrections so that you can use them for practice later.

3. As this chapter describes, signposts—words and phrases that tell your listeners what's coming—are very important in oral presentations. So are phrases that connect parts of your speech to earlier parts, such as "As I have previously mentioned, . . ." Review transitions in this handbook. (See 24c2.) Then check your written text to see where you might add words or phrases that link parts of your talk (for example, *on the other hand* to signal a contrasting point, *for instance* to introduce an example, *in summary* to signal your conclusion). Pause slightly after you use transitions for emphasis.

4. Speakers of some languages tend to speak more softly than English speakers. Also, some individuals naturally have soft voices. If someone appears to have trouble understanding you in English, it may not be because you are mispronouncing words, misusing vocabulary, or using incorrect grammar, but rather because you are speaking so softly that the person cannot hear you! You may want to ask a native English-speaking friend, a tutor, or your instructor to evaluate the loudness of your speech in an oral presentation. If your voice is too soft, try to increase the volume. Doing so may seem unnatural at first, but your listeners will appreciate your efforts.

58 **c** **Speaking in public**

Once your talk is prepared, you need to present it, usually at the front of the classroom, which means leaving your comfortable seat and moving front and center for attention. A recent poll identified public speaking as the greatest fear of most Americans. Even famous actors and speakers feel anxiety before performing before live audiences, and they learn to use their nervous energy to keep a sharp edge while performing. Nervousness is unavoidable; accept it and try to harness this energy to help your performance. The following suggestions may help to alleviate this fear.

Rehearse. Run through your oral presentation in the privacy of your room to check your understanding and to set your pace to make sure you can deliver the talk in the time allotted. Rehearsing your talk out loud several times beforehand will help you understand your own material better as well as give you confidence when you walk to the front of the room. And in rehearsing, don't be afraid to revise, edit, rearrange ideas that looked good on paper but now strike you as wrong for an oral delivery.

Make the room your own. Set up the room to suit the purpose of your presentation. If that means rearranging desks, tables, screens, or lecterns, then don't hesitate to do so. If there is a lectern front and center but you don't plan to use it, move it to one side. If you use the lectern, stand still and rest your hands on it—that will help you control any shaking. If you prefer your audience in a semicircle or in groups instead of straight rows, ask them to sit that way. Taking control of your space makes you comfortable and gives you ownership of your time in front of the class.

Maintain eye contact with friendly audience members. While it's important to look around at the whole audience and make everyone feel as if you are addressing him or her, return periodically to the faces most receptive to your words—to smiles or nods or friends—for these will boost your confidence and keep you going smoothly.

Speak point by point. The reason for sticking to your outline or note cards is to present information in an economical and orderly fashion. If your report is supposed to last ten minutes, jot the starting time on your notes and stick to ten minutes. If you speak too fast, the audience can't follow you; if you speak too slowly, they get restless—so strive for balance.

Leave time for questions. When giving oral reports, it is customary to allow your audience time to ask questions. Plan for this time, show your willingness to discuss further what you know, and always answer succinctly and honestly; if you don't know an answer, say so.

58 d Selecting creative options

Depending upon your task and time, you may want to enhance your presentation with some of the following materials or activities.

Use handouts. Many talks are augmented by handouts (outlines, poems, stories, ads, articles, illustrations) illustrating points made in the talk or as a text to attend to at some time during the presentation. Prepare handouts carefully, make sure they are legible, document them properly if they are borrowed from another source, and make enough for all in your audience.

Use prepared visual aids. Many talks are made more powerful when accompanied by illustrations or examples of what is being talked about. What aids you use will depend upon your purpose and topic, audience knowledge and size, and the physical setting available. Any of these visual aids may help: videos, films, maps, charts, sketches, photographs, posters, computer graphics, or overhead projectors. Carefully prepare the aids in advance, order machines if necessary, and mark in your speaking text where you plan to use them.

Use process visual aids. It often helps to illustrate something on the spot in front of your audience. This device may be especially effective during a question-and-answer session. Media that help you write or sketch things out include blackboards, flip charts, and overhead projectors. Arrange for these aids in advance.

Use an overhead projector. The single most versatile visual aid is the overhead projector (OHP), which facilitates the use of prepared material as well as on-the-spot composing. You might even consider putting your speaking outline on one or more transparencies (available along with water-soluble marking pens in bookstores), projecting to your classmates your topic, key words, organization, and specific facts. Using an OHP has several distinct advantages for oral presentation: (1) it makes your notes easy to read, (2) it provides a visual record to aid your audience in understanding, note-taking, and retention; and (3) it divides audience attention between you and the lighted screen, thereby relieving you of some of the pressure of public scrutiny.

Use audio aids. Some talks are best advanced when accompanied by music or oral recordings. Audience attention picks up noticeably when you introduce sounds or voices other than your own into your presentation. A sound or visual recording may be the featured text in your presentation, or it may provide useful accompaniment. Order any necessary recording equipment and rehearse in advance.

Ask your audience to write. If you want to engage your audience quickly and relax yourself at the same time, ask people to write briefly before you speak. For example, on the subject of "alcohol on campus," ask people to jot down their own experience with or knowledge of the subject on scratch paper, telling them it

---

 TIPS FOR PUBLIC SPEAKING

1. Plan. Know your purpose, analyze your audience, and allow time to create and discover the best ideas and approach to your talk.

2. Write. Whether you intend to read from text or notes, write your way through the planning, drafting, revision, and editing stages so that you understand fully what you are saying and how much time it will take.

3. Research. Add specific facts, observations, testimony, data, and ideas derived from library and field research to interest your audience and teach them something they don't already know.

4. Simplify. Your audience will hear you only one time, so edit, arrange, and condense to make your points and conclusion as clear, direct, and simple as possible.

5. Rehearse. To understand and pace your talk, practice it out loud in private before you deliver it in public.

6. Persuade. To make your audience understand and believe you, speak not only from knowledge but from personal conviction.

7. Illustrate. To increase audience interest and understanding, supplement your talk with visual and/or audio aids.

will remain private. After a few minutes, ask them to talk about—not read—their ideas with a neighbor for several more minutes. Writing for even five minutes pulls people into your topic by causing them to think personally about it. Talking aloud to seatmates pulls them in deeper still, and the oral buzz in the room makes everyone—especially you—more comfortable. To resume control, ask for several volunteer opinions and use these as a bridge to your own presentation.

A note to students and teachers: The best preparation for oral presentations is encouraging and regularly joining class discussions and asking questions out loud. The more you work in small groups, discuss with neighbors, and participate in all class discussion, the easier and more natural oral reporting will be.

PART EIGHT

Writing across the Curriculum

Good writing satisfies the expectations of an audience in form, style, and content. But different audiences come to a piece of writing with different expectations, so writing that is judged "good" by one audience may be judged "less good" by another. Although all college instructors value good writing, each area of study has its own set of criteria by which writing is judged. For instance, the loose form, informal style, and speculative content of a reflective essay that please an English instructor might not please an anthropology instructor, who expects form, style, and assertions to follow the more formal structures established in that discipline. This chapter provides a broad outline of these different criteria and points to some important similarities for writing across the curriculum.

59 a Understanding differences among the disciplines

As a rule, knowledge in the humanities focuses on texts and on individual ideas, speculations, insights, and imaginative connections. Interpretation in the humanities is thus relatively subjective. Accordingly, good writing in the humanities is characterized by personal involvement, lively language, and speculative or open-ended conclusions.

In contrast, knowledge in the social and physical sciences is likely to focus on data and on ideas that can be verified through observing, measuring, and testing. Interpretation in these disciplines needs to be objective. Accordingly, good writing in the social and physical sciences emphasizes inferences based on the careful study of data and downplays the personal opinion and speculation of the writer.

But boundaries between the disciplines are not absolute. For example, at some colleges history is considered one of the humanities, while at others it is classified as a social science. Geography is a social science when it looks at regions and how people live, but a physical science when it investigates the properties of rocks and glaciers. Colleges of business, engineering, health, education, and natural resources all draw on numerous disciplines as their sources of knowledge.

The field of English alone includes not only the study of literature, but also literary theory and history; not only composition, but also creative and technical writing. In addition, English departments often include linguistics, journalism, folklore, women's studies, Afro-American studies, and sometimes speech, film, and communications. In other words, within even one discipline, you might be asked to write several distinct types of papers: personal experience essays for a composition course; interpretations for a literature course; abstracts for a linguistics course; short stories for a creative writing course. Consequently, any observations about the different kinds of knowledge and the differing conventions for writing about them are only generalizations. The more carefully you study any one discipline, the more complex it becomes and the harder it is to make a generalization that doesn't have numerous exceptions.

59 b Understanding similarities among the disciplines

Regardless of discipline, certain principles of good writing hold true across all areas of academic study.

1 Knowledge

Each field of study attempts to develop knowledge about a particular aspect of the physical, social, or cultural world. For example, history courses focus on human beings living in particular time periods; sociology courses focus on human beings in groups; psychology courses focus on the operation and development of the individual human mind. In writing for a particular course, keep in mind the larger purpose of the field of study, especially when selecting, introducing, and concluding your investigation.

2 Method

Each field has accepted methods of investigation. Perhaps the best known is the scientific method, used in most of the physical and social sciences. One who uses the scientific method first asks a question, then poses a possible answer (a hypothesis), then carries out experiments to disprove this answer, and finally, if it cannot be disproved, concludes that the answer is correct. However, while research in the social sciences follows this scientific pattern, some disciplines, such as anthropology, rely instead on the more personal approach of ethnographic study. Literary research may be formal, historical, deconstructive, and so on. It is important to recognize that every discipline has its accepted—and its controversial—methods of study. Any conclusions you arrive at in writing should reflect that awareness.

3 Evidence

In every field, any claim you make about the subject of your study needs to be supported by evidence. If, in order to identify an unknown rock, you scrape it with a known rock in the geology laboratory, the scratch marks of the harder on the softer will be part of your evidence to support your claims about the unknown rock. If you analyze Holden Caulfield on the basis of his opening monologue in *The Catcher in the Rye*, his words will be evidence to support your interpretation. If you conduct a survey of students to examine college study habits, your findings will be evidence to support your conclusions. In other words, although the *nature* of evidence varies greatly from one discipline to another, the *need* for evidence is constant. In some cases, when you need to support an assertion, you will consult certain sources for evidence and will need to have clear documentation for these sources. (Chapters 18 and 61–65 provide detailed guidelines for documenting sources in various disciplines.)

4 Accuracy

Each field values precision and correctness, and each has its own specialized vocabulary for talking about knowledge. Writers are expected to use terms precisely and to spell them correctly. In addition, each discipline has developed formats in which to report information. You should know the difference in form between a literary analysis in English, a research report in sociology, and a laboratory report in chemistry. Each discipline also values conventional correctness in language. Your writing must always reflect standard use of grammar, punctuation, and mechanics.

60 | Writing Essay Examinations

Essay examinations are common writing assignments in the humanities, but they are important in the social and physical sciences as well. Such exams require students to sit and compose responses to instructors' questions about information, issues, and ideas covered in the course. Instructors assign essay exams instead of "objective" tests (multiple choice, matching, true/false) because they want students to go beyond identifying facts and to demonstrate mastery of concepts covered in the course.

The best preparation for taking an essay exam is to acquire a thorough knowledge of the subject matter. If you have attended all the classes, done all the assignments, and read all the texts, you should be in a good position to write such essays. If you have also kept journals, annotated your text, discussed course material with other students, and posed possible essay exam questions, you should be in even better shape for such writing. Equally important is your strategic thinking about the course and its syllabus. If the course was divided into different topics or themes, think of a general question on each one; if it has been arranged chronologically, create questions focusing on comparisons or cause-and-effect relations within a particular period or across periods. Consider, too, the amount of class time spent on each topic, and pay proportionately greater attention to emphasized areas.

While there is no substitute for careful preparation, using certain writing strategies will enhance your presentation of information in virtually any exam. This chapter outlines suggestions for writing under examination pressure.

60 a | Understanding the question

1 Read the whole examination

Before answering a single question, quickly read over the whole exam to assess its scope and focus. Answering three of four questions in 50 minutes requires a different approach than answering, say, five of eight questions in 75 minutes. If you are given a choice among several questions, select questions that together will demonstrate your knowledge of the whole course rather than answering two that might result in repetitious writing. Finally, decide which questions you are best prepared to answer, and respond to those first. Budget your time, however, so you can deal fully with the others later.

Starting with the questions you know you can answer relaxes you, warms you up intellectually, and often triggers knowledge about the others in the process.

2 Attend to direction words

Once you decide which questions you will answer, take a moment to analyze each one before you begin to write. Then focus closely on one particular question; read it several times. Underline the direction word that identifies the task you are to carry out, and understand what it is telling you to do.

Define or **identify** asks for the distinguishing traits of a term, subject, or event but does not require an interpretation or judgment. Use appropriate terminology learned in the course. For example, the question, "Define John Locke's concept of *tabula rasa*," is best answered by using some of Locke's terminology along with your own.

Describe may ask for a physical description ("Describe a typical performance in ancient Greek theater"), or it may be used more loosely to request an explanation of a process, phenomenon, or event ("Describe the culture and practices of the mound builders"). Such questions generally do not ask for interpretation or judgment but require abundant details and examples.

Summarize asks for an overview or a synthesis of the main points. Keep in mind that "Summarize the impact of the Battle of Gettysburg on the future conduct of the war" asks only that you hit the highlights; avoid getting bogged down in too much detail.

Compare and contrast suggests that you point out both similarities and differences, generally between two subjects but sometimes among three or more. Note that questions using other direction words may also ask for comparison or contrast: "Describe the differences between the works of Monet and Manet."

Analyze asks that you write about a subject in terms of its component parts. The subject may be concrete ("Analyze the typical seating plan of a symphony orchestra") or abstract ("Analyze the ethical ramifications of Kant's categorical imperative"). In general, your response should examine one part at a time.

Interpret asks for a discussion or analysis of a subject based on internal evidence and your own particular viewpoint: "Interpret Flannery O'Connor's short story 'Revelation' in terms of your understanding of her central religious and moral themes."

Explain asks what causes something or how something operates. Such questions may ask for an interpretation and an evaluation. "Explain the function of color in the work of Picasso," for example, clearly asks for interpretation of the artist's use of color; although it does not explicitly ask for a judgment, some judgment might be appropriate.

Evaluate or **critique** asks for a judgment based on clearly articulated analysis and reasoning. "Evaluate Plato's concept of the ideal state" and "Critique the methodology of this experiment," for example, ask for your opinions on these topics. Be analytical and lead up to a final statement, but don't feel that your conclusion must be completely one-sided. In many cases, you will also want to cite more experienced judgments to back up your own.

Discuss or **comment on** is a general request, which allows you considerable latitude. Your answers to questions such as "Discuss the effects of monetarist economic theories on current Third World development" often let you demonstrate what you know especially well. Use terms and ideas as they have been discussed during the semester, and add your own insights with care and thoughtfulness.

60 b Writing a good answer

Instructors give essay exams to find out not only how much students know about course content, but how thoroughly they understand and can discuss it. If they were interested in testing only for specific facts and information, they could give true/false or multiple choice tests. Therefore, the best essay answers will be accurate but also highly focused, carefully composed, and easy to follow. The following are two examples of answers to an essay question from a music history examination. Which do you think is the better answer?

Explain the origin and concept of neoclassicism, and identify a significant composer and works associated with the development of this music.

ESSAY #1   Neoclassicism in music is a return to the ideas of the classical period of earlier centuries. It is dry and emphasizes awkward and screeching sounds and does not appeal to the listener's emotions. It does not tell a story, but presents only a form. It is hard to listen to or understand compared to more romantic music such as Beethoven composed. Neoclassical music developed in the early part of the twentieth century. Stravinsky is the most famous composer who developed this difficult music.

ESSAY #2   Neoclassical music developed as a reaction against the romantic music of the nineteenth century. Stravinsky, the most famous neoclassical composer, took his style and themes from the eighteenth-century classical music of Bach, Handel, and Vivaldi rather than Beethoven or Brahms. Stravinsky emphasizes technique and form instead of story or image, with his atonal compositions appealing more to the intellect than the emotions. *Rite of Spring* (1913) and *Symphony of Psalms* (1940) are good examples.

Both answers are approximately the same length, and both are approximately correct. However, the second answer is stronger for the following reasons: It is more carefully organized (from general to specific); it includes more information (names, works, dates); it uses more careful disciplinary terms (*form, technique, image*); and it answers all parts of the question (the first answer omits the titles of works). It also does not digress into the writer's personal value judgments (that neoclassical is hard to listen to), which the question did not ask for.

The following strategies will help you write more carefully composed answers.

1 Planning and outlining

Take one or two minutes per question to make a potential outline of your answer. For example, if asked to compare and contrast three impressionist painters, decide in advance which three you will write about and in which order. While ideas will come as you start writing, having a plan of organization at the beginning allows you to write more effectively. If you create a quick outline in the margins of your paper or even just hold it in your head, your writing will include more focused information, presented in a more logical order (as in #2 above) rather than scattered randomly throughout (as in #1 above).

2 Leading with a thesis

The surest way to receive full credit on an essay question is to answer the question briefly and directly in your first sentence.

In other words, state your answer in a thesis statement which the rest of your essay explains, supports, and defends. In the example on page 788, essay #2 opens with a thesis statement: *Neoclassical music developed as a reaction against the romantic music of the nineteenth century.* The rest of the essay explains and supports this statement.

3 Writing with specific detail, examples, and illustrations

Remember that most good writing contains specific information that lets readers see for themselves the evidence for your position. Use as many supportive specifics as you can; memorize names, works, dates, and ideas as you prepare for the exam so you can recall them accurately if they are needed. Individual statistics alone are not worth much, but when used as evidence along with strong reasoning, these specifics make the difference between good and mediocre answers.

4 Providing context

In answering a question posed by an instructor who is an expert in the field, it is tempting to assume your instructor does not want a full explanation and thus to answer too briefly. However, you are being asked to demonstrate how much *you* understand, so view each question as an opportunity to show how much you know about the subject. Briefly explain any concepts or terms that are central to your answer. Take the time to fit any details into the larger scheme of the subject. In Essay #2 on page 788, for instance, it is clear that the second writer understood the relation of each musical movement to the century that produced it.

5 Using the technical terminology of the discipline

Be careful not to drop in names or terms gratuitously, unless these names and terms have been an integral part of the course. Make sure you define any other terms, use them appropriately, and spell them correctly. Essay exams also test your facility with the language and concepts peculiar to a particular discipline. In the music example on page 788, it pays to know the correct terms for historical periods (classical, romantic, neoclassical) as well as technical terms used in discussing music (image, tone).

6 Staying focused

Answer what the question asks. Attend to all parts of an answer, cover those parts, and once you have done that, do not digress or add extraneous information. While it may seem interesting to hear your other ideas on the subject at hand, some instructors may consider this digressing as reflecting unfocused attention.

STRATEGIES FOR WRITING ESSAY EXAMINATIONS

1. Skim the whole examination and block your time. Read quickly through the whole exam so that you know what you're being asked to do, and allot blocks of time for tackling each section.

2. Choose your essay questions carefully. The essay questions you answer should allow you to write on what you know best. Choose a mix of answers to show your range of knowledge.

3. Focus on direction words. For each question you have chosen, it is important to recognize what your instructor is really asking, for this understanding enables you to answer the question successfully.

4. Plan and outline each essay. Prepare a rough outline of your answer by identifying the key points you need to make and organizing them well.

5. Write thesis-first essays. Doing this illustrates your confidence in knowing the answer and setting out to prove it. (For more information on thesis-first organized essays, see 11f.)

6. Include specifics—details, examples, illustrations. Backing up statements with evidence shows your mastery of the subject matter. Include short, accurate, powerful quotes where relevant, citing each by author, title, and date, as relevant. To help you remember, focus on key words and jot them in the margins near your answer.

7. Use the terms and methods used by the discipline. Enter in the conversation of a particular discipline by using its accepted terms and methods.

8. Provide context but stay focused. Explain all your points as if your audience did not have the understanding your teacher does, but keep all your information focused on simply answering that one question. If you know more than time allows you to tell, end your answer with an outline of key points that you would discuss if you had more time.

9. Proofread your answers in the last five minutes before handing in the finished exam. Even this short step back from composing will allow you to spot errors and omissions.

61 Writing in Languages and Literature

This chapter describes the aims, style, and forms required for most kinds of writing in English, comparative literature, and foreign languages where the primary focus is on the study of texts. Many specialized areas, such as film and cultural studies, also follow the conventions described here. Papers in language and literature use the documentation system of the Modern Language Association (MLA) described in Chapter 18.

61 a The aims of writing in languages and literature

Language and literature courses are concerned with reading and writing about texts such as poems, novels, plays, and essays written by published authors as well as by students. (The term *text* is defined here broadly to include films, visual arts, advertisements—anything that can be read and interpreted.) What sets literary studies apart from most other disciplines, including others in the humanities, is the attention devoted to all elements of written language. In these courses, writing is not only the means of study but often the object of study as well: works are examined for their form and style as well as their content. Texts are read, listened to, discussed, and written about so students can discover what these texts are, how they work, what they mean, and what makes them exceptional or flawed. Moreover, literary studies often draw on ideas from other disciplines. For instance, reading a single novel such as Charles Dickens's *David Copperfield* or Toni Morrison's *Beloved* can teach readers a little about sociology, psychology, history, geography, architecture, political science, and economics as well as the esthetics of novel writing.

When you write in language and literature, you can examine texts from a variety of perspectives. You can focus on a text's ideas, authors, formal qualities, or themes. You can also consider the culture that produced the text, the text's relationship to other texts, its place in history, and its politics. Modern literary study may ask how to engage in any of five basic activities with texts.

1   You can **appreciate** texts. You can write about the text's most moving or interesting features, the beauty or strangeness of the setting, the character with whom you most identify, the plot as it winds from beginning to end, or the turns and rhythms of the language.

2   You can **analyze** texts, asking questions such as "How is it put together?" or "How does it work?" Analysis involves looking at a text's component parts (chapters) and the system that makes it work as a whole (plots), defining what they are, describing what they are like, and explaining how they function.

3   You can **interpret** texts, asking questions such as "What does it mean?" "How do I know what it means?" and "Why was it made?" Interpretations often vary widely from reader to reader and may provoke quite a bit of disagreement.

4   You can **evaluate** texts, asking questions such as "How good is it?" "What makes it worth reading?" and "How does it compare with other texts?" These are questions of judgment, based on criteria that might differ considerably from person to person. For example, you might judge a poem good because its pattern of rhythm and imagery is pleasing (esthetic criteria). Another reader may praise the same poem because it subverts common assumptions about power relationships (political criteria), and a third may do so because it evokes fond childhood memories (personal criteria). However, a fourth reader might dismiss the poem as sentimental (philosophical criteria), and a fifth might find it weak in contrast to another poet's work (comparative criteria).

5   You can **study the culture** that produced the text, asking such questions as "What are the values of the people depicted in the text?" and "How do the scenes, settings, and characters reveal the author's values?" To find answers to these and other questions, it is common to compare the text with other texts produced at the same or different times.

All of these activities come together when you are asked to write critical or analytical essays about the literature you read. (See 61c.) Learning to be critical—to think, read, and write critically—is one of the goals of all literary study. (See Chapters 2 and 12.) Critical essays answer questions such as "Is the idea or text clear?" "What does it mean?" "Is it true?" "Is the argument sound?" and "What are its assumptions and biases?"

61 **b** The style of writing in languages and literature

Writing in languages and literature demands clarity, variety, and vitality to create a strong connection between the writer and reader. Direct, unpretentious language and an engaging tone are valued over obscure terminology and an artificially formal style. Observing the standard conventions of grammar, punctuation, and mechanics is also expected.

All that said, greater freedom and variety of style are allowed in language and literature study than perhaps in any other discipline. Because literary studies center so closely on the multitude of ways readers approach texts, writing can range from the highly personal to the highly theoretical, from deeply impressionistic to sharply rational, from journalistic to experimental to political. Indeed, a single essay may knit together all these styles.

As a student, much of the writing you do in language and literature may be relatively conventional in style—asserting a thesis and supporting it with textual evidence and reasoned insight. But do not be surprised if you find yourself responding in different styles and voices for different kinds of assignments.

61 **c** Common forms of writing in languages and literature

As we said, there are five common aims of writing about texts: appreciation, analysis, interpretation, evaluation, and cultural study. Given any one of these aims, the essays you are assigned in language and literature courses are likely to fall into two categories: those in which you focus on your own responses to one or more texts without consulting any outside sources, and those in which you research and synthesize additional material before coming to your own conclusions about a particular text or texts. (See Chapter 12 for more on writing about texts.)

1 **Essays that focus on a writer's responses**

When you focus on your own responses to a text, you may be expected to be subjective and to incorporate your own experiences, cultural background, and gender in your analysis. Or you may be asked to be objective, basing your response exclusively on the way a text is put together, its form, and its imagery. (See 12d.)

GLOSSARY OF LITERARY TERMS

■ **Alliteration** The repetition of initial consonant sounds (*"On the bald street breaks the blank day."*).

■ **Antagonist** A character of force opposing the main character (*the protagonist*) in a story.

■ **Climax** A moment of emotional or intellectual intensity or a point in the plot where one opposing force overcomes another and the conflict is resolved.

■ **Epiphany** A flash of intuitive understanding by narrator or character in a story.

■ **Figurative language** Language that suggests special meanings or effects such as metaphors or similes; not literal language. (*"She stands like a tree, solid and rooted."*)

■ **Imagery** Language that appeals to one of the five senses; especially language that reproduces something the reader can see. (*"His heart was an open book, pages aflutter and crackling in the wind."*)

■ **Metaphor** A direct comparison between two things (*"He is a fox."*).

■ **Narrator** Someone who tells a story; a *character narrator* tells the story (Huckleberry Finn) while an *omniscient narrator* tells a story about other people.

■ **Persona** A *mask*, not the author's real self, worn by the author to present a story or poem.

■ **Plot** The sequence of events in a story or play.

■ **Point of view** The vantage point from which a story or event is perceived and told.

■ **Protagonist** The main character or hero of a plot.

■ **Rhyme** The repetition of sounds, usually at the ends of lines in poems, but also occurring at other intervals in a line (*moon, June, noon*).

■ **Rhythm** The rise and fall of stress sounds within sentences, paragraphs, and stanzas.

■ **Simile** An indirect comparison using the words "as" or "like" (*"He is like a fox."*).

■ **Symbol** An object which represents itself and something else at the same time. A *black rose* is both the color of the rose and the suggestion of something evil or death-like.

■ **Theme** The meaning or thesis of a text.

Either way, be sure to quote from the work directly whenever doing so can help clarify a point you are making.

Aim to go beyond summarizing the text or what may have already been covered in class discussions. Your particular insights into what a text means, how it works, and how well it works should constitute the body of any such paper. Your conclusions may be tentative and exploratory rather than assertive and conclusive, but they should always represent a careful, detailed reading.

2 Essays that incorporate secondary sources

Assignments that ask you to go beyond a primary text to consider secondary source material require you to read, evaluate, and synthesize what other critics have said about a work or to compare the work with other works or with historical events. In doing so, be careful not to let these additional sources overwhelm your own insights and viewpoint. You will be expected to develop your own thesis based on your close reading of the work, and to introduce secondary sources as a way of supporting, expanding, or contrasting your views with those of other critics.

You may also be required (or choose) to consult other kinds of sources: biographies, letters, journals, and interviews about the writer; studies and documents that provide historical or social context; popular responses to the text; or recordings and dramatizations of the text. Such sources should serve to help you develop and support a thesis or point of view that is ultimately your own. (For more information on synthesizing sources, see Chapter 17; for more information on using MLA documentation style, see Chapter 18; and for sample papers about literary texts using MLA documentation, see Chapters 12 and 19.)

62 Writing in the Humanities

This chapter describes the aims, style, forms, and documentation conventions associated with the humanities disciplines other than languages and literature: history, philosophy, religion, the fine arts. The Chicago Style (CMS) of documentation described in 62d differs substantially from the MLA documentation system (see Chapter 19) used in languages and literature studies.

62 a The aims of writing in the humanities

The purpose of studies in the humanities is to understand the human experience as it is expressed and interpreted in a variety of media. History examines the many documents that a civilization produces that provide clues to how its people thought and lived. Philosophy and religion examine the nature of humanity by scrutinizing texts produced by past thinkers and prophets. Studies in art and communications examine texts that are often nonverbal, including paintings, sculptures, and films.

In all humanities disciplines, writing is a primary means of interpreting meaning. Students of history and philosophy, for example, spend a lot of time reading texts, reading about texts, listening to lectures based on texts, and writing texts that demonstrate an understanding of historical or philosophical knowledge.

Studies in languages and literature have much in common with the other humanities. In all these disciplines, texts are analyzed, interpreted, and evaluated. (See 61a.) However, texts in history, philosophy, and the other humanities are more often a stepping-stone toward defining a broader context, a larger issue, or a fuller understanding of some aspect of human life or thought. They are seen as documents to be argued with.

Issues in the humanities seem matters of interpretation and debate rather than proofs and truths. Interpretive papers need to be carefully reasoned and well supported so that the work will be believed.

62 **b** The style of writing in the humanities

In the humanities, variety, vitality, and thoughtfulness of expression are especially important. Though writing in the humanities is often explicitly argumentative, your tone should be fair and objective, presenting issues or positions reasonably, completely, and with a minimum of bias and subjectivity. Neutral and analytical writing encourages readers to take your ideas seriously. When you treat a text objectively, even one with which you disagree, you lay the foundation for strong and believable criticism. Treating texts, ideas, or people fairly invites readers to listen more carefully when you do interpret or evaluate them in a critical fashion.

Although you should try to write fairly and rationally in the humanities, understand that the stylistic rules in the humanities are more variable than in most social science and science writing. In many of the humanities, individuality and uniqueness of expression are highly prized.

62 **c** Common forms of writing in the humanities

Two common forms of writing in the humanities are the critical analysis (or review) and the research paper.

☐ Critical analyses and reviews

As with language and literature studies, writing about texts in the other humanities requires analysis, interpretation, and evaluation. (See 61c.) However, essays in the humanities generally focus on nonliterary works, commenting on the persuasiveness or relevance of the ideas expressed in these texts.

Critical analyses require a thorough and objective summary of the ideas expressed in a text; such a summary often involves less direct quotation and more evaluation of the work. The writer questions connections among ideas, underlying assumptions, and contradictions within the text and notes persuasive or enlightening arguments. The thesis of the essay may be tentative or qualified, but it should be a clear assertion of a well-reasoned viewpoint.

Reviews most often focus on contemporary interpretations of events, ideas, or works. For example, you might review a dramatized version of a historic event or a biographical analysis of an artist's work. You will need to express an overall judgment based on your analysis of both strengths and weaknesses of your subject.

2 Research papers

Most research papers in the humanities require a **synthesis** of primary sources (such as original documents, historical accounts, and statements of ideas) and secondary sources (what other writers have said about those primary sources). The aim may be analytical (for example, tracing the effect of a particular invention on a society's economic or cultural life) or may be argumentative (for example, positing a radically different interpretation of a philosopher's beliefs). Whatever your aim, remember that the best research papers demonstrate originality of thought, suggest new insights, and point to further areas of study.

62 d Documentation and format conventions: Chicago (CMS) style

The most widely used documentation style in history, philosophy, religion, and fine arts is the traditional style found in *The Chicago Manual of Style*, 14th edition, published by the University of Chicago Press (Chicago: 1993). Although it is somewhat more cumbersome for writers and scholars than contemporary in-text citation systems, it hinders or distracts readers less than any other form of documentation. Sample pages using the Chicago style of documentation are provided at the end of this chapter.

1 Conventions for marking in-text citations

Each time you quote, paraphrase, or summarize source material in your text, you need to mark it by inserting a raised (superscript) Arabic number immediately after the sentence or clause containing the information. The superscript number must follow all punctuation except dashes. Each new reference to source material requires a new number, and numbers are arranged consecutively throughout the text.

Frank Lloyd Wright's "prairie style" was characterized initially by the houses he built around Chicago "with low horizontal lines echoing the landscape."[1] Vincent Scully sees the suburban building lots for which Wright was designing as one of the architect's most important influences.[2]

DIRECTORY FOR CHICAGO (CMS) DOCUMENTATION GUIDELINES

Each superscript number corresponds to a note at the end of the paper, or sometimes at the foot of the page on which the number appears.

1. "Wright, Frank Lloyd," The Concise Columbia Encyclopedia, 1st ed.

2. Vincent Scully, Architecture: The Natural and the Manmade (New York: St. Martin's, 1991), 340.

2 Conventions for positioning notes and bibliography

Endnotes are typed as a single list at the end of a text. Endnotes are easy to format since they can be typed separately on a sheet of paper without calculating the space needed on each page. Footnotes can be difficult to place, because the space taken up by the notes sometimes moves a footnote marker-number to the next page, requiring you to refigure the placement of your text. Some word processing programs have a built-in footnote-formatting function, but endnotes are more convenient—they allow you to use the full page for text rather than taking up space with footnotes. Also, endnotes can be added to or deleted from your paper without affecting the body of the text.

The **endnote page** follows the last page of text and is numbered in sequence with the rest of the paper. Title the first page of the endnote section "Notes"—centered, without quotation marks, and one inch from the top of the page. Double-space throughout—between this title and the first entry, within the notes or entries themselves, and between entries. Order your entries consecutively according to the note numbers in your paper. Indent the first line of each entry five spaces from the left margin, and place each subsequent entry line flush with the margin.

Footnotes are more convenient for readers, because instead of turning to the back of a text to check a numbered source, they can find the information simply by glancing at the bottom of the page they are reading. Footnotes must always be placed at the bottom of the same page on which the marker-number appears, four lines below the last line of text and single-spaced.

Some instructors and/or programs require a separate, alphabetically arranged list of sources, or **bibliography**, in addition to endnotes or footnotes. If so, follow the MLA guidelines for a list of Works Cited. (See 18c.) If you are asked to include in your bibliography *only* sources consulted in researching for your paper, you may title your bibliography list "Works Consulted."

3 Conventions for endnote and footnote format

Different style manuals offer a number of minor variations for the format of endnotes and footnotes. The following guidelines are based on *The Chicago Manual of Style*, which follows the endnote and footnote format also found in the *MLA Handbook for Writers of Research Papers*.

Numbers and spacing. Each entry is preceded by an Arabic number with a period that is indented five spaces and followed by a space. Any subsequent lines for an entry begin at the left margin. Double-space endnotes throughout. Single-space individual footnotes and double-space between footnotes.

Authors. List all authors' names first name first, spelling them as they appear in their book. You may spell out the first name or use initials.

Punctuation. Separate authors' names and all titles with commas, and enclose all book publication information and periodical dates in parentheses. Use colons to separate the place of publication from the publisher and commas to separate the publisher from the date. Colons should also be used to separate journal dates from page numbers. End all entries with a period.

Page numbers. Each entry for a book or periodical should end with the page number(s) on which the cited information can be found. (Note that according to the *Chicago Manual* style, "p." or "pp." is used with the actual page number for material from journals that do not use volume numbers.)

The following are examples of the most common endnote citations required in undergraduate humanities papers. See MLA guidelines (18c) for information about titles, publishers' names, dates and page numbers, and abbreviations. The section on MLA guidelines (18c) also includes more information on what to include in endnote entries.

DOCUMENTING BOOKS: FIRST REFERENCE

1. Book by one author

1. Jessica Benjamin, The Bonds of Love: Psychoanalysis, Feminism, and the Problem of Domination (New York: Prometheus, 1988), 76.

2. Book by two or more authors

2. Richard L. Zweigenhaft and G. William Domhoff, Blacks in the White Establishment (New Haven: Yale University Press, 1991), 113.

802 Writing in the humanities

For three or more authors, follow each name with a comma.

3. Revised edition of a book

3. S. I. Hayakawa, Language in Thought and Action, 4th ed. (New York: Harcourt, 1978), 77.

4. Edited book and one volume of a multivolume book

4. Tom Waldrep, ed., Writers on Writing, vol. 2 (New York: Random House, 1988), 123.

5. Translated book

5. Albert Camus, The Stranger, trans. Stuart Gilbert (New York: Random House, 1946), 12.

6. Reprinted book

6. Elizabeth E. G. Evans, The Abuse of Maternity (1875; reprint, New York: Arno, 1974), 74–78.

7. Work in an anthology or chapter in an edited collection

7. Mona Charen, "Much More Nasty Than They Should Be," in Popular Writing in America: The Interaction of Style and Audience, 5th ed., ed. Donald McQuade and Robert Atwan (New York: Oxford University Press, 1993), 207–8.

8. Article in a reference book

8. "Langella, Frank," International Television and Video Almanac, 40th ed. (New York: Quigley, 1995).

No page number is needed for an alphabetically arranged book. Begin the entry with the author's name, if available.

9. Anonymous book

9. The World Almanac and Book of Facts (New York: World Almanac-Funk & Wagnalls, 1995).

DOCUMENTING PERIODICALS: FIRST REFERENCE

10. Article, story, or poem in a monthly or bimonthly magazine

10. Matthew Hawn, "Stay on the Web: Make Your Internet Site Pay Off," Macworld, April 1996, 94–98.

11. Article, story, or poem in a weekly magazine

11. John Updike, "His Mother Inside Him," New Yorker, 20 April 1992, 34.

12. Article in a daily newspaper

12. Peter Finn, "Death of a U-Va. Student Raises Scrutiny of Off-Campus Drinking," Washington Post, 27 September 1995, Sec. D, p. 1.

13. Article in a journal paginated by volume

13. Jennie Nelson, "'This Was an Easy Assignment: Examining How Students Interpret Academic Writing Tasks," Research in the Teaching of English 34 (1990): 362–96.

14. Article in a journal paginated by issue

14. Helen Tiffin, "Post-Colonialism, Post-Modernism, and the Rehabilitation of Post Colonial History," Journal of Commonwealth Literature 23, no. 1 (1988): 169–81.

15. Review

15. Review of Bone, by Faye Myenne Ng, New Yorker, 8 February 1992, 113.

16. Steven Rosen, "Dissing 'HIStory,'" review of HIStory: Past, Present, and Future-Book I, by Michael Jackson, Denver Post, 3 July 1995, Sec. F, p. 8.

DOCUMENTING ELECTRONIC SOURCES: FIRST REFERENCE

Because the nature of electronic sources can vary so widely and because technology is so rapidly changing the ways in which research can be done, the following examples only begin to show documentation guidelines. Consult the *Chicago Manual,* if necessary, for more information.

16. Material on CD-ROM database, periodically updated

17. Oregon Trail II, Ver. 1.0 Mac. (Minneapolis: Educational Computing Corp., 1995), ERIC, CD-ROM, SilverPlatter, March 1996.

17. Material on diskette

18. Diane Greco, Cyborg: Engineering the Body Electric, (Watertown: Eastgate, 1996), diskette.

18. E-mail and other electronic messages

19. John Fallon, "Re: EECAP Summer Seminar," e-mail to John Clark, 6 February 1996.

19. Materials accessed via networks

20. Jerry Gray, "In Congress, G.O.P. Ponders Tactics to Regain the Edge," The New York Times on the Web [online] (25 February 1996), INTERNET.

21. Herman Melville, Moby Dick [online] (New York: Hendricks House, 1952), University of Virginia Library, 6 January 1996, INTERNET.

22. "Visible Human Project Fact Sheet," Visible Human Project [online] (Bethesda: National Library of Medicine, 1995), National Library of Medicine, 10 February 1996, INTERNET.

DOCUMENTING OTHER SOURCES: FIRST REFERENCE
20. Personal interview

23. John Morser, interview by author, Chicago, 15 December 1993.

21. Personal or unpublished letter

24. Paul Friedman, letter to author, 18 March 1992.

If the letter is in a collection, provide the pertinent information about where it may be found, after the date.

22. Work of art

25. Hans Holbein, Portrait of Erasmus, The Louvre, Paris, in The Louvre Museum, by Germain Bazin (New York: Abrams, n.d.), p. 148.

DOCUMENTING SUBSEQUENT REFERENCES TO THE SAME WORK

23. Subsequent references to a work

The second and any subsequent times you refer to a source, the Chicago style calls for you to include the author's last name, a comma, a shortened version of the title, another comma, and the page number(s).

26. Benjamin, <u>Bonds</u>, 76.

27. Evans, <u>The Abuse</u>, 74–78.

The traditional Latin abbreviations *ibid.* ("in the same place") and *op. cit.* ("in the work cited") are seldom used in contemporary scholarly writing.

62 e Sample page with endnotes

Owsley 2

recorded "in exultant tones the universal neglect that had over-taken pagan learning."[2] It would be some time, however, before Christian education would replace classical training, and by the fourth century, a lack of interest in learning and culture among the elite of Roman society was apparent. Attempting to check the demise of education, the later emperors established munici-pal schools, and universities of rhetoric and law were also estab-lished in major cites throughout the Empire.[3]

Owsley 12

Notes

1. Rosamond McKitterick, The Carolingians and the Written Word (Cambridge: Cambridge University Press, 1983), 61.

2. J. Bass Mullinger, The Schools of Charles the Great (New York: Stechert, 1911), 10.

3. James W. Thompson, The Literacy of the Laity in the Middle Ages (New York: Franklin, 1963), 17.

4. O. M. Dalton, introduction, The Letters of Sidonius (Oxford: Clarendon, 1915), cxiv.

5. Pierre Riche, Education and Culture in the Barbarian West (Columbia: University of South Carolina Press, 1976), 4.

6. Riche, Education and Culture, 6.

[Notes continue.]

Kelly 5

The Teatro Olímpico was completed in 1584, the statues, in-
scriptions, and bas-reliefs for the frons-scena being the last details completed. Meanwhile, careful plans were made for an inau-
gural which was to be a production of Oedipus in a new
translation.[10] Final decisions were made by the Academy in
February of 1585 for the seating of city officials, their wives, and
others, with the ruling that "no masked men or women would be
allowed in the theatre for the performance."[11]

The organization of the audience space was "unique among
Renaissance theaters, suggesting . . . its function as the theater
of a 'club of equals' rather than of a princely court."[12] The
Academy is celebrated and related to Roman grandeur by the
decorating over the monumental central opening, where its mot-
to, "Hoc Opus," appears.[13] It is difficult to make out the entrances

10. J. Thomas Oosting, Andrea Palladio's Teatro Olímpico
(Ann Arbor, MI: UMI Research Press, 1981), 118–19.

11. Oosting, Palladio's Teatro, 120.

12. Marvin Carlson, Places of Performance: The Semiotics of
Theater Architecture (Ithaca, N.Y.: Cornell University Press,
1989), 135.

13. Simon Tidworth, Theaters: An Architectural and
Cultural History (London: Praeger, 1973), 52.

This chapter describes the aims, style, forms, and documentation conventions associated with disciplines in the social sciences: psychology, sociology, anthropology, political science, and economics. The system of documentation described here is based on guidelines published by the American Psychological Association (APA).

63 a The aims of writing in the social sciences

The social sciences examine the fundamental structures and processes that make up the social world. Sociology examines social groups; political science examines the politics of social organizations; anthropology examines social cultures; economics examines the allocation and distribution of resources among social groups; and psychology examines the mind as both a biological and social construction. The social sciences use methodical and systematic inquiry to examine and analyze human behavior, commonly asking questions such as the following:

- What is society? Can it be isolated and observed? Can it be described?

- How do social and psychological systems function? What forces hold them together or lead to their breakdown?

- Why do social organizations and individuals behave the way they do? Can governing laws be identified, explained, and understood?

Most writing in the social sciences explains findings based on factual research: either the empirical research—that is, research based on firsthand observation and experimentation—or the wide reading that results in a literature review. Social scientists must also interpret their factual findings. As with any other field of academic study, individual interpretations and opinions must be carefully reasoned and based on clear evidence that is objectively presented.

As a student in the social sciences, you will be writing for professors and graduate students who are themselves social scientists and who are knowledgeable about the concepts and information you present. They will expect current, accurate information that is presented concisely and interpreted reasonably.

63 b The style of writing in the social sciences

Writing in the social sciences must be clearly organized. Connections among ideas should be explicitly stated. Language is expected to be precise—informal diction is discouraged. However, social science writing need not be dull or dry. Readers of the social sciences look for clarity, smoothness, and economy of expression. Writers should therefore avoid unnecessary jargon, wordiness, and redundancy. As you write and revise, keep the following guidelines in mind.

1 Write from a **third-person point of view**. (First-person experience is considered inappropriate for conveying empirical data because, in calling attention to the writer, it detracts from the information.)

2 Use the **past tense** to describe methods and results ("Individuals responded by . . ."); use the **past or past perfect tense** for literature reviews ("The study resulted in . . . ," "Jones has suggested . . ."); use the **present tense** to report established knowledge or to discuss conclusions ("The evidence indicates . . ."). Use tenses consistently.

3 Use the **technical language** of the discipline correctly, but avoid excessive jargon. Use plain, direct language. Choose synonyms with care.

4 Include **graphs, charts, and illustrations** when they convey information more readily than words. Label them clearly.

5 Incorporate **numbers, statistics, and equations** clearly and accurately. Include explanations.

63 c Common forms of writing in the social sciences

Two common forms of social science writing are reports of original research and reviews of published research.

1 **Research reports**

Empirical studies, those based on surveys and experiments, are common in the social sciences. In political science, a study might be based on an opinion poll about an election; in psychology, on the effects of a particular stimulus on behavior. The conventional form for research reports varies somewhat from discipline to discipline. However, many social science reports use the following basic structure.

Title page. The title should offer a concise summary of the paper and identify the theoretical issues or variables under study. Center the title on the page, and underneath it type your name, your instructor's name, the course title, and the date.

Abstract. An abstract is a brief (100 to 150 words) summary of the study and its results. It should be concise but comprehensive and self-contained, that is, complete in itself. It is best to write it after you complete the text itself. The abstract page follows the title page.

Introduction. Begin the report with an introduction that defines the problem you set out to study and that outlines your research strategy. In your introduction you should discuss the background of the problem. Include a brief literature review of any previously reported studies of the problem or issue. End by discussing your own purpose and rationale for the study and stating your hypothesis. The introduction has no heading.

Methods. The next section (headed "Methods") explains how your study was conducted. This section is often divided into three subsections: subjects (describing the type, number, and selection of participants in the study); apparatus (including any materials or statistical programs and their function); and procedure (summarizing the steps involved in conducting the study).

Results. In this section (headed "Results"), report the findings and conclusions of your study, including any findings that do not support your hypothesis. Use tables to present your results when doing so is clearer or more concise than a description in words. In this section, remain descriptive, not interpretive or evaluative.

Discussion. In this final section (headed "Discussion"), interpret what the results mean. Begin with a statement of whether or not your study supported your hypothesis. Consider what your work contributes to an understanding of the problem you set out to study. You may speculate on any theoretical implications or implications for further experiments. (This is the only section of a formal report in which the first person may be appropriate, as you may want to identify an opinion or theory as your own.)

References. List all the references cited in the report at the end on a separate page (headed "References"; see 64d2.)

2 Literature reviews

In addition to being included as part of research reports, literature reviews (sometimes called surveys) are often written as independent documents. Preparing a literature review will expose you to knowledge generated by social science methodology and will also acquaint you with the conventions of experimentation and documentation.

Reviews are generally written in the style of an essay, with one paragraph devoted to each article surveyed. While the precise form, length, and name of these papers may vary slightly in different disciplines, they will generally contain the following parts.

Title. Create a title that concisely describes the subject area that is surveyed in the paper.

Introduction. Begin the report with a brief introduction to the subject and a chronological listing of the articles to be reviewed.

Summary. Summarize the main conclusion of each article reviewed. Include brief quotations that succinctly state the researchers' findings, and make some suggestion of how you interpret their implications.

Conclusion. Conclude the report with a cumulative summary of the survey. Assess the most important articles in the review and suggest possible implications for further research.

References. List all the articles cited in the report on a separate page called "References." (See 63d3.)

63 d Documentation and format conventions: APA guidelines

Most disciplines in the social sciences—psychology, sociology, anthropology, political science, and economics—use the name-and-date system of documentation put forth by the American Psychological Association (APA). The disciplines of education and business also use this system. This citation style highlights dates of publication because the currency of published material is of primary importance in these disciplines. Also, listing *all* the authors is more strongly emphasized in the APA than in the MLA system; collaborative authoring is common in the social sciences, and it has been conventional to recognize the efforts of all collaborators. For more about the foundations and purposes of the APA system, see the *Publication Manual of the American Psychological Association,* 4th ed. (Washington, D.C.: APA, 1994). The numbered entries that follow introduce and explain some of the conventions of this system.

1 Conventions for in-text citations

1. Single work by one or more authors

Whenever you quote, paraphrase, or summarize material in your text, you should give both the author's last name and the date of the source. For direct quotations, you should also provide specific page numbers. You may also provide page references, as a convenience to your readers, whenever you suspect they might want to consult a source you have cited. Page references in the APA system are always preceded, in-text or in the reference list, by the abbreviation "p.," in the case of a single page, or "pp." in the case of multiple pages.

DIRECTORY FOR APA DOCUMENTATION GUIDELINES

CONVENTIONS FOR IN-TEXT CITATIONS (63d1)

1. Single work by one or more authors
2. Two or more works by the same author published in the same year
3. Unknown author
4. Corporate or organizational author
5. Authors with the same last name
6. Quote from an indirect source
7. More than one work in a citation
8. Long quote set off from text

CONVENTIONS FOR FOOTNOTES (63d2)

CONVENTIONS FOR THE REFERENCE LIST (63d3)

DOCUMENTING BOOKS

1. Book by one author
2. Book by two or more authors
3. More than one book by the same author
4. Book by a corporation, association, or organization
5. Revised edition of a book
6. Edited book

According to the APA system, authors' names, publication dates, and page numbers (when listed) should be placed in parentheses following citable material. If any of these elements are identified in the text referred to in the parenthetical citation, they are not repeated in the citation.

Exotoxins make some bacteria dangerous to humans (Thomas, 1974).

According to Thomas (1974), "Some bacteria are only harmful to us if they make exotoxins" (p. 76).

We need fear some bacteria only "if they make exotoxins" (Thomas, 1974, p. 76).

For a work by **two authors**, cite both names.

7. Book in more than one volume
8. Translated or reprinted book
9. Chapter or article in an edited book
10. Anonymous book
11. Government document

DOCUMENTING PERIODICALS

12. Article in a journal paginated by volume
13. Article in a journal paginated by issue
14. Magazine article
15. Newspaper article

DOCUMENTING ELECTRONIC SOURCES

16. General formats for documenting electronic sources
17. Abstract on CD-ROM
18. E-mail messages and other electronic conversations
19. Online abstract
20. Computer software or program
21. Online journal articles

DOCUMENTING OTHER SOURCES

22. Film, recording, and other nonprint media

Smith and Hawkins (1990) agree that all bacteria producing exotoxins are harmful to humans.

All known exotoxin-producing bacteria are harmful to humans (Smith & Hawkins, 1990).

The authors' names are joined by *and* within your text, but APA convention requires an ampersand (&) to join authors' names in parentheses.

For a work by **three to five authors**, identify all the authors by last name the first time you cite a source. In subsequent references identify only the first author followed by "et al." ("and others").

The most recent study supports the belief that alcohol abuse is on the rise (Dinkins, Dominic, Smith, Rogers, & White, 1989). . . . When homeless people were excluded from the study, the results were the same (Dinkins et al., 1989).

If you are citing a source by **six or more authors**, identify only the first author in all the references, followed by "et al."

2. Two or more works by the same author published in the same year

To distinguish between two or more works published in the same year by the same author or team of authors, place a lower-case letter (*a, b, c,* etc.) immediately after the date. This letter should correspond to that in the reference list, where the entries will be alphabetized by title. If two appear in one citation, repeat the year.

(Smith, 1992a, 1992b)

3. Unknown author

To cite the work of an unknown author, use the first two or three words of the entry as it is listed in the reference list (usually by the title). If the words *are* from the title, enclose them in quotation marks or underline them, whichever is appropriate.

Statistical Abstracts (1991) reports the literacy rate for Mexico at 75% for 1990, up 4% from census figures 10 years ago.

Many researchers now believe that treatment should not begin until other factors have been dealt with ("New Evidence Suggests," 1987).

4. Corporate or organizational author

If a citation refers to a work by a corporation, association, organization, or foundation, spell out the name of the authoring agency. If the name can be abbreviated and remain identifiable, you may spell out the name only the first time and put the abbreviation immediately after it, in brackets. For subsequent references to that source, you may use only the abbreviation.

(American Psychological Association [APA], 1993) . . . (APA, 1994)

5. Authors with the same last name

To avoid confusion in citing two or more authors with the same last name, include each author's initials in every citation.

(J. M. Clark, 1994)   (C. L. Clark, 1995)

6. Quote from an indirect source

Use the words "as cited in" to indicate when a quotation or any information in your source is originally from another source.

Lester Brown of Worldwatch believes international agriculture production has reached its limit and that "we're going to be in trouble on the food front before this decade is out" (as cited in Mann, 1993, p. 51).

7. More than one work in a citation

As a general guideline, list two or more sources within a single parenthetical reference in the same order in which they appear in your reference list. More than one work by the same author are listed in chronological order with the author's name mentioned once and the dates separated by commas: (Thomas, 1974, 1979). Works by different authors in the same parentheses are listed in alphabetical order by the author's last name, separated by semicolons:

(Miller, 1990; Webster & Rose, 1988)

8. Long quote set off from text

Start quotations of forty or more words on a new line and indent the block five spaces from the left margin. Indent the first line of the second or any subsequent paragraphs (but not the first paragraph) five additional spaces. Double-space all such quotations, omit quotation marks, and place the parenthetical citation after any end punctuation, with no period following the citation.

> Language is everywhere. It permeates our thoughts, mediates our relations with others, and even creeps into our dreams. The overwhelming bulk of human knowledge is stored and transmitted in language. Language is so ubiquitous that we take it for granted, but without it, society as we now know it would be impossible.

> Despite its prevalence in human affairs, language is poorly understood. (Langacker, 1968, p. 3)

2 Conventions for footnotes

Footnotes are used to provide additional information that cannot be worked into the main text, information highly likely to be of interest to some readers but also likely to slow down the pace of your text or obscure your point for other readers. Therefore, even the footnotes you do choose to provide should be as brief as possible; when the information you wish to add is extensive, it is better to present it in an appendix. Footnotes should be numbered consecutively, should follow the reference list on a page headed "Footnotes," should be double-spaced, and should have their first line indented five to seven spaces.

3 Conventions for the reference list

All works mentioned in a paper should be identified on a reference list according to the following general rules of the APA documentation system.

Format. After the final page of the paper, title a separate page "References," with no underline or quotation marks. Center the title an inch from the top of the page. Number the page in sequence with the last page of the paper.

Double-space between the title and the first entry. Set the first line flush with the left margin; the second and all subsequent lines of an entry should be indented three spaces from the left margin. This format, called a "hanging indent" format, is how the reference list will look typeset in books and journals. Note that APA asks writers to submit their manuscripts for publication using the paragraph indent format (with the first line indented five spaces and subsequent lines flush with the left margin) to help them with typesetting concerns. Most instructors prefer the hanging indent format for student papers since such papers are considered "final copy," but always check with your instructor first.

Also double-space both between and within entries. If your reference list exceeds one page, continue listing your references in sequence on an additional page or pages, but do not repeat the title "References."

Order of entries. Alphabetize the list of references according to authors' last names, using the first author's last name for works with multiple authors. For entries by an unknown author, alphabetize by the first word of the title, excepting nonsignificant words (e.g., *A, An, The*).

Format for entries. The three most common of several variations on general formats are the following.

GENERAL FORMAT FOR BOOKS

Author(s). (Year of publication). Book title. City of publication: Publisher.

GENERAL FORMAT FOR JOURNAL ARTICLES

Author(s). (Year of publication). Article title. Journal Title, volume number, inclusive page numbers.

GENERAL FORMAT FOR MAGAZINE AND NEWSPAPER ARTICLES

Author(s). (Year, month of publication). Article title. Publication Title, inclusive page numbers.

Authors. List the author's last name first, followed by a comma and the author's initials (not first names). When a work has more than one author, list all authors in this way, separating the names with a comma. When listing multiple authors for a single work, place an ampersand (&) before the last author's name. A period follows the author name(s).

Titles. List the complete titles and subtitles of books and articles, but capitalize only the first word of the title and any subtitle, as well as all proper nouns. Underline book titles and journal or publication titles, but do not underline article titles or place quotation marks around them. Place a period after the title.

Publishers. List publishers' names in shortened form, omitting words such as "Company." Spell out the names of university presses and organizations in full. For books, use a colon to separate the city of publication from the publisher.

Dates and page numbers. For magazines and newspapers, use commas to separate the year from the month and day, and enclose the publication dates in parentheses: (1954, May 25). Inclusive page numbers should be separated by a hyphen with no spaces: 361–375. Full sequences should be given for pages and dates: not 361–75. If pages do not follow consecutively (as in newspapers), include subsequent page numbers after a comma: pp. 1, 16. Note that "pp." precedes the page numbers for newspaper articles, but not for journal articles.

Abbreviations. State and country names are abbreviated, but months are not. Use U.S. postal abbreviations for state abbreviations.

Following are examples of the reference list format for a variety of source types.

DOCUMENTING BOOKS

1. Book by one author

Benjamin, J. (1988). The bonds of love: Psychoanalysis, feminism, and the problem of domination. New York: Prometheus.

2. Book by two or more authors

Zweigenhaft, R. L., & Domhoff, G. W. (1991). Blacks in the white establishment. New Haven, CT: Yale University Press.

Include all authors' names in the reference list, regardless of the number of authors associated with a particular work.

3. More than one book by the same author

List two or more works by the same author (or the same author team listed in the same order) chronologically by year in your reference list, with the earliest first. Arrange any such works published in the same year alphabetically by title, placing lowercase letters after the dates. In either case, give full identification of author(s) for each reference listing.

Bandura, A. (1969). Principles of behavior modification. New York: Holt, Rinehart, and Winston.

Bandura, A. (1977a). Self-efficacy: Toward a unifying theory of behavioral change. Psychological Review, 84, 191-215.

Bandura, A. (1977b). Social learning theory. Upper Saddle River, NJ: Prentice-Hall.

If the same author is named first but listed with different co-authors, alphabetize by the last name of the second author. Works by the first author alone are listed before works with co-authors.

4. Book by a corporation, association, or organization

American Psychological Association. (1994). Publication manual of the American
  Psychological Association (4th ed.). Washington, DC: Author.

Alphabetize corporate authors by the corporate name, excluding the articles *A*, *An*, and *The*. When the corporate author is also the publisher, designate the publisher as "Author."

5. Revised edition of a book

Peek, S. (1993). The game inventor's handbook (Rev. ed.). Cincinnati, OH:
  Betterway.

6. Edited book

Schaefer, Charles E., & Reid, S. E. (Eds.). (1986). Game play: Therapeutic use of
  childhood games. New York: Wiley.

Place "Ed." or "Eds.," capitalized, after the singular or plural name of the editor(s) of an edited book.

7. Book in more than one volume

Waldrep, T. (Ed.). (1985-1988). Writers on writing (Vols. 1-2). New York: Random
  House.

For a work with volumes published in different years, indicate the range of dates of publication. In citing only one volume of a multivolume work, indicate only the volume cited.

Waldrep, T. (Ed.). (1988). Writers on writing (Vol. 2). New York: Random House.

8. Translated or reprinted book

Freud, S. (1950). The interpretation of dreams (A. A. Brill, Trans.). New York: Modern
  Library-Random House. (Original work published 1900)

The date of the translation or reprint is in parentheses after the author's name. Indicate the original publication date parenthetically at the end of the citation, with no period. In the text, parenthetically cite the information with both dates: (Freud 1900/1950).

9. Chapter or article in an edited book

Telander, R. (1996). Senseless crimes. In C. I. Schuster & W. V. Van Pelt (Eds.), Speculations: Readings in culture, identity, and values (2nd ed., pp. 264–272). Upper Saddle River, NJ: Prentice-Hall.

The chapter or article title is not underlined or in quotation marks. Editors' names are listed in normal reading order (surname last). Inclusive page numbers, in parentheses, follow the title of the larger work.

10. Anonymous book

Stereotypes, distortions and omissions in U.S. history textbooks. (1977). New York: Council on Interracial Books for Children.

11. Government document

U.S. House of Representatives, Committee on Energy and Commerce. (1986). Ensuring access to programming for the backyard satellite dish owner (Serial No. 99–127). Washington, DC: U.S. Government Printing Office.

For government documents, provide the higher department or governing agency only when the office or agency that created the document is not readily recognizable. If a document number is available, list it after the document title in parentheses. Write out the name of the printing agency in full, as the publisher, rather than using the abbreviation "GPO."

DOCUMENTING PERIODICALS

In citing periodical articles, use the same format for listing author names as for books.

12. Article in a journal paginated by volume

Hartley, J. (1991). Psychology, writing, and computers: A review of research. Visible Language, 25, 339–375.

If page numbers are continuous throughout volumes in a year, use only the volume number, underlined, following the title of the periodical.

13. Article in a journal paginated by issue

Lowther, M. A. (1977). Career change in mid-life: Its impact on education. Innovator,

8 (7), 1, 9–11.

Include the issue number in parentheses if each issue of a journal is paginated separately.

14. Magazine article

Garreau, J. (1995, December). Edgier cities. Wired, 158–163, 232–234.

For nonprofessional periodicals, include the year and month (not abbreviated) after the author's name.

15. Newspaper article

Finn, P. (1995, September 27). Death of a U-Va. student raises scrutiny of off-campus

drinking. The Washington Post, pp. D1, D4.

If an author is listed for the article, begin with the author's name, then list the date (spell out the month); follow with the title of the newspaper. If there is a section, combine it with the page or pages, including continued page numbers as well.

DOCUMENTING ELECTRONIC SOURCES

16. General formats for documenting electronic sources

The fourth edition of the *Publication Manual of the American Psychological Association* (APA, 1994, pp. 218–219) provides three general formats for reference listings for online sources. The first of these formats is for a single-authored article/document in an online periodical.

Author, I. (date). Title of article. Name of Periodical [On-line], xx. Available: Specify

path

Note that this format follows almost exactly the format APA recommends for printed sources. If an author is named, the reference listing begins with the author's last name, a comma, and the author's initial(s). The title of the article comes next, with no quotation marks and only the first word of a title or subtitle capitalized. The title of the periodical follows, underlined and with all significant words capitalized. Then comes the description "On-line" in brackets, followed by a comma, *not* underlined, and then the volume number, underlined. APA recommends that you list a retrieval path for all online sources, preceded by the word "Available" and a colon. No period follows the retrieval path, in an effort to reduce address confusion. The protocol or access program used to locate the source should also be included, for readers' convenience, following the word "Available."

Available FTP: dartmouth.edu/pub/hypertexts

The second suggested format is for an article or chapter in an edited work.

Author, I., & Author, I. (date). Title of chapter. In Title of full work [On-line].
    Available: Specify path

APA's third general format suggestion is for an online book.

Author, I., Author, I., & Author, I. (date). Title of full work [On-line]. Available:
    Specify path

The *APA Publication Manual* (1994, p. 219) notes, "An availability statement replaces the location and name of a publisher typically provided for text references." Where a publication or version date is not available for an online source, the APA suggests that you provide the access date, or the date on which you read the material. Otherwise, reference listings for online sources should follow the conventions for their printed equivalents as closely as possible.

17. Abstract on CD-ROM

The most recent *APA Publication Manual* also provides a general format for making reference listings to abstracts on CD-ROM (APA, 1994, p. 221).

Author, I. (date). Title of article [CD-ROM]. Title of Journal, xx, xxx–xxx. Abstract
    from: Source and retrieval number

A specific example of this format is as follows:

Krauthammer, C. (1991). Why is America in a blue funk? [CD-ROM]. Time, 138, 83.

Abstract from: UMIACH file: Periodical Abstracts Item: 1126.00

18. E-mail messages and other electronic conversations

Current APA guidelines call for no reference listing for E-mail or other electronic conversations; instead you are asked to treat these "nonrecoverable" sources as you would any other form of personal communication, citing them in your text only. Give the initial(s) and the last name of the communicator in your in-text citation, in that order, followed by as exact a date for the communication as possible.

19. Online abstract

Szajna, B., & Mackay, J. M. (1995). Predictors of learning performance in a comput-

er-user training environment: A path-analytic study [On-line]. International

Journal of Human-Computer Interaction, 7, 167–185. Abstract from: DIALOG

file: PsycINFO Item: 83-09645

20. Computer software or program

HyperCard (Version 2.2) [Computer software]. (1993). Cupertino, CA: Apple

Computer.

Provide the version number, if available, in parentheses following the program or software name. Add the descriptive term "Computer software" in brackets and follow it with a period. Do not underline names of computer software or programs.

21. Online journal articles

Kapadia, S. (1995, November). A tribute to Mahatma Gandhi: His views on women

and social exchange [19 paragraphs]. Journal of South Asia Women's Studies

[On-line serial], 1 (1). Available: WWW: http://www.shore.net/~india/jsaws/

For online journal articles, indicate the number of paragraphs in brackets after the title of the article, and place the descriptor "On-line serial" in brackets (not underlined) between the journal name and the volume number. The issue number follows the volume number, in parentheses. Give standard search-path information for online sources, with no end punctuation.

DOCUMENTING OTHER SOURCES

22. Film, recording, and other nonprint media

Curtiz, M. (Director). (1942). <u>Casablanca</u> [Film]. Hollywood, CA: Warner Bros.

Alphabetize a film listing by the name of the person or persons with primary responsibility for the product. Identify the medium in brackets following the title, and indicate both location and name of the distributor (as publisher). Other identifying information should appear in parentheses.

64 Writing in the Physical Sciences

This chapter describes the general aims and style of scientific writing and provides an overview of common forms and specialized documentation systems shared by the scientific community. If you write extensively in the sciences, consult one of the more detailed style manuals listed in 64d.

64 a The aims of writing in the sciences

Scientific study examines the fundamental structures and processes of the natural world. In analyzing particular phenomena and organisms, scientists ask questions such as the following.

- What is it? Can it be isolated and observed? How can it be described?

- How does it function? What forces are in operation? How can these forces be explained?

- Why does it function the way it does? Can governing principles be identified, explained, and understood? Can predictions be made?

- What can be learned about other phenomena or organisms based on the evidence of particular studies?

Scientists approach and attempt to answer such questions using the **scientific method** of observation, prediction, experimentation, and analysis.

Observation. A chemist notices, for example, that when liquid A is mixed with liquid B, the solution of the two (C) has a higher temperature than A or B alone.

Prediction. On the basis of this observation, the chemist predicts that whenever these amounts of A and B are mixed together, C will always have a higher temperature. This prediction is called a *hypothesis*—a preliminary generalization or explanation based on the observed phenomena.

Experimentation. To test the hypothesis, the chemist devises an experiment (in this example, the mixing of the two liquids under controlled conditions), watches the results, and carefully notes what happens.

Analysis and conclusions. The results of the experiment may lead the scientist to conclude, "Yes, when specific amounts of A and B are mixed, reaction C occurs." This finding can be shared with other scientists and could provide the basis for further hypotheses. If the results are different from the hypothesis, new questions must be asked and new hypotheses formulated to explain why the results differed from the initial observations.

Writing plays a central role throughout the investigative and experimental process. To develop a hypothesis, scientists record observations, questions, and possible explanations. In conducting an experiment, scientists take full and accurate notes to keep a running account of methods, procedures, and results. To understand the significance of the results, scientists report or publish the results so other scientists can read about them and respond.

Scientific writing does not report the writer's opinions, values, or feelings; it aims for objectivity and accuracy when reporting observations and findings. When you write in the sciences, try to separate your observations from your expectations or biases. Record only what you see and hear and what the instruments tell you, not what you hope to discover. Keep in mind that your primary purpose is to present information accurately—not to persuade, argue, or entertain.

64 **b** The style of writing in the sciences

Most science writing seeks to convey information specifically, directly, economically, and accurately. But this common goal does not mean that the style of all science writing is uniform. For example, the form and style of a laboratory report is quite different from the laboratory notebook on which it is based. An article in *Scientific American* (written for a general readership) is quite different from one in *The Journal of Chemical Education* (written for college chemistry instructors). In writing in the sciences, keep the goals of clarity and directness in mind.

I   Choose **simple words** rather than complex words when the meaning is the same, and use disciplinary terminology carefully and accurately.

2   Prefer **simple sentences** to complex.

3   Maintain a **third-person point of view**, to avoid the pronoun *I*. Use the passive voice when necessary to describe procedures: *The liquids were brought to a temperature of 35°C.*

4   Use the **present tense** to refer to established knowledge or to discuss conclusions. Use the **past tense** to describe methods and results.

5   Insert **subheadings** to help readers predict what is coming.

6   Include **tables and figures** when they can help explain your methods or results. Label each of these clearly, and mention them at appropriate points in the text.

---

64 **c**   **Common forms of writing in the sciences**

Scientific reports have set forms that allow readers to locate information in predictable places. Two common forms of writing in college science courses are laboratory notebooks and laboratory reports.

▮ Laboratory notebooks

Lab notebooks are journals that scientists keep to monitor day-to-day laboratory work and experimentation. They are used to record data—dates, times, temperatures, quantities, measurements—as well as to aid memory and provide records. Lab notebooks are also used to speculate about the meaning of the data. These privately kept notes serve as the basis for the information made public in formal laboratory reports.

■   Lab notebook pages are usually numbered and bound rather than loose-leaf. This unalterable order guarantees an accurate record of exactly what happened in the laboratory, when it happened, and in what order.

■   Double-entry lab notebooks, with a vertical line down the center of each page, are especially useful. Record data on the left; on the right make notes and speculations about the data.

■   Lab notebooks must be complete and detailed. It is crucial to record all information about an experiment or observation.

2 Laboratory reports

Laboratory reports are formal reports that describe exactly what happened in any given experiment. The reader of a lab report should be able to replicate (or duplicate) the experiment by following the information in the report. While *labs* (as they are commonly called) vary slightly in format conventions from discipline to discipline, they all follow the following basic structure.

Introduction. The first section of the report defines the reasons for conducting the particular study, summarizes the findings of previous studies (a literature review), and states the researcher's hypothesis.

Methods and materials. Sometimes called "Procedure," this section details how the experiment was conducted and identifies all the equipment used. The experimental design is explained, and the methods of observation and measurement are described.

Results. Next, the researcher reports the specific factual findings of the study, describing the data and patterns that emerged but refraining from any judgment or interpretation.

Discussion. The final section of a lab report examines whether or not the results support the hypothesis. It can be somewhat speculative, focusing on the possible implications and limitations of the experiment and its results. It may also point out the relationship of the current study to other researchers' results, suggest further hypotheses that could be tested, and draw theoretical conclusions.

If you have mentioned published sources in your report, you need to include a list of **references cited**. (See 64d2.)

64 d Documentation and format conventions: number systems

The life sciences (biology, botany, zoology), the applied sciences (chemistry, computer science, mathematics, and physics), and the medical sciences (medicine, nursing, general health) all use a number system of documentation.

1 Conventions for number citation

In the number system of citation, writers alert readers to the use of other sources by citing a number, either in parentheses or with a "superscript" (a character raised a small space above the baseline of the surrounding text: [2]); as you can see, superscript numbers are also typically reduced in size two or more points (a **point** is 1/72 inch) for a neater appearance. This citation number corresponds to a numbered list of sources at the end of the paper. Math and life science disciplines generally prefer parenthetical numbers; chemistry, physics, the medical fields, and computer science disciplines generally prefer superscript numbers.

If in using the number system you use an author's name in a sentence, place the number immediately after the name, if possible.

Linhoffer (3) reported similar results.

Linhoffer[3] reported similar results.

If no author's name is used in the sentence, place the number immediately after the use of the source material. Science writers, using parenthetical numbers, have the option of including the author's last name before the number: (Smith 3).

According to the conventions of scientific writing, the numbers cited in the text can be organized either sequentially or alphabetically. In **sequential arrangement**, the first source cited in the text is numbered "1," the second cited source is numbered "2," and so on. Any subsequent reference to an already-cited source is given the same number. Sequential reference is preferred by writers in chemistry, computer science, physics, the life sciences, and medicine.

In **alphabetic arrangement**, writers assign numbers according to the alphabetical order of the authors' last names as they appear on the reference page(s). For example, a reference to an author named Smith, even if the first source cited in the text, should be accompanied by the number "12" if Smith is the twelfth name on the alphabetical list of references. Alphabetical arrangement is preferred in mathematical writing.

When using the sequential system, number the bibliography sequentially as you write and continue to use the same number each time you cite that authority. When using the alphabetical system, arrange your bibliography alphabetically and number accordingly.

2 Conventions for the list of references

The "Literature Cited" or "References" section provides publication information for all sources cited in the text.

830 **Writing in the physical sciences**

Each scientific discipline has it own format for documenting sources; select the style appropriate to your discipline or consult your instructor. The following brief examples are illustrative only; they suggest that minor differences occur from discipline to discipline within scientific fields. Should you need to write a substantial paper in any of these disciplines, consult the appropriate reference source listed below.

Life sciences

Biology, botany, zoology, anatomy, and physiology follow the documentation system recommended in the *CBE Style Manual*, 6th ed. (New York: Cambridge University Press, 1994), published by the Council of Biology Editors. In-text number citations are given sequentially in parentheses. Title the list of references "Literature Cited," "References Cited," or "References," and use the following general styles.

BOOK ENTRIES

1. Winfree, A. T. The timing of biological clocks. 2nd ed. New York: Scientific American Library; 1987:102–110.

Do not underline titles, and capitalize only the first word. Place a semicolon after the name of the publisher, and place a colon after the date if page numbers are given. Leave no space(s) on either side of the colon.

PERIODICAL ENTRIES

2. Brown, S. G.; Wagsten, M. V. Socialization processes in a female lowland gorilla. Zoo Biol. 1986; 5(12):269–280.

Do not place in quotation marks or underline article or journal titles. Use no space(s) between volume and page numbers, and place an issue number, if required, immediately after the volume number, in parentheses.

Chemistry

Documentation style in chemistry is based on the American Chemical Society's *The ABC Style Guide: A Manual for Authors and Editors* (Washington, DC: American Chemical Society, 1986). In-text citations should be superscript numbers and arranged either sequentially or by author name and date. For entries on the reference list, which should be titled "Literature Cited," use the following general styles.

BOOK ENTRIES

1. Siggia, S.; Hanna, J. G. Quantitative Organic Analysis via Functional Groups, 4th ed.; R. E. Krieger: Malabar, FL, 1988; pp. 55–60.

PERIODICAL ENTRIES

2. Scott, J. M. W. J. Chem. Ed. 1992,69,600–602.

For papers in the chemistry style, do not include article titles. If an issue number is required, place it immediately after the volume number ("69" in this example), in parentheses. Leave no spaces between date, volume, and page numbers for periodicals, and use all digits for page sequences.

Physics

Physics writing follows the style of the *AIP Style Manual*, 4th ed. (New York: American Institute of Physics, 1990). Following this citation style, number in-text citations in sequence and in superscript. In the reference page, which is titled "References," use the following styles.

BOOK ENTRIES

[1] Pagels, H. R. Perfect Symmetry: The Search for the Beginning of Time (Bantam, New York, 1986), pp. 78–86.

PERIODICAL ENTRIES

[2] Crawford, F. S. Am. J. Phys. 60, 751–752 (1992).

In the physics system of citation, article titles are not included in the entries. If issue numbers are required, place them immediately after the volume number, in parentheses, and follow them with a comma. Place the date last, with single spaces between volume, page number(s), and date.

This chapter describes the aims, style, and common forms of writing in the business and professional world. Like writing in the social and physical sciences, business writing puts a premium on information; like writing in the humanities, it is highly influenced by the relation between writer and reader.

65 a   The aims of writing in business

The guiding objectives of successful companies are efficiency, accuracy, and responsibility: Procedures are designed for minimal waste of time and energy, care is taken to avoid errors, and transactions are conducted fairly.

Communication in business mirrors these precepts. Business writing is primarily practical and instrumental, because its goal is to get things done. For efficiency, it should be simple, direct, and brief; for accuracy, it should convey correct information and conform to standard conventions; and for responsibility, it should be honest and courteous.

Business writers must be aware of their audience. They must ask: To whom is the communication being written? What information do they already have? What else do they need to know? What does this communication need to include in order to have its intended effect? What, if any, secondary audience is likely to read this communication? Business writers must also be concerned about presentation. To make a good impression, any piece of writing must be neat, clean, and correct.

65 b   The style of writing in business

Because clear communication is highly valued, writing for business purposes should be simple, direct, economical, and conventional. In general, the preferred tone is objective and fairly formal (although when addressing someone you know well, a more personal, informal tone may be appropriate). For most business writing, the following guidelines should be considered.

I **Start fast**. State the main point immediately, and avoid digression or repetition. In business your reader's time—as well as your own—is valuable.

2 **Write in simple, direct syntax**. Keep your sentences as straightforward and readable as possible.

3 **Choose the active voice** (*start fast*) rather than the passive voice (*fast starting is a principle to be followed*).

4 **Use** technical terminology or **jargon sparingly**. Write out complete names of companies, products, and titles. Explain any terms that could be misunderstood.

5 **Avoid** emotional or obviously **biased language** (sexist, racist) as well as stereotypes and clichés. Try to maintain a level of courtesy even when lodging a complaint.

6 **Use numbers**, bullets, or descriptive headings to help readers locate information quickly.

7 **Use graphs**, charts, and other illustrations when they convey information more clearly than verbal language.

65 **c** **Common forms of writing in business**

Common forms of writing in business include letters, résumés, and memos.

I **Business letters**

Business letters commonly are written to request, inform, or complain, in many cases to an audience unknown to the letter writer. State the purpose clearly and provide all information needed to make responding easy for the reader.

Business letters are typed on $8\frac{1}{2}'' \times 11''$ paper, one side only. Most business letters use *block* format, in which every element of the letter is typed flush with the left margin and paragraphs are not indented. All business letters contain the following elements.

Heading. The sender's address (but not name) and the date are typed single-spaced approximately one inch from the top of the first page of the letter. Spell out all street and town names and months in full; abbreviate state names using the standard postal abbreviations. Zip codes should be included.

If you are using letterhead stationery, type the date two line spaces below the letterhead address.

Inside address. Type the recipient's address two or more line spaces below the heading (depending on how much space is needed to center the letter on the page). Include the person's full name (and a courtesy title, if appropriate), followed by his or her position (if needed), the name of the division within the company, the company name, and the full street, city, and state address.

When writing to an unknown person, always try to find out the name, perhaps by calling the company switchboard. If doing this is impossible, use an appropriate title (*Personnel Director* or *Claims Manager*, for example) in place of a name.

Greeting. Type the opening salutation two line spaces below the inside address (*Dear Dr. Jones, Dear James Wong*) followed by a colon. If you and the recipient are on a first-name basis, it is appropriate to use only the first name. If you do not know the recipient's name, use *To Whom It May Concern:* or some variation of *Dear Claims Manager:* or *Attention: Director of Marketing* (the latter without a second colon). Avoid the old-fashioned *Dear Sir* or *Dear Sir or Madam.*

Body. Begin the body of the letter two line spaces below the greeting. Single-space within paragraphs; double-space between paragraphs. If your reason for writing is clear and simple, state it directly in the first paragraph. If it is absolutely necessary to detail a situation, to provide background, or to supply context, do so in the first paragraph or two, and then move on to describe your purpose in writing.

If your letter is more than one page long, type the addressee's last name, the date, and the page number flush with the right margin of each subsequent page.

Closing. Type the complimentary closing two spaces after the last line of the body of the letter. The most common closings are *Sincerely, Cordially, Yours truly, Respectfully yours* (formal), and *Best regards* (informal). Capitalize only the first word of the closing; follow it with a comma.

Signature. Type your full name, including any title, four line spaces below the closing. Sign the letter with your full name (or just first name if you have addressed the recipient by first name) in blue or black ink in the space above your typed name.

Additional information. You may provide additional brief information below your signature, flush with the left margin. Such information may include recipients of copies of the letter (*cc: Jennifer Rodriguez*); the word *Enclosures* (or the abbreviation *enc.*)

Business letter: block format on letterhead

Doyle Advertising Services
1011 Oakhollow Road
Norman, OK 73071   **LETTERHEAD**
405-555-1966 telephone
405-555-1982 fax

October 11, 19XX   **DATE**

Ms. Tamara Blackburn
Marketing Director
Tamlyn Foods   **INSIDE**
6850 Amberly Way   **ADDRESS**
Cordova, TN 38018

Dear Ms. Blackburn: **GREETING**
                                BODY, UNINDENTED

Tony Adamo, your account representative, asked that I
give you an update about the direct mail campaign for
Tamlyn's Muffin Chips.

During the week of September 1, our direct mail contractor sent mailings to approximately 7,500 homes in
the Oklahoma City/Little Rock test markets. As you
know, these mailings contained a sample-size package
of the chips, along with a postage-paid questionnaire
that recipients could return to receive a cents-off
coupon for other Tamlyn products.

As of October 9, 2,267 questionnaires had been returned, a very high response rate. We are currently
compiling the questionnaire results and should have
a formal report ready for you by October 15. The
cents-off coupons will be mailed out October 22.

If you have any other questions, please give me a
call at extension 557.

Sincerely,   **CLOSING**

Casey Dorris   **SIGNATURE**

Casey Dorris
Direct Mail Coordinator

Cover letter

405 Martin Street
Lexington, Kentucky 40508   **HEADING**
February 10, 19xx

Barbara McGarry, Director
Kentucky Council on the Arts **INSIDE ADDRESS**
953 Versailles Road
Box 335
Frankfort, Kentucky 40602

Dear Ms. McGarry: **GREETING**
                                                    BODY, UNINDENTED
John Huff, one of my professors at the University
of Kentucky, recommended that I write to you regarding openings in the Council's internship program
this summer. I would like to apply for one of these
positions and have enclosed my résumé for your consideration.

As you will note, my academic background combines a
primary concentration in business administration
with a minor in the fine arts. My interest in the
arts goes back to childhood when I first heard a
performance by the Lexington Symphony, and I have
continued to pursue that interest ever since. My
goal after graduation is a career in arts administration, focusing on fundraising and outreach for a
major public institution.

I hope you'll agree that my experience, particularly
my work with the local Community Concerts association, is strong preparation for an internship with
the Council. I would appreciate the opportunity to
discuss my qualifications with you in greater detail.

I will call your office within the next few weeks
to see about setting up an appointment to meet with
you. In the meantime, you can reach me at the above
address or by phone at 555-4033.

Thank you for your attention.

Sincerely,   **CLOSING**

Chris Aleandro   **SIGNATURE**

Chris Aleandro
enc.   **ADDITIONAL INFORMATION**

to indicate you are also enclosing additional material mentioned in the letter; and, if the letter was typed by someone other than the writer, both the writer's and the typist's initials (*TF/jlw*).

2 Résumés

A résumé is a brief summary of an applicant's qualifications for employment. It outlines education, work experience, and other activities and interests so a prospective employer can decide quickly whether or not an applicant is a good prospect for a particular job. Try to tailor your résumé for the position you are seeking by emphasizing experience that is most relevant to the position. Preparing a résumé on a computer lets you revise it easily and quickly.

Generally, a résumé is sent out with a cover letter that introduces the applicant, indicates the position applied for, and offers additional information that cannot be accommodated on the résumé itself. Examples of a résumé and cover letter appear on pages 838 and 836, respectively.

Résumés should be brief and to the point, preferably no more than a page long (if relevant experience is extensive, more than one page is acceptable). Résumé formats vary in minor ways, but most include the following information.

Personal information. Résumés begin with the applicant's name, address, and phone number, usually centered at the top.

Objective. Many résumés include a line summarizing the applicant's objective, naming either the specific job sought or describing a larger career goal.

Education. Most first-time job applicants list their educational background first, since their employment history is likely to be fairly limited. Name the last two or three schools attended (including dates of attendance and degrees), starting with the most recent. Indicate major areas of study, and highlight any relevant courses. Also consider including grade point average, awards, and anything else that shows you in a good light. When employment history is more detailed, educational background is often placed at the end of the résumé.

Work experience. Starting with the most recent, list all relevant jobs, including company name, dates of employment, and a brief job description. Use your judgment about listing jobs where you had difficulties with your employer.

Special skills or interests. It is often useful to mention special skills, interests, or activities that provide additional clues about your abilities and personality.

Résumé

Chris Aleandro
405 Martin Street
Lexington, Kentucky 40508
(606) 555-4033

Objective: Internship in arts administration.

Education

University of Kentucky: 1995 to present.
Currently a sophomore majoring in business administration with a minor in art history. Degree
expected May 1999.

Henry Clay High School (Lexington, KY): 1991 to 1995.
College preparatory curriculum, with emphasis
in art and music.

Related Work Experience

Community Concerts, Inc.: 1997 to present.
Part-time promotion assistant, reporting to local
director. Responsibilities include assisting with
scheduling, publicity, subscription/ticketing
procedures, and fund-raising. Position involves
general office duties as well as heavy contact
with subscribers and artists.

Habitat for Humanity: September to November 1997.
Co-chaired campus fundraising drive that included a benefit concert, raising $55,000.

Art in the Schools Program: 1995-1997.
Volunteer, through the Education Division of the
Lexington Center for the Arts. Trained to conduct hands-on art appreciation presentations in
grade school classrooms, visiting one school a
month.

Other Work Experience

Record City: 1994 to 1996 (part time and summers).
Sales clerk and assistant manager in a music
store.

Special skills: WordPerfect 5.1; desktop design of
brochures, programs, and other materials.

References

Professor John Huff	Ms. Joan Thomas
School of Business	Community Concerts,
Administration	Inc.
The University of Kentucky	1200 Fayette Street
Lexington, KY 40506	Lexington, KY 40513
(606) 555-3110	(606) 555-2900

References. Provide the names, addresses, and phone numbers of two or three people—teachers, supervisors, employers—whom you trust to give a good reference for you. (Make sure you get their permission first.) You may want instead to conclude with the line "References available on request."

3 Memos

Memo is short for *memorandum*, which is defined as a short note or reminder to someone to do something. Memos are used in business and college offices to suggest that actions be taken or to alert one or more people about a change in policy or an upcoming meeting. Part of the value of the memo is that the memo writer retains a record (a memory) that something was communicated to certain people on such and such a date.

Memo format is simple and direct. Names of both receiver and sender, along with the date and subject, are included at the top of the page so that the receiver knows instantly what this message is about:

Date flush right

To: name of person or persons to whom it will be sent

From: name of memo sender

Re: regarding what subject

Following is a typical memo:

January 25, 1996

To: Nancy, Bill, and Sue

From: Albert

Re: Curriculum Committee meeting

Our last meeting will be Tuesday (1/27) at 3:30 p.m. in Old Mill, room 117. The agenda is to plan discussion items for the spring semester.

65 d Documentation and format conventions

The format and style of documentation for business reports usually follow the guidelines of the American Psychological Association. (See 63d.)

PART NINE

A Grammar Reference

There are two basic approaches to English grammar. One looks at individual words and asks, "What kind of word is this?" This question leads to a consideration of words as **parts of speech**: nouns, pronouns, verbs, adjectives, prepositions, conjunctions, and interjections. The other approach examines sentence organization and asks, "What function does each word or group of words serve in the sentence?" This question leads to an analysis of **sentence elements**.

What part of speech a word is depends on its meaning and position in a sentence. Some words change parts depending on the context in which they appear. The word *ride*, for example, can be either a verb or a noun.

NOUN   They went for a *ride*.

VERB   They *ride* their horses.

To know what part of speech a word is, you must look not only at the word itself but also at its relation to other words in the sentence.

66 a Nouns

Nouns are words that name persons, animals, places, things, or ideas: *woman, Lassie, Grand Canyon, tree,* and *virtue* are all nouns.

Proper nouns name particular people, animals, places, or things: *Marie Curie, Black Beauty, Kentucky, USS Constitution, Catholicism.* They are almost always capitalized. (See 51c.) **Generic nouns,** or **common nouns,** can apply to any member of a class or group: *scientist, horse, state, ship, religion.* They are generally not capitalized.

Concrete nouns refer to things that can be seen, heard, touched, smelled, or tasted: *butterfly, telephone, ice, fudge.*

Abstract nouns refer to ideas or concepts that cannot be directly sensed: *nature, communication, temperature, temptation.* (For the uses of concrete and abstract nouns, see 28a.)

Count nouns refer to one or more individual items that can readily be counted: *one book, two books.* Count nouns usually name something concrete, though some are abstract: *one idea, several ideas.* **Noncount nouns** (or **mass nouns**) refer to entities that cannot be counted individually: *sand, water, oil.* These are seldom made plural.

Collective nouns, such as *crowd, couple,* and *flock,* refer to groups of similar things.

1 Singular and plural nouns

Nouns that refer to a single unit are **singular**: *boy, town, box.* Those that refer to two or more are **plural**: *boys, towns, boxes.*

Most nouns add *-s* or *-es* to the singular to create the plural. A few nouns change spelling in other ways to form the plural: *goose, geese; child, children; man, men; medium, media.* And a few stay the same regardless of number: *sheep, sheep.* Noncount nouns are almost never plural. (For more on forming plurals, see 47b.)

2 Possessive forms of nouns

Nouns change form to show possession, ownership, or connections, usually by adding an apostrophe and an *-s*: *the king's son, the town's mayor.* This form is called the **possessive case.** (For guidelines on forming possessives of plural nouns and nouns that end in *-s*, see 47a.)

66 b Pronouns

A **pronoun** is a word that substitutes for a noun or another pronoun. The word for which the pronoun substitutes is called its **antecedent.**

        antecedent   pronoun

Sean helped ⌐Aspasia¬ paint ⌐her¬ room.

       pronoun   antecedent

Because of ⌐its¬ construction, the ⌐boat¬ was unsinkable.

Usually an antecedent appears before the pronoun, but it may also follow shortly after the pronoun. (For a description of pronoun reference to clear antecedents, see 40a.) A pronoun must agree with (or correspond to) its antecedent in terms of person, number, and gender. (See Chapter 39.)

1 Kinds of pronouns

Personal pronouns

Personal pronouns, such as *me, you, their,* and *it,* refer to specific people, animals, places, things, or ideas.

I asked *you* to buy *it.*

Personal pronouns change their form to show **person.** First-person pronouns refer to the speaker or writer directly: *I, we.* Second-person pronouns refer to those being addressed: *you.* Third-person pronouns refer to someone other than the speaker or writer or those being addressed: *he, she, it, they.*

Personal pronouns also change form to show **number.** They are either singular (*I, he, she, it*) or plural (*we, they*). The pronoun *you* is the same whether it is plural or singular.

Singular personal pronouns change form to show **gender.** They are masculine (*he*), feminine (*she*), or neuter (*it*).

Personal pronouns also change form to show **case.** (See Chapter 41.)

Indefinite pronouns

Indefinite pronouns, such as *anyone, everybody, something, many, few,* and *none,* do not require an antecedent because they do not refer to any specific person, animal, place, thing, or idea. Often they are used to denote a quantity.

Many are called, but *few* are chosen.

Indefinite pronouns change form to indicate the possessive case by adding an apostrophe and an *-s: anyone's idea, everyone's preference.* They do not change form to show person, number, or gender. Most are either always singular (*someone*) or always plural (*many*). A few can be either singular or plural, depending on the context. (See 40d.)

Demonstrative pronouns

Demonstrative pronouns, such as *this*, *that*, *these*, and *those*, are used to identify or point out a specific person, place, or thing.

This is the largest one we have.

Demonstrative pronouns change form to show **number**: *this* and *that* are singular; *these* and *those* are plural.

These words are demonstrative pronouns only when they are not immediately followed by a noun, in which case they are adjectives: *I enjoyed reading this book.*

Relative pronouns

A relative pronoun, such as *who*, *which*, or *that*, introduces a dependent clause and "relates" that clause to an antecedent elsewhere in the sentence.

He chose the tool *that* worked best.

Some relative pronouns are also indefinite: *whoever*, *what*, *whatever*, *whichever*. Relative pronouns change form to show case. (See 66b2.)

Interrogative pronouns

Interrogative pronouns, such as *who*, *what*, and *whose*, are used to ask questions. They change form only to show case.

Who is there?

Reflexive and intensive pronouns

Pronouns ending in *-self*, or *-selves*, such as *myself*, *yourself*, and *themselves*, are **reflexive pronouns** when they refer back to, or "reflect," the subject of the sentence.

Dave cut *himself* while shaving.

The same pronouns are called **intensive pronouns** when they are used to emphasize, or "intensify," an antecedent.

I talked to the president *herself*.

846 Parts of speech

Unlike reflexive pronouns, intensive pronouns can be omitted without changing the sense of the sentence: *I talked to the president.*

Reflexive and intensive pronouns change form to show **person, number,** and **gender,** just as personal pronouns do.

PRONOUNS

PERSONAL
I, me, my, mine	it, its
you, your, yours	we, us, our, ours
he, him, his	they, them, their, theirs
she, her, hers	

INDEFINITE
all	each	many	none	some
any	either	more	no one	somebody
anybody	everybody	most	nothing	someone
anyone	everyone	much	one	something
anything	everything	neither	several	what
both	few	nobody		

DEMONSTRATIVE
this	that	these	those

RELATIVE
that	whatever	whichever	whoever	whomever
what	which	who	whom	whose

INTERROGATIVE
what	which	who	whom	whose
whatever	whichever	whoever	whomever	

REFLEXIVE AND INTENSIVE
myself	yourself	himself	herself	itself
ourselves	yourselves	themselves	oneself	

RECIPROCAL
each other	one another

Reciprocal pronouns

The reciprocal pronouns *each other* and *one another* are used to describe an action or state that is shared between two people, animals, places, things, or ideas.

The investigators helped *one another* with the research.

Reciprocal pronouns have possessive forms: *each other's*, *one another's*. Otherwise, they do not change form.

2 Pronoun case

Case indicates the role a word plays in a sentence, whether it is a subject, an object, or a possessive. To show the possessive case, nouns change form, usually by adding an apostrophe and -s to the end of the word. In the subjective and objective cases, nouns have the same form. Personal pronouns, indefinite pronouns, and the relative or interrogative pronouns *who* and *whoever* change form to show all three cases. Indefinite pronouns change form to show the possessive case by adding an apostrophe and -s, as nouns do.

subject	possessive	object
⌐Anne⌐ took	⌐Betty's⌐ book away from	⌐Michelle.⌐
She took	hers away from	her.

SUBJECTIVE		OBJECTIVE		POSSESSIVE	
SINGULAR	**PLURAL**	**SINGULAR**	**PLURAL**	**SINGULAR**	**PLURAL**
I	we	me	us	my, mine	our, ours
you	you	you	you	your, yours	your, yours
he	they	him	them	his	their, theirs
she	they	her	them	her, hers	their, theirs
it	they	it	them	its	their, theirs
who		whom		whose	
whoever		whomever			

The **subjective case** indicates that a pronoun is the subject of a clause or is a subject complement.

We should leave now.

It was *she who* wanted to leave.

The **objective case** indicates that a pronoun is the object of a verb, a preposition, or a verbal.

Whom did they choose?

The judging seemed unfair to *us*.

Seeing *her* made the holiday complete.

The **possessive case** indicates possession, ownership, or connection. Possessive personal pronouns have two forms: adjective forms (*my, your*) modify a noun or gerund; noun forms (*mine, yours*) stand alone as a subject or complement.

That is *my* hat.

The hat is *mine*.

(For more on choosing pronoun case, see Chapter 41.)

66 c Verbs

A **verb** describes an action or state of being.

The logger *chops* the tree.

The air *is* fragrant with the scent of pine.

The verb of a sentence changes form to show person, number, tense, voice, and mood. The **person** indicates who performed the action. The **number** indicates how many people performed the action. The **tense** indicates when the action was performed. The **voice** indicates whether the grammatical subject of the sentence acts or is acted upon. The **mood** indicates the speaker's reaction to or opinion of the action.

PERSON   I *write,* she *writes*

NUMBER   he *sings,* they *sing*

TENSE   she *argues,* she *argued*

VOICE   she *read* the book, the book *was read*

MOOD   I *am* a millionaire, if I *were* a millionaire

A verb with a specific person and number is called a **finite verb**. A verb form without these properties is called a **verbal**.

(See 66c5.) For complete information on verb person, number, tense, and mood, see Chapter 35. For information on verb voice, see 66c4.

In addition to one-word verbs, English has many **phrasal verbs** or **multiple-word verbs**. These consist of a verb plus a **particle**, a word that may serve as a preposition in other contexts but which is so important to the meaning of the phrasal verb that it is considered a part of it. Both the verb and the particle are necessary to convey the meaning of the phrasal verb, and that meaning usually cannot be determined by examining the parts individually. In the sentence, *That performance came off very well*, for example, *came off* is a phrasal verb; its meaning (*succeeded*) is not easy to determine by considering the separate meanings of the words *come* and *off*.

1 Auxiliary verbs

One sentence may have several verbs in it. The verb that expresses the action or state of the subject of the sentence is the **main verb**.

main verb

After swimming for an hour, he ⌐decided¬ to go home.

In some cases, the main verb of a sentence is preceded by one or more **auxiliary verbs** (or **helping verbs**). Together, the main verb and its auxiliaries form a **verb phrase**.

verb phrase

auxiliary verb   main verb

My oldest sister ⌐was⌐doing¬ a crossword puzzle.

Forms of the verbs *be*, *do*, and *have* are the most common auxiliary verbs. These auxiliaries are used to form certain tenses, add emphasis, ask questions, make negative statements, and form the passive voice. These verbs can also stand alone as main verbs. When used as auxiliaries, these verbs change to show person, number, and tense.

Certain auxiliary verbs, called **modal auxiliaries** or **modals**, add to the verb the meanings of desire, intent, permission, possibility, or obligation. Modals are not usually used alone as main verbs. English has both one-word modals and phrasal modals (or multiple-word modals).

850 Parts of speech

ONE-WORD MODALS

can	may	must	should	would
could	might	shall	will	

PHRASAL MODALS

be able to	be supposed to	have got to
be allowed to	had better	ought to
be going to	have to	used to

The one-word modals do not change form to show person, number, or tense: *I can sing, and you can dance.* Most of the phrasal modals do change form to show person, number, and tense: *I am able to sing, and you are able to dance.* The phrasal modals *had better, ought to,* and *used to* do not change form.

2 **Transitive and intransitive verbs**

Some verbs require a **direct object**, a word or words that indicate who or what received the action of the verb. (See 67c.)

direct object

She threw the ⌐ball.⌐

A verb that has a direct object is a **transitive verb.** A verb that does not have a direct object is an **intransitive verb.** Many verbs may be transitive or intransitive, depending on the context.

TRANSITIVE   Joey *grew* tomatoes last summer.

INTRANSITIVE   The tomatoes *grew* rapidly.

3 **Linking verbs**

Linking verbs include *be, become, seem,* and verbs describing sensations—*appear, look, feel, taste, smell, sound,* and so on. They link the subject of a sentence to an element, called a **subject complement**, that renames or identifies the subject. Subject complements can be nouns or adjectives. (See 67d.)

A linking verb, like an equal sign, links two equivalent terms.

Sue *is* nice.	Sue = nice
They *felt* tired.	they = tired
Jake *was* a recent graduate.	Jake = a recent graduate

4 Voice

Most transitive verbs may be used in either the active or the passive voice. In a sentence using the **active voice**, the subject of the sentence is the person or thing performing the action or state expressed by the verb. In a sentence using the **passive voice**, the subject of the sentence is the person or thing acted upon.

ACTIVE   The woman pushes the baby carriage.

PASSIVE   The baby carriage is pushed by the woman.

The passive voice is formed by using the past participle of the verb with a form of the verb *be* as an auxiliary verb. (See 66c1.) The object of the sentence in the active voice becomes the subject of the passive voice sentence. The subject of the active voice sentence, if it appears at all in the passive voice sentence, is usually an **agent** following the preposition *by*: *Movies are often seen by teenagers.* Some passive voice sentences do not have agents: *Movies are often seen at night.*

5 Verbals

A **verbal** is a special verb form. It does not change form to show person or number. There are three types of verbals.

1   **Infinitives:** the base form of the verb, usually preceded by the word *to*

2   **Gerunds:** the -ing form of the verb, functioning as a noun

3   **Participles:** either the past participle (usually ending in -ed or -d) or the present participle (ending in -ing)

The infinitive changes form to show tense.

PRESENT   *To sing* at Carnegie Hall is her ambition.
INFINITIVE

PAST   *To have sung* so well last night is something you
INFINITIVE   should be proud of.

After prepositions and certain verbs, the *to* of an infinitive does not appear: *He did everything except wash the floor. She let them visit their cousins.*

A verbal can function as a noun, an adjective, or an adverb, but it cannot function as the main verb of a sentence or clause.

NOUN *Jogging* is a great form of exercise.

ADJECTIVE We had *boiled* eggs for breakfast.

ADVERB This machine was designed *to self-destruct.*

Verbals can form **verbal phrases** by taking objects, complements, and modifiers. For more on verbal phrases, see 67e.

66 d Adjectives and adverbs

Adjectives and **adverbs** modify—that is, they further describe, identify, or limit the meaning of other words. They have many similar properties, so sometimes adjectives and adverbs are grouped together as **modifiers**. The difference between them lies in what they modify. Adjectives modify nouns, pronouns, or phrases and clauses used as nouns.

The tourist spotted *scarlet* tanagers. [Modifies noun *tanagers.*]

They were *beautiful.* [Modifies pronoun *they.*]

To see them would be *delightful.* [Modifies phrase *to see them.*]

Adverbs modify verbs, adjectives, verbals, or other adverbs; they can also modify clauses or entire sentences.

His judgment was made *hastily.* [Modifies verb *was made.*]

The feathers are *quite* beautiful. [Modifies adjective *beautiful.*]

Writing *well* takes practice. [Modifies verbal *writing.*]

She sings *very* nicely. [Modifies adverb *nicely.*]

Surprisingly, the band played for hours. [Modifies entire sentence.]

See 37a for more on distinguishing adjectives and adverbs.

Adjectives and adverbs come in three **degrees:** positive, comparative, and superlative. A modifier that makes no comparison is known as the **positive** form. A **comparative** adjective or adverb makes a comparison between two things. A **superlative** adjective or adverb distinguishes among three or more things.

POSITIVE   He lives in an *old* house.

COMPARATIVE   It is *older* than mine.

SUPERLATIVE   It is the *oldest* house in the county.

See 37e for more on forming comparatives and superlatives.

1 **Kinds of adjectives**

Adjectives that describe qualities or attributes are called **descriptive adjectives:** *gray* sky, *beautiful* garden. Adjectives that do not describe qualities but instead identify or specify the words they modify are called **limiting adjectives:** *this* sky, *my* garden.

Limiting adjectives include the **articles** *a*, *an*, and *the*. The word *the* is called the **definite article** because it identifies, or "defines," precisely which person or thing is being referred to. The words *a* and *an* are called **indefinite articles**. The choice between *a* and *an* depends on the initial sound of the following word: *a* precedes a consonant sound or a long *u* sound *(a monster, a university)* and *an* precedes any other vowel sound *(an apron)*.

Several types of **pronouns** can serve as limiting adjectives.

PERSONAL   She is going to buy *her* dog today.

RELATIVE   She hasn't decided *which* dog she will take.

DEMONSTRATIVE   She likes *that* dog very much.

INDEFINITE   But *every* dog looks good to her.

These words are considered adjectives only when they are directly followed by a noun. (See 66a.) **Numbers** can also be limiting adjectives when they are directly followed by a noun: *two dogs*.

Adjectives derived from proper nouns are called **proper adjectives**: *Alaskan, Shakespearean, British*. Like proper nouns, proper adjectives are always capitalized. (See 51c.)

Sometimes a noun is used as an adjective without any change of form. Such a noun is called a **noun modifier**.

He works as a *masonry* contractor and employs six *stone* masons.

The police dispersed the rioters with a *water* cannon.

2 Kinds of adverbs

In addition to the usual kind of descriptive adverb (*quickly, often*) there are several special groups of words that are classified as adverbs. The **negators** *no* and *not* are considered adverbs. **Conjunctive adverbs**, such as *however* and *therefore*, modify an entire clause and express its relationship to another clause. (For a list of common conjunctive adverbs, see Chapter 26.) **Relative adverbs**, such as *where, why*, and *when*, introduce adjective or adverb clauses. (See 67f.)

NEGATOR We were *not* ready.

CONJUNCTIVE ADVERB *However*, the train was leaving.

RELATIVE ADVERB We were visiting the house *where* I grew up.

66 e Prepositions

Words such as *to, with, by*, and *of* are **prepositions**. In addition to one-word prepositions such as these, English has several **phrasal prepositions** or **multiple-word prepositions**, which are made up of two or more words: *because of, except for, instead of.*

A preposition shows the relationship between a noun or pronoun—the **object** of the preposition—and other words in the sentence. The preposition, its object, and any associated modifiers are together called a **prepositional phrase**. In the sentence *I sat on the bed*, for example, *on* is a preposition, *bed* is the object of the preposition, and *on the bed* is a prepositional phrase. (For more on prepositional phrases, see 67e.)

A word is a preposition only if it introduces a phrase containing an object. Words that are commonly used as prepositions may also function as adverbs and as particles (parts of phrasal verbs).

PREPOSITION I looked *up* the street.

ADVERB The woman looked *up*.

PARTICLE He looked *up* the word in the dictionary.

(For more on adverbs, see 66d. For more on phrasal verbs, see 66c.)

 COMMON PREPOSITIONS

aboard	beneath	including	past
about	beside	in front of	regarding
above	besides	inside	since
according to	between	inside of	through
across	beyond	in spite of	throughout
after	but	into	till
against	by	like	to
ahead of	concerning	near	together with
along with	despite	next to	toward
among	down	notwithstanding	under
apart from	due to	of	underneath
around	during	off	unlike
as	except	on	until
as for	except for	onto	up
at	for	on top of	upon
away from	from	other than	up to
because of	in	out	via
before	in addition to	out of	with
behind	in back of	outside	within
below	in case of	over	without

---

66 **f** **Conjunctions**

The word **conjunction** comes from Latin words meaning "join" and "with." Conjunctions join two or more words, phrases, or clauses with one another. The **coordinating conjunctions**—*and, but, or, nor, for, so,* and *yet*—imply that the elements linked are equal or similar in importance.

Bill *and* I went shopping.

The bus will take you to the market *or* to the theater.

Correlative conjunctions always appear in pairs: *either . . . or, neither . . . nor, both . . . and, not only . . . but also, whether . . . or.* Correlative conjunctions join pairs of similar words, phrases, or clauses.

Neither Jack *nor* his brother was in school this morning.

She *not only* sings *but also* dances.

Subordinating conjunctions, such as *after, before, when, where, while, because, if, although,* and *unless,* introduce ideas in dependent clauses that are less important to the point of the passage than the ideas in main or independent clauses. (See 26b for a complete list of subordinating conjunctions.)

While you finish sewing, I will start dinner.

I left *because* I was angry.

Conjunctive adverbs, such as *however, therefore,* and *furthermore,* link independent clauses. The clauses they link must be separated by a semicolon or a period. (See 34b2 and 45a.)

I am finished; *therefore,* I am going home.

66 g Interjections

Interjections are words inserted, or "interjected," into a sentence. They may show surprise, dismay, or strong emotion. They most often appear in speech or dialogue, and their presence often calls for an exclamation point.

Ouch! That pipe is hot!

Gosh, you're muddy all over!

Yes, it does.

The principal elements of a sentence are the subject and the predicate. In general, the **subject** names who or what performs the action of the sentence or, if there is no action, whom or what the sentence is about. (Exceptions are sentences with verbs in the passive voice or the imperative mood. See 66c4.) The subject consists of a noun, a pronoun, or another word or group of words that can serve as a noun, along with all of its modifiers. The **predicate** contains the verb of the sentence, along with its objects, its modifiers, and any words that refer back to it. Both subject and predicate can be one word or many:

> predicate
>
> subject |
>
> ⌐Rain⌐fell.⌐

>   subject   predicate
>
> ⌐A women in a yellow raincoat⌐ran to catch the bus.⌐

As in these examples, the subject usually comes at the beginning of a sentence and the predicate at the end. Sometimes, as in questions, the subject may follow part of the predicate.

>   predicate
>
> ⌐subject⌐
>
> ⌐Do⌐you⌐know a good roofing contractor?⌐

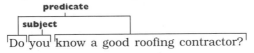

67 a   Subjects

Simple subject. The simple subject of a sentence is the person or thing that acts, is described, or is acted upon. Usually this is a noun or pronoun, but it can also be a verbal, a phrase, or a clause that is used as a noun.

NOUN   Long *shadows* crept along the lawn.

PRONOUN   *He* looked exactly like a cowboy.

VERBAL   *Singing* pleases Alan.

PHRASE   *To work hard* is our lot in life.

CLAUSE   *That LeeAnn could dance* amazed us all.

Complete subject. The complete subject consists of the simple subject and all words that modify or directly relate to it. Elements of a complete subject can be adjectives, adverbs, phrases, or clauses.

> *Winning the last game of a dreadful season that included injuries, losing streaks, and a strike* was small consolation to the team.

In this example, the simple subject is the gerund *Winning*. *The last game* is the object of *Winning*; the prepositional phrase *of a dreadful season* modifies *game*; and the clause *that included injuries, losing streaks, and a strike* modifies *season*.

Compound subject. A compound subject includes two or more subjects linked by a coordinating conjunction such as *and* or *or.*

> *Books, records,* and *videotapes* filled the room.

Implied subject. An implied subject is one that is not stated directly but may be understood.

> Come to the meeting to learn about the preschool program.

In this example, the subject is understood to be *you.* Commands with verbs in the imperative mood often have the implied subject *you.*

67 b   Predicates

Simple predicate. The simple predicate consists of the main verb of the sentence and any auxiliaries.

> The candidate who wins the debate *will win* the election.

Complete predicate. The complete predicate consists of the simple predicate and all words that modify or directly relate to it. Objects and complements are part of the predicate. Modifiers, including phrases, clauses, and single words, are part of the predicate if they modify the verb, object, or complement.

The farmer *gave the pigs enough food to last the weekend.*

The verb *gave* is the simple predicate. *Food* is the direct object of the verb and *pigs* is the indirect object of the verb. (See 67c.) The words *the* and *enough* modify *pigs* and *food,* respectively. The phrase *to last the weekend* also modifies *food.*

Compound predicate. A predicate in which two or more verbs have the same subject is a compound predicate. The following sentence has four verbs with the same subject.

At the beach we *ate* our picnic, *swam* in the surf, *read* to each other, and *walked* on the sand.

Ate, swam, read, and *walked* all have the subject *we.*

67 **c** **Objects of verbs**

A **direct object** completes the meaning of a transitive verb.

The company paid its *workers* earlier than usual.

Without the direct object *workers* and its modifiers, this sentence would be incomplete. If you read *The company paid,* you would not think it was a complete sentence expressing a complete thought. You would ask, *Whom or what did the company pay?* Asking a *Whom?* or *What?* question about the subject and verb of a sentence is a good way to find its direct object. (For more on transitive verbs, see 66c2.)

An **indirect object** is a person or thing to whom (or for whom) the action of the verb is directed. It must be a noun or a pronoun that precedes the direct object. It cannot be accompanied by a preposition (or it becomes the object of the preposition, not the object of the verb).

indirect object   direct object

The quarterback threw Lionel Fischer the ball.

To find an indirect object, identify the verb and the direct object and ask *To or for whom?* or *To or for what?* The answer is the indirect object. *He threw the ball to whom?* He threw it to *Lionel Fischer.*

67 d Complements

A **complement** renames or describes a subject or an object. A complement can be a noun, a pronoun, or an adjective.

A **subject complement** renames or describes the subject of a sentence. It follows a **linking verb**, a verb such as *be*, *become*, *seem*, or *appear*. (See 66c3.) A linking verb can be thought of as an equal sign, linking two equivalent terms. Whatever is on the left of the equal sign, before the linking verb, is the subject; whatever is on the right is the subject complement.

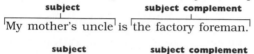

      subject   subject complement
My mother's uncle is the factory foreman.

      subject   subject complement
The factory foreman is my mother's uncle.

An **object complement** appears following a direct object, modifying it or renaming it.

Tonight we will paint the town *red.*

In this example, the adjective *red* describes the direct object *town.*

A noun or pronoun used as a complement is sometimes called a **predicate noun**. An adjective used as a complement is sometimes called a **predicate adjective**.

67 e Phrases

A group of related words lacking a subject, a predicate, or both is a **phrase**.

Verb phrase

A verb phrase consists of the main verb of a clause and its auxiliaries. It functions as the verb of a sentence.

           verb phrase
The college has been having a difficult year.

Noun phrase

A noun phrase consists of a noun, a pronoun, or an infinitive or gerund serving as a noun, and all its modifiers.

noun phrase

⌐The venerable and well-known institution˺ is bankrupt.

Noun phrases may function as subjects, objects, or complements.

SUBJECT   *The college's president* is distraught.

OBJECT   He addressed *the board of trustees.*

COMPLEMENT They became *a terrified mob.*

Prepositional phrase

A prepositional phrase consists of a preposition, its object, and any related modifiers.

prepositional phrase

The new book was hailed ⌐with great fanfare.˺

A prepositional phrase may function as an adjective or an adverb.

ADJECTIVE   He knows the difficulty *of the task.*

ADVERB   She arrived *at work* a little early.

Modifier phrase

A modifier phrase is any phrase that functions in a sentence as an adjective or an adverb. Prepositional phrases, infinitive phrases, participial phrases, and absolute phrases can be modifier phrases. Appositive phrases are sometimes considered modifier phrases.

Verbal phrase

A verbal phrase is one that contains a verbal plus any objects, complements, or modifiers. There are three kinds of verbals: infinitives, gerunds, and participles. (See 66c5.)

An **infinitive phrase** is one built around an infinitive, the base form of the verb usually preceded by *to.* Infinitive phrases can function as nouns, adjectives, or adverbs. When they function as nouns, they are usually subjects, complements, or direct objects.

862 **The elements of a sentence**

NOUN   *To raise a family* is a lofty goal.

ADJECTIVE   He has the duty *to protect his children.*

ADVERB   My father worked *to provide for his family.*

A **gerund phrase** is one built around a gerund, the *-ing* form of a verb functioning as a noun. Gerund phrases always function as nouns; they are usually subjects, subject complements, direct objects, or the objects of prepositions.

SUBJECT   *Studying these essays* takes a lot of time.

SUBJECT COMPLEMENT   The key to success is *reading all the assignments.*

DIRECT OBJECT   My roommate likes *reading novels.*

OBJECT OF PREPOSITION   She can forgive me *for preferring short stories.*

A **participial phrase** is one built around a participle, either the past participle (usually ending in *-ed* or *-d*) or the present participle (ending in *-ing*). A participial phrase always functions as an adjective.

ADJECTIVE   *Striking a blow for freedom,* the Minutemen fired the "shot heard round the world."

Appositive phrase

An appositive appears directly after a noun or pronoun and renames or further identifies it. (See 41b and 44c3.)

appositive phrase

Ralph Nader, ⌐a long-time consumer advocate,⌐ supports the new auto emissions proposal.

Absolute phrase

An absolute phrase modifies an entire sentence or clause. It consists of a noun or pronoun and a participle, together with any accompanying modifiers, objects, or complements.

absolute phrase

⌐The work done,⌐ the boss called for a celebration.

67 f Clauses

Any group of related words with a subject and a predicate is a **clause**. A clause that can stand alone as a complete sentence is called an **independent clause** or a **main clause**.

The moon rose.

The best candidate will win the election.

A clause that cannot stand by itself as a complete sentence is called a **dependent clause** or a **subordinate clause**. It is dependent because it is introduced by a subordinating word, usually either a subordinating conjunction (such as *because, when, unless*) or a relative pronoun (such as *who, which,* or *that*). (For lists of subordinating conjunctions and relative pronouns, see 26b.)

The little girl laughed *when the moon rose.*

I know *that the best candidate will win the election.*

Dependent clauses must be joined to independent clauses. They can be classified by the role they play in the sentence: they may be used as nouns, adjectives, or adverbs.

Noun clause

A noun clause is used as a noun would be—as a subject, an object, or a subject complement. A noun clause is usually introduced by a relative pronoun (such as *who, what,* or *which*) or by the subordinating conjunctions *how, when, where, whether,* or *why.*

SUBJECT   *What I want* is a good job.

DIRECT OBJECT   In class we learned *how we should write our résumés.*

OBJECT OF PREPOSITION   We wondered to *whom we should send them.*

SUBJECT COMPLEMENT   English history is *what I know best.*

864 The elements of a sentence

Adjective clause

An adjective clause modifies a noun or pronoun elsewhere in the sentence. Most adjective clauses begin with relative pronouns such as *who, whose,* or *that.* They can also begin with the relative adverbs *when, where,* or *why.* Adjective clauses are sometimes called **relative clauses**.

Because adjective clauses and noun clauses are introduced by similar words, they are often confused. Remember that a noun clause functions as a noun, while an adjective clause modifies a noun or pronoun. To determine if a dependent clause is an adjective clause, look for the noun or pronoun it modifies. Usually, an adjective clause directly follows the word it modifies.

The book that you reserved is now available.

The graduating seniors, who had just completed their exams, were full of high spirits.

Adjective clauses, along with adverb clauses, are also known as **modifier clauses.**

Adverb clause

An adverb clause modifies a verb, an adjective, an adverb, or an entire clause. Adverb clauses tell when, where, why, or how, or they specify a condition. They are introduced by subordinating conjunctions (such as *although, than,* or *since*).

The fish ride the tide as far as it will carry them.

Now they can be caught more easily than at any other time.

Adverb clauses, along with adjective clauses, are also known as **modifier clauses.**

Elliptical clauses

Clauses with words deliberately omitted are called elliptical clauses. The word left out of an elliptical clause may be the relative pronoun or subordinating conjunction introducing it, or it may be part of the predicate.

The man [that] I saw had one black shoe.

Marcia is as tall as I [am].

68 Sentence Classification and Sentence Patterns

Understanding how sentences are put together is particularly useful when you are editing for effectiveness and grammar. Sentences can be classified in two ways: by function and by grammatical structure. They can also be described in terms of their sentence patterns.

68 a Classifying sentences by function

Declarative sentences make statements.

The road is long.

The Pirates have won the Eastern Division.

The normal word order for a declarative sentence is subject followed by predicate, although this order is occasionally inverted: *At the top of the hill stood a tree.* (See 68c.)

Interrogative sentences ask questions.

Who goes there?

Is there life on Mars?

Can pigs really fly?

An interrogative sentence can be introduced by an interrogative pronoun, as in the first example. (See 66b.) Or the subject can follow part of the verb, as in the second and third examples.

Imperative sentences make commands or requests.

Drive slowly.

Signal before changing lanes.

In commands, the subject is *you*; it is usually not stated but is implied: [*You*] *drive slowly.* The verb form used is always the base form.

Exclamatory sentences exclaim (and usually end with an exclamation point).

Oh, how I hate to get up in the morning!

(See 27c for more on the uses of these different types of sentences.)

68 b **Classifying sentences by grammatical structure**

Sentences are classified by grammatical structure according to how many dependent and independent clauses they contain. (See 67f.)

A **simple sentence** consists of a single independent clause and no dependent clause. Some simple sentences are brief. Others, if they contain modifier phrases or compound subjects, verbs, or objects, can be quite long.

Marmosets eat bananas.

Benny and Griselda, marmosets at our local zoo, eat at least fifteen bananas a day, in addition to lettuce, nuts, and sometimes each other's tails.

A **compound sentence** has two or more independent clauses and no dependent clause.

independent   independent
⌐They grew tired of waiting,˺⌐so they finally hailed a taxicab.˺

A **complex sentence** contains one independent clause and at least one dependent clause.

independent   dependent
⌐The students assemble outside˺⌐when the bell rings.˺

A **compound-complex sentence** contains at least two independent clauses and at least one dependent clause.

independent

⌐The first motorcyclists to finish never ordered anything to eat;⌐

independent   dependent

⌐they just sat quietly⌐until their hands stopped shaking.⌐

68 **c** **Understanding sentence patterns**

Most independent clauses are built on one of five basic patterns. (See Chapter 67 for more on the sentence elements mentioned here.)

The simplest pattern has only two elements, a subject and a verb (S–V).

    s   **v**

Rain fell.

Even when expanded by modifying phrases, the basic pattern of an independent clause may still be only subject–verb.

           s   **v**

⌐Heavy tropical rain⌐ ⌐fell⌐ Tuesday and Wednesday in the Philippines, causing mud slides and killing hundreds of people.

In this example, *Tuesday and Wednesday in the Philippines* modifies the verb; *causing mud slides and killing hundreds of people* modifies the subject.

The next simplest pattern includes a subject, a verb, and a direct object (S–V–DO).

    s   **v**   **do**

Gloria read ⌐the book.⌐

    s   **v**   **do**

Robins eat worms.

A third pattern is subject, verb, indirect object, and direct object (S–V–IO–DO).

| S | V | IO | DO |

The committee sent the mayor its report.

| S | V | IO | DO |

The waiter brought her an appetizer.

A fourth pattern is subject, verb, and subject complement (S–V–SC).

| S | V | SC |

The commissioner seems worried.

| S | V | SC |

She is a Republican.

The fifth basic pattern is subject, verb, direct object, and object complement (S–V–DO–OC).

| S | V | DO | OC |

His friends call him an achiever.

| S | V | DO | OC |

That makes him proud.

Glossary of Usage

This glossary provides information about words that are frequently confused, words that are often used incorrectly, and words that are not considered appropriate for formal academic writing. If you are unsure about how to use a word or are having trouble choosing between words, try to find that word or words here.

Like any other aspect of editing, good usage is usually more than a matter of clear-cut distinctions and unvarying rules. Some usages described here would be considered incorrect by any knowledgeable speaker or writer in any context. For example, *discreet* means "prudent" and *discrete* means "separate"; no one who knows that these are two different words would argue that they are interchangeable. On the other hand, some usages are considered acceptable by some authorities but not by others. For example, some writers prefer to use *farther* only when referring to physical distances and *further* only when referring to the more abstract distances of time, quantity, or degree. However, respectable writers have been using them interchangeably for hundreds of years. To decide what is appropriate for your writing, carefully consider the expectations of your audience. In most cases, instructors will appreciate your using words as carefully and precisely as possible. This glossary identifies distinctions among words to enable you to do this.

Some of the usages described in this glossary are acceptable or common in contexts other than formal academic writing. For example, **nonstandard** usages (such as *anyways* instead of the standard *anyway*) reflect the speech patterns of a particular community but do not follow the conventions of the dominant American dialect. **Colloquial** usages (such as *flunk* meaning "to fail" or *awfully* meaning "very") are often heard in speech but are usually considered inappropriate for academic writing. **Informal** usages (such as using *can* and *may* interchangeably) may be acceptable in some papers but not in formal research essays or argument papers. Except where otherwise noted, the usages recommended in this glossary are those of standard written English as found in formal academic papers.

a, an   Use *a* before words that begin with a consonant sound (*a boy, a hero, a shining star*), even if the first letter of the word is a vowel (*a useful lesson*). Use *an* before words that begin with a vowel sound (*an antelope, an hour, an umbrella*).

accept, except   Accept is a verb meaning "to receive" or "to approve" (*I accept your offer*). *Except* is a verb meaning "to leave out" or "to exclude" (*He excepted all vegetables from his list of favorite foods*) or a preposition meaning "excluding" (*He liked to eat everything except vegetables*).

adapt, adopt   *Adapt* means "to adjust" or "to accommodate"; it is usually followed by to (*It is sometimes hard to adapt to college life*). *Adopt* means "to take into a relationship" (*My parents are adopting another child*) or "to take and use as one's own" (*I have adopted my roommate's habits*).

adverse, averse   *Adverse* is an adjective meaning "unfavorable" or "unpleasant," generally used to describe a thing or situation (*Adverse weather forced us to cancel the game*). *Averse*, also an adjective, means "opposed to" or "feeling a distaste for" and usually describes feelings about a thing or situation; it is usually followed by to (*We are averse to playing on a muddy field*).

advice, advise   *Advice* is a noun meaning "recommendation" or "information given"; *advise* is a verb meaning "to give advice to" (*I advise you to take my advice and study hard*).

affect, effect   *Affect* as a verb means "to influence" or "to produce an effect" (*That movie affected me deeply*). *Affect* as a noun means "feeling" or "emotion," especially in psychology. *Effect* is commonly used as a noun meaning "result," "consequence," or "outcome" (*That movie had a profound effect on me*); it is also sometimes used as a verb meaning "to bring about" (*Dr. Johnson effected important changes as president*).

aggravate   *Aggravate* is a verb meaning "to make worse." *Aggravate* is sometimes used colloquially to mean "to irritate" or "to annoy," but in formal writing use *irritate* or *annoy* (*I was irritated by my neighbors' loud stereo; my irritation was aggravated when they refused to turn it down*).

all ready, already   *All ready* means "fully prepared" (*The children were all ready for bed*). *Already* means "previously" (*The children were already in bed when the guests arrived*).

all right, alright   The two-word spelling is preferred; the one-word spelling is considered incorrect by many.

all together, altogether   *All together* means "all gathered in one place" (*The animals were all together in the ark*). *Altogether* means "thoroughly" or "completely" (*The ark was altogether too full of animals*).

allude, elude   *Allude* is a verb meaning "to refer to something indirectly"; it is followed by to (*Derek alluded to the rodent infestation by mentioning that he'd bought mousetraps*). *Elude* is a verb meaning "to escape" or "to avoid" (*The mouse eluded Derek at every turn*).

allusion, illusion   *Allusion* means "an indirect reference" or "the act of alluding to, or hinting at, something" (*Derek's allusion to lunchtime was not lost on his companions*). *Illusion* is a noun meaning "misapprehension" or "misleading image" (*Mr. Hodges created an optical illusion with two lines*).

a lot   *A lot* should be written as two words. Although *a lot* is used informally to mean "a large number," avoid using it in formal writing (*The prisoners had many* [not *a lot of*] *opportunities to escape*).

a.m., p.m. or A.M., P.M.   Use these abbreviations only with numbers to indicate time (6:30 p.m.). Do not use them as substitutes for *morning, afternoon, evening,* or *night.*

among, between   *Among* should be used when three or more individuals are being discussed (*It was difficult to choose among all the exotic plants*). *Between* is generally used when only two individuals are being discussed (*There were significant differences between the two candidates*).

amount, number   *Amount* should be used to refer to quantities that cannot be counted or cannot be expressed as a single number (*Fixing up the abandoned farmhouse took a great amount of work*). *Number* is used for quantities that can be counted (*A large number of volunteers showed up to clean out the abandoned farmhouse*).

an   See *a, an.*

and/or   *And/or* is used in technical and legal writing to connect two terms when either one or both apply (*Purchasers must select type and/or size*). Avoid this awkward phrasing by using the construction "*a* or *b* or both" (*Students may select chemistry or physics or both*).

anxious, eager   *Anxious* is an adjective meaning "worried" or "uneasy" (*Lynn is anxious about her mother's surgery*). Do not confuse it with *eager,* which means "enthusiastic," "impatient," or "marked by strong desire" (*I am eager* [not *anxious*] *to leave*).

anybody, anyone, any body, any one   *Anybody* and *anyone* are singular indefinite pronouns that refer to an unspecified person (*Anybody may apply for the new scholarship. Anyone on the hill could have seen our campfire*). *Any body* and *any one* are noun phrases consisting of the adjective *any* and the noun *body* or the pronoun *one*; they refer to a specific body or a single member of a group (*Each child may select any one toy from the toy box*).

anyplace, anywhere   In formal writing, do not use *anyplace*; use *anywhere* (*We could not find the game piece anywhere* [not *anyplace*]).

anyways, anywheres   Use the standard terms *anyway* and *anywhere* in writing.

as   *As* may be used to mean "because" (*We did not go ice skating as the lake was no longer frozen*), but only if no confusion will result. For example, *We canceled the meeting as only two people showed up* could mean that the meeting was canceled either at the moment when the two people showed up or because only two showed up.

as, as if, like   To indicate comparisons, *like* should be used only as a preposition followed by a noun or noun phrase to compare items that are similar but not equivalent (*Ken, like his brother, prefers to sleep late*). In formal writing, *like* should not be used as a conjunction linking two clauses. Use *as* or *as if* instead (*Anne talks as if* [not *like*] *she has read every book by Ernest Hemingway*).

assure, ensure, insure   *Assure* is a verb meaning "to reassure" or "to convince" (*The lawyer assured her client that the case was solid*). *Ensure* and *insure* both mean "to make sure, certain, or safe," but *insure* generally refers to financial certainty (*John hoped his college degree would ensure him a job, preferably one that would insure him in case of injury or illness*).

as to Do not use *as to* as a substitute for *about* (*We had questions about* [not *as to*] *the company's affirmative action policies*).

averse See *adverse, averse.*

awful, awfully *Awful* is an adjective meaning "inspiring awe." In formal writing, do not use it to mean "disagreeable" or "objectionable." Similarly, the adverb *awfully* means "in an awe-inspiring way"; in writing, do not use it in the colloquial sense of "very."

awhile, a while The one-word form *awhile* is an adverb that can be used to modify a verb (*We rested awhile*). Only the two-word form *a while*, a combination of the article *a* and the noun *while*, can be the object of a preposition (*We rested for a while*).

bad, badly *Bad* is an adjective, so it must modify a noun or follow a linking verb, such as *be, feel,* or *become* (*John felt bad about holding the picnic in bad weather*). *Badly* is an adverb, so it must modify a verb (*Pam played badly today*).

being as, being that *Being as* and *being that* are nonstandard expressions for *because* (*Anna withdrew from the tournament because* [not *being as*] *her shoulder was injured*).

beside, besides *Beside* is a preposition meaning "by the side of" or "next to" (*The book is beside the bed*). *Besides* can be used as a preposition meaning "other than" or "in addition to" (*No one besides Linda can build a good campfire*). *Besides* can also be used as an adverb meaning "furthermore," or "in addition" (*The weather is bad for hiking; besides, I have a cold*).

between See *among, between.*

breath, breathe *Breath* is a noun (*I had to stop to catch my breath*). *Breathe* is a verb (*It became difficult to breathe at higher elevations*).

bring, take The verb *bring* describes movement from a distant place to a nearer place; the verb *take* describes movement away from a place (*Dr. Gavin asked us to bring our rough sketches to class; she said we may take them home after class*).

but, however, yet Each of these words should be used alone, not in combination (*We finished painting the house, but* [not *but however*] *there is still much work to do*).

can, may In informal usage, *can* and *may* are often used interchangeably to indicate permission, but in formal writing, only *may* should be used this way (*May I borrow your dictionary?*). *May* is also used to indicate possibility (*It may snow tomorrow*). *Can* is used only to indicate ability (*I can see much better with my new glasses*).

capital, capitol *Capital* is an adjective meaning "punishable by death" (*capital punishment*) or is used to refer to uppercase letters (*A, B*). As a noun it means "accumulated wealth" (*We will calculate our capital at the end of the fiscal year*) or "a city serving as a seat of government" (*Albany is the capital of New York*). *Capitol* is a noun for the building in which lawmakers meet (*The civics class toured the capitol last week*).

censor, censure *Censor* is a noun or verb referring to the removal of material that is considered objectionable; *censure* is a verb meaning "to blame or condemn sternly" (*Plans to censor song lyrics have been censured by groups that support free speech*).

cite, site   *Cite* is a verb meaning "to quote for purposes of example, authority, or proof" (*Tracy cites several legal experts in her paper on capital punishment*). *Site* is usually used as a noun meaning "place or scene" (*Today we poured the foundation on the site of our future home*).

climactic, climatic   *Climactic* is an adjective derived from *climax*; it refers to a moment of greatest intensity (*In the climactic scene of the play, the murderer's identity is revealed*). *Climatic* is an adjective derived from the noun *climate*; it refers to weather conditions (*Some people fear that climatic changes are a sign of environmental dangers*).

compare to, compare with   *Compare to* means "to liken" or "to represent as similar" (*Jim compared our new puppy to an unruly child*). *Compare with* means "to examine to discover similarities or differences" (*We compared this month's ads with last month's*).

complement, compliment   *Complement* is a verb meaning "to fill out or complete"; it is also a noun meaning "something that completes or fits with" (*The bouquet of spring flowers complemented the table setting*). *Compliment* is a verb meaning "to express esteem or admiration" or a noun meaning "an expression of esteem or admiration" (*Russ complimented Nancy on her choice of flowers*).

compose, comprise   *Compose* means "to constitute or make up"; *comprise* means "to include or contain" (*Last year's club comprised fifteen members; only eight members compose this year's club*).

conscience, conscious   *Conscience* is a noun referring to a sense of right and wrong (*His conscience would not allow him to lie*). *Conscious* is an adjective meaning "marked by thought or will" or "acting with critical awareness" (*He made a conscious decision to be more honest*).

contact   *Contact* is often used informally as a verb meaning "to get in touch with." Avoid it in formal writing; use verbs such as *write* or *telephone*.

continual, continuous   *Continual* means "recurring" or "occurring repeatedly" (*Liz saw a doctor about her continual headaches*). *Continuous* means "uninterrupted in space, time, or sequence" (*Eventually we grew used to the continuous noise*).

council, counsel   *Council* is a noun meaning "a group meeting for advice, discussion, or government" (*The tribal council voted in favor of the new land rights law*). As a noun, *counsel* means "advice" or "a plan of action or behavior" (*The priest gave counsel to the young men considering the priesthood*). *Counsel* may also be used as a verb meaning "to advise or consult" (*The priest counseled the young man*).

criteria   *Criteria* is the plural of *criterion*, which means "a standard on which a judgment is based" (*Many criteria are used in selecting a president, but a candidate's hair color is not an appropriate criterion*).

data   *Data* is the plural of *datum*, which means "a fact" or "a result in research." Some writers now use *data* as both a singular and a plural noun; in formal usage it is still better to treat it as plural (*The data indicate that a low-fat diet may increase life expectancy*).

different from, different than   *Different from* is preferred to *different* than (*Hal's taste in music is different from his wife's*). But *different than* may be used to avoid awkward constructions (*Hal's taste in music is different than* [instead of *different from what*] *it was five years ago*).

differ from, differ with *Differ from* means "to be unlike" (*This year's parade differed from last year's in many ways*). *Differ with* means "to disagree with" (*Stephanie differed with Tom over which parade was better*).

discreet, discrete *Discreet* is an adjective meaning "prudent" or "modest" (*Most private donors were discreet about their contributions*). *Discrete* is an adjective meaning "separate" or "distinct" (*Professor Roberts divided the course into four discrete units*).

disinterested, uninterested *Disinterested* is an adjective meaning "unbiased" or "impartial" (*It will be difficult to find twelve disinterested jurors for such a highly publicized case*). *Uninterested* is an adjective meaning "indifferent" or "unconcerned" (*Most people were uninterested in the case until the police discovered surprising new evidence*).

don't *Don't* is a contraction for *do not*, not for *does not*. The contraction for *does not* is *doesn't* (*He doesn't* [not *don't*] *know where she's living now*).

due to *Due to* is an adjective phrase that is generally used after forms of the verb *be* (*The smaller classes were due to a decline in enrollment*). In formal writing, *due to* should not be used as a prepositional phrase meaning "because of" (*Class size decreased because of* [not *due to*] *a decline in enrollment*).

each *Each*—whether adjective or pronoun—is singular (*Each tool goes in its own place; each has to be put away properly*).

effect See *affect, effect.*

e.g. *E.g.* is the Latin abbreviation for *exempli gratia*, which means "for example." In formal writing, use *for example* or *for instance*.

elicit, illicit *Elicit* is a verb meaning "to draw forth" or "to bring out" (*The investigators could not elicit any new information*). *Illicit* is an adjective meaning "unlawful" or "not permitted" (*The investigators were looking for evidence of illicit drug sales*).

elude See *allude, elude.*

emigrate from, immigrate to *Emigrate* means "to leave one's country to live or reside elsewhere" (*His grandparents emigrated from Russia*). *Immigrate* means "to come into a new country to take up residence" (*His grandparents immigrated to the United States*).

eminent, imminent *Eminent* means "lofty" or "prominent" (*Her operation was performed by an eminent surgeon*). *Imminent* means "impending" or "about to take place" (*The hurricane's arrival is imminent*).

ensure See *assure, ensure, insure.*

enthused, enthusiastic In formal writing, *enthused*, a past-tense form of the verb *enthuse*, should not be used as an adjective; use *enthusiastic* (*Barb is enthusiastic* [not *enthused*] *about her music lessons*).

especially, specially *Especially* is an adverb meaning "particularly" or "unusually" (*The weather was especially cold this winter*). *Specially* is an adverb meaning "for a special reason" or "in a unique way" (*The cake was specially prepared for Sandy's birthday*).

etc. An abbreviation for the Latin expression *et cetera*, *etc.* means "and so forth." In formal writing, avoid ending a list with *etc.*; indicate that you are leaving items out of a list with *and so on* or *and so forth*. Use *etc.* alone, not with *and*, which is redundant.

eventually, ultimately   Although these words are often used interchangeably, *eventually* means "at an unspecified later time," while *ultimately* means "finally" or "in the end" (*He knew that he would have to stop running eventually, but he hoped that he would ultimately win a marathon*).

everybody, everyone, every body, every one   *Everybody* and *everyone* are singular indefinite pronouns that refer to an unspecified person (*Everybody wins in this game*). *Every body* and *every one* are noun phrases consisting of the adjective *every* and the noun *body* or the pronoun *one*; they refer to each individual body or each single member of a group (*Every one of these toys must be picked up*).

except   See *accept, except*.

expect   *Expect* means "to anticipate or look forward to." Avoid using it colloquially to mean "to think or suppose." (*I suppose* [not *expect*] *I should go study now*).

explicit, implicit   *Explicit* means "perfectly clear, direct, and unambiguous" (*Darrell gave me explicit directions to his house*). *Implicit* means "implied" or "revealed or expressed indirectly" (*His eagerness to see me was implicit in his cheerful tone of voice*).

farther, further   Although these words are often used interchangeably, some writers prefer to use *farther* to refer to physical distances (*Boston is farther than I thought*) and *further* to refer to quantity, time, or degree (*We tried to progress further on our research project*).

fewer, less   *Fewer* is an adjective used to refer to people or items that can be counted (*Because fewer people came to the conference this year, we needed fewer programs*). *Less* is used to refer to amounts that cannot be counted (*We also required less space and less food*).

finalize   Many writers avoid using *finalize* to mean "to make final." Use an alternative phrasing (*We needed to complete* [not *finalize*] *our plans*).

firstly, secondly, thirdly   These expressions are awkward; use *first, second, third*, and so on instead.

former, latter   *Former* is used to refer to the first of two people, items, or ideas being discussed, *latter* to refer to the second (*Monet and Picasso were both important painters; the former is associated with the impressionist school, the latter with cubism*). *Former* and *latter* should not be used when referring to more than two items.

further   See *farther, further*.

get   The verb *get* has many colloquial uses that should be avoided in formal writing. For example, *get* can means "to provoke or annoy" (*He gets to me*), "to start" (*We should get going on this project*), or "to become" (*She got worried when he didn't call*). *Have got to* should not be used in place of *must* (*I must* [not *have got to*] *finish by five o'clock*).

goes, says   The verb *goes* is sometimes used colloquially for *says*, but avoid this usage in formal writing (*When the coach says* [not *goes*] *"Now," everybody runs*).

good and   *Good and* should not be used for *very* in formal writing (*My shoes were very* [not *good and*] *wet after our walk*).

good, well   *Good* is an adjective; it should not be used in place of the adverb *well* in formal writing (*Mario is a good tennis player; he played well* [not *good*] *in the tournament*).

hanged, hung   *Hanged* is the past-tense and past-participle form of the verb *hang* meaning "to suspend by the neck until dead" (*Two Civil War prisoners were hanged at this spot*). *Hung* is the past-tense and past-participle form of the verb *hang* meaning "to suspend" or "to dangle" (*All her clothes were hung neatly in the closet*).

hardly, scarcely   *Hardly* and *scarcely* are adverbs meaning "barely," "only just." Do not use double negatives, such as *can't scarcely* and *not hardly*, in formal writing. (*I can scarcely* [not *can't scarcely*] *keep my eyes open*).

has got, have got   These are colloquial expressions; in formal writing use simply *has* or *have* (*He has* [not *has got*] *his books packed*).

have, of   The auxiliary verb *have* (not *of*) should be used in verb phrases beginning with modal auxiliaries such as *could, would,* and *might* (*We could have* [not *of*] *gone to the concert*).

he/she, his/her   When you require both female and male personal pronouns in formal writing, use *she or he* (or *he or she*) and *his or her* (or *her or his*) instead of a slash. For more on avoiding sexist language, see 32c.

herself, himself, itself, myself, ourselves, themselves, yourself, yourselves   These are reflexive or intensive pronouns and should be used only to reflect the action of a sentence back toward the subject (*He locked himself out of the apartment*) or to emphasize the subject (*I myself have no regrets*). Do not use these pronouns in place of personal pronouns such as *I, me, you, her,* or *him* (*He left an extra key with Bev and me* [not *myself*]).

hisself   *Hisself* is nonstandard; use *himself*.

hopefully   *Hopefully* is an adverb meaning "in a hopeful manner" (*The child looked hopefully out the window for her mother*). In formal writing, do not use *hopefully* to mean "I or we hope that" or "It is hoped that" (*I hope that* [not *hopefully*] *Bob will remember his camera*).

however   See *but, however, yet.*

hung   See *hanged, hung.*

i.e.   *I.e.* is an abbreviation for the Latin phrase *id est,* which means "that is." In formal writing, use *that is* instead of the abbreviation (*Hal is a Renaissance man; that is* [not *i.e.*], *he has many interests*).

if, whether   Use *if* in a clause that refers to a conditional situation (*I will wear my new boots if it snows tomorrow*). Use *whether* (or *whether or not*) in a clause that expresses or implies an alternative (*I will decide whether to wear my boots when I see what the weather is like*).

illicit   See *elicit, illicit.*

illusion   See *allusion, illusion.*

immigrate   See *emigrate from, immigrate to.*

imminent   See *eminent, imminent.*

implicit   See *explicit, implicit.*

imply, infer   *Imply* is a verb meaning "to express indirectly" or "to suggest"; *infer* is a verb meaning "to conclude" or "to surmise" (*Helen implied that she had time to visit with us, but we inferred from all the work on her desk that she was really too busy*).

incredible, incredulous   *Incredible* is an adjective meaning "hard to believe"; *incredulous* is an adjective meaning "skeptical" or "unbelieving" (*Joey was incredulous when I told him the incredible story*).

infer   See *imply, infer.*

ingenious, ingenuous   *Ingenious* means "resourceful" or "clever" (*Elaine came up with an ingenious plan*). *Ingenuous* means "innocent" or "simple" (*It was a surprisingly deceptive plan for such an ingenuous person*).

in regards to   *In regards to* is an incorrect combination of two phrases, *as regards* and *in regard to* (*In regard to* [or *As regards*] *the first question, refer to the guidelines you received*).

inside, inside of; outside, outside of   The prepositions *inside* and *outside* should not be followed by *of* (*The suspect is inside* [not *inside of*] *that building*).

insure   See *assure, ensure, insure.*

irregardless, regardless   *Irregardless* is often mistakenly used in place of *regardless* (*We will have the party regardless* [not *irregardless*] *of the weather*).

is when, is where   Avoid these awkward expressions in formal writing to define terms (*Sexual harassment refers to* [not *is when someone makes*] *inappropriate sexual advances or suggestions*).

its, it's   *Its* is the possessive form of the pronoun *it*; *it's* is a contraction for *it is* (*It's hard to tear a baby animal away from its mother*).

itself   See *herself, himself. . . .*

kind, sort, type   *Kind, sort,* and *type* are singular nouns; each should be used with *this* (not *these*) and a singular verb (*This kind of mushroom is* [not *These kind of mushrooms are*] *very expensive*). The plural forms—*kinds, sorts,* and *types*—should be used with *these* and with a plural verb (*These three types of envelopes are the only ones we need*).

kind of, sort of   In formal writing, avoid using the colloquial expressions *kind of* and *sort of* to mean "somewhat" or "rather" (*My paper is rather* [not *kind of*] *short; my research for it was somewhat* [not *sort of*] *rushed*).

later, latter   *Later* means "after some time"; *latter* refers to the second of two people, items, or ideas (*Later in the evening Jim announced that the latter of the two speakers was running late*). See also *former, latter.*

lay   See *lie, lay.*

lead, led   As a verb, *lead* means "to go first" or "to direct"; as a noun, it means "front position" (*Hollis took the lead in organizing the files*). *Lead* is also a noun for the metallic element. Be careful not to confuse this form of *lead* with *led*, which is pronounced the same way; *led* is the past-tense and past-participle form of the verb *lead* (*He led me to the cave*).

leave, let   *Leave* means "to depart"; it should not be used in place of *let*, which means "to allow" (*When you are ready to leave, let* [not *leave*] *me give you a ride*). The expressions *leave alone* and *let alone*, however, may be used interchangeably (*I asked Ben to leave* [or *let*] *me alone while I worked on my paper*).

led   See *lead, led.*

less   See *fewer, less.*

liable, likely   *Liable* means "inclined" or "tending," generally toward the negative (*If you do not shovel the sidewalk, you are liable to fall on the ice*). *Liable* is also a legal term meaning "responsible for" or "obligated under the law" (*The landlord is liable for the damage caused by the leak*). *Likely* is an adjective meaning "probable" or "promising" (*The school board is likely to cancel classes if the strike continues*).

lie, lay   The verb *lie* meaning "to recline" or "to rest in a horizontal position" has the principal forms *lie, lay, lain*. *Lie* should not be confused with the transitive verb *lay*, which means "to put or set down" and is followed by an object; the principal forms of *lay* are *lay, laid, laid* (*Lay the blanket on this spot and lie down; She laid the book next to the spot where he lay on the bed*).

like   See *as, as if, like*.

likely   See *liable, likely*.

loose, lose   *Loose* is an adjective meaning "not securely attached"; it should not be confused with the verb *lose*, which means "to misplace," "to fail to keep," or "to undergo defeat" (*Be careful not to lose that loose button on your jacket*).

lots, lots of   *Lots* and *lots of* are colloquial expressions meaning "many" or "much"; avoid them in formal writing (*The senator has much* [not *lots of*] *support, she is expected to win many* [not *lots of*] *votes*).

man, mankind   These terms were once used to refer to all human beings. Now such usage is considered sexist; use terms such as *people, humanity,* and *humankind* instead (*What has been the greatest invention in the history of humanity* [not *mankind*]?). See 32c.

may   See *can, may*.

may be, maybe   *May be* is a verb phrase (*Charles may be interested in a new job*); *maybe* is an adverb meaning "possibly" or "perhaps" (*Maybe I will speak to him about it*).

media   The term *media,* frequently used to refer to various forms of communication—newspapers, magazines, television, radio—is the plural form of the noun *medium*; it takes a plural verb (*Some people feel that the media were responsible for the candidate's loss*).

moral, morale   *Moral* is the message or lesson of a story or experience (*The moral is to treat others as you wish to be treated*). *Morale* is the mental condition or mood of a person or group (*The improvement in the weather lifted the crew's morale*).

most   In formal writing, do not use *most* to mean "almost" (*Prizes were given to almost* [not *most*] *all the participants*).

myself   See *herself, himself . . . .*

nor, or   *Nor* should be used with *neither* (*Neither Paul nor Sara guessed the right answer*); *or* should be used with *either* (*Either Paul or Sara will have to drive me home*).

number   See *amount, number*.

of   See *have, of*.

off of   Use *off* alone; *of* is not necessary (*The child fell off* [not *off of*] *the playground slide*).

OK, O.K., okay All three spellings are acceptable, but this colloquial term should be avoided in writing (*John's performance was all right* [or *adequate* or *tolerable*; not *okay*], *but it wasn't his best*).

on account of In formal writing, avoid *on account of* to mean "because of" (*The course was canceled because of* [not *on account of*] *lack of interest*). Also see *due to.*

outside, outside of See *inside, inside of; outside, outside of.*

passed, past *Passed* is the past-tense form of the verb *pass* (*She passed here several hours ago*). *Past* may be an adjective or a noun referring to a time before the present (*She has forgotten many details about her past life; the past is not important to her*).

per The Latin term *per* should be reserved for commercial or technical use (*miles per gallon, price per pound*). Avoid it in formal writing (*Kyle is exercising three times each* [not *per*] *week*).

percent, percentage The term *percent* (or *per cent*) refers to a specific fraction of one hundred; it is always used with a number (*We raised nearly 80 percent of our budget in one night*). Do not use the symbol % in formal writing. The term *percentage* is more general than *percent* and is not used with a specific number (*We raised a large percentage of our budget in one night*).

perspective, prospective *Perspective* is a noun meaning "a view"; it should not be confused with the adjective *prospective*, meaning "potential" or "likely" (*Mr. Harris's perspective on the new school changed when he met his son's prospective teacher*).

phenomena *Phenomena* is the plural of the noun *phenomenon*, meaning "an observed fact, occurrence, or circumstance" (*Last month's blizzard was an unusual phenomenon; there have been several such phenomena this year*).

plenty *Plenty* means "full" or "abundant"; in formal writing, do not use it to mean "very" or "quite" (*The sun was quite* [not *plenty*] *hot*).

plus *Plus* is a preposition meaning "increased by" or "with the addition of" (*With wool socks plus your heavy boots, your feet should be warm enough*). Do not use *plus* to link two independent clauses; use *besides* or *moreover* instead (*Brad is not prepared for the advanced class; moreover* [not *plus*], *he can't fit it in his schedule*).

p.m., a.m. P.M., A.M. See *a.m., p.m. or A.M., P.M.*

precede, proceed *Precede* is a verb meaning "to go or come before"; *proceed* is a verb meaning "to move forward or go on" or "to continue" (*The bridal attendants preceded the bride into the church; when the music started, they proceeded down the aisle*).

pretty In formal writing, avoid *pretty* to mean "quite" or "somewhat" (*Dave is quite* [not *pretty*] *tired this morning*).

principal, principle *Principal* is an adjective meaning "first" or "most important"; it is also a noun meaning "head" or "director" or "an amount of money" (*My principal reason for visiting Gettysburg was my interest in the Civil War; my high school principal suggested the trip*). *Principle* is a noun meaning "a rule of action or conduct" or "a basic law" (*I also want to learn more about the principles underlying the U.S. Constitution*).

proceed   See *precede, proceed*.

quotation, quote   *Quotation* is a noun, and *quote* is a verb. Avoid using *quote* as a noun (*Sue quoted Jefferson in her speech, hoping the quotation* [not *quote*] *would have a powerful effect on her audience*).

raise, rise   *Raise* is a transitive verb meaning "to lift" or "to increase"; it takes a direct object (*The store owner was forced to raise prices*). *Rise* is an intransitive verb meaning "to go up"; it does not take a direct object (*Prices will rise during periods of inflation*).

rarely ever   Do not use *rarely ever* to mean "hardly ever"; use *rarely* alone (*We rarely* [not *rarely ever*] *travel during the winter*).

real, really   *Real* is an adjective meaning "true" or "actual" (*The diamonds in that necklace are real*). *Really* is an adverb, used informally to mean "very" or "quite"; do not use *real* as an adverb (*Tim was really* [not *real*] *interested in buying Lana's old car*). In formal writing, it is generally best to avoid using *really* altogether.

reason is because   *Reason is because* is redundant; use *reason is that* or *because* instead (*The reason I am late is that* [not *because*] *I got stuck in traffic. Yesterday I was late because* [not *the reason I was late yesterday was because*] *I overslept*).

reason why   *Reason why* is redundant; use *reason* alone (*The reason* [not *The reason why*] *we canceled the dance is that no one volunteered to chaperone*).

regardless   See *irregardless, regardless*.

relation, relationship   *Relation* is a connection or association between things; *relationship* is a connection or involvement between people (*The analyst explained the relation between investment and interest. The relationship between a mother and child is complex*).

respectfully, respectively   The adverb *respectfully* means "in a respectful manner" (*The children listened to their teacher respectfully*). The adverb *respectively* means "in the order given" (*The sessions on Italian, French, and Spanish culture are scheduled for Tuesday, Wednesday, and Thursday, respectively*).

rise   See *raise, rise*.

says   See *goes, says*.

scarcely   See *hardly, scarcely*.

sensual, sensuous   *Sensual* means "arousing or exciting the senses or appetites"; it is often used in reference to sexual pleasure (*His scripts often featured titillating situations and sensual encounters*). *Sensuous* means "experienced through or affecting the senses," although it generally refers to esthetic enjoyment or pleasure (*Her sculpture was characterized by muted colors and sensuous curves*).

set, sit   *Set* is a transitive verb meaning "to put" or "to place"; it takes a direct object, and its principal forms are *set, set, set* (*Mary set her packages on the kitchen table*). *Sit* is an intransitive verb meaning "to be seated"; it does not take a direct object, and its principal forms are *sit, sat, sat* (*I sat in the only chair in the waiting room*).

shall, will   In the past, *shall* (instead of *will*) was used as a helping verb with the first-person subjects *I* and *we*. Now *will* is acceptable with all subjects (*We will invite several guests for dinner*). *Shall* is generally used in polite questions (*Shall we go inside now?*) or in legal writing (*Jurors shall refrain from all contact with the press*).

since   *Since* should be used to mean "continuing from a past time until the present" (*Carl has not gone skiing since he injured his knee*). Do not use *since* to mean "because" if there is any possibility that readers will be confused about your meaning. For example, in the sentence *Since she sold her bicycle, Lonnie has not been getting much exercise, since* could mean either "because" or "from the time that." Use *because* to avoid confusion.

sit   See *set, sit*.

site   See *cite, site*.

so, so that   The use of *so* to mean "very" can be vague; use *so* with a *that* clause of explanation (*Gayle was so depressed that she could not get out of bed*).

somebody, someone, something   These singular indefinite pronouns take singular verbs (*Somebody calls every night at midnight and hangs up; I hope something is done about this problem soon*).

someplace, somewhere   Do not use *someplace* in formal writing; use *somewhere* instead (*The answer must lie somewhere* [not *someplace*] *in the text*).

some time, sometime, sometimes   The phrase *some time* (an adjective and a noun) means "a length of time" (*We have not visited our grandparents in some time*). *Sometime* is an adverb meaning "at an indefinite time in the future" (*Let's get together sometime*); *sometimes* is an adverb meaning "on occasion" or "now and then" (*Sometimes we get together to talk about our assignments*).

sort   See *kind, sort, type*.

sort of   See *kind of, sort of*.

stationary, stationery   *Stationary* is an adjective meaning "not moving" (*All stationary vehicles will be towed*). *Stationery* is a noun meaning "writing materials" (*Karen is always running out of stationery*).

supposed to, used to   Both of these expressions consist of a past participle (*supposed, used*) followed by *to*. Do not use the base forms *suppose* and *use* (*Ben is supposed* [not *suppose*] *to take the garbage out; he is used* [not *use*] *to his mother's reminders by now*).

sure, surely   In formal writing, do not use the adjective *sure* to mean "certainly" or "undoubtedly"; use the adverb *surely* or *certainly* or *undoubtedly* instead (*It is certainly* [or *surely*; not *sure*] *cold today*).

sure and, try and   *Sure and* and *try and* are colloquial expressions for *sure to* and *try to*, respectively; avoid them in formal writing (*Be sure to* [not *and*] *come to the party; and try to* [not *and*] *be on time*).

take   See *bring, take*.

than, then   *Than* is a conjunction used in comparisons (*Dan is older than Eve*). *Then* is an adverb indicating time (*First pick up the files and then deliver them to the company office*).

that, which   A clause introduced by *that* is always a restrictive clause; it should not be set off by commas (*The historical event that interested him most was the Civil War*). Many writers use *which* only to introduce nonrestrictive clauses, which are set off by commas (*His textbook, which was written by an expert on the war, provided useful information*); however, *which* may also be used to introduce restrictive clauses (*The book which offered the most important information was an old reference book in the library*). See 39f.

their, there, they're   *Their* is the possessive form of the pronoun *they* (*Did they leave their books here?*). *There* is an adverb meaning "in or at that place" (*No, they left their books there*); it may also be used as an expletive with a form of the verb *be* (*There is no time to look for their books*). *They're* is a contraction of *they are* (*They're looking all over for their books*).

theirselves, themselves   *Theirselves* is nonstandard; always use *themselves*.

then   See *than, then*.

'til, till, until   *Till* and *until* are both acceptable spellings; *'til*, however, is a contraction and should be avoided in formal writing (*We will work until we are finished; you should not plan to leave till then*).

to, too, two   *To* is a preposition, often used to indicate movement or direction toward something (*Nancy is walking to the grocery store*). *Too* is an adverb meaning "also" (*Sam is walking too*). *Two* is a number (*The two of them are walking together*).

toward, towards   *Toward* is preferred, but both forms are acceptable.

try and   See *sure and, try and*.

type   In colloquial speech, *type* is sometimes used alone to mean "type of," but avoid this usage in formal writing (*What type of* [not *type*] *medicine did the doctor prescribe?*). Also see *kind, sort, type*.

ultimately   See *eventually, ultimately*.

uninterested   See *disinterested, uninterested*.

unique   *Unique* is an adjective meaning "being the only one" or "having no equal." Because it refers to an absolute, unvarying state, it should not be preceded by a word that indicates degree or amount (such as *most, less*, or *very*) (*Her pale blue eyes gave her a unique* [not *very unique*] *look*). The same is true of other adjectives that indicate an absolute state: *perfect, complete, round, straight*, and so on.

until   See *'til, till, until*.

usage, use   The noun *usage* means "an established and accepted practice or procedure" (*He consulted the glossary whenever he was unsure of the correct word choice or usage*). Do not substitute it for the noun *use*, which means "the act of putting into service" (*Park guidelines forbid the use* [not *usage*] *of gas grills*).

used to   See *supposed to, used to*.

utilize   The verb *utilize*, meaning "to put to use," is often considered inappropriately technical for formal writing; it is generally better to use *use* instead (*We were able to use* [not *utilize*] *the hotel kitchen to prepare our meals*).

wait for, wait on   *Wait for* means "to await" or "to be ready for." *Wait on* means "to serve"; in formal writing they are not interchangeable (*You are too old to wait for* [not *on*] *your mother to wait on you*).

way, ways   Do not use *ways* in place of *way* when referring to long distances (*Los Angeles is a long way* [not *ways*] *from San Francisco by car*).

well   See *good, well.*

where   *Where* is nonstandard when used in place of *that* (*I read that* [not *where*] *several of the company's plants will be closed in June*).

where . . . at, where . . . to   *Where* should be used alone, not in combination with *at* or *to* (*Where did you leave your coat?* [not *Where did you leave your coat at?*] *Where are you going next?* [not *Where are you going to next?*]).

whether   See *if, whether.*

which   See *that, which.*

which, who, that   Use the relative pronoun *which* to refer to places, things, or events; use *who* to refer to people or to animals with individual qualities or given names; use *that* to refer to places, things, or events or to groups of people (*The parade, which was rescheduled for Saturday, was a great success; the man who* [not *which*] *was grand marshal said it was the best parade that he could remember*). *That* is also occasionally used to refer to a single person (*Beth is like the sister that I never had*). See 39f.

who   See *which, who, that.*

who, whom, whoever, whomever   Use *who* and *whoever* for subjects and subject complements; use *whom* and *whomever* for objects and object complements (*Who revealed the murderer's identity? You may invite whomever you wish*). See 41f.

who's, whose   *Who's* is a contraction of *who is* (*Who's coming for dinner tonight?*). *Whose* is the possessive form of *who* (*Whose hat is lying on the table?*).

will   See *shall, will.*

-wise   The suffix *-wise* indicates position or direction in words such as *clockwise* and *lengthwise*. In formal writing, do not add it to words to mean "with regard to" (*My personal life is rather confused, but with regard to my job* [not *jobwise*], *things are fine*).

yet   See *but, however, yet.*

your, you're   *Your* is the possessive form of the pronoun *you* (*Your table is ready*). *You're* is a contraction of *you are* (*You're leaving before the best part of the show*). See 47d.

yourself, yourselves   See *herself, himself . . . .*

Glossary of Terms

absolute   A modifier indicating a quality that cannot be made larger or smaller (*entire, unique, superior*). An absolute does not have a comparative or superlative form. See 37e.

absolute phrase   A phrase that consists of a noun or pronoun and a participle and that modifies an entire sentence, not just one part of it. See 67e.

abstract word   A word referring to something that cannot be perceived by one of the five senses: *liberty, education, exciting*. See 28a, 66a.

acronym   An abbreviation that forms a word out of the initials of the name or title that it shortens: *LILCO, MoMA, MADD*. See 55e.

active voice   See *voice*.

adjective   A modifier that describes nouns and pronouns. There are three types of adjectives: **descriptive** (*green, tall*), **proper** (*Italian, Buddhist*), and **limiting** (*few, all, a, the*). See also *article* and *modifier*. See 28a, Chapter 37, 66d.

adjective clause   A dependent clause introduced by a relative pronoun (*who, which, that*) and functioning as an adjective. See 67f.

adverb   A modifier that describes a verb, adjective, another adverb, or a whole sentence. See also *modifier*. See Chapter 37, 66d.

adverb clause   A dependent clause introduced by a subordinating conjunction and functioning as an adverb. See 67f.

agreement   Grammatical correspondence in number, person, and gender between subjects and their verbs and between pronouns and their antecedents. See Chapter 36, Chapter 40.

analogy   See *figurative language*.

analytical essay   See *interpretive essay*.

antecedent   A noun, noun phrase or clause, or pronoun that a pronoun replaces. Pronouns agree with their antecedents in person, number, and gender. Also called *referent*. See also *agreement, gender, number*, and *person*. See Chapter 39, Chapter 40, 66b.

appositive   A word or phrase placed next to a noun or pronoun and used to describe or rename it: *Cliff, an old family friend, always helps out at harvest time*. See 41b, 44c.

argumentative research   Research undertaken to collect information to support a thesis. See also *informational research*. See 14d.

argumentative thesis   See *thesis*.

argument paper   An essay whose purpose is to persuade readers regarding one side of an issue or regarding one answer to a question. See also *interpretive essay, position paper*. See Chapter 11.

article   *A, an* **(indefinite articles)**, or *the* **(definite article)**. Considered adjectives and also called *determiners*. See 66d.

attributory words   Words that indicate the person who is quoted in a direct quotation: *I said, Jonathan wrote*. See 44g.

audience   The readers to whom a piece of writing is directed. See Chapter 7, 20d.

automatic phrase   A phrase that is used habitually but adds little to a sentence's meaning. See 29b.

auxiliary verb   A form of the verb *be, do,* or *have,* or the verb *can, could, may, might, must, shall, should, will,* or *would*. An auxiliary verb together with a main verb or a participle constitutes a *verb phrase*. Also called *helping verb*. See 35c, 66c.

base form   The first-person, singular, present-tense form of a verb: *go, stop, sit, stand*. Also called *plain form* or *simple form*. See 35a.

biased language   Writing in which meaning is expressed by connotation rather than by direct statements of opinion, fact, inference, or evidence. See Chapter 32.

bibliography   A complete list of works on a topic, or sources consulted in conducting research. See 15b, 18b.

brainstorming   An invention and discovery technique in which the writer makes a list of possible solutions to a problem or answers to a question. See 6a.

bureaucratese   Jargon or pretentious language that is typical of governmental or institutional writing. See *doublespeak, euphemism*. See 29e.

case   The form of a pronoun that shows whether it functions as a subject **(subjective case)** or an object **(objective case)** or whether it indicates ownership **(possessive case)**. Nouns change form only to show ownership (possessive case). See Chapter 41, 47a, 66a, 66b.

cause-and-effect analysis   A writing strategy in which the writer identifies the action or actions (cause) that bring about a certain condition (effect). See 9e, 10d.

chronological order   See *sequence of events*.

claim   A statement or assertion made in support of an argument. The argument's central claim is its *thesis*. A **counterclaim** is a claim made against the thesis. See 11a.

classification and division   A writing strategy in which the writer puts things or people in a category or class with similar things or people (classification) and identifies the constituent parts of something (division). See 10d.

clause   a group of words that includes both a subject and a predicate. See also *dependent clause, independent clause*. See 67f.

cliché   An expression used so often and for so long that it is no longer striking, vivid, or meaningful. See 31j.

clustering   An invention and discovery technique in which ideas are grouped nonlinearly, with relationships among them indicated by lines and circles. See 6f.

coherence   The clear connection between ideas which the writer establishes by using such strategies as introducing transitional expressions or sparingly repeating key words. See 24c.

collaborating　Working as a group with other writers. See Chapter 22, 23c.

collective noun　A singular noun that names a group of things or people: *fleet, team, family.* See 36f, 40c, 66a.

colloquialism　A term or expression used in spoken language but not precise enough or understandable enough for formal writing. See 31g.

command　See *imperative sentence.*

comma splice　The joining of two independent clauses with only a comma. See Chapter 34.

common noun　A noun that names a general person, place, or thing. Also called *generic noun.* See also *proper noun.* See 51c, 66a.

communicative writing　Writing whose primary purpose is to communicate information and ideas. The most common communicative purposes are to recount an experience, to report information, to explain an idea, and to argue a position. See 5b.

comparative form　See *modifier.*

comparison and contrast　A writing strategy in which the writer describes similarities between two or more things or people (comparison) and then the differences between them (contrast). See 10d.

complement　A word or phrase that renames a subject or object. A **subject complement** is an adjective or noun that follows a linking verb and renames the subject: *Tom is patient.* An **object complement** is an adjective or noun that follows an object and renames it: *They named him captain.* See also *linking verb.* See 36c, 37b, 44j, 67d.

complete predicate　See *predicate.*

complete subject　See *subject.*

complex sentence　A sentence that includes one independent clause and one or more dependent clauses. See 27c, 68b.

compound adjective　Two or more modifiers working as a unit with a single meaning: *freeloading, self-sufficient.* See 52c.

compound-complex sentence　A sentence containing two or more independent clauses and at least one dependent clause: *While you were gone, your mother called and the sink overflowed.* See 27c, 68b.

compound noun　Two or more words joined to create a noun: *football, trash can, jack-in-the-box.* See 52c.

compound predicate　Two or more predicates that share a subject and that are joined by a coordinating conjunction: *My uncle Ron shaved and got dressed.* See also *predicate.* See 67b.

compound sentence　A sentence containing two or more independent clauses and no dependent clauses: *I went to John's house, but he wasn't home.* See 26a, 27c, 68b.

compound subject　Two or more subjects that share a predicate and that are joined by a coordinating conjunction: *Her dog and her cat got sick.* See also *subject.* See 36d–e, 40a–b, 41a, 67a.

conclusion　The final section of a paper, in which the writer usually summarizes what has gone before and makes general statements about the topic that are needed to complete its purpose. See 20d, 25c, 25d.

concrete word   A word referring to something that can be perceived by the senses: *loud, sharp, computer.* See 28a, 66a.

conjunction   A word or pair of words that joins two sentence elements and sets up a relationship between them. A **coordinating conjunction** joins elements of equal grammatical weight: *and, but, or, nor, so, for, yet.* A **correlative conjunction** is a pair of words that joins grammatically equivalent elements: *both . . . and, either . . . or, neither . . . nor, not only . . . but also, whether . . . or.* A **subordinating conjunction** introduces a dependent clause and indicates its relationship to an independent clause. Subordinating conjunctions include *although, because, when,* and *while.* See also *conjunctive adverb.* See Chapter 26, 34a, 36d, 36e, 40a, 40b, 41a, 66f.

conjunctive adverb   A conjunctive adverb, together with a semicolon, joins two independent clauses: *however, therefore, furthermore.* It can also be used alone in an independent clause to express its connection to another independent clause. See 44b, 66f.

connotation   A word's associations in addition to its literal meaning. See also *denotation.* See 31d.

context   Background information provided for readers to understand a whole work. See 7b, 11c.

contraction   A word or phrase shortened by the omission of one or more letters, which are replaced with an apostrophe. See 30c, 47c.

contrast   See *comparison and contrast.*

coordinate adjectives   Two or more adjectives with distinct meanings modifying a noun or pronoun separately: *The tired, discouraged, disgusted ballplayer slumped on the bench.* Coordinate adjectives are separated by commas. See also *cumulative adjectives.* See 44d.

coordinating conjunction   See *conjunction.*

coordination   The grammatical connection of two or more ideas to give them equal emphasis and importance. See Chapter 26.

corelative conjunction   See *conjunction.*

counterclaim   See *claim.*

count noun   A noun that names something that can be counted by unit or instance: *fifty laps, thirty-nine flavors, two apples.* See also *mass noun.* See 66a.

creative writing   Writing whose primary purpose is the creation of a text that is enjoyable and rewarding in and of itself, apart from the information or ideas it conveys. Fiction, poetry, and drama are commonly identified as creative writing, but all writing can be creative. See 5c.

critical essay   See *interpretive essay.*

critical reading   An analysis of an author's assumptions, ideas, arguments, and conclusions to understand them better, test them, and determine their meaning in an overall sense. See Chapter 2.

cumulative adjectives   Two or more adjectives that build on one another and together modify a noun: *The unsightly green chair had been in the family for five generations.* See also *coordinate adjectives.* See 44d.

cumulative sentence   A sentence in which the main idea is stated at the beginning. See also *periodic sentence.* See 27c.

dangling modifier   A modifier, often a participle or participial phrase, that does not modify a clearly stated noun or pronoun: *Driving down the highway, the radar detector went off.* See 38c.

declarative sentence   A sentence that presents facts or assertions. See 27c, 68a.

deductive reasoning   Reasoning in which a general statement supports a conclusion about a specific case: *All cats purr. Rex is a cat. Rex must purr.* See also *inductive reasoning.*

definite article   See *article.*

definition   A writing strategy in which the writer describes something so that it can be distinguished from similar things. See 10d.

degree   See *modifier.*

demonstrative adjective   See *demonstrative pronoun.*

demonstrative pronoun   A pronoun that distinguishes its antecedent from similar things: *this, that, these, those.* When the word precedes a noun, it is a **demonstrative adjective:** *these apples.* See 66b.

denotation   A word's literal meaning. See also *connotation.* See 31d.

dependent clause   A clause containing a subject and a verb but introduced by a subordinating conjunction or a relative pronoun. A dependent clause cannot constitute a complete sentence. Also called *subordinate clause.* See 26b, 27c, 29c, 33b, 34e, 67f.

description   A writing strategy in which the writer creates an image of something, using words that appeal to the five senses. See 10d.

desktop publishing   The art of using computers and computer-based programs to design documents visually.   See Chapter 56.

determiner   See *article.*

direct address   A word or phrase that indicates a person or persons who are spoken to: *Don't forget, Amy, to lock the door.* See 44f.

direct discourse   See *quotation.*

direct object   See *object.*

direct question   A sentence that asks a question and ends with a question mark: *Will you marry me?* See also *indirect question, tag sentence.* See 43b.

direct quotation   See *quotation.*

discovery writing   Writing whose primary purpose is to uncover ideas and information stored in the writer's memory. See also *invention.* See 5a, Chapter 6.

disruptive modifier   A modifier placed in such a way as to make the phrase or clause it modifies difficult to follow. See also *split infinitive.* See 38d.

division   See *classification and division.*

documentation   The practice and procedures for crediting and identifying source materials used in research writing. See 17e, Chapter 18, 62d, 63d, 64d.

double negative   The nonstandard use of two negative modifiers that, in effect, cancel each other out. See 37d.

doublespeak   An extreme form of euphemism that purposely describes things so they seem the opposite of what they actually are. See 29f.

drafting.   The stage of the writing process in which the writer begins to produce a text. The complete text is called a **draft;** each subsequent revision of the piece of writing is considered a new draft. See also *editing, revising.* See 3c.

editing   The stage of the writing process in which the writer improves a draft by making sentences and words clearer, more powerful, and more precise. See also *revising.* See 3f.

effect   See *cause-and-effect analysis.*

effectiveness   The quality of writing that makes it clear, interesting, and readable. See 3f, Chapters 24–32.

ellipsis   The omission of one or more words from a quoted phrase or clause. An ellipsis must be indicated by ellipsis points (. . .). See also *elliptical construction.* See 49c.

elliptical construction   A phrase or clause from which one or more words are omitted and are assumed to be understood: *I ordered the shrimp; Angelo, the lobster.* See 26g, 27f.

euphemism   A polite term substituted for one considered unpleasant or impolite. See 29f.

evidence   Information presented in support of an argument. The most important types of evidence are facts, examples, inferences, informed opinions, and personal testimony. See 11b, 11e.

exclamatory sentence   A sentence that expresses strong feeling and that usually ends with an exclamation point. See 27c, 68a.

explanatory paper   An essay whose purpose is to present information and ideas that will help readers understand the subject. Sometimes called *informative paper, expository paper,* or *report.* See Chapter 10.

expletive construction   A sentence beginning with *it* or *there* (called an *expletive* when used in this manner), followed by a form of the verb *be* and the subject of the sentence: *There is a delay on Route 24 this morning.* See 28b, 29c.

expository paper   See *explanatory paper.*

fallacy   Incorrect logic or weak reasoning. See 11e.

faulty predication   A mixed construction in which the subject and verb do not make sense together. See 42b.

field research   Research conducted outside of the library by **interviewing** people who have information about a topic or by **observing** people and activities related to the topic. See Chapter 16.

figurative language   Any use of language that makes surprising comparisons or describes things in unexpected ways. The main types of figurative language are analogy, hyperbole, irony, metaphor, paradox, personification, simile, and understatement. See 10d, 31i, 61c.

finite verb   A verb that changes form to indicate person, number, tense, and mood. See also *verbal.* See 66c.

first person　See *person, point of view.*

flashback　See *sequence of events.*

fragment　A word group that is grammatically incomplete but that is punctuated as a sentence. See Chapter 33.

freewriting　An invention and discovery technique in which the writer writes quickly without stopping. See 2b, 6b.

fused sentence　Two or more independent clauses joined without any punctuation or a conjunction. Also called *run-on sentence.* See Chapter 34.

gender　(1) The categorization of a noun or pronoun as masculine, feminine, or neuter. See also *agreement.* See Chapter 40. (2) The categorization of a person as male or female. See Chapter 32. Pronouns must agree with their antecedents in gender.

general　Categorization of a word or statement that includes or refers to an entire group, type, or category. See also *specific.* See 28a.

generality　A very broad generalization that is essentially meaningless or empty. See 29a.

generalization　A conclusion based on a number of specific facts or instances. Sometimes called *inference.* When a generalization becomes so broad as to be empty or meaningless, it is called a *generality.* See 11e, 29a, Chapter 32.

generic noun　See *common noun.*

gerund　The *-ing* form of a verb functioning as a noun: *Painting is her life.* See also *present participle, verbal.* See 33a, 35b, 66c.

gerund phrase　A gerund, its modifiers, complements, and objects. See 67e.

grammar　A system for describing how sentences are organized and structured. See 23a, Chapters 33–42, 66–68.

helping verb　See *auxiliary verb.*

homonym　Words that sound alike but have different spellings and meanings. See 31e.

hyperbole　See *figurative language.*

idiom　A customary phrase or usage that does not make literal sense or follow strict rules. See 31f.

imperative mood　See *mood.*

imperative sentence　A sentence that gives an order or instruction. Also called *command.* See 27c, 68a.

implied subject　A subject that is not stated but that can be inferred from context. In imperative sentences (commands), the subject *you* is usually implied: *Shut the door.* See also *subject.* See 67a.

indefinite article　See *article.*

indefinite pronoun　A pronoun that refers to a nonspecific person or thing and therefore does not have a clear antecedent: *anybody, no one, everything, some, none.* See 36g, 40d, 66b.

independent clause　A clause that contains a subject and a predicate that can stand alone as a complete sentence because it is not introduced by a subordinating word. Also called *main clause*. See also *dependent clause*. See Chapter 33, Chapter 34, 67f.

indicative mood See *mood*.

indirect discourse See *quotation*.

indirect object See *object*.

indirect question A sentence that reports a question, usually in a dependent clause, and ends with a period: *She asked if I would marry her.* See also *direct question, tag sentence*. See 43b.

indirect quotation See *quotation*.

inductive reasoning Reasoning in which specific facts support a probable general conclusion: *The alarm has run at 8:30 on the past five mornings. The alarm will probably ring at 8:30 this morning.* See also *deductive reasoning*.

inference See *generalization*.

infinitive The base form of a verb preceded by *to*. An infinitive functions as a noun, adverb, or adjective. See also *verbal*. See 35b.

infinitive phrase An infinitive, its modifiers, and its objects or complements. See 67e.

informational research Research undertaken to collect information needed to answer a research question. See also *argumentative research*. See 14b.

informational thesis See *thesis*.

informative paper See *explanatory paper*.

intensive pronoun A pronoun ending in *-self* or *-selves* placed next to its antecedent for emphasis: *I myself prefer steak.* See also *reflexive pronoun*. See 66b.

interjection A term inserted into a sentence or standing alone that expresses strong feeling or reaction: *wow, jeepers.* See 66g.

interpretive community Any group that shares a set of beliefs or approaches to analyzing, discussing, and interpreting ideas. See 12c.

interpretive essay An essay whose purpose is to analyze a text and present a persuasive interpretation. Sometimes called *analytical essay, critical essay, literary interpretation,* or *review essay*. See Chapter 12.

interrogative pronoun A pronoun used to introduce a question: *who, whose.* See 41f, 66b.

interrogative sentence A sentence that asks a question. See also *direct question, indirect question, tag sentence*. See 27c, 68a.

interview See *field research*.

intransitive verbs See *transitive and intransitive verbs*.

invention Writing or other activities undertaken to help the writer develop solutions to questions and problems encountered in the writing process. See also *discovery writing*. See Chapter 6.

inverted word order The placement of words in a sentence in an unexpected sequence for emphasis. The most common inverted order is verb before subject. See 27c.

invisible writing An invention and discovery technique in which the writer uses a word processor for freewriting but darkens the screen so that the words on it are invisible. See 6b.

irony See *figurative language*.

irregular verb A verb that does not follow the usual -*d* or -*ed* pattern in spelling its past tense and past participle. See also *regular verb*. See 35b.

issue A topic that can be argued about, often stated in the form of a question. It raises a real question that has at least two distinct answers, one of which the writer is interested in advocating. See 11b.

jargon Terms and expressions that arise within a specialty or field, often essential language for people in that field but not understood by others. See 31h.

journal A record of a person's thoughts and ideas on any aspect of life, work, or studies. See Chapter 4.

level of formality A quality of language created by word choice and sentence structure and ranging from the very formal (or ceremonial) to the familiar. See 30c.

limiting modifier A modifier that distinguishes the word modified from other similar things. See 38a, 66d.

linking verb A verb that connects a subject to a complement, which is a word that renames or describes the subject. See also *complement*. See 36c, 37b, 66c.

literary interpretation See *interpretive essay*.

literary present The present tense used to describe the events of a literary work. See 35d.

looping An invention and discovery technique in which the writer creates a series of freewritings, each building on the most important idea uncovered in the previous one. Sometimes called *loop writing*. See also *freewriting*. See 6c.

main clause See *independent clause*.

mass noun A noun that names something concrete that cannot be counted and given a number: *silver, tobacco, information*. Also called *noncount noun*. See also *count noun*. See 66a.

mechanics The standardized features of written language, other than punctuation, that are used to clarify meaning. Elements of mechanics are spelling, capitalization, hyphenation, and italics. See Chapters 23, 50–55.

metaphor See *figurative language*.

misplaced modifier A modifier that is placed in a sentence in such a way that it is unclear what it describes or which word it modifies. See 38a.

mixed construction A sentence that combines two or more types of sentence structures that do not fit together grammatically. See 42b.

mixed metaphor An implied comparison in which unrelated elements are introduced from a different implied comparison: *We're all in the same boat, and the wing is broken*. See also *figurative language*. See 31i.

modal auxiliary An auxiliary verb that does not change form for person or number. The one-word modals are *can, could, may, might, must, shall, should, will*, and *would*. See 35c, 66c.

modifier   A word or group of words that describes a noun, verb, phrase, or clause. The most common modifiers are adjectives and adverbs. Modifiers have three degrees: **positive,** which simply states a quality (*He worked hard*); **comparative,** which compares the degree of that quality between two persons or things (*He worked harder than his sister*); and **superlative,** which compares the degree of the quality among three or more persons or things (*He worked hardest of all the company's employees*). See Chapter 37, Chapter 38, 66d.

modifier clause   A dependent clause that functions as an adjective or adverb. See 67f.

modifier phrase   A phrase that functions as an adjective or adverb. See 67e.

mood   The characteristic of a verb used to indicate whether it is stating fact **(indicative),** giving an order or instruction **(imperative mood),** or expressing a wish or condition contrary to fact **(subjunctive).** See 35f, 66c.

multiple-word verb   See *phrasal verb.*

nominalization   The construction of a noun from a verb root plus a suffix: *estrange* plus *-ment* equals the nominal *estrangement.* See 28b.

noncount noun   See *mass noun.*

nonfinite verb   See *verbal.*

nonrestrictive clause   See *restrictive and nonrestrictive clause.*

nonsexist language   See *sexist language.*

noun   A word that names a person, animal, place, or idea. See also *common noun, count noun, mass noun, proper noun.* See 66a.

noun clause   A dependent clause that functions as a noun (as a subject, object, or complement). See 67f.

noun cluster   A group of words consisting of a noun and several other nouns used as modifiers: *hardwood maple ballroom floor.* See 28d.

noun phrase   A noun and its modifiers functioning as a noun. See 67e.

number   The characteristic of a noun, pronoun, or verb that indicates whether it is *singular* (referring to one person or thing) or *plural* (referring to more than one). See also *agreement.* See Chapter 36, Chapter 40, 66b, 66c.

object   A noun, pronoun, or noun phrase or clause that receives the action of or is influenced by a verb, a verbal, or a preposition. A **direct object** receives the action of a verb or verbal: *She read the newspaper.* An **indirect object** indicates to or for whom or what the action of the verb is directed: *She gave him the newspaper.* The **object of a preposition** follows a preposition: *The newspaper had a story about the peace plan.* The preposition, its object, and any associated modifiers together form a **prepositional phrase:** *The newspaper had a story about the peace plan.* See 66e.

object complement   See *complement.*

objective case   See *case.*

objective stance   See *stance.*

observation   See *field research.*

opening   The beginning of an essay, which establishes the subject, the tone, and sometimes the theme or thesis of the essay. See 20d, 25a, 25b.

outline   Organized list showing the points made about a topic, the information supporting each point, and the organization of this material. Outlining is useful as an invention and discovery technique, a means of organizing materials before drafting, and a revision technique. See 6e, 17b, 20d.

paradox   See *figurative language.*

paragraph   A group of sentences about a single topic. Good paragraphs are unified, coherent, and well organized. See Chapter 24.

parallelism   Repetition of a grammatical element or structure—a word, phrase, clause, sentence, or paragraph—for emphasis. See 26f–g.

paraphrase   A restatement of the ideas of a written or spoken source in the writer's own words. See also *quotation, summary.* See 17d.

parenthetical element   A word or word group that comments on or adds information to a sentence but is not part of the sentence structure and does not alter the meaning of the sentence. Parenthetical elements appear between parentheses, commas, or dashes. See 44e, 49a, 49b.

participial phrase   A present or past participle, including its modifiers, that functions as an adjective. See 67e.

particle   See *phrasal verb.*

passive voice   See *voice.*

past participle   A verb form created by adding *-d* or *-ed* to the base form in regular verbs. In irregular verbs the past participle is formed differently for each verb. Used with an auxiliary verb, it can function as a main verb in a sentence. Used without an auxiliary verb, it functions as a modifier. See also *verbal.* See 35a, 66c.

past tense   See *tense.*

perfect progressive tense   See *tense.*

perfect tense   See *tense.*

periodic sentence   A sentence in which the main idea is placed at the end. See also *cumulative sentence.* See 27c.

person   The characteristic of a noun, pronoun, or a verb that indicates whether the subject or actor is the one speaking (**first person:** *I, we*), spoken to (**second person:** *you*), or spoken about (**third person:** *he, she, it, they*). See 35a, Chapter 36, Chapter 40, 66b, 66c.

personal experience paper   A common college writing assignment whose purpose is to recount events experienced by the writer in an interesting and enlightening manner. See Chapter 9.

personal pronoun   A pronoun that refers to a particular person, group, or thing. See 66b.

personification   See *figurative language.*

perspective   The vantage point from which a paper is written. Perspective is established through point of view, tense, emphasis, and level of formality. See also *point of view, stance, tone.* See 9c, 10f.

persuasion   See *argument paper.*

phrasal preposition   A group of words that work together as a single preposition: *except for, according to.* See 66e.

phrasal verb   A verb with more than one word. Phrasal verbs are formed by combining a one-word verb with one or more **particles** such as *to* or *off.* Together, the verb and the particle(s) create a meaning that is distinct from that of the original verb: *come to, come off.* Also called *two-word verb* or *multiple-word verb.* See 31f, 66c.

phrase   Two or more words that do not include a subject and a verb but that work as a grammatical unit, serving as a noun, verb, adjective, or adverb. See also *absolute phrase, modifier phrase, noun phrase, object, verbal phrase, verb phrase.* See 67e.

plagiarism   Any use of someone else's ideas or words without explicit and complete documentation or acknowledgment. See 15e, 17e.

plain form   See *base form.*

plural   See *number.*

point of view   An indication of the writer's proximity to or distance from his or her material. See also *person.* See 9c, 30b, 61c.

position paper   A type of argument paper that sets forth a position on an issue of local or national concern. See Chapter 11.

positive form   See *modifier.*

possessive case   See *case.*

predicate   The part of a sentence that specifies action or being. The **simple predicate** is the main verb of the sentence. The **complete predicate** is the simple predicate plus its modifiers, objects, and complements. See also *compound predicate.* See 67b.

predicate adjective   An adjective functioning as a complement. See also *complement.* See 67d.

predicate noun   A noun functioning as a complement. See also *complement.* See 67d.

prefix   A word segment attached to the beginning of a word root to change its meaning. See 31c.

preposition   A word that connects a noun or noun phrase (the **object** of the preposition) to another word, phrase, or clause and conveys a relation between the elements connected. See also *object.* See 66e.

prepositional phrase   See *object.*

present participle   A verb form created by adding *-ing* to the base form. Used with auxiliary verbs, it forms the progressive tenses. Used without an auxiliary verb, it is a modifier and functions as an adjective or it is a gerund and functions as a noun. See also *verbal.* See 35a, 35c, 66c.

pretentious language   Excessively formal, old-fashioned, or complicated words and expressions used not for their appropriateness but to impress the reader. See 29e.

primary and secondary sources   A primary source contains firsthand information and raw data on a topic. Many of the sources consulted in field research are primary sources. A secondary source contains interpretations of and arguments about firsthand information and raw data. Many of the sources consulted in library research are secondary sources. See 14e.

progressive tense   See *tense.*

pronoun   A word used in place of a noun or noun phrase. See also *agreement, antecedent, demonstrative pronoun, intensive pronoun, interrog-*

ative pronoun, personal pronoun, reciprocal pronoun, reflexive pronoun, relative pronoun. See Chapters 39–41, 66b.

proofreading   The final stage in a writing project; it involves rereading the final draft to catch small errors such as typographical errors, misspellings, and incorrect capitalization. See 3f.

proper adjective   See *adjective*.

proper noun   A name of a particular person, place, animal, organization, or thing. Proper nouns are capitalized. See also *common noun*. See 51c, 66a.

punctuation   A system of standardized marks used in written material to clarify meaning. The marks of punctuation used most often in English are the period, the exclamation point, the question mark, the comma, the semicolon, the colon, the apostrophe, quotation marks, the slash, the dash, ellipsis points, parentheses, and brackets. See Chapters 23, 43–49.

purpose   The reason for generating a piece of writing; the goal a writer wants to accomplish through writing. Three general purposes for writing are to discover, to communicate, and to create. See Chapter 5, 7b.

quotation   The reproduction of a writer's or speaker's exact words. In **direct quotation** (or **direct discourse**), a writer reproduces another person's words exactly and places them in quotation marks. In **indirect quotation** (or **indirect discourse**), a writer rephrases another person's words and integrates them grammatically and logically into his or her own sentence. See also *paraphrase, summary*. See 17d.

reciprocal pronoun   A two-word pronoun that refers to one part of a plural antecedent: *each other, one another*. See 66b.

recounting experience   See *personal experience paper*.

redundancy   The unnecessary repetition of key words or ideas. See 29d.

referent   See *antecedent*.

reflective essay   A common college writing assignment in which the writer reflects on a significant subject, raises questions about it, and speculates on possible answers but does not provide a strong argument. Sometimes called simply an *essay*. See Chapter 13.

reflexive pronoun   A pronoun ending in *-self* or *-selves* whose antecedent is the subject of the sentence it appears in: *I could kick myself*. See also *intensive pronoun*. See 41g, 66b.

regionalism   A form of language use that is common in one geographic area but not used elsewhere. See 31g.

register   See *level of formality*.

regular verb   A verb that forms its past tense and past participles by adding *-d* or *-ed* to the base form. See also *irregular verb*. See 35b.

relative adverb   An adverb that introduces an adjective clause. Common relative adverbs are *when, where*, and *how*. See 66d.

relative clause   A dependent clause that functions as an adjective. See 67f.

relative pronoun   A pronoun that introduces a dependent noun or adjective clause: *who, whose, which, what*. See 66b.

report   See *explanatory paper*.

reporter's questions   A set of questions that reporters use in gathering information and that can be used by any writer as an invention and discovery technique: *Who? What? Where? When? Why? How?* Also called *journalist's questions.* See 6d.

research essay   A common college writing assignment in which students conduct research and write about their findings. Research essays are generally longer, require more extensive research, use a more formal style and format, and take more time than other papers. Sometimes called *research paper* or *research report.* See Chapter 14.

researching   The stage of the writing process in which the writer gathers information and ideas about which to write. Research is a part of all writing assignments except those written completely from personal experience. See also *argumentative research, field research, informational research, research essay.* See 3d.

research question   The question that research is designed to answer. See 14a.

responding   The act of offering comments on a writer's material, ideals, or drafts. See *collaborating, writing group.* See Chapter 22.

restrictive and nonrestrictive clause   *Restrictive clauses* are adjective clauses that limit the nouns they modify and that are essential to the meaning of a sentence: *I bought the books that were assigned.* Restrictive clauses are not set off from the words they modify with commas. *Nonrestrictive clauses* do not limit the nouns they modify and are not essential to the meaning of a sentence: *The assigned books, which were on a special shelf, cost sixty dollars.* Nonrestrictive clauses are not set off with commas. See 39f, 44c.

review essay   See *interpretive essay.*

revising   The stage of the writing process in which the writer improves a draft by making changes to its direction, focus, argument, information, organization, or other important features. Revision generally occurs at the level of ideas. See also *editing.* See 3e.

root   The part of a word that stays the same as the word changes form with the addition of prefixes and suffixes. *Route* is the root of *routing, routine, reroute.* Also called **base word.** See 31c, 50b.

secondary source   See *primary and secondary sources.*

second person   See *person, point of view.*

sentence   A group of words containing a subject and a predicate and conveying a comprehensible, complete idea or thought.

sequence of events   The order in which events are related in an essay. The most straightforward sequence of events is *chronological order,* which presents events in the same order in which they happened. Another sequence of events is the *flashback,* in which earlier events are related after later ones. See 9e.

sequence of tenses   the relationship between the main verb and all the other verbs in a sentence. See also *governing tense* in **tense.** See 35e.

series   A list of words, phrases, or clauses separated by commas or semicolons. See 26f, 44d.

sexist language   Any language in which assumptions about gender are embedded: *policeman, each must do his best.* Nonsexist alternatives are *police officer* and *his* or *her best.* See Chapter 32.

shift   Any change in verb tense, number, or person within a sentence or between sentences that results in confusion for the reader. See 42a.

simile   See *figurative language.*

simple form   See *base form.*

simple predicate   See *predicate.*

simple sentence   A sentence that contains one independent clause. See 68b.

simple subject   See *subject.*

simple tense   See *tense.*

singular   See *number.*

slang   Colorful, irreverent expressions coined by small groups to describe their words and relationships. Slang is not appropriate in formal writing. See 31g.

specific   Categorization of a word or statement that refers to a single, particular thing. See also *general.* See 28a.

split infinitive   A construction in which words intervene between the infinitive marker *to* and the infinitive verb. See 38d.

squinting modifier   An ambiguously placed modifier that does not clearly modify one sentence element but could modify more than one. See 38b.

stance   The perspective adopted for a particular paper. An **objective stance** focuses on the topic under discussion rather than on the writer's own thoughts and feelings. A **subjective stance** incorporates the writer's thoughts and feelings into the account or analysis.

stereotype   Overgeneralization about a person or group based on gender, race, ethnicity, and so on. See 32a.

style   The distinctive way a writer expresses himself or herself, established primarily through the level of formality and the simplicity or complexity of words, sentences, and paragraphs. See also *level of formality.* See 7b, 8b.

subject   (1) The noun or pronoun that performs the action of the verb, is acted upon by the verb, or is described by the verb. The **simple subject** is the noun or pronoun alone. The **complete subject** is the noun or pronoun plus its modifiers. See also *compound subject, implied subject.* See 67a. (2) The idea or thing about which a paper is written. See also *topic.*

subject complement   See *complement.*

subjective case   See *case.*

subjective stance   See *stance.*

subjunctive mood   See *mood.*

subordinate clause   See *dependent clause.*

subordinating conjunction   See *conjunction.*

subordination   Connection of two or more ideas (usually clauses) to make one of them dominant and the other or others logically secondary or subordinate. See 26b–c, 34e.

suffix   A word segment attached to the end of a word root to change its meaning or form. See 31c, 50b.

summary   A distillation of a source's ideas into a brief statement phrased in the writer's own words. See also *paraphrase, quotation*. See 17d.

superlative form   See *modifier.*

synonym   Two or more different words with the same meaning.

synthesis   An element of critical thinking in which a writer or reader applies the process of summary, analysis, and interpretation to prior beliefs to produce new ideas. See also **thesis**. See 11a.

tag question   See *tag sentence.*

tag sentence   A brief sentence placed at the end of another sentence (after a comma) for the purpose of providing emphasis or eliciting a response. A tag sentence may be either a statement or a question: *Mark cannot join us, I'm afraid. You're tired, aren't you?* See 34b, 44f.

tense   The form a verb takes to show when its action occurs. **Simple tenses** show events that occur in the past, present, or future: *I walked, I am walking, I will walk.* **Perfect tenses** indicate action completed in the past (*had sat*), present (*have sat*), and future (*will have sat*). **Progressive tenses** indicate action happening continuously, and not necessarily ending, in the past (*was sitting*), present (*am sitting*), and future (*will be sitting*). **Perfect progressive tenses** express actions happening over a period of time and then ending in the past (*had been sitting*), the present (*have been sitting*), or in the future (*will have been sitting*). The **governing tense** is the tense used in verbs describing most of the actions in a paper or story. See 9b, 35d, 66c.

text   Any symbolic work constructed by humans that is open to interpretation, specifically written texts such as essays, novels, short stories, plays, and poems. See Chapter 12.

theme   The central idea of a personal or reflective essay. It is not necessarily stated outright but is more often strongly implied. See 12d, 61c.

thesis   A statement, usually made early in a research or persuasive essay, that asserts the point the writer hopes to make in the essay. A **working thesis** is a statement of the point a writer thinks his or her finished essay will make; it is useful in the research and drafting phases of writing and often changes during the writing process. An **argumentative thesis** expresses an opinion about the issue the writer is exploring; the essay then serves to support that opinion. An **informational thesis** presents a factual statement that will be fleshed out with explanation and detail. See 5a, 10d, 11a, 12d.

third person   See *person, point of view.*

tone   The writer's attitude toward the subject and audience, conveyed through the piece of writing. Tone is established primarily through word choice, point of view, and level of formality. See also *level of formality, point of view*. See 7b, Chapter 30.

topic The specific issue, idea, fact, or situation about which a paper is written. See also *subject*. Also called **main idea**. See 2a, 25a.

topic sentence The sentence that states the main idea of a paragraph. See 24a.

transitional expression A word or phrase that connects separate ideas or statements and describes the relationship between them: *for example, as a result*. See 24c, 44b, 44e.

transitive and intransitive verbs A **transitive verb** expresses an action that has an object or recipient; an **intransitive verb** expresses action or being with no object or recipient. Many verbs can be both transitive and intransitive: *I walked the dog* (transitive); *I walked to the store* (intransitive). See 66c.

two-word verb See *phrasal verb*.

understatement See *figurative language*.

verb A word that indicates action or existence, expressing what a subject does or is. See 66c. An **action verb** expresses motion or creates vivid images. See 28b. A **dynamic verb**, which usually appears in the –*ing* form, expresses actions, processes, or events that are in progress. See 35d. A **static verb** expresses a subject's existence rather than action: *be, seem, become*. See 28b.

verbal A verb form that does not function as the main verb of a sentence. See also *gerund, infinitive, past participle, present participle*. See 35b, 66c.

verbal phrase A verbal plus its modifiers, objects, and complements. See also *gerund phrase, infinitive phrase, participial phrase*. See 67e.

verb phrase A main verb plus any auxiliary verbs. See also *auxiliary verb*. See 67e.

voice (1) The sense of the writer, conveyed to the reader through a piece of writing. See Chapter 8, 9a. (2) In grammar, an attribute of a verb showing whether the action of the verb is performed by the sentence's subject **(active voice)** or is performed on the sentence's subject **(passive voice).** *Mary reads the book* (active); *The book is read by Mary* (passive). See 28c, 66c.

working thesis See *thesis*.

writing group A group of writers who work together to help one another improve their writing. Writers may respond to one another's work or they may collaborate on a piece of writing. See 22e.

writing process The set of activities writers go through to produce a finished piece of writing. Writing processes vary from person to person and from situation to situation. However, the typical writing process can be described as having five discrete but overlapping stages: planning, drafting, researching, revising, and editing. See Chapter 3.

ESL Index

Index

Please note that boldface type has been used to indicate page numbers for the main text discussion of a topic. For example, the listing, "Acronyms, 629, **748–49**, 884," shows that for the definition of and lists of acronyms, first consult pp. 748–49.

Editing symbols

ABB	abbreviation **55**	REF	pronoun reference **39**
AD	adjective/adverb **37**	REP	repetitious **29d**
AWK	awkward	S-V AGR	subject-verb agreement **36**
BIAS	biased language **32**	SHIFT	distracting shift **42a**
CAP	capital letter **51**	SLANG	slang **31g**
CASE	pronoun case **41**	SP	spelling **50**
CLICHÉ	cliché **31j**	SUB	subordination **26b–c**
COH	coherence **24c**	T	verb tense **35d–e**
CONCL	conclusion **25c–d**	TONE	tone **30**
COORD	coordination **26a–c**	TRANS	transition **24c**
CS	comma splice **34**	??	unclear
D	diction **28a–b, 31**	U	unity **24a**
DEV	development **9–13**	US	usage glossary
DIR	indirect **29e–f**	VAR	variety **27b–f**
DM	dangling modifier **38c**	VERB	verb **35**
DOC	documentation **18, 62–65**	VITAL	vitality **28**
EMPH	emphasis **27a**	W	wordy **29a–d**
FRAG	sentence fragment **33**	WC	word choice **31**
FS	fused sentence **34**	WW	wrong word **31**
GR	grammar **66–68**	'	apostrophe **47**
HYPH	hyphen **52**	[ ]	brackets **49d**
INC	incomplete construction **42c**	:	colon **46**
ITAL	italics (underlining) **53**	,	comma **44**
JARG	jargon **31h**	—	dash **49b**
LC	lowercase letter **51**	. . .	ellipsis points **49c**
LOG	logic **11e**	( )	parentheses **49a**
MIXED	mixed construction **42b**	.	period **43a**
MM	misplaced modifier **38a–b, d**	?	question mark **43b**
MOOD	verb mood **35f–g**	" "	quotation marks **48**
MS	manuscript format **56**	;	semicolon **45**
NUM	number **54**	/	slash **49e**
OPEN	opening **25a–b**	◯	close up
¶	paragraph **24**	#	add space
//	parallelism **26f–g**	^	insert
P	punctuation **43–49**	ℰ	delete
P-A AGR	pronoun-antecedent agreement **40**	∼	transpose
PASS	passive voice **28c**	X	obvious error